When we look hard into God's Word, we always learn something new about Jesus. Thanks, Philip, for pointing the way in your new book.

Joni Eareckson Tada
President, JAF Ministries

In the more than twenty years I've known Philip Yancey, he's shown a deep and persistent hunger for the truth in Jesus. I would rather read his words on Jesus than almost any other contemporary's, for I know that he speaks from deep learning and deep passion.

Tim Stafford

This is the best book about Jesus I have ever read, probably the best book about Jesus in the whole century. Yancey gently took away my blinders and blazed the trail through my own doubting fears, pious know-it-all, and critical balderdash until I saw the Savior anew and thought I heard him ask me, "Now whom do you say that I am?" and I understood the question as I never had before.

Lewis B. Smedes
Senior Professor
Fuller Seminary

In this, *The Jesus I Never Knew,* Philip Yancey is both more personal and more focused on Jesus than perhaps he has ever been before. He remembers the experiences of his childhood church with honest sight and astonishing insight—and then he holds himself and his reader to a true biblical and historical investigation of who this Jesus was (and is) after all. Jesus becomes, under his faithful eye, human and divine and powerfully present, in the text of Scripture and in our lives. It is this progression—from a view of our Lord too narrow for the full promises of the Bible to a presence both broad and blessed—which is the genuine gift of Yancey's book. I am grateful for the gift.

Walter Wangerin Jr.

Philip Yancey can always be counted on not only to tell the truth, but to pursue it with passion. In *The Jesus I Never Knew,* he continues the hunt.

Virginia Stem Owens
Kansas Newman College

Philip Yancey takes the reader with him on his very personal journey to Jesus. In *The Jesus I Never Knew*, I became convinced that the Jesus I met—in some ways for the first time—has known me all along. This book is destined to become a favorite—to recommend to those still seeking Jesus and to pass along to those who've met him, but long to know him more.

Elisa Morgan
President, MOPS International

In *The Jesus I Never Knew*, Yancey both educates and inspires the reader to take a closer look at the biblical Jesus and his motivations. In doing so, he helps us gain new perspective on what it truly means to be a follower of Christ. Even those who think they know Jesus well will find new information and meaning in this remarkable book.

Dale Hanson Bourke

In his unique, challenging, and careful way, Philip Yancey breaks through stale stereotypes to give us a powerful antidote to the "Prozac Jesus" and other inadequate images, to reveal the complex reality and impact of Jesus of Nazareth on all of life. A fresh and helpful book.

Roberta Hestenes
President, Eastern College

Yancey's flair for honest, vivid, well-informed down-to-earthness gives piercing power to these broodings on the gospel facts about Jesus Christ. In a day when novel ideas about Jesus are all the rage, Yancey's pages offer major help for seeing the Savior as he really was.

James I. Packer
Sangwoo Youtong Chee Professor of Theology

There is no writer in the evangelical world that I admire and appreciate more.

Billy Graham

Philip Yancey

THE
JESUS I
NEVER
KNEW

ZondervanPublishingHouse

Grand Rapids, Michigan

A Division of HarperCollinsPublishers

The Jesus I Never Knew
Copyright © 1995 by Philip Yancey

Requests for information should be addressed to:

🏭 ZondervanPublishingHouse
Grand Rapids, Michigan 49530

Library of Congress Cataloging-in-Publication Data

Yancey, Philip, 1949–
   The Jesus I never knew / Philip Yancey.
      p.   cm.
   Includes bibliographical references (p.   ).
   ISBN: 0-310-38570-9 (hardcover : alk. paper)
   1. Jesus Christ—Person and offices. 2. Jesus Christ—Biography. 3. Jesus Christ—
Teachings. I. Title.
BT202.Y33   1995
232—dc20   95-9395
                                                                                                          CIP

International Trade Paper Edition 0-310-20407-0

This edition printed on acid-free paper and meets the American National Standards Institute
Z39.48 standard.

Edited by John Sloan
Interior design by Sue Koppenol
Cover illustration: "The Lord's Image" by Heinrich Hoffman, courtesy of Superstock

Printed in the United States of America

96 97 98 99 / DH / 10 9 8 7

Contents

Thanks . . .

To the class I taught, and was taught by, at LaSalle Street Church in Chicago.

To Tim Stafford, Bud Ogle, and Walter Wangerin Jr., whose perceptive comments caused me to rewrite this book several more times than I would have on my own.

To Verlyn Verbrugge, for his careful technical editing on matters of biblical accuracy.

To my editor John Sloan, who patiently endured, and helped improve, all those drafts.

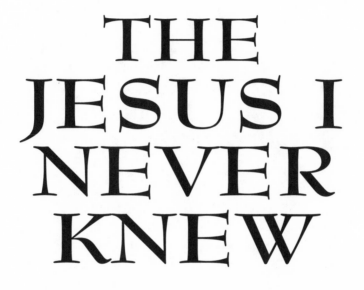

THE
JESUS I
NEVER
KNEW

Part One

Who He Was

1
The Jesus
I Thought I Knew

Suppose we hear an unknown man spoken of by many men.
Suppose we were puzzled to hear that some men said he was too tall
and some too short; some objected to his fatness, some lamented his
leanness; some thought him too dark, and some too fair. One
explanation . . . would be that he might be an odd shape. But there
is another explanation. He might be the right shape. . . . Perhaps
(in short) this extraordinary thing is really the ordinary thing; at
least the normal thing, the centre.

G. K. Chesterton

1
The Jesus
I Thought I Knew

I first got acquainted with Jesus when I was a child, singing "Jesus Loves Me" in Sunday school, addressing bedtime prayers to "Dear Lord Jesus," watching Bible Club teachers move cutout figures across a flannelgraph board. I associated Jesus with Kool-Aid and sugar cookies and gold stars for good attendance.

I remember especially one image from Sunday school, an oil painting that hung on the concrete block wall. Jesus had long, flowing hair, unlike that of any man I knew. His face was thin and handsome, his skin waxen and milky white. He wore a robe of scarlet, and the artist had taken pains to show the play of light on its folds. In his arms, Jesus cradled a small sleeping lamb. I imagined myself as that lamb, blessed beyond all telling.

Recently, I read a book that the elderly Charles Dickens had written to sum up the life of Jesus for his children. In it, the portrait emerges of a sweet Victorian nanny who pats the heads of boys and girls and offers such advice as, "Now, children, you must be nice to your mummy and daddy." With a start I recalled the Sunday school image of Jesus that I grew up with: someone kind and reassuring, with no sharp edges at all—a Mister Rogers before the age of children's television. As a child I felt comforted by such a person.

Later, while attending a Bible college, I encountered a different image. A painting popular in those days depicted Jesus, hands outstretched, suspended in a Dalí-like pose over the United Nations building in New York City. Here was the cosmic Christ, the One in whom all things inhere, the still point of the turning world. This world figure had come a long way from the lamb-toting shepherd of my childhood.

Still, students spoke of the cosmic Jesus with a shocking intimacy. The faculty urged us to develop a "personal relationship with Jesus Christ," and in chapel services we hymned our love for him in most familiar terms. One song told about walking beside him in a garden with dew still on the roses. Students testifying about their faith casually dropped in phrases like "The Lord told me...." My own faith hung in a kind of skeptical suspension during my time there. I was wary, confused, questioning.

Looking in retrospect on my years at Bible college, I see that, despite all the devotional intimacies, Jesus grew remote from me there. He became an object of scrutiny. I memorized the list of thirty-four specific miracles in the Gospels but missed the impact of just one miracle. I learned the Beatitudes yet never faced the fact that none of us—I above all—could make sense of those mysterious sayings, let alone live by them.

A little later, the decade of the 1960s (which actually reached me, along with most of the church, in the early 1970s) called everything into question. Jesus freaks—the very term would have been an oxymoron in the tranquil 1950s—suddenly appeared on the scene, as if deposited there by extraterrestrials. No longer were Jesus' followers well-scrubbed representatives of the middle class; some were unkempt, disheveled radicals. Liberation theologians began enshrining Jesus on posters in a troika along with Fidel Castro and Che Guevara.

It dawned on me that virtually all portrayals of Jesus, including the Good Shepherd of my Sunday school and the United Nations Jesus of my Bible college, showed him wearing a mustache and beard, both of which were strictly banned from the Bible college. Questions now loomed that had never occurred to me in childhood. For example, How would telling people to be nice to one another get a man crucified? What government would execute Mister Rogers or Captain Kangaroo? Thomas Paine said that no religion could be truly divine which has in it any doctrine that offends the sensibilities of a little child. Would the cross qualify?

In 1971 I first saw the movie *The Gospel According to St. Matthew*, directed by Italian filmmaker Pier Paolo Pasolini. Its release had scandalized not only the religious establishment, who barely recognized the Jesus on-screen, but also the film community, who knew Pasolini as an outspoken homosexual and Marxist. Pasolini wryly dedicated the film to Pope John XXIII, the man indirectly responsible for its creation. Trapped in an enormous traffic jam during a papal visit to Florence, Pasolini had checked into a hotel room where, bored, he picked up a copy of the New Testament from the bedside table and read through Matthew. What he discovered in those pages so startled him that he determined to make a film using no text but the actual words from Matthew's gospel.

Pasolini's film captures well the reappraisal of Jesus that took place in the 1960s. Shot in southern Italy on a tight budget, it evokes in chalky whites and dusty grays something of the Palestinian surroundings Jesus lived in. The Pharisees wear towering headpieces, and Herod's soldiers faintly resemble Fascist *squadristi*. The disciples act like bumbling raw recruits, but Jesus himself, with a steady gaze and a piercing intensity, seems fearless. The parables and other sayings, he fires in clipped phrases over his shoulder as he dashes from place to place.

The impact of Pasolini's film can only be understood by one who passed through adolescence during that tumultuous period. Back then it had the power to hush scoffing crowds at art theaters. Student radicals realized they were not the first to proclaim a message that was jarringly antimaterialistic, antihypocritical, pro-peace, and pro-love.

For me, the film helped to force a disturbing revaluation of my image of Jesus. In physical appearance, Jesus favored those who would have been kicked out of Bible college and rejected by most churches. Among his contemporaries he somehow gained a reputation as "a wine-bibber and a glutton." Those in authority, whether religious or political, regarded him as a troublemaker, a disturber of the peace. He spoke and acted like a revolutionary, scorning fame, family, property, and other traditional measures of success. I could not dodge the fact that the words in Pasolini's film were taken entirely from Matthew's gospel, yet their message clearly did not fit my prior conception of Jesus.

About this same time a Young Life worker named Bill Milliken, who had founded a commune in an inner-city neighborhood, wrote *So Long, Sweet Jesus*. The title of that book gave words to the change at work inside me. In those days I was employed as the editor of *Campus Life* magazine, an official publication of Youth For Christ. *Who was this Christ, after all?* I wondered. As I wrote, and edited the writing of others, a tiny dybbuk of doubt hovered just to my side. *Do you really believe that? Or are you merely dispensing the party line, what you're paid to believe? Have you joined the safe, conservative establishment—modern versions of the groups who felt so threatened by Jesus?*

As often as not I avoided writing directly about Jesus.

When I switched on my computer this morning, Microsoft Windows flashed the date, implicitly acknowledging that, whatever you may believe about it, the birth of Jesus was so important that it split history into two parts. Everything that has ever happened on this planet falls into a category of before Christ or after Christ.

Richard Nixon got carried away with excitement in 1969 when Apollo astronauts first landed on the moon. "It's the greatest day since Creation!" crowed the president, until Billy Graham solemnly reminded him of Christmas and Easter. By any measure of history Graham was right. This Galilean, who in his lifetime spoke to fewer people than would fill just one of the many stadia Graham has filled, changed the world more than any other person. He introduced a new force field into history, and now holds the allegiance of a third of all people on earth.

Today, people even use Jesus' name to curse by. How strange it would sound if, when a businessman missed a golf putt, he yelled, "Thomas Jefferson!" or if a plumber screamed "Mahatma Gandhi!" when his pipe wrench mashed a finger. We cannot get away from this man Jesus.

"More than 1900 years later," said H. G. Wells, "a historian like myself, who doesn't even call himself a Christian, finds the picture centering irresistibly around the life and character of this most significant man. . . . The historian's test of an individual's greatness is 'What did he leave to grow?' Did he start men to thinking along fresh lines with a vigor that persisted after him? By this test Jesus stands first." You can gauge the size of a ship that has passed out of sight by the huge wake it leaves behind.

And yet I am not writing a book about Jesus because he is a great man who changed history. I am not tempted to write about Julius Caesar or the Chinese emperor who built the Great Wall. I am drawn to Jesus, irresistibly, because he positioned himself as the dividing point of life—my life. "I tell you, whoever acknowledges me before men, the Son of Man will also acknowledge him before the angels of God," he said. According to Jesus, what I think about him and how I respond will determine my destiny for all eternity.

Sometimes I accept Jesus' audacious claim without question. Sometimes, I confess, I wonder what difference it should make to my life that a man lived two thousand years ago in a place called Galilee. Can I resolve this inner tension between doubter and lover?

I tend to write as a means of confronting my own doubts. My book titles—*Where Is God When It Hurts*, *Disappointment with God*—betray me. I return again and again to the same questions, as if fingering an old wound that never quite heals. Does God care about the misery down here? Do we really matter to God?

Once, for a two-week period, I was snowbound in a mountain cabin in Colorado. Blizzards closed all roads and, somewhat like Pasolini, I had nothing to do but read the Bible. I went through it slowly, page by page. In the Old Testament I found myself identifying with those who boldly stood up to God: Moses, Job, Jeremiah, Habakkuk, the psalmists. As I read, I felt I was watching a play with human characters who acted out their lives of small triumph and large tragedy onstage, while periodically calling to an unseen Stage Manager, "You don't know what it's like out here!" Job was most brazen, flinging to God this accusation: "Do you have eyes of flesh? Do you see as a mortal sees?"

Every so often I could hear the echo of a booming voice from far offstage, behind the curtain. "Yeah, and you don't know what it's like back here either!" it said, to Moses, to the prophets, most loudly to Job. When I got to the Gospels, however, the accusing voices stilled. God, if I may use such language, "found out" what life is like in the confines of planet earth. Jesus got acquainted with grief in person, in a brief, troubled life not far from the dusty plains where Job had travailed. Of the many reasons for Incarnation, surely one was to answer Job's accusation: Do you have eyes of flesh? For a time, God did.

If only I could hear the voice from the whirlwind and, like Job, hold a conversation with God himself! I sometimes think. And perhaps that is why I now choose to write about Jesus. God is not mute: the Word spoke, not out of a whirlwind, but out of the human larynx of a Palestinian Jew. In Jesus, God lay down on the dissection table, as it were, stretched out in cruciform posture for the scrutiny of all skeptics who have ever lived. Including me.

> *The vision of Christ that thou dost see*
> *Is my vision's greatest enemy:*
> *Thine has a great hook nose like thine,*
> *Mine has a snub nose like to mine....*
> *Both read the Bible day and night,*
> *But thou read'st black where I read white.*
> WILLIAM BLAKE

As I think about Jesus, an analogy from Karl Barth comes to mind. A man stands by a window gazing into the street. Outside, people are shading their eyes with their hands and looking up into the sky. Because of the overhang of the building though, the man cannot see what it is they are pointing toward. We who live two thousand years after Jesus have a viewpoint not unlike the man standing by the window. We hear the shouts of exclamation. We study the gestures and words in the Gospels and the many books they have spawned. Yet no amount of neck-craning will allow us a glimpse of Jesus in the flesh.

For this reason, as William Blake's poem expresses so well, sometimes those of us who look for Jesus cannot see past our own noses. The Lakota tribe, for example, refers to Jesus as "the buffalo calf of God." The Cuban government distributes a painting of Jesus with a carbine slung over his shoulder. During the wars of religion with France, the English used to shout, "The pope is French but Jesus Christ is English!"

Modern scholarship further muddies the picture. If you peruse the academic books available at a seminary bookstore you may encounter Jesus as a political revolutionary, as a magician who married Mary Magdalene, as a Galilean charismatic, a rabbi, a peasant Jewish Cynic, a Pharisee, an anti-Pharisee Essene, an eschatological prophet, a "hippie in a world of Augustan yuppies," and as the hallucinogenic leader of a sacred mushroom cult. Serious scholars write these works, with little sign of embarrassment.*

Athletes come up with creative portrayals of Jesus that elude modern scholarship. Norm Evans, former Miami Dolphins lineman, wrote in his book *On God's Squad*, "I guarantee you Christ would be the toughest guy who ever played this game. . . . If he were alive today I would picture a six-foot-six-inch 260-pound defensive tackle who would always make the big plays and would be hard to keep out of the backfield for offensive linemen like myself." Fritz Peterson, former New York Yankee, more easily fancies Jesus in a baseball uniform: "I firmly believe that if Jesus Christ was sliding into second base, he would knock the second baseman into left field to break up the double play. Christ might not throw a spitball, but he would play hard within the rules."

In the midst of such confusion, how do we answer the simple question, "Who was Jesus?" Secular history gives few clues. In a delicious irony, the figure who has changed history more than any other

---

*The U.S. public tends to ignore such trendy portrayals. A recent Gallup survey revealed that 84 percent of Americans believe Jesus Christ was God or the Son of God. Overwhelmingly Americans believe that Jesus was sinless, brave, and emotionally stable. By lesser margins they regard him as easy to understand (!), physically strong and attractive, practical, warm, and accepting.

managed to escape the attention of most scholars and historians of his own time. Even the four men who wrote the Gospels omitted much that would interest modern readers, skipping over nine-tenths of his life. Since none devotes a word to physical description, we know nothing about Jesus' shape or stature or eye color. Details of his family life are so scant that scholars still debate whether or not he had brothers and sisters. The facts of biography considered essential to modern readers simply did not concern the gospel writers.

Before beginning this book I spent several months in three seminary libraries—one Catholic, one liberal Protestant, one conservative evangelical—reading about Jesus. It was daunting in the extreme to walk in the first day and see not just shelves but entire walls devoted to books about Jesus. A scholar at the University of Chicago estimates that more has been written about Jesus in the last twenty years than in the previous nineteen centuries. I felt almost as if the hyperbolic comment at the end of John's gospel had come true: "Jesus did many other things as well. If every one of them were written down, I suppose that even the whole world would not have room for the books that would be written."

The agglomeration of scholarship began to have a numbing effect on me. I read scores of accounts of the etymology of Jesus' name, discussions of what languages he spoke, debates about how long he lived at Nazareth or Capernaum or Bethlehem. Any true-to-life image receded into a fuzzy, indistinct blur. I had a hunch that Jesus himself would be appalled by many of the portrayals I was reading.

At the same time, with great consistency I found that whenever I returned to the Gospels themselves the fog seemed to lift. J. B. Phillips wrote, after translating and paraphrasing the Gospels, "I have read, in Greek and Latin, scores of myths, but I did not find the slightest flavour of myth here.... No man could have set down such artless and vulnerable accounts as these unless some real Event lay behind them."

Some religious books have about them the sour smell of propaganda—but not the Gospels. Mark records what may be the most important event in all history, an event that theologians strive to interpret with words like "propitiation, atonement, sacrifice," in one sentence: "With a loud cry, Jesus breathed his last." Odd, unpredictable scenes show up, such as Jesus' family and neighbors trying to put him away under suspicion of insanity. Why include such scenes if you are writing hagiography? Jesus' most devoted followers usually come off as scratching their heads in wonderment—*Who is this guy?*—more baffled than conspiratorial.

Jesus himself, when challenged, did not offer airtight proofs of his identity. He dropped clues here and there, to be sure, but he also said, after appealing to the evidence, "Blessed is he who takes no offense at me." Reading the accounts, it is hard to find anyone who does not at some point or another take offense. To a remarkable degree the Gospels throw the decision back to the reader. They operate more like a "whodunit" (or as Alister McGrath has pointed out, a "whowashe") detective story than like a connect-the-dots drawing. I found fresh energy in this quality of the Gospels.

It occurs to me that all the contorted theories about Jesus that have been spontaneously generating since the day of his death merely confirm the awesome risk God took when he stretched himself out on the dissection table—a risk he seemed to welcome. Examine me. Test me. You decide.

The Italian movie *La Dolce Vita* opens with a shot of a helicopter ferrying a giant statue of Jesus to Rome. Arms outstretched, Jesus hangs in a sling, and as the helicopter passes over the landscape, people begin to recognize him. "Hey, it's Jesus!" shouts one old farmer, hopping off his tractor to race across the field. Nearer Rome, bikini-clad girls sunbathing around a swimming pool wave a friendly greeting, and the helicopter pilot swoops in for a closer look. Silent, with an almost doleful expression on his face, the concrete Jesus hovers incongruously above the modern world.

My search for Jesus took off in a new direction when the filmmaker Mel White loaned me a collection of fifteen movies on the life of Jesus. They ranged from *King of Kings*, the 1927 silent classic by Cecil B. DeMille, to musicals such as *Godspell* and *Cotton Patch Gospel* to the strikingly modern French-Canadian treatment *Jesus of Montreal*.

I reviewed these films carefully, outlining them scene by scene. Then, for the next two years, I taught a class on the life of Jesus, using the movies as a springboard for our discussion.

The class worked like this. As we came to a major event in Jesus' life, I would scout through the various films and from them select seven or eight treatments that seemed notable. As class began, I would show the two- to four-minute clips from each film, beginning with the comical and stiff renditions and working toward profound or evocative treatments. We found that the process of viewing the same event through the eyes of seven or eight filmmakers helped to strip away the patina of predictability that had built up over years of Sunday school and Bible reading. Obviously, some of the film interpretations had to be wrong—they blatantly contradicted each other—but which ones? What really happened? After reacting to the film clips we turned to the gospel accounts, and the discussion took off.

This class met at LaSalle Street Church, a lively congregation in downtown Chicago, which included Ph.D.'s from Northwestern as well as homeless men who used the hour in a warm room as a chance to catch up on sleep. Thanks largely to the class, I gradually underwent a transformation in how I viewed Jesus. Walter Kasper has said, "Extreme notions ... see God dressed as a Father Christmas, or slipping into human nature like someone putting on dungarees in order to repair the world after a breakdown. The biblical and church doctrine that Jesus was a complete man with a human intellect and human freedom, does not seem to prevail in the average Christian head." It did not prevail in my head, I admit, until I taught the class at LaSalle Street Church and sought to encounter the historical person Jesus.

Essentially, the films helped restore Jesus' humanity for me. The creeds repeated in churches tell about Christ's eternal preexistence and glorious afterlife, but largely ignore his earthly career. The Gospels themselves were written years after Jesus' death, from the far side of Easter, reporting on events as distant from the authors as the Korean War is from us today. The films helped me get further back, closer to a sense of Jesus' life as seen by his contemporaries. What would it have been like to hang on the edges of the crowd? How would I have responded to this man? Would I have invited him over for dinner, like

Zacchaeus? Turned away in sadness, like the rich young ruler? Betrayed him, like Judas and Peter?

Jesus, I found, bore little resemblance to the Mister Rogers figure I had met in Sunday school, and was remarkably unlike the person I had studied in Bible college. For one thing, he was far less tame. In my prior image, I realized, Jesus' personality matched that of a *Star Trek* Vulcan: he remained calm, cool, and collected as he strode like a robot among excitable human beings on spaceship earth. That is not what I found portrayed in the Gospels and in the better films. Other people affected Jesus deeply: obstinacy frustrated him, self-righteousness infuriated him, simple faith thrilled him. Indeed, he seemed more emotional and spontaneous than the average person, not less. More passionate, not less.

The more I studied Jesus, the more difficult it became to pigeonhole him. He said little about the Roman occupation, the main topic of conversation among his countrymen, and yet he took up a whip to drive petty profiteers from the Jewish temple. He urged obedience to the Mosaic law while acquiring the reputation as a lawbreaker. He could be stabbed by sympathy for a stranger, yet turn on his best friend with the flinty rebuke, "Get behind me, Satan!" He had uncompromising views on rich men and loose women, yet both types enjoyed his company.

One day miracles seemed to flow out of Jesus; the next day his power was blocked by people's lack of faith. One day he talked in detail of the Second Coming; another, he knew neither the day nor hour. He fled from arrest at one point and marched inexorably toward it at another. He spoke eloquently about peacemaking, then told his disciples to procure swords. His extravagant claims about himself kept him at the center of controversy, but when he did something truly miraculous he tended to hush it up. As Walter Wink has said, if Jesus had never lived, we would not have been able to invent him.

Two words one could never think of applying to the Jesus of the Gospels: boring and predictable. How is it, then, that the church has tamed such a character—has, in Dorothy Sayers' words, "very efficiently pared the claws of the Lion of Judah, certified Him as a fitting household pet for pale curates and pious old ladies"?

The Jesus I Never Knew

Pulitzer prize-winning historian Barbara Tuchman insists on one rule in writing history: no "flash-forwards." When she was writing about the Battle of the Bulge in World War II, for example, she resisted the temptation to include "Of course we all know how this turned out" asides. In point of fact, the Allied troops involved in the Battle of the Bulge did *not* know how the battle would turn out. From the look of things, they could well be driven right back to the beaches of Normandy where they had come from. A historian who wants to retain any semblance of tension and drama in events as they unfold dare not flash-forward to another, all-seeing point of view. Do so, and all tension melts away. Rather, a good historian re-creates for the reader the conditions of the history being described, conveying a sense that "you were there."

That, I concluded, is the problem with most of our writing and thinking about Jesus. We read the Gospels through the flash-forward lenses of church councils like Nicea and Chalcedon, through the church's studied attempts to make sense of him.

Jesus was a human being, a Jew in Galilee with a name and a family, a person who was in a way just like everyone else. Yet in another way he was something different than anyone who had ever lived on earth before. It took the church five centuries of active debate to agree on some sort of epistemological balance between "just like everyone else" and "something different." For those of us raised in the church, or even raised in a nominally Christian culture, the balance inevitably tilts toward "something different." As Pascal said, "The Church has had as much difficulty in showing that Jesus Christ was man, against those who denied it, as in showing that he was God; and the probabilities were equally great."

Let me make it clear that I affirm the creeds. But in this book I hope to go back beyond those formulations. I hope, as far as is possible, to look at Jesus' life "from below," as a spectator, one of the many who followed him around. If I were a Japanese filmmaker, given $50 million and no script but the Gospels' text, what kind of film would I make? I hope, in Luther's words, to "draw Christ as deep as possible into the flesh."

In the process, sometimes I have felt like a tourist walking around a great monument, awed and overwhelmed. I circle the monument of Jesus inspecting its constituent parts—the birth stories, the teachings, the miracles, the enemies and followers—in order to reflect on and try to comprehend the man who has changed history.

Other times I have felt like an art restorer stretched out on the scaffolding of the Sistine Chapel, swabbing away the grime of history with a moistened Q-tip. If I scrub hard enough, will I find the original beneath all those layers?

In this book I attempt to tell the story of Jesus, not my own story. Inevitably, though, a search for Jesus turns out to be one's own search. No one who meets Jesus ever stays the same. I have found that the doubts that afflict me from many sources—from science, from comparative religion, from an innate defect of skepticism, from aversion to the church—take on a new light when I bring those doubts to the man named Jesus. To say more at this stage, in this first chapter, would cause me to break Barbara Tuchman's cherished principle.

2
Birth:
The Visited Planet

The God of power, as he did ride
In his majestick robes of glorie
Resolv'd to light; and so one day
He did descend, undressing all the way.

George Herbert

2
Birth:
The Visited Planet

Sorting through the stack of cards that arrived at our house last Christmas, I note that all kinds of symbols have edged their way into the celebration. Overwhelmingly, the landscape scenes render New England towns buried in snow, usually with the added touch of a horse-drawn sleigh. On other cards, animals frolic: not only reindeer, but also chipmunks, raccoons, cardinals, and cute gray mice. One card shows an African lion reclining with a foreleg draped affectionately around a lamb.

Angels have made a huge comeback in recent years, and Hallmark and American Greetings now feature them prominently, though as demure, cuddly-looking creatures, not the type who would ever need to announce "Fear not!" The explicitly religious cards (a distinct minority) focus on the holy family, and you can tell at a glance these folks are different. They seem unruffled and serene. Bright gold halos, like crowns from another world, hover just above their heads.

Inside, the cards stress sunny words like love, goodwill, cheer, happiness, and warmth. It is a fine thing, I suppose, that we honor a sacred holiday with such homey sentiments. And yet when I turn to the gospel accounts of the first Christmas, I hear a very different tone and sense mainly disruption at work.

The Jesus I Never Knew

I recall watching an episode of the TV show *Thirtysomething* in which Hope, a Christian, argues with her Jewish husband, Michael, about the holidays. "Why do you even bother with Hanukkah?" she asks. "Do you really believe a handful of Jews held off a huge army by using a bunch of lamps that miraculously wouldn't run out of oil?"

Michael exploded. "Oh, and Christmas makes more sense? Do you really believe an angel appeared to some teenage girl who then got pregnant without ever having had sex and traveled on horseback to Bethlehem where she spent the night in a barn and had a baby who turned out to be the Savior of the world?"

Frankly, Michael's incredulity seems close to what I read in the Gospels. Mary and Joseph must face the shame and derision of family and neighbors, who react, well, much like Michael ("Do you really believe an angel appeared ...").

Even those who accept the supernatural version of events concede that big trouble will follow: an old uncle prays for "salvation from our enemies and from the hand of all who hate us"; Simeon darkly warns the virgin that "a sword will pierce your own soul too"; Mary's hymn of thanksgiving mentions rulers overthrown and proud men scattered.

In contrast to what the cards would have us believe, Christmas did not sentimentally simplify life on planet earth. Perhaps this is what I sense when Christmas rolls around and I turn from the cheeriness of the cards to the starkness of the Gospels.

Christmas art depicts Jesus' family as icons stamped in gold foil, with a calm Mary receiving the tidings of the Annunciation as a kind of benediction. But that is not at all how Luke tells the story. Mary was "greatly troubled" and "afraid" at the angel's appearance, and when the angel pronounced the sublime words about the Son of the Most High whose kingdom will never end, Mary had something far more mundane on her mind: *But I'm a virgin!*

Once, a young unmarried lawyer named Cynthia bravely stood before my church in Chicago and told of a sin we already knew about: we had seen her hyperactive son running up and down the aisles every

Sunday. Cynthia had taken the lonely road of bearing an illegitimate child and caring for him after his father decided to skip town. Cynthia's sin was no worse than many others, and yet, as she told us, it had such conspicuous consequences. She could not hide the result of that single act of passion, sticking out as it did from her abdomen for months until a child emerged to change every hour of every day of the rest of her life. No wonder the Jewish teenager Mary felt greatly troubled: she faced the same prospects even without the act of passion.

In the modern United States, where each year a million teenage girls get pregnant out of wedlock, Mary's predicament has undoubtedly lost some of its force, but in a closely knit Jewish community in the first century, the news an angel brought could not have been entirely welcome. The law regarded a betrothed woman who became pregnant as an adulteress, subject to death by stoning.

Matthew tells of Joseph magnanimously agreeing to divorce Mary in private rather than press charges, until an angel shows up to correct his perception of betrayal. Luke tells of a tremulous Mary hurrying off to the one person who could possibly understand what she was going through: her relative Elizabeth, who miraculously got pregnant in old age after another angelic annunciation. Elizabeth believes Mary and shares her joy, and yet the scene poignantly highlights the contrast between the two women: the whole countryside is talking about Elizabeth's healed womb even as Mary must hide the shame of her own miracle.

In a few months, the birth of John the Baptist took place amid great fanfare, complete with midwives, doting relatives, and the traditional village chorus celebrating the birth of a Jewish male. Six months later, Jesus was born far from home, with no midwife, extended family, or village chorus present. A male head of household would have sufficed for the Roman census; did Joseph drag his pregnant wife along to Bethlehem in order to spare her the ignominy of childbirth in her home village?

C. S. Lewis has written about God's plan, "The whole thing narrows and narrows, until at last it comes down to a little point, small as the point of a spear—a Jewish girl at her prayers." Today as I read the accounts of Jesus' birth I tremble to think of the fate of the world resting on the responses of two rural teenagers. How many times did Mary review the angel's words as she felt the Son of God kicking against the walls of her uterus? How many times did Joseph second-guess his own encounter with an angel—*just a dream?*—as he endured the hot shame of living among villagers who could plainly see the changing shape of his fiancée?

We know nothing of Jesus' grandparents. What must they have felt? Did they respond like so many parents of unmarried teenagers today, with an outburst of moral fury and then a period of sullen silence until at last the bright-eyed newborn arrives to melt the ice and arrange a fragile family truce? Or did they, like many inner-city grandparents today, graciously offer to take the child under their own roof?

Nine months of awkward explanations, the lingering scent of scandal—it seems that God arranged the most humiliating circumstances possible for his entrance, as if to avoid any charge of favoritism. I am impressed that when the Son of God became a human being he played by the rules, harsh rules: small towns do not treat kindly young boys who grow up with questionable paternity.

Malcolm Muggeridge observed that in our day, with family-planning clinics offering convenient ways to correct "mistakes" that might disgrace a family name, "It is, in point of fact, extremely improbable, under existing conditions, that Jesus would have been permitted to be born at all. Mary's pregnancy, in poor circumstances, and with the father unknown, would have been an obvious case for an abortion; and her talk of having conceived as a result of the intervention of the Holy Ghost would have pointed to the need for psychiatric treatment, and made the case for terminating her pregnancy even stronger. Thus our generation, needing a Savior more, perhaps, than any that has ever existed, would be too humane to allow one to be born."

The virgin Mary, though, whose parenthood was unplanned, had a different response. She heard the angel out, pondered the repercussions, and replied, "I am the Lord's servant. May it be to me as you have said." Often a work of God comes with two edges, great joy and great pain, and in that matter-of-fact response Mary embraced both. She was the first person to accept Jesus on his own terms, regardless of the personal cost.

* * *

When the Jesuit missionary Matteo Ricci went to China in the sixteenth century, he brought along samples of religious art to illustrate the Christian story for people who had never heard it. The Chinese readily adopted portraits of the Virgin Mary holding her child, but when he produced paintings of the crucifixion and tried to explain that the God-child had grown up only to be executed, the audience reacted with revulsion and horror. They much preferred the Virgin and insisted on worshiping her rather than the crucified God.

As I thumb once more through my stack of Christmas cards, I realize that we in Christian countries do much the same thing. We observe a mellow, domesticated holiday purged of any hint of scandal. Above all, we purge from it any reminder of how the story that began at Bethlehem turned out at Calvary.

In the birth stories of Luke and Matthew, only one person seems to grasp the mysterious nature of what God has set in motion: the old man Simeon, who recognized the baby as the Messiah, instinctively understood that conflict would surely follow. "This child is destined to cause the falling and rising of many in Israel, and to be a sign that will be spoken against . . ." he said, and then made the prediction that a sword would pierce Mary's own soul. Somehow Simeon sensed that though on the surface little had changed—the autocrat Herod still ruled, Roman troops were still stringing up patriots, Jerusalem still overflowed with beggars—underneath, everything had changed. A new force had arrived to undermine the world's powers.

At first, Jesus hardly seemed a threat to those powers. He was born under Caesar Augustus, at a time when hope wafted through the Roman Empire. More than any other ruler, Augustus raised the expectations of what a leader could accomplish and what a society could achieve. It was Augustus, in fact, who first borrowed the Greek word for "Gospel" or "Good News" and applied it as a label for the new world order represented by his reign. The empire declared him a god and established rites of worship. His enlightened and stable regime, many believed, would last forever, a final solution to the problem of government.

Meanwhile, in an obscure corner of Augustus's empire the birth of a baby named Jesus was overlooked by the chroniclers of the day. We know about him mainly through four books written years after his death, at a time when less than one-half of one percent of the Roman world had ever heard of him. Jesus' biographers would also borrow the word *gospel*, proclaiming a different kind of new world order altogether. They would mention Augustus only once, a passing reference to set the date of a census that ensured Jesus would be born in Bethlehem.

The earliest events in Jesus' life, though, give a menacing preview of the unlikely struggle now under way. Herod the Great, King of the Jews, enforced Roman rule at the local level, and in an irony of history we know Herod's name mainly because of the massacre of the innocents. I have never seen a Christmas card depicting that state-sponsored act of terror, but it too was a part of Christ's coming. Although secular history does not refer to the atrocity, no one acquainted with the life of Herod doubts him capable. He killed two brothers-in-law, his own wife Mariamne, and two of his own sons. Five days before his death he ordered the arrest of many citizens and decreed that they be executed on the day of his death, in order to guarantee a proper atmosphere of mourning in the country. For such a despot, a minor extermination procedure in Bethlehem posed no problem.

Scarcely a day passed, in fact, without an execution under Herod's regime. The political climate at the time of Jesus' birth resembled that of Russia in the 1930s under Stalin. Citizens could not gather in public meetings. Spies were everywhere. In Herod's mind, the command to slaughter Bethlehem's infants was probably an act of utmost rationality, a rearguard action to preserve the stability of his kingdom against a rumored invasion from another.

In *For the Time Being,* W. H. Auden projects what might have been going on inside Herod's mind as he mused about ordering the massacre:

> Today has been one of those perfect winter days, cold, brilliant, and utterly still, when the bark of a shepherd's dog carries for miles, and the great wild mountains come up quite close to the city walls, and the mind feels intensely awake, and this evening as I stand at this window high up in the citadel there is

nothing in the whole magnificent panorama of plain and mountains to indicate that the Empire is threatened by a danger more dreadful than any invasion of Tartar on racing camels or conspiracy of the Praetorian Guard. . . .

O dear, Why couldn't this wretched infant be born somewhere else?

And so Jesus the Christ entered the world amid strife and terror, and spent his infancy hidden in Egypt as a refugee. Matthew notes that local politics even determined where Jesus would grow up. When Herod the Great died, an angel reported to Joseph it was safe for him to return to Israel, but not to the region where Herod's son Archelaus had taken command. Joseph moved his family instead to Nazareth in the north, where they lived under the domain of another of Herod's sons, Antipas, the one Jesus would call "that fox," and also the one who would have John the Baptist beheaded.

A few years later the Romans took over direct command of the southern province that encompassed Jerusalem, and the cruelest and most notorious of these governors was a man named Pontius Pilate. Well-connected, Pilate had married the granddaughter of Augustus Caesar. According to Luke, Herod Antipas and the Roman governor Pilate regarded each other as enemies until the day fate brought them together to determine the destiny of Jesus. On that day they collaborated, hoping to succeed where Herod the Great had failed: by disposing of the strange pretender and thus preserving the kingdom.

From beginning to end, the conflict between Rome and Jesus appeared to be entirely one-sided. The execution of Jesus would put an apparent end to any threat, or so it was assumed at the time. Tyranny would win again. It occurred to no one that his stubborn followers just might outlast the Roman empire.

The facts of Christmas, rhymed in carols, recited by children in church plays, illustrated on cards, have become so familiar that it is easy to miss the message behind the facts. After reading the birth stories once more, I ask myself, *If Jesus came to reveal God to us, then what do I learn about God from that first Christmas?*

The word associations that come to mind as I ponder that question take me by surprise. Humble, approachable, underdog, courageous—these hardly seem appropriate words to apply to deity.

Humble. Before Jesus, almost no pagan author had used "humble" as a compliment. Yet the events of Christmas point inescapably to what seems like an oxymoron: a humble God. The God who came to earth came not in a raging whirlwind nor in a devouring fire. Unimaginably, the Maker of all things shrank down, down, down, so small as to become an ovum, a single fertilized egg barely visible to the naked eye, an egg that would divide and redivide until a fetus took shape, enlarging cell by cell inside a nervous teenager. "Immensity cloistered in thy dear womb," marveled the poet John Donne. He "made himself nothing ... he humbled himself," said the apostle Paul more prosaically.

I remember sitting one Christmas season in a beautiful auditorium in London listening to Handel's *Messiah*, with a full chorus singing about the day when "the glory of the Lord shall be revealed." I had spent the morning in museums viewing remnants of England's glory—the crown jewels, a solid gold ruler's mace, the Lord Mayor's gilded carriage—and it occurred to me that just such images of wealth and power must have filled the minds of Isaiah's contemporaries who first heard that promise. When the Jews read Isaiah's words, no doubt they thought back with sharp nostalgia to the glory days of Solomon, when "the king made silver as common in Jerusalem as stones."

The Messiah who showed up, however, wore a different kind of glory, the glory of humility. "'God is great,' the cry of the Moslems, is a truth which needed no supernatural being to teach men," writes Father Neville Figgis. "That *God is little*, that is the truth which Jesus taught man." The God who roared, who could order armies and empires about like pawns on a chessboard, this God emerged in Palestine as a baby who could not speak or eat solid food or control his bladder, who depended on a teenager for shelter, food, and love.

In London, looking toward the auditorium's royal box where the queen and her family sat, I caught glimpses of the more typical way rulers stride through the world: with bodyguards, and a trumpet fanfare, and a flourish of bright clothes and flashing jewelry. Queen Elizabeth II had recently visited the United States, and reporters delighted in spelling out the logistics involved: her four thousand pounds of luggage included two outfits for every occasion, a mourning outfit in case someone died, forty pints of plasma, and white kid leather toilet seat covers. She brought along her own hairdresser, two valets, and a host of other attendants. A brief visit of royalty to a foreign country can easily cost twenty million dollars.

In meek contrast, God's visit to earth took place in an animal shelter with no attendants present and nowhere to lay the newborn king but a feed trough. Indeed, the event that divided history, and even our calendars, into two parts may have had more animal than human witnesses. A mule could have stepped on him. "How silently, how silently, the wondrous gift is given."

For just an instant the sky grew luminous with angels, yet who saw that spectacle? Illiterate hirelings who watched the flocks of others, "nobodies" who failed to leave their names. Shepherds had such a randy reputation that proper Jews lumped them together with the "godless," restricting them to the outer courtyards of the temple. Fittingly, it was they whom God selected to help celebrate the birth of one who would be known as the friend of sinners.

In Auden's poem the wise men proclaim, "O here and now our endless journey stops." The shepherds say, "O here and now our endless journey starts." The search for worldly wisdom has ended; true life has just begun.

Approachable. Those of us raised in a tradition of informal or private prayer may not appreciate the change Jesus wrought in how human beings approach deity. Hindus offer sacrifices at the temple. Kneeling Muslims bow down so low that their foreheads touch the ground. In most religious traditions, in fact, *fear* is the primary emotion when one approaches God.

Certainly the Jews associated fear with worship. The burning bush of Moses, the hot coals of Isaiah, the extraterrestrial visions of Ezekiel—a person "blessed" with a direct encounter with God expected to come away scorched or glowing or maybe half-crippled like Jacob. These were the fortunate ones: Jewish children also learned stories of the sacred mountain in the desert that proved fatal to everyone who touched it. Mishandle the ark of the covenant, and you died. Enter the Most Holy Place, and you'd never come out alive.

Among people who walled off a separate sanctum for God in the temple and shrank from pronouncing or spelling out the name, God made a surprise appearance as a baby in a manger. What can be less scary than a newborn with his limbs wrapped tight against his body? In Jesus, God found a way of relating to human beings that did not involve fear.

In truth, fear had never worked very well. The Old Testament includes far more low points than high ones. A new approach was needed, a New Covenant, to use the words of the Bible, one that would not emphasize the vast gulf between God and humanity but instead would span it.

A friend of mine named Kathy was using a "Can you guess?" game to help her six-year-old learn the different animals. His turn: "I'm thinking of a mammal. He's big and he does magic." Kathy thought for a while and then gave up. "I don't know." "It's Jesus!" said her son in triumph. The answer seemed irreverent at the time, Kathy told me, but later as she thought about it she realized her son had hit upon an unsettling insight into the depths of incarnation: Jesus as a mammal!

I learned about incarnation when I kept a salt-water aquarium. Management of a marine aquarium, I discovered, is no easy task. I had to run a portable chemical laboratory to monitor the nitrate levels and the ammonia content. I pumped in vitamins and antibiotics and sulfa drugs and enough enzymes to make a rock grow. I filtered the water through glass fibers and charcoal, and exposed it to ultraviolet light. You would think, in view of all the energy expended on their behalf, that my fish would at least be grateful. Not so. Every time my shadow loomed above the tank they dove for cover into the nearest shell. They showed me one "emotion" only: fear. Although I opened the lid and dropped in food on a regular schedule, three times a day, they responded to each visit as a sure sign of my designs to torture them. I could not convince them of my true concern.

To my fish I was deity. I was too large for them, my actions too incomprehensible. My acts of mercy they saw as cruelty; my attempts at healing they viewed as destruction. To change their perceptions, I began to see, would require a form of incarnation. I would have to become a fish and "speak" to them in a language they could understand.

A human being becoming a fish is nothing compared to God becoming a baby. And yet according to the Gospels that is what happened at Bethlehem. The God who created matter took shape within it, as an artist might become a spot on a painting or a playwright a character within his own play. God wrote a story, only using real characters, on the pages of real history. The Word became flesh.

Underdog. I wince even as I write the word, especially in connection with Jesus. It's a crude word, probably derived from dogfighting and applied over time to predictable losers and victims of injustice. Yet as I read the birth stories about Jesus I cannot help but conclude that though the world may be tilted toward the rich and powerful, God is tilted toward the underdog. "He has brought down rulers from their thrones but has lifted up the humble. He has filled the hungry with good things but has sent the rich away empty," said Mary in her Magnificat hymn.

Laszlo Tokes, the Romanian pastor whose mistreatment outraged the country and prompted rebellion against the Communist ruler Ceausescu, tells of trying to prepare a Christmas sermon for the tiny mountain church to which he had been exiled. The state police were rounding up dissidents, and violence was breaking out across the country. Afraid for his life, Tokes bolted his doors, sat down, and read again the stories in Luke and Matthew. Unlike most pastors who would preach that Christmas, he chose as his text the verses describing Herod's massacre of the innocents. It was the single passage that spoke most directly to his parishioners. Oppression, fear, and violence, the daily plight of the underdog, they well understood.

The next day, Christmas, news broke that Ceausescu had been arrested. Church bells rang, and joy broke out all over Romania. Another King Herod had fallen. Tokes recalls, "All the events of the Christmas story now had a new, brilliant dimension for us, a dimension of history rooted in the reality of our lives.... For those of us who lived through them, the days of Christmas 1989 represented a rich, resonant embroidery of the Christmas story, a time when the providence of God and the foolishness of human wickedness seemed as easy to comprehend as the sun and the moon over the timeless Transylvanian hills." For the first time in four decades, Romania celebrated Christmas as a public holiday.

Perhaps the best way to perceive the "underdog" nature of the incarnation is to transpose it into terms we can relate to today. An unwed mother, homeless, was forced to look for shelter while traveling to meet the heavy taxation demands of a colonial government. She lived in a land recovering from violent civil wars and still in turmoil—a situation much like that in modern Bosnia, Rwanda, or Somalia. Like half of all mothers who deliver today, she gave birth in Asia, in its far western corner, the part of the world that would prove least receptive to the son she bore. That son became a refugee in Africa, the continent where most refugees can still be found.

I wonder what Mary thought about her militant Magnificat hymn during her harrowing years in Egypt. For a Jew, Egypt evoked bright memories of a powerful God who had flattened a pharaoh's army and brought liberation; now Mary fled there, desperate, a stranger in a strange land hiding from her own government. Could her baby, hunted, helpless, on the run, possibly fulfill the lavish hopes of his people?

Even the family's mother-tongue summoned up memories of their underdog status: Jesus spoke Aramaic, a trade language closely related to Arabic, a stinging reminder of the Jews' subjection to foreign empires. Some foreign astrologers (probably from the region that is now Iraq) had dropped by to visit Jesus, but these men were considered "unclean" by Jews of the day. Naturally, like all dignitaries they had checked first with the ruling king in Jerusalem, who knew nothing about a baby in Bethlehem. After they saw the child and realized who he was, these visitors engaged in an act of civil disobedience: they deceived Herod and went home another way, to protect the child. They had chosen Jesus' side, against the powerful.

Growing up, Jesus' sensibilities were affected most deeply by the poor, the powerless, the oppressed—in short, the underdogs. Today theologians debate the aptness of the phrase "God's preferential option for the poor" as a way of describing God's concern for the underdog. Since God arranged the circumstances in which to be born on planet earth—without power or wealth, without rights, without justice—his preferential options speak for themselves.

Courageous. In 1993 I read a news report about a "Messiah sighting" in the Crown Heights section of Brooklyn, New York. Twenty thousand Lubavitcher Hasidic Jews live in Crown Heights, and in 1993 many of them believed the Messiah was dwelling among them in the person of Rabbi Menachem Mendel Schneerson.

Word of the Rabbi's public appearance spread like a flash fire through the streets of Crown Heights, and Lubavitchers in their black coats and curly sideburns were soon dashing down the sidewalks toward the synagogue where the Rabbi customarily prayed. Those lucky enough to be connected to a network of beepers got a head start, sprinting toward the synagogue the instant they felt a slight vibration. They jammed by the hundreds into a main hall, elbowing each other and even climbing the pillars to create more room. The hall filled with an air of anticipation and frenzy normally found at a championship sporting event, not a religious service.

The Rabbi was ninety-one years old. He had suffered a stroke the year before and had not been able to speak since. When the curtain finally pulled back, those who had crowded into the synagogue saw a frail old man in a long beard who could do little but wave, tilt his head, and move his eyebrows. No one in the audience seemed to mind, though. "Long live our master, our teacher, and our rabbi, King, Messiah, forever and ever!" they sang in unison, over and over, building in volume until the Rabbi made a small, delphic gesture with his hand, and the curtain closed. They departed slowly, savoring the moment, in a state of ecstasy.*

When I first read the news account I nearly laughed out loud. Who are these people trying to kid—a nonagenarian mute Messiah in Brooklyn? And then it struck me: I was reacting to Rabbi Schneer-

---

*Rabbi Schneerson died in June 1994. Now many Lubavitchers are anticipating his bodily resurrection.

son exactly as people in the first century had reacted to Jesus. A Messiah from Galilee? A carpenter's kid, no less?

The scorn I felt as I read about the Rabbi and his fanatical followers gave me a clue to the responses Jesus faced throughout his life. His neighbors asked, "Isn't his mother's name Mary, and aren't his brothers James, Joseph, Simon, and Judas? Where did this man get this wisdom and these miraculous powers?" Other countrymen scoffed, "Nazareth! Can anything good come from there?" His own family tried to put him away, believing he was out of his mind. The religious experts sought to kill him. As for the whipsaw commoners, one moment they judged him "demon-possessed and raving mad," the next they forcibly tried to crown him king.

It took courage, I believe, for God to lay aside power and glory and to take a place among human beings who would greet him with the same mixture of haughtiness and skepticism that I felt when I first heard about Rabbi Schneerson of Brooklyn. It took courage to risk descent to a planet known for its clumsy violence, among a race known for rejecting its prophets. What more foolhardy thing could God have done?

The first night in Bethlehem required courage as well. How did God the Father feel that night, helpless as any human father, watching his Son emerge smeared with blood to face a harsh, cold world? Lines from two different Christmas carols play in my mind. One, "The little Lord Jesus, no crying he makes," seems to me a sanitized version of what took place in Bethlehem. I imagine Jesus cried like any other baby the night he entered the world, a world that would give him much reason to cry as an adult. The second, a line from "O Little Town of Bethlehem," seems as profoundly true today as it did two thousand years ago: "The hopes and fears of all the world do rest on thee tonight."

"Alone of all creeds, Christianity has added courage to the virtues of the Creator," said G. K. Chesterton. The need for such courage began with Jesus' first night on earth and did not end until his last.

There is one more view of Christmas I have never seen on a Christmas card, probably because no artist, not even William Blake, could do it justice. Revelation 12 pulls back the curtain to give us a glimpse of Christmas as it must have looked from somewhere far beyond Andromeda: Christmas from the angels' viewpoint.

The account differs radically from the birth stories in the Gospels. Revelation does not mention shepherds and an infanticidal king; rather, it pictures a dragon leading a ferocious struggle in heaven. A woman clothed with the sun and wearing a crown of twelve stars cries out in pain as she is about to give birth. Suddenly the enormous red dragon enters the picture, his tail sweeping a third of the stars out of the sky and flinging them to the earth. He crouches hungrily before the woman, anxious to devour her child the moment it is born. At the last second the infant is snatched away to safety, the woman flees into the desert, and all-out cosmic war begins.

Revelation is a strange book by any measure, and readers must understand its style to make sense of this extraordinary spectacle. In daily life two parallel histories occur simultaneously, one on earth and one in heaven. Revelation, however, views them together, allowing a quick look behind the scenes. On earth a baby was born, a king got wind of it, a chase ensued. In heaven the Great Invasion had begun, a daring raid by the ruler of the forces of good into the universe's seat of evil.

John Milton expressed this point of view majestically in *Paradise Lost* and *Paradise Regained*, poems which make heaven and hell the central focus and earth a mere battleground for their clashes. The modern author J. B. Phillips also attempted such a point of view, on a much less epic scale, and last Christmas I turned to Phillips's fantasy to try to escape my earthbound viewpoint.

In Phillips's version, a senior angel is showing a very young angel around the splendors of the universe. They view whirling galaxies and blazing suns, and then flit across the infinite distances of space until at last they enter one particular galaxy of 500 billion stars.

> As the two of them drew near to the star which we call our sun and to its circling planets, the senior angel pointed to a small and rather insignificant sphere turning very slowly on its axis. It looked as dull as a dirty tennis-ball to the little angel, whose mind was filled with the size and glory of what he had seen.

"I want you to watch that one particularly," said the senior angel, pointing with his finger.

"Well, it looks very small and rather dirty to me," said the little angel. "What's special about that one?"

When I read Phillips's fantasy, I thought of the pictures beamed back to earth from the Apollo astronauts, who described our planet as "whole and round and beautiful and small," a blue-green-and-tan globe suspended in space. Jim Lovell, reflecting on the scene later, said, "It was just another body, really, about four times bigger than the moon. But it held all the hope and all the life and all the things that the crew of Apollo 8 knew and loved. It was the most beautiful thing there was to see in all the heavens." That was the viewpoint of a human being.

To the little angel, though, earth did not seem so impressive. He listened in stunned disbelief as the senior angel told him that this planet, small and insignificant and not overly clean, was the renowned Visited Planet.

"Do you mean that our great and glorious Prince ... went down in Person to this fifth-rate little ball? Why should He do a thing like that?" ...

The little angel's face wrinkled in disgust. "Do you mean to tell me," he said, "that He stooped so low as to become one of those creeping, crawling creatures of that floating ball?"

"I do, and I don't think He would like you to call them 'creeping, crawling creatures' in that tone of voice. For, strange as it may seem to us, He loves them. He went down to visit them to lift them up to become like Him."

The little angel looked blank. Such a thought was almost beyond his comprehension.

It is almost beyond my comprehension too, and yet I accept that this notion is the key to understanding Christmas and is, in fact, the touchstone of my faith. As a Christian I believe that we live in parallel worlds. One world consists of hills and lakes and barns and politicians and shepherds watching their flocks by night. The other consists of angels and sinister forces and somewhere out there places called heaven and hell. One night in the cold, in the dark, among the wrinkled hills of Bethlehem, those two worlds came together at a dramatic point of intersection. God, who knows no before or after, entered time and space. God, who knows no boundaries took on the shocking confines of a baby's skin, the ominous restraints of mortality.

"He is the image of the invisible God, the firstborn over all creation," an apostle would later write; "He is before all things, and in him all things hold together." But the few eyewitnesses on Christmas night saw none of that. They saw an infant struggling to work never-before-used lungs.

Could it be true, this Bethlehem story of a Creator descending to be born on one small planet? If so, it is a story like no other. Never again need we wonder whether what happens on this dirty little tennis ball of a planet matters to the rest of the universe. Little wonder a choir of angels broke out in spontaneous song, disturbing not only a few shepherds but the entire universe.

3
Background:
Jewish Roots and Soil

This again is a great contradiction: though he was a Jew, his followers were not Jews.

Voltaire

3
Background: Jewish Roots and Soil

As a boy growing up in a WASP community in Atlanta, Georgia, I did not know a single Jew. I pictured Jews as foreigners with thick accents and strange hats who lived in Brooklyn or some such faraway place where they all studied to become psychiatrists and musicians. I knew the Jews had something to do with World War II, but I had heard little about the Holocaust. Certainly these people had no relation to my Jesus.

Not until my early twenties did I befriend a Jewish photographer who disabused me of many notions about his race. One night when we stayed up late talking, he described what it was like to lose twenty-seven members of his family to the Holocaust. Later, he acquainted me with Elie Wiesel, Chaim Potok, Martin Buber, and other Jewish writers, and after these encounters I began reading the New Testament through new eyes. How could I have missed it! Jesus' true-blue Jewishness leaps out from Matthew's very first sentence, which introduces him as "the son of David, son of Abraham."

In church we affirmed Jesus as "the only-begotten Son of God, begotten of his Father before all worlds ... Very God of Very God." Those creedal statements, though, are light-years removed from the Gospels' account of Jesus growing up in a Jewish family in the agricultural town of Nazareth. I later learned that not even converted

Jews—who might have rooted Jesus more solidly in Jewish soil—were invited to the Council of Chalcedon that composed the creed. We Gentiles face the constant danger of letting Jesus' Jewishness, and even his humanity, slip away.

In historical fact, we are the ones who have co-opted *their* Jesus. As I got to know Jesus, the realization sank in that he probably did not spend his life among Jews in the first century merely to save Americans in the twentieth. Alone of all people in history, he had the privilege of choosing where and when to be born, and he chose a pious Jewish family living in a backwater protectorate of a pagan empire. I can no more understand Jesus apart from his Jewishness than I can understand Gandhi apart from his Indianness. I need to go back, way back, and picture Jesus as a first-century Jew with a phylactery on his wrist and Palestinian dust on his sandals.

Martin Buber said, "We Jews know [Jesus] in a way—in the impulses and emotions of his essential Jewishness—that remains inaccessible to the Gentiles subject to him." He is right, of course. To know Jesus' story I must, in the same way I get to know anyone else's story, learn something of his culture, family, and background.

Following this principle, Matthew opens his gospel not as I might be tempted to begin, with a teaser on "How this book will change your life," but rather with a dry list of names, the genealogy of Jesus. Matthew chose a representative sampling from forty-two generations of Jesus in order to establish Jesus' royal bloodline. Much like the shabby descendants of deposed European royalty, the peasant family of Joseph and Mary could trace their lineage back to some impressive ancestors, including Israel's greatest king, David, and its original founder, Abraham.*

---

*Matthew's list of names also lets some skeletons out of the closet. Consider the women mentioned (a rarity in Jewish genealogies). At least three of the four were foreigners, which may have been Matthew's way of hinting that Jesus held out universal promise. The Jewish Messiah had gentile blood!

Tamar, a childless widow, had to dress like a prostitute and seduce her father-in-law in order to produce her contribution to Jesus' line. Rahab did not merely pre-

Jesus grew up during a time of resurgent "Jewish pride." In a backlash against the pressure to embrace Greek culture, families had recently begun adopting names that harked back to the times of the patriarchs and the Exodus from Egypt (not unlike ethnic Americans who choose African or Hispanic names for their children). Thus Mary was named for Miriam, the sister of Moses, and Joseph was named after one of the twelve sons of Jacob, as were Jesus' four brothers.

Jesus' own name comes from the word *Joshua*—"he shall save"— a common name in those days. (As major-league baseball rosters reveal, the name Jesus remains popular among Latin Americans.) Its very ordinariness, not unlike "Bob" or "Joe" today, must have grated on Jewish ears in the first century as they listened to Jesus' words. Jews did not pronounce the Honorable Name of GOD, save for the high priest one day a year, and even today Orthodox Jews carefully spell out G_D. For people raised in such a tradition, the idea that an ordinary person with a name like Jesus could be the Son of God and Savior of the world seemed utterly scandalous. Jesus was a man, for goodness' sake, Mary's boy.

Signs of Jesus' Jewishness surface throughout the Gospels. He was circumcised as a baby. Significantly, the one scene included from Jesus' childhood shows his family attending an obligatory festival in Jerusalem, several days' journey from their home. As an adult Jesus worshiped in the synagogue and temple, followed Jewish customs, and spoke in terms his fellow Jews would understand. Even his controversies with other Jews, such as the Pharisees, underscored the fact that they expected him to share their values and act more like them.

As the German theologian Jürgen Moltmann has pointed out, if Jesus had lived during the Third Reich, very likely he would have been branded like other Jews and shipped to the gas chambers. A pogrom of his own time, Herod's massacre of infants, was specifically targeted against Jesus.

---

tend, but actually made her living as a prostitute. And "Uriah's wife," or Bathsheba, was the object of David's lust, which led to the most famous royal scandal of the Old Testament. These shady ancestors show that Jesus entered human history in the raw, a willing descendant of its shame. In contrast, Herod the Great, reigning king at Jesus' birth, had his genealogical records destroyed out of vanity because he wanted no one to compare his background with others'.

A rabbi friend mentioned to me that Christians perceive Jesus' cry from the cross, "My God, my God why have you forsaken me?" as a profound moment of struggle between Father and Son; Jews, however, hear those words as the death cry of yet another Jewish victim. Jesus was not the first and certainly not the last Jew to cry out words from the Psalms at a time of torture.

Yet a strange reversal occurred within a few generations of Jesus' life. With rare exceptions, Jews stopped following him and the church became thoroughly Gentile. What happened? It seems clear to me that Jesus failed to meet the expectations of Messiah the Jews were awaiting.

It would be impossible to exaggerate the import of the word *Messiah* among faithful Jews. The Dead Sea Scrolls discovered in 1947 confirm that the Qumram community imminently expected a Messiah-like figure, setting aside an empty seat for him each day at the sacred meal. Audacious as it may be to dream that a tiny province wedged in among great powers would produce a worldwide ruler, nonetheless Jews believed just that. They staked their future on a king who would lead their nation back to glory.

During Jesus' lifetime, revolt was in the air. Pseudo-messiahs periodically emerged to lead rebellions, only to be crushed in ruthless crackdowns. To take just one example, a prophet known as "the Egyptian" attracted multitudes into the wilderness where he proclaimed that at his command the walls of Jerusalem would fall; the Roman governor sent a detachment of soldiers after them and killed four thousand of the rebels.

When another report spread that the long-awaited prophet had turned up in the desert, crowds flocked to see the wild man dressed in camel skin. "I am not the Christ [Messiah]," insisted John the Baptist, who then proceeded to raise hopes even higher by speaking in exalted terms of one who would soon appear. John's question of Jesus, "Are you the one who was to come, or shall we expect someone else?" was in a real sense the question of the age, whispered everywhere.

Every Hebrew prophet had taught that someday God would install his kingdom on earth, and that is why rumors about the "Son of David" so inflamed Jewish hopes. God would prove in person that he had not forsaken them. He would, as Isaiah had cried, "rend the heavens and come down, that the mountains would tremble before you! . . . come down to cause the nations to quake before you."

But let us be honest. When the one John pointed to arrived on the scene, neither the mountains trembled nor the nations quaked. Jesus did not come close to satisfying the lavish hopes of the Jews. The opposite happened: within a generation Roman soldiers razed Jerusalem to the ground. The young Christian church accepted the destruction of the temple as a sign of the end of the covenant between God and Israel, and after the first century very few Jews converted to Christianity. Christians appropriated Jewish Scriptures, renaming them "Old Testament," and put an end to most Jewish customs.

Rejected by the church, blamed for Jesus' death, some Jews began a counter-campaign against the Christians. They spread a rumor that Jesus was the illegitimate offspring of Mary's liaison with a Roman soldier, and wrote a cruel parody of the Gospels. Jesus was hanged on the eve of Passover, said one report, because "he hath practiced sorcery and beguiled and led astray Israel." The man whose birth angels celebrated with a proclamation of peace on earth became the great divide of human history.

A few years ago I met with ten Christians, ten Jews, and ten Muslims in New Orleans. The psychiatrist and author M. Scott Peck had invited us there to see if we could overcome our differences enough to produce some sort of community. Each faith held a worship service—Muslims on Friday, Jews on Saturday, Christians on Sunday—which the others were invited to observe. The services had striking similarities and reminded us how much the three faiths have in common. Perhaps the intensity of feeling among the three traditions stems from a common heritage: family disputes are always the stubbornest, and civil wars the bloodiest.

I learned a new word in New Orleans: *supersessionism.* The Jews resented the notion that Christian faith had superseded Judaism. "I feel like a curiosity of history, as if my religion should be put in a nursing home," said one. "It grates on me to hear the term 'Old Testament God' or even 'Old' Testament, for that matter." Christians had also taken over the word Messiah, or at least its Greek equivalent, "Christ." One rabbi told of growing up in the only Jewish household in a small Virginia town. Each year the Christians asked his father, a respected member of the community (and, as a Jew, impartial in judgment), to rank the displays of Christmas lights and decide which houses deserved prizes. As a young boy, this rabbi drove with his father past every house in town, staring with longing and incomprehension at the bright displays of *Christ*-mas lights: literally, "Messiah lights."

I had not realized that Muslims look on both faiths with a supersessionist attitude. As they see it, just as Christianity grew out of and incorporated parts of Judaism, Islam grew out of and incorporated parts of both religions. Abraham was a prophet, Jesus was a prophet, but Muhammad was The Prophet. The Old Testament has a place, as does the New Testament, but the Qur'an is "the final revelation." Hearing my own faith talked about in such paternalistic terms gave me insight into how Jews have felt for two millennia.

I also realized, after listening to three faiths articulate their differences, how deep is the divide that Jesus introduced. The Muslim worship service consisted mostly of reverential prayers to the Almighty. The Jewish service incorporated readings from Psalms and the Torah and some warmhearted singing. Any of those elements can be faithful in a Christian service. What divided us from the others was the celebration of the Lord's Supper. "This is my body, broken for you," our leader read, before distributing the bread—Christ's body, the divergence point.

When Muslims conquered Asia Minor they converted many Christian churches into mosques, carving this stern inscription for the admonition of any remaining Christians: "God did not beget and is not begotten." The same phrase could be painted on synagogue walls. The great divide of history traces back to Bethlehem and Jerusalem. Was Jesus really Messiah, the Son of God? As the Jews in New

Orleans explained, a Messiah who dies at the age of thirty-three, a nation that goes downhill after its Savior's death, a world that grows more fractured, not less—these facts do not seem to add up for the members of Jesus' own race.

Nevertheless, despite two thousand years of the great divide, despite all that has taken place in this century of violent anti-Semitism, interest in Jesus is resurging among the Jews. In 1925, when the Hebrew scholar Joseph Klausner decided to write a book about Jesus, he could find only three full-length treatments of Jesus' life by contemporary Jewish scholars. Now there are hundreds, including some of the most illuminating studies available. Modern Israeli schoolchildren learn that Jesus was a great teacher, perhaps the greatest Jewish teacher, who was subsequently "co-opted" by the Gentiles.

Is it possible to read the Gospels without blinders on? Jews read with suspicion, preparing to be scandalized. Christians read through the refracted lenses of church history. Both groups, I believe, would do well to pause and reflect on Matthew's first words, "A record of the genealogy of Jesus Christ, son of David, son of Abraham." The son of David speaks of Jesus' messianic line, which Jews should not ignore; "a title which he would not deny to save his life cannot have been without significance for him," notes C. H. Dodd. The son of Abraham speaks of Jesus' Jewish line, which we Christians dare not ignore either. Jaroslav Pelikan writes,

> Would there have been such anti-Semitism, would there have been so many pogroms, would there have been an Auschwitz, if every Christian church and every Christian home had focused its devotion and icons of Mary not only as Mother of God and Queen of Heaven but as the Jewish maiden and the new Miriam, and on icons of Christ not only as a Pantocrator but as *Rabbi Jeshua bar-Joseph*, Rabbi Jesus of Nazareth?

Growing up, I did not know a single Jew. I do now. I know something of their culture. The close ties that keep sacred holidays alive even for families who no longer believe in their meaning. The passionate arguments that at first intimidated me but soon attracted me as a style of personal engagement. The respect, even reverence, for legalism amid a society that mainly values autonomy. The tradition of scholarship that has helped sustain a culture despite others' relentless attempts to obliterate it. The ability to link arms and dance and sing and laugh even when the world offers scant reason for celebration.

This was the culture Jesus grew up in, a Jewish culture. Yes, he changed it, but always from his starting point as a Jew. Now when I find myself wondering what Jesus was like as a teenager, I think of Jewish boys I know in Chicago. And when the thought jars me, I remember that in his own day Jesus got the opposite reaction. A Jewish teenager, surely—but the Son of God?

Not only did Jesus choose a race, he also chose a time and place in which to be born. History became, in Bonhoeffer's phrase, "the womb of the birth of God." Why that particular history? I sometimes wonder why Jesus did not come in modern times, when he could have taken advantage of mass communications. Or back in Isaiah's day, when expectations for the Messiah also ran high and Israel was still an independent nation. What about the first century made it the right time to ease God into the world?

Every age has its prevailing mood: the sunny confidence of the nineteenth century, the violent chaos of the twentieth. In the era of Jesus' birth, at the height of the Roman Empire, hope and optimism held sway. As in the Soviet Union before its breakup or the British Empire in Queen Victoria's day, Rome kept peace at the point of a sword, but by and large even the conquered peoples cooperated. Except in Palestine, that is.

Anticipation soared for "a new order of the ages" at the time of Jesus' birth. The Roman poet Virgil coined that phrase, sounding like an Old Testament prophet as he declared that "a new human race is descending from the heights of heaven," a change that would come about due to "the birth of a child, with whom the iron age of humanity will end and the golden age begin." Virgil wrote these messianic words not about Jesus, however, but about Caesar Augustus, the "present deity," the "restorer of the world," who had managed to reunite the empire after the civil war sparked by Julius Caesar's assassination.

To loyal Roman subjects Augustus offered peace, security, and entertainment: in two words, bread and circuses. The Pax Romana assured that citizens had protection from outside enemies and enjoyed the benefits of Roman justice and civil government. Meanwhile, a Greek soul filled the Roman body politic. People throughout the empire dressed like the Greeks, built their buildings in the Greek style, played Greek sports, and spoke the Greek language. Except in Palestine.

Palestine, the one lump the anaconda could not digest, exasperated Rome to no end. Contrary to Roman tolerance for many gods, the Jews held tenaciously to the notion of one God, their God, who had revealed to them a distinct culture as the Chosen People. William Barclay describes what happened when these two societies collided. "It is the simple historical fact that in the thirty years from 67 to 37 B.C. before the emergence of Herod the Great, no fewer than one hundred and fifty thousand men perished in Palestine in revolutionary uprisings. There was no more explosive and inflammable country in the world than Palestine."

Jews resisted Hellenization (imposed Greek culture) as fiercely as they fought the Roman legions. Rabbis kept this aversion alive by reminding Jews of the attempts by a Seleucid madman named Antiochus to Hellenize the Jews more than a century before. Antiochus had compelled young boys to undergo reverse circumcision operations so they could appear nude in Greek athletic contests. He flogged an aged priest to death for refusing to eat pig's flesh, and butchered a mother and her seven children for not bowing down to an image. In a heinous act that became known as the "abomination of desolation," he invaded the Most Holy Place of the temple, sacrificed an unclean pig on the altar in honor of the Greek god Zeus, and smeared the sanctuary with its blood.

Antiochus's campaign failed miserably, driving Jews to an open revolt led by the Maccabeans. (Jews still celebrate Hanukkah in memory of this victory.) For nearly a century, in fact, the Maccabeans held off foreign invaders, until the Roman juggernaut rolled into Palestine. It took thirty years for Roman armies to quash all signs of rebellion; then they installed the local strongman Herod as their puppet "King of the Jews." As Herod watched the Romans killing women and children in their houses, markets, and even in the temple, he asked a general, "Would the Romans deprive the city of all its inhabitants and possessions and leave me a king of the wilderness?" Almost. By the time Herod ascended the throne, not only Jerusalem but the entire country lay in ruins.

Herod the Great still reigned when Jesus was born. Comparatively, Palestine stayed quiet under his iron thumb, for the long wars had drained both the spirit and resources of the Jews. An earthquake in 31 B.C. killed 30,000 people and much livestock, leading to more destitution. The Jews called such tragedies "pangs of the Messiah" and pled with God for a deliverer.

It is difficult to find a modern parallel, now that the Soviet empire has collapsed, to the brittle situation the Jews faced under Roman rule. Tibet under China perhaps? The blacks in South Africa before they gained freedom from minority rule? The most provocative suggestion comes from visitors to modern Israel, who cannot help noticing the similar plights of Galilean Jews in Jesus' day and Palestinians in modern times. Both served the economic interests of their richer neighbors. Both lived in small hamlets, or refugee camps, in the midst of a more modern and alien culture. Both were subject to curfews, crackdowns, and discrimination.

As Malcolm Muggeridge observed in the 1970s, "The role of the Roman legionnaires had been taken over by the Israeli army. Now it was the Arabs who were in the position of a subject people; entitled, like the Jews in Jesus' lifetime, to attend their mosques and practise their religion, but otherwise treated like second-class citizens."

Both groups, modern Palestinians and Galilean Jews, also share a susceptibility to hotheads who would call them to armed revolt. Think of the modern Middle East with all its violence, intrigues, and squabbling parties. Into such an incendiary environment, Jesus was born.

The journey from Judea to Galilee in springtime is a journey from brown to green, from an arid, rocky terrain to some of the lushest fields in the Mediterranean basin. Fruits and vegetables grow in abundance, fishermen work the Sea of Galilee, and beyond rolling hills to the west lies the shimmering blue of the Mediterranean itself. Jesus' hometown of Nazareth, so obscure that it does not make the list of sixty-three Galilean towns mentioned in the Talmud, sits on a hillside 1,300 feet above sea level. The view from a ridge allows a sweeping panorama all the way from Mt. Carmel by the ocean to the snowy peak of Mt. Hermon to the north.

With fertile land, beautiful vistas, and moderate climate, Galilee had its attractions, and clearly Jesus enjoyed his childhood there. The wildflowers and weeds growing among the crops, the laborious method of separating wheat and chaff, the fig trees and grapevines dotting the hillsides, the fields white unto harvest—all these would show up later in his parables and sayings. Just as telling, some obvious features of Galilee did not show up. A mere three miles north, in easy view of Nazareth, sat the gleaming city of Sepphoris, just then in the process of being rebuilt. Jesus' neighbors—perhaps his own father— were employed in building trades there.

For most of Jesus' life, construction crews worked on this beautiful Greco-Roman metropolis, which featured colonnaded streets, a forum, a palace, a bath and gymnasium, and luxurious villas, all constructed in white limestone and colored marble. In an imposing theater that seated four thousand, Greek actors, or *hypocritēs*, entertained the multinational crowds. (Jesus would later borrow the word to describe one who played a false role in public.) During Jesus' lifetime Sepphoris served as Galilee's capital, second in importance only to Jerusalem in all of Palestine. Not once, however, do the Gospels record that Jesus visited or even mentioned the city. Nor did he visit Tiberias, Herod's winter resort town situated nearby on the shore of Lake Galilee. He gave centers of wealth and political power a wide berth.

Although Herod the Great managed to make Galilee the most prosperous province in Palestine, only a few reaped the benefits. Landless peasants mainly served the interests of wealthy landlords (another fact that would surface in Jesus' parables). An illness or back-to-back seasons of bad weather would bring disaster to most families. We know that Jesus was raised in poverty: his family could not afford a lamb for the sacrifice at the temple and offered instead a pair of doves or two young pigeons.

Galilee had a reputation as a breeding ground for revolutionaries. In 4 B.C., around the time of Jesus' birth, a rebel broke into the arsenal in Sepphoris and looted it to arm his followers. Roman troops recaptured and burned the town—which explains why it had to be rebuilt—crucifying two thousand Jews who had participated in the uprising. Ten years later another rebel, named Judas, incited a revolt, urging his countrymen to pay no taxes to the pagan Roman emperor. He helped found the Zealot party which would harass Rome for the next six decades. Two of Judas's sons would be crucified after Jesus' death, and his last son would ultimately capture the stronghold of Masada from the Romans, vowing to defend it until every last Jew had died. In the end, 960 Jewish men, women, and children took their own lives rather than fall captive to the Romans. Galileans were freedom-lovers to the core.

For all its prosperity and political activism, Galilee got little respect from the rest of the country. It was the farthest province from Jerusalem and the most backward culturally. Rabbinic literature of the time portrays Galileans as bumpkins, fodder for ethnic jokes. Galileans who learned Hebrew pronounced it so crudely that they were not called on to read the Torah in other synagogues. Speaking the common language of Aramaic in a slipshod way was a telltale sign of Galilean roots (as Simon Peter would one day find out, betrayed in a courtyard by his rural accent). The Aramaic words preserved in the Gospels show that Jesus, too, spoke in that northern dialect, no doubt encouraging skepticism about him. "How can the Christ come from Galilee?" "Nazareth! Can anything good come from there?"

Other Jews regarded Galilee as lax about spiritual matters as well. One Pharisee, after eighteen fruitless years there, lamented, "Galilee, Galilee, you hate the Torah!" Nicodemus, who stuck up for Jesus, was silenced by the rebuke, "Are you from Galilee, too? Look into it, and you will find that a prophet does not come out of Galilee." Jesus' own brothers encouraged him, "You ought to leave here and go to Judea." From the perspective of the religious power base in Jerusalem, Galilee seemed a most unlikely place for the Messiah to arise.

As I read the Gospels, I try to project myself back into those times. How would I have responded to oppression? Would I strive to be a model citizen and keep out of trouble, to live and let live? Would I be tempted by fiery insurrectionists like the Zealots? Would I fight back in more devious ways, by avoiding taxes perhaps? Or would I throw my energies into a religious movement and shun political controversies? What kind of Jew would I have made in the first century?

Eight million Jews lived in the Roman Empire then, just over a quarter of them in Palestine itself,* and sometimes they stretched Roman forbearance to the breaking point. Romans branded Jews "atheists" for their refusal to honor Greek and Roman gods, and regarded them as social misfits because of their peculiar customs: Jews refused to eat the "unclean" food of their neighbors, eschewed all business on Friday evenings and Saturdays, and disdained civic office. Nevertheless, Rome had granted Judaism legal status.

In many ways the plight of Jewish leaders resembled that of the Russian churches under Stalin. They could cooperate, which meant submitting to government interference, or they could go their own way, which meant harsh persecution. Herod the Great fit the Stalin pattern well, keeping the religious community in a state of suspicion and terror through his network of spies. "His High Priests he changed as he might change his clothes," complained one Jewish writer.

In response, the Jews splintered into parties that followed different paths of collaboration or separatism. These were the parties who would follow Jesus around, listening to him, testing him, taking his measure.

The Essenes were the most separate of all. Pacifistic, they did not actively resist Herod or the Romans, but rather withdrew into monkish communities in the caves of a barren desert. Convinced that the Roman invasion had come as a punishment for their failure to keep the Law, they devoted themselves to purity. The Essenes took ritual baths every day, maintained a strict diet, did not defecate on the Sabbath, wore no jewelry, took no oaths, and held all material goods in common. They hoped their faithfulness would encourage the advent of the Messiah.

---

*Due largely to the Holocaust, the number of Jews is approximately the same nineteen centuries later, and the same proportion lives in Palestine.

Zealots, representing a different strategy of separatism, advocated armed revolt to throw out impure foreigners. One branch of the Zealots specialized in acts of political terrorism against the Romans while another operated as a kind of "morals police" to keep fellow Jews in line. In an early version of ethnic cleansing, the Zealots declared that anyone who married into another race should be lynched. During Jesus' years of ministry, observers surely would have noted that his group of disciples included Simon the Zealot. On the other hand, Jesus' social contacts with Gentiles and foreigners, not to mention parables like the Good Samaritan, would have driven the jingoistic Zealots to fury.

At the other extreme, collaborationists tried to work within the system. The Romans had granted limited authority to a Jewish council called the Sanhedrin, and in return for their privileges the Sanhedrin cooperated with Romans in scouting out any sign of insurrection. It was in their best interests to prevent uprisings and the harsh reprisals they would surely bring.

The Jewish historian Josephus tells of a mentally ill peasant who would cry out "Woe to Jerusalem!" in the midst of popular festivals, agitating the crowds. The Sanhedrin tried punishing him, to no avail, so they turned him over to the Roman governor for a proper flogging. He was flayed to the bone and peace was restored. In the same vein, the Sanhedrin sent representatives to examine John the Baptist and Jesus. Did they represent a true threat to the peace? If so, should they be turned in to the Romans? Caiphas, the high priest, perfectly captured the collaborationist point of view: "It is better for you that one man die for the people than that the whole nation perish."

Sadducees were the most blatant collaborationists. They had first Hellenized under the Greeks, and then cooperated in turn with Maccabeans, Romans, and now Herod. Humanistic in theology, the Sadducees did not believe in an afterlife or divine intervention on this earth. What happens, happens, and since there is no future system of reward and punishment, a person might as well enjoy the limited time on earth. From the palatial homes and silver and gold kitchen utensils that archaeologists have uncovered, it appears that Sadducees enjoyed life very well indeed. Of all parties in Palestine, the mandarin Sadducees had the most to lose from any threat to the status quo.

Pharisees, the popular party of the middle class, often found themselves on the fence, vacillating between separatism and collaboration. They held to high standards of purity, particularly on such matters as Sabbath observance, ritual cleanliness, and the exact time of feast days. They treated nonobservant Jews "as Gentiles," shutting them out of local councils, boycotting their businesses, and ostracizing them from meals and social affairs. Yet the Pharisees had already suffered their share of persecution: in one instance eight hundred Pharisees were crucified on a single day. Although they believed passionately in the Messiah, Pharisees hesitated to follow too quickly after any impostor or miracle worker who might bring disaster on the nation.

The Pharisees picked their battles carefully, putting their lives on the line only when necessary. Once, Pontius Pilate spurned a prior agreement with the Jews that Roman troops would not enter Jerusalem carrying standards that bore an image ("icon") of the emperor. The Pharisees regarded this act as idolatry. In protest a crowd of Jews, mostly Pharisees, stood outside Pilate's palace for five days and nights in a kind of sit-down strike, weeping and begging him to change. Pilate ordered them to the hippodrome, where soldiers lay in ambush, and threatened to put to death any who did not cease their begging. As one, they fell on their faces, bared their necks, and announced they were prepared to die rather than have their laws broken. Pilate backed down.

As I consider each one of these groups, I conclude that most likely I would have ended up in the party of Pharisees. I would have admired their pragmatic approach to the ruling government, balanced by their willingness to stand up for principle. Orderly people, the Pharisees produced good citizens.* Radicals like the Essenes and

---

*Scholars have debated why the Gospels record so much conflict between Jesus and the Pharisees, when actually he had more in common with them than with the Sadducees, Essenes, or Zealots. One explanation is that the Gospels were written several decades after Jesus' death. By then Jerusalem had been destroyed and the other parties had virtually disappeared. Understandably, the gospel writers focused on the sole surviving threat to Christians, the Pharisees.

Zealots would have made me nervous; the Sadducees I would have scorned as opportunists. Thus as a sympathizer of the Pharisees, I would have stood on the edge of Jesus' audience, watching him deal with the burning issues of the day.

Would Jesus have won me over? Much as I wish, I cannot easily answer that question. At one time or another, Jesus managed to confound and alienate each of the major groups in Palestine. He held out a third way, neither separation nor collaboration, radically changing the emphasis from the kingdom of Herod or Caesar to the kingdom of God.

Looking back now, it may seem difficult to sort out the nuances that divided one party from another, or to understand why controversy flared over minor aspects of Jesus' teaching. For all their differences, though, Essenes, Zealots, Pharisees, and even Sadducees shared one goal: to preserve what was distinctively Jewish, no matter what. To that goal, Jesus represented a threat, and I'm sure I would have perceived that threat.

The Jews were, in effect, erecting a fence around their culture in hopes of saving their tiny nation of high ideals from the pagans around them. Could God liberate them from Rome as he had once liberated them from Egypt? One tradition promised that if all Israel repented for an entire day, or if Israel kept two Sabbaths perfectly, then redemption by the Messiah would soon follow. Something of a spiritual revival was under way, spurred by a splendid new temple. Constructed on a huge platform that dominated the entire city of Jerusalem, the temple had become the focal point of national pride and hope for the future.

It was against this background that I, like other Jews, would have judged Jesus' statements about legalism, about Sabbath-keeping, and about the temple. How could I reconcile my respect for family values with a comment like, "If anyone comes to me and does not hate his father and mother, his wife and children, his brothers and sisters . . . he cannot be my disciple"? What could Jesus possibly mean? Similarly, to official Sanhedrin ears, a reported comment like "I am able to destroy the temple of God and rebuild it in three days" was no idle boast but a form of blasphemy and even treason, striking against the very thing that held Jews together. Jesus' offer to forgive a person's sin seemed to them as bizarrely inappropriate as a private individual today offering to issue someone a passport or a building permit. Who did he think he was, preempting the entire temple system?

As it turned out, Jewish fears about cultural suicide proved entirely justified. Not Jesus, but other charismatic figures would lead revolts that finally, in A.D. 70, provoked Rome to destroy the temple and level Jerusalem. The city would later be rebuilt as a Roman colony, with a temple to the god Jupiter occupying the site of the demolished Jewish temple. Jews were forbidden to enter the city on pain of death. Rome set in motion an exile that would not end until our own generation, and it changed the face of Judaism forever.

4
Temptation: Showdown in the Desert

Love consents to all and commands only those who consent. Love is abdication. God is abdication.

Simone Weil

4
Temptation: Showdown in the Desert

The Gospels assert that Jesus, the Jew who grew up in rural Galilee, was none other than God's own Son, dispatched from heaven to lead the fight against evil. With that mission in view, certain questions about Jesus' priorities immediately come to mind. At the top of the list, natural disasters: If Jesus had the power to cure illness and raise the dead, why not tackle a few macro-problems like earthquakes and hurricanes, or perhaps the whole sinister swarm of mutating viruses that plague the earth?

Philosophers and theologians blame many of the rest of earth's ills on the consequences of human freedom, which raises a whole new set of questions. Do we in fact enjoy too much freedom? We have the freedom to harm and kill each other, to fight global wars, to despoil our planet. We are even free to defy God, to live without restraints as though the other world did not exist. At the least, Jesus could have devised some irrefutable proof to silence all skeptics, tilting the odds decisively in God's favor. As it is, God seems easy to ignore or deny.

Jesus' first "official" act as an adult, when he went into the wilderness to meet the accuser face-to-face, gave him the occasion to address these problems. Satan himself tempted the Son of God to change the rules and achieve his goals by a dazzling, shortcut method. More than

Jesus' character was at stake on the sandy plains of Palestine; human history hung in the balance.

When John Milton wrote a sequel to his epic *Paradise Lost*, he made the Temptation, not the crucifixion, the hinge event in Jesus' effort to regain the world. In a garden, a man and woman had fallen for Satan's promise of a way to rise above their assigned state. Millennia later, another representative—the Second Adam, in Paul's phrase—faced a similar test, though curiously inverted. *Can you be like God?* the serpent had asked in Eden; *Can you be truly human?* asked the tempter in the desert.

As I read the Temptation story it occurs to me that, in the absence of eyewitnesses, all details must have come from Jesus himself. For some reason, Jesus felt obliged to disclose to his disciples this moment of struggle and personal weakness. I presume the Temptation was a genuine conflict, not a role Jesus acted out with a pre-arranged outcome. The same tempter who had found a fatal spot of vulnerability in Adam and Eve aimed his thrust against Jesus with deadly accuracy.

Luke sets the stage with a tone of understated drama. "Jesus, full of the Holy Spirit, returned from the Jordan and was led by the Spirit in the desert, where for forty days he was tempted by the devil. He ate nothing during those days, and at the end of them he was hungry." Like single combat warriors, two giants of the cosmos converged on a scene of desolation. One, just beginning his mission in enemy territory, arrived in a badly weakened state. The other, confident and on home turf, seized the initiative.

I puzzle over certain details of the Temptation. Satan asked Jesus to turn a stone into bread, offered him all the kingdoms of the world, and urged him to jump from a high place in order to test God's promise of physical safety. Where is the evil in these requests? The three temptations seem like Jesus' prerogatives, the very qualities to be expected in a Messiah. Would not Jesus go on to multiply bread for five thousand, a far more impressive display? He would also conquer death and rise again to become King of Kings. The three temptations do not seem evil in themselves—and yet clearly something pivotal happened in the desert.

The British poet Gerard Manley Hopkins presents the Temptation as something of a get-acquainted session between Jesus and Satan. In the dark about the Incarnation, Satan did not know for certain whether Jesus was an ordinary man or a theophany or perhaps an angel with limited powers like himself. He challenged Jesus to perform miracles as a means of scouting his adversary's powers. Martin Luther goes further, speculating that throughout his life Jesus "conducted himself so humbly and associated with sinful men and women, and as a consequence was not held in great esteem," on account of which "the devil overlooked him and did not recognize him. For the devil is farsighted; he looks only for what is big and high and attaches himself to that; he does not look at that which is low down and beneath himself."

In the gospel accounts, the single combat warriors treat each other with a kind of wary respect, like two boxers circling one another in the ring. For Jesus, the greatest strain was probably a willingness to put up with the Temptation in the first place. Why not simply destroy the tempter, saving human history from his evil plague? Jesus demurred.

For his part, Satan offered to trade away his dominion over the world in exchange for the satisfaction of prevailing over the Son of God. Although Satan posed the tests, in the end it was he who flunked them. In two tests he merely asked Jesus to prove himself; by the third he was demanding worship, something God would never accede to.

The Temptation unmasked Satan, while God remained masked. *If you are God,* said Satan, *then dazzle me. Act like God should act.* Jesus replied, *Only God makes those decisions, therefore I do nothing at your command.*

In Wim Wender's elegant films about angels (*Wings of Desire; Faraway, So Close*), celestial beings discuss together in childlike wonder what it must be like to drink coffee and digest food, to experience warmth and pain, to sense a skeleton moving as you walk, to feel the touch of another human being, to say "Ah!" and "Oh!" because not everything is known in advance, to live by minutes and hours and thus to encounter *now* instead of just forever. At the age of thirty or so, when Jesus first squared off with Satan in the desert, he had realized all those "advantages" of being human. He lived comfortably inside his suit of skin.

As I look back on the three temptations, I see that Satan proposed an enticing improvement. He tempted Jesus toward the good parts of being human without the bad: to savor the taste of bread without being subject to the fixed rules of hunger and of agriculture, to confront risk with no real danger, to enjoy fame and power without the prospect of painful rejection—in short, to wear a crown but not a cross. (The temptation that Jesus resisted, many of us, his followers, still long for.)

Apocryphal gospels, judged spurious by the church, suggest what it might have looked like had Jesus succumbed to Satan's temptations. These fantastic accounts show the child Jesus making clay sparrows that he could bring to life with a puff of breath, and dropping dried fish into water to see them miraculously start swimming. He turned his playmates into goats to teach them a lesson, and made people go blind or deaf just for the thrill of healing them. The apocryphal gospels are the second-century counterparts to modern comic books about Superboy and Batgirl. Their value lies mainly in the contrast they form with the actual Gospels, which reveal a Messiah who did not use miraculous powers to benefit himself. Beginning with the Temptation, Jesus showed a reluctance to bend the rules on earth.

Malcolm Muggeridge, while filming a documentary in Israel, found himself musing on the Temptation:

> Curiously enough, just at the right moment to begin filming, when the shadows were long enough and the light not too weak, I happened to notice near by a whole expanse of stones, all identical, and looking uncommonly like loaves well baked and brown. How easy for Jesus to have turned these stone loaves into edible ones, as, later, he would turn water into wine at a wedding feast! And, after all, why not? The Roman authorities distributed free bread to promote Caesar's kingdom, and Jesus could do the same to promote his. . . .

Jesus had but to give a nod of agreement and he could have constructed Christendom, not on four shaky Gospels and a defeated man nailed on a Cross, but on a basis of sound socio-economic planning and principles.... Every utopia could have been brought to pass, every hope have been realized and every dream been made to come true. What a benefactor, then, Jesus would have been. Acclaimed, equally, in the London School of Economics and the Harvard Business School; a statue in Parliament Square, and an even bigger one on Capitol Hill and in the Red Square.... Instead, he turned the offer down on the ground that only God should be worshipped.

As Muggeridge sees it, the Temptation revolved around the question uppermost in the minds of Jesus' countrymen: What should the Messiah look like? A People's Messiah who could turn stones into bread to feed the multitudes? A Torah Messiah, standing tall at the lofty pinnacle of the temple? A King Messiah, ruling over not just Israel but all the kingdoms of earth? In short, Satan was offering Jesus the chance to be the thundering Messiah we think we want. Certainly, I recognize in Muggeridge's description the Messiah I think I want.

We want anything but a Suffering Messiah—and so did Jesus, at one level. Satan hit closest to home with his suggestion that Jesus throw himself from a high place to test God's care. That temptation would surface again. Once, in a flash of anger Jesus gave Peter a strong rebuke. "Out of my sight, Satan!" he said. "You do not have in mind the things of God, but the things of men." Peter had recoiled at Jesus' prediction of suffering and death—"Never, Lord! This shall never happen to you!"—and that instinctively protective reaction had hit a nerve. In Peter's words, Jesus heard again the allure of Satan tempting him toward an easier way.

Nailed to the cross, Jesus would hear the last temptation repeated as a taunt. A criminal scoffed, "Aren't you the Christ? Save yourself and us." Spectators took up the cry: "Let him come down from the cross, and we will believe in him.... Let God rescue him now if he wants him." But there was no rescue, no miracle, no easy, painless path. For Jesus to save others, quite simply, he could not save himself. That fact, he must have known as he faced Satan in the desert.

* * *

My own temptations tend to involve common vices such as lust and greed. As I reflect on Jesus' temptations, though, I realize they centered on his reason for coming to earth, his "style" of working. Satan was, in effect, dangling before Jesus a speeded-up way of accomplishing his mission. He could win over the crowds by creating food on demand and then take control of the kingdoms of the world, all the while protecting himself from danger. "Why move thy feet so slow to what is best?" Satan jeered in Milton's version.

I first found this insight in the writings of Dostoevsky, who made the Temptation scene the centerpiece of his great novel *The Brothers Karamazov*. The agnostic brother Ivan Karamazov writes a poem called "The Grand Inquisitor" set in sixteenth-century Seville at the height of the Inquisition. In the poem, a disguised Jesus visits the city at a time when heretics are daily being burned at the stake. The Grand Inquisitor, a cardinal, "an old man, almost ninety, tall and erect, with a withered face and sunken eyes," recognizes Jesus and has him thrown into prison. There, the two visit in a scene intentionally reminiscent of the Temptation in the desert.

The Inquisitor has an accusation to make: by turning down the three temptations, Jesus forfeited the three greatest powers at his disposal, "miracle, mystery, and authority." He should have followed Satan's advice and performed the miracles on demand in order to increase his fame among the people. He should have welcomed the offer of authority and power. Did Jesus not realize that people want more than anything else to worship what is established beyond dispute? "Instead of taking possession of men's freedom, you increased it, and burdened the spiritual kingdom of mankind with its sufferings forever. You desired man's free love, that he should follow you freely, enticed and taken captive by you."

By resisting Satan's temptations to override human freedom, the Inquisitor maintains, Jesus made himself far too easy to reject. He surrendered his greatest advantage: the power to compel belief. Fortunately, continues the sly Inquisitor, the church recognized the error and corrected it, and has been relying on miracle, mystery, and authority ever since. For this reason, the Inquisitor must execute Jesus one more time, lest he hinder the church's work.

The scene from *Karamazov* has added poignancy because at the time of its composition, communist revolutionaries were organizing themselves in Russia. As Dostoevsky noted, they too would borrow techniques from the church. They promised to turn stones into bread and to guarantee safety and security for all citizens in exchange for one simple thing: their freedom. Communism would become the new church in Russia, one likewise founded on miracle, mystery, and authority.

More than a century after Dostoevsky wrote this chilling dialogue about power and freedom, I had the opportunity to visit his homeland and observe in person the results of seven decades of Communist rule. I went in November of 1991, when the Soviet empire was crumbling, Mikhail Gorbachev was giving way to Boris Yeltsin, and the entire nation was trying to rediscover itself. The iron grasp of power had loosened, and people were now reveling in the freedom to say whatever they wished.

I remember vividly a meeting with the editors of *Pravda*, formerly the official mouthpiece of the Communist Party. *Pravda* as much as any institution had slavishly served the Communist "church." Now, though, *Pravda*'s circulation was falling dramatically (from eleven million to 700,000) in concert with communism's fall from grace. The editors of *Pravda* seemed earnest, sincere, searching—and shaken to the core. So shaken that they were now asking advice from emissaries of a religion their founder had scorned as "the opiate of the people."

The editors remarked wistfully that Christianity and communism have many of the same ideals: equality, sharing, justice, and racial harmony. Yet they had to admit the Marxist pursuit of that vision had produced the worst nightmares the world has ever seen. Why?

"We don't know how to motivate people to show compassion," said the editor-in-chief. "We tried raising money for the children of Chernobyl, but the average Russian citizen would rather spend his money on drink. How do you reform and motivate people? How do you get them to be good?"

Seventy-four years of communism had proved beyond all doubt that goodness could not be legislated from the Kremlin and enforced at the point of a gun. In a heavy irony, attempts to compel morality tend to produce defiant subjects and tyrannical rulers who lose their moral core. I came away from Russia with the strong sense that we Christians would do well to relearn the basic lesson of the Temptation. Goodness cannot be imposed externally, from the top down; it must grow internally, from the bottom up.

The Temptation in the desert reveals a profound difference between God's power and Satan's power. Satan has the power to coerce, to dazzle, to force obedience, to destroy. Humans have learned much from that power, and governments draw deeply from its reservoir. With a bullwhip or a billy club or an AK−47, human beings can force other human beings to do just about anything they want. Satan's power is external and coercive.

God's power, in contrast, is internal and noncoercive. "You would not enslave man by a miracle, and craved faith given freely, not based on miracle," said the Inquisitor to Jesus in Dostoevsky's novel. Such power may seem at times like weakness. In its commitment to transform gently from the inside out and in its relentless dependence on human choice, God's power may resemble a kind of abdication. As every parent and every lover knows, love can be rendered powerless if the beloved chooses to spurn it.

"God is not a Nazi," said Thomas Merton. Indeed God is not. The Master of the universe would become its victim, powerless before a squad of soldiers in a garden. God made himself weak for one purpose: to let human beings choose freely for themselves what to do with him.*

Søren Kierkegaard wrote about God's light touch: "Omnipotence which can lay its hand so heavily upon the world can also make its touch so light that the creature receives independence." Sometimes, I concede, I wish that God used a heavier touch. My faith suffers from too much freedom, too many temptations to disbelieve. At times I

---

*In Dorothy Sayers' play *The Man Born to Be King*, King Herod tells the Magi, "You cannot rule men by love. When you find your king, tell him so. Only three things will govern a people—fear and greed and the promise of security." King Herod understood the management principles Satan operates by, the same ones Jesus declined in the wilderness.

want God to overwhelm me, to overcome my doubts with certainty, to give final proofs of his existence and his concern.

I want God to take a more active role in human affairs as well. If God had merely reached down and flicked Saddam Hussein off the throne, how many lives would have been saved in the Gulf War? If God had done the same with Hitler, how many Jews would have been spared? Why must God "sit on his hands"?

I want God to take a more active role in my personal history too. I want quick and spectacular answers to my prayers, healing for my diseases, protection and safety for my loved ones. I want a God without ambiguity, One to whom I can point for the sake of my doubting friends.

When I think these thoughts, I recognize in myself a thin, hollow echo of the challenge that Satan hurled at Jesus two thousand years ago. God resists those temptations now as Jesus resisted them on earth, settling instead for a slower, gentler way. In George MacDonald's words,

> Instead of crushing the power of evil by divine force; instead of compelling justice and destroying the wicked; instead of making peace on earth by the rule of a perfect prince; instead of gathering the children of Jerusalem under His wings whether they would or not, and saving them from the horrors that anguished His prophetic soul—He let evil work its will while it lived; He contented Himself with the slow unencouraging ways of help essential; making men good; casting out, not merely controlling Satan....
>
> To love righteousness is to make it grow, not to avenge it.... He resisted every impulse to work more rapidly for a lower good.

"O Jerusalem, Jerusalem," Jesus cried, in the scene MacDonald alludes to, "how often I have longed to gather your children together, as a hen gathers her chicks under her wings, but you were not willing." The disciples had proposed that Jesus call down fire on unrepentant cities; in contrast, Jesus uttered a cry of helplessness, an astonishing "if only" from the lips of the Son of God. He would not force himself on those who were not willing.

The more I get to know Jesus, the more impressed I am by what Ivan Karamazov called "the miracle of restraint." The miracles Satan suggested, the signs and wonders the Pharisees demanded, the final proofs I yearn for—these would offer no serious obstacle to an omnipotent God. More amazing is his *refusal* to perform and to overwhelm. God's terrible insistence on human freedom is so absolute that he granted us the power to live as though he did not exist, to spit in his face, to crucify him. All this Jesus must have known as he faced down the tempter in the desert, focusing his mighty power on the energy of restraint.

I believe God insists on such restraint because no pyrotechnic displays of omnipotence will achieve the response he desires. Although power can force obedience, only love can summon a response of love, which is the one thing God wants from us and the reason he created us. "I, when I am lifted up from the earth, will draw all men to myself," Jesus said. In case we miss the point John adds, "He said this to show the kind of death he was going to die." God's nature is self-giving; he bases his appeal on sacrificial love.

I remember one afternoon in Chicago sitting in an outdoor restaurant listening to a broken man relate the story of his prodigal son. Jake, the son, could not keep a job. He wasted all his money on drugs and alcohol. He rarely called home, and brought little joy and much grief to both parents. Jake's father described to me his feeling of helplessness in words not unlike those Jesus used about Jerusalem. "If only I could bring him back, and shelter him and try to show how much I love him," he said. He paused to gain control of his voice, then added, "The strange thing is, even though he rejects me, Jake's love means more to me than that of my other three, responsible children. Odd, isn't it? That's how love is."

I sense in that final four-word sentence more insight into the mystery of God's restraint than I have found in any book of theodicy. Why does God content himself with the slow, unencouraging way of making righteousness grow rather than avenging it? *That's how love is.* Love has its own power, the only power ultimately capable of conquering the human heart.

* * *

Though rebuffed in all three temptations, Satan may well have departed from the confrontation wearing a smirk. Jesus' steadfast refusal to play by Satan's rules meant that Satan himself could continue playing by those rules. He still had the kingdoms of the world at his disposal, after all, and now he had learned a lesson about God's restraint. Restraint by God creates opportunity for those opposed to God.

Other skirmishes would come, of course. Jesus would forcibly cast out demons, but the Spirit he replaced them with was far less possessive and depended always on the will of the one possessed. Occasions for mischief abounded: Jesus admitted as much in his analogy of the kingdom of God growing up in the midst of evil, like wheat among the weeds.

From Satan's perspective, the Temptation offered a new lease on life. The kids from *Lord of the Flies* could roam the island awhile longer, apparently free of adult authority. Furthermore, God could be blamed for what went wrong. If God insisted on sitting on his hands while devilment like the Crusades and the Holocaust went on, why not blame the Parent, not the kids?

It occurs to me that by turning down the temptations in the desert, Jesus put God's own reputation at risk. God has promised to restore earth to perfection one day, but what about the meantime? The swamp of human history, the brutality even of church history, the apocalypse to come—are all these worth the divine restraint? To put it bluntly, is human freedom worth the cost?

No one who lives in the midst of the restoration process, not at its end, can answer that question fairly. All I can do is recall that Jesus, a single combat warrior facing Evil head-on with the power to destroy it, chose a different way. For him, preserving the free will of a notoriously flawed species seemed worth the cost. The choice could not have been easy, for it involved his own pain as well as his followers'.

As I survey the rest of Jesus' life, I see that the pattern of restraint established in the desert persisted throughout his life. I never sense Jesus twisting a person's arm. Rather, he stated the consequences of a choice, then threw the decision back to the other party. He answered a wealthy man's question with uncompromising words and then let him walk away. Mark pointedly adds this comment: "Jesus looked at him and loved him." Jesus had a realistic view of how the world would respond to him: "Because of the increase of wickedness, the love of most will grow cold."

We sometimes use the term "savior complex" to describe an unhealthy syndrome of obsession over curing others' problems. The true Savior, however, seemed remarkably free of such a complex. He had no compulsion to convert the entire world in his lifetime or to cure people who were not ready to be cured. In Milton's words, Jesus "held it more humane, more heavenly first / By winning words to conquer willing hearts, / And make persuasion do the work of fear."

In short, Jesus showed an incredible respect for human freedom. When Satan asked for the chance to test Peter and sift him as wheat, even then Jesus did not refuse the request. His response: "I have prayed for you, Simon, that your faith may not fail." When the crowds turned away and many disciples deserted him, Jesus said to the Twelve, almost plaintively, "You do not want to leave too, do you?" As his life moved toward doom in Jerusalem, he exposed Judas but did not try to prevent his evil deed—that, too, a consequence of restraint.

"Take up your *cross* and follow me," Jesus said, in the least manipulative invitation that has ever been given.

This quality of restraint in Jesus—one could almost call it a divine shyness came over me slowly. I realized, as I absorbed the story of Jesus in the Gospels, that I had expected from him the same qualities I had met in the southern fundamentalist church of my childhood. There, I often felt the victim of emotional pressures. Doctrine was dished out in a "Believe and don't ask questions!" style. Wielding the power of miracle, mystery, and authority, the church left no place for doubt. I also learned manipulative techniques for "soul-winning," some of which involved misrepresenting myself to the person I was talking to. Yet now I am unable to find any of these qualities in the life of Jesus.

If I read church history correctly, many other followers of Jesus have yielded to the very temptations he resisted. Dostoevsky shrewdly replayed the Temptation scene in the torture cell of the Grand Inquisitor. How could a church founded by the One who withstood the Temptation carry out an Inquisition of forced belief that lasted half a millennium? Meanwhile, in a milder Protestant version in the city of Geneva, officials were making attendance at church compulsory and refusal to take the Eucharist a crime. Heretics there, too, were burned at the stake.

To its shame, Christian history reveals unrelieved attempts to improve on the way of Christ. Sometimes the church joins hands with a government that offers a shortcut path to power. "The worship of success is generally *the* form of idol worship which the devil cultivates most assiduously," wrote Helmut Thielicke about the German church's early infatuation with Adolf Hitler. "We could observe in the first years after 1933 the almost suggestive compulsion that emanates from great successes and how, under the influence of these successes, men, even Christians, stopped asking in whose name and at what price...."

Sometimes the church grows its own mini-Hitlers, men with names like Jim Jones and David Koresh, who understand all too well the power represented in miracle, mystery, and authority. And sometimes the church simply borrows the tools of manipulation perfected by politicians, salesmen, and advertising copywriters.

I am quick to diagnose these flaws. Yet when I turn from church history and examine myself, I find that I too am vulnerable to the Temptation. I lack the willpower to resist shortcut solutions to human needs. I lack the patience to allow God to work in a slow, "gentlemanly" way. I want to seize control myself, to compel others to help accomplish the causes I believe in. I am willing to trade away certain freedoms for the guarantee of safety and protection. I am willing to trade away even more for the chance to realize my ambitions.

When I feel those temptations rising within me, I return to the story of Jesus and Satan in the desert. Jesus' resistance against Satan's temptations preserved for me the very freedom I exercise when I face my own temptations. I pray for the same trust and patience that Jesus showed. And I rejoice that, as Hebrews said, "We do not have a high priest who is unable to sympathize with our weaknesses, but we have one who has been tempted in every way, just as we are—yet without sin. . . . Because he himself suffered when he was tempted, he is able to help those who are being tempted."

5
Profile: What Would I Have Noticed?

Everything in Christ astonishes me. His spirit overawes me, and his will confounds me. Between him and whoever else in the world, there is no possible term of comparison. He is truly a being by himself. . . . I search in vain in history to find the similar to Jesus Christ, or anything which can approach the gospel. Neither history, nor humanity, nor the ages, nor nature, offer me anything with which I am able to compare it or to explain it. Here everything is extraordinary.

Napoleon

5
Profile: What Would I Have Noticed?

The Apostles' Creed hustles through Jesus' life in one paragraph, beginning with his birth and skipping immediately to his death, descent into hell, and ascent into heaven. Wait a minute—isn't something missing? What happened in the interval between his being born of the Virgin Mary and his suffering under Pontius Pilate? Somehow everything Jesus said and did in thirty-three years on earth gets swept aside in the rush to interpret his life. How did he spend his time here?

Memories from Sunday school actually detract from my efforts to picture Jesus' everyday life, for he was rendered in lifeless flannel-board scenes. There he is teaching. That's him holding a lamb. Now he's talking with a Samaritan woman and, look, another conversation with a man named Nicodemus. The closest thing to action came when the disciples in their miniature sailboats bobbed across the blue flannelboard sea. I remember one scene of Jesus standing in the temple with a whip in his hand, but it matched nothing else I had learned about him. I certainly never saw him at a party. I may have learned facts about Jesus' life in Sunday school, but as a person he remained remote and two-dimensional.

Movies about Jesus helped bring him to life for me. Some of them, such as *Jesus of Nazareth* by Zeffirelli, take great pains to recreate settings faithful to the gospel accounts. Unlike the placid flannelgraph

scenes, the movies show Jesus in action, surrounded by unruly spectators who jostle each other for a better view and press their demands
on him.

As I watch these movies, and then return to the Gospels, I try to
place myself in my familiar role as a journalist, or at least the first-century equivalent. I stand on the margins, listening and taking notes, intent
to capture something of Jesus in my reports, while at the same time aware
he is having an effect on me personally. What do I see? What impresses
me? Disturbs me? How can I convey him to my readers?

I cannot begin where I normally begin in reporting on a person,
by describing what my subject looked like. No one knows. The first
semi-realistic portraits of Jesus did not come until the fifth century,
and these were pure speculation; until then the Greeks had portrayed
him as a young, beardless figure resembling the god Apollo.

In 1514 someone forged a document under the name of Publius
Lentulus, the Roman governor who succeeded Pontius Pilate, which
contained this description of Jesus:

> He is a tall man, well shaped and of an amiable and reverend
> aspect; his hair is of a color that can hardly be matched, falling into
> graceful curls ... parted on the crown of his head, running as a
> stream to the front after the fashion of the Nazarites; his forehead
> high, large and imposing; his cheeks without spot or wrinkle, beau-
> tiful with a lovely red; his nose and mouth formed with exquisite
> symmetry, like beard, and of a color suitable to his hair, reaching
> below his chin and parted in the middle like a fork; his eyes bright
> blue, clear and serene....

I recognize that Jesus from the oil paintings hanging on the
concrete-block walls of my childhood church. The forger gave himself away, however, with his next sentence: "No man has seen him
laugh." Was he reading the same Gospels that I read, documents that
say not a word about Jesus' physical appearance yet depict him per-
forming his first miracle at a wedding, giving playful nicknames to his
disciples, and somehow gaining a reputation as a "gluttonous man and

a wine-bibber"? When the pious criticized his disciples for their laxity in spiritual disciplines, Jesus replied, "How can the guests of the bridegroom fast while he is with them?" Of all the images he could have chosen for himself, Jesus settled on that of the groom whose radiance cheers up the entire wedding party.

I once showed to a class several dozen art slides portraying Jesus in a variety of forms—African, Korean, Chinese—and then asked the class to describe what they thought Jesus looked like. Virtually everyone suggested he was tall (unlikely for a first-century Jew), most said handsome, and no one said overweight. I showed a BBC film on the life of Christ that featured a pudgy actor in the title role, and some in the class found it offensive. We prefer a tall, handsome, and, above all, slender Jesus.

One tradition dating back to the second century suggested Jesus was a hunchback. In the Middle Ages, Christians widely believed that Jesus had suffered from leprosy. Most Christians today would find such notions repulsive and perhaps heretical. Was he not a perfect specimen of humanity? Yet in all the Bible I can find only one physical description of sorts, a prophecy written hundreds of years before Christ's birth. Here is Isaiah's portrayal, in the midst of a passage that the New Testament applies to the life of Jesus:

> Just as there were many who were appalled at him—his appearance was so disfigured beyond that of any man and his form marred beyond human likeness. . . . He had no beauty or majesty to attract us to him, nothing in his appearance that we should desire him. He was despised and rejected by men, a man of sorrows, and familiar with suffering. Like one from whom men hide their faces he was despised, and we esteemed him not.

Because of the Gospels' silence, we cannot answer with certainty the basic question of what Jesus looked like. That is a good thing, I believe. Our glamorized representations of Jesus say more about us than about him. He had no supernatural glow about him: John the Baptist admitted he never would have recognized Jesus apart from special revelation. According to Isaiah, we cannot point to his beauty or majesty or anything else in his appearance to explain his attraction. The key lies elsewhere.

* * *

I move beyond physical appearance to consider what Jesus was like as a person. How would he have scored on a personality profile test?

The personality that emerges from the Gospels differs radically from the image of Jesus I grew up with, an image I now recognize in some of the older Hollywood films about Jesus. In those films, Jesus recites his lines evenly and without emotion. He strides through life as the one calm character among a cast of flustered extras. Nothing rattles him. He dispenses wisdom in flat, measured tones. He is, in short, the Prozac Jesus.

In contrast, the Gospels present a man who has such charisma that people will sit three days straight, without food, just to hear his riveting words. He seems excitable, impulsively "moved with compassion" or "filled with pity." The Gospels reveal a range of Jesus' emotional responses: sudden sympathy for a person with leprosy, exuberance over his disciples' successes, a blast of anger at coldhearted legalists, grief over an unreceptive city, and then those awful cries of anguish in Gethsemane and on the cross. He had nearly inexhaustible patience with individuals but no patience at all with institutions and injustice.

I once attended a men's movement retreat designed to help men "get in touch with their emotions" and break out of restrictive stereotypes of masculinity. As I sat in a small group, listening to other men tell of their struggles to express themselves and to experience true intimacy, I realized that Jesus lived out an ideal for masculine fulfillment that nineteen centuries later still eludes most men. Three times, at least, he cried in front of his disciples. He did not hide his fears or hesitate to ask for help: "My soul is overwhelmed with sorrow to the point of death," he told them in Gethsemane; "Stay here and keep watch with me." How many strong leaders today would make themselves so vulnerable?

Unlike most men I know, Jesus also loved to praise other people. When he worked a miracle, he often deflected credit back on the recipient: "Your faith has healed you." He called Nathanael "a true Israelite, in whom there is nothing false." Of John the Baptist, he said there was none greater born of women. Volatile Peter he renamed "the Rock." When a cringing woman offered him an extravagant act of devotion, Jesus defended her against critics and said the story of her generosity would be told forever.

The Gospels show that Jesus quickly established intimacy with the people he met. Whether talking with a woman at a well, a religious leader in a garden, or a fisherman by a lake, he cut instantly to the heart of the matter, and after a few brief lines of conversation these people revealed to Jesus their innermost secrets. People of his day tended to keep rabbis and "holy men" at a respectful distance, but Jesus drew out something else, a hunger so deep that people crowded around him just to touch his clothes.

Novelist Mary Gordon mentions Jesus' sensitivity to women and children as one of the main qualities that attracted her: "Surely, He is the only affectionate hero in literature. Who can imagine an affectionate Odysseus, Aeneas?" To Jesus' aside to the daughters of Jerusalem, "Alas for women with child in those days," Gordon responds, "I knew I wanted children; I felt those words were for me. Now I think: how many men would take into consideration the hardships of pregnancy and nursing?"

Jesus did not mechanically follow a list of "Things I Gotta Do Today," and I doubt he would have appreciated our modern emphasis on punctuality and precise scheduling. He attended wedding feasts that lasted for days. He let himself get distracted by any "nobody" he came across, whether a hemorrhaging woman who shyly touched his robe or a blind beggar who made a nuisance of himself. Two of his most impressive miracles (the raising of Lazarus and of Jairus's daughter) took place because he arrived too late to heal the sick person.

Jesus was "the man for others," in Bonhoeffer's fine phrase. He kept himself free—free for the other person. He would accept almost anybody's invitation to dinner, and as a result no public figure had a more diverse list of friends, ranging from rich people, Roman centurions, and Pharisees to tax collectors, prostitutes, and leprosy victims. People *liked* being with Jesus; where he was, joy was.

And yet, for all these qualities that point toward what psychologists like to call self-actualization, Jesus broke the mold. As C. S.

Lewis puts it, "He was not at all like the psychologist's picture of the integrated, balanced, adjusted, happily married, employed, popular citizen. You can't really be very well 'adjusted' to your world if it says you 'have a devil' and ends by nailing you up naked to a stake of wood."

Like most of Jesus' contemporaries, no doubt I would have balked at the odd combination of extravagant claims coming from an ordinary-looking Jewish man. He claimed to be the Son of God, and yet he ate and drank like other men, and even got tired and lonely. What kind of creature was he?

In some ways Jesus seemed to feel "at home" here, and in other ways he felt unequivocally "not at home." I think of the single scene preserved from his adolescence, when he disappeared in Jerusalem and got scolded by his mother. The cryptic record of her Jewish-mother response, "Son, why have you treated us like this?" probably does not do justice to the scene—his parents had, after all, been searching for three days. Jesus replied, "Why were you searching for me? Didn't you know I had to be in my Father's house?" Already a cleft, a conflict of loyalties, was dividing Jesus and his family.

Living on a planet of free will and rebellion, Jesus often must have felt "not at home." At such times he went aside and prayed, as if to breathe pure air from a life-support system that would give him the strength to continue living on a polluted planet. Yet he did not always get formulaic answers to his prayers. Luke reports that he prayed all night before choosing the twelve disciples—even so, the group included a traitor. In Gethsemane he prayed at first that the cup of suffering be taken from him, but of course it was not. That scene in the garden shows a man desperately "not at home," yet resisting all temptations toward supernatural rescue.

For me, one scene in the Gospels brings together the "at home" and "not at home" nature of Jesus. A storm blew up on the Sea of Galilee, nearly capsizing the boat in which Jesus lay sleeping. He stood up and yelled into the wind and spray, "Quiet! Be still!" The disciples shrank back in terror. What kind of person could shout to the weather as if correcting an unruly child?

The display of power in the midst of a storm helped convince the disciples that Jesus was unlike any other man. Yet it also hints at the depths of Incarnation. "God is vulnerable," said the philosopher Jacques Maritain. Jesus had, after all, fallen asleep from sheer fatigue. Moreover, the Son of God was, but for this one instance of miracle, one of its victims: the creator of rain clouds was rained on, the maker of stars got hot and sweaty under the Palestine sun. Jesus subjected himself to natural laws even when, at some level, they went against his desires ("If it is possible, may this cup be taken from me"). He would live, and die, by the rules of earth.

* * *

He comes as yet unknown into a hamlet of Lower Galilee. He is watched by the cold, hard eyes of peasants living long enough at subsistence level to know exactly where the line is drawn between poverty and destitution. He looks like a beggar, yet his eyes lack the proper cringe, his voice the proper whine, his walk the proper shuffle. He speaks about the rule of God, and they listen as much from curiosity as anything else. They know all about rule and power, about kingdom and empire, but they know it in terms of tax and debt, malnutrition and sickness, agrarian oppression and demonic possession. What, they really want to know, can this kingdom of God do for a lame child, a blind parent, a demented soul screaming its tortured isolation among the graves that mark the edges of the village? (John Dominic Crossan)

Jesus' neighbors soon found out what he could do for them. He made the lame child walk and the blind parent see, and exorcised demons from the demented soul among the graves. When Jesus inaugurated his ministry of healing and teaching, his neighbors scratched their heads and asked, flabbergasted, "Isn't he Mary's boy, Joseph the carpenter's son? Where did he get such wisdom and such miraculous power?"

Initially, for perhaps a year, Jesus met with great success. So many people flocked to him that he sometimes had to flee to a boat offshore. Without doubt it was the physical healings that first put him on the map. The Jews, who believed the Devil caused illness and thus holy men could be channels for God's intervention, had a long history of miracle workers. (One named Honi lived just before Jesus' time and is mentioned by the historian Josephus.) Jesus apparently knew of some rivals, for he subdued his disciples' impulse to condemn them.

About a third of the Gospels' stories about Jesus involve physical healings, and by journalistic instinct I probably would have investigated these stories, searching out medical records and interviewing the families of those who claimed a miracle. The healings were diverse and fit no real pattern. At least one person Jesus healed long-distance; some were instant and some gradual; many required the healed person to follow specific instructions.

I would have noticed in Jesus a curious ambivalence about miracles. On the one hand, Jesus healed in spontaneous response to human need: he saw a suffering person before him, felt compassion, and healed the person. Not once did he turn down a direct request for help. On the other hand, Jesus certainly did not advertise his powers. He condemned the "wicked and adulterous generation" who clamored for signs and, just as he had in the desert, resisted all temptation toward spectacle. Mark records seven separate occasions when Jesus instructed a person he had healed, "Tell no one!" In regions where people had no faith, he did no miracles.

Probably I would have speculated about what a man with such powers might have accomplished in Rome, Athens, or Alexandria. Jesus' brothers proposed that at the least he should concentrate his work in Jerusalem, Israel's capital. Jesus himself, though, preferred to keep out of the spotlight. Distrusting crowds and public opinion, he spent most of his time in towns of small size and little importance.

Despite his ambivalence, Jesus did not hesitate to use the miracles as proof of who he was: "Believe me when I say that I am in the Father and the Father is in me; or at least believe on the evidence of the miracles themselves," he told his disciples. And when his cousin John the Baptist, languishing in a jail cell, entertained doubts about whether Jesus was indeed the Messiah, Jesus gave John's disciples this message (as paraphrased by Frederick Buechner):

> You go tell John what you've seen around here. Tell him there are people who have sold their seeing-eye dogs and taken up bird-watching. Tell him there are people who've traded in aluminum walkers for hiking boots. Tell him the down-and-out have turned into the up-and-coming and a lot of dead-beats are living it up for the first time in their lives.

* * *

If I had sought a one-word label to describe Jesus to his contemporaries, I would have chosen the word *rabbi*, or teacher. In the United States now I know of no parallels to Jesus' life. Surely his style had little in common with that of modern mass evangelists, with their tents and stadia, their advance teams and billboards and direct-mail campaigns, their electronically enhanced presentations. His little band of followers, possessing no permanent base of operations, wandered from town to town without much discernible strategy.

"Foxes have holes and birds of the air have nests, but the Son of Man has no place to lay his head," Jesus said. Were they living in modern times, with the crackdown on homelessness, Jesus and his disciples would likely be harassed by police and forced to move on. Ancient times, though, knew many such teachers (there was actually a school of philosophers called the Peripatetics based on this common style of wisdom-sharing on the run).

In India I had the chance to observe in person something like the life Jesus led. There, Christian evangelists follow in the path of itinerant Hindu and Buddhist "holy men." Some hang around train stations, introducing themselves to waiting travelers and asking if they want to know more about God. Some walk from town to town, accompanied by their disciples. Others invite disciples to meet with them in *ashrams*, where together they worship and study the Scriptures.

The group Jesus led functioned with no headquarters or other property and apparently no officers except a treasurer (Judas). Financially, it seems, they barely scraped by. In order to scrounge up money for taxes, Jesus sent Peter fishing. He borrowed a coin to make a point about Caesar and had to borrow a donkey the one time he opted against traveling on foot. As his disciples walked through fields they pulled off the heads of standing grain to eat the raw kernels, taking advantage of Mosaic laws that made allowances for the poor. When Jesus met with influential people like Nicodemus or the rich young ruler it never seemed to occur to him that a person with money and influence could be of potential use.

How did Jesus support himself? In the Middle East of that day, teachers lived off the gifts of appreciative listeners. Luke points out that certain women who had been healed by Jesus—including the wife of Herod's finance minister!—helped provide for him. Touchingly, some of these women made the long and dangerous journey from Galilee to Jerusalem at the time of the Passover Feast, and stayed by Jesus at the cross after his closest disciples had deserted him.

By any account, Jesus was a master teacher. Followers were drawn by the magnetic power of his words which, in poet John Berryman's description, were "short, precise, terrible, and full of refreshment." Jesus gave his most enduring lessons on the spot, in spontaneous response to questions. A woman had seven successive husbands: Whose wife will she be in the life to come? Is it lawful to pay taxes to pagan authorities? What must I do to inherit eternal life? Who is the greatest in the kingdom of heaven? How can a man be born when he is old?

Jaroslav Pelikan tells of an old rabbi asked by his pupil, "Why is it that you rabbis so often put your teaching in the form of a question?" The rabbi shot back, "So what's wrong with a question?" Very often Jesus too deflected the question back in Socratic style, pressing the seeker toward a crisis point. His answers cut to the heart of the question and to the hearts of his listeners. I doubt I would have left any encounter with Jesus feeling smug or self-satisfied.

I would have marveled at Jesus' parables, a form that became his trademark. Writers ever since have admired his skill in communicating profound truth through such everyday stories. A scolding woman wears down the patience of a judge. A king plunges into an ill-planned war. A group of children quarrel in the street. A man is mugged and left for dead by robbers. A single woman who loses a penny acts as if she has lost everything. There are no fanciful creatures and sinuous plots in Jesus' parables; he simply describes the life around him.

The parables served Jesus' purposes perfectly. Everyone likes a good story, and Jesus' knack for storytelling held the interest of a mostly illiterate society of farmers and fishermen. Since stories are easier to remember than concepts or outlines, the parables also helped preserve his message: years later, as people reflected on what Jesus had taught, his parables came to mind in vivid detail. It is one thing to talk in abstract terms about the infinite, boundless love of God. It is quite another to tell of a man who lays down his life for friends, or of a heartsick father who scans the horizon every night for some sign of a wayward son.

Jesus came to earth "full of grace and truth," says the gospel of John, and that phrase makes a good summary of his message. First, grace: in contrast to those who tried to complicate the faith and petrify it with legalism, Jesus preached a simple message of God's love. For no reason—certainly not because we deserve it—God has decided to extend to us love that comes free of charge, no strings attached, "on the house."

In a rabbinic story of the time, the owner of a farm went into town to hire temporary workers for the harvest. The day wore on, and as late as the eleventh hour he recruited one last batch of workers, who had a mere hour remaining to prove their worth. In the familiar version of the story, the latecomers made up for lost time by working so hard that the foreman decided to reward them with a whole day's pay. Jesus' version, though, says nothing about the diligence of the workers. He accents instead the generosity of the employer—God—who lavishes his grace on veterans and newcomers alike. No one gets cheated and everyone gets rewarded, far beyond what they deserve.

Despite this emphasis on grace, no one could accuse Jesus of watering down the holiness of God. I would likely have stumbled over the truth that Jesus proclaimed, a truth more uncompromising by far than that taught by the strictest rabbis of his day. Contemporary teachers strove to "not impose a restriction upon the community unless the majority of the community will be able to stand it." Jesus had no such reticence. He broadened murder to include anger, adultery to include lust, theft to include coveting. "Be perfect, therefore, as your heavenly Father is perfect," he said, setting down an ethical standard that no one could reach.

As Elton Trueblood has observed, all the major symbols that Jesus used had a severe, even offensive quality: the yoke of burden, the cup of suffering, the towel of servanthood, and finally the cross of execution. "Count the cost," Jesus said, giving fair warning to any who dared follow him.

A modern rabbi named Jacob Neusner, the world's preeminent scholar on Judaism of the early Christian era, devoted one of his five hundred books (*A Rabbi Talks with Jesus*) to the question of how he would have responded to Jesus. Neusner has great respect for Jesus and for Christianity, and he admits that such teaching as the Sermon on the Mount leaves him "impressed—and moved." It would have quickened enough interest, he says, that he likely would have joined the crowd who followed Jesus from place to place, feasting on his wisdom.

Ultimately, though, Neusner concludes he would have parted company with the rabbi from Nazareth. "Jesus takes an important step—in the wrong direction," he says, by moving the emphasis from "us" as a Jewish community to an "I." Neusner could not go along with the shift from the Torah to Jesus himself as the central authority. "At issue is the figure of Jesus, not the teachings at all. . . . In the end the master, Jesus, makes a demand that only God makes," Respectfully, Neusner turns away, unable to make that leap of faith.

Neusner is right that Jesus' content hardly fit the pattern of other rabbis, not to mention wandering masters such as Confucius or Socrates. He was not so much seeking truth as pointing to it, by pointing to himself. In Matthew's words, "he taught as one who had authority, and not as their teachers of the law." The scribes endeavored to offer no personal opinions, rather basing their remarks on the Scriptures and approved commentaries. Jesus had many personal opinions, and used Scripture as the commentary. "You have heard that it was said . . . but I tell you . . ." went his commanding refrain. *He* was the source, and as he spoke he made no distinction between his own words and God's. His listeners understood the implication clearly, even in rejecting it. "This fellow is blaspheming!" they said.

Fearless, Jesus never backed away from a conflict. He took on hecklers and scoffers of every stripe. Once, he stood down a mob intent on stoning an adulterous woman. Another time, when guards went to seize him, they returned to the temple empty-handed: "No one ever spoke the way this man does," they said, awed by his presence. Jesus even gave direct orders to demons: "Be quiet!" "You deaf and dumb spirit, I command you, come out of him and never enter him again!" (Interestingly, the demons never failed to recognize him as the "holy one of God" or "son of the Most High"; it was human beings who questioned his identity.)

Jesus' statements about himself (I and the Father are one; I have the power to forgive sins; I will rebuild the temple in three days) were unprecedented and got him into constant trouble. Indeed, his teaching was so entwined with his person that many of his words could not have outlived him; the grand claims died with him on the cross. Disciples who had followed him as a master returned to their former lives, muttering sadly, "We had hoped that he was the one who was going to redeem Israel." It took the Resurrection to turn the proclaimer of truth into the one proclaimed.

I have placed myself on the edges of the crowd in Jesus' day, as a sincere seeker captivated by the rabbi but reluctant to commit to him. If I turn my attention from Jesus himself to the constellation of people surrounding me, I would see several groupings of onlookers forming concentric rings around him.

Farthest away, in the outer circle, are the groundlings, curiosity-seekers and others who, like me, are trying to figure out Jesus. The very presence of this multitude serves to protect Jesus: grumbling that "the whole world has gone after him," his enemies hesitate to seize him. In the early days especially, Jewish patriots hang out as well, eager for Jesus to announce a revolt against Rome. I note that Jesus never caters to this outer group. Yet he does preach to them, and that in itself distinguishes him from the Essenes and other sects, who reserve their meetings for initiates only.

Closer in, I spot a group of maybe a hundred sincere followers. Many of these traveling companions, I know, have joined up after John the Baptist's arrest—John's disciples complained that "everyone" was going over to Jesus. Spurning popularity, Jesus directs most of his comments not to the masses but to these serious seekers. He constantly pushes them toward a deeper level of commitment, with strong words that would bring anyone up short. You cannot serve two masters, he says. Forsake the love of money and the pleasures the world has to offer. Deny yourself. Serve others. Take up your cross.

That last phrase is no idle metaphor: along the roads of Palestine, Romans regularly nail up the worst criminals as an object lesson to the Jews. What kind of image could these words of "invitation" summon up in his followers' minds? Is he to lead a procession of martyrs? Apparently so. Jesus repeats one saying more than any other: "Whoever finds his life will lose it, and whoever loses his life for my sake will find it."

I have heard the closest ring of followers, the Twelve, boast that they welcome such a sacrifice. "You don't know what you are asking," Jesus replied. "Can you drink the cup I am going to drink?" "We can," they insist in their naïveté.

I sometimes ask myself if I would have wanted to join the Twelve. No matter. Unlike other rabbis, Jesus handpicked his inner circle of disciples, rather than letting them choose him. Such was Jesus' magnetism that it took only a few phrases to persuade them to leave their jobs and families to join him. Two sets of brothers—James and John, and Peter and Andrew—worked as partners on fishing boats, and when he called them they abandoned the business (ironically, after Jesus gave them their most successful fishing day ever). All but Judas Iscariot come from Jesus' home province of Galilee; Judas hails from Judea, which shows how Jesus' reputation has spread across the country.

I would have puzzled over the strange mixture represented by the Twelve. Simon the Zealot belongs to the party violently opposing Rome, while Matthew the tax collector has recently been employed by Rome's puppet ruler. No scholars like Nicodemus or wealthy patrons like Joseph of Arimethea have made it into the Twelve. One must look hard to detect any strong leadership abilities.

In my observation, in fact, the disciples' most obvious trait seems to be their denseness. "Are you so dull?" Jesus asks, and again, "How long shall I put up with you?" While he is trying to teach them servant leadership, they are squabbling about who deserves the most favored position. Their gnomic faith exasperates Jesus. After every miracle, they fret anxiously about the next. Can he feed five thousand—what about four thousand? Much of the time a fog of incomprehension separates the Twelve from Jesus.

Why does Jesus invest so much in these apparent losers? To answer that, I turn to Mark's written account, which mentions Jesus' motives in choosing the Twelve: "that they might be with him and that he might send them out to preach."

That they might be with him. Jesus never tried to hide his loneliness and his dependence on other people. He chose his disciples not as servants but as friends. He shared moments of joy and grief with them, and asked for them in times of need. They became his family, his substitute mother and brothers and sisters. They gave up everything for him, as he had given up everything for them. He loved them, plain and simple.

That he might send them out. From his very first invitation to the Twelve, Jesus had in mind what would transpire one day on Calvary. He knew his time on earth was short, and the ultimate success of his mission depended not just on what he accomplished in a few years but on what the Twelve—then eleven, soon to be thousands and then millions—would do after he had left.

Oddly, as I look back on Jesus' time from the present perspective, it is the very ordinariness of the disciples that gives me hope. Jesus does not seem to choose his followers on the basis of native talent or perfectibility or potential for greatness. When he lived on earth he surrounded himself with ordinary people who misunderstood him, failed to exercise much spiritual power, and sometimes behaved like churlish school-children. Three followers in particular (the brothers James and John, and Peter) Jesus singled out for his strongest reprimands—yet two of these would become the most prominent leaders of the early Christians.

I cannot avoid the impression that Jesus prefers working with unpromising recruits. Once, after he had sent out seventy-two disciples on a training mission, Jesus rejoiced at the successes they reported back. No passage in the Gospels shows him more exuberant. "At that time Jesus, full of joy through the Holy Spirit, said, 'I praise you, Father, Lord of heaven and earth, because you have hidden these things from the wise and learned, and revealed them to little children. Yes, Father, for this was your good pleasure.'" From such a ragtag band Jesus founded a church that has not stopped growing in nineteen centuries.

Part Two

Why He Came

6

Beatitudes: Lucky Are the Unlucky

A saint is one who exaggerates what the world neglects.

G. K. Chesterton

6
Beatitudes: Lucky Are the Unlucky

The Sermon on the Mount haunted my adolescence. I would read a book like Charles Sheldon's *In His Steps*, solemnly vow to act "as Jesus would act," and turn to Matthew 5–7 for guidance. What to make of such advice! Should I mutilate myself after a wet dream? Offer my body to be pummeled by the motorcycle-riding "hoods" in school? Tear out my tongue after speaking a harsh word to my brother?

Once, I became so convicted about my addiction to material things that I gave away to a friend my prized collection of 1,100 baseball cards, including an original 1947 Jackie Robinson and a Mickey Mantle rookie card. Anticipating a divine reward for this renunciation, instead I had to endure the monumental injustice of watching my friend auction off the entire collection at a huge profit. "Blessed are those who are persecuted because of righteousness," I consoled myself.

Now that I am an adult, the crisis of the Sermon on the Mount still has not gone away. Though I have tried at times to dismiss it as rhetorical excess, the more I study Jesus, the more I realize that the statements contained here lie at the heart of his message. If I fail to understand this teaching, I fail to understand him.

Jesus delivered the famous sermon at a time when his popularity was soaring. Crowds pursued him wherever he went, obsessed with one question: *Has the Messiah come at last?* On this unusual occasion

Jesus skipped the parables and granted his audience a full-blown "philosophy of life," somewhat like a candidate unveiling a new political platform. What a platform.

When time came to teach the Beatitudes to my class at LaSalle Street Church in Chicago, I followed my regular routine of previewing the movies about Jesus. Since I drew from fifteen different movies, the task of locating and viewing all the right portions consumed several hours of my time each week, much of it spent waiting for the VCR to fast-forward or reverse to the appropriate scenes. To relieve boredom while the VCR whirred and clicked its way to the right places, I had CNN playing on the TV monitor in the foreground. As the machine sped, say, to the eight-minute-twenty-second mark of Cecil B. DeMille's *King of Kings*, I caught up on news from around the world. Then I hit the "play" button and was transported back into first-century Palestine.

A lot was happening in the world in 1991 the week I taught the Beatitudes. In a ground campaign that lasted a scant one hundred hours, allied forces had achieved a stunning victory over Iraq in the Gulf War. Like most Americans, I could hardly believe the long-feared war had ended so quickly, with so few American casualties. As my VCR searched through the celluloid frames of Jesus in the background, various commentators on-screen were illustrating with charts and maps exactly what had transpired in Kuwait. Then came General Norman Schwarzkopf.

CNN announced an interruption in scheduled programming: they would shift to live coverage of the morning-after press conference by the commander of allied forces. For a time I tried to continue preparing for my class. I watched five minutes of Pasolini's version of Jesus delivering the Beatitudes, then several minutes of General Schwarzkopf's version of allied troops bearing down on Kuwait City. Soon I abandoned the VCR altogether—Stormin' Norman proved entirely too engaging. He told of the "end run" around Iraq's elite Republican Guard, of a decoy invasion by sea, of the allied capability of marching all the way to Baghdad unopposed. He credited the Kuwaitis, the British, the Saudis, and every other participant in the multinational force. A general confident in his mission and immensely proud of the soldiers who had carried it out, Schwarzkopf gave a bravura performance. I remember thinking, *That's exactly the person you want to lead a war.*

The briefing ended, CNN switched to commercials, and I returned to the VCR tapes. Max von Sydow, a blond, pasty Jesus, was giving an improbable rendition of the Sermon on the Mount in *The Greatest Story Ever Told*. "Blessed ... are ... the ... poor ... in spirit," he intoned in a slow, thick Scandinavian accent, "for ... theirs ... is ... the ... kingdom ... of ... heaven." I had to adjust to the languid pace of the movie compared to General Schwarzkopf's briefing, and it took a few seconds for the irony to sink in: I had just been watching the Beatitudes in reverse!

Blessed are the strong, was the general's message. Blessed are the triumphant. Blessed are the armies wealthy enough to possess smart bombs and Patriot missiles. Blessed are the liberators, the conquering soldiers.

The bizarre juxtaposition of two speeches gave me a feeling for the shock waves the Sermon on the Mount must have caused among its original audience, Jews in first-century Palestine. Instead of General Schwarzkopf, they had Jesus, and to a downtrodden people yearning for emancipation from Roman rule, Jesus gave startling and unwelcome advice. If an enemy soldier slaps you, turn the other cheek. Rejoice in persecution. Be grateful for your poverty.

The Iraqis, chastened on the battlefield, got a nasty measure of revenge by setting fire to Kuwait's oil fields; Jesus enjoined not revenge but love for one's enemies. How long would a kingdom founded on such principles survive against Rome?

"Happy are the bombed-out and the homeless," Jesus might as well have said. "Blessed are the losers and those grieving for fallen comrades. Blessed are the Kurds still suffering under Iraqi rule." Any Greek scholar will tell you the word "blessed" is far too sedate and beatific to carry the percussive force Jesus intended. The Greek word conveys something like a short cry of joy, "Oh, you lucky person!"

"How lucky are the unlucky!" Jesus said in effect.

* * *

A few years after the Gulf War episode, I received an invitation to the White House. President Bill Clinton, alarmed about his low standing among evangelical Christians, summoned twelve of us to a private breakfast in order to hear our concerns. Each of us would have five minutes to say whatever we wanted the president and vice-president to hear. The question, "What would Jesus say in such a setting?" crossed my mind, and I realized with a start that the only time Jesus met with powerful political leaders, his hands were tied and his back was clotted with blood. Church and state have had an uneasy relationship ever since.

I turned to the Beatitudes and found myself startled anew. What if I translated their message into contemporary terms?

> Mr. President, first I want to advise you to stop worrying so much about the economy and jobs. A lower Gross National Product is actually good for the country. Don't you understand that the poor are the fortunate ones? The more poor we have in the U.S., the more blessed we are. Theirs is the kingdom of heaven.
>
> And don't devote so much time to health care. You see, Mr. President, those who mourn are blessed too, for they'll be comforted.
>
> I know you've heard from the Religious Right about the increasing secularization of our country. Prayer is no longer allowed in schools, and protesters against abortion are subject to arrest. Relay sir. Government oppression gives Christians an opportunity to be persecuted, and therefore blessed. Thank you for the expanded opportunities.

I did not deliver such a speech to President Clinton, choosing instead to represent the immediate concerns of American Christians, but I did come away from the experience puzzled afresh. What meaning can the Beatitudes have for a society that honors the self-assertive, confident, and rich? Blessed are the happy and the strong, we believe. Blessed are those who hunger and thirst for a good time, who look out for Number One.

Some psychologists and psychiatrists, following Freud's lead, point to the Beatitudes as proof of Jesus' imbalance. Said one distinguished British psychologist, in a speech prepared for the Royal Society of Medicine,

> The spirit of self-sacrifice which permeates Christianity, and is so highly prized in the Christian religious life, is masochism moderately indulged. A much stronger expression of it is to be found in Christ's teaching in the Sermon on the Mount. This blesses the poor, the meek, the persecuted; exhorts us not to resist evil but to offer the second cheek to the smiter; and to do good to them that hate you and forgive men their trespasses. All this breathes masochism.

Which is it, masochism or profound wisdom? Anyone who responds with a quick and easy answer probably has not taken the Beatitudes seriously enough.

To put the issue bluntly, are the Beatitudes true? If so, why doesn't the church encourage poverty and mourning and meekness and persecution instead of striving against them? What is the real meaning of the Beatitudes, this cryptic ethical core of Jesus' teaching?

If I had been sitting in the audience when Jesus first delivered the Beatitudes, I believe I would have left the event feeling confused or outraged, not comforted. Nineteen centuries later, I still struggle to make sense of them. Yet now, especially as I think back on my teenage days of frenzied legalism, I can see that my understanding has developed in stages.

I am not, and may never be, ready to declare, "This is what the Beatitudes mean." But gradually, almost osmotically, I have come to recognize them as important truths. To me, they apply on at least three levels.

Dangled Promises. In my first stage of understanding, I regarded the Beatitudes as a sop Jesus threw to the unfortunates: "Well, since you aren't rich, and your health is failing, and your face is wet with tears, I'll toss out a few nice phrases to make you feel better." Later, as cynicism faded and my faith strengthened, I came to see them as genuine promises central to Jesus' message.

Unlike medieval kings who threw coins to the masses (or modern politicians who make promises to the poor just before elections), Jesus had the ability to offer his audience lasting, even eternal rewards. Alone of all people on earth, Jesus had actually lived "on the other side," and he who came down from heaven knew well that the spoils of the kingdom of heaven can easily counterbalance whatever misery we might encounter in this life. Those who mourn *will be* comforted; the meek *will inherit the earth*; the hungry *will be filled*; the pure *will see God*. Jesus could make such promises with authority, for he had come to establish God's kingdom that would rule forever.

One summer I met with a group of Wycliffe Bible Translators at their austere headquarters in the Arizona desert. Many lived in mobile homes, and we convened in a concrete-block building with a metal roof. I was impressed with the dedication of these professional linguists who were preparing for a life of poverty and hardship in remote outposts. They loved to sing one song especially: "So send I you, to labor unrewarded, to serve unpaid, unloved, unsought, unknown. ..." Listening to them, the thought occurred to me that the song has it slightly wrong: these missionaries were not planning to labor unrewarded. Rather, they endured certain hardships with the prospect of other rewards in mind. They served God, trusting in turn that God would make it worth their while—if not here, then in eternity.

In the mornings, before the sun rose too high above the hilltops, I went jogging along dirt roads that coiled among the stalky stands of saguaro cacti. Wary of cacti with snakes and scorpions, I mostly kept my head down looking at the road, but one morning on a new route I glanced up to see a shimmering resort looming before me, almost like a mirage. I jogged closer and discovered two Olympic swimming pools, aerobic workout rooms, a cinder jogging trail, lush gardens, a baseball diamond, soccer fields, and horse stables. The facilities, I learned, belonged to a famous eating disorder clinic that caters to movie stars and athletes. The clinic features the latest twelve-step program techniques, has a staff well stocked with Ph.D.'s and M.D.'s, and charges its clients about $300 per day.

I jogged slowly back to the jumble of houses and buildings at the Wycliffe base, keenly aware of their contrast to the gleaming architecture of the eating disorder clinic. One institution endeavored to save souls, to prepare people to serve God here and in eternity; the other endeavored to save bodies, to prepare people to enjoy this life. It seemed obvious which institution the world honors.

In the Beatitudes, Jesus honored people who may not enjoy many privileges in this life. To the poor, the mourners, the meek, the hungry, the persecuted, the poor in heart, he offered assurance that their service would not go unrecognized. They would receive ample reward. "Indeed," wrote C. S. Lewis, "if we consider the unblushing promises of reward and the staggering nature of the rewards promised in the Gospels, it would seem that Our Lord finds our desires, not too strong, but too weak. We are half-hearted creatures, fooling about with drink and sex and ambition when infinite joy is offered us, like an ignorant child who wants to go on making mud pies in a slum because he cannot imagine what is meant by the offer of a holiday at the sea."

I know that among many Christians an emphasis on future rewards has fallen out of fashion. My former pastor Bill Leslie used to observe, "As churches grow wealthier and more successful, their preference in hymns changes from 'This world is not my home, I'm just a passin' through' to 'This is my father's world.'" In the United States, at least, Christians have grown so comfortable that we no longer identify with the humble conditions Jesus addressed in the Beatitudes—which may explain why they sound so strange to our ears.

Yet, as C. S. Lewis reminds us, we dare not discount the value of future rewards. One need only listen to the songs composed by American slaves to realize this consolation of belief. "Swing low, sweet chariot, comin' for to carry me home." "When I get to heaven, goin' to put on my robe, goin' to shout all over God's heaven." "We'll soon be free, we'll soon be free, when the Lord will call us home." If the slave masters had written these songs for the slaves to sing, they would be an obscenity; rather, they come from the mouths of the slaves themselves, people who had little hope in this world but abiding hope in a world to come. For them, all hope centered in Jesus. "Nobody knows the trouble I see, nobody knows but Jesus." "I'm gonna' lay all my troubles on Jesus' shoulder."

I no longer scorn the eternal rewards mentioned in the Beatitudes as "pie in the sky." What good does it do to hope for future rewards? What good did it do Terry Waite to believe that he would not spend the rest of his life chained to a door in a filthy Beirut apartment, but that a world of family and friends and mercy and love and music and food and good books awaited him if he could just find the strength to hang on a little longer? What good did it do the slaves to believe that God was not satisfied with a world that included back-breaking labor and masters armed with bullwhips and lynching ropes? To believe in future rewards is to believe that the long arm of the Lord bends toward justice, to believe that one day the proud will be overthrown and the humble raised up and the hungry filled with good things.

The prospect of future rewards in no way cancels out our need to fight for justice now, in this life. Yet it is a plain fact of history that for convicts in the Soviet Gulag and slaves in America and Christians in Roman cages awaiting their turn with the wild beasts, the promise of reward was a source not of shame but of hope. It keeps you alive. It allows you to believe in a just God after all. Like a bell tolling from another world, Jesus' promise of rewards proclaims that no matter how things appear, there is no future in evil, only in good.

My wife, Janet, worked with senior citizens near a Chicago housing project judged the poorest community in the United States. About half her clients were white, half were black. All of them had lived through harsh times—two world wars, the Great Depression, social upheavals—and all of them, in their seventies and eighties, lived in awareness of death. Yet Janet noted a striking difference in the way the whites and the blacks faced death. There were exceptions, of course, but the trend was this: many of the whites became increasingly fearful and anxious. They complained about their lives, their families, and their deteriorating health. The blacks, in contrast, maintained a good humor and triumphant spirit even though they had more apparent reason for bitterness and despair.

What caused the difference in outlooks? Janet concluded the answer was hope, a hope that traced directly to the blacks' bedrock belief in heaven. If you want to hear contemporary images of heaven, attend a few black funerals. With characteristic eloquence, the preachers paint word pictures of a life so serene and sensuous that everyone in the congregation starts fidgeting to go there. The mourners feel grief, naturally, but in its proper place: as an interruption, a temporary setback in a battle whose end has already been determined.

I am convinced that for these neglected saints, who learned to anticipate and enjoy God in spite of the difficulties of their lives on earth, heaven will seem more like a long-awaited homecoming than a visit to a new place. In their lives, the Beatitudes have become true. To people who are trapped in pain, in broken homes, in economic chaos, in hatred and fear, in violence—to these, Jesus offers a promise of a time, far longer and more substantial than this time on earth, of health and wholeness and pleasure and peace. A time of reward.

The Great Reversal. Over time I learned to respect, and even long for, the rewards Jesus promised. Even so, these rewards lay somewhere in the future, and dangled promises do not satisfy immediate needs. Along the way, I have also come to believe that the Beatitudes describe the present as well as the future. They neatly contrast how to succeed in the kingdom of heaven as opposed to the kingdom of this world.

J. B. Phillips rendered the Beatitudes that apply in the kingdom of this world:

> Happy are the "pushers": for they get on in the world.
> Happy are the hard-boiled: for they never let life hurt them.
> Happy are they who complain: for they get their own way
>   in the end.
> Happy are the blasé: for they never worry over their sins.
> Happy are the slave-drivers: for they get results.
> Happy are the knowledgeable men of the world: for they know
>   their way around.
> Happy are the trouble-makers: for they make people take notice
>   of them.*

---

*Indeed, it appears that Jesus adapted a form of proverbs common in his day to make the opposite point. According to Walter Kasper, Greek and Jewish wisdom

Modern society lives by the rules of survival of the fittest. "The one who dies with the most toys wins," reads one bumper sticker. So does the nation with the best weapons and the largest gross national product. The owner of the Chicago Bulls gave a compact summary of the rules governing the visible world on the occasion of Michael Jordan's (temporary) retirement. "He's living the American Dream," said Jerry Reinsdorf. "The American Dream is to reach a point in your life where you don't have to do anything you don't want to do and can do everything that you do want to do."

That may be the American Dream, but it decidedly is not Jesus' dream as revealed in the Beatitudes. The Beatitudes express quite plainly that God views this world through a different set of lenses. God seems to prefer the poor and those who mourn to the Fortune 500 and supermodels who frolic on the beach. Oddly, God may prefer South Central L. A. to Malibu Beach, and Rwanda to Monte Carlo. In fact, one could almost subtitle the Sermon on the Mount not "survival of the fittest" but "triumph of the victims."

Various scenes in the Gospels give a good picture of the kind of people who impressed Jesus. A widow who placed her last two cents in the offering. A dishonest tax collector so riddled with anxiety that he climbed a tree to get a better view of Jesus. A nameless, nondescript child. A woman with a string of five unhappy marriages. A blind beggar. An adulteress. A man with leprosy. Strength, good looks, connections, and the competitive instinct may bring a person success in a society like ours, but those very qualities may block entrance to the kingdom of heaven. Dependence, sorrow, repentance, a longing to change—these are the gates to God's kingdom.

"Blessed are the poor in spirit," said Jesus. One commentary translates that "Blessed are the desperate." With nowhere else to turn, the desperate just may turn to Jesus, the only one who can offer the deliverance they long for. Jesus really believed that a person who is poor in spirit, or mourning, or persecuted, or hungry and thirsty for righteousness has a peculiar "advantage" over the rest of us. Maybe,

---

literature describes as blessed the man who has obedient children, a good wife, faithful friends, is successful, and so forth. Jesus added a contrarian twist to what the audience expected.

just maybe, the desperate person will cry out to God for help. If so, that person is truly blessed.

Catholic scholars coined the phrase "God's preferential option for the poor" to describe a phenomenon they found throughout both the Old and New Testaments: God's partiality toward the poor and the disadvantaged. *Why would God single out the poor for special attention over any other group?* I used to wonder. What makes the poor deserving of God's concern? I received help on this issue from a writer named Monika Hellwig, who lists the following "advantages" to being poor:

1. The poor know they are in urgent need of redemption.
2. The poor know not only their dependence on God and on powerful people but also their interdependence with one another.
3. The poor rest their security not on things but on people.
4. The poor have no exaggerated sense of their own importance, and no exaggerated need of privacy.
5. The poor expect little from competition and much from cooperation.
6. The poor can distinguish between necessities and luxuries.
7. The poor can wait, because they have acquired a kind of dogged patience born of acknowledged dependence.
8. The fears of the poor are more realistic and less exaggerated, because they already know that one can survive great suffering and want.
9. When the poor have the Gospel preached to them, it sounds like good news and not like a threat or a scolding.
10. The poor can respond to the call of the Gospel with a certain abandonment and uncomplicated totality because they have so little to lose and are ready for anything.

In summary, through no choice of their own—they may urgently wish otherwise—poor people find themselves in a posture that befits the grace of God. In their state of neediness, dependence, and dissatisfaction with life, they may welcome God's free gift of love.

As an exercise I went back over Monika Hellwig's list, substituting the word "rich" for "poor," and changing each sentence to its opposite. "The rich do not know they are in urgent need of redemption. . . . The rich rest their security not on people but on things. . . ." (Jesus did something similar in Luke's version of the Beatitudes, but that portion gets much less attention: "But woe to you who are rich, for you have already received your comfort. . . .")

✤ Next, I tried something far more threatening: I substituted the word "I." Reviewing each of the ten statements, I asked myself if my own attitudes more resembled those of the poor or of the rich. Do I easily acknowledge my needs? Do I readily depend on God and on other people? Where does my security rest? Am I more likely to compete or cooperate? Can I distinguish between necessities and luxuries? Am I patient? Do the Beatitudes sound to me like good news or like a scolding?

As I did this exercise I began to realize why so many saints voluntarily submit to the discipline of poverty. Dependence, humility, simplicity, cooperation, and a sense of abandon are qualities greatly prized in the spiritual life, but extremely elusive for people who live in comfort. There may be other ways to God but, oh, they are hard—as hard as a camel squeezing through the eye of a needle. In the Great Reversal of God's kingdom, prosperous saints are very rare.

I do not believe the poor to be more virtuous than anyone else (though I have found them more compassionate and often more generous), but they are less likely to *pretend* to be virtuous. They have not the arrogance of the middle class, who can skillfully disguise their problems under a facade of self-righteousness. They are more naturally dependent, because they have no choice; they must depend on others simply to survive.

I now view the Beatitudes not as patronizing slogans, but as profound insights into the mystery of human existence. God's kingdom turns the tables upside down. The poor, the hungry, the mourners, and the oppressed truly are blessed. Not because of their miserable states, of course—Jesus spent much of his life trying to remedy those miseries. Rather, they are blessed because of an innate advantage they hold over those more comfortable and self-sufficient. People who are rich, successful, and beautiful may well go through life relying on their natural gifts. People who lack such natural advantages, hence underqualified for success in the kingdom of this world, just might turn to God in their time of need.

Human beings do not readily admit desperation. When they do, the kingdom of heaven draws near.

Psychological Reality. More recently, I have come to see a third level of truth in the Beatitudes. Not only did Jesus offer an ideal for us to strive toward, with appropriate rewards in view; not only did he turn the tables on our success-addicted society; he also set forth a plain formula of psychological truth, the deepest level of truth that we can know on earth.

The Beatitudes reveal that what succeeds in the kingdom of heaven also benefits us most in this life here and now. It has taken me many years to recognize this fact, and only now am I beginning to understand the Beatitudes. They still jar me every time I read them, but they jar me because I recognize in them a richness that unmasks my own poverty.

Blessed are the poor in spirit . . . Blessed are the meek. A book like Paul Johnson's *Intellectuals* sets out in convincing detail what all of us know to be true: the people we laud, strive to emulate, and feature on the covers of popular magazines are not the fulfilled, happy, balanced persons we might imagine. Although Johnson's subjects (Ernest Hemingway, Bertrand Russell, Jean-Paul Sartre, Edmund Wilson, Bertolt Brecht, et al.) would be judged successful by any modern standard, it would be difficult to assemble a more miserable, egomaniacal, abusive company.

My career as a journalist has afforded me opportunities to interview "stars," including NFL football greats, movie actors, music performers, best-selling authors, politicians, and TV personalities. These are the people who dominate the media. We fawn over them, poring over the minutiae of their lives: the clothes they wear, the food they eat, the aerobic routines they follow, the people they love, the toothpaste they use. Yet I must tell you that, in my limited experience, I have found Paul Johnson's principle to hold true: our "idols" are as miserable a group of people as I have ever met. Most have troubled or broken marriages. Nearly all are incurably dependent on psychotherapy. In a heavy irony, these larger-than-life heroes seem tormented by self-doubt.

I have also spent time with people I call "servants." Doctors and nurses who work among the ultimate outcasts, leprosy patients in rural India. A Princeton graduate who runs a hotel for the homeless in Chicago. Health workers who have left high-paying jobs to serve in a backwater town of Mississippi. Relief workers in Somalia, Sudan, Ethiopia, Bangladesh, and other repositories of human suffering. The Ph.D.s I met in Arizona, who are now scattered throughout jungles of South America translating the Bible into obscure languages.

I was prepared to honor and admire these servants, to hold them up as inspiring examples. I was not prepared to envy them. Yet as I now reflect on the two groups side by side, stars and servants, the servants clearly emerge as the favored ones, the graced ones. Without question, I would rather spend time among the servants than among the stars: they possess qualities of depth and richness and even joy that I have not found elsewhere. Servants work for low pay, long hours, and no applause, "wasting" their talents and skills among the poor and uneducated. Somehow, though, in the process of losing their lives they find them.

The poor in spirit and the meek are indeed blessed, I now believe. Theirs is the kingdom of heaven, and it is they who will inherit the earth.

Blessed are the pure in heart. During a period of my life when I was battling sexual temptation, I came across an article that referred me to a thin book, *What I Believe*, by the French Catholic writer François Mauriac. It surprised me that Mauriac, an old man, devoted considerable space to a discussion of his own lust. He explained, "Old age risks being a period of redoubled testing because the imagination in an old man is substituted in a horrible way for what nature refuses him."

I knew that Mauriac understood lust. *Viper's Tangle* and *A Kiss for the Leper*, novels which helped win him the Nobel prize in literature, portray lust, repression, and sexual anger as well as anything I have ever read. For Mauriac, sexual temptation was a familiar battleground.

Mauriac dismissed most of the arguments in favor of sexual purity that he had been taught in his Catholic upbringing. "Marriage will cure lust": it did not for Mauriac, as it has not for so many others, because lust involves the attraction of unknown creatures and the taste for adventure and chance meetings. "With self-discipline you can master lust": Mauriac found that sexual desire is like a tidal wave powerful enough to bear away all the best intentions. "True fulfillment can only be found in monogamy": this may be true, but it certainly does not *seem* true to someone who finds no slackening of sexual urges even in monogamy. Thus he weighed the traditional arguments for purity and found them wanting.

Mauriac concluded that self-discipline, repression, and rational argument are inadequate weapons to use in fighting the impulse toward impurity. In the end, he could find only one reason to be pure, and that is what Jesus presented in the Beatitudes: "Blessed are the pure in heart, for they will see God." In Mauriac's words, "Impurity separates us from God. The spiritual life obeys laws as verifiable as those of the physical world.... Purity is the condition for a higher love—for a possession superior to all possessions: that of God. Yes, this is what is at stake, and nothing less."

Reading François Mauriac's words did not end my struggle with lust. But I must say beyond all doubt that I have found his analysis to be true. The love God holds out to us requires that our faculties be cleansed and purified before we can receive a higher love, one attainable in no other way. That is the motive to stay pure. By harboring lust, I limit my own intimacy with God.

The pure in heart are truly blessed, for they will see God. It is as simple, and as difficult, as that.

Blessed are the merciful. I learned the truth of this Beatitude from Henri Nouwen, a priest who used to teach at Harvard University. At the height of his career, Nouwen moved from Harvard to a community called Daybreak, near Toronto, in order to take on the demanding chores required by his friendship with a man named Adam. Nouwen now ministers not to intellectuals but to a young man who is considered by many a useless person who should have been aborted.

Nouwen describes his friend:

Adam is a 25-year-old man who cannot speak, cannot dress or undress himself, cannot walk alone, cannot eat without much help. He does not cry or laugh. Only occasionally does he make eye contact. His back is distorted. His arm and leg movements are twisted. He suffers from severe epilepsy and, despite heavy medication, sees few days without grand-mal seizures. Sometimes, as he grows suddenly rigid, he utters a howling groan. On a few occasions I've seen one big tear roll down his cheek.

It takes me about an hour and a half to wake Adam up, give him his medication, carry him into his bath, wash him, shave him, clean his teeth, dress him, walk him to the kitchen, give him his breakfast, put him in his wheelchair and bring him to the place where he spends most of the day with therapeutic exercises.

On a visit to Nouwen in Toronto, I watched him perform that routine with Adam, and I must admit I had a fleeting doubt as to whether this was the best use of his time. I have heard Henri Nouwen speak, and have read many of his books. He has much to offer. Could not someone else take over the menial task of caring for Adam? When I cautiously broached the subject with Nouwen himself, he informed me that I had completely misinterpreted what was going on. "I am not giving up anything," he insisted. "It is *I*, not Adam, who gets the main benefit from our friendship."

Then Nouwen began listing for me all the benefits he has gained. The hours spent with Adam, he said, have given him an inner peace so fulfilling that it makes most of his other, more high-minded tasks seem boring and superficial by contrast. Early on, as he sat beside that helpless child-man, he realized how marked with rivalry and competition, how obsessive, was his drive for success in academia and Christian ministry. Adam taught him that "what makes us human is not our mind but our heart, not our ability to think but our ability to love." From Adam's simple nature, he had glimpsed the "emptiness" necessary before one can be filled by God—the kind of emptiness that desert monks achieved only after much searching and discipline.

All during the rest of our interview, Henri Nouwen circled back to my question, as if he could not believe I could ask such a thing. He kept thinking of other ways he had benefited from his relationship with Adam. Truly, he was enjoying a new kind of spiritual peace, acquired not within the stately quadrangles of Harvard, but by the bedside of incontinent Adam. I left Daybreak convicted of my own spiritual poverty, I who so carefully arrange my writer's life to make it efficient and single-focused. The merciful are indeed blessed, I learned, for they will be shown mercy.

Blessed are the peacemakers ... Blessed are those who are persecuted for the sake of righteousness. This truth came to me in a roundabout way. The great novelist Leo Tolstoy tried to follow it, but his irascible temper kept getting in the way of peacemaking. Tolstoy did write eloquently about the Sermon on the Mount, however, and half a century later a Hindu ascetic named Mohandas Gandhi read *The Kingdom of God Is Within You* by Tolstoy and decided to live by the literal principles of the Sermon on the Mount.

The movie *Gandhi* contains a fine scene in which Gandhi tries to explain his philosophy to the Presbyterian missionary Charlie Andrews. Walking together in a South African city, the two suddenly find their way blocked by young thugs. The Reverend Andrews takes one look at the menacing gangsters and decides to run for it. Gandhi stops him. "Doesn't the New Testament say if an enemy strikes you on the right cheek you should offer him the left?" Andrews mumbles that he thought the phrase was used metaphorically. "I'm not so sure," Gandhi replies. "I suspect he meant you must show courage—be willing to take a blow, several blows, to show you will not strike back nor will you be turned aside. And when you do that it calls on something in human nature, something that makes his hatred decrease and his respect increase. I think Christ grasped that and I have seen it work."

Years later an American minister, Martin Luther King Jr., studied Gandhi's tactics and decided to put them into practice in the United States. Many blacks abandoned King over the issue of nonviolence and drifted toward "black power" rhetoric. After you've been hit on the head with a policeman's nightstick for the dozenth time and received yet another jolt from a jailer's cattle prod, you begin to question the effectiveness of nonviolence. But King himself never wavered.

As riots broke out in places like Los Angeles, Chicago, and Harlem, King traveled from city to city trying to cool tempers, forcefully reminding demonstrators that moral change is not accomplished through immoral means. He had learned that principle from the Sermon on the Mount and from Gandhi, and almost all his speeches reiterated the message. "Christianity," he said, "has always insisted that the cross we bear precedes the crown we wear. To be a Christian one must take up his cross, with all its difficulties and agonizing and tension-packed content, and carry it until that very cross leaves its mark upon us and redeems us to that more excellent way which comes only through suffering."

Martin Luther King Jr. had some weaknesses, but one thing he got right. Against all odds, against all instincts of self-preservation, he stayed true to the principle of peacemaking. He did not strike back. Where others called for revenge, he called for love. The civil rights marchers put their bodies on the line before sheriffs with nightsticks and fire hoses and snarling German shepherds. That, in fact, was what brought them the victory they had been seeking so long. Historians point to one event as the single moment in which the movement attained a critical mass of public support for its cause. It occurred on a bridge outside Selma, Alabama, when Sheriff Jim Clark turned his policemen loose on unarmed black demonstrators. The American public, horrified by the scene of violent injustice, at last gave assent to passage of a civil rights bill.

I grew up in Atlanta, across town from Martin Luther King Jr., and I confess with some shame that while he was leading marches in places like Selma and Montgomery and Memphis, I was on the side of the white sheriffs with the nightsticks and German shepherds. I was quick to pounce on his moral flaws and slow to recognize my own blind sin. But because he stayed faithful, by offering his body as a target but never as a weapon, he broke through my moral calluses.

The real goal, King used to say, was not to defeat the white man, but "to awaken a sense of shame within the oppressor and challenge his false sense of superiority.... The end is reconciliation; the end is redemption; the end is the creation of the beloved community." And that is what Martin Luther King Jr. finally set into motion, even in racists like me.

King, like Gandhi before him, died a martyr. After his death, more and more people began adopting the principle of nonviolent protest as a way to demand justice. In the Philippines, after Benigno Aquino's martyrdom, ordinary people brought down a government by gathering in the streets to pray; army tanks rolled to a stop before the kneeling Filipinos as if blocked by an invisible force. Later, in the remarkable year of 1989, in Poland, Hungary, Czechoslovakia, East Germany, Bulgaria, Yugoslavia, Romania, Mongolia, Albania, the Soviet Union, Nepal, and Chile, more than half a billion people threw off the yoke of oppression through nonviolent means. In many of these places, especially the nations of Eastern Europe, the Christian church led the way. Protesters marched through the streets carrying candles, singing hymns, and praying. As in Joshua's day, the walls came tumbling down.

Peacemakers will be called sons and daughters of God. Blessed also are those who are persecuted because of righteousness, for theirs is the kingdom of heaven.

Blessed are those who mourn. Because I have written books with titles like *Where Is God When It Hurts?* and *Disappointment with God*, I have spent time among mourners. They intimidated me at first. I had few answers for the questions they were asking, and I felt awkward in the presence of their grief. I remember especially one year when, at the invitation of a neighbor, I joined a therapy group at a nearby hospital. This group, called Make Today Count, consisted of people who were dying, and I accompanied my neighbor to their meetings for a year.

Certainly I cannot say that I "enjoyed" the gatherings; that would be the wrong word. Yet the meetings became for me one of the most meaningful events of each month. In contrast to a party, where participants try to impress each other with signs of status and power, in this group no one was trying to impress. Clothes, fashions, apartment furnishings, job titles, new cars—what do these things mean to people who are preparing to die? More than any other people I had met, the Make Today Count group members concentrated on ultimate issues. I found myself wishing that some of my shallow, hedonistic friends would attend a meeting.

Later, when I wrote about what I had learned from grieving and suffering people, I began hearing from strangers. I have three folders, each one several inches thick, filled with these letters. They are among my most precious possessions. One letter, twenty-six pages long, was written on blue-lined note paper by a mother sitting in a lounge outside a room where surgeons were operating on her four-year-old daughter's brain tumor. Another came from a quadriplegic who "wrote" by making puffs of air into a tube, which a computer translated into letters on a printer.

Many of the people who have written me have no happy endings to their stories. Some still feel abandoned by God. Few have found answers to the "Why?" questions. But I have seen enough grief that I have gained faith in Jesus' promise that those who mourn will be comforted.

I know two small-scale ministries, run from private homes, that have developed out of grief. The first came into being when a woman in California discovered that her son, the apple of her eye, was dying of AIDS. She got little sympathy and support from her church and community because of the young man's homosexuality. She felt so alone and needy that she decided to start a newsletter that now brings together a network of parents of gay people. Although she offers little professional help and promises no magic cures, now hundreds of other parents view this courageous woman as a lifesaver.

Another woman, in Wisconsin, lost her only son in a Marine Corps helicopter crash. For years she could not escape the dark cloud of grief. She kept her son's room intact just as he had left it. Eventually, she began to notice how frequently helicopter crashes were reported on the news. She kept thinking of other families facing tragedies like hers, and wondering whether she could do something to help. Now, whenever a military helicopter crashes, she sends a packet of letters and helpful materials to an officer in the Defense Department who forwards the packet on to the affected family. About half of them strike up a regular correspondence, and in her retirement this Wisconsin woman directs her own "community of suffering." The activity has not solved the grief for her son, of course, but it has given her a sense of meaning, and she no longer feels helpless against that grief.

There is no more effective healer, I have found, than what Henri Nouwen calls "a wounded healer." Blessed are those who mourn, for they will be comforted.

Blessed are those who hunger and thirst for righteousness. In a sense, everyone I have mentioned in this litany of the Beatitudes manifests this final promise of Jesus. The "servants" who invest their lives among the poor and needy, François Mauriac striving to stay pure, Henri Nouwen bathing and dressing Adam, Martin Luther King Jr. and the disciples of nonviolence, mothers of gay men and Marine pilots who reach out beyond their grief—all these are responding to pangs of hunger and thirst for righteousness. All of them have received a reward, not only in the life to come, but in this life as well.

An Albanian nun spent sixteen years in an exclusive convent teaching geography to the wealthiest Bengali and British daughters of Calcutta. One day, on a railway trip to the Himalayas, she heard a voice calling her to change paths and minister to the poorest of the poor. Can anyone really doubt that Mother Teresa has found more personal fulfillment in her latter occupation than in her former? I have seen this principle borne out in saints and in ordinary people so often that I now easily understand why the Gospels repeat the one saying of Jesus more than any other: "Whoever wants to save his life will lose it, but whoever loses his life for my sake will find it."

Jesus came, he told us, not to destroy life but that we may have it more abundantly, "life . . . to the full." Paradoxically, we get this abundant life in ways we may not have counted on. We get it by investing in others, by taking courageous stands for justice, by ministering to the weak and needy, by pursuing God and not self. I would not dare feel pity for any of the people I have just mentioned, though all have lived with hardship. For all their "sacrifices," they seem to me more fully alive, not less. Those who hunger and thirst for righteousness get filled.

In the Beatitudes, strange sayings that at first glance seem absurd, Jesus offers a paradoxical key to abundant life. The kingdom of heaven, he said elsewhere, is like a treasure of such value that any shrewd investor would "in his joy" sell all he has in order to buy it. It represents value far more real and permanent than anything the world has to offer, for this treasure will pay dividends both here on earth and also in the life to come. Jesus places the emphasis not on what we give up but on what we receive. Is it not in our own self-interest to pursue such a treasure?

When I first heard the Beatitudes, they sounded to me like impossible ideals given by some dreamy mystic. Now, though, I see them as truths proclaimed by a realist every bit as pragmatic as General Norman Schwarzkopf. Jesus knew how life works, in the kingdom of heaven as well as the kingdom of this world. In a life characterized by poverty, mourning, meekness, a hunger for righteousness, mercy, purity, peacemaking, and persecution, Jesus himself embodied the Beatitudes. Perhaps he even conceived the Beatitudes as a sermon to himself as well as to the rest of us, for he would have much opportunity to practice these hard truths.

7

Message:
A Sermon of Offense

The test of observance of Christ's teachings is our consciousness of our failure to attain an ideal perfection. The degree to which we draw near this perfection cannot be seen; all we can see is the extent of our deviation.

Leo Tolstoy

7

Message: A Sermon of Offense

The Beatitudes represent only the first step toward understanding the Sermon on the Mount. Long after I came to recognize the enduring truth of the Beatitudes, I still brooded over the uncompromising harshness of the rest of Jesus' sermon. Its absolutist quality left me gasping. "Be perfect, therefore, as your heavenly Father is perfect," Jesus said, his statement tucked almost casually between commands to love enemies and give away money. Be perfect like God? Whatever did he mean?

I cannot easily dismiss this extremism, because it turns up elsewhere in the Gospels. When a rich man asked Jesus what he should do to ensure eternal life, Jesus told him to give his money away—not 10 percent or 18.5 percent or even 50 percent, but all of it. When a disciple asked if he should forgive his brother seven times, Jesus replied, "I tell you, not seven times, but seventy-seven times." Other religions taught variations of the "Golden Rule," but stated in a more limited, negative form: "Don't do to others what you wouldn't want them to do to you." Jesus expanded the Rule into its unbounded form, "In everything, do to others what you would have them do to you."

Has anyone ever lived a life as perfect as God's? Has anyone ever followed the Golden Rule? How can we even respond to such impossible ideals? We humans prefer common sense and balance, something closer to Aristotle's Golden Mean than Jesus' Golden Rule.

* * *

A friend of mine named Virginia Stem Owens assigned the Sermon on the Mount to her composition class at Texas A&M University, asking the students to write a short essay. She had expected them to have a basic respect for the text, since the Bible Belt extends right across Texas, but her students' reactions soon disabused her of that notion. "In my opinion religion is one big hoax," wrote one. "There is an old saying that 'you shouldn't believe everything you read' and it applies in this case," wrote another.

Virginia recalled her own introduction to the Sermon on the Mount in Sunday school, where pastel poster illustrations showed Jesus sitting on a green hillside surrounded by eager, pink children. It never occurred to her to react with anger or disgust. Her students thought otherwise:

> The stuff the churches preach is extremely strict and allows for almost no fun without thinking it is a sin or not.

> I did not like the essay "Sermon on the Mount." It was hard to read and made me feel like I had to be perfect and no one is.

> The things asked in this sermon are absurd. To look at a woman is adultery. That is the most extreme, stupid, unhuman statement that I have ever heard.

"At this point," Virginia wrote about the experience, "I began to be encouraged. There is something exquisitely innocent about not realizing you shouldn't call Jesus stupid.... This was the real thing, a pristine response to the gospel, unfiltered through a two-millennia cultural haze.... I find it strangely heartening that the Bible remains offensive to honest, ignorant ears, just as it was in the first century. For me, that somehow validates its significance. Whereas the scriptures almost lost their characteristically astringent flavor during the past century, the current widespread biblical illiteracy should catapult us into a situation more nearly approximating that of their original, first-century audience."

Offensive, astringent—yes, these are apt words to apply to the Sermon on the Mount. As I viewed fifteen movie treatments of the scene, only one seemed to capture anything like the offense of the original. A low-budget BBC production entitled *Son of Man* sets the Sermon on the Mount against a background of chaos and violence. Roman soldiers have just invaded a Galilean village to exact vengeance for some trespass against the empire. They have strung up Jewish men of fighting age, shoved their hysterical wives to the ground, even speared babies in order to "teach these Jews a lesson." Into that tumultuous scene of blood and tears and keening for the dead strides Jesus with eyes ablaze.

> I tell you: Love your enemies and pray for those that persecute you.
>
> An eye for an eye, a tooth for a tooth, right? So our forefathers said. Love your kinsmen, hate your enemies, right? But I say it's easy to love your own brother, to love those who love you. Even tax collectors do that! You want me to congratulate you for loving your own kinsmen? No, Love your *enemy*.
>
> Love the man who would kick you and spit at you. Love the soldier who would drive his sword in your belly. Love the brigand who robs and tortures you.
>
> Listen to me! Love your enemy! If a Roman soldiers hits you on the left cheek, offer him the right one. If a man in authority orders you to walk one mile, walk two miles. If a man sues you for your coat, give him the shirt off your back.
>
> Listen! I tell you, it is hard to follow me. What I'm saying to you hasn't been said since the world began!

You can imagine the villagers' response to such unwelcome advice. The Sermon on the Mount did not puzzle them; it infuriated them.

Early in the Sermon on the Mount, Jesus addressed head-on a question that worried most of his listeners: Was he a revolutionary or an authentic Jewish prophet? Here is Jesus' own description of his relationship to the Torah:

> Do not think that I have come to abolish the Law or the Prophets; I have not come to abolish them but to fulfill them. . . .

> For I tell you that unless your righteousness surpasses that of the Pharisees and the teachers of the law, you will certainly not enter the kingdom of heaven.

That last statement surely made the crowd sit up and take notice. Pharisees and teachers of the law competed with one another in strictness. They had atomized God's law into 613 rules—248 commands and 365 prohibitions—and bolstered these rules with 1,521 emendations. To avoid breaking the third commandment, "You shall not misuse the name of the LORD," they refused to pronounce God's name at all. To avoid sexual temptation they had a practice of lowering their heads and not even looking at women (the most scrupulous of these were known as "bleeding Pharisees" because of frequent collisions with walls and other obstacles). To avoid defiling the Sabbath they outlawed thirty-nine activities that might be construed as "work." How could an ordinary person's righteousness ever *surpass* that of such professional holy men?

The Sermon on the Mount details exactly what Jesus meant, and this explication is what seemed so absurd to twentieth-century students at Texas A&M as well as first-century Jews in Palestine. Using the Torah as a starting point, Jesus pushed the law in the same direction, further than any Pharisee had dared push it, further than any monk has dared live it. The Sermon on the Mount introduced a new moon in the moral universe that has exerted its own force of gravity ever since.

Jesus made the law impossible for anyone to keep and then charged us to keep it. Consider some examples.

Every human society in history has had a law against murder. There are variations, of course: the U.S. allows killing in self-defense or in unusual circumstances such as spouse abuse. But no society has come up with anything like Jesus' enlarged definition of murder: "I tell you that anyone who is angry with his brother will be subject to judgment. . . . anyone who says 'You fool!' will be in danger of the fire of hell." Growing up with an older brother, I fretted over this verse. Can two brothers weather the storms of adolescence without relying on words such as "stupid" and "fool"?

Every society also has taboos against sexual promiscuity. Today at least one college requires male students to ask females' permission for each stage of sexual contact. Meanwhile, some feminist groups are trying to forge a legal link between pornography and crimes against women. But no society has ever proposed a rule as strict as Jesus': "I tell you that anyone who looks at a woman lustfully has already committed adultery with her in his heart. If your right eye causes you to sin, gouge it out and throw it away. It is better for you to lose one part of your body than for your whole body to be thrown into hell."

I have heard calls for castration of serial rapists, but never have I heard a proposal for facial mutilation on account of lust. Indeed, lust in America is an established national pastime, celebrated in ads for blue jeans and beer, in the annual *Sports Illustrated* swimming suit issue, and in the twenty million copies of pornographic magazines sold each month. When presidential candidate Jimmy Carter tried to explain this verse in a *Playboy* magazine interview, the press reacted with what John Updike described as "nervous hilarity." "How strangely on modern ears," said Updike, "falls the notion that lust—sexual desire that wells up in us as involuntarily as saliva—in itself is wicked!"

As for divorce, in Jesus' day the Pharisees heatedly debated how to interpret the Old Testament rules. The prominent rabbi Hillel taught that a man could divorce his wife if she did anything at all to displease him, even something as trivial as burning his food; a husband needed only to pronounce "I divorce you" three times to make the divorce final. Jesus countered, "I tell you that anyone who divorces his wife, except for marital unfaithfulness, causes her to become an adulteress, and anyone who marries the divorced woman commits adultery."

Finally, Jesus spelled out the principle of nonviolence. Who could even survive with the rule Jesus laid down: "Do not resist an evil person. If someone strikes you on the right cheek, turn to him the other also. And if someone wants to sue you and take your tunic, let him have your cloak as well."

I stare at these and the other strict commands of the Sermon on the Mount and ask myself how to respond. Does Jesus really expect me to give to every panhandler who crosses my path? Should I abandon all insistence on consumer rights? Cancel my insurance policies and trust God for the future? Discard my television to avoid temptations to lust? How can I possibly translate such ethical ideals into my everyday life?

* * *

I once went on a reading binge in search of the "key" to understanding the Sermon on the Mount, and it brought some consolation to learn I was not the first to flounder over its high ideals. Throughout church history, people have found canny ways to reconcile Jesus' absolute demands with the grim reality of human delinquency.

Thomas Aquinas divided Jesus' teaching into Precepts and Counsels, which in more modern language we might rename Requirements and Suggestions. Precepts encompassed universal moral laws like the Ten Commandments. But for the more idealistic commands, such as Jesus' statements about anger and lust, Aquinas applied a different standard: though we should accept them as a good model and strive to fulfill them, they have not the moral force of Precepts. The Roman Catholic Church later codified Aquinas's distinctions into lists of "mortal" and "venial" sins.

Martin Luther interpreted the Sermon on the Mount in light of Jesus' formula "Give to Caesar what is Caesar's and to God what is God's." Christians maintain a dual citizenship, he said: one in the kingdom of Christ and one in the kingdom of the world. The extremism in the Sermon on the Mount applies absolutely to Christ's kingdom, but not to the world's. Take the commands to "Love your enemies" and "Do not resist an evil person"; of course these do not apply to the state! In order to prevent anarchy, a government must resist evil and repel enemies. Therefore, a Christian should learn to separate the office from the person; a Christian soldier, say, must carry out orders to fight and kill even while following Christ's law of love for enemies in his heart.

In Luther's day, various Anabaptist movements chose a radically different approach. All such attempts to water down Jesus' straightforward commands are misguided, they said. Had not the early church cited Christ's command to "love your enemies" more often than any other during its first four centuries? Simply read the Sermon on the Mount. Jesus does not differentiate between Precepts and Counsels, or the office and the person. He says don't resist an evil person, don't take oaths, give to the needy, love your enemies. We should follow his commands in the most literal way possible. For this reason some groups vowed to hold no personal property. Others, like the Quakers, refused to take oaths or doff their hats to a public official, and opposed having an army or even a police force. Subsequently, thousands of Anabaptists were killed in Europe, England, and Russia; many of the survivors made their way across the ocean to America, where they attempted to found colonies and communes based on the principles of the Sermon on the Mount.*

In nineteenth-century America a theological movement emerged with a new spin on the Sermon on the Mount. Dispensationalism explained such teaching as the last vestige of the age of Law, soon to be displaced by the age of Grace after Jesus' death and resurrection. Hence we need not follow its strict commands. The popular Scofield Bible described the sermon as "pure law" but with "beautiful moral application to the Christian."

Still another interpretation came from Albert Schweitzer, who saw the Sermon on the Mount as a set of interim demands for unusual times. Convinced that the world would soon end in the apocalypse, Jesus was setting into motion a kind of "martial law." Since the world did not end, we must now view his instructions differently.

Assiduously I studied all these movements, trying to understand the Sermon on the Mount from their vantage point—and, I must admit, trying to find a way to wriggle out from under its stern demands. Each school of thought contributed important insights, yet each also seemed to have a blind spot. Like most of the good doctor's elucidations, Aquinas's categories of Precepts and Counsels made fine common sense, but his was not a distinction Jesus made. Jesus seemed rather to equate the Precept "Do not commit adultery" with the Counsel " . . . anyone who looks at a woman lustfully has already committed adultery with her in his heart." Luther's solution seemed ingenious and wise, but World War II demonstrated the schizophrenic abuse it may allow. Many Lutheran Christians served in Hitler's army with a clear conscience: "just following orders," they carried out the office of the state while maintaining an inner allegiance to Christ.

---

*In response to Anabaptists, Luther scornfully wrote about a Christian who let lice nibble on him because he would not kill the vermin and thus risk defying the command "Resist not evil."

As for Anabaptists and other literalists, their nonviolent response to persecution stands as one of the shining moments in church history. Yet they themselves admitted their failure to fulfill literally every command in the Sermon on the Mount. Quakers, for example, found ways to circumvent the rules in order to help the cause of the American Revolution. And what of Jesus' unbending statements against anger and lust? Origen had taken the warning against lust to its literal extreme many centuries before, but the church, horrified, then banned his solution of castration.

Dispensationalists and apocalyptists found clever ways to dodge the harder requirements of Jesus' sermon, but they seemed to me just that: ways to dodge. Jesus himself gave no indication that his commands applied only for a short period or in special circumstances. He delivered them with authority ("But I say unto you . . .") and severity ("Anyone who breaks one of the least of these commandments and teaches others to do the same will be called least in the kingdom of heaven . . .").

No matter how hard I tried, I could not find an easy way around or through the Sermon on the Mount. Like a low-grade case of depression, my cognitive dissonance over Jesus' words kept me in a state of spiritual restlessness. If the Sermon on the Mount sets forth God's standard of holiness, I concluded, then I may as well resign from the start. The Sermon on the Mount did not help me improve; it simply revealed all the ways I had not.

Ultimately I found a key to understanding the Sermon on the Mount, not in the writings of great theologians but in a more unlikely place: the writings of two nineteenth-century Russian novelists. From them I have gained my own view of the Sermon on the Mount and its mosaic of law and grace, consisting of one-half Tolstoy and one-half Dostoevsky.*

---

*In the early 1970s Malcolm Muggeridge was surprised to hear that members of the intellectual elite in the Soviet Union were experiencing a spiritual revival. Anatoli Kuznetsov, living in exile in England, told him there was scarcely a single

From Tolstoy I learned a deep respect for God's inflexible, absolute Ideal. The ethical ideals Tolstoy encountered in the Gospels attracted him like a flame, though his failure to live up to those ideals ultimately consumed him. Like the Anabaptists, Tolstoy strove to follow the Sermon on the Mount literally, and his intensity soon caused his family to feel like victims of his quest for holiness. For instance, after reading Jesus' command to the rich man to give away everything, Tolstoy decided to free serfs, give away his copyrights, and dispose of his vast estate. He wore peasant clothes, made his own shoes, and began working in the fields. His wife, Sonya, seeing the family's financial security about to vaporize, protested petulantly until he made some concessions.

As I read Tolstoy's diaries, I see flashbacks of my own lunges toward perfectionism. The diaries record many struggles between Tolstoy and his family, but many more between Tolstoy and himself. In an attempt to reach perfection he kept devising new lists of rules. He gave up hunting, smoking, drinking, and meat. He drafted "Rules for developing the emotional will. Rules for developing lofty feelings and eliminating base ones." Yet he could never achieve the self-discipline necessary to keep the rules. More than once, Tolstoy took a public vow of chastity and asked for separate bedrooms. He could never keep the vow for long, and much to his shame, Sonya's sixteen pregnancies broadcast to the world that inability.

Sometimes Tolstoy managed to accomplish great good. For example, after a long hiatus he wrote one last novel, *Resurrection*, at the age of seventy-one, in support of the Doukhobors—an Anabaptist group undergoing persecution by the tsar—donating all proceeds to finance their emigration to Canada. And, as I have mentioned, Tolstoy's philosophy of nonviolence, lifted directly from the Sermon on the Mount, had an impact that long outlived him, in ideological descendants like Gandhi and Martin Luther King Jr.

---

writer or artist or musician in the U.S.S.R. who was not exploring spiritual issues. Muggeridge said, "I asked him [Kuznetsov] how this could have happened, given the enormous anti-religious brainwashing job done on the citizenry, and the absence of all Christian literature, including the Gospels. His reply was memorable; the authorities, he said, forgot to suppress the works of Tolstoy and Dostoevsky, the most perfect expositions of the Christian faith of modern times."

For every Gandhi stirred by such high-minded ideals, though, there is a critic or biographer repelled by how miserably Tolstoy himself failed to meet those ideals. Frankly, he failed to practice what he preached. His wife put it well (in an obviously biased account):

> There is so little genuine warmth about him; his kindness does not come from his heart, but merely from his principles. His biographies will tell of how he helped the laborers to carry buckets of water, but no one will ever know that he never gave his wife a rest and never—in all these thirty-two years—gave his child a drink of water or spent five minutes by his bedside to give me a chance to rest a little from all my labors.

Tolstoy's ardent strides toward perfection never resulted in any semblance of peace or serenity. Up to the moment of his death the diaries and letters kept circling back to the rueful theme of failure. When he wrote about his religious faith, or attempted to live out that faith, the antagonism between the real and the ideal haunted him like a dybbuk. Too honest for self-deception, he could not silence the conscience that convicted him because he knew his conscience to be true.

Leo Tolstoy was a deeply unhappy man. He fulminated against the corrupt Russian Orthodox Church of his day and earned their excommunication. His schemes for self-improvement all foundered. He had to hide all the ropes on his estate and put away his guns in order to resist the temptation toward suicide. In the end, Tolstoy fled from his fame, his family, his estate, his identity; he died like a vagrant in a rural railroad station.

What, then, do I learn from the tragic life of Leo Tolstoy? I have read many of his religious writings, and without fail I come away inspired by his penetrating insight into God's Ideal. I have learned that, contrary to those who say the gospel solves our problems, in many ways—justice issues, money issues, race issues—the gospel actually adds to our burdens. Tolstoy saw this, and never lowered the ideals of the gospel. A man willing to free his serfs and give away his possessions in simple obedience to Christ's command is not easy to dismiss. If only he could live up to those ideals—if only I could live up to them.

To his critics Tolstoy replied, Don't judge God's holy ideals by my inability to meet them. Don't judge Christ by those of us who imperfectly bear his name. One passage especially, taken from a personal letter, shows how Tolstoy responded to such critics toward the end of his life. It stands as a summary of his spiritual pilgrimage, at once a ringing affirmation of the truth that he believed with all his heart and a plangent appeal for grace that he never fully realized.

"What about you, Lev Nikolayevich, you preach very well, but do you carry out what you preach?" This is the most natural of questions and one that is always asked of me; it is usually asked victoriously, as though it were a way of stopping my mouth. "You preach, but how do you live?" And I answer that I do not preach, that I am not able to preach, although I passionately wish to. I can preach only through my actions, and my actions are vile.... And I answer that I am guilty, and vile, and worthy of contempt for my failure to carry them out.

At the same time, not in order to justify, but simply in order to explain my lack of consistency, I say: "Look at my present life and then at my former life, and you will see that I do attempt to carry them out. It is true that I have not fulfilled one thousandth part of them [Christian precepts], and I am ashamed of this, but I have failed to fulfill them not because I did not wish to, but because I was unable to. Teach me how to escape from the net of temptations that surrounds me, help me and I will fulfill them; even without help I wish and hope to fulfill them.

"Attack me, I do this myself, but attack *me* rather than the path I follow and which I point out to anyone who asks me where I think it lies. If I know the way home and am walking along it drunkenly, is it any less the right way because I am staggering from side to side! If it is not the right way, then show me another way; but if I stagger and lose the way, you must help me, you must keep me on the true path, just as I am ready to support you. Do not mislead me, do not be glad that I have got lost, do not shout out joyfully: 'Look at him! He said he was going home, but there he is crawling into a bog!' No, do not gloat, but give me your help and support."

I feel sad as I read Tolstoy's religious writings. The X-ray vision into the human heart that made him a great novelist also made him a tortured Christian. Like a spawning salmon, he fought upstream all his life, in the end collapsing from moral exhaustion.

Yet I also feel grateful to Tolstoy, for his relentless pursuit of authentic faith has made an indelible impression upon me. I first came across his novels during a period when I was suffering the delayed effects of "biblical child abuse." The churches I grew up in contained too many frauds, or at least that is how I saw it in the arrogance of youth. When I observed the huge gap between the ideals of the gospel and the flaws of its followers, I was sorely tempted to abandon those ideals as hopelessly unattainable.

Then I discovered Tolstoy. He was the first author who, for me, accomplished that most difficult of tasks: to make Good as believable and appealing as Evil. I found in his novels, fables, and short stories a Vesuvian source of moral power. Unfailingly, he raised my sights.

A. N. Wilson, a biographer of Tolstoy, remarks that Tolstoy suffered from a "fundamental theological inability to understand the Incarnation. His religion was ultimately a thing of Law rather than of Grace, a scheme for human betterment rather than a vision of God penetrating a fallen world." With crystalline clarity Tolstoy could see his own inadequacy in the light of God's Ideal. But he could not take the further step of trusting God's grace to overcome that inadequacy.

Shortly after reading Tolstoy I discovered his countryman Fyodor Dostoevsky. These two, the most famous and accomplished of all Russian writers, lived and worked during the same period of history. Oddly, they never met, and perhaps it was just as well—they were opposites in every way. Where Tolstoy wrote bright, sunny novels, Dostoevsky wrote dark and brooding ones. Where Tolstoy worked out ascetic schemes for self-improvement, Dostoevsky periodically squandered his health and fortune on alcohol and gambling. Dostoevsky got many things wrong, but he got one thing right: His novels communicate grace and forgiveness with a Tolstoyan force.

Early in his life, Dostoevsky underwent a virtual resurrection. He had been arrested for belonging to a group judged treasonous by Tsar

Nicholas I, who, to impress upon the young parlor radicals the gravity of their errors, sentenced them to death and staged a mock execution. The conspirators were dressed in white death gowns and led to a public square where a firing squad awaited them. Blindfolded, robed in white burial shrouds, hands bound tightly behind them, they were paraded before a gawking crowd and then tied to posts. At the very last instant, as the order, "Ready, aim!" was heard and rifles were cocked and lifted upward, a horseman galloped up with a pre-arranged message from the tsar: he would mercifully commute their sentences to hard labor.

Dostoevsky never recovered from this experience. He had peered into the jaws of death, and from that moment life became for him precious beyond all calculation. "Now my life will change," he said; "I shall be born again in a new form." As he boarded the convict train toward Siberia, a devout woman handed him a New Testament, the only book allowed in prison. Believing that God had given him a second chance to fulfill his calling, Dostoevsky pored over that New Testament during his confinement. After ten years he emerged from exile with unshakable Christian convictions, as expressed in one famous passage, "If anyone proved to me that Christ was outside the truth . . . then I would prefer to remain with Christ than with the truth."

Prison offered Dostoevsky another opportunity as well. It forced him to live at close quarters with thieves, murderers, and drunken peasants. His shared life with these people later led to unmatched characterizations in his novels, such as that of the murderer Raskolnikov in *Crime and Punishment*. Dostoevsky's liberal view of the inherent goodness in humanity shattered in collision with the granitic evil he found in his cellmates. Yet over time he also glimpsed the image of God in even the lowest of prisoners. He came to believe that only through being loved is a human being capable of love; "We love because he [God] first loved us," as the apostle John says.

I encountered grace in the novels of Dostoevsky. *Crime and Punishment* portrays a despicable human being who commits a despicable crime. Yet grace enters Raskolnikov's life as well, through the person of the converted prostitute Sonia, who follows him all the way to Siberia and leads him to redemption. *The Brothers Karamazov*, perhaps the greatest novel ever written, draws a contrast between Ivan the brilliant agnostic and his devout brother Alyosha. Ivan can critique the failures of humankind and every political system devised to deal with those failures, but he can offer no solutions. Alyosha has no solutions for the intellectual problems Ivan raises, but he has a solution for humanity: love. "I do not know the answer to the problem of evil," said Alyosha, "but I do know love." Finally, in the magical novel *The Idiot*, Dostoevsky presents a Christ figure in the form of an epileptic prince. Quietly, mysteriously, Prince Myshkin moves among the circles of Russia's upper class, exposing their hypocrisy while also illuminating their lives with goodness and truth.

Taken together, these two Russians became for me, at a crucial time in my Christian pilgrimage, spiritual directors. They helped me come to terms with a central paradox of the Christian life. From Tolstoy I learned the need to look inside, to the kingdom of God that is within me. I saw how miserably I had failed the high ideals of the gospel. But from Dostoevsky I learned the full extent of grace. Not only the kingdom of God is within me; Christ himself dwells there. "Where sin increased, grace increased all the more," is how Paul expressed it in Romans.

There is only one way for any of us to resolve the tension between the high ideals of the gospel and the grim reality of ourselves: to accept that we will never measure up, but that we do not have to. We are judged by the righteousness of the Christ who lives within, not our own. Tolstoy got it halfway right: anything that makes me feel comfort with God's moral standard, anything that makes me feel, "At last I have arrived," is a cruel deception. But Dostoevsky got the other half right: anything that makes me feel discomfort with God's forgiving love is also a cruel deception. "There is now no condemnation for those who are in Christ Jesus": that message, Leo Tolstoy never fully grasped.

Absolute ideals and absolute grace: after learning that dual message from Russian novelists, I returned to Jesus and found that it suffuses his teaching throughout the Gospels and especially in the Sermon on the Mount. In his response to the rich young ruler, in the parable of the Good Samaritan, in his comments about divorce, money, or any other moral issue, Jesus never lowered God's Ideal. "Be perfect, therefore, as your heavenly Father is perfect," he said. "Love the Lord your God with all your heart and with all your soul and with all your mind." Not Tolstoy, not Francis of Assisi, not Mother Teresa, not anyone has completely fulfilled those commands.

Yet the same Jesus tenderly offered absolute grace. Jesus forgave an adulteress, a thief on the cross, a disciple who had denied ever knowing him. He tapped that traitorous disciple, Peter, to found his church and for the next advance turned to a man named Saul, who had made his mark persecuting Christians. Grace is absolute, inflexible, all-encompassing. It extends even to the people who nailed Jesus to the cross: "Father, forgive them, for they do not know what they are doing" were among the last words Jesus spoke on earth.

For years I had felt so unworthy before the absolute ideals of the Sermon on the Mount that I had missed in it any notion of grace. Once I understood the dual message, however, I went back and found that the message of grace gusts through the entire speech. It begins with the Beatitudes—Blessed are the poor in spirit, those who mourn, the meek; blessed are the desperate—and it moves toward the Lord's Prayer: "Forgive us our debts ... deliver us from the evil one." Jesus began this great sermon with gentle words for those in need and continued on with a prayer that has formed a model for all twelve-step groups. "One day at a time," say the alcoholics in AA; "Give us this day our daily bread," say the Christians. Grace is for the desperate, the needy, the broken, those who cannot make it on their own. Grace is for all of us.

For years I had thought of the Sermon on the Mount as a blueprint for human behavior that no one could possibly follow. Reading it again, I found that Jesus gave these words not to cumber us, but to tell us what *God* is like. The character of God is the urtext of the Sermon on the Mount. Why should we love our enemies? Because our clement Father causes his sun to rise on the evil and the good. Why be perfect? Because God is perfect. Why store up treasures in heaven? Because the Father lives there and will lavishly reward us. Why live without fear and worry? Because the same God who clothes the lilies and the grass of the field has promised to take care of us. Why pray?

If an earthly father gives his son bread or fish, how much more will the Father in heaven give good gifts to those who ask him.

How could I have missed it? Jesus did not proclaim the Sermon on the Mount so that we would, Tolstoy-like, furrow our brows in despair over our failure to achieve perfection. He gave it to impart to us God's Ideal toward which we should never stop striving, but also to show that none of us will ever reach that Ideal. The Sermon on the Mount forces us to recognize the great distance between God and us, and any attempt to reduce that distance by somehow moderating its demands misses the point altogether.

The worst tragedy would be to turn the Sermon on the Mount into another form of legalism; it should rather put an end to all legalism. Legalism like the Pharisees' will always fail, not because it is too strict but because it is not strict enough. Thunderously, inarguably, the Sermon on the Mount proves that before God we all stand on level ground: murderers and temper-throwers, adulterers and lusters, thieves and coveters. We are all desperate, and that is in fact the only state appropriate to a human being who wants to know God. Having fallen from the absolute Ideal, we have nowhere to land but in the safety net of absolute grace.

8
Mission: A Revolution of Grace

The quality of mercy is not strained.
It droppeth as the gentle rain from heaven ...
And earthly power doth then show likest God's
When mercy seasons justice.

Shakespeare, The Merchant of Venice

8

Mission:
A Revolution of Grace

As my class in Chicago read the Gospels and watched movies about Jesus' life, we noticed a striking pattern: the more unsavory the characters, the more at ease they seemed to feel around Jesus. People like these found Jesus appealing: a Samaritan social outcast, a military officer of the tyrant Herod, a quisling tax collector, a recent hostess to seven demons.

In contrast, Jesus got a chilly response from more respectable types. Pious Pharisees thought him uncouth and worldly, a rich young ruler walked away shaking his head, and even the open-minded Nicodemus sought a meeting under the cover of darkness.

I remarked to the class how strange this pattern seemed, since the Christian church now attracts respectable types who closely resemble the people most suspicious of Jesus on earth. What has happened to reverse the pattern of Jesus' day? Why don't sinners *like* being around us?

I recounted a story told me by a friend who works with the down-and-out in Chicago. A prostitute came to him in wretched straits, homeless, her health failing, unable to buy food for her two-year-old daughter. Her eyes awash with tears, she confessed that she had been renting out her daughter—two years old!—to men interested in kinky sex, in order to support her own drug habit. My friend could hardly bear hearing the sordid details of her story. He sat in silence, not knowing what to say. At last he asked if she had ever thought of going to a church for help. "I will never forget the look of pure astonishment that crossed her face," he later told me. "'Church!' she cried. 'Why would I ever go there? They'd just make me feel even worse than I already do!'"

Somehow we have created a community of respectability in the church, I told my class. The down-and-out, who flocked to Jesus when he lived on earth, no longer feel welcome. How did Jesus, the only perfect person in history, manage to attract the notoriously imperfect? And what keeps us from following in his steps today?

Someone in the class suggested that legalism in the church had created a barrier of strict rules that made non-Christians feel uncomfortable. The class discussion abruptly lurched in a new direction, as survivors of Christian colleges and fundamentalist churches began swapping war stories. I told of my own bemusement in the early seventies when the redoubtable Moody Bible Institute, located just four blocks down the street from our church, was banning all beards, mustaches, and hair below the ears of male students—though each day students filed past a large oil painting of Dwight L. Moody, hirsute breaker of all three rules.

Everyone laughed. Everyone except Greg, that is, who fidgeted in his seat and smoldered. I could see his face flush red, then blanch with anger. Finally Greg raised his hand, and rage and indignation spilled out. He was almost stammering. "I feel like walking out of this place," he said, and all of a sudden the room hushed. "You criticize others for being Pharisees, I'll tell you who the real Pharisees are. They're you [he pointed at me] and the rest of you people in this class. You think you're so high and mighty and mature. I became a Christian because of Moody Church. You find a group to look down on, to feel more spiritual than, and you talk about them behind their backs. That's what a Pharisee does. You're all Pharisees."

All eyes in the class turned to me for a reply, but I had none to offer. Greg had caught us red-handed. In a twist of spiritual arrogance, we were now looking down on other people for being Pharisees. I glanced at the clock, hoping for a reprieve. No such luck: It showed fifteen minutes of class time remaining. I waited for a flash of inspiration, but none came. The silence grew louder. I felt embarrassed and trapped.

Then Bob raised his hand. Bob was new to the class, and until the day I die I will always be grateful to him for rescuing me. He began softly, disarmingly, "I'm glad you didn't walk out, Greg. We need you here. I'm glad you're here, and I'd like to tell you why I come to this church.

"Frankly, I identify with the Chicago prostitute Philip mentioned. I was addicted to drugs, and in a million years it wouldn't have occurred to me to approach a church for help. Every Tuesday, though, this church lets an Alcoholics Anonymous chapter meet in the basement room we're sitting in right now. I started attending that group, and after a while I decided a church that welcomes an AA group—cigarette butts, coffee spills, and all—can't be too bad, so I made a point to visit a service.

"I've got to tell you, the people upstairs were threatening to me at first. They seemed like they had it all together while I was barely hanging on. People here dress pretty casually, I guess, but the best clothes I owned were blue jeans and T-shirts. I managed to swallow my pride, though, and started coming on Sunday mornings as well as Tuesday nights. People didn't shun me. They reached out to me. It's here that I met Jesus."

As if someone had opened an air lock, all tension discharged from the room during Bob's speech of simple eloquence. Greg relaxed, I mumbled an apology for my own Pharisaism, and the class ended on a note of unity. Bob had brought us back to common ground, as sinners equally desperate in our need of God.

What would it take, I asked in closing, for church to become a place where prostitutes, tax collectors, and even guilt-tinged Pharisees would gladly gather?

Jesus was the friend of sinners. They liked being around him and longed for his company. Meanwhile, legalists found him shocking, even revolting. What was Jesus' secret that we have lost?

"You can know a person by the company he keeps," the proverb goes. Imagine the consternation of people in first-century Palestine who tried to apply that principle to Jesus of Nazareth. The Gospels mention eight occasions when Jesus accepted an invitation to dinner. Three of these (the wedding at Cana, hospitality by Mary and Martha, and the interrupted meal in Emmaus after his resurrection) were normal social occasions among friends. The other five, however, defy all rules of social propriety.

Once, Jesus dined with Simon the Leper. Because of my work with Dr. Paul Brand, a leprosy specialist, I too have dined with leprosy patients, and I can tell you that two thousand years of medical progress have done little to lessen the social stigma of the disease. One refined, educated man in India told me of the day he sat weeping in a car outside a church as his daughter got married within. He dared not show his disfigured face, lest all the guests leave. Nor could he host the traditional wedding banquet, for who would enter the home of a leper?

In Palestine, stern laws enforced the stigma against leprosy: the afflicted had to live outside city walls and yell "Unclean!" when they approached anyone. Yet Jesus ignored those rules and reclined at the table of a man who wore that stigma as part of his name. To make matters worse, during the course of the meal a disreputable woman poured expensive perfume on Jesus' head. According to Mark, Judas Iscariot left the meal in disgust and went straight to the chief priests to betray Jesus.

In a different scene with some striking parallels, Jesus shared a meal with another man named Simon, and here too a woman anointed Jesus with perfume, wiping his feet with her hair and her tears. This Simon, though, being a proper Pharisee, recoiled at the indiscretion. Jesus gave a searing reply that helps explain why he preferred the company of "sinners and tax collectors" over outstanding citizens like Simon:

> Do you see this woman? I came into your house. You did not give me any water for my feet, but she wet my feet with her tears and wiped them with her hair. You did not give me a kiss, but this woman, from the time I entered, has not stopped kissing my feet. You did not put oil on my head, but she has poured perfume on my feet. Therefore, I tell you, her many sins have been forgiven—for she loved much. But he who has been forgiven little loves little.

At least one other time Jesus accepted hospitality from a prominent Pharisee. Like double agents, the religious leaders were following him around and inviting him to meals while scrutinizing his every move. Provocatively, despite it being the Sabbath, Jesus healed a man from dropsy, and then he drew a stinging contrast between the social-climbing banquets of the Pharisees and God's banquet spread for "the poor, the crippled, the blind and the lame." The Gospels record no other meals with prominent citizens, and I can easily understand why: Jesus hardly made for a soothing dinner guest.*

The last two meals we know about took place in the homes of "publicans," or tax collectors, a class of people unpopular in any age but especially so in Jesus' day. They collected taxes on a commission basis, pocketing whatever profits they could extort from the locals, and most Jews viewed them as traitors serving the Roman Empire. The word *publican* became synonymous with robber, brigand, murderer, and reprobate. Jewish courts considered a tax collector's evidence as invalid, and his money could not be accepted as alms for the poor or used in exchange since it had been acquired by such despicable means.

Pointedly, Jesus invited himself to the homes of both tax collectors. When he noticed the ostracized Zacchaeus, so short he had to climb a tree to see Jesus, he called the man down and asked to stay at his house. The crowd muttered disapproval, but Jesus shrugged off their complaints: "For the Son of Man came to seek and to save what was lost." Another such reprobate, Levi, Jesus met at a booth in the very act of collecting the hated taxes. "It is not the healthy who need a doctor, but the sick," he told the crowd that time.

Reading about Jesus' assorted dinner companions, I search for a clue that might explain why Jesus made one group (sinners) feel so comfortable and the other group (pious) feel so uncomfortable. I find such a clue in one more scene from the Gospels that brings together Pharisees and a blatant sinner simultaneously. The Pharisees have

*Pharisees thought of their dining table as a kind of "little temple," which explains why they refused to dine with Gentiles or sinners. Perhaps Jesus understood his dining table as a little temple as well, which explains why he ate with such a motley assortment of dining companions. The great banquet, he proclaimed, is now open to all, not merely those who have been through proper purification.

caught a woman in the very act of adultery, a crime that calls for the death penalty. What would Jesus have them do? they ask, hoping to trap him in a conflict between morality and mercy.

Jesus pauses, writes on the ground for a moment, then says to the accusers, "If any one of you is without sin, let him be the first to throw a stone at her." When all of them have filed away, Jesus turns to the cringing woman. "Where are they? Has no one condemned you?" he asks. "Then neither do I condemn you. Go now and leave your life of sin."

This tense scene reveals a clear principle in Jesus' life: he brings to the surface repressed sin, yet forgives any freely acknowledged sin. The adulteress went away forgiven, with a new lease on life; the Pharisees slunk away, stabbed to the heart.

Perhaps prostitutes, tax collectors, and other known sinners responded to Jesus so readily because at some level they knew they were wrong and to them God's forgiveness looked very appealing. As C. S. Lewis has said, "Prostitutes are in no danger of finding their present life so satisfactory that they cannot turn to God: the proud, the avaricious, the self-righteous, are in that danger."

Jesus' message met a mixed response among first-century Jews, many of whom preferred the style of John the Baptist, with his insect diet and his stern message of judgment and wrath, to Jesus' message of grace and a banquet spread for all. I can understand this odd preference for the law because of the legalistic environment I grew up in. Grace was slippery, evanescent, hard to get my mind around. Sin was concrete, visible, an easy target to pounce on. Under law, I always knew where I ranked.

Wendy Kaminer, a modern Jew trying to comprehend Christianity, confesses that "as an article of faith, this doctrine of salvation by grace and grace alone is remarkably unappealing to me. It takes, I think, remarkable disregard for justice to idealize a God who so values belief over action. I prefer the God who looks down upon us (in a very old joke) and says, 'I wish they'd stop worrying about whether or not I exist and start obeying my commandments.'"

In truth we Christians, too, may find it easier to follow a God who simply says, "Start obeying my commandments."

Jews in Jesus' day envisioned a ladder reaching higher and higher towards God, a hierarchy expressed in the very architecture of the temple. Gentiles and "half-breeds" like the Samaritans were permitted only in the outer Court of the Gentiles; a wall separated them from the next partition, which admitted Jewish women. Jewish men could proceed one stage further, but only priests could enter the sacred areas. Finally, only one priest, the high priest, could enter the Most Holy Place, and that just once a year on the day of Yom Kippur.

The society was, in effect, a religious caste system based on steps toward holiness, and the Pharisees' scrupulosity reinforced the system daily. All their rules on washing hands and avoiding defilement were an attempt to make themselves acceptable to God. Had not God set forth lists of desirable (spotless) and undesirable (flawed, unclean) animals for use in sacrifice? Had not God banned sinners, menstruating women, the physically deformed, and other "undesirables" from the temple? The Qumram community of the Essenes made a firm rule, "No madman, or lunatic, or simpleton, or fool, no blind man, or maimed, or lame, or deaf man, and no minor, shall enter into the Community."

In the midst of this religious caste system, Jesus appeared. To the Pharisees' dismay he had no qualms about socializing with children or sinners or even Samaritans. He touched, or was touched by, the "unclean": those with leprosy, the deformed, a hemorrhaging woman, the lunatic and possessed. Although Levitical laws prescribed a day of purification after touching a sick person, Jesus conducted mass healings in which he touched scores of sick people; he never concerned himself with the rules of defilement after contact with the sick or even the dead.

To take just one example of the revolutionary changes Jesus set in motion, consider Jesus' attitude toward women. In those days, at every synagogue service Jewish men prayed, "Blessed art thou, O Lord, who hast not made me a woman." Women sat in a separate section, were not counted in quorums, and were rarely taught the Torah. In social life, few women would talk to men outside of their families, and a woman was to touch no man but her spouse. Yet Jesus associated freely with women and taught some as his disciples. A Samaritan woman who had been through five husbands, Jesus tapped to lead a spiritual revival (notably, he began the conversation by asking *her* for help). A prostitute's anointing, he accepted with gratitude. Women traveled with his band of followers, no doubt stirring up much gossip. Women populated Jesus' parables and illustrations, and frequently he did miracles on their behalf. According to biblical scholar Walter Wink, Jesus violated the mores of his time in every single encounter with women recorded in the four Gospels. Truly, as Paul would later say, in Christ "There is neither Jew nor Greek, slave nor free, male nor female. ...."*

Indeed, for women and other oppressed people, Jesus turned upside down the accepted wisdom of the day. Pharisees believed that touching an unclean person polluted the one who touched. But when Jesus touched a person with leprosy, Jesus did not become soiled—the leprous became clean. When an immoral woman washed Jesus' feet, *she* went away forgiven and transformed. When he defied custom to enter a pagan's house, the pagan's servant was healed. In word and in deed Jesus was proclaiming a radically new gospel of grace: to get clean a person did not have to journey to Jerusalem, offer sacrifices, and undergo purification rituals. All a person had to do was follow Jesus. As Walter Wink puts it, "The contagion of holiness overcomes the contagion of uncleanness."

---

*Dorothy Sayers expands the point: "Perhaps it is no wonder that the women were first at the Cradle and last at the Cross. They had never known a man like this Man there had never been such another. A prophet and teacher who never nagged at them, who never flattered or coaxed or patronized; who never made arch jokes about them, never treated them either as 'The women, God help us!' or 'The ladies, God bless them!'; who rebuked without querulousness and praised without condescension; who took their questions and arguments seriously, who never mapped out their sphere for them, never urged them to be feminine or jeered at them for being female; who had no ax to grind and no uneasy male dignity to defend; who took them as he found them and was completely unselfconscious.

"There is no act, no sermon, no parable in the whole Gospel that borrows its pungency from female perversity; nobody could possibly guess from the words of Jesus that there was anything 'funny' about woman's nature.

"But we might easily deduce it from His contemporaries, and from His prophets before Him, and from His Church to this day."

In short, Jesus moved the emphasis from God's holiness (exclusive) to God's mercy (inclusive). Instead of the message "No undesirables allowed," he proclaimed, "In God's kingdom there are no undesirables." By going out of his way to meet with Gentiles, eat with sinners, and touch the sick, he extended the realm of God's mercy. To Jewish leaders, Jesus' actions jeopardized the very existence of their religious caste system—no wonder the Gospels mention more than twenty occasions when they conspired against Jesus.

One of Jesus' stories, contrasting a pious Pharisee with a remorseful tax collector, captures the inclusive gospel of grace in a nutshell. The Pharisee, who fasted twice a week and tithed on schedule, piously thanked God that he was above robbers, evildoers, and adulterers—and far above the tax collector standing to the side. The tax collector, too humiliated even to raise his eyes to heaven, prayed the simplest prayer possible, "God, have mercy on me, a sinner." Jesus drew the conclusion, "I tell you that this man, rather than the other, went home justified before God."

Can we infer from Jesus' story that behavior does not matter, that there is no moral difference between a disciplined legalist and a robber, evildoer, and adulterer. Of course not. Behavior matters in many ways; it simply is not how to get accepted by God. The skeptic A. N. Wilson comments on Jesus' parable of the Pharisee and tax collector, "It is a shocking, morally anarchic story. All that matters in the story appears to be God's capacity to forgive." Precisely.

In his own social interactions, Jesus was putting into practice "the great reversal" heralded in the Beatitudes. Normally in this world we look up to the rich, the beautiful, the successful. Grace, however, introduces a world of new logic. Because God loves the poor, the suffering, the persecuted, so should we. Because God sees no undesirables, neither should we. By his own example, Jesus challenged us to look at the world through what Irenaeus would call "grace-healed eyes."

Jesus' parables underscored that mission, for often he made the poor and oppressed the heroes of his stories. One such story featured a poor man, Lazarus—the only named person in Jesus' parables—who was being exploited by a rich man. At first the rich man enjoyed sumptuous clothes and food while the beggar Lazarus, covered with scars, lay outside his gate with the dogs. Death, though, stunningly reversed their fortunes. The rich man heard from Abraham, "Son, remember that in your lifetime you received your good things, while Lazarus received bad things, but now he is comforted here and you are in agony."

That trenchant story sank deep into the consciousness of early Christians, many of whom belonged to lower economic classes. Rich and poor Christians struck a bargain: the rich agreed to fund charities in exchange for the poor praying for their souls. Surely God was more inclined toward the prayers of the poor, they reasoned. (Even today at funerals Benedictine monks pray that "Lazarus will know" their fallen colleague, following the tradition that Lazarus, not Peter, guards the entrance into heaven.)

For a while, the church worked hard to follow this new logic, and as a result, early Christians were renowned within the Roman Empire for their support of the poor and suffering. The Christians, unlike their pagan neighbors, readily ransomed their friends from barbarian captors, and when plague hit, the Christians tended their sufferers whereas the pagans abandoned the sick at the first symptoms. For the first few centuries, at least, the church took literally Christ's commands to receive strangers, clothe the naked, feed the hungry, and visit those in prison.*

As I read the stories of Jesus and study the history of the early church, I feel both inspired and troubled. The question I first raised with my class in Chicago returns to convict me. In view of Jesus' clear example, how is it that the church has now become a community of respectability, where the down-and-out no longer feel welcome?

I presently live in Colorado, where I attend a church in which most people come from the same race (white) and the same social class (middle). It startles me to open the New Testament and see in what mixed soil the early church took root. The middle-class church many

---

*According to church historians, this good work continued until the triumph of Constantine, who legalized the faith and established an official imperial church. From that point on the church tended to spiritualize poverty and leave "welfare" to the emperor. Over time the church itself became part of the wealthy establishment.

of us know today bears little resemblance to the diverse group of social rejects described in the Gospels and the book of Acts.

Projecting myself back into Jesus' time, I try to picture the scene. The poor, the sick, the tax collectors, sinners, and prostitutes crowd around Jesus, stirred by his message of healing and forgiveness. The rich and powerful stand on the sidelines, testing him, spying, trying to entrap him. I know these facts about Jesus' time, and yet, from the comfort of a middle-class church in a wealthy country like the U.S., I easily lose sight of the radical core of Jesus' message.

To help correct my vision, I have read sermons that come out of the Christian base communities in the Third World. The gospel through Third World eyes looks very different from the gospel as preached in many U.S. churches. The poor and the unlearned cannot always identify Jesus' mission statement (" . . . he has anointed me to preach good news to the poor . . . to proclaim freedom for the captives and release for the prisoners . . .") as a quotation from Isaiah, but they hear it as good news indeed. They understand the great reversal not as an abstraction but as God's promise of defiant hope and Jesus' challenge to his followers. Regardless of how the world treats them, the poor and the sick have assurance, because of Jesus, that God knows no undesirables.

It took the writings of a Japanese novelist named Shusaku Endo to impress on me that the phenomenon of reversal lay at the very heart of Jesus' mission.

In a country where the church comprises less than one percent of the population, Endo was raised by a devout Christian mother and baptized at the age of eleven. Growing up as a Christian in prewar Japan, he felt a constant sense of alienation and was sometimes bullied by classmates for his association with a "Western" religion. After World War II ended he traveled to France, hoping there to find spiritual soulmates. Again he faced persecution, this time on account of race, not religion. As one of the first Japanese exchange students in an

Allied country, Endo found himself the target of racial abuse. "Slanty-eyed gook," some called him.

Rejected in his homeland, rejected in his spiritual homeland, Endo underwent a grave crisis of faith. He began visiting Palestine to research the life of Jesus, and while there he made a transforming discovery: Jesus too knew rejection. More, Jesus' life was *defined* by rejection. His neighbors laughed at him, his family questioned his sanity, his closest friends betrayed him, and his countrymen traded his life for that of a terrorist. Throughout his ministry, Jesus gravitated toward the poor and the rejected ones, the riffraff.

This new insight into Jesus hit Endo with the force of revelation. From his faraway vantage point in Japan he had viewed Christianity as a triumphant, Constantinian faith. He had studied the Holy Roman Empire and the glittering Crusades, had admired photos of the grand cathedrals of Europe, had dreamed of living in a nation where one could be a Christian without disgrace. Now, as he studied the Bible, he saw that Christ himself had not avoided "dis-grace." Jesus was the Suffering Servant, as depicted by Isaiah: "despised and rejected by men, a man of sorrows, and familiar with suffering. Like one from whom men hide their faces. ..." Endo felt that surely this Jesus, if anyone, could understand the rejection he himself was going through.

As Shusaku Endo sees it, Jesus brought the message of mother-love to balance the father-love of the Old Testament.* Of course mercy appears in the Old Testament as well, but it easily gets lost amid the overwhelming emphasis on judgment and law. Addressing a culture raised on those strict demands of the Torah, Jesus told of a God who prefers the pleas of an ordinary sinner to the supplications of a religious professional. He likened God to a shepherd who leaves ninety-nine sheep inside the fence and hunts frantically for one stray; to a father who can't stop thinking about his rebellious ingrate of a son though he has another who's

---

*Therapist Erich Fromm says that a child from a balanced family receives two kinds of love. Mother-love tends to be unconditional, accepting the child no matter what, regardless of behavior. Father-love tends to be more provisional, bestowing approval as the child meets certain standards of behavior. Ideally, says Fromm, a child should receive and internalize both kinds of love. According to Endo, Japan, a nation of authoritarian fathers, has understood the father-love of God, but not the mother-love.

respectful and obedient; to a rich host who opens the doors of the banquet hall to a menagerie of bag ladies and bums.

Jesus was often "moved by compassion," and in New Testament times that very word was used maternally to express what a mother feels for her child in her womb. Jesus went out of his way to embrace the unloved and unworthy, the folks who matter not at all to the rest of society—they embarrass us, we wish they'd go away—to prove that even "nobodies" matter infinitely to God. One unclean woman, too shy and full of shame to approach Jesus face-to-face, grabbed his robe, hoping he would not notice. He did notice. She learned, like so many other "nobodies," that you cannot easily escape Jesus' gaze.

Jesus proved in person that God loves people not as a race or species, but as individuals. We *matter* to God. "By loving the unlovable," said Augustine, "You made me lovable."

At times, I do not find it easy to believe in the love of God. I do not live in poverty, like the Christians in the Third World. Nor have I known a life of rejection, like Shusaku Endo. But I have known my share of suffering, a fact of life that cuts across all racial and economic boundaries. Suffering people also need grace-healed eyes.

One terrible week two people called me on successive days to talk about one of my books. The first, a youth pastor in Colorado, had just learned his wife and baby daughter were dying of AIDS. "How can I possibly talk to my youth group about a loving God after what has happened to me?" he asked. The next day I heard from a blind man who, several months before, had invited a recovering drug addict into his home as an act of mercy. Recently he had discovered that the recovering addict was carrying on an affair with his wife, under his own roof. "Why is God punishing me for trying to serve him?" he asked. Just then he ran out of quarters, the phone went dead, and I never heard from the man again.

I have learned not even to attempt an answer to the "Why?" questions. Why did the youth pastor's wife happen to get the one tainted bottle of blood? Why do some good people get persecuted for their deeds while some evil people live to healthy old age? Why do so few of the millions of prayers for physical healing get answered? I do not know.

One question, however, no longer gnaws at me as it once did, a question that I believe lurks behind most of our issues with God: "Does God care?" I know of only one way to answer that question, and it has come through my study of the life of Jesus. In Jesus, God gave us a face, and I can read directly in that face how God feels about people like the youth pastor and the blind man who never gave me his name. By no means did Jesus eliminate all suffering—he healed only a few in one small patch of the globe—but he did signify an answer to the question of whether God cares.

Three times that we know of, suffering drove Jesus to tears. He wept when his friend Lazarus died. I remember one dreadful year when three of my friends died in quick succession. Grief, I found, is not something you get used to. My experience of the first two deaths did nothing to prepare me for the third. Grief hit like a freight train, flattening me. It left me gasping for breath, and I could do nothing but cry. Somehow, I find it comforting that Jesus felt something similar when his friend Lazarus died. That gives a startling clue into how God must have felt about my three friends, whom he also loved.

Another time, tears came to Jesus when he looked out over Jerusalem and realized the fate awaiting that fabled city. He let out a cry of what Shusaku Endo has called mother-love: "O Jerusalem, Jerusalem, you who kill the prophets and stone those sent to you, how often I have longed to gather your children together, as a hen gathers her chicks under her wings, but you were not willing." I sense in that spasm of emotional pain something akin to what a parent feels when a son or daughter goes astray, flaunting freedom, rejecting everything he or she was brought up to believe. Or the pain of a man or woman who has just learned a spouse has left—the pain of a jilted lover. It is a helpless, crushing pain of futility, and it staggers me to realize that the Son of God himself emitted a cry of helplessness in the face of human freedom. Not even God, with all his power, can force a human being to love.

Finally, Hebrews tells us, Jesus "offered up ... loud cries and tears to the one who could save him from death." But of course he was not saved from death. Is it too much to say that Jesus himself asked the question that haunts me, that haunts most of us at one time or another: Does God care? What else can be the meaning of his quotation from that dark psalm, "My God, my God, why have you forsaken me?"

Again, I find it strangely comforting that when Jesus faced pain he responded much as I do. He did not pray in the garden, "Oh, Lord, I am so grateful that you have chosen me to suffer on your behalf. I rejoice in the privilege!" No, he experienced sorrow, fear, abandonment, and something approaching even desperation. Still, he endured because he knew that at the center of the universe lived his Father, a God of love he could trust regardless of how things appeared at the time.

Jesus' response to suffering people and to "nobodies" provides a glimpse into the heart of God. God is not the unmoved Absolute, but rather the Loving One who draws near. God looks on me in all my weakness, I believe, as Jesus looked on the widow standing by her son's bier, and on Simon the Leper, and on another Simon, Peter, who cursed him yet even so was commissioned to found and lead his church, a community that need always find a place for rejects.

9

Miracles: Snapshots of the Supernatural

The genuine realist, if he is an unbeliever, will always find strength and ability to disbelieve in the miraculous, and if he is confronted with a miracle as an irrefutable fact he would rather disbelieve his own senses than admit the fact. Faith does not . . . spring from the miracle, but the miracle from faith.

Fyodor Dostoevsky

9

Miracles: Snapshots of the Supernatural

The atmosphere I grew up in was humid with miracles. Most Sundays people in our church would testify about marvelous answers to prayer they had received the preceding week. God found parking places for mothers who drove their children to the doctor. Lost fountain pens mysteriously reappeared. Tumors shrank away the day before scheduled surgery.

In those days I envisioned Jesus as the Great Magician and, fittingly, the story of his walking on water especially impressed me. If only I could pull off such a stunt in my school, just once! How I would love to fly through the room like an angel, silencing with levitation all who scoffed at me and other religious types. How I would love to walk unscathed through the bullies at the bus stop, as Jesus had walked through an angry crowd in his hometown.

I never managed to fly through the classroom, though, and bullies continued to torment me no matter how hard I prayed. Even the "answers to prayer" confused me. Sometimes, after all, parking places did not open up and fountain pens stayed lost. Sometimes church people lost their jobs. Sometimes they died. A great shadow darkened my own life: my father had died of polio just after my first birthday, despite a round-the-clock prayer vigil involving hundreds of dedicated Christians. Where was God then?

I have spent much of my adult life coming to terms with questions first stirred up during my youth. Prayer, I have found, does not work like a vending machine: insert request, receive answer. Miracles are just that, *miracles*, not "ordinaries" common to daily experience. My view of Jesus too has changed. As I now reflect on his life, miracles play a less prominent role than what I had imagined as a child. Superman, he was not.

Yes, Jesus performed miracles—around three dozen, depending on how you count them—but the Gospels actually downplay them. Often Jesus asked those who had seen a miracle not to tell anyone else. Some miracles, such as the Transfiguration or the raising of a twelve-year-old dead girl, he let only his closest disciples watch, with strict orders to keep things quiet. Though he never denied someone who asked for physical healing, he always turned down requests for a demonstration to amaze the crowds and impress important people. Jesus recognized early on that the excitement generated by miracles did not readily convert into life-changing faith.

Some skeptics, of course, have no place for miracles, and for them any account of a supernatural event must by definition be discarded. The Smithsonian museum in Washington displays a leather-bound book in which Thomas Jefferson pasted all the passages from the Gospels that contain no miraculous element. This was the Bible he read every day toward the end of his life, a more palatable gospel of Jesus the teacher but not the miracle worker.

Thomas Jefferson's approach is a historical echo of what happened in Jesus' own day. Then too rationalists pondered Jesus' teaching and scrutinized his miracles. Sometimes they denied the plain evidence in front of them and sometimes they sought alternative explanations (magic, the Devil's power). Rarely did people find it easy to believe in miracles; they seemed as peculiar in the first century as they would seem if performed today. Then, as now, miracles aroused suspicion, contempt, and only occasionally faith.

Because I accept Jesus as God's Son, who came to earth "trailing clouds of glory," I accept the miracles he performed as a natural complement to his work. Even so, the miracles raise big questions for me. Why are there so few? Why any at all? Why these particular miracles and not others? I am a journalist, not a theologian, so in my search for clues I look at the miracles not in systematic categories but rather as individual scenes, impressionistic snapshots from the life of Jesus.

Jesus' first miracle was perhaps the strangest of all. He never repeated anything quite like it, and the miracle seemed to take Jesus by surprise as much as anyone else.

At the age of thirty or so Jesus showed up at a wedding with his newly formed band of disciples. His mother came too, probably accompanied by other members of the family. In the village life of Galilee, a wedding brought celebration into an otherwise drab existence. The bridegroom and his men made a gala procession through the streets to fetch the bride's party by torchlight, then everyone rushed to the groom's house for a feast worthy of royalty. Think of happy scenes from *Fiddler on the Roof*: of peasant Jewish families dancing across the courtyard in their finest embroidered clothes, of music and laughter, of banquet tables laden with clay platters of food and jugs of wine. The feast might go on for as long as a week, as long as the food and wine and good cheer held out. Truly a wedding was a time of high joy.

Jesus' disciples must have blinked in disbelief at the raucous scene, especially those who had come over to him from John the Baptist with his desert diet and animal-skin clothes. Did these ascetics now dance with the Jewish girls and gorge themselves on culinary delights? Did townsfolk quiz them about the Baptist, the closest thing to a prophet Israel had seen in four hundred years? John's gospel does not say. It only tells us that in a moment of social crisis the whole feast nearly ground to a halt. The wine ran out.

As emergencies go, this one falls well down the list. It caused embarrassment, to be sure, but need a Messiah who had come to heal the sick and liberate the captives concern himself with a social *faux pas*? "Dear woman, why do you involve me?" Jesus replied when his mother mentioned the problem. "My time has not yet come."

We can only guess what went through Jesus' mind during those next few seconds as he weighed Mary's request. If he acted, that would mean his time *had* come, and from that moment on life would change. If word of his powers leaked, he would soon hear pleas from needy people from Tyre to Jerusalem. Crowds would flock: epileptics, paralytics, deaf-mutes, the demon-possessed, not to mention any street beggar who wanted a free glass of wine. Investigators would be dispatched from the capital. A clock would start ticking that would not stop until Calvary.

Then Jesus, the same person who while fasting in the desert a scant time before had rebuffed Satan's challenge to turn stones into bread, reached a decision. For the first but surely not the last time in his public life, he changed his plans to accommodate someone else. "Fill the jars with water," he told the servants. Water went in and miraculously wine—the best wine, the choice wine usually served early on when palates are most discriminating and guests most impressionable—flowed out. The feast kicked into gear again, the host relaxed, the bridal party returned to serious celebrating.

John gives no indication that the guests or even the host knew about the little drama behind the scenes. Mary knew, of course, as did the servants. And Jesus' disciples knew: "He thus revealed his glory and his disciples put their faith in him."

What can we learn from this odd incident? The writers George MacDonald and C. S. Lewis see in it a reminder of God's common grace, focused in this instance in a narrow beam like solar rays through a magnifying glass. Jesus' miracles, they note, do not usually contradict natural law, but rather replicate the normal activity of creation at a different speed and on a smaller scale. "Some of the miracles do locally what God has already done universally," writes Lewis. "God creates the vine and teaches it to draw up water by its roots and, with the aid of the sun, to turn that water into a juice which will ferment and take on certain qualities. Thus every year, from Noah's time till ours, God turns water into wine." Similarly, antibodies and antigens conduct miracles of healing in our bodies every day, but in a slower, less sensational manner than the kinds of healings Jesus would go on to perform.

Yes, but what about the underlying meaning? What did this strange first miracle signify? In a departure from custom, John fails to interpret for us the miraculous "sign," which for him almost always means a symbol, a kind of acted parable. Some commentators see in it a preview of the Last Supper, when Jesus transforms not water into wine but wine into blood, his blood, shed for all humanity. Maybe.

I prefer a more whimsical interpretation. Tellingly, John notes that the wine came from huge (twenty- to thirty-gallon) jugs that stood full of water at the front of the house, vessels that were used by observant Jews to fulfill the rules on ceremonial washing. Even a wedding feast had to honor the burdensome rituals of cleansing. Jesus, perhaps with a twinkle in his eye, transformed those jugs, ponderous symbols of the old way, into wineskins, harbingers of the new. From purified water of the Pharisees came the choice new wine of a whole new era. The time for ritual cleansing had passed; the time for celebration had begun.

Prophets like John the Baptist preached judgment, and indeed many miracles of the Old Testament expressed that sense of stern judgment. Jesus' first miracle, though, was one of tender mercy. The lesson was not lost on the disciples who joined him at the wedding that night in Cana—especially the recent recruits from the Baptist.

The miracle of changing water into wine, a one-time event, occurred out of the spotlight in an obscure town whose location archaeologists cannot even agree on. Before long, though, Jesus was exercising miraculous powers in broad daylight before enthusiastic crowds. As is true today, the miracles of physical healing captured the most attention, and John 9 tells of one such miracle in Jerusalem, the capital city and heart of opposition to Jesus. John devotes an entire chapter to the story, sketching a classic portrayal of what happens when Jesus disturbs the accepted order.

The story starts where many sick people start, with the question of cause. *Why me? What is God trying to tell me?* In Jesus' day people assumed that tragedy hit people who deserved it.* "There is no death

---

*I have noticed a remarkable change since Jesus' time in how people think about calamity. Nowadays we tend to blame God, both for the cataclysmic (which insurance companies call "acts of God") and for the trivial. At the 1994 Winter

without sin, and there is no suffering without iniquity," taught the Pharisees, who saw the hand of punishment in natural disasters, birth defects, and such long-term conditions as blindness and paralysis. Here is where "the man blind from birth" entered the picture. Steeped in good Jewish tradition, Jesus' disciples debated what could account for such a birth defect. Had the man somehow sinned *in utero*? Or was he suffering the consequences of his parents' sin—a prospect easier to imagine but patently unfair.

Jesus responded by overturning common notions about how God views sick and disabled people. He denied that the man's blindness came from any sin, just as he dismissed the common opinion that tragedies happen to those who deserve them (see Luke 13:1–5). Jesus wanted the sick to know they are especially loved, not cursed, by God. Every one of his miracles of healing, in fact, undercut the rabbinic tradition of "You deserved it."

The disciples were looking backward, to find out "Why?" Jesus redirected their attention forward, answering a different question: "To what end?" His answer: "Neither this man nor his parents sinned, but this happened so that the work of God might be displayed in his life."

What began as a tragic tale of one man's blindness ends as a surreal tale of everyone else's blindness. The man's neighbors make him prove his identity, the Pharisees subject him to formal interrogations, and his own parents (who had been callous enough to let him lead a life of begging, after all) waffle under all the pressure. As for the once-blind man, he has little time for such theoretical musings: "Whether he is a sinner or not, I don't know," he testifies about Jesus, "One thing I do know. I was blind but now I see!"

In Jerusalem, where Jesus had been censured as a heretic, a clear-cut miracle, especially one performed on the Sabbath, posed a grave threat to official doctrine. Although the Pharisees could not disprove

---

Olympics, when speed-skater Dan Janssen scraped the ice and lost the 500-meter race once again, his wife, Robin, cried out instinctively, "Why, God, again? God can't be that cruel!" A few months later a young woman wrote Dr. James Dobson this letter, "Four years ago, I was dating a man and became pregnant. I was devastated! I asked God, 'Why have You allowed this to happen to me?'" Exactly what role, I cannot help but wonder, did God play in an ice-skater losing control on a turn and a young couple losing control on a date?

the miracle—a blind beggar was now looking them in the eye and taunting them in open court—in the end they clung to their time-worn theories of punishment. "You were steeped in sin at birth; how dare you lecture us!" they snapped at the man. Theological blinders do not easily fall off.

The response to this miracle, as well as most of the others reported in the Gospels, bears out a striking principle of faith: Although faith may produce miracles, miracles do not necessarily produce faith.

You can view disease as a mechanical breakdown of bodily cells, or you can view it in a broader sense as a state of dis-ease involving body, mind, and soul. I learned this from the patients of Dr. Paul Brand, the leprosy specialist whose books I have coauthored. Except in very early stages, the leprosy patient does not feel physical pain. That, in fact, is the problem: after leprosy bacilli deaden nerve cells, patients no longer alert to danger proceed to damage their own bodies. A leprosy patient may walk all day on a sharp metal screw, or use a splintery hammer, or scratch an infected spot on the eyeball. Each of these acts destroys tissue and may eventually lead to loss of limb or vision, but at no point does the leprosy patient *hurt*.

Though they may not hurt, leprosy patients surely *suffer*, as much as any people I have ever known. Almost all the pain they feel comes from outside, the pain of rejection imposed on them by the surrounding community. Dr. Brand told me of one bright young man he was treating in India. In the course of the examination Brand laid his hand on the patient's shoulder and informed him through a translator of the treatment that lay ahead. To his surprise the man began to shake with muffled sobs. "Have I said something wrong?" Brand asked his translator. She quizzed the patient in a spurt of Tamil and reported, "No, doctor. He says he is crying because you put your hand around his shoulder. Until he came here no one had touched him for many years."

In modern Western countries, where leprosy is rare, a new disease has taken over much of its moral and social stigma. "AIDS is the modern-day leprosy," says former Surgeon General C. Everett Koop. "There are people who have the same attitude toward AIDS patients today that many people had toward leprosy patients one hundred years ago." I know of one AIDS patient who traveled eleven hundred miles to be with his family in Michigan for Thanksgiving dinner. He had not seen them in seven years. The parents welcomed him warily, and when dinner was served everyone got a heaping portion of turkey and all the trimmings on the best Wedgewood china plates—except for their son the AIDS patient, who was served on Chinette, with plastic utensils.

Jesus knew all about the social stigma that accompanies a disease like AIDS or leprosy. Levitical laws decreed that a person with leprosy live outside the town, keep a six-foot distance from everyone else, and wear the clothes of a mourner going to a burial service. I can easily imagine indignation rippling through the crowd when one such outcast walked through them, no doubt given a wide berth, and threw himself at the feet of Jesus. "Lord, if you are willing, you can make me clean," he said.

Matthew, Mark, and Luke give varying accounts of the scene, but all three include the same explosive sentence: "Jesus reached out his hand and touched the man." The crowd must have gasped—had not Moses' law forbidden such an act? The leprosy victim may have flinched. For how many months or years had he been deprived of the sensation of warm human flesh against his own? That one touch from Jesus brought his state of dis-ease to an end. Shalom was restored.

Jesus' response to disease set a pattern for the church that formed around him, and Christians proceeded to follow his example of caring for the sick, the poor, and the outcast. In the case of leprosy, although the church sometimes added to the misery with its "curse of God" message, at the same time individuals rose up to lead the way in treatment. Religious orders dedicated themselves to the care of leprosy, and scientific breakthroughs on the disease tended to come from missionaries because they were the only ones willing to work with leprosy patients.* Similarly,

---

*A bizarre belief in the Middle Ages spurred the church's outreach to leprosy patients. Due to a mistranslation by Jerome, church leaders came to believe that Isaiah's description of the Suffering Servant as "afflicted," or "familiar with suffering"

Christians are now involved in ministries to AIDS patients and in hospice, a modern movement devoted to those who have little hope of physical healing but much need for love and care.

Mother Teresa, whose sisters in Calcutta run both a hospice and a clinic for leprosy patients, once said, "We have drugs for people with diseases like leprosy. But these drugs do not treat the main problem, the disease of being *unwanted*. That's what my sisters hope to provide." The sick and the poor, she said, suffer even more from rejection than material want. "An alcoholic in Australia told me that when he is walking along the street he hears the footsteps of everyone coming toward him or passing him becoming faster. Loneliness and the feeling of being unwanted is the most terrible poverty." One need not be a doctor or a miracle worker to meet that need.

A delightful story that directly follows the leprosy healing in the Gospels shows the difference friends can make for an afflicted person. A paralyzed man, who by necessity had to rely on others for food, bathing, and even help with sanitation, now needed assistance in acting on his faith.

I remember my destructive impulses being aroused the first time I heard the story in Sunday school. This paralytic wanted so desperately to meet Jesus that he talked four friends into digging up a roof and lowering him through the hole! The man who had spent his life horizontal would have one moment of vertical fame. Biblical commentators take pains to mention that the thatch and tile roofs of Palestine were much easier to disassemble and repair than the roofs that adorn our houses today. They miss the point: a hole in the roof is hardly the normal way to

meant he was actually stricken with leprosy. Thus in the twelfth and thirteenth centuries people jumped to the conclusion that Jesus must have had leprosy. This belief led to a complete reversal of how leprosy was regarded: no longer a curse of God, it was now a "Holy Disease." Crusaders who returned with leprosy were treated with great reverence, and "lazar houses" to treat the disease (named for Lazarus the beggar) sprang up everywhere, nearly two thousand in France alone. This historical movement stands as a novel example of the church following literally Jesus' command to treat "the least of these brothers of mine" as they would treat Christ himself.

enter a house. Moreover, no matter how flimsy the roof, ripping a hole in it will surely disrupt what goes on underneath. Dust flies, bits of straw and clay fall on the guests, noise and chaos interrupt the meeting.*

The crowd whose very presence had created the accessibility problem had two rude shocks. First was the messy way the paralytics' friends solved it. Then came Jesus' completely unexpected reaction. When Jesus saw *their* faith—plural, emphasizing the four friends' role in the healing—he said, "Take heart, son; your sins are forgiven." "Son, be of good cheer," the *King James Version* translates that first phrase. Literally, "Cheer up!"

Apparently, Jesus rather enjoyed the interruption. Outstanding faith never failed to impress him, and certainly the four-man demolition crew had demonstrated that. Yet his response baffled the observers. Who said anything about sins? And who was Jesus to forgive them? In typical fashion, the religious experts started arguing about Jesus' right to forgive sins, all the while ignoring the disabled man lying in the debris.

Jesus hushed the debate with enigmatic words that seem to sum up his general attitude toward physical healing: "Which is easier, to say to the paralytic, 'Your sins are forgiven,' or to say, 'Get up, take your mat and walk'?" Although he let the question hang there for the moment, his entire ministry provides an answer. Physical healing was far easier, without question. As if to prove the point, Jesus merely gave a word and the paralyzed man stood to his feet, rolled up his mat, and walked—or perhaps skipped—home.

Jesus never met a disease he could not cure, a birth defect he could not reverse, a demon he could not exorcise. But he did meet skeptics he could not convince and sinners he could not convert. Forgiveness of sins requires an act of will on the receiver's part, and some

*A priest named Donald Senior made an observation about this story that I had never before noticed, concerning the issue of accessibility for the disabled. Senior writes, "Any disabled person can supply lots of stories like this one—entering a church through the sacristy (or, worse, having to be carried up the front steps like a child), coming into a lecture hall by means of a freight elevator and then through the kitchen or utility room before being able to join the 'normal' people who come in the front door."

who heard Jesus' strongest words about grace and forgiveness turned away unrepentant.

"But that you may know that the Son of Man has authority on earth to forgive sins …" Jesus announced to the skeptics as he healed the man, a clear illustration of the "lower" serving the "higher." Jesus knew that spiritual dis-ease has a more devastating effect than any mere physical ailment. Every healed person ultimately dies—then what? He had not come primarily to heal the world's cells, but to heal its souls.

How easily do we who live in material bodies devalue the world of spirit. It occurs to me that although Jesus spent much time on issues such as hypocrisy, legalism, and pride, I know of no television ministries devoted to healing those "spiritual" problems; yet I know of many that center on physical ailments. Just as I begin feeling smug, however, I remember how easily I feel tormented by the slightest bout with physical suffering, and how seldom I feel tormented by sin.

When it comes to miracles, Jesus has a different set of priorities than most of his followers.

Only one miracle made it into all four Gospels. It transpired on the grassy hills by the shores of the Sea of Galilee at a time when Jesus' popularity—and also his vulnerability—was cresting. Wherever he went, a throng that included many deranged and afflicted trailed behind.

The day before the big miracle, Jesus crossed the lake to elude the masses. Herod had just executed John the Baptist, Jesus' relative, his forerunner and friend, and Jesus needed time alone to grieve. Doubtless, John's death provoked somber thoughts of the fate awaiting him.

Alas, there would be no secluded retreat. A huge swarm of yesterday's multitude made the ten-mile journey around the lake and soon hundreds, even thousands of people clamored around Jesus. "He had compassion on them," says Mark, "because they were like sheep without a shepherd." Instead of spending the day renewing his spirit, Jesus spent it healing the sick, always an energy drain, and speaking to a crowd large enough to fill a modern basketball arena.

The issue of food came up. *What to do? There are at least five thousand men, not to mention the women and children!* Send them away, suggested one disciple. Buy them dinner, said Jesus. *What? Is he kidding? We're talking eight months' wages!*

Then Jesus took command in a way none of them had seen before. Have the people sit down in groups of fifty, he said. It was like a political rally—festive, orderly, hierarchical—exactly what one might expect from a Messiah figure.

Unavoidably, we moderns read Jesus' life backwards, knowing how it turns out. That day, no one but Jesus had a clue. Murmurs rustled through the groups on the packed hillside. *Is he the one? Could it be?* In the wilderness, Satan had dangled before Jesus the prospects of a crowd-pleasing miracle. Now, not to please a crowd but merely to settle their stomachs, Jesus took two salted fish and five small loaves of bread and performed the miracle everyone was waiting for.

Three of the Gospels leave it at that. "They all ate and were satisfied, and the disciples picked up twelve basketfuls of broken pieces of bread and fish," reports Mark with masterful understatement. Only John tells what happened next. Jesus got his time alone, at last. As the disciples rowed back across the lake, fighting a storm all the way, Jesus spent the night on a mountain, alone in prayer. Later that night he rejoined them by walking across the water.

The next morning, in a near-comic chase scene, the crowd commandeered boats and sailed in hot pursuit, like a shoal of fish chasing a curiosity around the lake. After a day to savor one miracle, they were spoiling for more. Jesus detected the mob's true intent: to seize him by force and crown him king. *All the kingdoms of the world I will give you,* Satan had promised.

A conversation ensued between two parties who might as well have been speaking different languages. Jesus was unusually brusque, accusing the crowd of greedy motives, of desiring only food for their bellies. He made provocative statements, such as "I am the bread of life" and "I have come down from heaven." He said incomprehensible things like, " ... unless you eat the flesh of the Son of Man and drink his blood, you have no life in you."

Like a Greek chorus, the audience gave a dramatic response to each of these tough words. They grumbled. They argued. Not easily would they give up their dream, however. An old Jewish tradition taught that the Messiah would renew Moses' practice of serving manna, and had not Jesus done that very thing the day before? With yesterday's miracle still digesting in their bellies, they asked for yet another miraculous sign. They were addicted.

In the end, Jesus "won" the argument. He was not their kind of Messiah after all: he would not provide bread and circuses on demand. The large, restless crowd filed away, and Jesus' own disciples began grumbling among themselves. "This is a hard teaching. Who can accept it?" they said. Many deserted him, a breakup of disciples mentioned only by John. "You do not want to leave too, do you?" Jesus sadly asked the Twelve.

The feeding of the five thousand illustrates why Jesus, with all the supernatural powers at his command, showed such ambivalence toward miracles. They attracted crowds and applause, yes, but rarely encouraged repentance and long-term faith. He was bringing a hard message of obedience and sacrifice, not a sideshow for gawkers and sensation-seekers.

From that day on, Jesus' teaching had a different twist. As if the back-to-back scenes of acclamation and rejection had clarified his future, he began to talk much more openly about his death. The odd figures of speech he had used against the crowd began to make more sense. The bread of life was not magic, like manna; it came down from heaven in order to be broken, and mixed with blood. He was talking about his own body. In the words of Robert Farrar Capon, "the Messiah was not going to save the world by miraculous, Band-Aid interventions: a storm calmed here, a crowd fed there, a mother-in-law cured back down the road. Rather, it was going to be saved by means of a deeper, darker, left-handed mystery, at the center of which lay his own death."

Jesus passed a kind of test that day on the grassy knoll by the lake. Satan had given him a preview in the desert, but that temptation was more theoretical. This was the real thing, a test of proffered kingship to which he had every right—and which he declined, in favor of a harder, humbler way.

"A wicked and adulterous generation asks for a miraculous sign!" Jesus would say when someone else asked for a display of his powers.

And in Jerusalem, the capital, though many people saw the miracles he did and believed in him, "he would not entrust himself to them," for he knew what was in their hearts.

A sign is not the same thing as proof; a sign is merely a marker for someone who is looking in the right direction.

The last great "sign" in John appears in the exact center of his book, chapter 11, and forms a narrative hinge for all that precedes and follows. John points to the miracle involving Lazarus as the event that turned the religious establishment fatally against Jesus. His account also offers a neat summary of what miracles did, and did not, accomplish in Jesus' time on earth.

The story of Lazarus has a unique "staged" quality about it. Usually when Jesus got word of a sick person he responded immediately, sometimes changing plans in order to accommodate the request. This time, after receiving word of the illness of one of his good friends, he lingered in another town for two more days. He did so intentionally, in full knowledge that the delay would result in Lazarus's death. John includes Jesus' cryptic explanation to his disciples, "Lazarus is dead, and for your sake I am glad I was not there, so that you may believe." Deliberately, he let Lazarus die and his family grieve.

In another context Luke contrasts the personality types of Lazarus's two sisters: Martha, the obsessive hostess who scurries about the kitchen, and Mary the contemplative, content to sit at the feet of Jesus. In a time of tragedy, the personality types held true. Martha rushed down the road to meet Jesus' party outside the village. "Lord," she chided him, "if you had been here, my brother would not have died." Some time later Mary caught up and, poignantly, said exactly the same words: "Lord, if you had been here, my brother would not have died."

The sisters' words carry the tone of accusation, the indictment of a God who did not answer prayer. No matter how hard we try, those of us who grieve cannot avoid words like "if only." *If only he had missed that flight. If only she had quit smoking. If only I had taken time to say "Good-bye."*

In this case, Mary and Martha had a clear target for their "if onlys": the Son of God himself, their friend, who could have prevented the death.

Lack of faith was not to blame. Martha assured Jesus that she believed in the afterlife, and, remarkably, she even proclaimed Jesus the Messiah, the Son of God. That childlike faith lay at the heart of the issue: Why had Jesus not honored it? Friends and relatives asked curtly, "Could not he who opened the eyes of the blind man have kept this man from dying?"

Martha was crying. Mary was crying. All the mourners were crying. Finally, Jesus himself, "deeply moved in spirit and troubled," broke into tears. John does not say why Jesus wept. Since he had already revealed his plans to raise Lazarus from the dead, he surely did not feel the same grief as the devastated mourners. Still, something got to him. As he approached the tomb, again he felt a spasm, "groaning in spirit" as some translations have it.

Death had never bothered Jesus before. Effortlessly he restored a son to the widow of Nain, stopping a funeral prosession in its tracks. He returned Jairus's daughter to life with an almost playful command, "My child, get up!"—like a parent announcing the end of nap time. With Lazarus's family, though, he seemed troubled, affected, distressed.

Jesus' prayer at the tombside gives a clue: "Father, I thank you that you have heard me. I knew that you always hear me, but I said this for the benefit of the people standing here, that they may believe that you sent me." Nowhere else had Jesus prayed with an over-the-shoulder audience in mind, like a Shakespearean actor who turns to the crowd to deliver an aside. At this moment Jesus seemed self-consciously aware of his dual identity, simultaneously the One who came down from heaven and the Son of Man born on earth.

The public prayer, the loud voice, the gestures—these have all the marks of a spiritual battle under way. Jesus was making a point, working out a "sign" in full public view, and here as nowhere else he acknowledged the in-between state of God's creation. Jesus knew, of course, that Lazarus was now whole and content, in every way better for having shuffled off this mortal coil. Martha and Mary knew as much too, theoretically. But unlike Jesus and unlike Lazarus, they had never heard the sounds of laughter from the other side of death. Belief in God's power and love was for the moment overwhelmed by grief. All they knew was loss, all they felt was pain.

That in-between state of loss and pain perhaps explains the source of Jesus' tears. Greek scholars say that the word translated "deeply moved" conveys more than distress; it implies anger, even rage. At that very moment Jesus himself hung between two worlds. Standing before a tomb stinking of death gave a portent of what lay before him in this damned—literally damned—world. That his own death would also end in resurrection did not reduce the fear or the pain. He was human: he had to pass through Golgotha to reach the other side.

Lazarus's story, seen in full cycle, gives not only a preview of Jesus' future but also a compressed view of the entire planet. All of us live out our days in the in-between time, the interval of chaos and confusion between Lazarus's death and reappearance. Although such a time may be temporary, and may pale into insignificance alongside the glorious future that awaits us, right now it is all we know, and that is enough to bring tears to our eyes—enough to bring tears to Jesus' eyes.

The resurrection of one man, Lazarus, would not solve the dilemma of planet earth. For that, it would take one man's death. John adds the startling, ironic detail that the miracle of Lazarus sealed Jesus' fate. "So from that day on they plotted to take his life." And from that day on, significantly, Jesus' signs and wonders ceased.

As I now read the accounts of selected miracles from Jesus' time, I find in them a very different message.

As a child, I saw the miracles as absolute proofs of Jesus' claims. In the Gospels, however, miracles never offered such certitude even to those who saw the wonders in person. "If they do not listen to Moses and the Prophets, they will not be convinced even if someone rises from the dead," Jesus said of skeptics. Probably Jesus had his own resurrection in mind, but the sequel to Lazarus's story proves the same point: bizarrely, the chief priests sought to cover up the miracle by killing off poor Lazarus again! With hard evidence of a spectacular miracle walking around free in the person of Lazarus, they balefully conspired to destroy that evidence. In no event did the miracles bowl people over and "steam-roller" them into belief. Otherwise, there would be no room for faith.

As a child, I saw the miracles as guarantees of personal safety. Did not Jesus promise, " . . . not one [sparrow] will fall to the ground apart from the will of your Father"? Later, I learned that this promise appears in the midst of a series of dire warnings to the twelve disciples, in which Jesus predicts their arrest, persecution, and death. According to tradition, the eleven disciples who survived Judas all died martyrs' deaths. Jesus suffered, as did the apostle Paul and most early Christian leaders. Faith is not an insurance policy. Or, as Eddie Askew suggests, maybe it is: insurance does not prevent accidents, but rather gives a secure base from which to face their consequences.

As a child, I strove for ever more faith. Adults urged me to develop faith, and I had few clues as to how to proceed. Reading all the healing stories together, I now detect in the Gospels a kind of "ladder of faith." At the top of the ladder stand those people who impressed Jesus with bold, unshakable faith: a centurion, an impertinent blind beggar, a persistent Canaanite woman. These stories of gristly faith threaten me, because seldom do I have such faith. I am easily discouraged by the silence of God. When my prayers are not answered, I am tempted to give up and not ask again. For this reason, I look down the ladder to find people of lesser faith, and it heartens me to learn that Jesus seemed willing to work with whatever tiny glimmer of faith came to light. I cling to the tender accounts of how Jesus treated the disciples who forsook and then doubted him. The same Jesus who praised the bold faith of those high up the ladder also gently quickened the flagging faith of his disciples. And I take special comfort in the confession of the father of a demon-possessed boy who said to Jesus, "I do believe; help me overcome my unbelief!" Even that wavering man got his request granted.

As a child, I saw miracles everywhere. Now I see them rarely, and they seem ambiguous, susceptible to different interpretations. My childlike vision has doubtless grown cloudy with age, and I feel this as a loss. Yet surely the baffling selectivity of miracles was no easier to understand in Jesus' day than it is today. A man who could walk on water did it only once. What self-restraint! Yes, he brought Lazarus back from death and dried the tears of his sisters—but what about the many other sisters and wives and daughters and mothers who were grieving that day for their own loved ones? When Jesus himself discussed miracles directly, he stressed their *infrequency*.

As a child, I saw miracles as magic. Now, I see them as signs. When John the Baptist languished in prison, Jesus sent him reports of healings and resurrections to prove that he was "the one"; a short time later, though, John himself died at an executioner's hand. Jesus' message to John did nothing to alleviate his physical condition, and we do not know what effect it might have had on his faith. Regardless, the message did express the character of the kingdom Jesus had come to set in motion. It was a kingdom of liberation in which the blind would see, the lame would leap, the deaf would hear, the leprous would be cleansed, and the poor set free. For some (in three dozen miraculous instances that we know of), liberation occurred while Jesus walked the roads of Galilee and Judea. Others have realized liberation through the dedicated service of Jesus' followers. But others, John the Baptist among them, did not achieve such liberation on earth at all.

Why, then, any miracles? Did they make any difference? I readily concede that Jesus, with a few dozen healings and a handful of resurrections from the dead, did little to solve the problem of pain on this planet. That is not why he came. Nevertheless, it was in Jesus' nature to counteract the effects of the fallen world during his time on earth. As he strode through life Jesus used supernatural power to set right what was wrong. Every physical healing pointed back to a time in Eden when physical bodies did not go blind, get crippled, or bleed nonstop for twelve years—and also pointed forward to a time of re-creation to come. The miracles he did perform, breaking as they did the chains of sickness and death, give me a glimpse of what the world was meant to be and instill hope that one day God will right its wrongs. To put it mildly, God is no more satisfied with this earth than we are; Jesus' miracles offer a hint of what God intends to do about it.

Some see miracles as an implausible suspension of the laws of the physical universe. As signs, though, they serve just the opposite function. Death, decay, entropy, and destruction are the true suspensions of God's laws; miracles are the early glimpses of restoration. In the words of Jürgen Moltmann, "Jesus' healings are not supernatural miracles in a natural world. They are the only truly 'natural' things in a world that is unnatural, demonized and wounded."

10
Death:
The Final Week

Why did Providence hide its face "at the most critical moment"...
as though voluntarily submitting to the blind, dumb, pitiless laws
of nature?

Fyodor Dostoevsky

10
Death:
The Final Week

The church I grew up in skipped past the events of Holy Week in a rush to hear the cymbal sounds of Easter. We never held a service on Good Friday. We celebrated the Lord's Supper only once per quarter, an awkward ceremony in which solemn ushers monitored the progress of trays bearing thimble-cups and broken Saltine crackers.

Roman Catholics did not believe in the Resurrection, I was told, which explained why Catholic girls wore crosses "with the little man on them." Mass, I learned, they celebrated with burning candles in a kind of cultic ritual, a symptom of their fixation with death. We Protestants were different. We saved our best clothes, our rousing hymns, and our few sanctuary decorations for Easter.

When I began to study theology and church history I found that my church was wrong about the Catholics, who believed in Easter as strongly as we did and in fact wrote many of the creeds best expressing that belief. From the Gospels I also learned that, unlike my church, the biblical record slows down rather than speeds up when it gets to Holy Week. The Gospels, said one early Christian commentator, are chronicles of Jesus' final week with increasingly longer introductions.

Of the biographies I have read, few devote more than ten percent of their pages to the subject's death—including biographies of men like Martin Luther King Jr. and Mahatma Gandhi, who died violent and politically significant deaths. The Gospels, though, devote nearly a third of their length to the climactic last week of Jesus' life. Matthew, Mark, Luke, and John saw death as the central mystery of Jesus.

Only two of the Gospels mention the events of his birth, and all four offer only a few pages on his resurrection, but each chronicler gives a detailed account of the events leading to Jesus' death. Nothing remotely like it had happened before. Celestial beings had slipped in and out of our dimension prior to the Incarnation (remember Jacob's wrestler and Abraham's visitors), and a few humans had even waked from the dead. But when the Son of God died on planet earth—how could it be that a Messiah should face defeat, a God get crucified? Nature itself convulsed at the deed: the ground shook, rocks cracked open, the sky went black.

For several years, as Holy Week approaches, I have read all the gospel accounts together, sometimes back-to-back, sometimes inter-woven in a "harmony of the Gospels" format. Each time I feel swept away by the sheer drama. The simple, unadorned rendering has a grinding power, and I can almost hear a bass drum beating dolefully in the background. No miracles break in, no supernatural rescue attempts. This is tragedy beyond Sophocles or Shakespeare.

The might of the world, the most sophisticated religious system of its time allied with the most powerful political empire, arrays itself against a solitary figure, the only perfect man who has ever lived. Though he is mocked by the powers and abandoned by his friends, yet the Gospels give the strong, ironic sense that he himself is overseeing the whole long process. He has resolutely set his face for Jerusalem, knowing the fate that awaits him. The cross has been his goal all along. Now, as death nears, he calls the shots.

One year I came to the gospel narratives just after reading the entire Old Testament. Working my way through the books of history, poetry, and prophecy, I had got to know a God of muscular power. Heads rolled, empires toppled, entire nations disappeared from the earth. Every year the Jews paused as a nation to remember God's great feat of deliverance from Egypt, an event replete with miracles. I felt aftershocks of the Exodus all through the psalms and prophets, cues to a beleaguered tribe that the God who had answered their prayers once might do so again.

With those accounts still ringing in my ears, I arrived at Matthew's scene-by-scene description of Jesus' final week. Once more Jews had gathered in Jerusalem to remember the Exodus and celebrate the Passover. Once more hope sprang eternal: *Messiah has come!* ran one rumor. And then, like an arrow shot into the heart of hope, came Jesus' betrayal, trial, and death.

How can we who know the outcome in advance ever recapture the dire end-of-the-world feeling that descended upon Jesus' followers? Over the centuries the story has grown familiar, and I cannot comprehend, much less re-create, the impact of that final week on those who lived through it. I will merely record what stands out to me as I review the Passion story one more time.

Triumphal Entry. All four Gospels mention this event, which at first glance seems the one departure from Jesus' aversion to acclaim. Crowds spread clothes and tree branches across the road to show their adoration. "Blessed is the king who comes in the name of the Lord!" they cried. Though Jesus usually recoiled from such displays of fanaticism, this time he let them yell. To indignant Pharisees he explained, "I tell you, if they keep quiet, the stones will cry out."

Was the prophet from Galilee now being vindicated in Jerusalem? "Look how the whole world has gone after him!" exclaimed the Pharisees in alarm. At that moment, with several hundred thousand pilgrims assembled in Jerusalem, it looked for all the world as if the King had arrived in force to claim his rightful throne.

I remember as a child riding home from Palm Sunday service, absentmindedly tearing apart the palm fronds, skimming ahead in the Sunday school quarterly to the next week's topic. It made no sense. With such a throng throwing themselves at his feet one week, how did Jesus get arrested and killed the next?

Now when I read the Gospels I see undercurrents that help explain the shift. On Palm Sunday a group from Bethany surrounded him, still exultant over the miracle of Lazarus. No doubt pilgrims from Galilee, who knew him well, comprised another large portion of the crowd. Matthew points out that further support came from the blind, the lame, and the children. Beyond that constituency, however, lurked danger. Religious authorities resented Jesus, and Roman legions brought in to control the festival crowds would heed the Sanhedrin's assessment of who might present a threat to order.

Jesus himself had mixed feelings during the clamorous parade. Luke reports that as he approached the city he began to weep. He knew how easily a mob could turn. Voices who shout "Hosanna!" one week can shriek "Crucify him!" the next.

The triumphal entry has about it an aura of ambivalence, and as I read all the accounts together, what stands out to me now is the slapstick nature of the affair. I imagine a Roman officer galloping up to check on the disturbance. He has attended processions in Rome, where they do it right. The conquering general sits in a chariot of gold, with stallions straining at the reins and wheel spikes flashing in the sunlight. Behind him, officers in polished armor display the banners captured from vanquished armies. At the rear comes a ragtag procession of slaves and prisoners in chains, living proof of what happens to those who defy Rome.

In Jesus' triumphal entry, the adoring crowd makes up the ragtag procession: the lame, the blind, the children, the peasants from Galilee and Bethany. When the officer looks for the object of their attention he spies a forlorn figure, *weeping*, riding on no stallion or chariot but on the back of a baby donkey, a borrowed coat draped across its backbone serving as his saddle.

Yes, there was a whiff of triumph on Palm Sunday, but not the kind of triumph that might impress Rome and not the kind that impressed crowds in Jerusalem for long either. What manner of king was this?

The Last Supper. Every time I read John's account I am startled by its "modern" tone. Here, as nowhere else, a writer of the Gospels provides a realistic, slow-motion portrayal. John quotes long stretches of dialogue and notes the emotional interplay between Jesus and his disciples. We have, in John 13–17, an intimate memoir of Jesus' most anguished night on earth.

There were many surprises in store for the disciples that evening as they moved through the Passover ritual, laden with symbolism. When Jesus read aloud the story of the Exodus, the disciples' minds may have understandably substituted "Rome" for "Egypt." What better plan than for God to duplicate that tour de force at such a moment, with all the pilgrims congregated in Jerusalem. Jesus' sweeping pronouncement excited their wildest dreams: "I confer on you a kingdom," he said magisterially, and "I have overcome the world."

As I read John's account, I keep coming back to a peculiar incident that interrupts the progress of the meal. "Jesus knew that the Father had put all things under his power," John begins with a flourish and then adds this incongruous completion: "so he got up from the meal, took off his outer clothing, and wrapped a towel around his waist." In the garb of a slave, he then bent over and washed the grime of Jerusalem from the disciples' feet.

What a strange way for the guest of honor to act during a final meal with his friends. What incomprehensible behavior from a ruler who would momentarily announce, "I confer on you a kingdom." In those days, foot washing was considered so degrading that a master could not require it of a Jewish slave. Peter blanched at the provocation.

The scene of the foot washing stands out to author M. Scott Peck as one of the most significant events of Jesus' life. "Until that moment the whole point of things had been for someone to get on top, and once he had gotten on top to stay on top or else attempt to get farther up. But here this man already on top—who was rabbi, teacher, master—suddenly got down on the bottom and began to wash the feet of his followers. In that one act Jesus symbolically overturned the whole social order. Hardly comprehending what was happening, even his own disciples were almost horrified by his behavior."

Jesus asked us his followers to do three things to remember him. He asked us to baptize others, just as he had been baptized by John. He asked to us remember the meal he shared that very evening with the disciples. Finally, he asked us to wash one another's feet. The church has always honored two of those commands, although with much dispute about what they mean and how best to fulfill them. But today we tend to associate the third, foot washing, with small denominations tucked away in the hills of Appalachia. Only a few denominations carry on the practice of foot washing; for the rest, the whole notion seems primitive, rural, unsophisticated. One can debate about whether Jesus intended his command only for the twelve disciples or for all of us to come, but there is no evidence that the Twelve followed instructions either.

Later that same evening a dispute arose among the disciples as to which of them was considered to be greatest. Pointedly, Jesus did not deny the human instinct of competition and ambition. He simply redirected it: "the greatest among you should be like the youngest, and the one who rules like the one who serves." That is when he proclaimed, "I confer on you a kingdom"—a kingdom, in other words, based on service and humility. In the foot washing, the disciples had seen a living tableau of what he meant. Following that example has not gotten any easier in two thousand years.

Betrayal. In the midst of this intimate evening with his closest friends, Jesus dropped a bombshell: One of the twelve men gathered around him would, that night, betray him to the authorities. The disciples "stared at one another, at a loss to know which of them he meant," and began to interrogate each other.

Jesus had hit a nerve. "Surely not I?" the disciples responded in turn, exposing their underlying doubts. Betrayal was no new thought. In conspiratorial Jerusalem, who knows how many disciples had been approached by Jesus' enemies, probing for access. The Last Supper itself was shrouded in danger, the upstairs room arranged clandestinely with a mystery man carrying a jar of water.

A few moments after Jesus' bombshell, Judas quietly left the room, arousing no suspicion. Naturally the group's treasurer may have to excuse himself to purchase supplies or perhaps run an errand of charity.

The name "Judas," once common, has all but disappeared. No parent wants to name a child after the most notorious traitor in history. And yet now, to my own surprise, as I read the gospel accounts it is Judas's *ordinariness*, not his villainy, that stands out. He, like other disciples, had been handpicked by Jesus after a long night of prayer. As treasurer, he obviously held the others' trust. Even at the Last Supper he sat in an honored place near Jesus. The Gospels contain no hint that Judas had been a "mole" infiltrating the inner circle to plan this perfidy.

How, then, could Judas betray the Son of God? Even as I ask the question I think of the remaining disciples fleeing from Jesus in Gethsemane and of Peter swearing, "I don't know the man!" when pressured in a courtyard and of the Eleven stubbornly refusing to believe reports of Jesus' resurrection. Judas's act of betrayal differed in degree, but not in kind, from many other disloyalties.

Curious as to how Hollywood would render the act of betrayal, I watched fifteen movie treatments of Judas. Theories abounded. According to some, he was money hungry. Others showed him as fearful, deciding to strike a deal as Jesus' enemies closed in. Some portrayed him as disillusioned—why did Jesus cleanse the sacred temple with a whip instead of raising an army against Rome? Perhaps he had grown annoyed at Jesus' "softness": like militants in modern Palestine or Northern Ireland, Judas had no patience for a slow, nonviolent revolution. Or, on the contrary, was he hoping to force Jesus' hand? If Judas arranged an arrest, surely that would prompt Jesus to declare himself and install his kingdom.

Hollywood prefers casting Judas as a complex, heroic rebel; the Bible states simply, "Satan entered into him" as he left the table to do the deed. In any event, Judas's disenchantment differed, again, only in degree from what other disciples had felt. When it became clear that Jesus' kind of kingdom led to a cross, not a throne, each one of them slunk away into the darkness.

Judas was not the first or the last person to betray Jesus, merely the most famous. Shusaku Endo, the Christian novelist in Japan, centered many of his novels on the theme of betrayal. *Silence*, his best known, tells of Japanese Christians who recanted their faith under persecution by the shoguns. Endo had read many thrilling stories about the Christian martyrs, but none about the Christian traitors. How could he? None had been written. Yet, to Endo, the most powerful message of Jesus was his unquenchable love even for—*especially* for—people who betrayed him. When Judas led a lynch mob into the garden, Jesus addressed him as "Friend." The other disciples deserted him but still he loved them. His nation had him executed; yet while stretched out naked in the posture of ultimate disgrace, Jesus roused himself for the cry, "Father, forgive them...."

I know of no more poignant contrast between two human destinies than that of Peter and Judas. Both assumed leadership within the group of Jesus' disciples. Both saw and heard wondrous things. Both went through the same dithery cycle of hope, fear, and disillusionment. As the stakes increased, both denied their Master. There, the similarity breaks off. Judas, remorseful but apparently unrepentant, accepted the logical consequences of his deed, took his own life, and went down as the greatest traitor in history. He died unwilling to receive what Jesus had come to offer him. Peter, humiliated but still open to Jesus' message of grace and forgiveness, went on to lead a revival in Jerusalem and did not stop until he had reached Rome.

Gethsemane. From an upstairs room in Jerusalem, stuffy with the smells of lamb, bitter herbs, and sweaty bodies, Jesus and his band of eleven arose and headed for the cool open air, wending their way through a garden called Gethsemane. Spring was in full bloom, the night air fragrant with blossoms. Reclining under the moon and stars in a peaceful setting outside the bustle of the city, the disciples quickly drifted asleep.

Jesus, however, felt no such peace. "He began to be sorrowful and troubled," says Matthew. He felt "deeply distressed," adds Mark. Both writers record his plaintive words to the disciples: "My soul is overwhelmed with sorrow to the point of death. Stay here and keep watch with me." Often Jesus had gone off by himself to pray, sometimes sending the disciples away in a boat so he could spend the night alone with the Father. This night, though, he needed their presence.

By instinct, we humans want someone by our side in the hospital the night before surgery, in the nursing home as death looms near, in any great moment of crisis. We need the reassuring touch of human presence—solitary confinement is the worst punishment our species has devised. I detect in the Gospels' account of Gethsemane a profound depth of loneliness that Jesus had never before encountered.

Perhaps if women had been included in the Last Supper, Jesus would not have spent those hours alone. Jesus' mother, presciently, had come to Jerusalem—her first mention in the Gospels since early in her son's ministry. The same women who would stand by the cross, and wrap his stiff body, and hurry to the tomb at daybreak surely would have sat with him in the garden, held his head, wiped away his tears. But only male friends accompanied Jesus. Drowsy with dinner and wine, they slept while Jesus endured the crucible, alone.

When the disciples failed him, Jesus did not try to conceal the hurt: "Could you not keep watch for one hour?" His words suggest something more ominous than loneliness. Is it possible that for the first time ever he did not want to be alone with the Father?

A great struggle was under way, and the Gospels describe Jesus' torment in a way quite unlike Jewish and Christian stories of martyrdom. "Take this cup from me," he pled. These were no pious, formal prayers: "being in anguish, he prayed more earnestly, and his sweat was like drops of blood falling to the ground." What was the struggle, exactly? Fear of pain and death? Of course. Jesus no more relished the prospects than you or I do. But there was more at work as well, a new experience for Jesus that can only be called God-forsakenness. At its core Gethsemane depicts, after all, the story of an unanswered prayer. The cup of suffering was not removed.

The world had rejected Jesus: proof came in the torchlight parade then snaking through the pathways of the garden. Soon the disciples would forsake him. During the prayers, the anguished prayers that met a stone wall of no response, it surely must have felt as if God, too, had turned away.

John Howard Yoder speculates on what might have happened if God had intervened to grant the request "Take this cup from me." Jesus was by no means powerless. If he had insisted on his will and not the

Father's, he could have called down twelve legions of angels (72,000) to fight a Holy War on his behalf. In Gethsemane, Jesus relived Satan's temptation in the desert. Either time he could have solved the problem of evil by force, with a quick stab of the accuser in the desert or a fierce battle in the garden. There would be no church history—no church, for that matter—as all human history would come to a halt and the present age would end. All this lay within Jesus' power if he merely said the word, skipped the personal sacrifice, and traded away the messy future of redemption. No kingdom would advance like a mustard seed; the kingdom would rather descend like a hailstorm.

Yet, as Yoder reminds us, the cross, the "cup" that now seemed so terrifying, was the very reason Jesus had come to earth. "Here at the cross is the man who loves his enemies, the man whose righteousness is greater than that of the Pharisees, who being rich became poor, who gives his robe to those who took his cloak, who prays for those who despitefully use him. The cross is not a detour or a hurdle on the way to the kingdom, nor is it even the way to the kingdom; it is the kingdom come."

After several hours of torturous prayer, Jesus came to a resolution. His will and the Father's converged. "Did not the Christ have to suffer these things?" is how he would later put it. He woke his slumberous friends one last time and marched boldly through the darkness toward the ones intent on killing him.

The Trials. These days television programs and best-selling novels make familiar the once-arcane world of legal procedure. For those who desire greater realism, a cable channel broadcasts live the grisliest murder trials and sexiest harassment cases. Time after time the American public has watched with fascination as lawyers craft clever defenses to get famous people off the hook when everyone watching knows the defendants are guilty as sin.

In a span of less than twenty-four hours, Jesus faced as many as six interrogations, some conducted by the Jews and some by the Romans. In the end an exasperated governor pronounced the harshest verdict permitted under Roman law. As I read the trial transcripts, Jesus' *defenselessness* stands out. Not a single witness rose to his defense. No leader had the nerve to speak out against injustice. Not even Jesus tried to defend himself. Throughout, God the Father said not a word.

The trial sequence has a "pass-the-buck" quality. No one seems willing to accept full responsibility for executing Jesus, yet everyone wants him disposed of. Scholars have written thousands of words to determine precisely what share of the blame for Jesus' death belongs to Rome and what share to the Jews.* In fact, both parties participated in the decision. Focusing on all the irregularities in the trials risks missing the main point: Jesus posed a genuine threat to the establishment in Jerusalem.

As a charismatic leader with a large following, Jesus had long aroused the suspicion of Herod in Galilee and the Sanhedrin in Jerusalem. They misunderstood the nature of his kingdom, it is true, but shortly before his arrest Jesus had indeed used force to drive moneychangers out of the temple. To a puppet Sanhedrin government intent on keeping "peace at any cost" for their Roman masters, such an event raised alarm. In addition, a rumor had spread that Jesus claimed he could destroy the temple and rebuild it in three days. Jewish leaders had trouble getting witnesses to agree on the exact wording of Jesus' statement, but their alarm is understandable. Imagine the reaction today if an Arab ran through the streets of New York City shouting, "The World Trade Center will blow up, and I can rebuild it in three days."

---

*To hold the Jewish race as a whole responsible for Jesus' death is one of the great slanders of history. No one thinks of holding modern Italians responsible for what *their* forebears did nineteen centuries ago. Joseph Klausner writes, "The Jews, *as a nation*, were far less guilty of the death of Jesus than the Greeks, as a nation, were guilty of the death of Socrates; but who now would think of avenging the blood of Socrates the Greek upon his countrymen, the present Greek race? Yet these nineteen hundred years past, the world has gone on avenging the blood of Jesus the Jew upon his countrymen, the Jews, who have already paid the penalty, and still go on paying the penalty in rivers and torrents of blood." This despite the fact that Jesus said he had come to "the lost sheep of Israel," and despite the fact that almost all of the first Christians were Jews.

To the priests and the pious, these political threats paled before the reports of Jesus' religious claims. The Pharisees had often blanched at Jesus' boldness in unilaterally forgiving sins and in calling God his own Father. His seeming disregard for the Sabbath scandalized them; Moses' law made Sabbath-breaking a capital offense. Jesus represented a threat to the Law, the sacrificial system, the temple, kosher food regulations, and the many distinctions between clean and unclean.

Finally, at the trial, the high priest appealed to the solemn Oath of the Testimony—"I charge you under oath by the living God"—to ask a question that Jesus as the defendant was required by law to answer. "Tell us if you are the Christ [Messiah], the Son of God." At last Jesus broke his silence: "Yes, it is as you say."

The accused went on to speak in exalted terms of the Son of Man coming on the clouds of heaven. It was too much. To a faithful Jew, Jesus' words sounded blasphemous by any stretch of justice. "Why do we need any more witnesses?" said the high priest, tearing his clothes.

There was only one alternative to blasphemy and the death sentence it carried: that Jesus' words were true and he really was the Messiah. How could that be? Bound, surrounded by armed guards, the very picture of helplessness, Jesus looked to be the least Messiah-like figure in all of Israel.

Blasphemy meant little to the Romans, though, who preferred to stay aloof from local religious disputes. On the way to the Roman judges, the implications of the *Messiah* claim changed from blasphemy to sedition. The word did mean king, after all, and Rome had no tolerance for any agitator who professed such a title.

Before Herod, the same ruler who had hacked off the head of John the Baptist and had long wanted to examine Jesus in person, Jesus maintained a serene silence. Only Pilate could get any kind of confession out of him. "Are you the king of the Jews?" Pilate asked. Once again Jesus, hands tied behind his back, face puffy with sleeplessness, soldiers' palm prints impressed on his cheeks, replied simply, "Yes, it is as you say."

Many times before, Jesus had turned down the chance to declare himself. When healed people, disciples, and even demons recognized him as Messiah, he had hushed them up. In the days of popularity, when crowds chased him around the lake like fanatics pursuing a celebrity, he had fled. When these fans caught him, eager to coronate him on the spot, he preached a sermon so troublesome that all but a few turned away.

Only on this day, first before the religious establishment and then before the political, only when his claims would seem the height of absurdity, did he admit to who he was. "The Son of God," he told the religious powers, who had him in their grasp. "A king," he told a Roman governor, who must have laughed aloud. A pitiful specimen, he probably reminded Pilate of one of Rome's deranged who claimed to be Caesar.

Weak, rejected, doomed, utterly alone—only then did Jesus think it safe to reveal himself and accept the title "Christ." As Karl Barth comments, "He does not confess his Messiahship until the moment when the danger of founding a religion is finally past."

Such a notion was an offense, Paul would later say. A stumbling block—the kind of rock tossed aside as useless, a nuisance on the construction site. But such a rock can form, with God's kind of power, the cornerstone of a new kingdom.

Calvary. In a memoir of the years before World War II, Pierre Van Paassen tells of an act of humiliation by Nazi storm troopers who had seized an elderly Jewish rabbi and dragged him to headquarters. In the far end of the same room, two colleagues were beating another Jew to death, but the captors of the rabbi decided to have some fun with him. They stripped him naked and commanded that he preach the sermon he had prepared for the coming Sabbath in the synagogue. The rabbi asked if he could wear his yarmulke, and the Nazis, grinning, agreed. It added to the joke. The trembling rabbi proceeded to deliver in a raspy voice his sermon on what it means to walk humbly before God, all the while being poked and prodded by the hooting Nazis, and all the while hearing the last cries of his neighbor at the end of the room.

When I read the gospel accounts of the imprisonment, torture, and execution of Jesus, I think of that naked rabbi standing humiliated in a police station. Even after watching scores of movies on the subject, and reading the Gospels over and over, I still cannot fathom the indignity, the *shame* endured by God's Son on earth, stripped naked, flogged, spat on, struck in the face, garlanded with thorns.

Jewish leaders as well as Romans intended the mockery to parody the crime for which the victim had been condemned. *Messiah, huh? Great, let's hear a prophecy.* Wham. *Who hit you, huh?* Thunk. *C'mon, tell us, spit it out, Mr. Prophet. For a Messiah, you don't know much, do you?*

You say you're a king? Hey, Captain, get a load of this. We have us a regular king here, don't we. Well, then, let's all kneel down before hizzoner. What's this? A king without a crown? Oh, that will never do. Here, Mr. King, we'll fix you a crown, we will. Crunch. *How's that? A little crooked? I'll fix that. Hey, hold still! My, look how modest we are. Well, how about a robe then—something to cover that bloody mess on your back. What happened, did your majesty have a little tumble?*

It went like that all day long, from the bullying game of Blind Man's Bluff in the high priest's courtyard, to the professional thuggery of Pilate's and Herod's guards, to the catcalls of spectators turned out to jeer the criminals stumbling up the long road to Calvary, and finally to the cross itself where Jesus heard a stream of taunts from the ground below and even from the cross alongside. *You call yourself a Messiah? Well, then come down from that cross. How you gonna save us if you can't even save yourself?*

I have marveled at, and sometimes openly questioned, the self-restraint God has shown throughout history, allowing the Genghis Khans and the Hitlers and the Stalins to have their way. But nothing—nothing—compares to the self-restraint shown that dark Friday in Jerusalem. With every lash of the whip, every fibrous crunch of fist against flesh, Jesus must have mentally replayed the Temptation in the wilderness and in Gethsemane. Legions of angels awaited his command. One word, and the ordeal would end.

"The idea of the cross should never come near the bodies of Roman citizens," said Cicero; "it should never pass through their thoughts, eyes or ears." For the Romans, crucifixion was the cruelest form of capital punishment, reserved for murder, slave revolts, and other heinous crimes in the colonies. Roman citizens were beheaded, not crucified. Jews shared their revulsion—"anyone who is hung on a tree is under God's curse," said Deuteronomy—and preferred stoning when they had authority to carry out executions.

Evangelists, archaeologists, and medical experts have described the grim details of crucifixion so thoroughly that I see no need to iterate them here. Besides, if the "seven last words of Christ" are any indication, Jesus himself had other things on his mind than the pain. The closest to a physical complaint was his cry, "I thirst!" and even then he turned down the vinegar wine offered as an anesthetic. (The irony of one who had made gallons of wine for a wedding party, who had spoken of living water that would quench all thirst forever, dying with a swollen tongue and the sour smell of spilled vinegar on his beard.)

As always, Jesus was thinking about others. He forgave the men who had done the deed. He arranged care for his mother. He welcomed a shriven thief into paradise.

The Gospels record different snatches of conversation from Calvary, and only two agree on Jesus' very last words. Luke has him saying, "Father, into your hands I commit my spirit," a final act of trust before he died. John has the cryptic summation of his entire mission to earth, "It is finished." But Matthew and Mark have the most mysterious saying of all, the woeful quotation, "My God, my God, why have you forsaken me?"*

This time only, of all his prayers in the Gospels, Jesus used the formal, distant word "God" rather than "Abba" or "Father." He was quoting from a psalm, of course, but he was also expressing a grave sense of estrangement. Some inconceivable split had opened up in the Godhead. The Son felt abandoned by the Father.

"The 'hiddenness' of God perhaps presses most painfully on those who are in another way nearest to Him, and therefore God Himself, made man, will of all men be by God most forsaken," wrote C. S. Lewis. No doubt he is right. It matters little if I am rebuffed by the checkout girl at the supermarket or even by a neighbor two blocks down the street. But if my wife, with whom I've spent my entire adult life, suddenly cuts off all communication with me—that matters.

No theologian can adequately explain the nature of what took place within the Trinity on that day at Calvary. All we have is a cry of pain from a child who felt forsaken. Did it help that Jesus had antici-

---

*Commentators have observed that the record in Matthew and Mark is one of the strongest proofs that we have an authentic account of what took place on Calvary. For what reason would the founders of a new religion put such despairing words in the mouth of their dying hero—unless that's precisely what he said.

pated that his mission on earth would include such a death? Did it help Isaac to know his father Abraham was just following orders when he tied him to the altar? What if no angel had appeared and Abraham had plunged a knife into the heart of his son, his only son, whom he loved? What then? That is what happened on Calvary, and to the Son it felt like abandonment.

We are not told what God the Father cried out at that moment. We can only imagine. The Son became "a curse for us," said Paul in Galatians, and "God made him who had no sin to be sin for us," he wrote the Corinthians. We know how God feels about sin; the sense of abandonment likely cut both ways.

Dorothy Sayers writes, "He is the only God who has a date in history.... There is no more astonishing collocation of phrases than that which, in the Nicene Creed, sets these two statements flatly side by side: 'Very God of Very God ... He suffered under Pontius Pilate.' All over the world, thousands of times a day, Christians recite the name of a rather undistinguished Roman proconsul ... merely because that name fixes within a few years the date of the death of God."

Despite the shame and sadness of it all, somehow what took place on a hill called Calvary became arguably the most important fact of Jesus' life—for the writers of the Gospels and Epistles, for the church, and, as far as we can speculate, for and to Father, for God as well.

It took time for the church to come to terms with the ignominy of the cross. Church fathers forbade its depiction in art until the reign of the Roman emperor Constantine, who had seen a vision of the cross and who also banned it as a method of execution.* Thus not until the fourth century did the cross become a symbol of the faith. (As C. S.

*According to historian Michael Grant, Constantine had little interest in the person of Jesus himself and found the crucifixion an embarrassment. In a remarkable irony, seeing "the Cross not so much as an emblem of suffering but as a magic totem confirming his own victoriousness," Constantine transformed the cross from a symbol of sacrificial love and humiliation into a symbol of triumph: he had it painted on the shields of his soldiers.

Lewis points out, the crucifixion did not become common in art until all who had seen a real one died off.)

Now, though, the symbol is everywhere: artists beat gold into the shape of the Roman execution device, baseball players cross themselves before batting, and candy confectioners even make chocolate crosses for the faithful to eat during Holy Week. Strange as it may seem, Christianity has become a religion of the cross—the gallows, the electric chair, the gas chamber, in modern terms.

Normally we think of someone who dies a criminal's death as a failure. Yet the apostle Paul would later reflect about Jesus, "Having disarmed the powers and authorities, he made a public spectacle of them, triumphing over them by the cross." What could he mean?

On one level I think of individuals in our own time who disarm the powers. The racist sheriffs who locked Martin Luther King Jr. in jail cells, the Soviets who deported Solzhenitsyn, the Czechs who imprisoned Václav Havel, the Filipinos who murdered Benigno Aquino, the South African authorities who imprisoned Nelson Mandela—all these thought they were solving a problem, yet instead all ended up unmasking their own violence and injustice. Moral power can have a disarming effect.

When Jesus died, even a gruff Roman soldier was moved to exclaim, "Surely this man was the Son of God!" He saw the contrast all too clearly between his brutish colleagues and their victim, who forgave them in his dying gasp. The pale figure nailed to a crossbeam revealed the ruling powers of the world as false gods who broke their own lofty promises of piety and justice. Religion, not irreligion, accused Jesus; the law, not lawlessness, had him executed. By their rigged trials, their scourgings, their violent opposition to Jesus, the political and religious authorities of that day exposed themselves for what they were: upholders of the status quo, defenders of their own power only. Each assault on Jesus laid bare their illegitimacy.

Thieves crucified on either side of Jesus showed two possible responses. One mocked Jesus' powerlessness: *A Messiah who can't even save himself?* The other recognized a different kind of power. Taking the risk of faith, he asked Jesus to "remember me when you come into your kingdom." No one else, except in mockery, had addressed Jesus as a king. The dying thief saw more clearly than anyone else the nature of Jesus' kingdom.

In a sense, the paired thieves present the choice that all history has had to decide about the cross. Do we look at Jesus' powerlessness as an example of God's impotence or as proof of God's love? The Romans, bred on power deities like Jupiter, could recognize little godlikeness in a crumpled corpse hanging on a tree. Devout Jews, bred on stories of a power Jehovah, saw little to be admired in this god who died in weakness and in shame. As Justin Martyr's "Dialogue with the Jew Tryphon" shows, Jesus' death on a cross made a decisive case against his Messiahship for the Jews; crucifixion had fulfilled the curse of the law.

Even so, over time it was the cross on the hill that changed the moral landscape of the world. M. Scott Peck writes,

> I cannot be any more specific about the methodology of love than to quote these words of an old priest who spent many years in the battle: "There are dozens of ways to deal with evil and several ways to conquer it. All of them are facets of the truth that the only ultimate way to conquer evil is to let it be smothered within a willing, living human being. When it is absorbed there like blood in a sponge or a spear into one's heart, it loses its power and goes no further."
>
> The healing of evil—scientifically or otherwise—can be accomplished only by the love of individuals. A willing sacrifice is required ... I do not know how this occurs. But I know that it does ... Whenever this happens there is a slight shift in the balance of power in the world.

The balance of power shifted more than slightly that day on Calvary because of who it was that absorbed the evil. If Jesus of Nazareth had been one more innocent victim, like King, Mandela, Havel, and Solzhenitsyn, he would have made his mark in history and faded from the scene. No religion would have sprung up around him. What changed history was the disciples' dawning awareness (it took the Resurrection to convince them) that God himself had chosen the way of weakness. The cross redefines God as One who was willing to relinquish power for the sake of love. Jesus became, in Dorothy Sölle's phrase, "God's unilateral disarmament."

Power, no matter how well-intentioned, tends to cause suffering. Love, being vulnerable, absorbs it. In a point of convergence on a hill called Calvary, God renounced the one for the sake of the other.

11
Resurrection:
A Morning Beyond Belief

I find that Holy Week is draining; no matter how many times I have
lived through his crucifixion, my anxiety about his resurrection
is undiminished—I am terrified that, this year, it won't happen; that,
that year, it didn't. Anyone can be sentimental about the Nativity;
any fool can feel like a Christian at Christmas. But Easter
is the main event; if you don't believe in the resurrection,
you're not a believer.

John Irving, A Prayer for Owen Meany

11
Resurrection:
A Morning Beyond Belief

In early childhood I associated Easter with death, not resurrection, because of what happened one sunny Easter Sunday to the only cat I ever owned. Boots was a six-week-old kitten, solid black except for white "boots" on each of her legs, as if she had daintily stepped in a shallow dish of paint. She lived in a cardboard box on the screened porch and slept on a pillow stuffed with cedar shavings. My mother, insisting that Boots must learn to defend herself before sampling the huge outdoors, had fixed a firm date of Easter Sunday for the kitten's big test.

At last the day arrived. Georgia sunshine had already coaxed spring into full bloom. Boots sniffed her first blade of grass that day, batted at her first daffodil, and stalked her first butterfly, leaping high in the air and missing. She kept us joyously entertained until neighbor kids came over for an Easter egg hunt.

When our next-door playmates arrived, the unthinkable happened. Their pet Boston terrier Pugs, following them into our yard, spied Boots, let out a low growl, and charged. I screamed, and we all ran toward Boots. Already Pugs had the tiny kitten in its mouth, shaking it like a sock. We kids encircled the scene, shrieking and jumping up and down to scare Pugs off. Helpless, we watched a whirl of flashing teeth and flying tufts of fur. Finally Pugs dropped the limp kitten on the grass and trotted off.

I could not have articulated it at the time, but what I learned that Easter under the noonday sun was the ugly word *irreversible*. All afternoon I prayed for a miracle. *No! It can't be! Tell me it's not true!* Maybe Boots would come back—hadn't the Sunday school teacher told such a story about Jesus? Or maybe the whole morning could somehow be erased, rewound, and played over again minus that horrid scene. We could keep Boots on the screen porch forever, never allowing her outside. Or we could talk our neighbors into building a fence for Pugs. A thousand schemes ran through my mind over the next days until reality won out and I accepted at last that Boots was dead. Irreversibly dead.

From then on, Easter Sundays in my childhood were stained by the memory of that death in the grass. As the years increased, I would learn much more about the word irreversible.

Not so long ago, as I have mentioned, three of my friends died in quick succession. One, a retired man in excellent health, fell over dead in a parking lot after dining out with his wife. Another, a young woman of forty, died in flames on the way to a church missions conference when a tanker truck rear-ended her car in the fog. A third, my friend Bob, died scuba diving at the bottom of Lake Michigan. Life came to a halt three times that year. I spoke at all three funerals, and each time as I struggled with what to say the old, ugly word *irreversible* came flooding back, with greater force than I had ever known. Nothing I could say, nothing I could do would accomplish what I wanted above all else, to get my friends back.

On the day Bob made his last dive I was sitting, oblivious, in a café at the University of Chicago, reading *My Quest for Beauty* by Rollo May. In that book the famous therapist recalls scenes from his lifelong search for beauty, especially a visit to Mt. Athos, a peninsula of monasteries attached to Greece. There, he happened to stumble upon an all-night celebration of Greek Orthodox Easter. Incense hung in the air. The only light came from candles. At the climax of that service, the priest gave everyone three Easter eggs, splendidly decorated and wrapped in a veil. "Christos Anesti!" he said—"Christ is Risen!" Each person present, including Rollo May, replied according to custom, "He is risen indeed!"

Rollo May writes, "I was seized then by a moment of spiritual reality: what would it mean for our world if He had truly risen?" I read that passage just before returning home to learn that Bob had died, and Rollo May's question kept floating around in my mind, hauntingly, after I heard the terrible news. What did it mean for our world that Christ had risen?

In the cloud of grief over Bob's death, I began to see the meaning of Easter in a new light. As a five-year-old on Easter Sunday I had learned the harsh lesson of irreversibility. Now, as an adult, I saw that Easter actually held out the awesome promise of reversibility. Nothing—no, not even death—was final. Even that could be reversed.

When I spoke at Bob's funeral, I rephrased Rollo May's question in the terms of our particular grief. What would it mean for us if Bob rose again? We were sitting in a chapel, numbed by three days of sorrow, death bearing down upon us like a crushing weight. How would it be to walk outside to the parking lot and there, to our utter astonishment, find Bob. *Bob!* With his bounding walk, his crooked grin, his clear gray eyes. It could be no one else but Bob, alive again!

That image gave me a hint of what Jesus' disciples felt on the first Easter. They too had grieved for three days. On Sunday they heard a new, euphonious sound, clear as a bell struck in mountain air. Easter hits a new note of hope and faith that what God did once in a graveyard in Jerusalem, he can and will repeat on grand scale. For Bob. For us. For the world. Against all odds, the irreversible will be reversed.

The first Christians staked everything on the Resurrection, so much so that the apostle Paul told the Corinthians, "And if Christ has not been raised, our preaching is useless and so is your faith." Did it really happen, this event apart from which our faith is useless? How can we be sure?

People who discount the resurrection of Jesus tend to portray the disciples in one of two ways: either as gullible rubes with a weakness for ghost stories, or as shrewd conspirators who conceived a resurrection plot as a way to jump-start their new religion. The Bible paints a distinctly different picture.

As for the first theory, the Gospels portray Jesus' followers themselves as the ones most leery of rumors about a risen Jesus. One disciple especially, "doubting Thomas," has gained the reputation as a skeptic, but in truth all the disciples showed a lack of faith. None of them believed the wild report the women brought back from the empty tomb; "nonsense" they called it. Even after Jesus appeared to them in person, says Matthew, "some doubted." The eleven, whom Jesus had to rebuke for a stubborn refusal to believe, can hardly be called gullible.

The alternative, a conspiracy theory, falls apart on close examination for, if the disciples had set out to concoct a seamless cover-up story, they failed miserably. Chuck Colson, who participated in a feckless conspiracy after the Watergate break-in, says that cover-ups only work if all participants maintain a unified front of assurance and competence. That, the disciples surely did not do.

The Gospels show the disciples cringing in locked rooms, terrified that the same thing that happened to Jesus might happen to them. Too afraid even to attend Jesus' burial, they left it to a couple of women to care for his body. (Ironically, for Jesus had fought Sabbath restrictions against works of mercy, the dutiful women waited until Sunday morning to finish the embalming process.) The disciples seemed utterly incapable of faking a resurrection or risking their lives by stealing a body; nor did it occur to them in their state of despair.

According to all four Gospels, women were the first witnesses of the resurrection, a fact that no conspirator in the first century would have invented. Jewish courts did not even accept the testimony of female witnesses. A deliberate cover-up would have put Peter or John or, better yet, Nicodemus in the spotlight, not built its case around reports from women. Since the Gospels were written several decades after the events, the authors had plenty of time to straighten out such an anomaly—unless, of course, they were not concocting a legend but recording the plain facts.

A conspiracy also would have tidied up the first witnesses' stories. Were there two white-clad figures or just one? Why did Mary Magdalene mistake Jesus for a gardener? Was she alone or with

Salome and another Mary? Accounts of the discovery of the empty tomb sound breathless and fragmentary. The women were "afraid yet filled with joy," says Matthew; "trembling and bewildered," says Mark. Jesus makes no dramatic, well-orchestrated entrance to quell all doubts; the early reports seem wispy, mysterious, confused. Surely conspirators could have done a neater job of depicting what they would later claim to be the hinge event of history.

In short, the Gospels do not present the resurrection of Jesus in the manner of apologetics, with arguments arranged to prove each main point, but rather as a shocking intrusion that no one was expecting, least of all Jesus' timorous disciples. The first witnesses reacted as any of us would react—as I would react if I answered the doorbell and suddenly saw my friend Bob standing on my front porch: with fear and great joy. Fear is the reflexive human response to an encounter with the supernatural. The fear, though, was overpowered by joy because the news they heard was news too good to be true yet news so good it had to be true. Jesus was alive! Dreams of a Messiah came surging back as the women ran, on legs of fear and joy, to tell the disciples the news.

There actually was a conspiracy, of course, one set in motion not by Jesus' disciples but by the authorities who had to deal with the embarrassing fact of the empty tomb. They could have put a stop to all the wild rumors about a resurrection merely by pointing to a sealed tomb or producing a body. But the seal was broken and the body missing, hence the need for an official plot. Even as the women ran to report their discovery, soldiers were rehearsing an alibi, their role in the scheme of damage-control.

Soldiers standing guard outside Jesus' tomb were the only eyewitnesses of the greatest miracle in history. Matthew says that when the earth quaked and an angel appeared, bright as lightning, they shook and became like dead men.* But here is an astounding fact: later

---

*The Resurrection actually constituted an act of civil disobedience, since it involved breaking Pilate's seal and striking down the official guards. In this case, triumphing over the powers meant active resistance.

The apocryphal Gospel of Peter gives a fanciful version of what took place at the tomb. Two figures descended in a cloud of light, so luminous that many eyewitnesses gathered round to watch. The stone rolled away all by itself, and the two

that afternoon the soldiers who had seen proof of the resurrection with their own eyes changed their story to a lie, parroting the priests' line that "His disciples came during the night and stole him away while we were asleep." The alibi had obvious weaknesses (a huge stone rolled away without disturbing sleep? And how could they identify the disciples if asleep?), but at least it kept the guards out of trouble.

Like everything else in Jesus' life, the resurrection drew forth contrasting responses. Those who believed were transformed; infused with hope and courage, they went out to change the world. Those who did not believe found ways to ignore strong evidence. Jesus had predicted as much: "If they do not listen to Moses and the Prophets, they will not be convinced even if someone rises from the dead."

We who read the Gospels from the other side of Easter, who have the day printed on our calendars, forget how *hard* it was for the disciples to believe. In itself the empty tomb did not convince them: that fact only demonstrated "He is not here," not "He is risen." Convincing these skeptics would require intimate, personal encounters with the one who had been their Master for three years, and over the next six weeks Jesus provided exactly that.

Author Frederick Buechner is struck by the unglamorous quality of Jesus' appearances after resurrection Sunday. There were no angels in the sky singing choruses, no kings from afar bearing gifts. Jesus showed up in the most ordinary circumstances: a private dinner, two men walking along a road, a woman weeping in a garden, some fishermen working a lake.

I see in the appearances a whimsical quality, as if Jesus is enjoying the bird-like freedom of his resurrection body. Luke, for example, gives a touching account of Jesus' sudden arrival alongside two forlorn followers on a road to Emmaus. They know about the women's

glowing figures emerged from the tomb supporting a third figure, followed by a magical cross. The heads of the two "reached into heaven ... but of him that was led by them ... it overpassed the heavens." It is this kind of sensationalism that the authentic Gospels conspicuously avoid.

discovery of the empty tomb, and Peter's eyewitness confirmation. But who can believe such rumors? Is not death by definition irreversible? "We had hoped that he was the one who was going to redeem Israel," one of them says with obvious disappointment.

A short time later, at mealtime, the stranger makes a riveting gesture, breaking bread, and a link snaps into pace. It is Jesus who has been walking beside them and now sits at their table! Most strangely, the instant they recognize their guest, he disappears.

When the two rush back to Jerusalem, they find the Eleven meeting behind locked doors. They spill out their incredible story, which corroborates what Peter has already learned: Jesus is out there somewhere, alive. Without warning, even as the doubters argue the point, Jesus himself shows up in their midst. *I am no ghost*, he declares. *Touch my scars. It is I myself!* Even then the doubts persist, until Jesus volunteers to eat a piece of broiled fish. Ghosts don't eat fish; a mirage cannot cause food to disappear.

Life continues in that vein for nearly six weeks: Jesus is there, then he's gone. The appearances are not spectral, but flesh-and-blood encounters. Jesus can always prove his identity—no other living person bears the scars of crucifixion—yet often the disciples fail to recognize him right away. Painstakingly, he condescends to meet the level of their skepticism. For suspicious Thomas, it means a personal invitation to finger the scars. For the humiliated Peter, it means a bittersweet scene of rehabilitation in front of six friends.

The appearances, approximately a dozen, show a definite pattern: Jesus visited small groups of people in a remote area or closeted indoors. Although these private rendezvous bolstered the faith of those who already believed in Jesus, as far as we know not a single unbeliever saw Jesus after his death.

Reading the accounts of execution and resurrection back-to-back, I have sometimes wondered why Jesus did not make even more appearances. Why limit visitations to his friends? Why not reappear on Pilate's porch or before the Sanhedrin, this time with a withering blast against those who had condemned him? Perhaps a clue to strategy can be found in his words to Thomas, on the day Thomas's skepticism melted away forever. "Because you have seen me, you have believed; blessed are those who have not seen and yet have believed."

In the six-week interlude between Resurrection and Ascension, Jesus, if one may use such language, "broke his own rules" about faith. He made his identity so obvious that no disciple could ever deny him again (and none did). In a word, Jesus overwhelmed the witnesses' faith: anyone who saw the resurrected Jesus lost the freedom of choice to believe or disbelieve. Jesus was now irrefutable. Even Jesus' brother James, always a holdout, capitulated after one of the appearances—enough so that he became a leader of the church in Jerusalem and, according to Josephus, died as one of the early Christian martyrs.

"Because you have seen me, you have believed," said Jesus. These privileged few could hardly disbelieve. But what about the others? Very soon, as Jesus well knew, his personal appearances would come to a halt, leaving only "those who have not seen." The church would stand or fall based on how persuasive these eyewitnesses would be for all—including us today—who have not seen. Jesus had six weeks in which to establish his identity for all time.

That Jesus succeeded in changing a snuffling band of unreliable followers into fearless evangelists, that eleven men who had deserted him at death now went to martyrs' graves avowing their faith in a resurrected Christ, that these few witnesses managed to set loose a force that would overcome violent opposition first in Jerusalem and then in Rome—this remarkable sequence of transformation offers the most convincing evidence for the Resurrection. What else explains the whiplash change in men known for their cowardice and instability?

Others—at least fifteen Jews within a hundred years of Jesus—had made Messiah claims, only to flare and then fade like a dying star. Fanatic loyalty to Jesus, though, did not end with his death. Something had happened, something beyond all precedent. Surely the disciples would not lay down their lives for the sake of a cobbled-together conspiracy theory. Surely it would have been easier, and more natural, to honor a dead Jesus as one of the martyr-prophets whose tombs were so venerated by the Jews.

One need only read the Gospels' descriptions of disciples huddling behind locked doors and then proceed to the descriptions in Acts of the same men proclaiming Christ openly in the streets and in jail cells to perceive the seismic significance of what took place on Easter Sunday. The Resurrection is the epicenter of belief. It is, says C. H. Dodd, "not a belief that grew up within the church; it is the belief around which the church itself grew up, and the 'given' upon which its faith was based." Novelist John Updike states the same truth more poetically:

> *Make no mistake: if He rose at all*
> *it was as His body;*
> *if the cells' dissolution did not reverse, the molecules*
> *reknit, the amino acids rekindle,*
> *the Church will fall.*

"Blessed are those who have not seen and yet have believed," Jesus said to doubting Thomas after silencing his doubts with tangible proof of the Easter miracle. Except for the five hundred or so people to whom the resurrected Jesus appeared, every Christian who has ever lived falls into the category of "blessed." I ask myself, *Why do I believe?*—I, who resemble Thomas more than any other disciple in my skepticism and slowness to accept what cannot be proved beyond doubt.

I have weighed the arguments in favor of the resurrection, and they are indeed impressive. The English journalist Frank Morison dealt with most of these arguments in the classic *Who Moved the Stone?* Although Morison had set out to discount the resurrection as a myth, the evidence convinced him otherwise. Yet I also know that many intelligent people have looked at the same evidence and found it impossible to believe. Although much about the Resurrection invites belief, nothing compels it. Faith requires the possibility of rejection, or it is not faith. What, then, gives me Easter faith?

One reason I am open to belief, I admit, is that at a very deep level I want the Easter story to be true. Faith grows out of a subsoil of yearning, and something primal in human beings cries out against the reign of death. Whether hope takes the form of Egyptian pharaohs stashing their jewels and chariots in pyramids, or the modern American obsession with keeping bodies alive until the last possible nanosecond and then preserving them with embalming fluids in double-sealed caskets, we humans resist the idea of death having a final say. We want to believe otherwise.

I remember the year I lost my three friends. Above all else, I want Easter to be true because of its promise that someday I will get my friends back. I want to abolish that word *irreversible* forever.

I suppose you could say I want to believe in fairy tales. I am not alone. Has any age not produced fairy tales? We first hear them in our cribs from parents and grandparents, and repeat them to our children who will tell them to their children, and on it goes. Even in this scientific age, some of the highest-grossing movies are variations of fairy tales: *Star Wars*, *Aladdin*, *The Lion King*. Astonishingly in light of human history, most fairy tales have a happy ending. That old instinct, hope, billows up. Like life, fairy tales include much struggle and pain, yet even so they manage to resolve in a way that replaces tears with smiles. Easter does that too, and for this as well as many other reasons, it rings true.*

The crowd at Jesus' crucifixion challenged him to prove himself by climbing down from the cross, but not one person thought of what actually would happen: that he would die and then come back. Once the scenario played out, though, to those who knew Jesus best it made perfect sense. The style fit God's pattern and character. God has always chosen the slow and difficult way, respecting human freedom regardless of cost. "God did not abolish the fact of evil: He transformed it," wrote Dorothy Sayers. "He did not stop the crucifixion: He rose from the dead." The hero bore all consequences, yet somehow triumphed.

I believe in the Resurrection primarily because I have gotten to know God. I know that God is love, and I also know that we human beings want to keep alive those whom we love. I do not let my friends die; they live on in my memory and my heart long after I have stopped seeing them. For whatever reason—human freedom lies at the core, I

---

*J. R. R. Tolkien, perhaps this century's greatest creator of fairy tales, often faced the charge that fantasy is an "escapist" way of shifting attention away from the pressures of the "real world." His reply was simple: Everything depends on that from which one is escaping. We view the flight of a deserter and the escape of a prisoner very differently. "Why should a man be scorned if, finding himself in prison, he tries to get out and go home?"

imagine—God allows a planet where a man dies scuba diving in the prime of life and a woman dies in a fiery crash on the way to a church missions conference. But I believe—if I did not believe this, I would not believe in a loving God—that God is not satisfied with such a blighted planet. Divine love will find a way to overcome. "Death, be not proud," wrote John Donne: God will not let death win.

One detail in the Easter stories has always intrigued me: Why did Jesus keep the scars from his crucifixion? Presumably he could have had any resurrected body he wanted, and yet he chose one identifiable mainly by scars that could be seen and touched. Why?

I believe the story of Easter would be incomplete without those scars on the hands, the feet, and the side of Jesus. When human beings fantasize, we dream of pearly straight teeth and wrinkle-free skin and sexy ideal shapes. We dream of an unnatural state: the perfect body. But for Jesus, being confined in a skeleton and human skin *was* the unnatural state. The scars are, to him, an emblem of life on our planet, a permanent reminder of those days of confinement and suffering.

I take hope in Jesus' scars. From the perspective of heaven, they represent the most horrible event that has ever happened in the history of the universe. Even that event, though—the crucifixion—Easter turned into a memory. Because of Easter, I can hope that the tears we shed, the blows we receive, the emotional pain, the heartache over lost friends and loved ones, all these will become memories, like Jesus' scars. Scars never completely go away, but neither do they hurt any longer. We will have re-created bodies, a re-created heaven and earth. We will have a new start, an Easter start.

There are two ways to look at human history, I have concluded. One way is to focus on the wars and violence, the squalor, the pain and tragedy and death. From such a point of view, Easter seems a fairy-tale exception, a stunning contradiction in the name of God. That gives some solace, although I confess that when my friends died, grief was so overpowering that any hope in an after-life seemed somehow thin and insubstantial.

There is another way to look at the world. If I take Easter as the starting point, the one incontrovertible fact about how God treats those whom he loves, then human history becomes the contradiction and Easter a preview of ultimate reality. Hope then flows like lava beneath the crust of daily life.

This, perhaps, describes the change in the disciples' perspective as they sat in locked rooms discussing the incomprehensible events of Easter Sunday. In one sense nothing had changed: Rome still occupied Palestine, religious authorities still had a bounty on their heads, death and evil still reigned outside. Gradually, however, the shock of recognition gave way to a long slow undertow of joy. If God could do that ...

Part Three

What He Left Behind

12
Ascension: A Blank Blue Sky

But God's own descent
Into flesh was meant
As a demonstration . . .
Spirit enters flesh and for all it's worth
Charges into earth in birth after birth
Ever fresh and fresh.

Robert Frost

12
Ascension:
A Blank Blue Sky

Sometimes I think about how different the world would be had Jesus not resurrected from the dead. Although the disciples would not risk their lives trumpeting a new faith in the streets of Jerusalem, neither would they forget him. They had given three years to Jesus. He may not be the Messiah (not without Easter), but he had impressed them as the wisest teacher ever and had demonstrated powers that no one could explain.

After time, as emotional wounds began to heal, the disciples would seek some way to memorialize Jesus. Perhaps they would collect his sayings in a written form akin to one of our Gospels, though with the more sensational claims excised. Or, along with Jews from that period who were honoring other martyr-prophets, they might build a monument to Jesus' life. If so, we who live in modern times could still visit that monument and learn about the carpenter/philosopher from Nazareth. We could sift through his sayings, taking or leaving whatever we liked. Worldwide, Jesus would be esteemed in the same way Confucius or Socrates is esteemed.

In many respects I would find an unresurrected Jesus easier to accept. Easter makes him dangerous. Because of Easter I have to listen to his extravagant claims and can no longer pick and choose from his sayings. Moreover, Easter means he must be loose out there somewhere. Like the disciples, I never know where Jesus might turn up, how he might speak to me, what he might ask of me. As Frederick Buechner says, Easter means "we can never nail him down, not even if the nails we use are real and the thing we nail him to is a cross."

Easter puts Jesus' life in a whole new light. Apart from Easter I would think it a tragedy that Jesus died young after a few short years of ministry. What a waste for him to leave so soon, having affected so few people in such a small part of the world! Yet, viewing that same life through the lens of Easter, I see that was Jesus' plan all along. He stayed just long enough to gather around him followers who could carry the message to others. Killing Jesus, says Walter Wink, was like trying to destroy a dandelion seed-head by blowing on it.

When Jesus returned after death to vaporize all doubts among the remnant of believers, he tarried a mere forty days before vanishing for good. The time between Resurrection and Ascension was an interlude, nothing more.

If Easter Sunday was the most exciting day of the disciples' lives, for Jesus it was probably the day of Ascension. He the Creator, who had descended so far and given up so much, was now heading home. Like a soldier returning across the ocean from a long and bloody war. Like an astronaut shedding his spacesuit to gulp in the familiar atmosphere of earth. Home at last.

Jesus' prayer at the Last Supper with his disciples reveals something of this point of view. "I have brought you glory on earth by completing the work you gave me to do," Jesus prayed, "And now, Father, glorify me in your presence with the glory I had with you before the world began." Before the world began! Like an old man reminiscing—no, like an ageless God reminiscing—Jesus, who sat in a stuffy room in Jerusalem, was letting his mind wander back to a time before the Milky Way and Andromeda. On an earthly night dark with fear and menace, Jesus was making preparations to return home, to assume again the glory he had set aside.

On the day Jesus ascended, the disciples stood around dumbfounded, like children who have lost their parent. Two angels sent to calm them asked the obvious question, "Men of Galilee, why do you stand here looking into the sky?" The sky was blank, empty. Still they stood and gazed, not knowing how to go on or what to do next.

So many times in the course of writing this book I have felt like one of those disciples, peering intently at a blank blue sky. I look for some sign of Jesus, some visual clue. When I glance around me at the church he left behind, I want to avert my eyes. Like the disciples' eyes, mine ache for a pure glimpse of the One who ascended. Why, I ask again, did he have to leave?

But as I go back through the Gospels, trying to envision how Jesus himself viewed his time on earth, it seems obvious he planned this departure from the beginning. Nothing pleased Jesus more than the successes of his disciples; nothing disturbed him more than their failures. He had come to earth with the goal of leaving again, after transferring his mission to others. The angels' gentle rebuke might as well have been his own: "Why do you stand here looking into the sky?"

The first time Jesus sent the disciples out alone, he warned them about opposition that would likely take the form of floggings and public torture. "I am sending you out like sheep among wolves," he said. Reading these dire warnings, I cannot push from my mind a harrowing scene from Shusako Endo's novel *Silence*. A Portuguese missionary priest, bound, is forced to watch as samurai guards torture Japanese Christians, one by one, and throw them into the sea. The samurai swear they will keep on killing Christians until the priest renounces his faith. "He had come to this country to lay down his life for other men, but instead of that the Japanese were laying down their lives one by one for him."

What was it like for Jesus, who saw with piercing vision the terrible consequences of what he had set loose in the world, not only for himself but for the huddled few around him, his best friends in all the world? "Brother will betray brother to death, and a father his child ... All men will hate you because of me. ..."

I struggle to reconcile that point of view—a parent consigning her children to the gangs, a general ordering his troops into the line of fire—with what took place at the Last Supper. There, as Jesus disclosed plans for his departure in terms no one could mistake, he said,

"But I tell you the truth: It is for your good that I am going away." All along he had planned to depart in order to carry on his work in other bodies. Their bodies. Our bodies. The new body of Christ.

At the time the disciples had no idea what Jesus meant. *How can it be good that he is going away?* They ate the "body, broken for you" without comprehending the drastic change, that the mission God had assigned to the Son, the Son was now entrusting to them. "As you sent me into the world, I have sent them into the world," Jesus prayed.

Jesus left few traces of himself on earth. He wrote no books or even pamphlets. A wanderer, he left no home or even belongings that could be enshrined in a museum. He did not marry, settle down, and begin a dynasty. We would, in fact, know nothing about him except for the traces he left in human beings. That was his design. The law and the prophets had focused like a beam of light on the One who was to come, and now that light, as if hitting a prism, would fracture and shoot out in a human spectrum of waves and colors.

Six weeks later, the disciples would find out what Jesus had meant by the words *for your good*. As Augustine put it, "You ascended from before our eyes, and we turned back grieving, only to find you in our hearts."

Would it be too much to say that, ever since the Ascension, Jesus has sought other bodies in which to begin again the life he lived on earth? The church serves as an extension of the Incarnation, God's primary way of establishing presence in the world. We are "After Christ," in Gerard Manley Hopkins's coinage:

> . . . *for Christ plays in ten thousand places,*
> *Lovely in eyes, and lovely in limbs not his*
> *To the Father through the features of men's faces.*

The church is where God lives. What Jesus brought to a few—healing, grace, the good-news message of God's love—the church can now bring to all. That was the challenge, or Great Commission, that Jesus gave just before vanishing from the numbed disciples' sight. "Unless a kernel of wheat falls to the ground and dies," he had explained earlier, "it remains only a single seed. But if it dies, it produces many seeds." Propagation by the dandelion method.

Such is the theory, at least. In truth, I must, though, place myself with the disciples who watch with jaws agape as Jesus lifts into the air like some wingless creature defying gravity. "Lord, are you at this time going to restore the kingdom to Israel?" they have just asked—and now this. He's gone! I sympathize with their bewilderment, because I too yearn for a power-Messiah to impose order on a world of evil and violence and poverty. Living two millennia after the disciples, I look back and marvel at how little difference the church has made in such a world. Why did Jesus leave us alone to fight the battles? How can it be good that he went away?

I have concluded, in fact, that the Ascension represents my greatest struggle of faith—not whether it happened, but why. It challenges me more than the problem of pain, more than the difficulty of harmonizing science and the Bible, more than belief in the Resurrection and other miracles. It seems odd to admit such a notion—I have never read a book or article conceived to answer doubts about the Ascension—yet for me what has happened since Jesus' departure strikes at the core of my faith. Would it not have been better if the Ascension had never happened? If Jesus had stayed on earth, he could answer our questions, solve our doubts, mediate our disputes of doctrine and policy.

I find it much easier to accept the fact of God incarnating in Jesus of Nazareth than in the people who attend my local church—and in me. Yet that is what we are asked to believe; that is how we are asked to live. The New Testament declares that the future of the cosmos is being determined by the church (see Romans 8:19–21; Ephesians 3:10). Jesus played his part and then left. Now it is up to us.

"It is a serious thing," wrote C. S. Lewis, "to live in a society of possible gods and goddesses, to remember that the dullest and most uninteresting person you talk to may one day be a creature which, if you saw it now, you would be strongly tempted to worship, or else a horror and a corruption such as you now meet, if at all, only in a nightmare. All day long we are, in some degree, helping each other to one or another of these destinations."

Ancient religions, such as the Roman paganism of Jesus' day, believed that the actions of gods in the heavens above affected the earth below. If Zeus got angry, thunderbolts shot out. Like kids dropping rocks off highway bridges onto the cars below, the gods rained cataclysm onto the earth. "As above, so below," went the ancient formula. Jesus, though, inverted that formula: "As below, so above." "He who listens to you listens to me," Jesus told his followers; "he who rejects you rejects me." A believer prays, and heaven responds; a sinner repents, and the angels rejoice; a mission succeeds, and Satan falls like lightning; a believer rebels, and the Holy Spirit is grieved. What we humans do here decisively affects the cosmos.

I believe these things, and yet somehow I keep "forgetting" them. I forget that my prayers matter to God. I forget that I am helping my neighbors to their eternal destinations. I forget that the choices I make today bring delight—or grief—to the Lord of the Universe. I live in a world of trees and telephones and fax machines, and the reality of this material universe tends to overwhelm my faith in a spiritual universe suffusing it all. I look into the blank blue sky and see nothing.

By ascending, Jesus took the risk of being forgotten.

Not long ago, as I was reading through Matthew, I noticed with a start that Jesus himself foresaw the very predicament of being forgotten. Four parables toward the end of Matthew, among the last that Jesus gave, have a common theme lurking in the background. An owner leaves his house vacant, an absentee landlord puts his servant in charge, a bridegroom arrives so late the guests grow drowsy and fall asleep, a master distributes talents among his servants and takes off—all these circle around the theme of the departed God.

In effect, Jesus' stories anticipated the central question of the modern era: "Where is God now?" The modern answer, from the likes of Nietzsche, Freud, Marx, Camus, and Beckett, is that the landlord has abandoned us, leaving us free to set our own rules. *Deus absconditus*. In places like Auschwitz and Rwanda, we have seen living versions of those parables, graphic examples of how some will act when they stop believing in a sovereign landlord. If there is no God, as Dostoevsky said, then anything is permissible.

Reading on, I came to one more parable, the Sheep and the Goats, probably the last one Jesus taught.

> When the Son of Man comes in his glory, and all the angels with him, he will sit on his throne in heavenly glory. All the nations will be gathered before him, and he will separate the people one from another as a shepherd separates the sheep from the goats. He will put the sheep on his right and the goats on his left.
>
> Then the King will say to those on his right, "Come, you who are blessed by my Father; take your inheritance, the kingdom prepared for you since the creation of the world. For I was hungry and you gave me something to eat, I was thirsty and you gave me something to drink, I was a stranger and you invited me in, I needed clothes and you clothed me, I was sick and you looked after me, I was in prison and you came to visit me."
>
> Then the righteous will answer him, "Lord, when did we see you hungry and feed you, or thirsty and give you something to drink? When did we see you a stranger and invite you in, or needing clothes and clothe you? When did we see you sick or in prison and go to visit you?"
>
> The King will reply, "I tell you the truth, whatever you did for one of the least of these brothers of mine, you did for me."
>
> Then he will say to those on his left, "Depart from me, you who are cursed, into the eternal fire prepared for the devil and his angels. For I was hungry and you gave me nothing to eat, I was thirsty and you gave me nothing to drink, I was a stranger and you did not invite me in, I needed clothes and you did not clothe me, I was sick and in prison and you did not look after me."
>
> They also will answer, "Lord, when did we see you hungry or thirsty or a stranger or needing clothes or sick or in prison, and did not help you?"
>
> He will reply, "I tell you the truth, whatever you did not do for one of the least of these, you did not do for me."
>
> Then they will go away to eternal punishment, but the righteous to eternal life.

I knew this last parable well. It is as potent and disturbing as anything Jesus ever said. But I had never before noticed its logical connection with the four parables that precede it.

In two ways the parable of the Sheep and the Goats directly addresses the question raised by the others: the issue of the absentee landlord, the missing God. First, it gives a glimpse of the landlord's return on judgment day, when there will be hell to pay—literally. The departed One will return, this time in power and in glory, to settle accounts for all that has happened on earth. "Men of Galilee," said the angels, "why do you stand here looking into the sky? This same Jesus, who has been taken from you into heaven, will come back in the same way you have seen him go into heaven."

Second, the parable refers to the meantime, the centuries-long interval we live in now, the time when God seems absent. The answer to that most modern question is at once profound and shocking. God has not absconded at all. Rather, he has taken on a disguise, a most unlikely disguise of the stranger, the poor, the hungry, the prisoner, the sick, the ragged ones of earth: "I tell you the truth, whatever you did for one of the least of these brothers of mine, you did it for me." If we cannot detect God's presence in the world, it may be that we have been looking in the wrong places.

Commenting on this passage, the great American theologian Jonathan Edwards said that God has designated the poor as his "receivers." Since we cannot express our love by doing anything to profit God directly, God wants us to do something profitable for the poor, who have been delegated the task of receiving Christian love.

One night I was absently flipping the channels of television when I came across what seemed to be a children's movie, starring the young Hayley Mills. I settled back and watched the plot unfold. She and two friends, while playing in a country barn, stumbled across a vagrant (Alan Bates) sleeping in the straw. "Who are you?" Mills demanded. The vagrant jerked awake and, seeing the children, muttered, "Jesus Christ!"

What he meant as an expletive, the children took as the truth. They actually believed the man to be Jesus Christ. For the rest of the movie (*Whistle Down the Wind*), they treated the vagrant with awe, respect, and love. They brought him food and blankets, sat and talked with him, and told him about their lives. In time their tenderness transformed the vagrant, an escaped convict who had never before known such mercy.

Mills's mother, who wrote the story, intended it as an allegory of what might happen if all of us took literally Jesus' words about the poor and the needy. By serving them, we serve Jesus. "We are a contemplative order," Mother Teresa told a rich American visitor who could not comprehend her fierce commitment to the dregs of Calcutta. "First we meditate on Jesus, and then we go out and look for him in disguise."

As I reflected on the last parable in Matthew 25, I became aware that many of my own questions of God are actually boomerang questions that come right back to me. Why does God allow babies to be born in Brooklyn ghettoes and by a river of death in Rwanda? Why does God allow prisons and homeless shelters and hospitals and refugee camps? Why did Jesus not clean up the world's messes in the years he lived here?

According to this parable, Jesus knew that the world he left behind would include the poor, the hungry, the prisoners, the sick. The decrepit state of the world did not surprise him. He made plans to cope with it: a long-range plan and a short-range plan. The long-range plan involves his return, in power and great glory, to straighten out planet earth. The short-range plan means turning it over to the ones who will ultimately usher in the liberation of the cosmos. He ascended so that we would take his place.

"Where is God when it hurts?" I have often asked. The answer is another question, "Where is the church when it hurts?"

That last question, of course, is the problem of history in a nutshell, and also the reason why I say the Ascension represents my greatest struggle of faith. When Jesus departed, he left the keys of the kingdom in our fumbling hands.

All through my own quest for Jesus has run a counterpoint theme: my need to strip away layers of dust and grime applied *by the church itself.* In my case the image of Jesus was obscured by the racism, intolerance, and petty legalism of fundamentalist churches in the South. A Russian or a European Catholic confronts a very different restoration process. "For not only dust, but also too much gold can cover up the true figure," wrote the German Hans Küng about his own search. Many, far too many, abandon the quest entirely; repelled by the church, they never make it to Jesus.

"What a pity that so hard on the heels of Christ come the Christians," observes Annie Dillard. Her statement reminds me of a T-shirt that can be spotted at contemporary political rallies: "Jesus save us ... from your followers." And of a line from the New Zealand film *Heavenly Creatures* in which two girls describe their imaginary kingdom: "It's like heaven only better—there aren't any Christians!"

The problem showed itself early on. Commenting on the church in Corinth, Frederick Buechner writes, "They were in fact Christ's body, as Paul wrote to them here in one of his most enduring metaphors—Christ's eyes, ears, hands—but the way they were carrying on, that could only leave Christ bloodshot, ass-eared, all thumbs, to carry on God's work in a fallen world." In the fourth century an exasperated St. Augustine wrote about the fractious church, "The clouds roll with thunder that the House of the Lord shall be built throughout the earth; and these frogs sit in their marsh and croak— 'We are the only Christians!'"

I could fill several pages with such colorful quotations, all of which underscore the risk involved in entrusting God's own reputation to the likes of us. Unlike Jesus, we do not perfectly express the Word. We speak in garbled syntax, stuttering, mixing languages together, putting accent marks in wrong places. When the world looks for Christ it sees, like the cave-dwellers in Plato's allegory, only shadows created by the light, not the light itself.

Why don't we look more like the church Jesus described? Why does the body of Christ so faintly resemble him? If Jesus could foresee such disasters as the Crusades, the Inquisition, the Christian slave trade, apartheid, why did he ascend in the first place?

I cannot provide a confident answer to such questions, for I am part of the problem. Examined closely, my query takes on a distressingly personal cast: Why do *I* so poorly resemble him? I merely offer three observations that help me come to terms with what has transpired since Jesus' ascension.

First, the church has brought light as well as darkness. In the name of Jesus, St. Francis kissed the beggar and took off his robes,

Mother Teresa founded the Home for the Dying, Wilberforce freed the slaves, General Booth established an urban Army of Salvation, and Dorothy Day fed the hungry. Such work continues: as a journalist I have met educators, urban ministers, doctors and nurses, linguists, relief workers, and ecologists serving all over the world for little pay and less fame, all in the name of Jesus. In other ways, Michelangelo, Bach, Rembrandt, the masons of cathedrals, and many like them offered up the best of their creation "for the glory of God alone." God's hands on earth have reached wider since the Ascension.

I see no point in tallying up a balance sheet to weigh the church's failures against its successes. The final word will come from God's own judgment. The first few chapters of Revelation show how realistically God views the church, and yet elsewhere the New Testament makes clear that God takes pleasure in us: we are "peculiar treasures," a "pleasing aroma," "gifts that he delights in." I cannot fathom such statements; I merely accept them on faith. God alone knows what pleases God.

Second, Jesus takes full responsibility for the constituent parts of his body. "You did not choose me, but I chose you," he told his disciples, and these were the very scalawags who so exasperated him and would soon desert him at his hour of greatest need. I think of Peter, whose bluster, love, hot-headedness, misdirected passion, and faithless betrayal preview in embryo form nineteen centuries of church history. On "rocks" like him, Jesus built his church, and he promised that the gates of hell would not prevail against it.*

I take hope as I observe Jesus together with his disciples. Never did they disappoint him more than on the night of his betrayal. Yet it was then, says John, that Jesus "showed them the full extent of his love," and then that he conferred on them a kingdom.

Finally, the problem of the church is no different than the problem of one solitary Christian. How can an unholy assortment of men and women be the body of Christ? I answer with a different question:

---

*Charles Williams comments that Jesus "does not seem, to judge by his comments on the religious leaders of his day, ever to have hoped much from officers of a church. The most he would do was to promise that the gates of hell should not *prevail* against it. It is about all that, looking on the history of the Church, one can feel they have not done."

How can one sinful man, myself, be accepted as a child of God? One miracle makes possible the other.

I remind myself that the apostle Paul's soaring words about the bride of Christ and the temple of God were addressed to groups of hideously flawed individuals in places like Corinth. "We have this treasure in jars of clay to show that this all-surpassing power is from God and not from us," wrote Paul in one of the most accurate statements ever penned.

The novelist Flannery O'Connor, who could never be accused of glossing over human depravity, once answered a letter from a reader complaining about the state of the church. "All your dissatisfaction with the Church seems to me to come from an incomplete understanding of sin," O'Connor began:

> ... what you seem actually to demand is that the Church put the kingdom of heaven on earth right here now, that the Holy Ghost be translated at once into all flesh. The Holy Spirit rarely shows Himself on the surface of anything. You are asking that man return at once to the state God created him in, you are leaving out the terrible radical human pride that causes death. Christ was crucified on earth and the Church is crucified in time ... The Church is founded on Peter who denied Christ three times and who couldn't walk on the water by himself. You are expecting his successors to walk on the water. All human nature vigorously resists grace because grace changes us and the change is painful. Priests resist it as well as others. To have the Church be what you want it to be would require the continuous miraculous meddling of God in human affairs ...

In two memorable phrases, O'Connor has captured the choices God faced, looking out on human history: to engage in "the continuous miraculous meddling in human affairs" or to allow himself to be "crucified in time" as his Son was on earth. With a few exceptions, God, whose nature is self-living love, has chosen the second option. Christ bears the wounds of the church, his body, just as he bore the wounds of crucifixion. I sometimes wonder which have hurt worse.

13
Kingdom:
Wheat Among the Weeds

The human comedy doesn't attract me enough. I am not entirely of this world. . . . I am from elsewhere. And it is worth finding this elsewhere beyond the walls. But where is it?

Eugene Ionesco

13
Kingdom:
Wheat Among the Weeds

Each fall the childhood church I attended sponsored a prophecy conference. Silver-haired men of national repute would stretch their prophecy charts—stitched bedsheets covered with Day-Glo renditions of beasts and armies—across the platform and expound on "the last days" we were living in.

I listened in fear and fascination as they drew a straight line south from Moscow to Jerusalem and sketched in the movements of million-strong armies who would soon converge on Israel. I learned that the ten members of Europe's Common Market had recently fulfilled Daniel's prophecy about the beast with ten horns. Soon all of us would wear a number stamped on our foreheads, the mark of the beast, and be registered in a computer somewhere in Belgium. Nuclear war would break out and the planet would teeter on the brink of annihilation, until at the last second Jesus himself would return to lead the armies of righteousness.

That scenario seems far less likely now that Russia has declined and the Common Market (now European Union) has expanded beyond ten members. What sticks with me, though, is not so much the particulars of prophecy as their emotional effect on me. I grew up at once terrified and desperately hopeful. In high school I took courses in Chinese and my brother studied Russian so that one of us could communicate with invading armies from either direction. My uncle went further, packing up his family and moving to Australia. Yet in the midst of this terror we also had hope: though I felt certain the world would soon end, nevertheless I banked all my childhood faith on the belief that somehow Jesus would conquer.

Later, as I read church history, I learned that often before—during the first decades of Christianity, the end of the tenth century, the late 1300s, the Napoleonic era, World War I, the Axis of Hitler and Mussolini—visions of the end times had bubbled to the surface. As recently as the 1991 Gulf War, Saddam Hussein was being branded the Antichrist, the new trigger-man for the apocalypse. Each time, Christians went through a passionate cycle of fear, hope, and sheepish disillusionment. The end times had not arrived after all.

I also learned that the Jewish race has repeatedly undergone the exact same cycle, never more poignantly than in the first century A.D. At that time many Jews expected the Messiah to arise and liberate them from the terrors of Rome, a hope that the man from Nazareth at first ignited, and then dashed. To understand Jesus and the mission he left behind after his ascension, I need to return once more to his own era, to place myself again in his time, to listen to him speak on the topic he favored more than any other: the kingdom of God. What he said about God's kingdom in the first century has great relevance to me today in the twentieth.

In Jesus' day, Jews were poring over the same passages from Daniel and Ezekiel that would later figure so prominently in the prophecy conferences of my childhood.* We disagreed on some details—Northern Europe was then a forest full of barbarians not a Common Market, and Russia was unknown—yet our visions of the Messiah matched: we expected a conquering hero. Anyone

---

*The scribes who pored so assiduously over Old Testament prophecies did not recognize Jesus as the fulfillment of those prophecies. Should not their failure to interpret signs of the first coming sound a note of caution to those today who so confidently proclaim signs of the Second Coming?

who declared "The kingdom of God has come upon you!" would surely awaken in his listeners' minds the image of a political leader who would arise, take charge, and defeat the most powerful empire ever known.

In such an environment, Jesus well understood the explosive power of the word *Messiah*. In William Barclay's judgment, "If Jesus had publicly claimed to be Messiah, nothing could have stopped a useless flood tide of slaughter." Although Jesus did not use the title himself, he accepted it when others called him Messiah, and the Gospels show a gradual dawning on his disciples that their teacher was none other than the long-awaited King.

Jesus encouraged such beliefs by using the word that quickened the pulse of his people. "The *kingdom* of heaven is near," he proclaimed in his very first message. Each time he spoke it, that word stirred memories to life: bright banners, glittering armies, the gold and ivory of Solomon's day, the nation of Israel restored. What was about to happen, Jesus said, would far surpass anything from the past: "For I tell you that many prophets and kings wanted to see what you see but did not see it, and to hear what you hear but did not hear it." On another occasion he announced provocatively, "Now one greater than Solomon is here."

Zealots stood at the edge of Jesus' audience, armed and well-organized guerrillas spoiling for a fight against Rome, but to their consternation the signal for revolt never came. In time, Jesus' pattern of behavior disappointed all who sought a leader in the traditional mold. He tended to flee from, rather than cater to, large groups. He insulted the memory of Israel's glory days, comparing King Solomon to a common day lily. The one time a crowd tried to crown him king by force, he mysteriously withdrew. And when Peter finally did wield a sword on his behalf, Jesus healed the victim's wounds.

To the crowds' dismay, it became clear that Jesus was talking about a strangely different kind of kingdom. The Jews wanted what people have always wanted from a visible kingdom: a chicken in every pot, full employment, a strong army to deter invaders. Jesus announced a kingdom that meant denying yourself, taking up a cross, renouncing wealth, even loving your enemies. As he elaborated, the crowd's expectations crumbled.

By the time Jesus was nailed to wooden crossbeams, everyone had lost hope and fallen away. Scholars report that first-century Jews had no concept of a suffering Messiah. As for the Twelve, no matter how often or how plainly Jesus warned them of his impending death, it never sank in. No one could imagine a Messiah dying.

The word *kingdom* meant one thing to Jesus and quite another to the crowd. Jesus was rejected, in large part, because he did not measure up to a national image of what a Messiah was supposed to look like.

A question has long puzzled me. In view of their expectations, why did Jesus keep arousing his followers' hopes with the word *kingdom*? (It appears fifty-three times in Matthew's gospel alone.) He insisted on associating himself with a term that everyone seemed to misunderstand. What did Jesus mean by the *kingdom of God*?

It is a great irony that the one who so failed the expectations of his people became known to all history as a king—so much so that a form of the word became his "last name." Christ, or *Christos* in Greek, translates the Hebrew word *Messiah*, which means anointed and refers to the ancient manner of coronating kings. Now, all of us who call ourselves *Christ*-ians carry an echo of the word that so baffled the people of Jesus' day. I wonder, Do we understand the kingdom of God any better?

Jesus never offered a clear definition of the kingdom, instead he imparted his vision of it indirectly through a series of stories. His choice of images is telling: everyday sketches of farming, fishing, women baking bread, merchants buying pearls.

The kingdom of heaven is like a farmer going out to sow his seed. As every farmer knows, not all the seed you plant ends up yielding crops. Some falls among rocks, some gets eaten by birds and field mice, some gets crowded out by weeds. All this seems natural to a farmer, but heretical to a traditional kingdom-builder. Are not kings judged by their power, their ability to impose their will on a populace, their strength in repelling enemies? Jesus was indicating that the kingdom of God comes with a resistible power. It is humble and unobtrusive and coexistent with evil—a message that surely did not please patriotic Jews intent on revolt.

Consider the mustard seed, a seed so tiny it can fall to the ground and lie unnoticed by human beings and birds alike. Given time, though, the seed may sprout into a bush that overtakes every other plant in the garden, a bush so large and verdant that birds come and nest in its branches. God's kingdom works like that. It begins so small that people scorn it and give it no chance for success. Against all odds, God's kingdom will grow and spread throughout the world, bringing shade to the sick, the poor, the imprisoned, the unloved.

The kingdom of heaven is like a businessman who specializes in rare gems. One day he finds a pearl gorgeous enough to make princesses drool with envy. Recognizing its value, he liquidates his entire business in order to buy it. Although the purchase costs everything he owns, not for a moment does he regret it. He makes the trade with joy, as the crowning achievement of his life: the treasure will outlive him, enduring long after the family name has disappeared. God's kingdom works like that. The sacrifice—deny yourself, take up your cross—turns out to be a shrewd investment, its outcome not remorse but joy beyond all telling.

These are the stories Jesus told. As I review the parables of the kingdom, though, I realize how far my own understanding has drifted from such homespun images. I tend to envision the same kind of kingdom the Jews did: a visible, powerful kingdom. I think of Constantine leading his troops, crosses emblazoned on their armor, with the slogan "By this sign conquer." I think of the armies marching across the bedsheets at the prophecy conferences. Obviously, I need to listen again to Jesus' description of the kingdom of God.

Those of us in the twentieth century, an era that has few literal "kings," conceive of kingdoms in terms of power and polarization. We are the children of revolution. Two centuries ago in the U.S. and France the oppressed rose up and overturned the reigning powers.

Later, in places like Russia and China, Marxists led revolts with an ideology that became a kind of religion: they began, in fact, to view all history as an outgrowth of class struggle, or dialectical materialism. "Workers, unite! Throw off your chains!" cried Marx, and so they did for much of our bloody century.

For a period of time I tried to read the Gospels through the eyes of liberation theology. Ultimately I had to conclude that, whatever else it is, the kingdom of God is decidedly not a call to violent revolution. First-century Jews were doubtless looking for such an upheaval. Battle lines were clear: oppressed Jews versus the bad-guy Romans—pagans who collected taxes, trafficked in slaves, regulated religion, and quashed dissent. Under these conditions the Zealots issued a call much like Marx's: "Jews, unite! Throw off your chains!" But Jesus' message of the kingdom had little in common with the politics of polarization.

As I read the Gospels, Jesus seems to speak a two-pronged message. To the oppressors, he had words of warning and judgment. He treated the powers of government with an attitude of mild contempt, dismissing Herod as "that fox" (a Jewish expression for a worthless or insignificant person) and agreeing to pay a temple tax "so that we may not offend them." He placed little store in politics; it was government, after all, that tried to exterminate him.

To the oppressed, his primary audience, Jesus offered a message of comfort and consolation. He called the poor and the persecuted "blessed." Never did he incite the oppressed to rise up and throw off their chains. In words that must have galled the Zealots, he com-manded, "Love your enemies." The kingdom advances not by power: love, not coercion.

People who looked to Jesus as their political savior were constantly befuddled by his choice of companions. He became known as a friend of tax collectors, a group clearly identified with the foreign exploiters, not the exploited. Though he denounced the religious system of his day, he treated a leader like Nicodemus with respect, and though he spoke against the dangers of money and of violence, he showed love and compassion toward a rich young ruler and a Roman centurion.

In short, Jesus honored the dignity of people, whether he agreed with them or not. He would not found his kingdom on the basis of race or class or other such divisions. Anyone, even a half-breed with five husbands or a thief dying on a cross, was welcome to join his kingdom. The person was more important than any category or label.

I feel convicted by this quality of Jesus every time I get involved in a cause I strongly believe in. How easy it is to join the politics of polarization, to find myself shouting across the picket lines at the "enemy" on the other side. How hard it is to remember that the kingdom of God calls me to love the woman who has just emerged from the abortion clinic (and, yes, even her doctor), the promiscuous person who is dying of AIDS, the wealthy landowner who is exploiting God's creation. If I cannot show love to such people, then I must question whether I have truly understood Jesus' gospel.

A political movement by nature draws lines, makes distinctions, pronounces judgment; in contrast, Jesus' love cuts across lines, transcends distinctions, and dispenses grace. Regardless of the merits of a given issue—whether a pro-life lobby out of the Right or a peace-and-justice lobby out of the Left—political movements risk pulling onto themselves the mantle of power that smothers love. From Jesus I learn that, whatever activism I get involved in, it must not drive out love and humility, or otherwise I betray the kingdom of heaven.

If I am tempted to see the kingdom of God as one more power structure, I need only turn to the account of the trial in Jerusalem, a scene that brings together the two kingdoms in striking apposition. On that climactic day the rulers of the "kingdom of this world" confronted Jesus and his kingdom face-to-face.

Two kings, Herod and Jesus, personified very different kinds of power. Herod had legions of Roman soldiers to enforce his will, and history records how Herod used his power: he stole his brother's wife, locked up all dissenters, beheaded John the Baptist as a party trick. Jesus too had power, but he used it compassionately, to feed the hungry and heal the sick. Herod had a gold crown, palaces, guards, and all the visible tokens of royalty. For Jesus, the closest thing to a formal coronation, or Messiah's "anointing," occurred in an embarrassing scene when a disreputable woman poured perfume over his head. He got the title "King of the Jews" as a criminal sentence. His "crown," made of thorns, was merely one more source of pain. And though he could have called on a legion of angels for protection, he declined.

Consistently, Jesus refused to use coercive power. He knowingly let one of his disciples betray him and then surrendered himself without protest to his captors. It never ceases to amaze me that Christian hope rests on a man whose message was rejected and whose love was spurned, who was condemned as a criminal and given a sentence of capital punishment.

Despite Jesus' plain example, many of his followers have been unable to resist choosing the way of Herod over that of Jesus. The Crusaders who pillaged the Near East, the conquistadors who converted the New World at the point of a sword, the Christian explorers in Africa who cooperated with the slave trade—we are still feeling aftershocks from their mistakes. History shows that when the church uses the tools of the world's kingdom, it becomes as ineffectual, or as tyrannical, as any other power structure. And whenever the church has intermingled with the state (the Holy Roman Empire, Cromwell's England, Calvin's Geneva), the appeal of the faith suffers as well. Ironically, our respect in the world declines in proportion to how vigorously we attempt to force others to adopt our point of view.

Sheep among wolves, a tiny seed in the garden, yeast in bread dough, salt in meat: Jesus' own metaphors of the kingdom describe a kind of "secret force" that works from within. He said nothing of a triumphant church sharing power with the authorities. The kingdom of God appears to work best as a minority movement, in opposition to the kingdom of this world. When it grows beyond that, the kingdom subtly changes in nature.

For this reason, I must say in an aside, I worry about the recent surge of power among U.S. Christians, who seem to be focusing more and more on political means. Once Christians were ignored or scorned; now they are courted by every savvy politician. Evangelicals especially are identified with a certain political stance, so much so that the news media use the terms "evangelical" and "religious right" interchangeably. When I ask a stranger, "What is an evangelical Christian?" I get an answer something like this: "Someone who supports family values and opposes homosexual rights and abortion."

This trend troubles me because the gospel of Jesus was not primarily a political platform. The issues that confront Christians in a secular society must be faced and addressed and legislated, and a democracy gives Christians every right to express themselves. But we dare not invest so much in the kingdom of this world that we neglect our main task of introducing people to a different kind of kingdom, one based solely on God's grace and forgiveness. Passing laws to enforce morality serves a necessary function, to dam up evil, but it never solves human problems. If a century from now all that historians can say about evangelicals of the 1990s is that they stood for family values, then we will have failed the mission Jesus gave us to accomplish: to communicate God's reconciling love to *sinners*.

Jesus did not say, "All men will know you are my disciples ... if you just pass laws, suppress immorality, and restore decency to family and government," but rather " ... if you love one another." He made that statement the night before his death, a night when human power, represented by the might of Rome and the full force of Jewish religious authorities, collided head-on with God's power. All his life, Jesus had been involved in a form of "culture wars" against a rigid religious establishment and a pagan empire, yet he responded by giving his life for those who opposed him. On the cross, he forgave them. He had come, above all, to demonstrate love: "For God so loved the world that he gave his one and only Son ..."

When the Roman governor Pilate asked Jesus point-blank whether he was king of the Jews, he replied, "My kingdom is not of this world. If it were, my servants would fight to prevent my arrest by the Jews. But now my kingdom is from another place." Allegiance to a kingdom "not of this world" has emboldened Christian martyrs who, ever since the death of their founder, have met resistance from kingdoms that are of this world. Unarmed believers used that text against their Roman persecutors in the Colosseum, Tolstoy used it to undermine the authority of the tsars, and civil rights marchers used it to challenge apartheid laws in the southern United States and in South Africa. It speaks of a reign that transcends the boundaries—and sometimes the laws—of nation and empire.

On another occasion, Jesus was asked by the Pharisees when the kingdom of God would come. He replied, "The kingdom of God does not come with your careful observation, nor will people say, 'Here it is,' or 'There it is,' because the kingdom of God is within you."

Clearly, the kingdom of God operates by a set of rules different from any earthly kingdom's. God's kingdom has no geographical borders, no capital city, no parliament building, no royal trappings that you can see. Its followers live right among their enemies, not separated from them by a border fence or a wall. It lives, and grows, on the inside of human beings.

Those of us who follow Jesus thus possess a kind of dual citizenship. We live in an external kingdom of family and cities and nationhood, while at the same time belonging to the kingdom of God. In his command, "Give to Caesar what is Caesar's, and to God what is God's," Jesus underscored the fundamental tension that can result. For the early Christians, loyalty to God's kingdom sometimes meant a fatal clash with Caesar's visible kingdom. Historian Will Durant, in *The Story of Civilization*, concludes:

> There is no greater drama in human record than the sight of a few Christians, scorned and oppressed by a succession of emperors, bearing all trials with a fierce tenacity, multiplying quietly, building order while their enemies generated chaos, fighting the sword with the word, brutality with hope, and at last defeating the strongest state that history has known. Caesar and Christ had met in the arena, and Christ had won.

We have seen vivid demonstrations of the clash of kingdoms in our own time. In communist countries—Albania, the U.S.S.R., China—the government forced the Christian church to go underground so that it became, quite literally, invisible. In waves of persecution during the 1960s and 1970s, for instance, Chinese believers were fined, imprisoned, and tortured, and local regulations prohibited most religious activities. Yet despite this government oppression, a spiritual revival broke out that could well be the largest in the history of the church. As many as fifty million believers gave their allegiance to an invisible kingdom even as the visible kingdom made them suffer for it.

In fact, problems seem to arise when the church becomes too external, and gets too cozy with government. As one U.S. legislative aide said after a tour of China, "I believe there is a word of caution for us in the apolitical nature of China's underground church. They fervently pray for their leaders but maintain a careful independence. We are privileged to live in a participatory democracy, but having worked in American politics for almost a decade, I have seen more than a few believers trade in their Christian birthright for a mess of earthly pottage. We must continually ask ourselves: Is our first aim to change our government or to see lives in and out of government changed for Christ?"

To rephrase her question, Is our first aim to change the external, political kingdom or to further God's transcendent kingdom? In a nation like the U.S., the two easily get confused.

I grew up in a church that proudly displayed the "Christian flag" next to the Stars and Stripes, and we would pledge allegiance to both. People would apply to the United States passages from the Old Testament that were obviously intended for a time when God worked through a visible kingdom on earth, the nation of Israel. For example, I often heard this verse quoted as a formula for national revival: "If my people, who are called by my name, will humble themselves and pray and seek my face and turn from their wicked ways, then will I hear from heaven and will forgive their sin and will heal their land." The principle may apply in a general way, of course, but the specific national promise was given as part of God's covenant relationship with the ancient Hebrews; its occasion was the dedication of Solomon's temple, God's dwelling place on earth. Have we any reason to assume God has a similar covenant arrangement with the U.S.?

Indeed, have we any indication that God now judges the U.S. or any other country *as a national entity*? Jesus told his parables of the kingdom in part to correct such nationalistic notions. God is working not primarily through nations, but through a kingdom that transcends nations.

As I now reflect on Jesus' stories of the kingdom, I sense that much uneasiness among Christians today stems from a confusion of the two kingdoms, visible and invisible. Each time an election rolls around, Christians debate whether this or that candidate is "God's man" for the White House. Projecting myself back into Jesus' time, I have difficulty imagining him pondering whether Tiberius, Octavius, or Julius Caesar was "God's man" for the empire. The politics of Rome were virtually irrelevant to the kingdom of God.

Nowadays, as the U.S. grows increasingly secularized, it appears that church and state are heading in different directions. The more I understand Jesus' message of the kingdom of God, the less alarm I feel over that trend. Our real challenge, the focus of our energy, should not be to Christianize the United States (always a losing battle) but rather to strive to be God's kingdom in an increasingly hostile world. As Karl Barth said, "[The Church] exists ... to set up in the world a new sign which is radically dissimilar to [the world's] own manner and which contradicts it in a way which is full of promise."

Ironically, if the United States is truly sliding down a slippery moral slope, that may better allow the church—as it did in Rome and also in China—to set up "a new sign ... which is full of promise." I would prefer, I must admit, to live in a country where the majority of people follow the Ten Commandments, act with civility toward each other, and bow their heads once a day for a bland, nonpartisan prayer. I feel a certain nostalgia for the social climate of the 1950s in which I grew up. But if that environment does not return, I will not lose any sleep. As an American citizen, I will work and pray for the kingdom of God to advance. If the gates of hell cannot prevail against the church, the contemporary political scene hardly offers much threat.

In Stuttgart, Germany, in 1933 Martin Buber held a discussion with a New Testament scholar on why he, a Jew who admired Jesus, nevertheless could not accept him. To Christians, he began, Jews must seem stubborn as they steadfastly wait for a Messiah to come. Why not acknowledge Jesus as Messiah? "The church rests on its faith that the Christ has come, and that this is the redemption which God has bestowed on mankind. We, Israel, are not able to believe this.... We know more deeply, more truly, that world history has not been turned upside down to its very foundations—that the world is not redeemed. We *sense* its unredeemedness." Buber's classic statement took on added poignancy in the next few years, for 1933 was the year Adolf Hitler came to power in Germany, putting to rest any doubts about the unredeemed character of the world. How could a true Messiah allow such a world to continue?

The only possible explanation lies in Jesus' teaching that the kingdom of God comes in stages. It is "Now" and also "Not yet," present and also future. Sometimes Jesus stressed the present aspect, as when he said the kingdom is "at hand" or "within you." At other times he suggested the kingdom lay in the future as when he taught his disciples to pray, "Your kingdom come, your will be done, on earth as it is in heaven." Martin Buber is correct to observe that God's will is apparently not being done on earth as it is in heaven. In some important ways, the kingdom has not fully come.

Probably Jesus himself would have agreed with Buber's assessment of the state of the world. "In this world, you will have trouble," he told his disciples. He also warned of impending disasters: "You will hear of wars and rumors of wars, but see to it that you are not alarmed. Such things must happen, but the end is still to come." The presence of evil guarantees that history will be full of strife and that the world will look unredeemed. For a period of time, the kingdom of God must exist alongside an active rebellion against God. God's kingdom advances slowly, humbly, like a secret invasion force operating within the kingdoms ruled by Satan.

As C. S. Lewis expressed it,

> Why is God landing in this enemy-occupied world in disguise and starting a sort of secret society to undermine the devil? Why is He not landing in force, invading it? Is it that He is not strong enough? Well, Christians think He is going to land in force; we do not know when. But we can guess why He is delaying: He wants to give us the chance of joining His side freely.... God will invade. But I wonder whether people who ask God to

interfere openly and directly in our world quite realise what it will be like when He does. When that happens, it is the end of the world. When the author walks on to the stage the play is over.

Jesus' closest disciples had difficulty grasping this double view of the kingdom. After his death and resurrection, when they understood at last that the Messiah had come not as a conquering king but as one clothed in humility and weakness, even then one thought obsessed them: "Lord, are you at this time going to restore the kingdom to Israel?" No doubt they were thinking of a visible kingdom to replace the rule of Rome. Jesus brushed aside the question and commanded them to carry word of him to the ends of the earth. That is when, to their amazement, he ascended out of sight and when, a few moments later, the angels explained, "This same Jesus, who has been taken from you into heaven, *will come back* in the same way you have seen him go into heaven." The kind of kingdom they yearned for would indeed come, but not yet.

I must confess that for many years I avoided thinking about the Second Coming of Jesus—partly, I'm sure, as a reaction to the prophecy mania of my childhood church. The doctrine seemed an embarrassment, the kind of talk that attracted people who believed in flying saucers. I still have little certainty about details of the Second Coming, but I now see it as the necessary culmination of the kingdom of God. To the degree that the church loses faith in Christ's return and contents itself to be a comfortable part of this world and not the advance guard of a kingdom from another world, to that degree we risk losing faith in a sovereign God.

God has put his reputation on the line. The New Testament points to a time when "every knee should bow . . . and every tongue confess that Jesus Christ is Lord." Obviously, that has not yet happened. Several decades after Easter, the apostle Paul spoke of the whole creation groaning in labor pains for a redemption not yet realized. Jesus' first coming did not solve the problems of planet earth, rather it presented a vision of God's kingdom to help break the earthly spell of delusion.

Only at Christ's second coming will the kingdom of God appear in all its fullness. In the meantime we work toward a better future, always glancing back to the Gospels for a template of what that future will be like. Jürgen Moltmann has observed that the phrase "Day of the Lord" in the Old Testament inspired fear; but in the New Testament it inspires confidence, because those authors had come to know the Lord whose Day it was. They now knew what to expect.

When Jesus lived on earth he made the blind to see and the lame to walk; he will return to rule over a kingdom that has no disease or disability. On earth he died and was resurrected; at his return, death will be no more. On earth he cast out demons; at his return, he will destroy the Evil One. On earth he came as a baby born in a manger; he will return as the blazing figure described in the book of Revelation. The kingdom he set in motion on earth was not the end, only the beginning of the end.

Indeed, the kingdom of God will grow on earth as the church creates an alternative society demonstrating what the world is *not*, but one day will be: Barth's prescription of "a new sign which is radically dissimilar to [the world's] own manner and which contradicts it in a way which is full of promise." A society that welcomes people of all races and social classes, that is characterized by love and not polarization, that cares most for its weakest members, that stands for justice and righteousness in a world enamored with selfishness and decadence, a society in which members compete for the privilege of serving one another—this is what Jesus meant by the kingdom of God.

The Four Horsemen of the Apocalypse give a preview of how the world will end: in war, famine, sickness, and death. But Jesus gave a personal preview of how the world will be restored, by reversing the deeds of the Four Horsemen: he made peace, fed the hungry, healed the sick, and brought the dead to life. He made the message of God's kingdom powerful by living it, by bringing it to reality among the people around him. The prophets' fairy-tale predictions of a world free of pain and tears and death referred to no mythical world, but rather to *this* world.

We in the church, Jesus' successors, are left with the task of displaying the signs of the kingdom of God, and the watching world will judge the merits of the kingdom by us. We live in a transition time— a transition from death to life, from human injustice to divine justice, from the old to the new—tragically incomplete yet marked here and there, now and then, with clues of what God will someday achieve in perfection. The reign of God is breaking into the world, and we can be its heralds.

14
The Difference He Makes

The other gods were strong; but Thou wast weak;
They rode, but Thou didst stumble to a throne;
But to our wounds only God's wounds can speak,
And not a god has wounds but Thou alone.

Edward Shillito

14
The Difference He Makes

Scott Peck writes that he first approached the Gospels skeptically, suspecting he would find public-relations accounts written by authors who had tied together loose ends and embellished their biographies of Jesus. The Gospels themselves quickly disabused him of that notion.

> I was absolutely thunderstruck by the extraordinary *reality* of the man I found in the Gospels. I discovered a man who was almost continually frustrated. His frustration leaps out of virtually every page: "What do I have to say to you? How many times do I have to say it? What do I have to do to get through to you?" I also discovered a man who was frequently sad and sometimes depressed, frequently anxious and scared.... A man who was terribly, terribly lonely, yet often desperately needed to be alone. I discovered a man so incredibly real that no one could have made Him up.
>
> It occurred to me then that if the Gospel writers had been into PR and embellishment, as I had assumed, they would have created the kind of Jesus three quarters of Christians still seem to be trying to create ... portrayed with a sweet, unending smile on His face, patting little children on the head, just strolling the earth with this unflappable, unshakable equanimity.... But the Jesus of the Gospels—who some suggest is the best-kept secret of Christianity—did not have much "peace of mind," as we ordinarily think of peace of mind in the world's terms, and insofar as we can be His followers, perhaps we won't either.

How can we know the "real Jesus" of whom Scott Peck got a glimpse? I have made a conscious attempt to view Jesus "from below," to grasp as best I can what it must have been like to observe in person the extraordinary events unfolding in Galilee and Judea. Like Scott Peck, I too feel thunderstruck by what I have found.

Icons of the Orthodox Church, stained-glass windows in European cathedrals, and Sunday school art in low-church America all depict on flat planes a placid, "tame" Jesus, yet the Jesus I met in the Gospels was anything but tame. His searing honesty made him seem downright tactless in some settings. Few people felt comfortable around him; those who did were the type no one else felt comfortable around. He was notoriously difficult to predict, pin down, or even understand.

I conclude my survey of Jesus with as many questions as answers. I certainly have not succeeded in taming him, for myself, let alone for anyone else. I now have a built-in suspicion against all attempts to categorize Jesus, to box him in. Jesus is radically unlike anyone else who has ever lived. The difference, in Charles Williams' phrase, is the difference between "one who is an example of living and one who is the life itself."

To sum up what I have learned about Jesus, I offer a series of impressions. They do not form a whole picture by any means, but these are the facets of Jesus' life that challenge me and, I suspect, will never cease to challenge me.

A Sinless Friend of Sinners. When Jesus came to earth, demons recognized him, the sick flocked to him, and sinners doused his feet and head with perfume. Meanwhile he offended pious Jews with their strict preconceptions of what God should be like. Their rejection makes me wonder, Could religious types be doing just the reverse now? Could we be perpetuating an image of Jesus that fits our pious expectations but does not match the person portrayed so vividly in the Gospels?

Jesus was the friend of sinners. He commended a groveling tax collector over a God-fearing Pharisee. The first person to whom he openly revealed himself as Messiah was a Samaritan woman who had a history of five failed marriages and was currently living with yet another man. With his dying breath he pardoned a thief who would have zero opportunity for spiritual growth.

Yet Jesus himself was not a sinner. "Unless your righteousness surpasses that of the Pharisees and the teachers of the law, you will certainly not enter the kingdom of heaven," he taught. The Pharisees themselves searched in vain for proof that he had broken the law of Moses. He had defied certain of their traditions, yes, but at his formal trial the only "crime" that stuck was the one he finally acknowledged, his claim to be Messiah.

I view with amazement Jesus' uncompromising blend of graciousness toward sinners and hostility toward sin, because in much of church history I see virtually the opposite. We give lip service to "hate the sin while loving the sinner," but how well do we practice this principle?

The Christian church has always found ways to soften Jesus' strong words on morality. For three centuries Christians tended to take literally his command to "Resist not evil," but eventually the church developed a doctrine of "just war" and even "holy war." At various times small groups of Christians have followed Jesus' words about disposing of wealth, but most of these have lived on the fringe of a wealthy church establishment. Nowadays many of the same Christians who hotly condemn homosexuality, which Jesus did not mention, disregard his straightforward commands against divorce. We keep redefining sin and changing the emphasis.

At the same time, the institutional church expends much energy positioning itself against the sinful world outside. (A term like "Moral Majority" only sounds appealing to someone already included in it.) I recently attended a play based on stories from a support group comprising people with AIDS. The theater director said he decided to stage the play after hearing a local minister state that he celebrated each time he read an obituary of a young single man, believing each death to be yet another sign of God's disapproval. Increasingly, I fear, the church is viewed as an enemy of sinners.

All too often, sinners feel unloved by a church that, in turn, keeps altering its definition of sin—exactly the opposite of Jesus' pattern. Something has gone awry.

In one of his earlier books, *Shame,* Salman Rushdie said that the true battle of history is fought not between rich and poor, socialist and capitalist, or black and white, but between what he termed the epicure and the puritan. The pendulum of society swings back and forth between those who say, "Anything goes," and those who say, "Oh, no you don't!": the Restoration versus Cromwell, the ACLU versus the religious right, modern secularists versus Islamic fundamentalists. As if to prove his point, soon afterward Iran set a million-dollar bounty on Rushdie's head; he had crossed a line.

History gives ample precedent for legalism and also for decadence. But how does one hold to high standards of moral purity while at the same time showing grace to those who fail those standards? How to embrace the sinner without encouraging sin? Christian history offers few facsimiles of the pattern Jesus laid down.

While I was researching the life of Jesus, I also read several lengthy studies of the first three centuries of the faith. The early church began well, placing a high premium on moral purity. Baptismal candidates had to undergo long periods of instruction, and church discipline was rigorously enforced. Sporadic persecution by Roman emperors helped to purge the church of "lukewarm" Christians. Yet even pagan observers were attracted to the way Christians reached out to others by caring for the oppressed and devoting themselves to the sick and the poor.

A major change took place with the emperor Constantine, who first legalized Christianity and made it a state-subsidized religion. At the time his reign appeared to be the faith's greatest triumph, for the emperor was now using state funds to build churches and sponsor theological conferences rather than to persecute Christians. Alas, the triumph did not come without cost: the two kingdoms got confused. The state began appointing bishops and other church offices, and soon a hierarchy grew up that neatly replicated the hierarchy of the empire itself. As for their part, Christian bishops began imposing morality on society at large, not just the church.

Ever since Constantine, the church has faced the temptation of becoming the "morals police" of society. The Catholic Church in the Middle Ages, Calvin's Geneva, Cromwell's England, Winthrop's New

England, the Russian Orthodox Church—each of these has attempted to legislate a form of Christian morality, and each has in its own way found it hard to communicate grace.

I realize, as I look at the life of Jesus, how far we have come from the divine balance he set out for us. Listening to the sermons and reading the writings of the contemporary church in the U.S., I sometimes detect more of Constantine than of Jesus. The man from Nazareth was a sinless friend of sinners, a pattern that should convict us on both counts.

The God-Man. It would be easier, I sometimes think, if God had given us a set of ideas to mull over and kick around and decide whether to accept or reject. He did not. He gave us himself in the form of a person.

"Jesus saves," announce the bumper stickers—imagine how ridiculous it would sound if you substituted Socrates or Napoleon or Marx. The Buddha gave his disciples permission to forget him as long as they honored his teaching and followed his path. Plato said something similar of Socrates. Jesus, though, pointed to himself and said "*I am the way.*"

Looking at Jesus' life primarily "from below," I have not stressed such concepts as preexistence and divine essence and dual nature, which take up so much space in theology books. It required five centuries for the church to work out the details of Jesus' divinity/humanity, and I have deliberately stayed close to the viewpoint presented by Matthew, Mark, Luke, and John, not the interpretive screen provided by the rest of the New Testament and formalized by the councils of Nicea and Chalcedon.

Even so, the Gospels themselves present the mystery of Jesus' dual identity. How did this Galilean Jew with a family and hometown come to be worshiped as "Very God of Very God"? Simple: Read the Gospels, especially John. Jesus accepted Peter's prostrate worship. To a lame man and an adulterous woman and many others he said commandingly, "I forgive your sins." To Jerusalem he remarked, "I am sending you prophets and wise men and teachers," as if he was not a rabbi standing before them but the sovereign God of history. When challenged, Jesus answered bluntly, "I and the Father are one." "Before Abraham was born, *I am*," he said on another occasion, uttering the sacred Hebrew word for God in case they missed the point. Devout Jews did not miss the point; several times they picked up stones to punish him for blasphemy.

Jesus' audacious claims about himself pose what may be the central problem of all history, the dividing point between Christianity and other religions. Although Muslims and, increasingly, Jews respect Jesus as a great teacher and prophet, no Muslim can imagine Mohammed claiming to be Allah any more than a Jew can imagine Moses claiming to be Yahweh. Likewise, Hindus believe in many incarnations but not one Incarnation, while Buddhists have no categories in which to conceive of a sovereign God becoming a human being.

Could Jesus' disciples have back-filled his teaching to include such brazen claims as part of their conspiracy to launch a new religion? Unlikely. The disciples, as we have seen, were inept conspirators, and in fact the Gospels portray them as resistant to the very idea of Jesus' divinity. Every disciple, after all, belonged to the most fiercely monotheistic race on earth. As late as Jesus' last night with them, after they had heard all the claims and seen all the miracles, one of them asked the Teacher, "Show us the Father." Still they could not grasp it. Jesus was never clearer in his response: "Anyone who has seen me has seen the Father."

It is an incontestable fact of history that Jesus' followers, the same ones who were scratching their heads over his words at the Last Supper, a few weeks later were proclaiming him as the "Holy and Righteous One," the "Lord," the "author of life." By the time the Gospels were written they regarded him as the Word who was God, through whom all things were made. In a later letter John took pains to point out "That which was from the beginning, which we have heard, which we have seen with our eyes, which we have looked at and our hands have touched—this we proclaim concerning the Word of life." The book of Revelation describes Jesus as a blazing figure whose face "was like the sun shining in all its brilliance," but always the author connected this Cosmic Christ to the actual Galilean man the disciples had heard and seen and touched.

Why would Jesus' disciples invent these notions? Followers of Mohammed or Buddha, willing to lay down their lives for their master, did not make such a jump in logic. Why would Jesus' disciples, so slow to accept it themselves, require of us a belief so difficult to swallow? Why make it harder rather than easier to accept Jesus?

The alternative to a conspiracy theory, regarding Jesus himself as the source of the audacious claims, only magnifies the problem. As I read through the Gospels, I sometimes try to view them as an outsider might, in the same way I read the Qur'an or the *Upanishads*. When I take up that perspective I find myself repeatedly startled, even offended, by the arrogance of one who says, "I am the way, the truth and the life. No one comes to the Father except through me." I can read only a few pages before stumbling across one of these statements that seem outlandishly to undercut all his wise teaching and good deeds. If Jesus is not God, then he is badly deluded.

C. S. Lewis made this point forcefully. "The discrepancy between the depth and sanity and (let me add) *shrewdness* of His moral teaching and the rampant megalomania which must lie behind His theological teaching unless He is indeed God, has never been satisfactorily got over," he wrote in *Miracles*. Lewis phrased the argument more colorfully in a famous passage in *Mere Christianity*: "A man who was merely a man and said the sort of things Jesus said would not be a great moral teacher. He would either be a lunatic—on the level with the man who says he is a poached egg—or else he would be the Devil of Hell. You must make your choice. Either this man was, and is, the Son of God; or else a madman or something worse."

I remember reading that quote from *Mere Christianity* in college and thinking it a gross exaggeration. I knew many people who respected Jesus as a great moral teacher but judged him neither the Son of God nor a lunatic. That was, in fact, my own view at the time. As I have studied the Gospels, though, I have come to agree with Lewis. Jesus never temporized or waffled about his identity. He was either the Son of God sent to save the world or an impostor deserving of crucifixion. The people of his day understood the binary choice precisely.

I now see that Jesus' entire life stands or falls on his claim to be God. I cannot trust his promised forgiveness unless he has the authority to back up such an offer. I cannot trust his words about the other side ("I go to prepare a place for you ...") unless I believe what he said about having come from the Father and returning to the Father. Most important, unless he was in some way God, I must view the cross as an act of divine cruelty rather than sacrificial love.

Sidney Carter wrote this disturbing poem:

> *But God is up in heaven*
> *And he doesn't do a thing,*
> *With a million angels watching,*
> *And they never move a wing. ...*
> *It's God they ought to crucify*
> *Instead of you and me,*
> *I said to this Carpenter*
> *A-hanging on the tree.*

Theologically, the only answer to Carter's accusation is the mysterious doctrine that, in Paul's words, "God was in Christ reconciling the world to himself." In an incomprehensible way, God personally experienced the cross. Otherwise, Calvary would go down in history as a form of cosmic child abuse, rather than a day we call Good Friday.*

Portrait of God. George Buttrick, former chaplain at Harvard, recalls that students would come into his office, plop down on a chair and declare, "I don't believe in God." Buttrick would give this disarming reply: "Sit down and tell me what kind of God you don't believe in. I probably don't believe in that God either." And then he would talk about Jesus, the corrective to all our assumptions about God.

---

*In Frederick Buechner's words, "What is new about the New Covenant, therefore, is not the idea that God loves the world enough to bleed for it but the claim that here he is actually putting his money where his mouth is. Like a father saying about his sick child, 'I'd do anything to make you well,' God finally calls his own bluff and does it. Jesus Christ is what God does, and the cross where he did it is the central symbol of New Covenant faith."

Books of theology tend to define God by what he is not: God is *im*mortal, *in*visible, *in*finite. But what is God like, positively? For the Christian, Jesus answers such all-important questions. The apostle Paul boldly called Jesus "the image of the invisible God." Jesus was God's exact replica: "For God was pleased to have all his fullness dwell in him."

God is, in a word, Christlike. Jesus presents a God with skin on whom we can take or leave, love or ignore. In this visible, scaled-down model we can discern God's features more clearly.

I must admit that Jesus has revised in flesh many of my harsh and unpalatable notions about God. *Why am I a Christian?* I sometimes ask myself, and to be perfectly honest the reasons reduce to two: (1) the lack of good alternatives, and (2) Jesus. Brilliant, untamed, tender, creative, slippery, irreducible, paradoxically humble—Jesus stands up to scrutiny. He is who I want my God to be.

Martin Luther encouraged his students to flee the hidden God and run to Christ, and I now know why. If I use a magnifying glass to examine a fine painting, the object in the center of the glass stays crisp and clear, while around the edges the view grows increasingly distorted. For me, Jesus has become the focal point. When I speculate about such imponderables as the problem of pain or providence versus free will, everything becomes fuzzy. But if I look at Jesus himself, at how he treated actual people in pain, at his calls to free and diligent action, clarity is restored. I can worry myself into a state of spiritual ennui over questions like "What good does it do to pray if God already knows everything?" Jesus silences such questions: he prayed, so should we.

During my work on *The Student Bible* I spent several years immersed in the Old Testament. With a steady diet of "the Old Covenant," I absorbed something like the attitude of an Orthodox Jew. The Old Testament underscores the vast gulf between God and humanity. God is supreme, omnipotent, transcendent, and any limited contact with him puts human beings at risk. The worship instructions in a book like Leviticus remind me of a manual on handling radioactive material. Bring only spotless lambs to the tabernacle. Do not touch the Ark. Always let smoke cover it; if you look at the ark, you'll die. Never enter the Most Holy Place, except for the high priest on the one permitted day of the year. On that day, Yom Kippur, fasten a rope around his ankle, and a bell, so that if he makes a mistake and dies inside, his corpse can be dragged out.

Jesus' disciples grew up in such an environment, never pronouncing God's name, complying with the intricate code of cleanliness, heeding the requirements of Mosaic law. They took for granted, as did most other religions of the time, that worship must include sacrifice: something had to die. Their God had forbidden human sacrifice, and so on a festival day Jerusalem was filled with the bleats and cries of a quarter million animals destined for the temple altar. The noise and smell of sacrifice were sharp sensory reminders of the great gulf between God and themselves.

I worked in the Old Testament for so long that, when one day I skipped over to the book of Acts, the contrast jolted me. Now God's followers, good Jews most of them, were meeting in private homes, singing hymns, and addressing God with the informal *Abba*. Where was the fear, and the solemn protocol required of anyone who dared approach *mysterium tremendum*? No one brought animals to sacrifice; death did not enter into worship except for the solemn moment when they broke bread and drank wine together, reflecting on the once-for-all sacrifice Jesus had made.

In these ways, Jesus introduced profound changes in how we view God. Mainly, he brought God near. To Jews who knew a distant, ineffable God, Jesus brought the message that God cares for the grass of the field, feeds the sparrows, numbers the hairs on a person's head. To Jews who dared not pronounce the Name, Jesus brought the shocking intimacy of the Aramaic word *Abba*. It was a familiar term of family affection, onomatopoeic like "Dada," the first word many children spoke. Before Jesus, no one would have thought of applying such a word to Yahweh, the Sovereign Lord of the universe. After him, it became a standard term of address even in Greek-speaking congregations; imitating Jesus, they borrowed the foreign word to express their own intimacy with the Father.

An event happened as Jesus hung on the cross that seemed to seal the new intimacy for the young church. Mark records that just as Jesus breathed his last, "The curtain of the temple was torn in two from top to bottom." This massive curtain had served to wall off the Most Holy

Place, where God's presence dwelled. As the author of Hebrews would later note, the tearing of this curtain showed beyond doubt exactly what was accomplished by Jesus' death. No more sacrifices would ever be required. No high priest need tremble to enter the sacred room.

Those of us in modern times have lived under the new intimacy for so long that we take it for granted. We sing choruses to God and converse in casual prayers. To us, the notion of sacrifice seems primitive. Too easily we forget what it cost Jesus to win for us all—ordinary people, not just priests—immediate access to God's presence. We know God as *Abba*, the loving Father, only because of Jesus.

The Lover. Left on my own, I would come up with a very different notion of God. My God would be static, unchanging; I would not conceive of God "coming" and "going." My God would control all things with power, stamping out opposition swiftly and decisively. As a Muslim boy told psychiatrist Robert Coles, "Allah would tell the world, everyone, 'God is great, very great' . . . He would make everyone believe in Him, and if someone refused, he'd die—that's what would happen if Allah came here."

Because of Jesus, however, I must adjust my instinctive notions about God. (Perhaps that lay at the heart of his mission?) Jesus reveals a God who comes in search of us, a God who makes room for our freedom even when it costs the Son's life, a God who is vulnerable. Above all, Jesus reveals a God who is love.

On our own, would any of us come up with the notion of a God who loves and yearns to be loved? Those raised in a Christian tradition may miss the shock of Jesus' message, but in truth love has never been a normal way of describing what happens between human beings and their God. Not once does the Qur'an apply the word love to God. Aristotle stated bluntly, "It would be eccentric for anyone to claim that he loved Zeus"—or that Zeus loved a human being, for that matter. In dazzling contrast, the Christian Bible affirms, "God *is* love," and cites love as the main reason Jesus came to earth: "This is how God showed his love among us: He sent his one and only Son into the world that we might live through him."

As Søren Kierkegaard wrote, "The bird on the branch, the lily in the meadow, the stag in the forest, the fish in the sea, and countless joyful people sing: God is love! But under all these sopranos, as if it were a sustained bass part, sounds the *de profundis* of the sacrificed: God is love."

Jesus' own stories about God's love express a quality almost of desperation. In Luke 15 he tells of a woman who searches all night until she finds a valuable coin and of a shepherd who hunts in the darkness until he finds the one sheep who has wandered astray. Each parable concludes with a scene of rejoicing, a celestial party that erupts over the news of another sinner welcomed home. Finally, building to an emotional climax, Jesus tells the story of the lost son, a prodigal who spurns the love of his father and squanders his inheritance in a far country.

The priest Henri Nouwen sat in the Hermitage Museum in St. Petersburg, Russia, for many hours meditating on Rembrandt's great painting *Return of the Prodigal Son*. While staring at the painting, Nouwen gained a new insight into the parable: the mystery that Jesus himself became something of a prodigal son for our sakes. "He left the house of his heavenly Father, came to a foreign country, gave away all that he had, and returned through a cross to his Father's home. All of this he did, not as a rebellious son, but as the obedient son, sent out to bring home all the lost children of God ... Jesus is the prodigal son of the prodigal Father who gave away everything the Father had entrusted to him so that I could become like him and return with him to his Father's home."

In a nutshell, the Bible from Genesis 3 to Revelation 22 tells the story of a God reckless with desire to get his family back. God struck the decisive blow of reconciliation when he sent the Son on the long journey to planet earth. The Bible's last scene, like the parable of the lost son, ends in jubilation, the family united once again.

Elsewhere, the Gospels comment on the extent to which God went to accomplish that rescue plan of love.

> This is love: not that we loved God, but that he loved us and sent his Son as an atoning sacrifice for our sins.
> Greater love has no one than this, that he lay down his life for his friends.

> For God so loved the world that he gave his one and only
> Son...

I remember a long night sitting in uncomfortable Naugahyde chairs in O'Hare Airport, waiting impatiently for a flight that was delayed for five hours. I happened to be next to a wise woman who was traveling to the same conference. The long delay and the late hour combined to create a melancholy mood, and in five hours we had time to share all the dysfunctions of childhood, our disappointments with the church, our questions of faith. I was writing the book *Disappointment with God* at the time, and I felt burdened by other people's pains and sorrows, doubts and unanswered prayers.

My companion listened to me in silence for a very long time, and then out of nowhere she asked a question that has always stayed with me. "Philip, do you ever just let God love you?" she said. "It's pretty important, I think."

I realized with a start that she had brought to light a gaping hole in my spiritual life. For all my absorption in the Christian faith, I had missed the most important message of all. The story of Jesus is the story of a celebration, a story of love. It involves pain and disappointment, yes, for God as well as for us. But Jesus embodies the promise of a God who will go to any length to win us back. Not the least of Jesus' accomplishments is that he made us somehow lovable to God.

The novelist and literary critic Reynolds Price put it this way: "He says in the clearest voice we have the sentence that mankind craves from stories—*The Maker of all things loves and wants me* ... In no other book our culture owns can we see a clearer graph of that need, that tall enormous radiant arc—fragile creatures made by God's hand, hurled into space, then caught at last by a man in some ways like ourselves."

Portrait of Humanity. When a light is brought into a room, what was a window becomes also a mirror reflecting back the contents of that room. In Jesus not only do we have a window to God, we also have a mirror of ourselves, a reflection of what God had in mind when he created this "poor, bare, forked animal." Human beings were, after all, created in the image of God; Jesus reveals what that image should look like.

"The Incarnation shows man the greatness of his misery by the greatness of the remedy which he required," said Pascal. In a most unsettling way Jesus exposed our failures as human beings. We tend to excuse our many faults by saying, "That's just human." A man gets drunk, a woman has an affair, a child tortures an animal, a nation goes to war: that's just human. Jesus put a stop to such talk. By enacting what we ought to be like, he showed who we were meant to be and how far we miss the mark.

"Behold the man!" Pilate cried. Behold the best example yet of humanity. Yet look at what it got him. Jesus unmasked for all time the jealousy, the lust for power, the violence that infects this planet like a virus. In a weird sort of way, that was the intent of the Incarnation. Jesus knew what he was getting into by coming to this planet; his death had been decreed from the beginning. He came to make an exchange of the most preposterous kind, as described in the Epistles:

> ... though he was rich, yet for your sakes he became poor, so that you through his poverty might become rich.
>
> Who, being in very nature God ... made himself nothing, taking the very nature of a servant, being made in human likeness.
>
> God made him who had no sin to be sin for us, so that in him we might become the righteousness of God.
>
> And he died for all, that those who live should no longer live for themselves but for him who died for them and was raised again.

Our riches for poverty, deity for servanthood, perfection for sin, his death for our life—the exchange seems entirely one-sided. But elsewhere in the Epistles can be found intriguing hints that the Incarnation had meaning for God as well as for human beings. Indeed, the suffering endured on earth served as a kind of "learning experience" for God. Such words sound faintly heretical, but I am merely following Hebrews: "Although he was a son, he learned obedience from what he suffered." Elsewhere, that book tells us that the author of our salvation was "made perfect" through suffering. Commentaries often avoid these phrases, for they are difficult to reconcile with traditional notions of an unchanging

God. To me, they demonstrate certain "changes" that had to take place within the Godhead before we could be reconciled.

During that wrinkle in time known as the Incarnation, God experienced what it is like to be a human being. In thirty-three years on earth God's Son learned about poverty and about family squabbles and social rejection and verbal abuse and betrayal. He learned, too, about pain. What it feels like to have an accuser leave the red imprint of his fingers on your face. What it feels like to have a whip studded with metal lashed across your back. What it feels like to have a crude iron spike pounded through muscle, tendon, and bone. On earth, God's Son "learned" all that.

God's character did not permit the option of simply declaring about this defective planet, "It doesn't matter." God's Son had to encounter evil personally in a way that perfect deity had never before encountered evil. He had to forgive sin by taking on our sin. He had to defeat death by dying. He had to learn sympathy for human beings by becoming one. The author of Hebrews reports that Jesus became a "sympathetic" advocate for us. There is only one way to learn sympathy, as signified by the Greek roots of the word, *syn pathos*, "to feel or suffer with." Because of the Incarnation, Hebrews implies, God hears our prayers in a new way, having lived here and having prayed as a weak and vulnerable human being.*

In one of his last statements before dying, Jesus prayed, "Father, forgive them"—all of them, the Roman soldiers, the religious leaders, his disciples who had fled in darkness, you, me, who have denied him in so many ways—"forgive them, for they do not know what they are doing." Only by becoming a human being could the Son of God truly say with understanding, "They do not know what they are doing." He had lived among us. Now, he understood.

* * *

---

*As a doctor who works in hospice told me, "When my patients pray, they are talking to someone who has actually died—something that's not true of any other adviser, counselor, or death expert."

The Wounded Healer. Goethe asked, "There the cross stands, thickly wreathed in roses. Who put the roses on the cross?"

In my travels to foreign countries, I have noticed the striking differences of the symbols used by the great religions. In India, where the four largest religions coexist, I took a brisk walk through the large city of Bombay in the course of which I came upon worship centers of all four.

Hindu temples were everywhere, even portable temples on mobile carts such as sidewalk vendors use, and each had an elaboration of carved, brightly painted images depicting some of the thousands of gods and goddesses in the Hindu pantheon. In stark contrast, a large Muslim mosque in the center of the city contained no images; a soaring spire or minaret pointed skyward, toward the one God, Allah, who could never be reduced to a graven image. Looking at Hindu and Muslim buildings, virtually side by side, I could better understand why each religion finds the other so incomprehensible.

I also visited a Buddhist center that afternoon. Compared to the crowded, noisy streets outside, it offered an atmosphere of serenity. Monks in saffron robes knelt in prayer in the dark, quiet room suffused with the smell of incense. A gilded statue of the Buddha dominated the room, his sly smile expressing the Buddhist belief that the key to contentment lies in developing inner strength that allows one to surmount any suffering in life.

And then I came across a Christian church, a Protestant church of a kind that discouraged images. It most closely resembled the Muslim mosque, with one exception: atop the spire above the church stood a large, ornate cross.

In a foreign country, uprooted from my own culture, I saw the cross with new eyes, and suddenly it struck me as bizarre. What possessed Christians to seize upon this execution device as a symbol for faith? Why not do everything within our power to squelch the memory of the scandalous injustice? We could stress the Resurrection, mentioning the cross only as an unfortunate footnote of history. Why make it the centerpiece of the faith? "Why, that picture might make some people lose their faith!" cried one of Dostoevsky's characters after viewing Holbein's painting of the crucified Christ.

There is, of course, the plain fact that Jesus commanded us to remember his death when we gather together in worship. He did not need to say, "This do in remembrance of me," about Palm Sunday or Easter, but clearly he did not want us to forget what happened on Calvary. Christians have not forgotten. In John Updike's words, the cross "profoundly offended the Greeks with their playful, beautiful, invulnerable pantheon and the Jews with their traditional expectations of a regal Messiah. Yet it answered, as it were, to the facts, to something deep within men. God crucified formed a bridge between our human perception of a cruelly imperfect and indifferent world and our human need for God, our human sense that God is present."

I realized, as I stood on a Bombay street corner with pedestrians, bicyclists, and farm animals swarming around me, why the cross had come to mean so much to Christians, why it had come to mean so much to me. The cross enacts for us deep truths that would make no sense apart from it. The cross gives hope when there is no hope.

The apostle Paul heard from God, "My [God's] power is made perfect in weakness," and then concluded about himself, "When I am weak, then I am strong." "That is why," he added, "I delight in weakness, in insults, in hardships, in persecutions, in difficulties." He was pointing to a mystery which goes several steps beyond the Buddhist way of coming to terms with suffering and hardship. Paul spoke not of resignation but of transformation. The very things that make us feel inadequate, the very things that plunder hope, these are what God uses to accomplish his work. For proof, look at the cross.

I wish someone with the talents of Milton or Dante would render the scene that must have transpired in hell on the day that Jesus died. No doubt an infernal celebration broke out. The snake of Genesis had struck at the heel of God; the dragon of Revelation had devoured the child at last. God's Son, sent to earth on a rescue mission, had ended up dangling from a cross like some ragged scarecrow. Oh, what a diabolical victory!

Oh, what a short-lived victory. In the most ironic twist of all history, what Satan meant for evil, God meant for good. Jesus' death on the cross bridged the gap between a perfect God and a fatally flawed humanity. On the day we call Good Friday, God defeated sin, routed death, triumphed over Satan, and got his family back. In that act of transformation, God took the worst deed of history and turned it into the greatest victory. No wonder the symbol never went away; no wonder Jesus commanded that we never forget.

Because of the cross, I have hope. It is through the Servant's wounds that we are healed, said Isaiah—not his miracles. If God can wrest such triumph out of the jaws of apparent defeat, can draw strength from a moment of ultimate weakness, what might God do with the apparent failures and hardships of my own life?

Nothing—not even the murder of God's own Son—can end the relationship between God and human beings. In the alchemy of redemption, that most villainous crime becomes our healing strength.

The fatally wounded healer came back on Easter, the day that gives a sneak preview of how all history will look from the vantage point of eternity, when every scar, every hurt, every disappointment will be seen in a different light. Our faith begins where it might have seemed to end. Between the cross and the empty tomb hovers the promise of history: hope for the world, and hope for each one of us who lives in it.

The German theologian Jürgen Moltmann expresses in a single sentence the great span from Good Friday to Easter. It is, in fact, a summary of human history, past, present, and future: "God weeps with us so that we may someday laugh with him."

The author and preacher Tony Campolo delivers a stirring sermon adapted from an elderly black pastor at his church in Philadelphia. "It's Friday, but Sunday's Comin'" is the title of the sermon, and once you know the title you know the whole sermon. In a cadence that increases in tempo and in volume, Campolo contrasts how the world looked on Friday—when the forces of evil won over the forces of good, when every friend and disciple fled in fear, when the Son of God died on a cross—with how it looked on Easter Sunday. The disciples who lived through both days, Friday and Sunday, never doubted God again. They had learned that when God seems most absent he may be closest of all, when God looks most powerless he may be most powerful, when God looks most dead he may be coming back to life. They had learned never to count God out.

Campolo skipped one day in his sermon, though. The other two days have earned names on the church calendar: Good Friday and Easter Sunday. Yet in a real sense we live on Saturday, the day with no name. What the disciples experienced in small scale—three days, in grief over one man who had died on a cross—we now live through on cosmic scale. Human history grinds on, between the time of promise and fulfillment. Can we trust that God can make something holy and beautiful and good out of a world that includes Bosnia and Rwanda, and inner-city ghettoes and jammed prisons in the richest nation on earth? It's Saturday on planet earth; will Sunday ever come?

That dark, Golgothan Friday can only be called Good because of what happened on Easter Sunday, a day which gives a tantalizing clue to the riddle of the universe. Easter opened up a crack in a universe winding down toward entropy and decay, sealing the promise that someday God will enlarge the miracle of Easter to cosmic scale.

It is a good thing to remember that in the cosmic drama, we live out our days on Saturday, the in-between day with no name. I know a woman whose grandmother lies buried under 150-year-old live oak trees in the cemetery of an Episcopal church in rural Louisiana. In accordance with the grandmother's instructions, only one word is carved on the tombstone: "Waiting."

Sources

Chapter 1

13: *Dickens*: Charles Dickens, *The Life of Our Lord*. London: Associated Newspapers Ltd., 1934.

15: *Pasolini*: Richard H. Campbell and Michael R. Pitts, *The Bible on Film*. Metuchen, N.J.: The Scarecrow Press, 1981, p. 54.

16: *Milliken*: Bill Milliken, *So Long, Sweet Jesus*. New York: Prometheus Press, n.d.

17: *H. G. Wells*: Quoted from *The Greatest Men in History* in Mark Link, S.J., *He Is the Still Point of the Turning World*. Chicago: Argus Communications, 1971, p. 111.

17: *"I tell you, whoever"*: Luke 12:8.

17: *"Do you have eyes"*: Job 10:4.

18: *Blake*: William Blake, "The Everlasting Gospel," *The Portable Blake*. New York: The Viking Press, 1968, p. 612.

18: *Barth*: Karl Barth, *The Word of God and the Word of Man*. New York: Harper & Row, Publishers, 1957, p. 62.

19: *Lakota*: Cullen Murphy, "Who Do Men Say That I Am?" *The Atlantic Monthly*, December 1986, p. 58.

19: *Norm Evans*: Quoted in "Making It Big," *The Reformed Journal*, December 1986, p. 4.

19: *Fritz Peterson*: Quoted in *The Chicago Tribune*, May 24, 1981.

20: *"scholar at the University of Chicago"*: David Tracy, quoted in Murphy, "Who Do Men Say That I Am?" op cit., p. 38.

20: *Phillips*: J. B. Phillips, *Ring of Truth*. Wheaton, Ill.: Harold Shaw Publishers, 1977, p. 79.

20: *"With a loud cry"*: Mark 15:37.

21: *"Blessed is he"*: Matthew 11:6, RSV.

21: *McGrath*: Alister McGrath, *Understanding Jesus*. Grand Rapids: Zondervan Publishing House, 1987, p. 52.

22: *Kasper*: Walter Kasper, *Jesus the Christ*. New York: Paulist Press, 1977, p. 46.

23: *"Get behind me"*: Matthew 16:23.

23: *Wink*: Walter Wink, *Engaging the Powers*. Minneapolis: Fortress Press, 1992, p. 129.

23: *Sayers*: Dorothy Sayers, *Christian Letters to a Post-Christian World*. Grand Rapids: William B. Eerdmans Publishing Company, 1969, p. 15.

24: *Tuchman*: Barbara Tuchman, *Practicing History*. New York: Alfred A. Knopf, 1981, p. 22.

24: *Pascal*: Blaise Pascal, *Pensées*. New York: E. P. Dutton, Inc., 1958, p. 228.

24: *Luther*: Quoted in Jürgen Moltmann, *The Way of Jesus Christ*. San Francisco: HarperSanFrancisco, 1990, p. 84.

Chapter 2

30: *"salvation from"*: Luke 1:71.

30: *"sword will pierce"*: Luke 2:35.

31: *Lewis*: C. S. Lewis, "The Grand Miracle," in *God in the Dock: Essays on Theology and Ethics*. Grand Rapids: William B. Eerdmans Publishing Company, 1972, p. 84.

32: *Muggeridge*: Malcolm Muggeridge, *Jesus: the Man Who Lives*. New York: Harper & Row, 1975, p. 19.

32: *"I am the Lord's"*: Luke 1:38.

33: *Ricci*: Jonathan D. Spence, *The Memory Palace of Matteo Ricci*. New York: Penguin Books, 1984, p. 245.

33: *"This child is destined"*: Luke 2:34.

33: *Augustus*: John Dominic Crossan, *The Historical Jesus: The Life of a Mediterranean Jewish Peasant*. San Francisco: HarperCollins Publishers, 1991, p. 31.

34, see also p. 57: *Herod the Great*: Joseph Klausner, *Jesus of Nazareth: His Life, Times, and Teaching*. London: George Allen & Unwin, Ltd, 1925, p. 146.

34: *Auden*: *The Collected Poetry of W. H. Auden*. New York: Random House, 1945, p. 455.

36: *Donne*: John Donne, "Nativity," *The Complete English Poems*. New York: Penguin Books, 1971, p. 307.

36: *"made himself nothing"*: Philippians 2:7.

36: *"silver as common"*: 1 Kings 10:27.

36: *Figgis*: Neville Figgis, *The Gospel and Human Needs*. London: Longmans, Green, 1909, p. 11.

37: *"O here and now"*: W. H. Auden, *The Collected Poetry*, op cit., pp. 443–44.

39: *"brought down rulers"*: Luke 1:52.

39: *Tokes*: Laszlo Tokes, *The Fall of Tyrants*. Wheaton, Ill.: Crossway Books, 1990, p. 186.

41: *Lubavitcher*: David Remnick, "Waiting for the Apocalypse in Crown Heights," *The New Yorker*, December 21, 1992, p. 52ff.

42: *"Isn't his mother's name"*: Matthew 13:54–55.

42: *"Nazareth!"*: John 1:46.

42: *"demon-possessed"*: John 10:20.

42: *Chesterton*: G. K. Chesterton, *Orthodoxy*, Garden City, N.Y.: Doubleday/Image Books, 1959, p. 137.

43: *Phillips*: J. B. Phillips, *New Testament Christianity*. London: Hodder & Stoughton, 1958, pp. 27–33.

44: *Apollo astronauts*: Quoted in William M. Justice, *Our Visited Planet*. New York: Vantage Press, 1973, p. 167.

45: *"He is the image"*: Colossians 1:15, 17.

Chapter 3

50: *Buber*: Quoted in Geza Vermes, *Jesus the Jew: A Historian's Reading of the Gospels*. London: Collins, 1973, p. 9.

51: *Moltmann*: Jürgen Moltmann, *The Way of Jesus Christ*, op cit., p. 168.

52: *"My God, my God"*: Matthew 27:46.

52: *"I am not"*: John 3:28.

52: *"Are you the one"*: Matthew 11:3.

53: *"rend the heavens"*: Isaiah 64:1.

53: *"he hath practised sorcery"*: Joseph Klausner, *Jesus of Nazareth*, op cit., p. 27.

54: *"God did not beget"*: Jürgen Moltmann, *The Crucified God*. New York: Harper & Row, 1974, p. 235.

55: *Dodd*: C. H. Dodd, *The Founder of Christianity*. London: The Macmillan Company, 1970, p. 103.

55: *Pelikan*: Jaroslav Pelikan, *Jesus Through the Centuries*. New Haven, Conn.: Yale University Press, 1985, p. 20.

56: *Bonhoeffer*: Dietrich Bonhoeffer, *Christ the Center*. San Francisco: Harper & Row, Publishers, 1978, p. 61.

56: *Virgil*: Quoted in Jaroslav Pelikan, *Jesus Through the Centuries*, op cit., p. 35.

57: *Barclay*: Quoted in Malcolm Muggeridge, *Jesus: the Man Who Lives*, op cit., p. 74.

57: *Antiochus*: Donald B. Kraybill, *The Upside-Down Kingdom*. Scottsdale, Pa.: The Herald Press, 1990, p. 38.

57: *"Would the Romans"*: Joseph Klausner, *Jesus of Nazareth*, op cit., p. 144.

58: *Muggeridge*: Malcolm Muggeridge, *Jesus: the Man Who Lives*, op cit., p. 13.

60: *"How can the Christ"*: John 7:41.

60: *"Nazareth!"*: John 1:46.

60: *"Galilee, Galilee, you hate"*: Vermes, *Jesus the Jew*, op cit., p. 53.

60: *"Are you from Galilee"*: John 7:52.

60: *"You ought to leave"*: John 7:3.

61: *"His high priests"*: Joseph Klausner, *Jesus of Nazareth*, op cit., p. 151.

62: *Josephus*: A. N. Wilson, *Jesus*. New York: W. W. Norton & Company, 1992, p. xii.

62: *"It is better"*: John 11:50.

64: *"If anyone comes"*: Luke 14:26.

64: *"I am able"*: Matthew 26:61.

Chapter 4

70: *"Jesus, full of the Holy Spirit"*: Luke 4:1–2.

71: *Hopkins*: The Sermons and Devotional Writings of Gerard Manley Hopkins. London: Oxford University Press, 1959, pp. 180–83.

71: *Luther*: Quoted in F. Forrester Church, *Entertaining Angels*. San Francisco: Harper & Row, Publishers, 1987, p. 54.

72: *Muggeridge*: Malcolm Muggeridge, *Jesus: the Man Who Lives*, op cit., p. 52ff.

73: *"Out of my sight"*: Matthew 16:23.

73: *"Never, Lord"*: Matthew 16:22.

73: *"Aren't you"*: Luke 23:39.

73: *"Let him come down"*: Matthew 27:42–43.

74: *Milton*: "Paradise Regained," *The Complete Poems of John Milton*. New York: Washington Square Press, Inc., 1964, p. 393.

74: *Karamazov*: Fyodor Dostoevsky, *The Brothers Karamazov*. Garden City, N.Y.: Nelson Doubleday, Inc., n.d., pp. 229–39.

76n.: *Sayers*: Dorothy Sayers, *The Man Born to Be King*. Grand Rapids: William B. Eerdmans Publishing Company, n.d., p. 35.

76: *Kierkegaard*: Quoted in D. R. Davies, *On to Orthodoxy*. London: Hodder and Stoughton, 1939, p. 162.

77: *MacDonald*: George MacDonald, *Life Essential, The Hope of the Gospel*. Wheaton, Ill.: Harold Shaw Publishers, 1974, pp. 24–25.

77: *"O Jerusalem"*: Matthew 23:37.

78: *"I, when I am"*: John 12:32–33.

80: *"Jesus looked at him"*: Mark 10:21.

80: *"Because of the increase"*: Matthew 24:12.

80: *"held it more humane"*: Milton, "Paradise Regained," op cit., 368.

80: *"I have prayed"*: Luke 22:32.

80: *"You do not"*: John 6:67.

80: *"Take up your cross"*: Matthew 16:24.

81: *Thielicke*: Helmut Thielicke, *Our Heavenly Father*. Grand Rapids: Baker Book House, 1974, p. 123.

81: "*We do not have*": Hebrews 4:15; 2:18.

Chapter 5

86: *Lentulus*: Sherwood Wirt, *Jesus, Man of Joy*. Nashville: Thomas Nelson, 1991, p. 28.

86: "*a gluttonous man*": Luke 7:34, KJV.

87: "*How can the guests*": Mark 2:19.

87: "*Just as there were many*": Isaiah 52:14; 53:2–3.

87: *John the Baptist admitted*: John 1:33.

88: "*My soul is*": Matthew 26:38.

88: "*Your faith*": Matthew 9:22.

88: "*a true Israelite*": John 1:47.

89: *Mary Gordon*: Alfred Corn, ed., *Incarnation: Contemporary Writers on the New Testament*. New York: Viking Penguin, 1990, p. 21.

90: *Lewis*: C. S. Lewis, *The Four Loves*. London: Geoffrey Bles, 1960, p. 67.

90: "*Son, why*": Luke 2:48–49.

90: "*Quiet!*": Mark 4:39.

91: *Maritain*: Quoted in John S. Dunne, *The Church of the Poor Devil*. New York: Macmillan Publishing Co., Inc., 1982, p.111.

91: "*If it is possible*": Matthew 26:39.

91: *Crossan*: John Dominic Crossan, *The Historical Jesus*, op cit., p. xi.

91: "*Isn't he*": Matthew 13:54–55, paraphrased.

92: "*wicked and adulterous*": Matthew 12:39.

92: "*Believe me*": John 14:11.

93: *Buechner*: Frederick Buechner, *Peculiar Treasures*. San Francisco: Harper & Row, Publishers, 1979, p. 70.

93: "*Foxes*": Matthew 8:20.

94: *Berryman*: John Berryman, "Eleven Addresses to the Lord," in *Love & Fame*. New York: Farrar, Straus and Giroux, 1970, p. 92.

94: *Pelikan*: Jaroslav Pelikan, *Jesus Through the Centuries*, op cit., p. 13.

95: "*full of grace*": John 1:14.

95: "*not impose*": Joseph Klausner, *From Jesus to Paul*, quoted in Everett F. Harrison, *A Short Life of Christ*. Grand Rapids: Wm. B. Eerdmans Publishing Company, 1968, p. 98.

96: *Trueblood*: Elton Trueblood, *The Yoke of Christ and Other Sermons*. Waco, Tex.: Word Books, 1958, p. 113.

96: "*Count the cost*": Luke 14:28, RSV.

96: *Neusner*: Jacob Neusner, *A Rabbi Talks with Jesus*. New York: Doubleday, 1993, pp. 24, 29, 31, 53.

96: "*he taught*": Matthew 7:29.

96: "*You have heard*": Matthew 5:21, et al.

97: "*This fellow*": Matthew 9:3.

97: "*No one ever*": John 7:46.

97: "*Be quiet*": Mark 1:25.

97: "*You deaf*": Mark 9:25.

97: "*We had hoped*": Luke 24:21.

97: "*the whole world*": John 12:19.

98: "*Whoever finds*": Matthew 10:39.

98: *"You don't know"*: Matthew 20:22.
99: *"Are you so dull"*: Mark 7:18.
99: *"How long"*: Matthew 17:17.
99: *"that they might"*: Mark 3:14.
100: *"At that time"*: Luke 10:21.

Chapter 6
105: *"Blessed are . . ."*: All Beatitudes taken from Matthew 5.
109: *"The spirit of self-sacrifice"*: Quoted in Alister Hardy, *The Biology of God*. New York: Taplinger Publishing Company, 1975, p. 146.
111: *Lewis*: C. S. Lewis, *The Weight of Glory*. Grand Rapids: William B. Eerdmans Publishing Company, 1965, pp. 1–2.
113: *Phillips*: J. B. Phillips, *Good News*. London: Geoffrey Bles, 1964, pp. 33–4.
113n.: *Kasper*: Walter Kasper, *Jesus the Christ*, op cit., p. 84.
115: *Hellwig*: Monika Hellwig, "Good News to the Poor: Do They Understand It Better?" in *Tracing the Spirit*, James E. Hug, ed. Mahwah, N.J.: Paulist Press, 1983, p. 145.
118: *Mauriac*: François Mauriac, *What I Believe*. New York: Farrar, Straus and Company, 1963, pp. 47–56.
120: *"Adam is a 25-year-old"*: Henri Nouwen, "Adam's Peace," in *World Vision Magazine*, August-September 1988, pp. 4–7.
122: *"Christianity has always insisted"*: Martin Luther King Jr. Quoted in David J. Garrow, *Bearing the Cross*. New York: William Morrow and Company, Inc., 1986, p. 532.
122: *"to awaken a sense"*: Ibid, p. 81.
125: *"Whoever wants"*: Matthew 16:25, et al.
125: *"life to the full"*: John 10:10.
125: *"in his joy"*: Matthew 13:44.

Chapter 7
129: *"Be perfect"*: Matthew 5:48.
129: *"I tell you, not seven"*: Matthew 18:22.
129: *"In everything"*: Matthew 7:12.
130: *Owens*: Virginia Stem Owens, "God and Man at Texas A&M," in *The Reformed Journal*, November 1987, pp. 3–4.
131: *"Do not think"*: Matthew 5:17, 20.
132: *"You shall not misuse"*: Exodus 20:7.
132: *bleeding Pharisees*: Mary Stewart Van Leeuwen, "Why Christians Should Take the Men's Movement Seriously," in *Radix*, Vol. 21, no. 3, p. 6.
133: *"I tell you . . ."*: All such statements taken from Sermon on the Mount, Matthew 5–7.
133: *Updike*: John Updike, "Even the Bible Is Soft on Sex," in *The New York Times Book Review*, June 20, 1993, p. 3.
134: *"Give to Caesar"*: Matthew 22:21.
136n.: *Muggeridge*: Malcolm Muggeridge, "Books," in *Esquire*, April 1972, p. 39.
137: *Tolstoy*: See William L. Shirer, *Love and Hatred: The Stormy Marriage of Lev and Sonya Tolstoy*. New York: Simon & Schuster, 1994.
138: *"There is so little genuine warmth"*: From Sonya Tolstoy's diary, January 26, 1895.
139: *"What about you"*: Quoted in A. N. Wilson, *The Lion and the Honeycomb: The Religious Writings of Tolstoy*. San Francisco: Harper & Row, Publishers, pp. 147–8.
140: *Wilson*: Ibid, p. 17.

140: *Dostoevsky*: See Joseph Frank: *Dostoevsky, The Years of Ordeal, 1850–1859*. Princeton, N.J.: Princeton University Press, 1983.

141: *"We love because"*: 1 John 4:19.

142: *"Where sin increased"*: Romans 5:20.

142: *"There is now no"*: Romans 8:1.

143: *"Be perfect"*: Matthew 5:48.

143: *"Love the Lord"*: Matthew 22:37.

143: *"Father, forgive"*: Luke 23:34.

Chapter 8

150: *"Do you see"*: Luke 7:44–47.

151: *"the poor, the crippled"*: Luke 14:21.

151: *"For the Son"*: Luke 19:10.

151: *"It is not"*: Matthew 9:12.

152: *"If any one of you"*: John 8:7–11.

152: *Lewis*: C. S. Lewis, *The Problem of Pain*. New York: The Macmillan Company, 1962, p. 98.

152: *Kaminer*: Wendy Kaminer, from *By the Book: America's Self-Help Habit*, quoted in "Saving Therapy: Exploring the Religious Self-Help Literature," *Theology Today*, October 1991, p. 301.

153: *"No madman"*: Hans Küng, *On Being a Christian*. Garden City, N.Y.: Doubleday & Company, Inc., 1976, p. 235.

153: *"Blessed art thou"*: Marcus J. Borg, *Jesus, A New Vision*. San Francisco: Harper & Row, 1987, 133–34.

154: *Wink*: Wink, *Engaging the Powers*, op cit., p. 129.

154: *"There is neither"*: Galatians 3:28.

154n.: *Sayers*: Dorothy L. Sayers, *Are Women Human*. Downers Grove, Ill.: InterVarsity Press, 1971, p. 47.

154: *Wink*: Wink, *Engaging the Powers*, op cit., p. 130.

155: *"God, have mercy"*: Luke 18:13–14.

155: *Wilson*: A. N. Wilson, *Jesus*, op cit., p. 30.

156: *"Son, remember"*: Luke 16:25.

156n.: *Constantine, early Christians*: See Robin Lane Fox, *Pagans and Christians*. New York: Alfred A. Knopf, 1989.

157: *Third World base communities*: See Robert McAfee Brown, *Unexpected News: Reading the Bible with Third World Eyes*. Philadelphia: The Westminster Press, 1984.

157: *"he has anointed"*: Isaiah 61:1.

158: *Endo*: See Shusaku Endo, *A Life of Jesus*. New York: Paulist Press, 1973.

160: *"O Jerusalem"*: Matthew 23:37.

160: *"offered up loud"*: Hebrews 5:7.

161: *"My God"*: Matthew 27:46.

Chapter 9

167: *Miracle of water into wine*: John 2:1–11

168: *Lewis*: C. S. Lewis, "Miracles," in *God in the Dock*, op cit., p. 29.

169: *"There is no death"*: Footnote to John 9:2 in *The NIV Study Bible*. Grand Rapids: Zondervan Publishing House, 1985, p. 1614.

170: *Miracle of healed blindness*: John 9: 1–41.

171: *Koop*: From personal interview.

172: *Miracle of healed leprosy*: Matthew 8:1–4; Mark 1:40–44; Luke 5:12–14.

173n.: *"Holy Disease"*: Patrick Feeny, *The Fight Against Leprosy*. New York: American Leprosy Mission, 1964, pp. 25, 32.

173: *Teresa*: From television interview.

173: *Miracle of healed paralysis*: Matthew 9:1–8; Mark 2:1–12; Luke 5:17–26.

174n.: *"Any disabled person"*: Donald Senior, C. P., "With New Eyes," in *Stauros Notebook*, vol. 9, no. 2, p. 1.

176: *Miracle of feeding five thousand*: Matthew 14:13–21; Mark 6:30–44; Luke 9:10–17; John 6:5–71.

177: *Capon*: Robert Farrar Capon, *Parables of the Kingdom*. Grand Rapids: Zondervan Publishing House, 1985, p. 27.

177: *"A wicked and adulterous"*: Matthew 12:39.

178: *"he would not entrust"*: John 2:24.

178: *Miracle of raising Lazarus*: John 11:1–54.

181: *"If they do not listen"*: Luke 16:31.

181: *"not one [sparrow]"*: Matthew 10:29.

181: *Askew*: Eddie Askew, *Disguises of Love*. London: The Leprosy Mission International, 1983, p. 50.

181: *"I do believe"*: Mark 9:24.

182: *John the Baptist*: Matthew 11:1–7.

183: *Moltmann*: Jürgen Moltmann, *The Way of Jesus Christ*, op cit., p. 99.

Chapter 10

189: *"Blessed is the king"*: Luke 19:38.

189: *"I tell you"*: Luke 19:40.

189: *"Look how"*: John 12:19.

191: *"I confer on you"*: Luke 22:29.

191: *"I have overcome"*: John 16:33.

191: *"Jesus knew"*: John 13:3–4.

191: *Peck*: M. Scott Peck, *The Different Drum*. New York: Touchstone/Simon & Schuster, 1988, p. 293.

192: *"the greatest"*: Luke 22:26.

192: *"stared at one another"*: John 13:22.

192: *"Surely not I?"*: Mark 14:19.

193: *"I don't know"*: Matthew 26:74.

193: *"Satan entered"*: John 13:27.

194: *"Father, forgive"*: Luke 23:34.

194: *Gethsemane*: Matthew 26:36–56; Mark 14:32–52; Luke 22:39–53.

195: *Yoder*: John Howard Yoder, *The Politics of Jesus*. Grand Rapids: William B. Eerdmans Publishing Company, 1972, pp. 55–56, 61.

196: *"Did not the Christ"*: Luke 24:26.

197n.: *Klausner*: Joseph Klausner, *Jesus of Nazareth*, op cit., p. 348.

198: *"I charge you . . ."*: Matthew 26:63–65.

198: *"Are you the king"*: Luke 23:3.

199: *Barth*: Karl Barth, *The Word of God and the Word of Man*, op cit., p. 82.

200: *Cicero*: Quoted in Walter Kasper, *Jesus the Christ*, op cit., p. 113.

200: *"anyone who is hung"*: Deuteronomy 21:23.

201: *"I thirst"*: John 19:28, KJV.

201: *"Father, into"*: Luke 23:45.

201: *"It is finished"*: John 19:30.

201: *"My God, my God"*: Matthew 27:46; Mark 15:33.
201: *Lewis*: C. S. Lewis, *Letters to Malcolm: Chiefly on Prayer*. London: Geoffrey Bles, 1964, p. 65.
202: *"a curse for us"*: Galatians 3:13.
202: *"God made him"*: 2 Corinthians 5:21.
202: *Sayers*: Sayers, *The Man Born to Be King*, op cit., p. 5.
20n.: *Constantine*: Michael Grant, *Constantine the Great*. New York: Charles Scribner's Sons, 1994, pp. 149, 222.
203: *Lewis: Letters to Malcolm: Chiefly on Prayer*, op cit., p. 113.
203: *"Having disarmed"*: Colossians 2:15.
203: *"Surely this man"*: Mark 15:39.
203: *"remember me"*: Luke 23:42.
204: *Justin Martyr*: Hans Küng, *On Being a Christian*, op cit, p. 339.
204: *Peck*: M. Scott Peck, *People of the Lie*. New York: Simon and Schuster, 1983, p. 269.
205: *Sölle*: Dorothy Sölle, *Of War and Love*. Maryknoll, N.Y.: Orbis Books, 1984, p. 97.

Chapter 11
210: *May*: Rollo May, *My Quest for Beauty*. Dallas: Saybrook Publishing Company, 1985, p. 60.
211: *"And if Christ"*: 1 Corinthians 15:14.
212: *"nonsense"*: Luke 24:11.
212: *"some doubted"*: Matthew 28:17.
213: *"afraid yet"*: Matthew 28:8.
213: *"trembling and bewildered"*: Mark 16:8.
213: *Gospel of Peter*: Quoted in Frederick Buechner, *The Faces of Jesus*. San Francisco: Harper & Row Publishers, 1989, p. 218.
214: *"His disciples came"*: Matthew 28:13.
214: *"If they do not listen"*: Luke 16:31.
214: *"He is not here"*: Cited in Hans Küng, *On Being a Christian*, op cit, p. 365.
214: *Buechner*: Frederick Buechner, *Whistling in the Dark*. San Francisco: Harper & Row Publishers, 1988, p. 42.
214: *Emmaus story*: Luke 24:13–49
216: *"Because you have seen"*: John 20:29.
217: *Dodd*: C. H. Dodd, *The Founder of Christianity*, op cit., p. 163.
217: *Updike John Updike* "Seven Stanzas at Easter" in *Telephone Poems 1954–1961* New York: Alfred A. Knopf, 1993, p. 20. Used by permission.
218n. *Tolkien*: J. R. R. Tolkien, "On Fairy Tales," quoted in Robert McAfee Brown, *Persuade Us to Rejoice*. Louisville, Ky.: Westminster/John Knox Press, 1992, p. 145.
218: *Sayers*: Dorothy L. Sayers, *The Mind of the Maker*. London: Methuen & Co. Ltd., 1959, p. 67.

Chapter 12
226: *Buechner*: Frederick Buechner, *The Magnificent Defeat*. New York: The Seabury Press, 1979, p. 86.
226: *Wink*: Walter Wink, *Engaging the Powers*, op cit., p. 143.
226: *"I have brought you glory…"*: John 17:4–5.
227: *"Men of Galilee"*: Acts 1:11.
227: *"I am sending"*: Matthew 10:16.
227: *Endo*: Shusaku Endo, *Silence*. New York: Taplinger Publishing Company, 1979, p. 203.

227: *"Brother will betray"*: Matthew 10:21–22.

228: *"But I tell you"*: John 16:7.

228: *"As you sent"*: John 17:18.

228: *Hopkins*: "Inversnaid," in Gerard Manley Hopkins, *Poems and Prose*. Baltimore, Md.: Penguin Books, 1953, p. 51.

228: *"Unless a kernel"*: John 12:24.

229: *"Lord, are you at this time"*: Acts 1:6.

229: *Lewis*: C. S. Lewis, *The Weight of Glory*, op cit., p. 15.

230: *"He who listens"*: Luke 10:16.

231: *"When the Son"*: Matthew 25:31–46.

232: *"Men of Galilee"*: Acts 1:11.

232: *Edwards*: Gerald R. McDermott, "What Jonathan Edwards Can Teach Us About Politics," *Christianity Today*, July 18, 1994, p. 35.

234: *Küng*: Hans Küng, *On Being a Christian*, op cit., p. 132.

234: *Dillard*: Alfred Corn, *Incarnation*, op cit., p. 36.

234: *Buechner*: Ibid, p. 123.

234: *Augustine*: Quoted in Paul Johnson, *A History of Christianity*. New York: Atheneum, 1976, p. 115.

235: *"You did not choose"*: John 15:16.

235n.: *Williams*: Charles Williams, *He Came Down from Heaven*. London: William Heinemann Ltd., 1938, p. 108.

235: *"showed them the full"*: John 13:1.

236: *"We have this treasure"*: 2 Corinthians 4:7.

236: *O'Connor*: Flannery O'Connor, *The Habit of Being*. New York: Vintage Books, 1979, p. 307.

Chapter 13

241: *"The kingdom of God"*: Matthew 12:28.

241: *Barclay*: Quoted in Malcolm Muggeridge, *Jesus: the Man Who Lives*, op cit., p. 74.

241: *"The kingdom of heaven"*: Matthew 3:2.

241: *"For I tell you"*: Luke 10:24.

241: *"Now one greater"*: Matthew 12:42.

244: *"that fox"*: Luke 13:32.

244: *"so that we may not offend"*: Matthew 17:27.

244: *"Love your enemies"*: Matthew 5:44.

247: *"All men will know"*: John 13:35.

247: *"For God so loved"*: John 3:16.

247: *"My kingdom is not"*: John 18:36.

248: *"The kingdom of God does not come"*: Luke 17:20.

248: *"Give to Caesar"*: Matthew 22:21.

248: *Durant*: Will Durant, *The Story of Civilization Part III: Caesar and Christ*. New York: Simon & Schuster, 1944, p. 652.

249: *Legislative aide in China*: Karen M. Feaver, "Chinese Lessons," *Christianity Today*, May 16, 1994, p. 33.

249: *"If my people"*: 2 Chronicles 7:14.

250: *Barth*: Karl Barth, from *Church Dogmatics*, quoted in Stanley Hauerwas and William H. Willimon, *Resident Aliens*. Nashville: Abingdon Press, 1989, p. 83.

250: *Buber*: Quoted in Jürgen Moltmann, *The Way of Jesus Christ*, op cit., p. 28.

251: *"Your kingdom come"*: Matthew 6:10.

251: *"In this world"*: John 16:33.

251: *"You will hear of wars"*: Matthew 24:6.

251: *Lewis*: C. S. Lewis, *Mere Christianity*. New York: The Macmillan Company, 1960, p. 65.

252: *"Lord, are you at this time"*: Acts 1:6.

252: *"This same Jesus"*: Acts 1:11.

252: *"every knee should bow"*: Philippians 2:10–11.

Chapter 14

257: *Peck*: M. Scott Peck, *Further Along the Road Less Traveled*. New York: Simon & Schuster, 1993, p. 160.

259: *"Unless your righteousness"*: Matthew 5:20.

261: *"I am the way"*: John 14:6.

261: *"I am sending"*: Matthew 23:34.

262: *"I and the Father"*: John 10:30.

262: *"Before Abraham"*: John 8:58.

262: *"Show us"*: John 14:8.

262: *"Anyone who has seen"*: John 14:9.

262: *"That which was"*: 1 John 1:1.

262: *"was like the sun"*: Revelation 1:16.

263: *"I am the way"*: John 14:6.

263: *Lewis*: C. S. Lewis, *Miracles*. New York: The Macmillan Company, 1947, p. 113.

263: *Lewis*: *Mere Christianity*, op cit., p. 56.

264: *"I go to prepare"*: John 14:2, KJV.

264: *Carter*: Quoted in Gordon Bridger, *A Day That Changed the World*. Downers Grove, Ill.: InterVarsity Press, 1975, p. 56.

264n.: *Buechner*: Frederick Buechner, *Wishful Thinking*. San Francisco: Harper & Row Publishers, p. 17.

265: *"image of the invisible"*: Colossians 1:15.

265: *"For God was pleased"*: Colossians 1:19.

266: *"The curtain"*: Mark 15:38.

267: *Coles*: Robert Coles, *The Spiritual Life of Children*. Boston: Houghton Mifflin Company, 1990, p. 231.

267: *Aristotle*: Aristotle, *Magna Moralia*, Quoted in Diogenes Allen, *Love*. Cambridge, Mass.: Cowley Publications, 1987, p. 115.

267: *"God is love"*: 1 John 4:8.

267: *"This is how God showed"*: 1 John 4:9.

268: *Kierkegaard*: Quoted in Karl Barth, *The Word of God and the Word of Man*, p. 84.

268: *Nouwen*: Henri J. M. Nouwen, *The Return of the Prodigal Son*. New York: Image Books/Doubleday, 1994, p. 55.

268: *"This is love"*: 1 John 4:10.

268: *"Greater love"*: John 15:13.

269: *"For God so loved"*: John 3:16.

269: *Price*: Quoted in Alfred Corn, *Incarnation*, op cit., p. 72.

270: *Pascal*: Blaise Pascal, *Pensées*, op cit., p. 143.

270: *"Behold the man"*: John 19:5.

270: *"though he was rich"*: 2 Corinthians 8:9, KJV.

270: *"Who, being in very nature"*: Philippians 2:6–7.

270: *"God made him"*: 2 Corinthians 5:21.

270: *"And he died for all"*: 2 Corinthians 5:15.

270: *"Although he was a son"*: Hebrews 5:8.

271: *"Father, forgive them"*: Luke 23:34.
272: *Goethe*: Quoted in Walter Kasper, *Jesus the Christ*, op cit., p. 182.
272: *Dostoevsky*: Quoted in Hans Küng, *On Being a Christian*, op cit., p. 142.
273: *Updike*: Alfred Corn, *Incarnation*, op cit., p. 10.
273: *"my power is made perfect"*: 2 Corinthians 12:9–10.
274: *Moltmann*: Jürgen Moltmann, *The Way of Jesus Christ*, op cit., p. 322.

Others

In addition to the specific citations above, I must express gratitude to the following authors for helping me understand Jesus better:

Anderson, Sir Norman. *Jesus Christ: the Witness of History*. Downers Grove, Ill.: InterVarsity Press, 1985.

Baillie, John. *The Place of Jesus Christ in Modern Christianity*. Edinburgh: T&T Clark, 1929.

Bainton, Roland H. *Behold the Christ*. New York: Harper & Row, 1974.

Baker, John Austin. *The Foolishness of God*. Atlanta: John Knox Press, 1970.

Barclay, William. *Jesus As They Saw Him*. Grand Rapids: William B. Eerdmans Publishing Company, 1962.

Barton, Bruce. *The Man Nobody Knows*. New York: Macmillan Publishing Company, 1987.

Batey, Richard. *Jesus and the Poor*. San Francisco: Harper & Row, Publishers, 1972.

Berkhof, Hendrik. *Christ and the Powers*. Scottsdale, Pa.: Herald Press, 1977.

Bright, John. *The Kingdom of God*. Nashville: Abingdon, 1980.

Brown, Colin. *Miracles and the Critical Mind*. Grand Rapids: William B. Eerdmans Publishing Company, 1984.

Bruce, F. F. *Jesus and Christian Origins Outside the New Testament*. Grand Rapids: William B. Eerdmans Publishing Company, 1974.

Bruce, F. F. *What the Bible Teaches About What Jesus Did*. Wheaton, Ill.: Tyndale House Publishers, 1979.

Capon, Robert Farrar. *Hunting the Divine Fox*. New York: The Seabury Press, 1974.

Cullman, Oscar. *Jesus and the Revolutionaries*. New York: Harper & Row, Publishers, 1970.

Ellul, Jacques. *The Subversion of Christianity*. Grand Rapids: William B. Eerdmans Publishing Company, 1986.

Falk, Harvey. *Jesus the Pharisee: A New Look at the Jewishness of Jesus*. New York: Paulist Press, 1985.

Fretheim, Terence E. *The Suffering of God*. Philadelphia: Fortress Press, 1984.

Guardini, Romano. *The Lord*. Chicago: Regnery Gateway, Inc., 1954.

Guthrie, Donald. *A Shorter Life of Christ*. Grand Rapids: Zondervan Publishing, 1970.

Hellwig, Monika. *Jesus, The Compassion of God*. Wilmington, Del.: Michael Glazier, Inc., 1983.

Hengel, Martin. *The Charismatic Leader and His Followers*. New York: Crossroad, 1981.

Kierkegaard, Søren, *Training in Christianity*. Princeton, N.J.: Princeton University Press, 1947.

Ladd, George Eldon. *The Gospel of the Kingdom*. Grand Rapids: William B. Eerdmans Publishing Company, 1959.

Macquarrie, John. *The Humility of God*. Philadelphia: The Westminster Press, 1978.

Macquarrie, John. *Jesus Christ in Modern Thought*. Philadelphia: Trinity Press International, 1990.

Mason, Steve. *Josephus and the New Testament*. Peabody, Mass.: Hendrickson Publishers, 1992.

McGrath, Alister. *Understanding Jesus.* Grand Rapids: Zondervan Publishing House, 1988.

Meier, John P. *A Marginal Jew.* New York: Doubleday, 1991.

Moltmann, Jurgen. *The Trinity and the Kingdom.* San Francisco: Harper & Row Publishers, 1981.

Morison, Frank. *Who Moved the Stone?* London: Faber and Faber Limited, 1944.

Niebuhr, H. Richard. *Christ and Culture.* New York: Harper & Brothers Publishers, 1956.

Oppenheimer, Helen. *Incarnation and Immanence.* London: Hodder and Stoughton, 1973.

Pfeiffer, Charles. *Between the Testaments.* Grand Rapids: Baker Book House, 1959.

Stott, John. *Christian Counter-Culture: The Message of the Sermon on the Mount.* Downers Grove, Ill.: InterVarsity Press, 1978.

van Buren, Paul M. *A Theology of the Jewish-Christian Reality: Part III, Christ in Context.* San Francisco: Harper & Row, 1988.

Willis, Wendell, ed. *The Kingdom of God in 20th-Century Interpretation.* Peabody, Mass.: Hendrickson Publishers, 1987.

Wright, N. T. *Who Was Jesus?* Grand Rapids: William B. Eerdmans Publishing Company, 1992.

Ziolkowski, Theodore. *Fictional Transfigurations of Jesus.* Princeton, N.J.: Princeton University Press, 1972.

Ecology of
Salt Marshes
and Sand Dunes

Ecology of Salt Marshes and Sand Dunes

D. S. RANWELL

*Head of the Coastal Ecology
Research Station (Nature Conservancy)
Norwich*

LONDON
CHAPMAN AND HALL

First published 1972
by Chapman and Hall Ltd
11 New Fetter Lane, London EC4P 4EE
Printed in Great Britain by
Cox & Wyman Ltd., Fakenham

SBN 412 10500 4

Contents

List of Plates

Preface

Some attempt has been made in this book to bring together recent knowledge of the ecology of salt marshes and sand dunes and to relate it to current work on associated subjects.

What could be a greater contrast than the flatness and wetness of a marsh and the hilliness and dryness of a dune? Yet in both there are interesting parallels in the ways in which plants and animals achieve mastery over these initially inhospitable environments as well as in the obvious contrasts.

The extreme differences in the two habitats have influenced approaches to the study of each in the past. This has led to emphasis on study of salinity in the salt marsh and lack of appreciation of the significance of drought near the upper limits of the marsh. Emphasis on the study of drought effects on the dunes has resulted in neglect of moisture effects in the damp slacks between them.

Individual habitats, or parts of them, have been studied in isolation in the past. Now, with increasing knowledge and better facilities, it is possible and essential to study whole systems and the relationships between salt marshes and sand dunes and their associated environments.

With the increasing pace of human activities on and near the coast it is vital for the coastal ecologist to gain a more balanced understanding of these habitats and to develop effective predictive models of the processes at work in them.

I hope that this book will help to encourage new studies where they are most needed, not only in existing marshes and dunes, but also in the design of the new coastal environments derived from the exciting coastal engineering schemes now on the drawing boards. We should no longer submit to a defensive protection of coastal wildlife resources, but insist that due regard for a rightful place for these be built into the new environments to come and ensure that adequate stepping stones are preserved to allow them to take this place alongside their human neighbours.

The book is planned in four parts: the first (Chapters 1 to 3) and last (Chapters 12 and 13), synthetic in character; the two central parts (Chapters 4 to 11) analytical. The first part concerns general relationships of both habitats, the second and the third parts contain separate treatments of the ecology of salt marshes and sand dunes, while the fourth part deals with human influences and management.

Coastal Ecology Research Station,   D.S.R.
(Nature Conservancy),
Norwich

February 1972

Acknowledgements

I am very much aware of the dependence of this book on the guidance and help I have received from teachers and colleagues in the past, but I should make it clear that the responsibility for opinions expressed is solely my own.

In particular I am grateful to Professor W. T. Williams and Professor T. A. Bennet-Clark F.R.S., who taught me respect for the discipline of plant physiology; Dr G. Metcalfe and Dr J. M. Lambert who encouraged my initial ecological interest; Professor J. A. Steers who encouraged my interest in coastal physiology; and especially Professor P. W. Richards who supervised my first studies in coastal ecology with a wisdom which I still appreciate. I would like to thank also colleagues who helped with my work and influenced my thinking: Dr M. V. Brian, Dr D. A. Ratcliffe, Mrs B. Brummitt, Mr R. E. Stebbings, Mr J. C. E. Hubbard and Dr E. C. F. Bird. I am especially grateful to Dr R. L. Jefferies for much helpful advice on Chapter 3 and to the many others too numerous to mention who have helped in many ways. Special thanks are due to Miss E. J. Reeve and Mrs S. van Piere for help in typing the manuscript, and to Mr P. G. Ainsworth, Miss S. S. Anderson and Mr B. H. Grimes for assistance with a number of the illustrations and photographs.

I should also like to thank the following for permission to use various quotations: Dr A. J. Brereton; the American Society of Limnology and Oceanography; the British Entomological and Natural History Society; the Institution of Civil Engineers; the New York Botanical Garden; Academic Press Inc. (London) Ltd.; G. Bell and Sons Ltd.; Blackwell Scientific Publications Ltd.; and the University of Chicago Press. Grateful acknowledgement is made to those who have granted permission to reproduce figures and tables; the source in each case is given at the end of the caption or table title.

Finally I would like to record my gratitude to the editor, Mr D. C. Ingram, for much helpful advice and to my wife for her constant encouragement throughout.

D.S.R.

PART ONE General Relationships

1 Climatic Restraints

Distributions and Climate

World patterns

There is a certain similarity in the appearance of the vegetation of salt marshes or of sand dunes in whatever part of the world they are found. Each is subjected to two overriding physical restraints which control the type of growth they can support. For the salt marsh these are silt and saline water; for the dune, sand and wind.

Given these physical restrictions, the kinds of plants and animals which can survive in any particular part of the world is then largely governed by prevailing climate. Whether they actually occur there or not depends on chance factors of migration or introduction. Opportunities for widespread dispersal are in fact much better for coastal plants than for other kinds because the transporting powers of the sea, migratory birds and ships all help to promote this.

It follows that we might expect to find among coastal plants some of the most widely distributed species in the world; species whose distribution most nearly reflects the absolute climatic limits they can withstand. So, we find for example that *Phragmites communis*, accredited to be perhaps the most widely distributed species in the world (Ridley 1930), is an element of the coastal flora on moderately saline coastal soils. The submerged coastal aquatics *Ruppia maritima* and *Zostera marina*, which occur respectively at the upper and lower limits of estuaries, and the brackish marsh species *Scirpus maritimus*, are among the most widely distributed species in the northern hemisphere. The recent discovery of *Zostera marina* beneath 1 m of winter ice at nearly 65°N in the Bering Sea, Alaska, is a remarkable further extension of the known range of this species (McRoy, 1969).

B

But we must bear in mind the limitations of the species concept when considering widely distributed species spanning major climatic zones. Such widely distributed plants as *Phragmites*, though relatively uniform in appearance and behaviour throughout its range, will undoubtedly be broken down eventually into a complex of closely related forms each adapted to special conditions. For example coastal *Phragmites* of the Red Sea area is known to tolerate a much higher soil salinity than temperate forms of *Phragmites* (Kassas – in litt.).

The absence of large accumulations of blown sand on tropical coasts was noted by Hitchcock (1904). He concluded that in these latitudes the long growing season is especially favourable to vegetation allowing it to colonize closer to high water mark than in more temperate zones. It therefore covers up sites from which sand dunes would normally receive their sand supply. Jennings (1964) has recently reached a similar conclusion from a study of literature on tropical coasts, but adds that the humid climate may also limit the extent to which sand can be blown. Special local conditions may account for exceptions such as the large dune accumulations in south Java. On corraline strands, the angularity of fragments may lock them into a more wind resistant surface (Oosting 1954). It seems likely that, as Van Steenis (1958) claims, genuine dunes tend to be restricted to regions with a seasonal climate in the more temperate parts of the world.

While it is true that salt marshes throughout the world are generally similar in appearance, even a layman would place himself in the tropics if set down in a mangrove marsh. These coastal marsh trees form a very distinctive group of some half a dozen genera whose main distribution falls neatly within the tropic zone. Their absolute limits are at 28°N and 25°S in the New World and 28°N and 38°S in the Old World (MacNae 1968, Good 1966, Clark and Hannon 1967, and Chapman and Ronaldson 1958). Frost damage occurs both at their north limit in Florida (Webber 1895 and Davis 1940) and at their south limit (Chapman 1944) in New Zealand. Their restriction to these limits is thought to be controlled largely by frost incidence.

The mangrove (*Rhizophora mangle*) forms dense growths on mainland and island shores as far north as Ormond (29° 22′N), Florida. It was killed during the 1894–95 winter (minimum temperature Ormond 29 December 1894, –7.7°C) as far south as Lake Worth (26° 40′N), except in cases where plants grew on the south side of large stretches of water. On the west shore of the Florida peninsula at Myers (26° 40′N) mangroves *were* killed on the south shore of the Calosabatchee river estuary (Webber 1895). The points of interest here are the width, over 200 miles (320 km), of the damage belt at the mangrove northern limit, and the pockets of survival related to local topography lying within it. This illustrates the difficulty of applying precision to the concept of a climatic limit although it may be clearly significant for the plant or animal concerned.

The latitudinal temperature gradient in the sea is very gradual because here fluctuations in climate are literally damped down. Work on the distribution of marine Angiosperms in relation to temperature has suggested that the distribution of these plants is likely to be controlled by temperature and the following main world zones have been distinguished on this basis. (Table 1)

Table 1. Marine temperature zones (after Setchell 1920).

Zone	Mean maximum temperature range °C
Upper Boreal	0–10
Lower Boreal	10–15
Temperate	15–20
Subtropical	20–25
Tropical	25–30

Crisp (see Johnson and Smith 1965) observes, 'Our success in relating intertidal population changes to climatic fluctuations may result from the fact that the main factor, temperature, is easily measured. The lack of comparable evidence from land plants may perhaps be due to the intervention of interaction of other factors (such as rainfall, sunlight, day length) which tend to obscure correlations. Are we clear about what limits the distribution of land plants?'

The answer to this is certainly no at the present time, but it does suggest that we may have a better chance of finding limits which are climatically controlled in intertidal salt marsh plants than in dune plants beyond tidal influence.

Assumptions about climatic limits are best tested by transplants to find out potential range. This is a useful preliminary to more critical work in the growth cabinet and field. Success and failure results for world-wide transplants of the salt marsh grass *Spartina anglica* probably give a true indication of the climatic limits of this species (Fig.1). The northern limit of *S. anglica* in the northern hemisphere (57°N), like mangrove, seems to be controlled by frost frequency. Frost killed 99 per cent of transplants in plantations in northern Holland; those in southern Holland were virtually unaffected. The northern limit of the species in the southern hemisphere

(35°S) may be controlled by day length as the plant does not flower under short day conditions (Hubbard 1969). However, Chapman (1964 *in litt.*) has suggested that winter temperatures may be too high at 35°S for normal development and notes that little seed is set at this latitude in New Zealand.

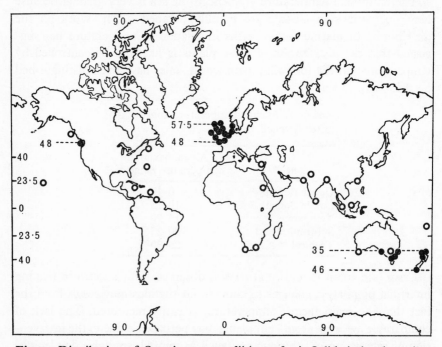

Fig. 1. Distribution of *Spartina townsendii* (*sensu lato*). Solid circles show sites where plants were known to be established in 1965. Open circles show sites where plantings are known to have failed. There are records of many other introductions, but the fate of these is unknown (from Ranwell 1967).

pean coasts, has been planted successfully in N. America, South Africa, New Zealand. It thrives from the boreal to subtropical zones (Cooper 1958). No similar study of its world distribution and climatic requirements seems to have been made in spite of its acknowledged success as a foredune builder and aid to coastal protection.

Regional patterns

We are so ignorant of what limits individual species of plants and animals to particular parts of the world that great care must be taken not to make any assumptions about the extent to which climate controls the individual components of regional floras and faunas. Indeed the very constitution of the coastal dune and salt marsh floras (let alone faunas) of many parts of the world are still very incompletely known. This does not only apply to the remoter shores of South America or Asia, but also in surprising measure to shorelines like the Mediterranean close to major centres of civilization.

Chapman (1960) distinguishes nine major regional salt marsh floras adapted to the particular climate conditions where they occur:

Arctic	Chinese, Japanese and Pacific Siberian
North European	South American
Mediterranean	Tropical
Eastern North American	Australia and New Zealand
Western North American	

Within each group are certain characteristic species of relatively wide range which impart some degree of inherent homogeneity to the group as a whole (e.g. *Puccinellia phryganodes* in Arctic salt marshes).

No similar attempt has been made to classify the dune floras of the world. These are much more variable in species composition than salt marshes partly because their distribution tends to be much more discontinuous and less freely linked by any major agent of dispersal like the sea.

Matthews (1937) showed how the British flora could be clumped into recognizable geographical groups. He found that some 600 species out of 1500 native or well naturalized species could be classified in distinctive geographical groups. The rest were generally distributed. Since his analysis was based on the known absolute distribution of the species concerned it seemed reasonable to assume that climatic factors were predominant in determining the flora of these groupings.

In fact an analysis of species reaching coastal limits in the British Isles (based on data from Perring and Walters 1962) shows a background of continuous replacement with evidence of disjunction at certain points clearly related as much to geographical barriers as to climatic zones (Fig. 2). Further analysis of the species reaching limits at points of concentration shows that less than half of them fall into Matthew's groups, the remainder being presumably capable of much wider distribution round the coast and to that extent relatively independent of climatic restraints.

Mörzer-Bruijns and Westhoff (1951) have shown how the Netherlands can be divided into climatic areas using indices based on extremes of climate over the course of a decade. These climatic areas can be correlated with biogeographical regions as determined by the distribution of insects

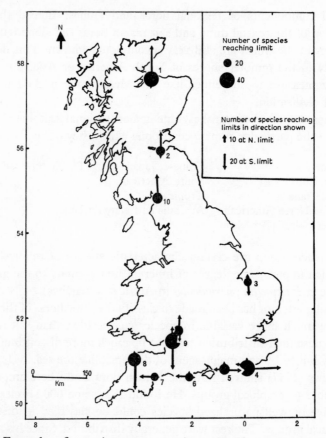

Fig. 2. Examples of some important meeting points for geographical elements of the Coastal flora in Great Britain.

1. Moray Firth
2. Forth of Firth
3. Wash
4. Durlay Illau
5. Arun

6. Poole Harbour
7. Exe
8. Taw-Torridge
9. Juvvam
10. Solway Firth

Results are derived from records of all species recorded in coastal 10 Km squares in the Atlas of the British Flora (1962) and show numbers of species reaching north and south limits on east and west coasts, and north, east and west limits on the south coast, for only those squares in which 20 or more species reach such limits. There are two exceptions: (1) Beachy Head to Sussex Ouse, two contiguous squares each with more than 20 species at limits which have been combined to make the map record clearer. (2) Exe estuary with only 16 species at limits, included because other evidence, not considered here, suggests it is an important meeting point of eastern and western elements of the flora (from Ranwell 1968).

and plants. Beeftink (1965) has produced a comprehensive classification of European halophytic higher plant communities related to geographic regions.

Studies of this type help to narrow down the field to specific locations and particular species where intensive study of the biology of the plants or animals concerned in relation to key climatic factors is likely to prove rewarding (Plate 2). They do not in themselves tell us exactly how climatic factors control survival.

Oceanicity

Troll (1963) points out that: 'the greatest modification of the latitudinal zonation of thermal seasons in temperate latitudes is due to the distribution of oceans and continents'. Reduction of annual fluctuation of temperature is a measure of oceanicity. It is achieved by the greater heat storage capacity of water compared with land and the possibilities of convective heat exchange between warm water surface and colder land surface.

Thermophilous species such as *Samolus valerandi* are capable of surviving in inland localities of England and Wales but are restricted to the coast in Scotland (Fig. 3) and in Scandinavia. The more oceanic climate of the north-west coast of the North American continent allows *Spartina anglica* to survive at least 2° of latitude further north than on the north-east coast where the incidence of frost in the more continental climate prevents its survival.

Faegri (1958 and 1960) gives useful discussions of the climatic demands of oceanic plants. He concludes that many oceanic or maritime plants are sensitive to winter frosts, and that summer warmth for the successful ripening of seeds may be an additional limiting factor. The northernmost limit of oceanic species frequently follows winter isotherms closely up to a certain point then crosses them to follow particular summer isotherms. This suggests that a point has been reached where summer temperature has become more critical than that of winter. Rising lower altitude limits towards the south (such as *Dryas octopetala* shows in Britain) suggest that humidity may be critical for certain species. Ratcliffe's (1968) studies of Atlantic bryophytes also stress the importance of humidity and demonstrate interaction with varying soil tolerances. The concept of oceanicity is not a simple one and involves the interaction of at least three important climatic factors (temperature, wind and humidity) together with other environmental restraints.

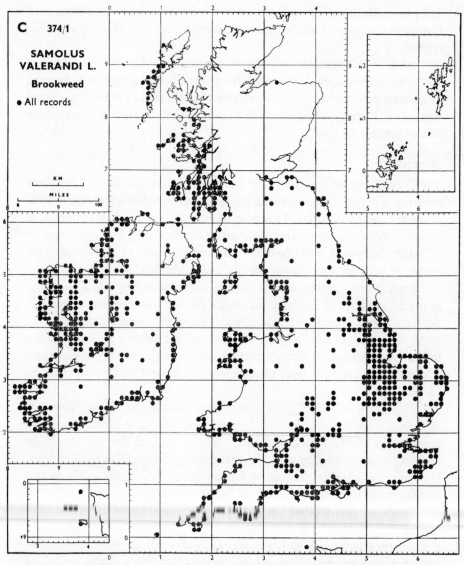

C 374/1

SAMOLUS
VALERANDI L.

Brookweed

● All records

KM

MILES

BOTANICAL SOCIETY OF THE BRITISH ISLES DISTRIBUTION MAPS SCHEME

Fig. 3. Distribution of *Samolus valerandi* in the British Isles showing trend to
strictly coastal distribution in the northern part of its range (from *Atlas of the
British Flora*, F. H. Perring and S. M. Walter, T. Nelson & Sons Ltd., 1962).

Specific Climatic Factors

Local variations

It will be useful at this point to consider the effects of sunlight, temperature, rain and wind on dune and marsh, because they differ profoundly in each habitat. In particular, climatic factors operate much more uniformly over the flat surface of a marsh than over the broken terrain of a dune system. Climatic variability tends to be unidirectional across a marsh surface from seawards to landwards and is a contributory factor to the marked zonation of vegetation apparent in this direction (Fig. 4). Much greater diversity of microclimate is detectable in the different parts of a dune system according to local shelter effects and proximity to the water table (Fig. 5). This is reflected in much more complex mosaic patterns of the vegetation.

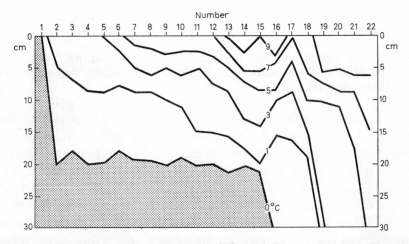

Fig. 4. Soil temperature 0–30 cm deep in different habitats at Liminka, Finland. 18. V. 1968 at 12–14 o'clock. The shaded area is below 0°C. No. 1. *Carex nigra* var. *juncea*, 2. *Phragmites communis*, 3. *arable land*, 4. wood of *Vaccinium – Myrtillus* type (VMT), shaded by spruce, 5. *Juncus gerardii – Odontites litoralis*, 6. *Carex aquatilis*, 7–9. *Carex mackenziei*, 10. *Salix phylicifolia* shrubs, 11. *Juncus gerardii – Primula finmarchica*, 12. *Eleocharis palustris*, 13. *Alnus incana* wood, 14 – 15. *Phragmites communis*, 16. *Eleocharis palustris*, 17. VMT wood (open location), 18. *Triglochin maritimum* (a depression in the Carices distigmaticae zone), 19–20. *Deschampsia caespitosa*, 21. *Betula pubescens* wood, 22. field drainage ditch. All readings correspond to littoral zones, except numbers 3, 4, 17, 19 and 22, which were taken on the epilittoral 5 km from the water boundary (from Siira 1970). N.B. Communities not in zonal sequence.

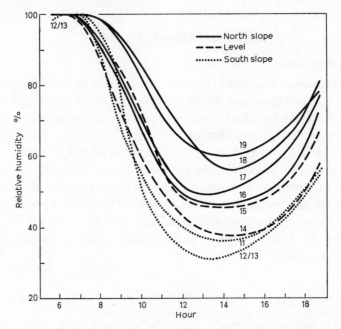

Fig. 5. Course of relative humidity just above soil surface at sites investigated between 05.30 and 18.40 hours on 23 August in the Wassenaar dunes, Holland (from Boerboom 1964).

It is a remarkable fact that climate or specific climatic factors are not the primary theme in any of the nearly 400 references in the bibliography to Chapman's (1960) monograph on salt marshes. This reflects how relatively little work has been done on climatic factors in relation to salt marsh plant growth. In contrast, significant advances have been made in the study of microclimate in dune vegetation by a number of authors, notably Salisbury (1933, 1952), Stoutjesdijke (1961) and Boerboom (1964). Comprehensive ~~experimental study of climatic factors limiting growth and reproduction~~ still remains to be carried out for the majority of the commoner salt marsh and dune species which make up the bulk of the floras of these two habitats.

Stoutjesdijke (1961) discusses thermo-electric measuring techniques suitable for use on dunes and in dune vegetation. He obtained simultaneous measurements of temperature and absolute humidity of the air, wind velocity, radiation intensity and soil temperature in dune grass and scrub vegetation.

Miniaturization at the sensor end and direct linkage to computer analysis at the other would be the best way to reveal the complex micro-meteorological patterns prevailing in salt marsh and sand dune communities.

Light

Cottam and Munro (1954) record that *Zostera marina var. latifolia* survives at the 'almost incredible' depths of 100 ft (30m) on the slopes of La Jolla submarine canyon in the clear waters off southern California. Beneath the relatively turbid waters over mudflats around European shores *Zostera marina* is usually confined to water depths of less than 20 ft (6m). Transplants of *Zostera marina var. angustifolia* made in the upper reaches of Poole Harbour a few years ago died gradually *in situ* at levels normally within the tidal range of this species, apparently for lack of adequate light. Johnson and York (1915) have shown that the anatomical leaf structure of *Zostera* and *Ruppia* is similar to that of shade tolerant plants. Day (1951) notes that in the turbid waters of the Berg estuary, South Africa, *Zostera* (*Z. capensis*) is limited to inter-tidal banks, but in the clear waters of the Knysa estuary it extends at least 3 ft (1m) below low tide mark. He summarizes techniques of measuring turbidity and gives a useful brief discussion of this factor.

Much work has been done to show how salt marsh plant zonation may be correlated with duration of tidal submergence (Chapman 1938, Adams 1963, Hinde 1954), but practically none on the survival of individual species subjected to submergence experimentally. *Spartina anglica* has been shown to survive continuous submergence in clear sea water in greenhouse conditions without apparent harm for $4\frac{1}{2}$ months. This is far beyond the maximum possible duration of submergence it receives in its normal intertidal habitat. Growth chamber studies have demonstrated that this species tillers but does not flower in short days (Hubbard 1969) and flowering may be inhibited by limitations on the supply of light during submergence at its lower limit. Flowering is generally poor at this limit, but this may be due to mechanical damage as well as reduced light.

The effects of reduced light on salt marsh plants is very noticeable beneath the shade of overhanging oaks in estuaries like the Fal, Cornwall or Beaulieu estuary, Hampshire. Here the growth of *Glaux maritima*, *Aster tripolium* or *Triglochin maritima* becomes very straggly and attenuated. It would be interesting to measure light values, morphological responses and the sequence of survival as shade increases in such situations.

Not all salt marsh plants require high light intensities, however, and *Althaea officinalis* appears to thrive best in the half shade of oaks near high water mark on wooded shores of Hampshire and Sussex. Lack of light may limit growth at both ends of the salt marsh. At the seaward end turbidity may be operative, and at the landward end the growth of taller plants shades out shorter plants where the marshes are ungrazed.

Thus in a mixed boundary where *Phragmites* was invading *Spartina anglica* marsh in Poole Harbour, it was found that *Spartina* was first drawn up in the taller growth, then ceased to flower, then lost its ability to tiller, became aetiolated, and finally died out some 25 m landward of the seaward limit of *Phragmites*. Merely cutting the stems of *Phragmites* near the extinction point of *Spartina* in no more than 1 metre square was sufficient to enable *Spartina* to recommence both tillering and flowering again.

It might be assumed that the light requirements of pioneer plants on the open sand of dunes would be high. In fact this is not necessarily so. It is intriguing to find for example that *Carex arenaria*, which we associate with the very high light conditions of open sand, is one of the last species to survive beneath the quite dense shade of mature pines on the dunes at Holkham in Norfolk. Once again no study appears to have been made of the shade-tolerance of dune plants and this would be of particular interest in view of the current trend towards scrub on dunes since 1954 when rabbit populations in Britain were greatly reduced by the virus disease known as myxomatosis.

Temperature

Little information is available about the field temperature controls on the germination, establishment, growth and flowering of salt marsh plants. There must certainly be far lower temperature ranges and smaller rates of fluctuation in lower marshes subject to regular inundation by the sea than in higher marshes free from its influence for days or even weeks at a time. Duff and Teal (1965) provide evidence supporting this in *Spartina alterniflora* marsh. *Cochlearia anglica* grows on both lower and higher shore in the Orne estuary, France. Binet (1965a) shows that on the lower shore seed germination is delayed and growth slowed down in winter in this species compared to germination and growth on the higher shore, but he does not relate these differences to temperature differences. Species like *Halimione portulacoides* and *Agropyron pungens* are often generally abundant in English and Welsh salt marshes, but absent from Scotland north of a line from the Solway to the Forth and in the more northerly parts of Europe. The abrupt disappearance of common species such as these at certain latitudes strongly suggests that their limits are controlled by some climatic factor, but just how and at what stage in the life cycle this happens we do not know. Iverson (1954) records the rapid spread of *Halimione portulacoides* at Skallingen, Denmark between 1931 and 1954 and this may be partly in response to ameliorated climatic conditions. The species was clearly damaged by frost in Holland in 1963. *Limonium vulgare* on the other hand is not particularly frost sensitive (Boorman 1968) and it seems more likely that day length requirements for flowering may be a controlling factor near its northern limit in Scandinavia.

Binet (1965b) has shown that seeds of *Cochlearia anglica* germinate best at relatively low temperatures between 5° – 15°C while those of *Plantago maritima* will scarcely germinate at all at these temperatures, but will do so at 25°C, though even better in diurnal alternations of 5°C and 25°C.

It is extremely difficult to get a clear indication of the way in which temperature may limit survival because of its complex interactions with photoperiod and salinity which is itself affected by rainfall. Tsopa (1939), Chapman (1942) and more recently, Binet (1964 a and b, 1965 a, b, c, d, e, and 1966) have made important contributions in this field in relation to germination requirements of salt marsh species, while Seneca (1969) has studied the germination responses of dune grasses. Chapman (1960, p. 315) points out that the germination of seeds of most salt marsh species occurs at times of reduced salinity, that is when low temperatures combine with high rainfall.

Stubbings and Houghton (1964) have shown that the cooling effect in winter and heating effect in summer which takes place in the harbour shallows of Chichester Harbour, Sussex, is of the order of 2°C below or above the open surface water temperature of the Harbour.

In contrast to the ameliorating effect of more or less permanently moist ground on temperature fluctuation in salt marshes, extremely wide and rapid temperature fluctuations are characteristic of the dune habitat. For example at Newborough Warren in Anglesey the temperature of the sand surface rose 14°C between 4.30 and 10.0 a.m. on a clear day in August. Salisbury (1952) notes that temperatures of over 60°C occur at the surface of bare sand on a hot summer day and diurnal fluctuations of 30°C were common. Such fluctuations are much reduced in damp dune slacks compared with dunes. In the generally cooler climate of damp slacks leafing of *Salix repens* may be delayed up to a fortnight after that on nearby dunes. Boerboom (1964) noted the persistence of late frosts in dune slacks in Dutch dunes in June 1957. *Juncus acutus* suffered over 80 per cent mortality in open drier slacks, but less than 50 per cent mortality locally in closed wetter slacks to landward in the 1962–1963 cold winter at Braunton Burrows, Devon (Hewett 1971).

Soil temperature fluctuation is markedly reduced beneath dune scrub, compared with bare sand (Fig. 6). Stoutjesdijk (1961) notes that the heat storage capacity of the soil beneath open sand was able to compensate for the net radiation loss from the surface during the night and there was no dew formation. By contrast, beneath *Hippophaë* scrub the much lower heat storage of the soil was only able to compensate for about one third of the net radiation loss so that the remainder was compensated by heat taken up from the air either as sensible heat or as heat of condensation resulting in strong dew formation on the *Hippophaë* surfaces. Further studies related to dew formation are considered in Chapter 9.

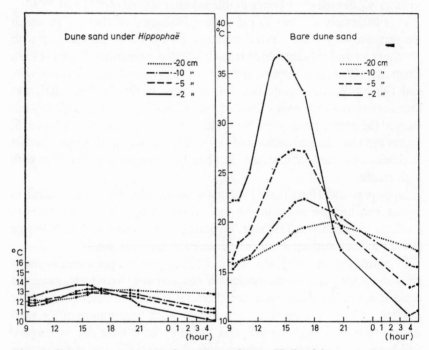

Fig. 6. Soil temperatures on Oostvoorne dunes, Holland between 9 a.m. on 16 June and 5 a.m. on 17 June (from Stoutjesdijke 1961).

The sand dune flora is notable for its high proportion of annual plants. These, unlike those of arable land, tend to pass through the hot summer period as seed and grow during cooler months, some germinating in autumn to grow as winter annuals. Salisbury (1934) has shown that the air close to leaves of annual dune species in April may be around 10°C higher in temperature than that of the general ambient air temperature. This could allow rapid photosynthesis in annuals at a time when low temperature was preventing photosynthesis in other species. Following the earlier work of Salisbury there is renewed interest in the temperature and light controls on the germination and growth of these species at the present time (Bakker *et al*, 1966). The variable topography of dunes produces striking climatic contrasts according to aspect. For example *Tortula ruralis* carpets may differ in temperature as much as 9°C on north and south aspects of Dutch dunes (Boerboom 1946). Such contrasts provide a juxtaposition of almost regionally distinct climatic zones in the form of mosaic units a few metres apart.

Rainfall

There is a very characteristic difference in the appearance of salt marsh vegetation as one goes south from North Europe to the sub-tropics. This is shown by the increasing openness of the vegetation dependent on the degree to which evapo-transpiration exceeds precipitation for substantial periods of time. In general the vegetation of north European marshes forms a more or less continuous sward (except in the pioneer zone), interrupted only by discontinuities in the surface. In the Camargue, France, Bigot (1958) notes that cover in the main salt marsh areas is often less than 80 per cent and some times as low as 50 per cent and here evapo-transpiration exceeds precipitation during much of the summer (Plate 1). On the borders of the Red Sea vegetation cover rarely exceeds 70 per cent and is mostly below 50 per cent, though this is partly due to the incidence of grazing in addition to the desert-type climate (Kassas 1957). In Gambia (in the tropical zone) where the rainy season is confined to June to October, the remaining months are in general hot and very dry and Giglioli and Thornton (1965) note that this results in extensive areas of barren mud within the mangrove swamps. There is marked interaction between seasonal and season to season rainfall and salinity. Indeed it is the incidence and amount of rainfall and not tidal influence which dominates salinity concentrations in upper salt marsh levels (Ranwell *et al* 1964).

Plants of the higher salt marsh are generally tolerant of the highest salinities likely to obtain in the climate of north European coasts. Growth room studies have shown that *Spartina anglica* for example can survive salinities up to twice that of sea water, a value much in excess of any recorded in 162 field samples measured. *Glaux maritima* and *Limonium vulgare* are also known to be tolerant of salinities in excess of sea water. Yet, in periods of summer drought these plants may die back extensively as they did on the northern Irish coast for example in the dry summer of 1968. Little study seems to have been made of the drought tolerance of salt marsh plants and this would be well worth investigation for it might help to explain the successive replacement of species in progressively higher zones of marsh. Boorman (1967) has demonstrated by transplant experiments that drought is a limiting factor of growth for *Limonium vulgare* on sandy soil at the upper levels of a marsh.

As mentioned earlier, species characteristic of the montane element in the British flora such as *Dryas octopetala, Trollius europaeus* and *Saxifraga aizoides* descend to the coast and are able to survive on north and west Scottish dunes. Further south they are confined to montane regions. These plants are characteristic of high rainfall in their mountain habitats and it is probably the more humid climate on the northern dunes which allows them to survive there.

Mosses normally found in dune slacks further south, grow on dunes at Luskentyre in the Outer Hebrides and Gimingham *et al* (1948) suggest this may be correlated with the relatively uniformly rainy climate of the area. Similar moisture-loving mosses occur in *Ammophila* tussocks in north-west Sutherland. In both of these sites the average annual potential water deficit is less than 0·5 ins (13 mm), among the lowest for any coastal site in Great Britain, one of the wettest parts of Europe (Green 1964).

Wind

There is much historical evidence (from the burial of human settlements), of pronounced dune activity on European coasts in Mediaeval times during periods of exceptionally stormy weather, e.g. from Penhale, Corn- wall (Steers 1964); South Wales (Higgins, 1933); Newborough, Anglesey (Ranwell, 1959); Forvie, Aberdeenshire (Barkley, 1955), and many other sites on the European coast from the Baltic dunes to those of The Landes in France. Attempts have been made to link exceptional periods of stormi- ness with recurrent astronomical events affecting tidal maxima (Petterssen, 1914; Brooks, 1949) and there does seem to be some evidence in the above of pronounced dune activity at times of major (1700 year cycle) and minor (90 year cycle) tidal maxima. According to Petterssen's hypothesis the last major maximum was in 1433 A.D. and we should be reaching the next minor maximum in the 1970 to 1980 period, when it might be expected that the storminess noted at the end of the nineteenth century may be repeated. Lamb (1970 *a* and *b*) has recently drawn together evidence of climatic periodicity which suggests that cycles of 5, 10, 20, 90, 200 years may also be operative.

The direct effect of wind on plant growth in salt marshes has not been investigated, but it must curtail both height and extent of growth in more exposed sites. There is a noticeable reduction in height of *Phragmites* growth at the windward edge of clones invading *Spartina* marsh in Poole Harbour, Dorset, but this may be partly due to competition for water or nutrients. Lines (1957) has shown how wind exposure may be compared from site to site using tatter flags.

Wind exerts a profound influence on the growth of dune plants, on the redistribution of organic and inorganic nutrients, on the amount of salt received, on the distribution of propagules, and above all shapes the very ground on which they grow. These different influences are discussed in Chapter 8 and subsequently.

Response to Climatic Changes

While it is true as Major (in Shaw 1967) points out that: '. . . ecologists ascribe to climate major importance in differentiating the kinds of vegetation on earth' it is also paradoxically true as he says, '. . . it is difficult even to rank the relative importance of a climatic difference in relation to other site factors.'

The problem becomes less acute perhaps if individual species rather than vegetation types are considered. Especially those species which by their powers of regeneration, superior height or dominating influence in one form or another gain ascendancy and exert such influence as to control to a large extent the type of habitat and even survival of accompanying plants and animals. In fact one searches the literature in vain for critical studies of the performance of such species near the limits of their range. Experimental transplants beyond such limits have scarcely been attempted let alone monitored to see how prevailing climate affects their growth.

Many botanists are reluctant to deliberately move plants outside their existing range. They are keenly aware of the risks of liberating potentially invasive species in a new environment. However the case against introductions is frequently based on the argument that they may interfere with studies on geographical distributions. In fact such studies often reveal only correlations of doubtful significance between range and climatic factors. Properly controlled introductions provide information of real predictive value and are a powerful tool for those who are asked to make a practical contribution to advice on vegetation management.

Lethal and sub-lethal damage.

Wholesale damage to *Spartina anglica* and *Halimione portulacoides* was noted in Holland near the northern limit of range of these species after the cold winter of 1963. But in fact despite this setback *Halimione* has apparently extended its range northwards in Denmark.

The 1963 winter froze *Spartina anglica* marsh soil to a depth of 10 cm

c

(the main rooting level) at the height of the frost, and surface growth was much diminished in the following summer at Poole Harbour, Dorset. There was full recovery in lower *Spartina* marsh in 1964, but near the upper limit of *Spartina* growth species such as *Agropyron pungens* and *Aster tripolium* invaded and persisted, occupying much of the ground formerly covered by *Spartina*. This differential effect of severe frost on plants in optimum, compared with sub-optimum growth conditions, underlines the need to examine climatic effects on the same species in different habitats.

Suaeda fruticosa near the northern limit of its range in Europe at Blakeney Point, Norfolk lost all its leaves after the 1962–1963 cold winter, but some buds on higher twigs survived to put out new growth which however mostly came from the base of plants (White 1967). This illustrates how extremely local even severe climatic effects can be.

Zoologists use the level at which 50 per cent of the population is killed by any particular factor operating over unit time as an indication of lethal dose (L.D. 50). Crisp (1965) for example gives L.D. 50's for low temperature operating for 18 hours for a range of shore organisms many of which were severely affected by 1962–1963 frosts. It would be of great interest to have similar information on low temperature lethal limits for salt marsh and dune plants of predominantly southern distribution in the British Isles. *Festuca arundinacea*, though by no means confined to these habitats, does occur in dune grassland and in upper estuarine brackish marsh grassland. It also shows a marked coastal trend in northern Scotland. Recent work by Robson and Jewiss (1968) demonstrates an inverse relationship between winter growth and winter hardiness in forms of this species. In culture the L.D. 50 for Mediterranean varieties occurs at temperatures of −13°C and for more northerly varieties at −16°C. Their work illustrates the further complexity of interaction between climate and genetic adaptation.

Population response to climatic changes

The nature of the limit in relation to a plant population must be considered as the combination of internal and external environmental factors which regularly result in L.D. 50, rather than in reference to any one factor in particular.

As we saw in the case of the Florida mangrove, local pockets of the species may persist in sheltered refuges (perhaps for a century or more), so a frequency value needs to be added to the L.D. 50 to make it meaningful for a climatically controlled limit.

Study of microclimates at refuge limits could characterize climatic tolerances where these are believed to be limiting to growth, reproduction or survival. They would be representative of the effective adaptive limits but not necessarily of the potential adaptive limits of the species as a whole. For example, Sakai (1970) has recently drawn attention to the latent genetic potential of tropical willows to withstand freezing to very low temperatures.

There is little evidence of climatically induced population changes in the British sand dune flora, with a few notable exceptions. Prior to 1930 *Otanthus maritimus* occurred as far north as Anglesey and Suffolk, but now survives only in Cornwall in Great Britain. *Eryngium maritimum*, formerly in the Shetlands, now survives only south of a line from the Hebrides to south Yorkshire, while *Glaucium flavum* appears to have retreated south from its Scottish habitats. The latter is a continental southern species which may require hot dry summers and therefore not be favoured by the increasing trend towards higher rainfall evident up to at least the 1950's, (Lamb in Johnson and Smith, 1965). *Parnassia palustris* on the other hand, a plant of the continental northern flora, has disappeared from several coastal habitats including dune slacks in southern England, possibly in response to the generally warmer winters which have characterized our climate in the first half of the twentieth century.

It is now becoming evident (Lamb 1969) that climatic trends may be quite short-lived and that records over periods as short as a decade may give a better indication of current trends, than longer runs of records. We are only beginning to see how rapidly there may be an adaptive adjustment in species populations where other factors related to establishment and selection operate in favour or against a species. Adaptation to climatic change is clearly a product of inherent variability and where this is low in a rare species, ground lost by the species may not be regained for very long periods of time, even though climatic trends once more favour its growth in the site.

2 Physiography and Hydrology

As the sum of knowledge grows in different disciplines it becomes possible to break down the isolation between them, to see relevant connections and work towards a synthesis which in turn opens up new lines of study and unsuspected possibilities for the practical use of knowledge gained. Understandably in the past both ecological and physiographic studies have tended to concentrate on the immediate influences at work in particular sites, and this has led to a distinctly piecemeal approach to advice on problems of coastal protection or coast land reclamation. For example the benefits in terms of raised shore levels obtained by groyning at one site may be gained at the expense of lowered shorelines in another. Again, a low water training bank to hold a deep water channel for shipping on one side of an estuary may result in silting on the other side of the estuary and loss of beach recreational facilities.

Now there are welcome signs that we are moving towards a synthesis of coastal physiographic knowledge and in this chapter some attempt is made to link up the complex of forces which controls the disposition, type and development of salt marshes and sand dunes on the British coast as a whole. Sources of sediment supply come from erosion of the land surface, the edge of the coast or the sea bed mainly during periods of high wind or high rainfall; deposition occurs mainly in calm weather conditions.

Physiographic Influences

Rock-type influences

Primary geological effects on the distribution of marshes and dunes are particularly evident in a country like Great Britain because its small size and unusually diverse series of rock types bring out striking differences between one part of the coast and another.

There is an obvious natural division for example between highland and lowland Britain. To the north and west of a line from the Tees to the Exe hard rocks predominate in relatively high-lying country. To south and east of this line soft rocks predominate in relatively low-lying country. This is reflected in the predominance of coarse sediment deposits in the north and west which form the building material of dunes. Finer sediments have accumulated to form the extensive marshlands of the south and east and also in the three isolated soft rock outlets on the west coast: the Bristol Channel, the Dee-Mersey area, and the Solway.

Apart from any contributions of sedimentary material brought down by rivers which we shall consider shortly, the erodibility and lime status of coastal rocks partly governs the particle size and particle type of adjoining sedimentary deposits. It is not easy to sort out the various contributions from country rock, glacial material and soil erosion which go to make up marsh and dune sediments and this is a field that would repay much further study. Clues to the origins of sediments can be obtained from heavy mineral analysis, X-ray diffraction and differential thermal analysis of clay minerals (Guilcher and Berthois, 1957), and more recently from electron micrography studies of particle surface textures (e.g. Biederman, 1962; Porter, 1962 and Krinsley and Funnell, 1965). There are one or two sites where direct connections between adjoining rock strata and dune type can be made with some confidence. The Spurn Head dunes, Yorkshire, are clearly influenced in their high lime status by the extensive exposures of chalk on the Yorkshire coast. The lime deficient dunes of Studland, Dorset (an area not subject to glaciation), must owe their relatively recent origin to erosion of the adjoining lime-deficient Bagshot sand deposits of Poole Bay.

Indented cliff coasts of lime-deficient rocks, though not themselves a source of lime, provide innumerable sites for molluscs which derive lime for their shells from the adequate supplies in sea water. Much of the beach material for building dunes on these hard coasts is therefore in the form of broken shell material often comprising more than 50 per cent of the sand, as at Penhale, Cornwall, the dunes of the Outer Hebrides, or the shell sand beaches of the west coast of Scotland.

The legacy of glacial deposits

Superimposed on the rock formations of northern Europe are varying quantities of glacial material of mixed and derived origin. Its deposition occurred rapidly in the form of out-wash fans from the main centres of glaciation as the glaciers themselves began to melt and retreat northwards some 20,000 years ago. These glacial deposits, re-worked by the sea at the time of the last major land and sea level adjustment some 7,000 years ago, probably form the structural basis of many of our present-day marshes and dunes. They also form a bank of material, easily eroded at the coast and in the immediately offshore zones, from which supplies are drawn to help feed accreting coastal systems today. We do not know the size of this bank, nor, what is more important, its capacity to supply withdrawals, but both are clearly limited.

Long term changes in the relationship of land and sea level modify the distribution of salt marshes and sand dunes by exposing or submerging the foreshore deposits from which they are built according to varying amounts of wind or wave action. The pattern of the present configuration of the coast and its adjoining inter-tidal flats was established about 6,000 years ago when sea level is believed to have attained its present level. Since that time there have been only minor oscillations (Fairbridge 1961). Land subsidence or elevation operates more locally and it may increase or reduce the relative sea level rise in any particular part of the coast.

It is not certain whether the sand in Caernarvon Bay is of glacial or pre-glacial origin, but there is evidence (Ranwell 1955) that there has been a steady deepening of the bay during the past 250 years. During that time very considerable quantities of sand have been blown from the shore onto land beyond reach of tides. This clearly must have come from the bay.

Studies in the Danish Waddensea have shown that there is a net input of sedimentary material to the system and the bulk of this is believed to be derived from off-shore deposits of glacial or pre-glacial material. The movement of submarine material can be studied indirectly by means of sea bed drifters (Perkins et al 1963), or more directly by the use of radio-active tracers (Perkins and Williams (1965)), but much of this work has been confined to littoral deposits and we are largely ignorant about the extent to which storms can stir up and transport deeper sea bed deposits, and incidentally, potential pollutants dumped off-shore.

Topographic relationships

Coastal sedimentary material derives ultimately from aerial or marine erosion of the land surfaces and forms a discontinuous belt of various thickness and width on either side of the shoreline.

The disposition of material is related to the vertical angles and horizontal distributions of the 'rocks' across and along the shoreline which in turn is governed by the nature of these rocks. These topographical relationships control rates of river and sea-water flow in which loose sediments are carried when it is fast, or deposited when it is slow.

The type of material available for transport or deposition varies according to the texture of the rocks eroded: harder rocks producing coarser-particled material and softer rocks finer-particled material.

It follows that of the two habitats with which we are concerned, sand deposits are characteristic of the inlets and embayments of the hard rock cliffed coast of Northern Scotland; silt deposits of the graded soft coastline of south and east England. Elsewhere the conjunction of both types of rock provides both sand and silt for deposition side by side according to local shelter and the sorting action imposed by differential rates of water flow.

Only at the extreme heads of the most sheltered inlets on the rugged north and west coasts of Scotland (e.g. Kyle of Tongue, Sutherland), can one find vestigial salt marshes on silt. This contrasts with the widespread occurrence of salt marsh in the estuaries of lowland coasts further south and even extending onto the open coasts of Essex shores (e.g. at Dengie and Foulness). These are the two extremes. More commonly estuaries are found with silt in the sheltered upper reaches and sand accumulations in the form of various types of spits and cusps on one or both sides of the estuary mouth.

Before considering the different types of dune and marsh systems we need to consider external hydrological factors operating on them from the larger systems of which they form a part: on the landward side, the catchment area, and to seawards, its effective counterpart, the tidal basin.

Hydrological Influences

Influences from the land catchment

In the past, as we have seen, the bulk of European coastal deposits are believed to have derived from glacial deposits distributed by glacial melt-water erosion of the land surface. At the present time available evidence and deductions from river volume and flow rates, suggests that relatively small amounts of material are derived from the land surface (excluding for the moment the contribution from coastal erosion), and these mainly at times of bank-full river conditions during heavy rain. Nevertheless catchment type, size, vegetative cover and management, together make discernible contributions, particularly to upper estuarine marshes. The catchment influences deserve much fuller study than they have yet received, and a few examples will help to make this clear.

Catchment types with predominantly basic rocks and soils derived from them in the south of England provide nutrients which favour the growth of *Artemisia maritima*, *Carex divisa*, *Inula crithmoides* and many other species absent from salt marsh soils deficient in lime. At Langstone Harbour, Hampshire, chalk bed-rock outcrops in the inter-tidal zone and freshwater springs from it help to keep the chalk surface exposed and free from mud locally. These lime-rich waters, quite brackish at low tide, favour growths of *Zostera angustifolia* and some of the biggest marsh populations of *Inula crithmoides* found in Britain. Permeable sandy marshes and those with only a thin layer of silt overlying permeable deposits or bedrock may be strongly influenced in this way by sub-surface fresh water drained from the catchment.

A relatively high-lying catchment commanding high rainfall such as that of the River Tay in Scotland, which produces a greater discharge than any other in Britain, markedly reduces the estuarine salinity. This allows species such as *Scirpus maritimus* (normally a pioneer of upper estuarine muds), to extend its range as a pioneer to much nearer the estuarine mouth than normal.

A large catchment like that of the Mississippi produces great quantities of silt and characteristic deltaic marshes. Some tendency towards deltaic marsh development is evident in the Thames with its reclaimed marsh islands (Canvey, Grain), lying at the mouth.

Vegetative cover in the form of blanket bog and hard rocks resistant to erosion provide little sediment in the rivers of north and west Scotland. Much more sediment is transported from catchments with a high proportion of agricultural land, notably catchments from the Humber to the Thames. Little quantitative information is available in this country on catchment erosion, but Gottschalk and James (1955) estimate that soil loss from arable land is about 500 times that from grassland. Recent estuarine barrage feasibility studies (Anon 1966 a, b and c) for freshwater reservoirs provide rough comparative estimates of the river-borne sediment supplies to the Solway and Morecambe Bay. Those to the Solway are sufficiently high to influence decisions in favour of selecting Morecambe Bay as a potential barrage site rather than the Solway.

Currently the enormous increase in the use of fertilizers, herbicides and pesticides in agricultural catchments is also changing the chemical quality of water and silt coming from the land. Westlake (1968) calculates that 500 metric tons per year of nitrate nitrogen at an average concentration of 2 mg/1, and about 20 metric tons per year of phosphate phosphorus at an average concentration of 0·09 mg/1, are currently discharged to the sea by the River Frome, Dorset, a small well-graded river. Relationships with catchment activities on the one hand and contributions of silt and nutrients from these sources to the marshes on the other, have yet to be made. However it is recorded that the amount of nitrogen applied as fertilizer to agricultural land in England and Wales has doubled in the 7 years from 1962 to 1969 (Anon 1970 c).

Tidal basin influences

One way of considering the marine contribution to the hydrology and physiography of marsh and dune systems is to think in terms of the tidal basin. Like the catchment for the land, this is a convenient, though much less discrete unit of the sea. Superimposed on both, of course, are the effects of aerial weather systems and one can foresee that with better understanding it may eventually be possible to relate contributions from land, sea and air in some unit form to the modelling of coastal systems.

As an example of this type of approach, Phillips' (1964) studies on the Yorkshire coast is of outstanding interest. She studied beach features known as 'ords' which develop on the Yorkshire coasts between Flamborough Head and Hornsea. Where protection of Flamborough Head is no longer effective, strong northerly winds directly on shore generate big waves which may initiate upper beach erosion to form an 'ord'. 'Ords' are about 45 to 55 m long and may lower the top beach by as much as 3 m. They travel southwards as units at an average rate of about 1·6 km per year and enable storm waves to erode embryo dunes or coast defence works, whichever is present. Their movement as a unit is only initiated when winds of over 15 knots (7·7 m/s) blow from the northerly quarter for at least several hours. Such winds are usually associated with a deep depression centred over southern Scandinavia. These conditions produce not only powerful waves developed in the long fetch available to the north west, but also a storm surge which causes a temporary oscillatory rise in sea level in the North Sea basin. Under most other wind conditions the beach tends to become built up in form. Once developed, 'ords' and the higher sections of beach between them, move as a unit since, as Phillips points out, the rate of longshore movement on this only slightly curving stretch of coast would tend to be uniform. The importance of this work lies in the link-up and interaction of major environmental systems, the distinctive threshold effect that produces such beach features, and the very short time periods that may be involved in beach re-structuring. Concerning the latter, Groves (in Steers 1960) records that even under relatively calm conditions

en found that the level of a shore feeding a dune system may alter uch as 0·3 m over the greater part of the profile within as little as rs. Clearly beach profiles should be sampled in relation to weather ations rather than at regular time intervals.

Tides are produced in the oceans by the gravitational pull of planetary bodies, primarily the sun, the moon and the earth. Because these are moving in relation to each other the gravitational forces change. Constraints to movement formed by land boundaries result in water basins within which oscillations are set up and rotated by Coriolis forces about nodal or amphidromic points, points or areas of no significant tidal rise or fall (Defant, 1964). Around these points tidal range increases concentrically. Fig. 7 shows the distribution of tidal basins around British coasts. The minimum tidal ranges of the Solent area are, as one might expect, close to an amphidromic point in that region. Maximum tidal ranges on the west coast in the Bristol Channel region lie towards the outer edge of the much larger Atlantic Ocean tidal basin.

The vertical range in level of a salt marsh is primarily related to tidal range and secondarily to turbidity of the water. If the turbidity of the water is high, this reduces the potential vertical range of growth of salt marsh plants. In the maximum tide range of 12 m in the Bristol Channel, salt marsh growth ranges vertically over 4 m; in the small tidal range of 1·8 m in Poole Harbour salt marsh growth is telescoped into a vertical range of about 1 m. Marshes within a large tidal range tend to be more steeply sloping and consequently have more clearly zoned vegetation and sharper drainage systems normal to the shore. Marshes within a small tidal range have less clearly zoned vegetation and sluggish drainage on the ebb which produces a more complex network of winding and much-branched creeks. The Poole Harbour to Chichester Harbour salt marshes in a minimum tide zone have these distinctive features of complex drainage patterns and mosaics of indistinctly zoned vegetation. It is true also that long established high level marshes tend to flatten near the limit at which tidal submergence (and therefore silting), becomes insignificant. In such regions zonation again becomes indistinct and vegetation mosaics are common.

Water in the tidal basin moves in response to tidal streams and currents which may have their origin within or outside the basin and, to winds which generate waves. While the former may transport material in the vicinity of coasts, it is waves under the influence of wind which predominate in moving material along the shore or add material to the shore from supplies immediately off-shore or by erosion of the coastline (Steers, 1964).

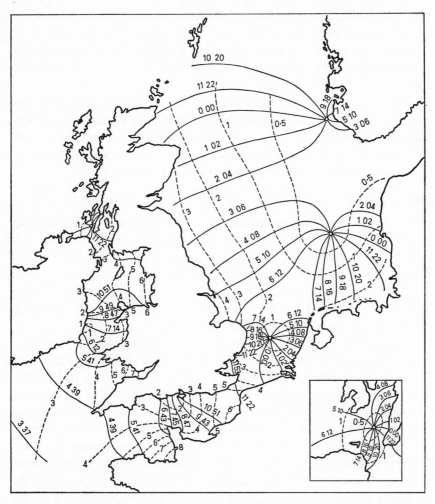

Fig. 7. Co-tidal and range lines for the North Sea tides. (Based on BA chart no 5058 with the sanction of the Controller, H.M. Stationery Office and of the Hydrographer of the Navy, from *Beaches and Coasts*, C. King, Edward Arnold Ltd. 1972.)

Robinson (1966) concluded from marine surveys, observations of current movements and drogue runs, that residual ebb/flood currents were important in determining off-shore bottom topography on the East Anglian coast. In addition to waves, tidal streams also influenced coastal topography. The tidal basin of the southern North Sea gives a decrease of tidal range along the Norfolk coast southwards leading to a tendency for the flood residual to be dominant. South of Yarmouth the situation is reversed and the ebb residual current is likely to be more effective. These inequalities of tidal range affect the tidal streams which have velocities capable of transporting the sea-bed sediment. In this area sand is in constant circulation throughout the shallow water zone down to at least 18 m according to Robinson.

Compared with the land, human activities within the tidal basin are minimal, though in the cases of offshore dredging and dumping of pollutants, not negligible. By contrast, human activities at the land edges of the tidal basin may have profound effects on the longshore movement of beach material as a glance at any groyne system demonstrates.

Wave action

Waves are usually generated by the wind, and their size is governed partly by the strength of the wind and partly by the size of the water body over which the wind operates, the 'fetch', e.g. the Atlantic 'rollers' which fall upon our western shores under the influence of the prevailing and dominant west or south-westerly winds. On the east coast of Britain the prevailing wind is off-shore and it is the dominant winds from the north-east which occur most frequently on these shores.

When a wave breaks upon the shore it has a forward action up the shore, the 'swash', and a backward action downwards, the 'backwash'. More often than not the angle of wave approach is oblique to the shore, while that of its retreat under gravity is normal to the shore (Fig. 8). Material disturbed by the wave is consequently carried along shore by this process of beach drifting. Material carried in this way tends to pile up against objects in its path whether this be a groyne or a natural coastal deposit. Under the influence of north easterly winds material thus tends to move southward down the east coast or on the south coast eastward under the influence of south-westerly drift. Contrary winds frequently reverse the directional flow.

Certain types of waves throw up more material than they comb down off the beach (constructive waves), others remove more material than they supply (destructive waves). The conditions under which these different types of waves occur are not yet fully understood, further discussion of the subject is given in King (1972) and Steers (1964). Certainly storm waves can be of either type, and undoubtedly the shore profile on their approach path (whether well or poorly stocked with material) must influence this. Efficient sampling methods for estimating mean particle size of beach samples, are discussed by Krumbein and Slack (1956). Where the whole sample population is used, careful choice of size grades enables the results

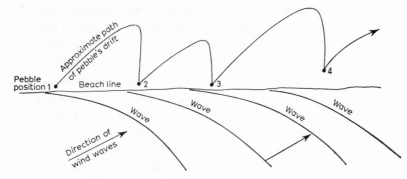

Fig. 8. Beach-drifting (from Steers 1964).

to be plotted on a logarithmic basis and departures from the smooth curve give clues to the presence and possible origins of unsorted material newly deposited on the shore.

Kestner (1961) points out that two groups of processes, sorting and mixing are continually going on in estuaries. Suspended load travel sorts particle sizes so that fine material is transported up or downstream in tidal flow and can only settle in fairly still water. Mixing processes include side erosion, scour and bed movement. From his studies on the Lune estuary, Lancashire and elsewhere, Kestner distinguishes three types of loose boundary transport.

Silt (particles below 0·1 mm diameter) forms loose boundary surfaces which are flat and unrippled. The material has arrived in suspension, is highly cohesive and resistant to surface scour; it is most likely to be eroded by some form of side erosion.

Fine sand between 0·1 and 0·2 mm can be very highly mobile and capable of moving with equal ease either in suspension or along the bed. Changing current velocities rather than high velocity itself may be responsible for starting this material into movement. Since more of this material is carried in the flood than on the ebb tide it may be responsible for rapid upstream shoaling especially where fresh water flow is reduced.

Medium and coarser sands above 0·2 mm may not be in suspension and sand banks of this material tend to move along the bed as units.

Kestner (1963) has demonstrated from suspended load sampling in the Wash that the important material for mudflat and therefore salt marsh development is a coarse silt or fine sand around 0·64–0·128 mm particle size. He notes that quite a small addition of finer particles makes it very cohesive. Clearly these threshold effects are highly relevant to both animal and plant establishment.

Experiments with radio-active tracers have demonstrated the rate at which silt or sand can be moved in estuaries. For example silt has been shown to move 10 miles (16 km) downstream in a matter of hours in the Thames estuary (Inglis and Allen 1957). Sand may move upstream up to 500 ft (152 m) per tide in the Mersey estuary (Price and Kendrick 1963). The speed of such changes and the distances involved underline the difficulties of investigating these movements and the need to extend studies (and plans for dealing with coastal erosion problems) far beyond the immediate vicinity of the coastal area being investigated. Just as whole catchment studies are necessary to understanding changes in an estuary, so studies based on whole tidal basins are likely to be needed to understand forces moulding estuary mouths and adjoining open coasts.

Habitat Series

The salt marsh series

Both salt marsh and dune physiographic series are best classified in relation to their maritime or terrestrial affinities.

The most maritime of all salt marshes are those which develop on relatively open coast conditions. Those in the lee of small islands offshore from low coasts backed by low hills are bathed in almost full strength sea water since the island fresh water catchment is negligible and drainage from the land catchment minimal. Some of the best examples of these marshes in Europe are found in association with the shingle and dune islands and spits off the north Norfolk coast, e.g. at Scolt Head Island. Marshes attached to the open coastline are developed on relatively coarse-particled sediments, as one might expect in the conditions of relatively strong water flow. They occur where broad expanses of inter-tidal sediments are found e.g. off the North Norfolk coast or on the Danish, German and Dutch Wadden coasts.

Next in the series are estuarine mouth marshes. These usually form in the lee of coastal spits, tend to be more coarse-particled than those further up estuary, and subject to stronger saline influence though less so than the open coast marshes. Estuarine mouth marshes such as those on the Dovey or Burry estuaries in Wales occupy about one fifth of the marsh area in any estuary.

Marshes of the more maritime type are characteristically rich in algae including free-living diminutive forms of *Fucus* species derived from normal forms attached to rocks or stones in the neighbourhood of the marshes.

Embayed marshes themselves form series according to the depth of the embayment and degree of fresh water flushing they receive. Shallowly embayed marshes are often extensive in area and developed on relatively freely-draining sandy silt of relatively high salinity as at Morecambe Bay in Lancashire for example. Marshes at the head of lochs tend to be small in area and subject to much fresh water flushing for silt is in short supply, but land drainage water abundant in the rocky terrain where they occur. Narrow-mouthed deep embayments are more sheltered and allow deposition of finer particles, producing salt marshes with intricate drainage systems on poorly drained clay and silt soils as at Hamford Water, Essex, Poole Harbour, Dorset or Chichester Harbour, Sussex. The salinity of embayed marshes depends on the amount of fresh water inflow. At Hamford Water and Chichester Harbour very little surface-drained fresh water reaches the marshes. At Poole Harbour two sizable rivers enter the upper reaches and reduce marsh salinity.

This brings us to the final group of marshes associated with the mid and upper reaches of estuaries which are progressively more terrestrial in affinity and increasingly influenced by fresh, rather than salt water tidal flooding.

Mid estuary marshes are extensive in area, occupying some three fifths of the total marsh area of an estuary. They are usually developed on silt and much subject to alternate periods of advance or retreat on any mid-estuarine shore under the influence of swings of the low water channel where this has not been trained in a particular direction. Studies on the Wyre-Lune estuary provide evidence that these fluctuations are self maintaining (Kestner and Inglis 1956). The important thing to bear in mind here is the relative impermanence of at least the lower levels of mid-estuarine marshes.

Upper estuarine marshes are the most sheltered of all and develop on clay-silt in regions of reduced salinity.

Any particular marsh may be intermediate in character between the three main types distinguished: spit-associated marshes; embayed marshes; estuarine marshes. So long as the various gradients: exposure; soil particle size; salinity; are kept in mind there should be no difficulty in placing the marsh in the ecosystem of which it forms a part. It is essential to consider the system as a whole when interpreting results obtained from the study of any part of it.

Transitional habitats

Before considering the dune series it is logical at this point to refer briefly to habitats transitonal between salt marshes and dunes, and between either of these two and any other coastal habitats.

The important point to bear in mind is that special conditions obtain in the transition zone dependent on interactions between the two or more coastal habitats represented.

Take the case of the horizontal transition between high level sand flats and high level mudflats. The primary colonist of such regions on European coasts is *Puccinellia maritima* which characteristically forms dome-shaped hummocks under the joint influence of contributions of wind-borne sand and water-borne sand and silt (Plate 3). These transitions usually occur either in sand-floored bays with silt deposits in the more sheltered inlets to landward (e.g. Morecambe Bay, Lancashire or Baie de la Frenaye, Côtes du Nord, France) or near the mouths of estuaries where the mud deposits of upper and mid estuary give way to sand deposits at the estuary mouth (e.g. Burry estuary, Glamorgan or the Dovey estuary, Cardiganshire). In all these cases the resultant marshes are rich in pans whose development is clearly traceable to a primary origin dependent on the formation of *Puccinellia maritima* hummocks, and the associated hollows between them.

The development of vegetation on these transitional tidal flats increases surface roughness, reduces rates of flow of tidal water and encourages deposition of increasing amounts of fine-particled material. Consequently the original sandy flat becomes overlaid with silt and gradually converted to a more uniform level salt marsh. In the early stages when only a thin layer of silt overlies sand the habitat is transitional not only in the horizontal, but also in the vertical plane and certain species (e.g. *Armeria maritima*), favoured by relatively well-aerated marsh soil conditions, are characteristic of this phase. In open bays with limited supplies of silt, marshes of the transitional type may persist through to maturity. In estuaries, gradually increasing silt aggradation insulates the marsh from such surface sand effects (e.g. improved drainage, aeration, and percolation of fresh water from land drainage) and a typical silt or silt and clay marsh flora develops.

Similar horizontal and vertical transitions occur between salt marsh or sand dune and shingle to produce special relationships of drainage and aeration and characteristic floras and faunas. The tendency to fresh water flooding in dune slacks is usually presumptive evidence of an impermeable silt or clay sub-surface below the sand. However, in the case of island dunes on shingle there may be a tidal influence on the water table due to the high permeability of the underlying shingle.

Study of these transitional habitats and the complexities resulting from interaction of different coastal habitat systems is still in its infancy but it is central to an understanding of much of the pattern of diversity which distinguishes minor variants in the salt marsh or sand dune series.

In the case of the sand-silt flat transition one useful line of laboratory investigation would be to study seedling displacement from sand and silt mixtures in relation to rates of water and wind flow. In the field it might be possible to estimate strain forces at work using anchored fibres of different breaking-strain strengths attached to seedlings.

The dune series

Six main physiographic types of dune system are distinguished on the basis of position in relation to the shoreline. Three of these types: offshore islands, spits, and nesses, project seawards from the shoreline and are generally of a prograding nature. They are best collectively described as Frontshore systems and are more characteristic of sheltered shores including those where the prevailing and dominant winds are at least partially in opposition.

The other three types of dune systems distinguished here are bay dunes, hindshore dunes (usually with well developed slacks) and hindshore sand plains, or 'machairs' as they are known in western Scotland where the latter characteristically occur. These last three systems, progressively more terrestrial in position, may be collectively called Hindshore systems though their point of origin is of course on the shoreline itself. Bay dunes may have equally developed frontshore and hindshore components and form an intermediate link between the more maritime frontshore systems and the more terrestrial hindshore systems. The latter are particularly associated with more exposed shorelines where prevailing and dominant winds reinforce each other.

For a dune to form at all there must be some obstacle, natural or artificial around which wind blown sand can accumulate. In the absence of significant amounts of tidal litter or other wind-stilling barriers, but where abundant supplies of sand at the backshore level occur, the backshore flats may become colonized *in situ* and the whole system develops as a rapidly prograding vegetated sand plain with minimal dune formation. Where sections of lower-lying backshore levels become enclosed by higher-lying backshore levels to seawards, primary slacks develop in parallel with the shore line and they often carry elements of the sandy salt marsh facies due to occasional incursions of sea water or a brackish water table. The low-relief vegetated sand plain, Morrich More, Ross is a good example of this rather unusual rapidly prograding Frontshore system.

D

The effect of a solitary obstacle placed on backshore flats just high enough to accommodate the growth of strandline plants is well illustrated at Holkham, Norfolk. Here an abandoned military vehicle left on the backshore is said to have accumulated an isolated dune some 5 or 6 m high in about 20 years.

More usually tidal litter initiates sand accumulation at the top of backshore. This becomes colonized first by annual species and then by perennial grasses capable of growing up through sand accretion to form dunes of varying height according to the level at which sand loss exceeds sand supply.

Dunes up to 100 m high occur in the Coto Doñana, Spain. On British coasts they rarely exceed 30 m though sand may be blown to higher levels over rock outcrops in the hinterland e.g. at Penhale in Cornwall. Dunes with low relief may either occur in more sheltered areas with rapid progradation and stabilization, or in sites so exposed that strong winds never allow growth of high dunes at all e.g. Shetland Island dunes.

Sand or shingle spits built by beach drifting form a foundation on which dunes can accumulate, fan-wise by apposition of new material to seawards, or terminally as the spit lengthens alongshore. Storm conditions may throw material at the exposed tip landwards intermittently so that the linear growth alongshore is interrupted by a series of spur-like recurves. Systems such as these at Scolt Head Island or Blakeney, Norfolk tend to achieve stabilization in the position of formation of main dune ridges. This results in a series of dune zones of increasing age from the distal to the proximal end of a spit, or in the case of nesses, a series of apposition ridges of increasing age from seaward to landward.

This tendency to stabilize *in situ* is dependent on reduced wind strengths found on sheltered coasts and reduced frequency of higher wind strengths in any one particular direction. In other words coasts where the stronger winds tend to cancel out each others effects.

Bay dunes generally occur as a narrow strip of dunes at the head of the bay with some penetration back onto the land surface. Relatively small bay systems set in cliffed coast are much influenced by fixed shelter factors of the surrounding topography. This greatly modifies the prevailing and dominant wind pattern of the general area so that dune systems only a few miles apart may be controlled by dominant winds from totally different directions. Ritchie and Mather (1969) have calculated the Exposure Index (pattern of wind incidence and direction) for a number of Scottish dune sites (Figs 9 and 10). Melvich Bay and Strathy Bay, both facing north on the north shore of Sutherland and, only 5 km apart, have dominant winds from the south and north west respectively. Sand supply

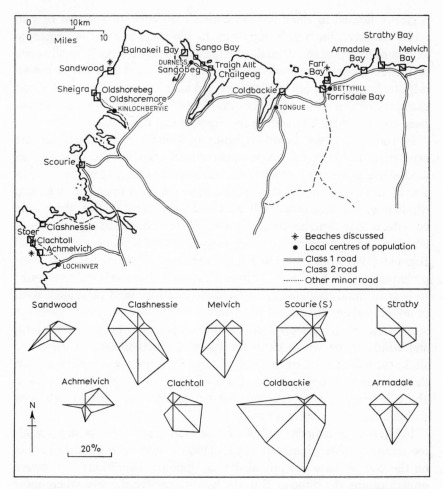

Fig. 9. Location of beaches in Sutherland, Scotland where Ritchie and Mather calculated exposure index as given in Fig. 10. (After Ritchie and Mather 1971)

Fig. 10. Exposure index for a selection of sites in Sutherland, Scotland as given in Fig. 9 (from Ritchie and Mather 1969)

is clearly limited in small bays in cliffed coast such as this, not only in actual resources, but also in supply as the bay headlands act as barriers to longshore transport of material. In large shallow open bays (virtually open coastline), growth of a dune system, may be limited to a single coastal ridge by limited supplies of backshore and high level foreshore sand. Good examples of this type of system are found along the Northumberland coast e.g. Druridge Bay and on the Scottish east coast.

In contrast, where broad expanses of backshore and foreshore are exposed in the inter-tidal zone opportunities exist for the largest of all sand dune systems to develop. In addition to the prograding systems already discussed, such shores orientated so that prevailing and dominant winds reinforce each others influence in an onshore direction, drive sand onto the land to form hindshore systems. The mechanics of vegetated dune building and movement are much in need of study along the lines that Bagnold (1941) has explored for un-vegetated desert dunes, but some preliminary work on this is given in Chapter 8. Here it is only necessary to bear in mind that just as Bagnold showed that sand movement itself profoundly alters the state of the wind, so the dune system itself alters the state of the wind. This produces continuous feedback between dune form and wind regime which expresses itself in differentiation of dune and slack, the basic land form units of all large hindshore dune systems. Note the contrast here between the effects of *fixed* topography as referred to above in small bay systems in cliffed coast and the *plastic* topography within a large dune system itself.

In effect what happens with abundant sand supplies but onshore winds too strong to allow significant progradation is that dune building grasses on the coastal dune are provided with optimum conditions for upward growth raising the dune level to the height limit for the area where more sand is lost than gained at the crest from wind erosion, and at the seaward toe, from wave erosion. Hereafter, the marine coastal dune, unable to repair the continuously eroding vertical faces on its seaward side, is eroded back to make way for new embryo dunes to develop on tidal litter cast to the limit of storm tides. Such a dune once set in motion continues inland until it is sufficiently flattened and sheltered to stabilize while a new coast dune builds vertically again. Between the two, erosion persists to the damp sand level where it stops and a slack surface is available for colonization. The ridge structure may be broken up into a series of parabola-shaped mobile dunes. Landsberg (1956) has developed formulae which give good correlation between orientation of the long axis of these parabolas and calculated wind resultant.

Perhaps the most significant distinction between these active hindshore systems and prograding systems stabilized *in situ* is the periodic re-exposure of bare sand at intervals in the mobile part of the system and the tendency to cyclic alternation of dune and slack at any particular point within it. Braunton Burrows, Devon, Newborough Warren, Anglesey and Ainsdale, Lancashire are among the best examples of hindshore systems in Britain. Full stabilization is only achieved when the landwardmost ridges are deflated to an almost flat plain at the dry slack level.

The last system in the dune series is really an extreme example of the hindshore system and has close affinity with its stable stage. Under extreme conditions of exposure on the north west coast of Scotland where the full force of Atlantic gales reach low lying islands, the height limit of dune building is so low that much of the sand from the shore is swept inland to form low lying sandy plains. The universal influence of open range sheep grazing or of cultivation of the lime-rich sandy pastures further limit the possibilities of dune development. Towards the landward side of these sandy plains or 'machairs' lime-rich sand thinly overlies lime-deficient moorland peat providing contrasting conditions for great variety of plant species.

Many salt marshes and sand dune systems are of course intermediate between the types distinguished on the maritime to terrestrial gradient. Familiarity with the series as a whole soon enables intermediate and apparent anomalies to be placed in the general framework described. We begin to see these plastic deposits of the coast moulded into recognizable forms by the four great agents, wind, water, land and living things, operating simultaneously upon them.

3   Mineral Nutrient Relations

The essential nutritional problem for plants that grow on salt marsh or calcareous dune soils is one of adaptation to growth on soils, with elevated levels of certain ionic species. Such adaptation is intimately concerned with osmotic effects. These partly control ionic concentrations either side of cell membranes and also the capacity of plants to function in the presence of elevated ionic levels, particularly of sodium. Although these adaptations can be studied at a variety of organizational levels; within the cell, within the whole plant, or within the community, they must be related to the capacity of a plant to survive, grow and reproduce in the habitat where selection operates at all levels in the life cycle; on individuals, populations and at the species level.

While elevated levels of sodium ions are the main problem for salt marsh plant growth, there is increasing evidence that high levels of calcium ions in addition exert profound effects on the tolerance of certain species to sodium and on the actual species composition of the salt marsh flora.

The sodium ion problem is only critical for a small but important element of the dune flora in at the coast where communities mainly at the species confined to the dune habitat occur. Elsewhere in the dune system the main nutritional problems for dune plants are either, growth in elevated levels of calcium ions or, the more widespread problem of general mineral deficiency.

The presence of high ionic levels makes it essential to discuss a number of soil physical parameters related to soil evolution, development, and structure since they have big effects on availability of ions for plants. It must be remembered also that ionic exchange is not confined to the soil and root boundary, but also to the leaf and water, or leaf and air boundaries. For example ionic exchange in *Zostera* occurs primarily through the leaf cuticle and salt may be exuded through leaf glands as in *Spartina* in addition to exchange through cuticle and stomata. Consideration of osmotic effects follows logically discussion of soil physical parameters. This in turn sets the scene for discussion of chemical parameters associated with nutrient uptake, salt tolerance mechanisms and ionic balance. This chapter concludes with a brief account of nutrient levels and availability in the two habitats. Nutrient supply and nutrient cycling at the community level are mentioned in passing but considered in more detail in appropriate places in the sections dealing with salt marshes and sand dunes separately.

Physical Constraints on the Chemical System

Effects of particle size composition

Kelley (1951) notes that the amount of growth of plants is much more seriously affected by exchangeable sodium in the soil than by equal amount in true solution. The yield of beans (*Phaseolus vulgaris*) for example has been shown to be much reduced by quite low levels of exchangeable sodium in the soil, but is maintained in the presence of soluble sodium at much higher concentrations (Bernstein and Pearson 1956). Now Lopez-Gonzales and Jenny (1959) have demonstrated with the aid of cation-exchange resin discs in contact and apart, that contact exchange of ions occurs much more rapidly than that by mass transfer of ions through the solution when discs were separated. As Heimann (1958) points out this suggests an explanation for the different effects of sodium in soil and solution on plant growth. In soil it seems likely that contact exchange mechanisms may operate additionally to mass flow under the influence of transpiration or diffusion mechanisms. If so, then ionic readjustments of equilibrium disturbed at the root surface by selective uptake may well be more rapidly compensated by the common pool of ions where solution mechanisms are at work than where less readily compensated contact exchange mechanisms are in operation. The ecologist might advance knowledge in this field by comparing the salinity tolerance of clonal material of different species in mud, sand and culture solution. It is clear that we should beware of concluding that tolerances in culture are immediately relevant to field conditions. Equally, in reporting field tolerances it is evidently important to specify the clay and organic matter content of the soil. The lengthy procedures associated with mechanical analysis have been a barrier to this, but water holding capacity of the soil can be quite rapidly measured and Glopper (1964) has shown this is closely correlated with the clay and organic matter content.

It is relevant at this point to recall the early experiments of Joseph and Oakley (1929) on the structural improvements to soil with impeded drainage produced by charging their exchange complexes with calcium or potassium ions. With either, this results in at least a halving of the water retaining capacity and a capillary rise of water increased by at least a factor of 40 compared with sodium-charged exchange complexes. These effects may not be important in lower salt marshes subject to regular inundation by sea-water, but they are likely to be important in improving both the nutrient environment and the amelioration of salinity at higher marsh levels.

Soil macrostructure

Salt marsh and sand dune soils form an extreme contrast so far as texture is concerned. Improvements in texture (and nutrient availability) in the salt marsh soil depend on factors *increasing* pore space; in contrast in sand dune soil factors *decreasing* pore space are instrumental in improving texture and nutrient availability.

Reduced incidence of flooding in higher marsh levels does not automatically improve texture as dried out sodium clays are mechanically difficult for roots to penetrate. Cracking of the surface helps, but only in a very localized way. Far more important are the biological effects of roots and the larger soil animals in opening up cavities. Green and Askew (1965) have investigated the activities of roots, ants, and earthworms in reclaimed marsh soils at Romney Marsh, Sussex, using infiltration techniques. They attribute the high fertility of these soils to improvements in drainage caused in this way.

Olson (1958 *a*) notes the improvements of exchange capacity with buildup of the clay fraction in an inland dune system and incidentally notes the value of dune soils for studies on dust fall and weathering.

Base exchange characteristics of salt marsh and sand dune soils

In young salt marsh muds there may be very little organic matter (less than 5 per cent) and the bulk of adsorbed ions will be associated with the clay mineral lattices which would be fully saturated with ions, presumably mainly sodium ions. The cation exchange capacity of different clay minerals varies considerably. For kaolinite it is approximately 3 to 15 mE; for illite and chlorite 10 to 40 mE; for montmorillonite 80 to 150 mE. (Grim 1953). Equivalence (E) is defined here as 1 mole of electronic charge (i.e. 96 487 coulombs) on the clay lattice complex. There have been very few analyses of the clay mineral composition of salt marsh muds, but Guilcher and

Berthois (1957) investigating the possible origin of salt marsh muds in Brittany showed that illite was the dominant clay mineral in that area. Unpublished work by Stebbings and Ball indicated that in muds at Poole Harbour, Dorset, and Bridgwater Bay, Somerset, illite and chlorite were dominant while in the upper reaches of the Fal estuary, Cornwall, the fine clay fraction was practically pure kaolinite. Now it is interesting that on the Fal estuary, *Scirpus maritimus* exhibits much poorer growth and flowering than in Bridgwater Bay, and Poole Harbour. At Bridgwater Bay it is true that the exceptionally strong growths there are also no doubt influenced by greatly increased nutrient supply and abundant calcium both of which may be limiting factors in the other two environments. However, the point to be made is that salt marsh muds do differ by as much as a factor of 10 in cation exchange capacity and this may well be partly responsible for differences in productivity.

Nutrient-deficient muds like those of the Fal estuary, could profitably be used as an experimental medium for studies on the effects of adding nutrients in relation to salt marsh plant growth. It would also be interesting to know the total cation exchange capacity of these muds in relation to the amount of organic matter as this might shed light on that part of the exchange capacity dependent on organic matter.

Sand dune soils with free carbonate are invariably base-saturated, but the total cation exchange capacity is itself low due to the very low clay and organic matter contents of the soil. In dune soils it is of the order of 10–15 mE. per 100 g and in dune slacks from 15–30 mE. per 100 g (Ranwell 1959). In dune sands devoid of free carbonate, either initially or through leaching, the exchange complexes are frequently partly unsaturated and this may occur even where the soil reaction is neutral (Table 2). We can see these figures in perspective against Renger's (1965) observations derived from over 1,500 soil samples estimating the mE. per 100 g of: organic matter (168 to 249); clay (38 to 51); silt (2 to 22) and sand (0·7 to 6·5).

Ecologists can make a useful contribution by studying field sites where a particular environmental factor is likely to exert an extreme influence. So far as nutrient deficiencies are concerned, the kaolin muds of the Fal estuary, Cornwall and the base deficient dunes of Winterton, Norfolk or Studland, Dorset are therefore recommended for study.

Osmotic Effects

Plant cells must maintain internal osmotic potential lower than the external osmotic potential or they lose water. The osmotic effect only becomes

Table 2. Base status of stable dune and slack soils at Newborough Warren, Anglesey beneath *Salix repens* associes. Equivalence (E) is defined as 1 mole of electronic charge (i.e. 96,487 coulombs) on the soil/organic complex (from Ranwell 1959).

Sample site	Sample depth (cm)	Exch. bases in mE/100 g oven-dry soil	Exch. H_2 in mE/100 g oven-dry soil	Total cation exch. cap. in mE/100 g oven-dry soil	% Base saturation	CaO as % of total exch. bases	CO_3 as % of weight of oven-dry soil	pH value Water	pH value KCl	Water table (free) depth (cm)
Fixed dune	8	12·02	0	12·02	100	79·07	0·03	7·8	7·3	> 200
Salicetum	30	19·09	0	19·09	100	60·82	0·23	8·8	8·2	
Fixed dry slack	8	2·76	0·61	3·37	81·9	67·11	0	5·3	5·0	104
turf	30	7·10	0·08	7·18	98·9	89·04	0	7·1	7·2	
Fixed dry slack	8	2·85	4·38	6·23	45·7	61·58	0	4·4	4·1	84
Salicetum	30	17·78	0·76	18·54	95·9	7·71	0	4·9	4·7	
Fixed wet slack	8	18·84	0	18·84	100	63·16	0·22	7·2	7·1	64
Salicetum	30	27·36	0	27·36	100	39·66	0·77	7·3	8·1	
Fixed wet-dry	8 (i)	17·09	2·46	19·55	87·4	86·22	0	6·1	6·3	
slack Salicetum	(ii)	16·12		18·58	86·8	89·76				
(+ *Calluna*)	30 (i)	27·54	0	27·54	100	48·51	0·61	7·5	8·0	79
	(ii)	32·75		32·75	100	59·91				

serious for non-halophytes at high external concentrations of salt in the order of 0·05 M (e.g. one tenth sea water strength) or more, corresponding to osmotic potentials around two bars (Epstein 1969). It is of interest that concentrations of salt of this order occur in the water flooding the seaward limit of tidal woodland in Europe marking a major change in the flora from few halophytes to many non-halophytes (see Stebbings 1971). Obligate halophytes subject to salinities at full strength sea water need to develop osmotic pressures greater than 20 bars to survive. Arnold's (1955) results (Table 3) show in fact that they do. The two exceptions (*Glaux maritima* and *Scirpus maritimus*) are facultative halophytes and persist for centuries in effectively non-saline habitats e.g. in dune slacks or old reclaimed marshland.

Table 3. Osmotic pressures of cell-sap of various halophytes and proportion due to chloride ion. One atm. is equal to 101325 Nm^{-2} (from Arnold 1955).

Species	No. of determinations	O.P. sap (atm.)	Proportion O.P. sap due to Cl^- (atm.)	Cl^- as per cent O.P. sap
Atriplex patula var. *hastata*	6	31·6	13·3	42
Suaeda fruticosa	15	35·2	15·3	43
Glaux maritima	2	14·6	7·4	51
Distichlis spicata	10	29·3	15·1	52
Juncus gerardi	3	27·8	15·5	56
Iva frutescens var. *oraria*	4	23·9	13·8	58
Suaeda nigra	2	41·1	24·7	60
Spartina glabra	4	27·0	16·9	62
Triglochin maritima	10	24·6	16·1	66
Scirpus maritimus	2	14·7	10·4	71
Salicornia rubra	11	44·3	31·5	71
Limonium carolinianum	4	29·2	21·4	73
Spartina patens	4	20·9	15·7	75
Salicornia ambigua	6	42·5	34·1	80
Salicornia stricta (*herbacea*)	10	39·7	35·9	91
Salicornia mucronata	3	34·0	31·5	93
	Av.	32·6	21·1	65 ± 11·2

There are four main effects of high external osmotic potential according to Slatyer (1967).

(1) It depresses growth and therefore yield of either the whole plant or parts of it and this effect occurs even with halophytes.

(2) It may depress transpiration initially, but not to the extent that growth is depressed. The extent to which this occurs depends in part on stomatal behaviour.

(3) It may have similar effects to low soil water content and reduce water availability.

(4) It induces excess ion accumulation in tissues which may combine with reduced uptake of essential mineral elements.

In the past workers have tended to give undue weight to the effect of osmotic pressure of the soil solution and pay little attention to the effect of soil matric pressure. The soil water potential (soil water stress) is now recognized to be a combination of these forces. However, the osmotic relations within the plant are modified by uptake of soil solutes and entry of excess salts. Therefore the effects of osmotic pressure of the soil solution and those of the soil matric pressure do not have equivalent effects on the internal osmotic relations of the plant tissue.

Experimental studies suggest that some reduction of metabolic function may be attributable to direct osmotic effects on internal water deficits, but this does not appear to be as pronounced as that caused by a similar reduction in substratum water potential caused by a reduction in soil water content. However these are short term responses to imposed salinity. The main long term effects of salinity are associated with ion accumulation (and therefore mineral uptake disturbance or toxic ion effects) in the plant rather than with reduced water availability in the substratum, as earlier workers tended to assume.

It follows that tolerance to elevated ionic levels therefore requires a high degree of selectivity in ion uptake. Excess accumulation of electrolytes in plant cells, particularly of sodium or chloride ions, is likely to result in progressive changes in protein hydration and conformation and enhancement or depression of enzyme activity resulting in gradual dislocation of metabolism.

Less tolerant species with less efficient ion discriminatory mechanisms may expend more respiratory energy, resulting in reduction of net assimilation rate and growth suppression, than more tolerant species with more efficient discriminatory mechanisms.

There is faster recovery from soil water stress than from salinity stress not only because of the more serious metabolic disturbances induced by the latter, but also as a result of the time required for excess ion accumulation within the plant to be diluted by new growth.

Mannitol has a large organic molecule which enters the cells of higher plants extremely slowly. A solution of mannitol can therefore be used to simulate osmotic effects similar to those produced by a solution of electrolytes, but without an immediate direct chemical effect on cell physiology.

However, mannitol is slowly metabolized and this must be kept in mind in the interpretation of experimental results. Parham (1970) has used solutions of mannitol to separate osmotic and ionic effects of saline solutions on the germination of halophyte seeds and this seems a very promising application of the technique. His results indicated that germination of *Plantago coronopus*, *P. lanceolata* and *P. major* seeds was inhibited by high ionic concentrations rather than high osmotic pressures. Germination of the halophytes *Plantago maritima* and *Triglochin maritima* and the non-halophyte *Triglochin palustris* occurred in high ionic concentrations, but was apparently inhibited by osmotic effects at salinities equivalent to a 70 per cent solution of sea water. However, it was shown that continued growth of the halophyte seedlings was better in solutions of sodium chloride than mannitol, while the reverse was found with the non-halophyte *Triglochin palustris*.

Chemical Problems of Nutrition in Elevated Ionic Environments

Nutrients essential for the growth of plants

At least 16 elements are required for the growth of all higher plants. They include: hydrogen, oxygen, carbon, potassium, calcium, magnesium, nitrogen, phosphorus, sulphur, iron, manganese, zinc, copper, chlorine, boron and molybdenum.

Cobalt is required for symbiotic nitrogen fixation in root nodules of legumes (Bollard and Butler 1966), and also for nitrogen fixation in blue-green algae. Diatoms have a specific requirement for silicon and there is evidence that the presence of silicon increases resistance to blast fungus disease in rice (Okuda and Takahashi 1965).

This is not the place to consider specific roles of mineral nutrients and Evans and Sorger (1966) have produced an excellent review of this subject. However, it is of some interest to see how concentrations of physiologically important elements are distributed in marine organisms compared with their distribution in sea water and Kalle's (1958) results for this are given in Table 4.

Other elements may be accumulated by sand dune or salt marsh plants without having any obvious nutritional role. For example *Lycium* species which occur on dunes and in other coastal habitats though not confined to the coast, accumulate especially high levels of lithium even when lithium is not abundant in the soil and the levels remain high throughout the growth period (Bollard and Butler 1966).

Table 4. Distribution of physiologically important elements in sea water organisms (from Kalle 1958).

Plastic Elements	Content of			Catalytic elements	Content of		
	100 g organism (dry) N	1 ml sea water 35% S, A	Ratio A/N		100 g organisms (dry) N	1 ml sea water 35% S, A	Ratio A/N
Hydrogen	7 g	10·75 kg		Copper	5 mg	10 mg	2
Sodium	3 g	390 g	3,600	Zinc	20 mg	5 mg	4
Potassium	1 g	390 g	390	Boron	2 mg	5 g	2,500
Magnesium	0·4 g	1·3 kg	3,300	Vanadium	3 mg	0·3 mg	0·1
Calcium	0·5 g	416 g	830	Arsenic	0·1 mg	15 mg	150
Carbon	30 g	28 g	1	Manganese	2 mg	5 mg	2·5
Silicon a	0·5 g	500 mg	1	Fluorine	1 mg	1·4 g	1,400
Silicon b	10 g	500 mg	0·05	Bromine	2·5 mg	66 g	26,000
Nitrogen	5 g	300 mg	0·06	Iron a	1 g	50 mg	0·05
Phosphorus	0·6 g	30 mg	0·05	Iron b	40 mg	50 mg	1·3
Oxygen as O_2 and CO_2	47 g	90 g	2	Cobalt	0·05 mg	0·1 mg	2
				Aluminium	1 mg	120 mg	120
				Titanium	100 mg		
Sulphur	1 g	900 g	900	Radium	$4 \cdot 10^{-12}$ g	10^{-10} g	25
Chlorine	4 g	19·3 kg	4,800				

Iodine has been shown to be incorporated in amino acids in *Salicornia perennis* and *Aster tripolium* (Fowden 1959) and it is well known that iodine often accumulates in marine algae, but it is not known to be essential for growth. The mangrove *Rhizophora harrisonii* accumulates aluminium and up to 10 per cent of the aluminium in the mud is in the form of a complex with organic matter beneath stands of this species.

Certain halophytes have been shown to have a specific requirement for sodium. *Atriplex vesicaria* grown in the absence of sodium in water culture showed severe growth retardation and chlorosis but recovered when sodium was added to the culture solution (Brownell 1965). *Salicornia perennis* and *Suaeda maritima* grow larger with sodium well in excess of amounts needed by non-halophytes (Pigott in Rorison 1969). These effects seem to be characteristic of mature plants for, as mentioned in Chapter 1, in general halophytes germinate more freely in lower than in high salinities.

Salt tolerance mechanisms

The study of nutrition in coastal plants is still in its infancy. Much more work has been done on the nutrition of crop plants grown with the aid of irrigation in the very extensive salinized soils of central continental areas. A vast literature on this subject exists and perhaps because of this, the problem of salinity in relation to coastal plants tends to be given undue prominence at the expense of other nutritional aspects equally vital to their growth.

Much of the work on crop plants is not directly relevant to halophytes, because the crop species have only a marginal as opposed to full salinity tolerance. Much of the crop plant work also rests on short period studies and does not shed light on the adaptive phenomena associated with halophytism. Of far greater relevance is work associated with extreme forms of salt tolerance.

There are certain bacteria (*Halobacteria*) which cannot survive in sodium chloride concentrations *less than* 2 M and show optimum growth at the extremely high concentration of 4·3 M sodium chloride. They have been the subject of intensive study and it is of particular interest that even these highly specialized organisms are believed to have metabolic pathways not basically different from those in non-halophilic bacteria (Larsen 1967). It follows that we would not expect to find the basic metabolism of salt marsh plants very different from that of plants in non-saline environments and this seems to be so. But it is remarkable the number of ways in which halophytes have become adapted to high salinity environments. Since they shed light on the central problem of nutrition, the maintenance of balanced ionic environment in the plant cell in the face of temporary or permanent imbalance with relation to the external medium, they are worth considering in more detail. Without this background, the ecologist cannot fully appreciate for example the significance of measurements of salinity tolerance in relation to soil physical and chemical structure, or narrow down his selection of field situations for experimental study to sites where nutritional factors are paramount for the survival of particular species.

There are at least four ways in which halophytes have become adapted to enable normal metabolic functioning in high sodium environments: ion selection; ion extrusion; ion accumulation and ion dilution. Many halophytes exhibit more than one of these adaptations simultaneously and the relative importance of each in any particular species may vary according to the stage of growth and environmental conditions.

As we have seen, the extreme form of adaptation in which organisms can only function in the presence of abnormally high sodium levels occurs in the *Halobacteria* and marine algae, both of which are capable of a high degree of selective ion absorption (of potassium for example) in the presence of high sodium concentrations in the external medium.

Recently Parham (1970) has shown that in this respect certain flowering plant halophytes exhibit such marine algal-type properties. Maximum uptake of potassium into the roots of *Triglochin maritima* was shown to occur only when the concentration of both sodium and potassium in the external solution was high and moreover this uptake was shown to be metabolically mediated. This species, like *Salicornia* and *Suaeda maritima*, is therefore in the true sense an obligate halophyte.

Many species such as *Avicennia* and *Spartina* have long been known to practise ion extrusion via special salt glands on the shoots and there is evidence of sodium ion 'out pumps' in submerged halophytes and algae (Pollard and Butler 1970.)

Ion accumulation in parts of the plant where concentrations may be stored away from active metabolic sites is probably a feature of most halophytes. For example *Agropyron elongatum* accumulates chlorides in the roots which, as in most grasses, are shed annually together with accumulated ions. Similarly it is commonly observed that in periods of drought on high marsh levels the leaves of *Limonium* die off prematurely shedding accumulated ions as they do so.

The development of succulence is another feature common to many halophytes (e.g. *Aster*) and this has the effect of increasing ion dilution by increasing the volume to surface area ratio of the plant.

Ionic balance

Gutnecht and Dainty (1968) suggest that the evolution of a sodium 'out-pump' may have developed in the earliest living systems in response to the need to control osmosis and that subsequently, with the development of a mechanically resistant cell wall, the sodium pump remained primarily for nutritional purposes. With elegant reasoning they go on to postulate that since extrusion of sodium ions results in high intracellular concentrations of potassium ions this would lead to enzyme adaptation to a high potassium ion environment and evolution of the inward potassium ion pumps. Sodium may also stimulate the growth of many organisms under conditions where potassium is deficient (Evans and Sorger 1966).

Several recent authors have drawn attention to the importance of calcium in enabling plants to grow in saline conditions (e.g. *Avicennia* (Macnae 1966) and *Agropyron* species (Elzam and Epstein 1969)). The sodium concentrations in leaves of *Phaseolus* fell by a factor of 16 over a range of calcium sulphate from 1×10^{-4}M to 3×10^{-3}M in 5×10^{-2}M sodium chloride solutions indicating a massive breakthrough of sodium to leaves in calcium sulphate concentrations below 3×10^{-3}M (i.e. 0·01 per cent calcium). It is suggested that calcium is essential for the maintenance of the integrity of selective ion transport mechanisms (especially selective absorption of potassium in the presence of sodium) at the surface of the absorbing cells of the roots where the entry of ions into the roots is governed.

Ionic balance and hydrogen ion concentration

In salt marsh soils the ionic balance is dominated by sodium. In dune soils landward of significant sea spray influence, the concentration of cations in solution is determined, either by a dominant calcium inflow (from shell fragments) or (in calcium-deficient sands), by the concentrations of nitrate, sulphate and bicarbonate anions resulting from (in part) microbial activity (Black 1968). The salt spray effect imposes a very localised nutritional regime at the dune coast well illustrated by the results of Gorham (1958), Willis et al (1959) and Sloet van Oldruitenborgh (1969) in respect of sodium, magnesium, and chloride (Tables 5 and 6). Its effects on the dune flora are masked by the severe limitations on the number of species that can occur because of high soil mobility. The nutritional effect of salt spray is much more readily appreciated on low coastal cliffs on acid soil where heath is replaced by a narrow band of grassland in the spray-dominated zone (e.g. in low offshore islands like the Isles of Scilly).

The salt effect is negligible in dune soils further inland from the coast.

E

Table 5. Soluble materials in dune sands from Blakeney Point, Norfolk. Equivalence (E) is defined as 1 mole of electronic charge (i.e. 96,487 coulombs) (from Gorham 1958 a).

	1 Embryo dunes	2 Sand hills (Ammophila)	3 Face of main ridge (Ammophila)	4 Laboratory dunes (Ammophila-Festuca)	5 Laboratory dunes (Carex arenaria)	6 Long Hills (Ammophila-Festuca)	7 The Hood (Ammophila-Carex arenaria)	8 Lifeboat House well 1957	9 Lifeboat House well 1955 (analysed 1957)
pH (original)	8·2	8·1	7·9	6·2	5·7	6·1	5·7	7·9	8·6
(aerated)	7·9	7·9	7·8	7·7	7·0	7·6	7·1	8·6	8·7
Specific conductivity (micromhos at 20°C)	10	53	54	45	28	51	50	551	656
Sum of cations	0·18	0·60	0·61	0·52	0·29	0·57	0·52	6·57	7·73
Sodium	0·46	0·08	0·08	0·04	0·04	0·07	0·15	3·65	4·94
Potassium	0·05	0·03	0·04	0·04	0·04	0·07	0·11	0·20	0·24
Calcium	0·49	0·42	0·43	0·21	0·08	0·23	0·08	1·53	1·30
Magnesium	0·17	0·07	0·05	0·15	0·07	0·09	0·08	1·18	1·25
Ammonium (mE/200 g dry sand)	0·006	0·004	0·008	0·08	0·06	0·11	0·10	0·009	nil
Bicarbonate	0·49	0·47	0·47	0·35	0·12	0·29	0·15	3·56	3·95
Chloride	0·42	0·05	0·06	0·01	0·02	0·04	0·08	2·16	2·91
Sulphate	0·21	0·07	0·06	0·07	0·08	0·12	0·17	0·80	0·87
Phosphate	0·004	0·004	0·006	0·05	0·05	0·11	0·11	0·004	<0·001
Nitrate	0·011	0·005	0·004	0·001	<0·001	<0·001	<0·001	0·019	0·009
Silica (p.p.m. SiO$_2$)	1·6	1·6	1·5	1·0	1·0	1·1	1·0	8·1	8·1
Optical density (log $\frac{I_0}{I}$ at 320 mμ, 10 cm cells)	0·5	0·5	0·6	2·0	2·4	2·7	3·9	0·5	0·5
Na/Cl ratio	1·1	1·6	1·3	4·0	2·0	1·8	1·9	1·7	1·7
Mg/Cl ratio	0·4	1·4	0·8	15·0	3·5	2·3	1·0	0·6	0·4
Ca/HCO$_2$ ratio	1·0	0·9	0·9	0·6	0·7	0·8	0·5	0·4	0·3
*CaCO$_3$ (% dry wt. of soil)		0·28–0·61		nil–0·64		nil–0·05	nil–0·05		
*Ignition loss (% dry wt. of soil, corrected for carbonates)		0·2–0·5		0·3–0·9		0·6–2·7	0·6–6·3		

*Soil data from Salisbury (1922).

Table 6. Chemical analyses of the soils from different types of vegetation at Braunton Burrows, Devon (from Willis *et al* 1959)

The results are expressed per gm dry weight of soil.

	Dry dunes							Slacks and hollows						
	Ammophila fore dunes	Pure Ammophiletum (main dunes)	Mixed Ammophiletum	Dry dune pasture	Stable pasture with lichens	Pteridietum	Dune scrub	Slack near sea	Plantago-Leontodon community	Festuca-Agrostis pasture	Festuca-Carex flacca pasture	Caricetum nigrae	Salicetum repentis	Salicetum atrocinereae
pH	9·05	9·06	8·79	8·70	8·66	8·60	8·18	8·99	8·73	8·42	8·22	8·12	8·11	8·06
Organic Carbon mg	0·52	0·19	0·94	0·74	2·44	4·47	12·60	0·41	1·39	5·82	9·23	22·93	13·55	19·47
Total Nitrogen mg	0·18	0·11	0·20	0·23	0·41	0·67	2·15	0·15	0·26	0·81	1·36	2·38	1·38	2·82
Calcium mg	70·4	69·5	62·3	57·3	60·6	49·2	33·9	64·4	66·1	49·1	62·0	46·8	50·4	45·2
Magnesium µg	2,270	990	1,070	1,060	880	980	220	1,570	1,470	770	970	570	280	240
Sodium µg	528	14	11	6	11	14	55	15	25	17	24	50	26	81
Potassium µg	50	6	9	7	7	12	13	11	14	18	6	26	15	17
Carbonate mg	119·6	115·4	103·9	92·8	98·2	78·4	51·0	109·7	112·1	75·9	96·6	73·5	78·3	68·4
Phosphate-P µg	109	110	98	107	59	91	148	112	110	103	108	133	110	131
Chloride µg	845	14	7	3	3	3	10	10	25	14	17	29	22	39

In these regions, the hydrogen ion concentrations of the soil solution exerts profound effects on both nutrient availability and on concentrations of ions which may have toxic effects in the soil solution.

At high pH values for example there may be a decrease in availability of potassium, phosphorus and iron due in part to competition for sites on soil ion exchange complexes. The solubilities of metallic cations vary markedly at different hydrogen ion concentrations (Sparling 1967). In general they tend to increase with increasing hydrogen ion concentrations (i.e. at lower pH values). This effect is particularly marked with aluminium which may be released in soluble form in toxic concentrations at pH values around 4. There is also a marked increase in the solubilities of many other metallic cations around pH 7.

High levels of soluble aluminium may interfere with uptake of calcium, phosphorus and iron at low pH values. In toxic concentrations aluminium inhibits root growth, particularly in seedlings (Bollard and Butler 1966), so it would be interesting to experiment with calcicole members of the dune flora to see how their seedlings respond to varying aluminium levels where these species become eliminated from the more leached parts of a dune system.

Nutrient Levels and Availability

We are now in a better position to appreciate the significance of the general nutrient levels in salt marsh and dune soils in relation to availability. It must be stressed however that much of the older data is of limited value because of inadequacies of sampling and methodology. In view of this, emphasis is given to more recent work.

General levels of the commoner nutrients in salt marsh soils are given by Chapman (1960); Zonneveld (1960); Goodman and Williams (1961); Ranwell (1961 a, b) and Piggott (in Harrison 1966), and in dune dune soils by Gimingham (1951); Gorham (1958 a); Olsen (1958 a); Ranwell (1959); Willis et al (1959); Willis and Yemm (1961); and Freijsen (1964). The nutrient supply from rainfall, a source of particular importance to dune plants, has been analysed by Gorham (1958 b), Allen et al (1968), and Parham (1970).

Macro-nutrients

Both sea water and shore sand are very deficient in nitrogen, but so far as pioneer salt marsh plants are concerned this may be a distinct advantage as lush, brittle growth induced by high nitrogen levels would be subject to severe damage from wave action. Supplies in marsh mud are probably augmented by fixation of atmospheric nitrogen by blue-green algae the precursors of salt marsh growth. Gorham (1958 *a*) shows that nitrate nitrogen is distinctly higher in the embryo dunes subject to spray than further landward, but organic matter in tidal litter is undoubtedly an important source of nitrogen in this region. Also, Metcalfe (*pers. comm.*) has shown that *Azotobacter* is widely distributed in dune soils and again fixation of atmospheric nitrogen by this means is probably an important nitrogen source for the younger dune communities (see Chapter 9).

It is well known that organic carbon, and with it total nitrogen, augments with increasing age and increasing density of plant cover on dunes. The rate of increase in damp slacks due to inflow of nutrients from leaching and reduced rate of organic matter breakdown in the wetter soils, is faster than on dunes (Ranwell 1959; Willis *et al* 1959). Little is known about the changes in total nitrogen from seaward to landward in salt marshes, but evidence from newly accreted surface layers at Bridgwater Bay show an increasing trend in nitrogen (Table 7) from bare mud to marsh levels near high water mark. A similar trend was also found in Poole Harbour marshes. Since both marshes are dominated by *Spartina anglica* we can see also how the much higher soil moisture levels at Poole dependent on a high clay content result in almost twice as much organic carbon and total nitrogen compared with the more freely draining coarser-particled marsh soil at Bridgwater Bay.

Table 7. Nutrient content of newly accreted silt, 0 to 0·5 cm depth, from *Spartina anglica* marsh, Bridgwater Bay, Somerset, sampled 7 Nov. 1962 (from Ranwell 1964 *b*).

Sampling site	Distance seaward (m)	% oven dry weight of silt					% volume of wet silt				
		K	Ca	P	N	Organic carbon	K	Ca	P	N	Organic carbon
Level *Spartina*	30	2·2	5·11	0·11	0·30	5·66	1·27	2·94	0·06	0·17	3·26
Level *Spartina*	150	2·1	5·17	0·10	0·29	6·39	1·26	3·11	0·02	0·17	3·85
Spartina on ridge	230	1·3	5·62	0·08	0·14	4·68	1·38	5·55	0·08	0·14	4·63
Bare mud on ridge	230	1·1	6·11	0·07	0·11	3·80	1·03	5·74	0·07	0·10	3·57

Hesse (1961) however has shown that organic matter type may override soil conditions, for example he finds greater accumulation of organic matter beneath *Rhizophora* than *Avicennia* even though the soil of the latter had a higher clay content.

Total nitrogen does not of course tell us much about availability and inorganic nitrogen added to *Rhizophora* mud was rapidly immobilized (Table 8), presumably through bacterial consumption since the carbon/nitrogen ratio of 36 was extremely high. In dune soils the C/N ratio is usually less than 10 (Willis *et al* 1959) though Olson (1958) did find a ratio of 20 in ancient inland dune forest soils. In salt marsh soils the ratio usually lies between 10 and 20 but it may be higher at least for short periods where tidal litter accumulates. In spite of the frequent references to nitrophilous species being associated with tidal litter deposits, one of the commonest (*Atriplex hastata*) has been shown to grow on highly nitrogen-deficient substrata (Weston 1964).

Table 8. The immobilization of nitrogen by fibrous mangrove-swamp soil. Results on an oven-dry basis (from Hesse 1961).

Soil	ppm NH$_4$-N		ppm NO$_3$-N	
	Initial	After 15 days	Initial	After 15 days
Mud alone	12·5	14·0	0	1·6
Mud + (NH$_4$)$_2$SO$_4$ at 2 cwt/acre 6″	32·0	10·2	0	2·2

Some extremely interesting studies have been carried out recently on nitrogen availability to *Suaeda maritima* in Conway estuary marshes, North Wales (Stewart *et al* 1972). They have shown that total nitrogen, soluble amino acids, and nitrate show a well marked gradient which decreased in *Suaeda* tissue from seaward to landward up the marsh. Using an enzyme bio-assay technique they showed that nitrate reductase levels in *Suaeda maritima* were found to be as much as 40 to 50 times higher in plants from low-lying seaward parts, as opposed to higher-lying landward parts, of the salt marsh (Table 9). This adaptive behaviour of the enzyme system is an intriguing example of physiological plasticity. We know very little about this in salt marsh plants. The results also suggest that the actual through-put of nitrate as a result of daily incursions of the tide in lower marsh levels is very much higher than the supply at higher marsh levels rarely reached by the tide, even though the total nitrogen values of the soil are highest in the latter.

Table 9. Nitrate reductase activity in samples of *Suaeda maritima* from different levels in a salt marsh on the Conway estuary, Caernarvonshire. Figures in brackets refer to number of samples taken randomly at each site (from Stewart *et al* 1972).

| Site | μ moles NO_2/h/g fresh wt. | | μ moles NO_2/h/mg protein |
	Average value	Range of values	Average value
1 (Seaward)	5·55 (8)	4·86–6·14	0·62
2	2·45 (6)	2·01–2·69	0·40
3	1·84 (12)	1·09–2·49	0·21
4	0·81 (5)	0·41–1·19	0·11
5 (Landward)	0·11 (8)	0·08–0·16	0·01

Hesse (1963) has studied the forms in which phosphate occurs and their distribution in mangrove swamp mud (Fig. 11). He gives a useful discussion of the complexities associated with phosphate availability in saline muds.

The responses of salt marsh species from low marsh and high marsh levels to nitrogen and phosphate fertilisers have been examined by Pigott (in Rorison 1969). *Salicornia* species and *Suaeda maritima* grown on their own marsh soils with and without fertilizer all showed response to nitrogen

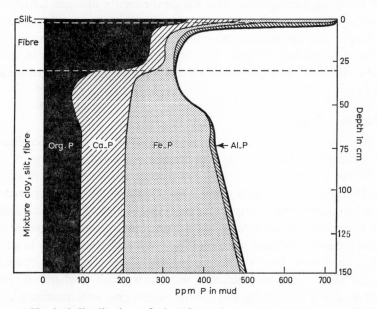

Fig. 11. Vertical distribution of phosphorus in mangrove-swamp mud (from Hesse 1963).

and phosphate fertilizer at higher marsh levels. In the case of the pioneer species *Salicornia dolichostachya,* growth on cores of bare mud was rapid with or without the addition of nitrogen. It was also shown that *Halimione portulacoides* taken from sub-optimal growth sites responded to nitrogen and phosphate. The apparent nutrient deficiency symptoms found in high marsh plants might be due in part to deficient water supply and soil mechanical restrictions on rooting since high marsh levels may dry out considerably in summer as Pigott points out.

Willis and Yemm (1961) used turf transplants and tomato culture to reveal that nitrogen, phosphate, and potassium were deficient in the soils of a calcareous dune system. Big responses to complete fertilizer applications were also found in both dune and slack vegetation resulting in a marked increase in grasses at the expense of lower-growing herbs and bryophytes (Willis 1963). The changes were in fact remarkably similar to those occurring in dune vegetation following myxomatosis, (Ranwell 1960 *b*). This illustrates the improved nutritional status that conservation of organic matter beneath taller vegetation can bring to these relatively arid soils. One notable effect of mineral deficiency is to restrain growth of fast growing species resulting in the maintenance of high species diversity.

Both Brown and Hafenrichter (1948) and Augustine *et al* (1964) found that ammonium compounds were the most effective nitrogen fertilizers in experiments concerned with promoting growth of *Ammophila* plantations on dunes. The controlled release fertilizer magnesium ammonium phosphate with potassium added, gave highly significant increases in growth over controls in *Ammophila arenaria* and *A. breviligulata*. (Augustine *et al* 1964).

Micro-nutrients

Willis (1963) found no significant response to trace element fertilization (iron, sodium, manganese, zinc, copper or molybdenum) in dunes.

Gorham and Gorham (1965) record that ash from salt marsh plants was 2 to 10 times greater than in plants from other habitats. However, iron was from $\frac{1}{3}$ to $\frac{1}{15}$, and manganese from $\frac{1}{7}$ to $\frac{1}{25}$ that of plants from other habitats. It is suggested that ion antagonism may prevent iron and manganese ions, mobilized in the reduced state, entering salt marsh plants freely in an ion-rich environment. Adams (1963) found that plants of *Spartina alterniflora* became chlorotic in iron-deficient soils where high level marsh species such as *Distichalis spicata* and *Juncus roemerianus* were unaffected. The *Spartina* responded to experimental foliar applications of ferrous sulphate or the addition of iron to a saline nutrient solution. Now *Spartina alterniflora* is restricted to low marsh where the mean soluble iron content is in excess of 4 p.p.m. Adams suggests that iron deficiency may limit the growth of *Spartina* in high level marsh. He also notes that iron becomes available through the action of anaerobic iron-reducing bacteria and observed that *Spartina alterniflora* shows the greatest tendency towards chlorosis in better-drained, rather than wetter sites at the high marsh level.

PART TWO   Salt Marshes

4 Salt Marshes:
Tidal Influence

Salt marsh formation normally begins at a level subject to salt water tidal inundation twice daily. The upper level of the tidal influence, where salt marsh is replaced by fresh-water marsh, is subject to tidal inundation only a few times a year at the spring and autumn equinoxes, and then by almost fresh water. Between these two extremes organisms are zoned according to the range of conditions they can withstand; conditions dominated by the tide at lower levels, but almost independent of them at the highest levels.

It follows that efforts to explain zonation as a whole in relation to any one factor such as duration of tidal submergence or salinity is bound to fail not only in relation to different species, but even in relation to upper and lower limits of the same species where these have wide vertical ranges.

So far as survival, growth and reproduction of organisms in the inter-tidal zone is concerned, tidal factors of particular importance include: intensity and frequency of *mechanical disturbance* due to tidal action; the *vertical range* over which the tide operates which controls tidal flooding depths and the vertical extent of salt marsh; the *form of tidal cycle* which controls frequency and duration of submergence and emergence, and *water quality* which controls the amount of light reaching submerged growths and the salinity to which they are subjected.

Tidal Parameters

Tidal disturbance

Forward colonization of a salt marsh only takes place in relatively sheltered inlets or behind broad expanses of tidal flats where much of the energy of waves has already been dissipated. Under these conditions waves are relatively low in height and do not exert much force in their downward plunge on breaking. On these relatively level shores the swash, or landward motion of the water, tends to be more powerful than the backwash. The aerial parts of a pioneer plant are first pulled landward strongly and then pulled seaward less strongly as a wave completes its breaking.

There is much evidence (Ragotskie 1959, Møller 1964 and Pestrong 1965) that ebb flow reaches higher velocities than flood flow and controls drainage patterns in tidal channels on salt marshes and this is a subject we shall return to in Chapter 5. However, it is of interest to note here that Bradley (in Ragotskie 1959) found that tidal velocities of flood currents 3 cm above a tidal flat were consistently 15 to 20 per cent higher than those of the ebb.

No attempts appear to have been made to measure the strength of the water-borne forces required to break salt marsh plants or uproot them and this would be a profitable line of study of fundamental importance to an understanding of conditions required for salt marsh formation.

Clearly, as well as the force, the frequency with which a plant is rocked back and forth by the water affects its chances of survival. Wave force and frequency varies with both distant and local weather conditions but the maximum incidence of wave break tends to occur on a salt marsh at the

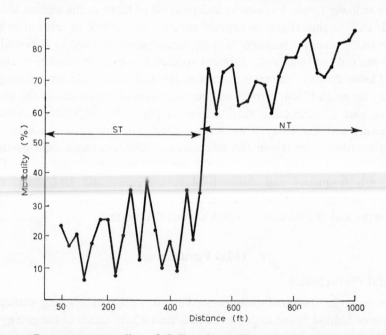

Fig. 12. Percentage mortality of *Salicornia* seedlings in the spring tide (ST) zone and the neap tide (NT) zone (From Chapman 1960, after Wiehe 1935).

level of mean high water neap tides because most tides pass over or reach this point and more waves have time to break there while the tide is on the turn.

Wiehe (1935) has shown that the density of *Salicornia* seedlings in the spring tide zone increases from 2 to 6 times that in the neap tide zone and that a two fold increase in density occurs within a 30 m distance above the top of the neap tide zone. In his work on the Dovey estuary in Wales he found *Salicornia* seedling mortalities of 60 per cent or more in the neap tide zone but less than 40 per cent in the spring tide zone (Fig. 12). As Chapman (1960) points out in relation to these observations, the sharp rise in seedling mortality occurs at the level flooded daily by the tides and mortality is a direct result of tidal water washing out a high percentage of the seedlings.

Brereton (1965) found that during the first half of the period March to June *Salicornia* seeds continue to germinate at a rate sufficient to offset losses due to up-rooting by the tide so that seedling density increases. In

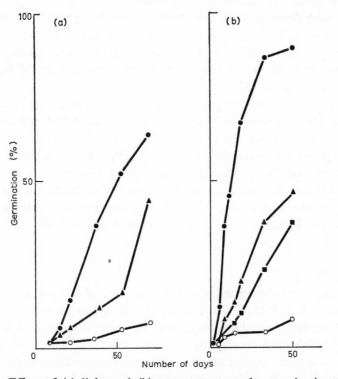

Fig. 13. Effect of (a) light and (b) temperature on the germination of seed of *Spartina anglica*. Light: ●, dark; ▲, 8 h; ○, 16 h. Temperature: ●, 25°C; ▲, 20°C; ■, 15°C; ○, 7°C. (from Hubbard 1970).

the second half of this period the rate of germination falls off but the uprooting effect of the tide does not and seedling density decreases.

Chapman (1960) suggests that pioneer species need a specific period of time of continuous emergence of the marsh surface so that seedlings are not swept away by the tides. In fact newly germinated seedlings of *Spartina anglica* at the seaward edge of the marsh at Bridgwater Bay, Somerset were invariably found with seed cases and/or stem collars from 2 to 10 cm below the mud surface. The seeds must have germinated below the surface and Hubbard (1970) has shown that both rate and amount of germination of this species is greater in the dark than in the light (Fig. 13). It follows that the period of continuous submergence is more likely to be related to the light requirements of the emerging seedling shoot than to mud surface stability given that wave action is sufficiently moderate to allow establishment to occur at all. Experimental work on the establishment of pioneer species from ripe seed buried at different depths and on the light requirements of newly emerged seedlings is indicated.

It is interesting to note that Stevenson and Emery (1958) obtained germination of *Salicornia bigelowii* in seeds completely submerged in sea water. Also tests on the seeds of five Australian salt marsh species showed that none were prevented from germination beneath 5 cm of tap water (Clarke and Hannon 1970).

The density of *Spartina anglica* seedlings in the neap tide zone at the seaward edge of a marsh in Bridgwater Bay, Somerset was at a maximum opposite the centre of the marsh and diminished regularly towards the more exposed and disturbed ends of the marsh. This again suggested that mechanical disturbance was regulating seedling density. Even in the most favourable zone for establishment 40 per cent of seedlings marked in July 1964 were missing after one month. Of the young plants wintering 50 per cent survived to become established clumps by the following August (Table 10).

Tide range

Tidal range varies enormously in different parts of the world from a few centimetres (e.g. in the Baltic and the Mediterranean) to nearly 19 metres (e.g. in the Bay of Fundy, Nova Scotia). However, the period of tidal cycle from one high water level to the next has a fixed period of about 12 hours predetermined by regular astronomical events. Consequently the vertical range in which salt marsh formation can take place is very much greater in the big tide range areas than in the smallest ones. Further in the big tide range areas there is room for a series of communities zoned according to the tidal conditions. In the smallest tide range (e.g. in the Baltic) tidal movements may be strongly modified by over-riding weather effects, nevertheless distinctive vegetational zonation related to duration of submergence is still found in such situations (Tyler 1971). Changes in atmospheric pressure alone are sufficient to depress or increase water level by as much as 30 cm in the Danish Wadden sea (Jacobsen, N.K. *pers. comm*); on west Swedish coasts where the tidal range is about 30 cm, changes in wind direction and atmospheric pressure give non-periodic water level ranges up to 170 cm (Gillner 1965).

Table 10. Survival of newly germinated *Spartina anglica* seedlings on open mud at the seaward limit of the Bridgwater Bay marsh, Somerset. Seedlings were searched for within a mudflat area 450 × 150 m (long axis parallel to the shore) and marked with a bamboo cane 1 m away.

Date	No. of marked sites (out of 50 originally marked) located	No. of marked seedlings still present	Survival %
13/7/64	50	50	100
17/8/64	48	30	62
23/9/64	47	22	46
14/6/65	45	10	22
27/8/65	45	9	20

Tide curve modifications

It is an observed fact that the tidal curve steepens up estuary though its ultimate amplitude of course diminishes eventually to zero. It was noted that the lower limits of *Spartina anglica* marsh in Poole Harbour, Dorset were higher at successive intervals up estuary (Ranwell *et al* 1964), though the differences were small and only just significant. However, Beeftink (1966) has shown on the Scheldt estuary in Holland that different species do retreat to higher levels upstream apparently proportionate to the steepening of the tidal curve.

Contrasted Habitats in Submergence and Emergence Zones

Tidal submergence

If the duration of tidal submergence per annum is plotted against vertical level within the tide range, the curve obtained is typically S-shaped (Fig. 14). In Poole Harbour, Dorset a difference in marsh level of 10 cm near high water spring tides gives difference of only about 100 hours submergence per year. In contrast, a difference in marsh level of 10 cm near high

F

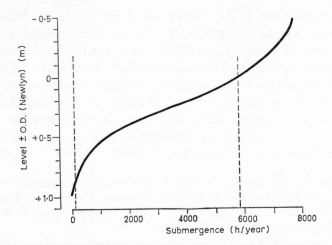

Fig. 14. Duration of submergence per annum in relation to O.D. levels. Broken lines mark upper and lower limits of *Spartina*. Derived from tide gauge records at Poole Bridge, Poole Harbour, July 1962 to July 1963 (from Ranwell *et al* 1964).

water neap tides gives a difference of about 700 hours submergence per year. In other words level is much more sensitively related to submergence at the marsh seaward limit than at its landward limit.

Now it is common knowledge that many salt marsh plants can survive much longer periods of submergence in the quiet waters of sheltered brackish lagoons than they are ever likely to experience at their seaward limits of growth in open marsh conditions. Hubbard (1969) has shown that *Spartina anglica* may be submerged throughout daylight hours during certain neap tide periods (Fig. 15) and it can also withstand submergence in the laboratory for at least $4\frac{1}{2}$ months. So submergence itself is not critical for survival of these, the lowest growing salt marsh species.

Apart from any mechanical effect, the big difference between quiet saline water and tidal water flooding an open marsh is that the former tends to be clear while the latter is turbid with silt in suspension and this cuts down the length of time available for photosynthesis. It is remarkable that virtually no work seems to have been done on light as a limiting factor for establishment, growth, and survival of salt marsh plants, though shading effects are obvious wherever a salt marsh is overhung by trees.

The most turbid non-toxic tidal waters in Britain are found in Cornish estuaries clouded by sediment derived from china clay mining activities in the catchment. In the upper estuary of the River Fal this results in a

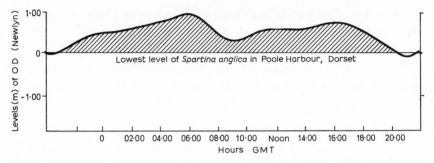

Fig. 15. Tidal curve showing the lowest level of *Spartina anglica* in Poole Harbour and the extent of its immersion (hatched area) by a neap tide on 5 November 1962. Readings obtained from the tide gauge on Poole Harbour, Dorset (from Hubbard 1969).

truncation of salt marsh zonation which precludes entirely the development of lower marsh levels. *Puccinellia maritima* growth is confined to the extreme upper limit of its vertical range where it shares a pioneer role with *Triglochin maritima* and other species of higher marsh levels.

Effects of turbidity on photosynthetic activity might be investigated using algal culture techniques (see Hopkins 1962).

Pioneer salt marsh plants capable of withstanding regular submergence must also withstand extremely low oxygen levels especially in marsh soils with a high clay content. However even in the exceptionally poorly drained soils associated with 'die-back' in *Spartina anglica* marsh, Goodman and Williams (1961) were unable to find direct evidence of damage primarily due to anaerobiosis.

Submergence and Emergence marshes

From extensive studies in British and American marshes on frequency and duration of submergence, Chapman (1960) concludes there is a fundamental distinction between lower marshes and higher marshes with the line of demarcation at about mean high water level. He notes that 'lower marshes commonly undergo more than 360 submergences per annum, their *maximum* period of continuous exposure never exceeds nine days, whilst there is more than 1·2 hours submergence *per diem* in daylight. Upper marshes on the other hand undergo less than 360 submergences annually, their *minimum* period of continuous exposure exceeds ten days, and there is less than one hour's submergence daily during daylight.'

However, as Chapman points out, this does not hold for the San Francisco Bay marshes studied by Hinde (1954). Moreover data on zonation and numbers of both algae and phanerogams given by Chapman (in Steers 1960) in his study area at Scolt Head Island, Norfolk, show no really significant disjunction at the proposed demarcation line (Figs 16 and 17).

Numbers of phanerogam species augment rapidly from seaward to landward, because only very few are adapted to regular submergence.

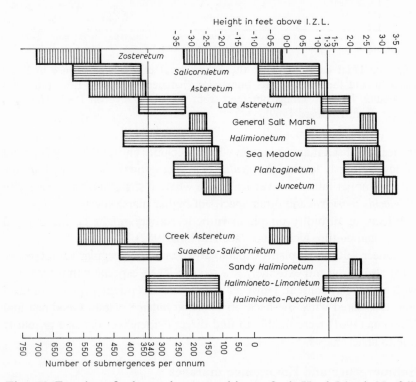

Fig. 16. Zonation of salt marsh communities at Scolt Head Island, Norfolk. Levels and number of tidal submergences per annum (0 OD = 1.2 ft O.D. Newlyn). The lines at 1·30 ft and 340 submergences per annum mark the approximate division between Submergence and Emergence marsh (from Chapman in Steers, 1960).

It is of particular interest that Chapman (1940) found that it was characteristic of American salt marsh species that 'the further south they spread on the continent the more tolerant they are of submergence (i.e. the lower they go in the tidal plane).' Although he adduces temperature as the factor possibly responsible for this it seems more likely that stronger light intensities and temperature act together to allow photosynthesis at deeper levels of submergence further south.

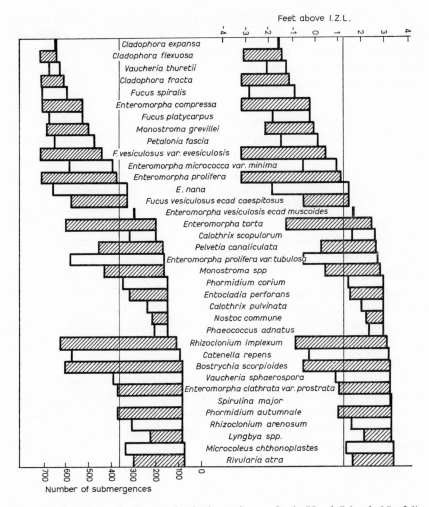

Feet above I.Z.L.

Cladophora expansa
Cladophora flexuosa
Vaucheria thuretii
Cladophora fracta
Fucus spiralis
Enteromorpha compressa
Fucus platycarpus
Monostroma grevillei
Petalonia fascia
F. vesiculosus var. evesiculosis
Enteromorpha micrococca var. minima
Enteromorpha prolifera
E. nana
Fucus vesiculosus ecad caespitosus
Enteromorpha vesiculosis ecad muscoides
Enteromorpha torta
Calothrix scopulorum
Pelvetia canaliculata
Enteromorpha prolifera var. tubulosa
Monostroma spp
Phormidium corium
Entocladia perforans
Calothrix pulvinata
Nostoc commune
Phaeococcus adnatus
Rhizoclonium implexum
Catenella repens
Bostrychia scorpioides
Vaucheria sphaerospora
Enteromorpha clathrata var. prostrata
Spirulina major
Phormidium autumnale
Rhizoclonium arenosum
Lyngbya spp.
Microcoleus chthonoplastes
Rivularia atra

Number of submergences

Fig. 17. Zonation of salt marsh algal species at Scolt Head Island, Norfolk. Levels and number of tidal submergences per annum (0·0 ft I.Z.L. = + 7 ft O. D. Newlyn). The lines at 1·30 ft and 340 submergences per annum mark the approximate division between Submergence and Emergence marsh (from Chapman in Steers 1960).

Nevertheless, Chapman has drawn attention to an important distinction which, even if it cannot be critically defined, is none the less real. Lower marshes are dominated by factors associated with submergence and, as we shall see, upper marshes are dominated by factors associated with emergence. Lower marsh from about mean high water neaps to mean high water is best described as *Submergence marsh*, and upper marsh from mean high water to mean high water springs, as *Emergence marsh*. Bearing in mind that turbidity, insolation, temperature, fresh water input, grazing and adaptive ecotypes will all play a part in modifying the exact limits of species both at a site and at any particular time within a site it should be recognized that boundaries between these marsh zones cannot be exactly defined since they are bound to vary from site to site and are anyway oscillatory in nature. What might be achieved and would be most useful in practice would be a balance sheet of limiting submergence and emergence factors for particular species so that their true affinities for Submergence and Emergence marsh could be more effectively assessed. Already it is evident that species spanning the transition zone are likely to have their lower limits controlled by submergence factors and their upper limits by emergence factors. The extreme example is *Spartina anglica* whose clones are known to persist for at least 50 years without significant seedling recruitment from the seaward limit of salt marsh growth to the zone around mean high water spring tides. The Bridgwater Bay marsh gives us an opportunity to see how the performance of this one species varies across the Submergence and Emergence zones. There is some evidence of discontinuity between these zones so far as height of *Spartina anglica* growth is concerned (Fig. 18).

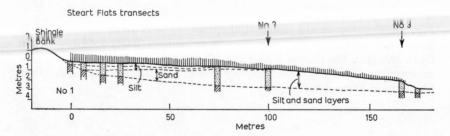

Fig. 18. Vertical height of shoots of *Spartina anglica* from landward (left) to seaward (right) at Bridgwater Bay, Somerset. Note the quite distinct change in height (indicated by closely spaced vertical lines) just to the left of arrow No. 2. Growth in Emergence marsh is much taller than in Submergence marsh (after Braybrooks 1958).

Mechanical effects on Emergence marsh

The incidence of mechanical disturbance from the tide is much reduced on Emergence marsh compared with that affecting establishment and growth on Submergence marsh. It is greatest at higher marsh levels around mean high water spring tides where wave presence often persists, prolonged by onshore winds delaying the ebb. Tidal litter accumulates at this level, crushes weak growths, and temporarily reduces, or cuts off the light supply (Plate 4). This produces the characteristic open ground of the strandline near the landward limit of the marsh favoured by temporary colonists like the annual species of *Atriplex*. Kidson and Carr (1961) recorded disturbance of shingle markers at Bridgwater Bay, Somerset and showed that significant movement was limited to a narrow zone near high water mark. Measurements are needed of mechanical disturbance in different salt marsh zones and fracture devices involving threads of different breaking strains might be employed. It is evident from the gradient of normal tide curves that flood and ebb tides pass relatively swiftly over marsh levels between mean high water neap and mean high water spring tides and mechanical disturbance should be reduced there.

Submergence, or reduced light due to submergence, is unlikely to be a limiting factor for plants of Emergence marsh except at the very lowest levels, because the duration of submergence is too short to seriously impede photosynthesis.

Field Salinity in Relation to Tidal Action

Salinity in Submergence and Emergence marshes

The one common factor that does affect all plants of Emergence salt marsh and precludes the growth of non-halophytic terrestrial species is of course the high level of salinity maintained persistently by the tides. Salinities in Submergence marsh rarely rise above that of the tidal water with which it is regularly and frequently bathed, Emergence marsh however can develop much higher salinities in the soil solution than that of the tidal water as a result of water evaporation during dry inter-tidal periods. Hannon and Bradshaw (1968) have in fact demonstrated that upper marsh populations of *Festuca rubra* are more salt tolerant than those of lower marsh.

Gillham (1957) took advantage of a drought in 1955 to record extreme high salinities in the soil solution of many species regarded as non-halophytes in Emergence marsh on the shores of islands off the west coast of Scotland. Her results (Fig. 19) show that in addition to the normal halophytes, non-

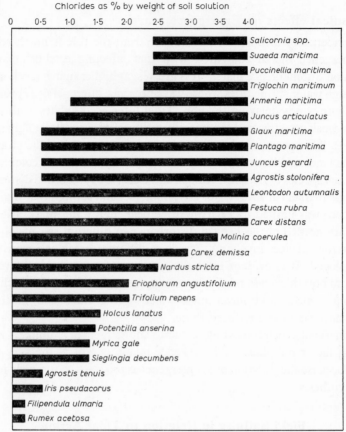

Chlorides as % by weight of soil solution

0   0·5   1·0   1·5   2·0   2·5   3·0   3·5   4·0

Salicornia spp.
Suaeda maritima
Puccinellia maritima
Triglochin maritimum
Armeria maritima
Juncus articulatus
Glaux maritima
Plantago maritima
Juncus gerardi
Agrostis stolonifera
Leontodon autumnalis
Festuca rubra
Carex distans
Molinia coerulea
Carex demissa
Nardus stricta
Eriophorum angustifolium
Trifolium repens
Holcus lanatus
Potentilla anserina
Myrica gale
Sieglingia decumbens
Agrostis tenuis
Iris pseudacorus
Filipendula ulmaria
Rumex acetosa

Range of tolerance of soil salinity

Fig. 19. Distribution of common lochside species in relation to salt-tolerance. Combined data from three west coast lochs, Mull. Samples taken during the drought of August 1955. Note the downshore penetration of moorland plants into soils having as much as 3·5 per cent salt in the soil solution (i.e. full sea strength). Moorland dominants which are apparently intolerant of salt are *Calluna, Erica* spp., *Trichophorum, Juncus acutiflorus* and *Sphagnum* spp. (from Gillham 1957).

halophytes such as *Carex demissa*, *Molinia coerulea* and *Nardus stricta* were surviving chlorinity levels of 2·1 per cent by weight of soil solution (equivalent to full strength sea water salinities), without apparent harm to growth. In addition facultative halophytes like *Agrostis stolonifera*, *Carex distans* and *Juncus articulatus* were surviving hyper-saline conditions of up to 4 per cent chlorinity. Judging from the distribution of these species at the extreme upper limits of Emergence marsh where they are more likely to come under the influence of regular fresh water flushing than these exceptionally high salinities, they would be unlikely to survive the latter for more than brief periods. We need to know much more about the time factor in relation to salinity tolerance than we do at present.

Salinity control of *Phragmites* growth

Field measurements of salinity rarely catch these extreme conditions where levels rise close to a species limit of tolerance. It follows that for much of the time, salinity is not limiting for the growth of many salt marsh plants or facultative halophytes. Only where persistently high levels occur close to a species limit of tolerance does salinity become limiting. Since these conditions occur in quite a narrow sector of the estuarine gradient, where the species may become discontinuous due to other limiting factors, the location of a site where salinity is an operative limiting factor is difficult to find or may not occur at all in particular estuarine marsh systems. If we take the case of *Phragmites communis* in Poole Harbour, the great majority of 87 samples taken in dry summer conditions at the seaward limit of *Phragmites* growth gave salinities well within the tolerance of this species. Limiting values were only found at the point where the seaward limit of growth coincided with the limit of penetration down-estuary of *Phragmites* in salt marsh. The field limit of 1·3 per cent chlorinity of the soil solution at 10 cm depth (Ranwell *et al* 1964) was very close to the experimentally determined limit of 1·25 per cent found by Taylor (1939).

There is little evidence that salinity limits the growth of true halophytes in Cool Temperate zone marshes. It is more likely to do so in Warm Temperate and Sub-Tropical zones where evaporation regularly exceeds precipitation. Purer (1942) records salinities of 17 to 23 per cent on Californian marshes and notes that plant growth is inhibited where salt efflorescence occurs.

However, there is growing evidence that the seaward penetration of facultative halophytes in the Cool Temperate zone is often limited by salinity although other limiting factors such as grazing may prevent a species growing to the limit of its salinity tolerance.

Inversions of zonation

Complexities arise in the highest part of estuaries where inversions of zonation occur (see Gillham 1957 and Beeftink 1966). A similar phenomenon has been observed in the upper parts of the Humber estuary Yorkshire. *Puccinellia maritima* zoned below *Agrostis stolonifera* in the lower estuary retreats to the tops of hummocks above *Agrostis stolonifera* in the upper parts of the estuary where it seems likely that temporarily high salinity or drought in dry weather may exclude *Agrostis*.

Clearly whatever conclusions may be drawn about the relation of species zonation to tidal submergence in the more marine bay marshes or lower estuary marshes, these do not necessarily hold in the special conditions existing in the up-estuary regions.

As marsh levels rise under the influence of tide-borne sediments many factors other than those directly dependent on tidal action control the zonation and growth of the increasing number of species which colonize Emergence marsh. In particular physical soil factors: structure, particle size, aeration and moisture become significant. It is convenient to deal with sedimentation in association with these factors in the next chapter and to discuss biological factors in the two that follow.

5 Salt Marshes: Sedimentation, Drainage and Soil Physical Development

Salt Marsh Precursors

Biological activity on and in tidal mud flats starts off the processes of soil formation from mineral sediments, and salt marsh development accelerates these processes. We have little quantitative information about the role played by tidal flat organisms but there are a number of ways in which these precursors favour salt marsh formation once the flats are formed in sufficiently sheltered conditions, and high enough in relation to tides, for salt marsh plants to grow.

Ginsberg and Lowenstam (1958) review evidence of the stabilizing and silt trapping powers of filamentous algae and marine phanerogams in shallow lagoonal waters. Ginsberg *et al* (1954) also found that a culture of the algae *Phormidium* could re-establish a surface mat through as much as 4 mm of sediment in 24 hours. The burrows of invertebrate animals improve soil aeration, for example those of worms (e.g. *Nereis* sp.) are often lined with a layer of oxidized iron, reddish in colour in contrast to adjoining grey-blackish reduced mud. Colonies of molluscs like the Horse Mussel in San Francisco Bay (Gillham 1957) provide surface roughness which promotes sedimentation. On the sandy-silt flats adjoining Holy Island, Northumberland, *Enteromorpha* first colonizes on loose shells of *Cardium* in more mobile sites. Growth encourages silt deposition. The filament bases of the algae become embedded and ultimately lose their attachment to the now buried shells. Stronger growths of algae on the silt increase stability and accretion for the subsequent establishment of salt marsh species.

Kamps (1962) has shown that molluscs reconstitute clay into faecal pellets which settle quicker than unmodified clay flakes and help to promote accretion. His paper deserves much wider recognition than it has achieved for it gives much valuable quantitative information about the movement of clay in inter-tidal waters and its dependence on wind-induced waves and on the effects of inter-tidal organisms on silt movement in the Dutch Wadden sea.

Sedimentation

Techniques of measurement of salt marsh accretion

Kestner has developed an effective method for measuring changes in surface level of tidal flats using as a marker a creamed suspension of silica flour poured into cored out holes in the mudflats (Inglis and Kestner 1958). Where very high levels of accretion (several cm per year) occur, deeply embedded bamboo canes with about 15 cm sticking out of the surface enable repeated measurements to be made without destruction of the sampling site. They give reliable results when checked against natural markers like depth to previous years rosettes in perennials or successive seed case layers of annual species in the marsh soil profile (Ranwell 1964 a). In marshes with very low accretion rates it is necessary to lay down coloured marker layers (sand, coal dust, brick dust etc.) and record their depth of burial after several years (Jakobsen et al 1955, Steers 1964).

Rates of accretion

True accretion is the depth of sediment deposited in unit time minus the reduction in thickness of the accreted layer due to settlement factors. The latter become increasingly important at the higher levels of Emergence marsh where accretion diminishes, organic matter increases, and drying out occurs more frequently. Stearns and MacCreary (1957) for example found that settlement factors effectively compensated for an annual accretion of 0·64 cm on a high level marsh carrying Scirpus olneyi, Spartina patens and Eleocharis rostellata so that over a 20 year period there was no significant rise in marsh level. However, even over this sort of period, changes in land and sea level can be important and net increase in marsh level has to be considered in relation to them.

Chapman and Ronaldson (1958) found less than 0·2 mm per year accretion on a tropical mangrove marsh where roots and rhizomes are too widely spaced to retain much mud washed between them. In the pioneer zone of temperate marshes Salicornia accretion may be as much as 3 cm per year (Oliver 1929) and Puccinellia maritima can accrete sandy silt at a rate of 10 cm per year (Jakobsen et al 1955). Pioneer Spartina anglica can

Table 11. Values of correlation coefficients and their statistical significance for relationships between accretion, topography and vegetation at Bridgwater Bay, Somerset (from Ranwell 1964 *a*).

* P = 0·05, r = 0·2839
** P = 0·01, r = 0·3676
*** P = 0·001, r = 0·4594
With 46 degrees of freedom

	Dependent variate				Independent variates						
	Mean annual accretion (cm)			Mean height of site	Distance seaward	Creek depth	Shoot density	Mean height of vegetation	Air dry weight of vegetation	Dry weight/Density (mean shoot weight)	Dry weight per shoot/Mean height
	1960–61	1961–62	1960–62								
Mean annual vertical accretion (cm) 1960–61		+0·8799 ***		+0·4133 **	−0·4101 **	−0·3316 *	N.S.	+0·5098 ***	+0·5030 ***	+0·3825 **	N.S.
1961–62			+0·8668 ***	+0·4074 **	−0·3955 **	N.S.	−0·3279 *	+0·4372 **	+0·3025 *	+0·3408 *	N.S.
1960–62				+0·4751 ***	−0·4692 ***	−0·3115 *	−0·3277 *	+0·5418 **	+0·4626 ***	+0·4181 **	N.S.
Mean height of site above O.D. (m)					−0·9724 ***	−0·7571 ***	−0·4120 **	+0·6898 ***	+0·5062 ***	+0·7081 ***	N.S.
Distance seaward from landward limit of marsh (m)						+0·6742 ***	+0·4511 **	−0·6474 ***	−0·4866 ***	−0·7006 ***	N.S.
Creek depth (highest minus lowest O.D. level at site) (m)							N.S.	−0·4585 **	−0·3286 *	−0·4118 **	N.S.
Shoot density of vegetation (per m²)								−0·4366 **	N.S.	−0·5143 ***	N.S.
Mean height of vegetation (cm)									+0·7635 ***	+0·8644 ***	N.S.
Total air dry weight of vegetation (g/m²)										+0·7350 ***	N.S.
Dry weight/Density (mean shoot weight)											+0·2992 *
Dry weight per shoot/Mean height											

accrete 5 to 10 cm per year and at higher levels has been recorded as regularly accreting 15 cm of silt per year under exceptionally favourable conditions (Ranwell 1964 a). In general however accretion on temperate European and North-East American marshes in the Emergence zone is between 0·2 and 1 cm per year, and is unlikely to be a limiting factor for survival of salt marsh plants.

Pattern of accretion

In a study of accretion on an exceptionally rapidly accreting marsh at Bridgwater Bay, Somerset it was possible to show how annual accretion varied in different parts of the marsh (Ranwell 1964 a). Maximum accretion occurred in the centre section of the marsh which is not grazed; accretion diminished towards the ends of the marsh which were more exposed and grazed. The seaward to landward pattern (Fig. 20) showed maximum accretion about 50 m seawards of the landward limit of the marsh and minimum accretion at the seaward edge. Richards (1934) found that maximum accretion rates on the Dovey marshes occurred nearer the seaward limit. Now the Bridgwater Bay marsh was young and actively developing at all levels while the Dovey marsh was mature and more or less static at its seaward limit. Flattening out of marsh level occurs just landward of the zone of maximum accretion (evident in Fig. 20). This zone must migrate seawards as the marsh reaches maturity. Analysis of the Bridgwater Bay results suggested that rise in accretion rate was positively correlated with marsh height and the height or weight of the vegetation, and negatively correlated with distance seaward and the density of the vegetation (Table 11). The individual effects of the variables could not be separated and this emphasises the intimate nature of the phytogeomorphological processes at work. The positive correlation of accretion with marsh height only holds for young actively developing marshes. Evidently one significant feature of marsh system development is a change in surface angle from a slope to seaward to a more level surface and consequently a less readily drained one.

Mechanism of accretion

Because of the high rate of accretion at Bridgwater Bay it also proved possible to identify distinct seasonal changes in the pattern of mud supply to the marsh (Fig. 21). It seems that mud builds up at the seaward edge of the marsh during spring and summer, accretion is at a maximum over the whole marsh in the autumn, while in winter there is either no change or a slight trend towards erosion.

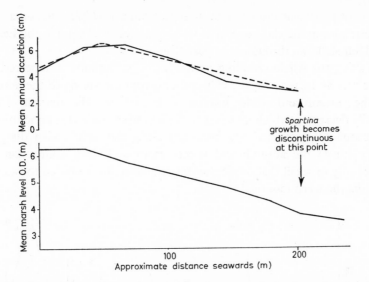

Fig. 20. Annual accretion and marsh-level curves derived as the means of results from five transects combined, Bridgwater Bay, Somerset (from Ranwell 1964 *a*).

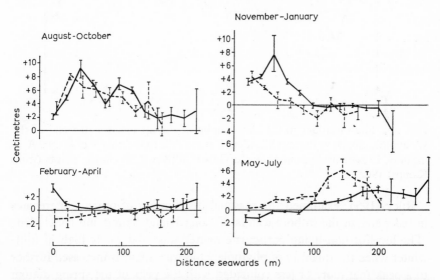

Fig. 21. Seasonal pattern of accretion and erosion on Transects 3 (solid line) and 4 (broken line), 1960–61. Transect 4 results have been slightly offset to the right for clarity. Vertical lines show plus or minus twice the standard error of the mean. *Spartina* growth becomes discontinuous at about 200 m seaward. Bridgwater Bay, Somerset (from Ranwell, 1964 *a*).

It is of particular interest here to note Kamps (1962) results on a study of variations in the clay content of the surface layers of mud in the Eastern Wadden shallows throughout a year (Fig. 22):

'Taking the whole sampling period into consideration it appeared that there was an increase in the clay content from the spring to the autumn. In the autumn and winter months it seemed that the amount of mud rapidly decreases, which means that during the spring and summer months large quantities of mud are deposited along the coast which disappear again during the autumn and winter months. In this connection it is interesting to recall that the former owners of the Banks called the autumn months the warp months.'

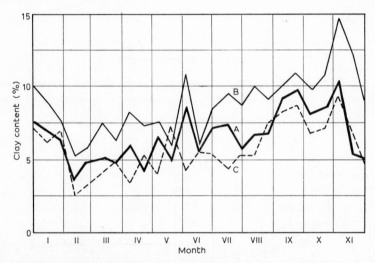

Fig. 22. The variations in the clay content of the upper layer (0·5 cm) of the Westpolder Shallow, Eastern Wadden, Netherlands in the course of a year. A = mean of 15 measuring points; B and C two individual measuring points (from Kamps, 1962).

Riley (1963) examined the seasonal distribution of organic aggregates in sea-water in the inshore waters of Long Island Sound and concluded: 'The level of non-living particulate matter was moderately high in mid-winter when the quantity of phytoplankton was small. It increased further to a peak that more or less coincided with the peak of the spring diatom flowering and thence declined to the lowest point of the year at about the time of the termination of the flowering. The quantity was relatively small during most of the summer and autumn.'

One further relevant factor is the flocculation effect of salt water on silt which Price and Kendrick (1963) believe may explain seasonal changes in suspended silt in the Thames and other estuarine areas:

'In the summer of 1959 the water became unusually free of silt and visibility increased from 6 in to 2 ft (15 to 60 cm). During the late autumn and early winter the deposits again became muddy. This may be explained as follows: In the dry summer of 1959 fresh water flow was minimal, hence salinity upstream was higher than usual. Charges on the silt particles neutralized by the electrolyte salt water caused flocculation and deposition of silt higher upstream than usual. When the fresh water flow returned to normal it is possible that the charges on the deposited silt could be restored mobilizing it again.'

The pattern of seasonal events in relation to marsh accretion seems to be as follows: In spring and summer large quantities of mud are deposited adjoining seaward edges of sheltered salt marshes as a combined result of flocculation due to high salinity and coagulation of particles through increased biological activity. In autumn the reverse effects occur as salinity declines with increased rainfall and biological activity declines with lowered temperatures. Under the influence of autumn storms mobilized silt arrives over the marsh and settles in maximum amount because the fully grown vegetation is at maximum trapping capacity. In winter fresh supplies of silt are mobilized under conditions of minimal salinity and biological activity, to settle once more against marsh edges in the following spring.

It is worth noting that Jakobsen (1961) using a simple siphon sampler found that under dense salt marsh vegetation not more than half the material suspended in tidal water was deposited.

If the top-most layer of newly accreted autumn silt is analysed for its chemical constituents in samples taken successively from landward to seaward, trends are apparent, at least on a dry weight basis (see Table 7). This suggests that the mud supply to higher marsh zones is derived from those successively lower. In other words the source of silt for accretion seems to be immediately adjacent and to seaward of the site concerned.

If the above interpretation is correct we have here some at least of the elements for a mathematical model of the accretion system. It will not be easy to get measurements of some of the parameters in this complex physico-biological system, but one begins to see the need for continuous monitoring of salinity and temperature and for critical studies on silt coagulation through biological activity in order to understand it.

G

Meanwhile it may be of interest to note that a regression equation has been calculated for the Bridgwater Bay marsh as follows:

Accretion = 0·643 (mean height of site above O.D.) + 0·0462 (mean height of vegetation) + 0·00135 (air dry weight of vegetation) − 1·143.

Stratigraphy and the Age of Marshes

Deep level stratigraphy of marshes is a study more in the province of the physiographer than the ecologist and has little relevance to current ecological processes at the surface which is the concern of this book. But it does have relevance to past land and sea level changes and calculations of the age of marshes.

Rising coastlines

On rising coastlines (e.g. such as parts of the Swedish and Scottish coasts are believed to be) there is little opportunity for salt marsh development to occur and the vertical extent of marsh deposits may be less than the tidal range would permit on a stable coastline. Where the coast is stable, sheltered inlets silt up with marsh deposits to a depth equivalent to that part of the tidal range where salt marsh growth is possible i.e. from about mean high water neaps to extreme high water spring tides.

Falling coastlines

On a subsiding coastline (e.g. south-east England) or one on which the sea level is rising, marsh formation can continue so long as its rate is not exceeded by the isostatic adjustment for as long as this occurs. In this way depths of marsh sediment far in excess of that permissible within the tidal range can accumulate.

The history of the marsh changes can be read from fragments preserved in the marsh soils. The reconstruction of the ontogeny of the Barnstaple marsh, New England by Redfield (1965) is an elegant example, and that of Jacobsen (1960 and 1964) in Denmark another.

Techniques for measuring the age of marshes

Three ways of measuring marsh age have been used: direct records, calculation from existing vertical zonation of plants and accretion rates

Table 12. Minimum rates of development of salt marshes to maturity.

Site	Type of marsh	Method of age estimation	Minimum age to maturity in years	Author
Malltraeth, Anglesey	Part enclosed	Direct observation	10	Ranwell (*pers comm.*)
Bridgwater Bay, Somerset	Open	Accretion rates	40	Ranwell (*pers comm.*)
St. Cyrus, Scotland	Part enclosed	Documentary records	70	Gimingham (1953)
Newport Bay, New England	Part enclosed	D. records	90	Stevenson and Emery (1958)
Fal, Cornwall	Part enclosed	Map records	100	Ranwell (*pers comm.*)
Baltrum Island	Open	Map records	100	Tuxen (1956)
Skallingen, Denmark	Open	Accretion rates	100	Nielsen (1935)
North Bull Island, Eire	Part enclosed	Documentary records	125	Chapman (1960)
Scolt Head Island, Norfolk	Open	Accretion rates	200	Chapman (1960)
Dovey, Wales	Open	Accretion rates	330	Chapman (1960)

corrected for subsidence and settlement, and radio-carbon dating. We need to distinguish between minimum age for reaching maturity and marshes whose life is extended indefinitely by the rejuvenating effect of subsidence at a rate less than that of the accretion rate.

Some minimum ages for marshes reaching maturity (which might be defined as the point where settlement tends to balance accretion) are given in Table 12. In general, part-enclosed marshes develop more rapidly than open coast marshes and the minimum order of time to reach maturity on the majority of marshes is about 100 years. What these estimates do not take into account is the level of the tidal flats when salt marsh formation originally took place. If for example tidal flats are significantly above the submergence limit for the pioneer species to begin with, and salt marsh formation is prevented by too high mobility, they will have a head start on salt marsh formation starting on lower level but less mobile flats if mobility is suddenly reduced by an artificial or natural barrier partly enclosing them. The extremely rapid development of the marsh on the Malltraeth estuary, Anglesey is a case in point. Here high level sand flats suddenly became more stable due to the artificially aided growth of a sand barrier and only 10 years were needed to build from pioneer *Puccinellia maritima* to a mature stage with *Juncus maritimus* (Packham and Liddle 1970). In the case of the Bridgwater Bay marsh, exceptionally silt-laden tidal water combined with the vigorous growth of *Spartina anglica* to speed up marsh development. At Scolt Head Island, Norfolk silt supplies are limited and marsh growth occurs at a much slower rate than normal (Chapman 1960).

Radio-carbon dating of deep level salt marsh deposits has been used by Godwin *et al* (1958) and Newman and Rusnak (1966) to estimate the eustatic rise in sea level and by Redfield and Rubin (1962) in connection with his studies of the Barnstaple marsh.

Stratigraphic studies are of more immediate concern to the ecologist. They enable comparisons to be made between the vertical zonation of the living plant at the surface and the depth of its organic remains in the soil profile (Fig. 23). Such studies also provide direct evidence of successional relationships that have occurred in the past and that are likely to be occurring at the present time (Fig. 24). Any species present in quantity is likely to leave distinctive remains in the profile. An end can often be put to speculation about successional relationships with the aid of a trowel and a sieve. Subsurface discontinuities in sediments which may profoundly affect soil moisture supplies for growth are also revealed by stratigraphic work.

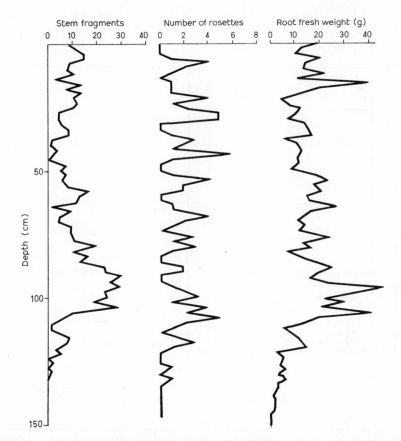

Fig. 23. Distribution of organic remains (*Spartina*) in the marsh profile near the site of the first plantings of *Spartina* in 1929, Bridgwater Bay. Samples were taken every 2 cm down the profile in summer 1962. Note that stem fragments, rosettes and root remains lie progressively deeper at the bottom of the profile as death in the natural position would be expected to leave them. Also, high values obtained near the bottom of the profile and the sudden tailing off of all three items measured near the same general level suggests that the true base level of *Spartina* has been reached and that the results are not significantly affected by loss of material due to decay in the lower half of the profile (from Ranwell 1964 *a*).

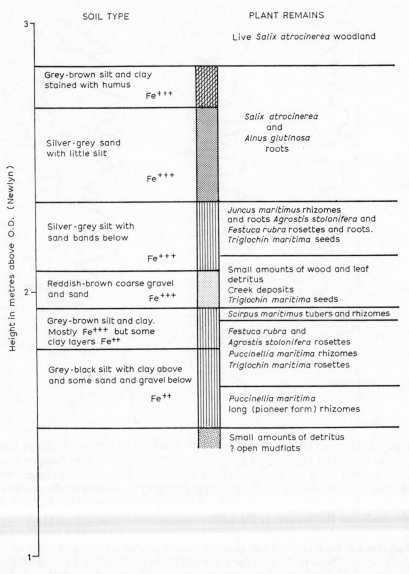

Fig. 24. Soil profile 150 m to landward of the present seaward limit of tidal woodland with evidence from plant remains of direct succession from pioneer salt marsh to tidal woodland. Fal estuary, Cornwall.

Marsh Formation, Drainage and Re-cycling

Marsh relief

Marsh morphology is dominated initially by the surface relief and hydrology of the tidal flats on which it takes place. Localized flood and ebb tide effects in relation to growth form of pioneer species and sedimentation has been studied by Jakobsen (1964) and Møller (1963 and 1964). In general it seems that flood tide effects may dominate under storm conditions while ebb tide effects are dominant in calmer conditions. Flood tide features in higher order creeks with two-way flow are also confined normally to the seaward edge of the marsh, for example the flood bars

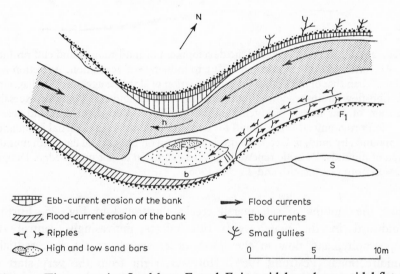

Ebb-current erosion of the bank   Flood currents
Flood-current erosion of the bank   Ebb currents
Ripples   Small gullies
High and low sand bars   0   5   10m

Fig. 25. The successive flood-bars F_1 and F_2 in a tidal creek on a tidal flat at Hojer. The salt marsh plants appear on the tidal flats, and the tidal creek is changing into a salt marsh creek. The flood-bar F_1 was formed in the original wadden gully. The flood-bar has made a barring for the flood-current in the flood-channel which is now a swamp (S). The flood-current now runs round the flood-bar forming ripples and eroding the outside of the bar. In the lower part of the original flood-channel the right side is eroded by the flood-current which forms an isolated flood-bar F_2 to the left. Because of the closing of the original flood-channel and the forming of a new bar the ebb-current is forced to erode the right side of the wadden gully forming a bigger ebb-channel meander. 1. Ebb-current erosion of the bank. 2. Flood-current erosion of the bank. 3. Ripples. 4. High and low sand bars. 5. Flood-currents. 6. Ebb-currents. 7. Small gullies. (from Jakobsen 1964).

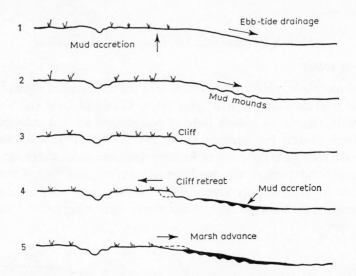

Fig. 26. Theoretical stages in the development of mud-mound and cliff profiles. 1. Accretion of mud on salt marsh due to influence of vegetation. Accretion rate higher than that of adjacent tidal flats. Creation of slope (exaggerated in diagram). 2. Ebb-flow drainage down slope creating mud-mounds. 3. Phase of excessive erosion of salt marsh producing cliffed profile. 4. Retreat of cliff and marsh erosion providing additional mud for deposition on tidal flats. Partial inundation of mounds by mud. 5. Excessive mud deposition on upper tidal flats with inundation of mounds. Possible renewed seaward extension of salt marsh edge. Dengie, Essex (from Greensmith and Tucker 1966).

near the mouths of salt marsh creeks illustrated in Fig. 25. Further landward in the marsh, ebb tide effects increasingly control the topography, and flow in the lower order marsh creeks is essentially unidirectional (Pestrong 1965). However, right from the very start of marsh formation the two opposing processes of accretion and erosion are at work side by side, and one after another, in fashioning the form of the marsh.

Usually one or other of these processes is clearly in the ascendancy. The change from a predominantly accreting situation to one of erosion and vice versa is usually quite rapid. However, Greensmith and Tucker (1966) have made a fascinating study of an Essex marsh where the processes of erosion and accretion are much more neatly balanced than usual (though erosion is believed to be dominant at the present time) and their theoretical conclusions on the cycle of events is summarized in Fig. 26.

Several recent authors (Ragotskie (1959), Redfield (in Ragotskie 1959) and Beeftink (1966)) have described the general changes in relief which accompany marsh genesis as follows:

(1) A change from the convex contours of the open mud flat surface to a concave marsh surface due to better growth at edges and hence levee formation through accretion.
(2) A general levelling of the relief as the marsh approaches maturity and its higher parts receive less and less accretion while the lower parts with more catch up to their level.
(3) A tendency to dissection of large marsh units into small ones, dependent on creek head ramification induced by ebb run-off.

Drainage

Pestrong (1965) has shown that hydraulic velocities and discharge are highest just after the onset of the ebb, and notes that vegetation dominates the hydraulic geometry of the marsh. Using multivariate analysis he concludes that moisture content and particle size exert most control over erodibility.

As studies on loose boundary hydraulics like those of Kestner (1961) become integrated with those on tidal marsh hydraulic geometry (e.g. Myrick and Leopold 1963, Ragotskie 1959 and Pestrong 1965) the approach to mathematical model analogues of the tidal marsh system comes closer. The contributions of physiographer and ecologist still tend to be largely descriptive though much more comprehensive in scope than in the past as shown for example in a study of marsh structure, mud origin, and re-cycling of deposits in Breton estuaries (Guilcher and Berthois 1951). There seems no reason why the various vegetation types and their trapping power for silt and the distinct physiographic units with which they are associated: flats, levees pans, flood bars, slumped blocks and cliff edges should not be analysed (e.g. with the aid of air photographs) separately, quantified, and then re-associated with hydraulic parameters like drainage density to create useful models for predictive purposes.

Re-cycling of sediments

Apart from the small scale re-cycling that accompanies marsh genesis it is a common feature of middle estuary regions that periodic swings of the river channel cause large scale re-cycling of marsh deposits over relatively short periods of time. Studies on a 1,500 acre salt marsh at Caerlaverock, Dumfries led to the conclusion that virtually the whole of it had developed, 'in something less than 140 years, large parts of it in much less' (Marshall

1963). Because of this relatively short period of time, Marshall concludes there would not have been long enough to allow isostatic change to be primarily responsible for the terracing characteristic of these marshes at one time believed to be an indication of a rising coastline.

Soil Composition, Aeration and Water-logging

Soil physical variation and growth

The majority of common salt marsh plants can grow on an extremely wide range of salt marsh soils of highly varied physical structure and composition. For example it is possible to find *Aster tripolium, Plantago maritima,* or *Triglochin maritima* equally on the clay-rich muds of south English coast harbours or on almost purely sandy gravel marshes in western Scottish coast sites. Leaving aside for the moment the possibilities of genetically controlled adaptation, it would be wrong to conclude from this that soil physical factors were of minor importance in relation to the salt marsh flora. While each species may have considerable latitude in survival on a wide range of soil types, performance and abundance are very markedly affected by physical factors and their dependent variates such as soil aeration. For this reason, floristic analyses which depend on presence and absence records alone may often give a misleading impression of uniformity in any comparison of marsh vegetation types.

Soil aeration

Adriani (1945) found air contents of 2–4 per cent in *Salicornia – Spartina* marsh and 25–45 per cent in *Salicornia fruticosa – Halimione* marsh. Chapman (1960) found that by poking a hole through the mud surface of submerged salt marsh, gas with significant oxygen trapped below the mud surface was released. His results (Table 13) also show an increase in oxygen content of marsh soils going from pioneer to longer established and higher-lying plant communities.

Chapman noted that at root depth soil biological remains were abundant and that the aerated layer was especially associated with them. Green and Askew (1965) have examined soil macropores in reclaimed marshland at Romney marsh in Kent using latex infiltrant techniques. They found fine pores up to 1 mm in diameter were especially associated with roots, *Enchytraeid* worms and *Gammarus* sp. Small cavities and tunnels 2–3 mm or more in diameter were associated with ant activities (*Laesius flavus*). The pore system suggested long periods of activities rather than intensity of current use and the pores and cavities were evidently highly persistent.

Table 13. Composition of salt marsh soil gas (from Chapman 1960).

Region	Marsh	% CO_2*	% O_2	% residual
	Aster marsh a^1	2·99	1·61	95·4
	Aster marsh a^2	2·53	0·82	96·63
Norfolk	Aster marsh a^3	3·26	0·71	96·03
(England)	Aster marsh b	4·22	1·42	94·36
	Limonium marsh 1	1·46	10·5	88·04
	Limonium marsh 2	0·93	17·5	81·57
Romney	Spartina glabra 1	1·79	3·42	94·79
	Spartina glabra 2	3·23	8·28	88·49
(New England)	Spartina patens	0·58	17·3	82·12
	Distichlis	1·17	17·3	81·53
New Zealand	Juncus, Leptocarpus	2·95	17·34	max.
marshes	Juncus, Leptocarpus	0·49	10·05	min.
	Juncus, Leptocarpus	1·75	12·7	av. (12 values)

* The method of analysis (absorption by KOH) also measures any hydrogen sulphide that may be present. This, however, is only likely to be a small percentage.

The mud of pioneer zones of salt marsh contains few large cavities due primarily to activities of *Arenicola* and *Nereid* worms, molluscs (especially *Cardium*), and finer more superficial cavities associated with *Corophium* and *Hydrobia*. A marked increase in finer cavity structure develops as a result of root growth. The persistence of biological effects on soil structure is immediately apparent wherever salt marsh soils show erosion faces.

Air is replenished in these cavities by biological activity (e.g. *Arenicola* air holes) and at higher levels by fissuring of clay soils in dry weather in summer. Air is trapped in these cavities by surface sealing with deposited clay (especially in autumn), and mucilaginous algal growths at the surface in winter and spring.

Clarke and Hannon (1967) have demonstrated with ring infiltrometers just how low the infiltration rate of even highly sandy marsh soils can be (Table 14). They suggest that sodium in the soil may disperse the small amounts of silt and clay so impeding infiltration. However, in a later paper Clarke and Hannon (1969) report that the aerated soil layer is not universal and tends to occur mainly in finer grained, less permeable sediments. Possibly this is because macropores are more abundant and persistent than in sandy soils. Tidal flooding was found to cause water table rise to surface in sandier soils. Penetration of tidal water may be either through solution of crystalline salt, reduction of soil surface salinity, and clay flocculation and/or by lateral seepage due to saturated flow.

Table 14. Infiltration rates in sandy mangrove and salt marsh soils (from Clarke and Hannon 1967).

Species	Infiltration rate 100 cm/hour		% Coarse + fine sand at surface
	Dry period	Wet period	
Avicennia marina	0–8	2–4	79
Arthrocnemum australasicum	25–67	2–42	78
Juncus maritimus var. australis	46–149	14–36	69
Casuarina glauca	240	150	70

Stevenson and Emery (1958) note the large bulk storage of air in shoots of *Spartina* (see also Baker 1970 *a*) and suggest this may account for its success in colonizing frequently submerged zones of fine-particled mud. The same may be true for *Aster tripolium*.

Using Poel's (1960) polarographic apparatus to measure oxygen diffusion rate in sandy salt marsh soils, Brereton (1965) showed that in spite of the increasing water retaining capacity of soils with increasing silt contents associated with rise in altitude, conditions with respect to waterlogging improved. Oxygen diffusion rate rose from 6·1 μA in pioneer *Salicornia* to 8·6 to 13·2 μA in *Puccinellia* zones.

According to Brereton (1965), 'initially population structure is a reflection of the dominant influence of a high water-table which produces a highly plastic marsh surface accompanied by water-logged conditions. Later as the water-table falls population structure is a reflection of point to point variations in soil composition.'

He concludes 'an examination of environmental features show that soil water relations as controlled by drainage (through altitude), and soil physical characters, are primarily responsible for producing differences in species performance between stands and within stands respectively'.

Effects of water-logging

Very little experimental work has been done on the effects of water-logging on salt marsh plants, but Brereton (1971) concludes from his work on *Salicornia* that the main factor affecting *Salicornia* during the succession appears to be aeration. This controlled both germination and growth rates, but there was interaction with salinity. While *Salicornia* shows a preference for soils having high redox levels and shows tolerance of high salt levels, *Puccinellia maritima* shows the opposite. *Puccinellia* performance is improved in water-logged soils of relatively low salt status. *Salicornia* shows the opposite. Field and laboratory culture data confirmed these relationships.

More recently Clarke and Hannon (1970) found that none of the Australian species (*Arthrocnemum australasicum, Suaeda australis, Triglochin striata, Juncus maritimus* var *australiensis* and *Casuarina glauca*) were prevented from germination by submergence in 4 mm of water, but coverage by 5 cm of water retarded and reduced germination. These species and *Sporobolus virginicus* were grown experimentally at three water levels from water-logged to free-drained but damp. All except *Suaeda* and *Casuarina* grew satisfactorily under water-logged conditions, but there is evidence that *Arthrocnemum* and *Aegiceras* seedlings are more intolerant of water-logging than mature plants.

As mentioned in Chapter 4, Goodman and Williams (1961) studying *Spartina* 'die-back' soils found no direct evidence of plant damage due primarily to anaerobiosis. Mineral studies moreover showed no evidence of nutrient unbalance. Since ion accumulation requires oxygen this is further evidence that anaerobiosis is not seriously limiting. They conclude that death is brought about by a toxic reduced ion, but could not definitely establish sulphide as the responsible ion. It might be interesting to compare the tolerance of salt marsh species to different sulphide concentrations side by side with treatments providing a similar level of anaerobiosis, but without sulphide.

While at the present time we seem to be faced again and again with the close interaction of significant factors in the study of causative phenomena in ecology (as illustrated all too apparently in this account of aeration in relation to saltmarsh plant growth) we are at least beginning to understand how the parts of the system are connected even if we do not know exactly how it works.

6 Salt Marshes:
Species Strategies

Autecological Limits

Each species on a salt marsh has evolved its own particular strategy for dispersal, establishment and growth; each has its own dimensional limits of age, height and potential clonal size.

Strategies are controlled by the range of environments in which a species can survive and the kinds of change the environments have undergone in the past and are undergoing now acting on the somatic and genetic material of which the species is composed. Perhaps we should remind ourselves right from the start that 'for sexual organisms, it is the local interbreeding population and not the species that is clearly the evolutionary unit of importance' (Ehrlich and Raven 1969).

The salt marsh habitat as a whole imposes certain limits on the kinds of plant that survive in it: all for example must be tolerant of high salinity and some of the ways in which this has been achieved have already been discussed. In addition each sub-habitat of the salt marsh imposes specific additional limits so that certain species survive in them preferentially. So in this chapter we will see how life in different zones on the salt marsh and in the types of habitats within them has been solved by different species. Autecological studies help us to understand how the various species dovetail into the complex tapestry of populations of which salt marsh plant communities are composed.

Grime (1965) has drawn attention to the necessity of studying and experimenting with events in the field rather than trying to draw nebulous conclusions from data correlations. He also emphasizes the value of looking for susceptibility limits and trying to discover '. . . of what adaptation is the susceptibility a consequence.' This approach is being increasingly adopted with success by workers concerned with the practical application of autecological knowledge and examples are selected for discussion here with this in mind.

Algal Strategies

A small number of red, filamentous green, and dwarf brown algae have become adapted to the salt marsh habitat. Chapman (in Steers 1960) has made a special study of the distribution of some of these in time and space on an English marsh at Scolt Head Island, Norfolk (Fig. 27 and 28).

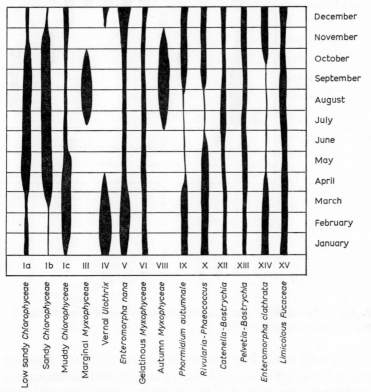

Fig. 27. Distribution of the Norfolk salt marsh algal communities in time (from Chapman in Steers, 1960).

Little is yet known about the autecology of these species and indeed their taxonomic relations are still in some cases little understood. But Chapman's studies reveal clearly some of the distinctive strategies, which enable algae to colonize salt marshes.

Mobile strategies

Certain *Enteromorpha* species (*E. prolifera*) which occur on sandy ground in the pioneer marsh zone have adopted a mobile strategy. They are moved

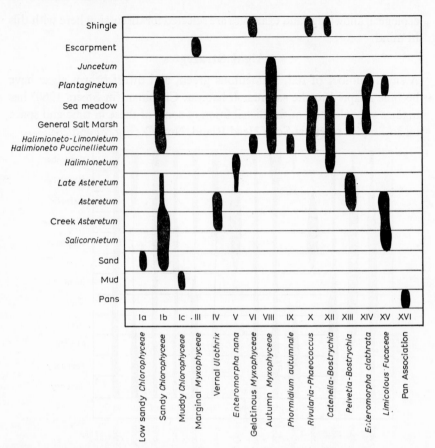

Fig. 28. Distribution of the Norfolk salt marsh algal communities in space (from Chapman in Steers 1960).

bodily by tidal action from one site to another while still retaining their 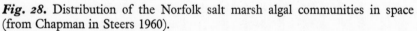 mobility. These opportunists may end up in more stable situations entangled around the stem bases of salt marsh plants or as part of the ephemeral algal mixtures stranded in temporarily flooded salt marsh pans. *Pelvetia canaliculata* also produces free-floating forms which accumulate in pans e.g. at Tyninghame marsh, East Lothian, Scotland.

Fixed strategies

Then there are species like *Vaucheria thurettii* and other filamentous bluegreen algae whose gelatinous secretions are sufficiently binding on mud surfaces to enable growth to occur on the steep banks of creeks where no other plants can grow, what one might call an adhesive strategy.

Many algae (e.g. *Ulothrix speciosa* in spring, and *Oscillatoria sancta* in autumn) have developed optimal growth patterns outside the season favourable to the growth of most salt marsh plants. This enables them to take advantage of improved light conditions beneath taller salt marsh plants at the ends of the normal growth season when it is still warm enough for algal metabolism. This is effectively an off-peak seasonal growth strategy.

Yet others adopt a shelter-hold strategy (e.g. *Bostrychia scorpioides*, *Catenella repens*, dwarf *Fucus* species) embedded in mud accreted in the shelter formed by salt marsh plant growth. A few show an epiphyte strategy (e.g. *Catanella repens* or *Enteromorpha nana*), growing on the stems of other plants. This confers advantages of improved light compared with those growing in more shaded conditions at ground level.

Flowering Plant Strategies

Salt marshes are often thought of as an open habitat. If this were true one would expect a high proportion of annuals in the flora, but in fact this is not so. Certainly the pioneer zone is open and is kept open by high incidence of wave break since it is located around mean high water neap tides. Similarly at mean high water spring tides the high incidence of wave break and local smothering of vegetation by tidal litter maintains an open habitat. A few species of annuals (e.g. *Salicornia* sp. in the pioneer zone; *Atriplex* sp. on the strandline) are abundant in these two zones but the zones where annual species are dominant are relatively narrow in width. Between them the bulk of the salt marsh vegetation, whether grazed or ungrazed covers most of the ground when viewed from above and shows little more well-lit bare ground than in an inland grazed pasture for example.

It is not surprising to find therefore that the majority of salt marsh species are perennial and in fact relatively few species of annuals have become adapted to the true salt marsh habitat. Many casual species not specific to the salt marsh flora occur on the strandline and this might account for the relatively high values for Therophytes quoted in Chapman's analyses (Chapman 1960, Table 30). However, he does conclude that 'on the basis of the percentage of total species it is clear that the salt marsh is fundamentally a Hemicryptophyte area'.

Annual Strategies

The majority of salt marsh annuals are members of one family, the Chenopodiaceae. Many of the 500 species comprising this family show a high

H

degree of tolerance to high salinities, but most of them are adapted to relatively stable inland salines: only a few to the very specialized saline *and* tidally-disturbed salt marsh conditions. The genera *Atriplex, Suaeda,* and *Salicornia* have all produced annual species adapted to survival on salt marshes.

Salt tolerance

Hunt (1965) has shown that the improvement in salt tolerance of selected seedlings of *Agropyron intermedium* averaged 100 per cent and exceeded 500 per cent in several of the 20 clonal lines examined, indicating it was a highly heritable character. Gutnecht and Dainty (1968) have shown how the appropriate ion systems to utilize high sodium environments could have evolved. In the case of *Salicornia*, selection appears to have run its course to produce species which not only tolerate high salinity, but ones in which the capacity for persistence in fresh water conditions has been either 'bred-out' or is so low that re-invasion of open fresh-water muds is no longer a possibility. It would be interesting to measure any residual capacity for fresh water growth adaptation to see just how low the improvement capacity might be as compared with Hunt's figures for the improvement of salt tolerance as given above.

Resistance to mechanical damage

Boyce (1954) and Oosting (1954) point out the relationship between salt, succulence, and resistance to mechanical damage. It seems there may be a syndrome in which a succulent leaf shape (characteristic of salt marsh Chenopodiaceae and other salt marsh plants) is better resistant to mechanical damage (e.g. by wind and tide on coastal flats) and reduced mechanical damage in turn reduces injury from salt (or in particular the Chloride ion), which stimulates the development of succulence.

The annual strategy in the pioneer zone on a salt marsh demands high resistance to mechanical damage. *Salicornia* shows reduction to a phylloclade form and this presents minimum leaf appendanges for tearing by wave action, but an adequate photosynthetic surface in the high-light open habitats where it occurs.

Tolerance of water-logged conditions

The lowest zones of salt marshes are characteristically water-logged and as Brereton (1965) has shown have low oxygen diffusion rates. But he also points out that *Salicornia* shows a preference for soils having a high redox potential, compared for example with *Puccinellia maritima*. In fact high level tidal flats where *Salicornia* can grow are frequently colonized by algal blooms in spring and summer and it is not uncommon to see a silvery texture on the surface of water-logged mud formed by millions of tiny oxygen bubbles produced by the diatom *Pleurosigma* in early summer. Newly germinating *Salicornia* in April and May may take advantage of this oxygen source and the annual growth strategy in fact takes advantage of the potentially better aerated conditions in summer and passes the unfavourable winter season in seed.

Dispersal

Annual salt marsh species commonly produce seeds of from 1 to 3 mm diameter and not uncommonly the fruit itself (e.g. in *Atriplex*) or even the fruiting head forms the dispersal propagule. Thus Dalby (1963) has shown that the fruiting head with from 4–10 seeds may be dispersed as a whole in *Salicornia pusilla* and can float for up to 3 months in sea water before germination. Stevenson and Emery (1958) found that 10 per cent of seeds of *Salicornia bigelowii* (a Californian species) floated for at least 19 days although Praeger (1913) found that Irish *Salicornia* seeds sank within a minute. Ball and Brown (1970) noted that in *Salicornia europaea* and *S. dolichostachya* some ripe seeds fell out of plants, but in many cases seeds were retained on plants and germinated *in situ*. It seems that dispersal strategy is variable in *Salicornia*. Retention of at least a proportion of propagules occurs in the pioneer zone, some are strewn throughout the marsh by the tide, while a high proportion are carried to the strandline at the upper limits of the marsh. It is of interest here to note that Ball and Brown (1970) found that *Salicornia dolichostachya*, characteristic of the pioneer zone, has larger seeds and a more rapid rate of elongation of the radicle on germination than *S. europaea*, characteristic of more closed marsh habitats (Fig. 29). Moreover *S. dolichostachya* was not capable of maturing seeds in the more shaded sites where *S. europaea* could still achieve maturity.

Phenotypic and genotypic variability

There is a high degree of plasticity within species of *Salicornia* and Ball and Brown (1970) could not find any single character of 14 examined (other than chromosome number) to distinguish the *Salicornia europaea* and *S. dolichostachya*. *Salicornia ramosissima* can survive as isolated depauperate plants beneath tall *Spartina anglica* growth. Extremely vigorous plants of this species developed when the *Spartina* growth was killed in

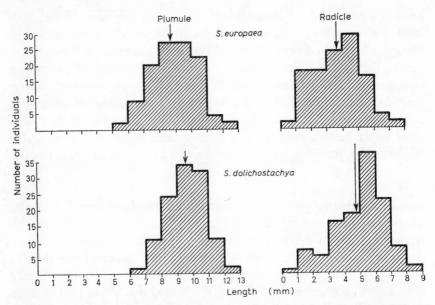

Fig. 29. Frequency distribution of the length of the plumule and radicle of *Salicornia* seedlings 4 days after germination (After Ball and Brown 1970).

herbicide experiments at Bridgwater Bay, Somerset (Ranwell and Downing 1960).

Dalby (1962) has brought together evidence showing that both diploid and tetraploid species occur among British *Salicornia* and that the tetraploids (e.g. *S. dolichostachya*) tend to be heavier seeded than the diploids. There is strong evidence (Fig. 30) that wind-pollination occurs, but plants have been shown to set a high proportion of seed by self-fertilization. This pattern of variation could result in the propagation of micro-species and also segregates from occasional crosses between lines to produce new lines,

Short-Lived Perennial Strategies

Flowering behaviour in *Aster* in relation to clines

Aster tripolium is a short-lived perennial widespread on most European and Mediterranean salt marshes. It is also found in inland salines in Europe and Western Asia. Gray (1971) has distinguished geographical and topographical clines in flowering behaviour. In the southern part of its range flowering occurs in the first year; in the northern part of its range flowering may be delayed up to 4 years or more. The topographical cline expressed by flowering behaviour is associated with a tendency for peren-

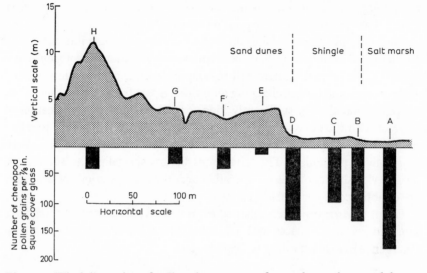

Fig. 30. Wind dispersion of pollen along transect from salt marsh to sand dunes, Blakeney, Norfolk. The lines marking the sampling points, A to H are not drawn to scale vertically (After Dalby 1962).

nial (and therefore earlier-maturing) plants, to occur in Submergence marsh, while annual (and therefore later-maturing) plants, occur more frequently in Emergence marsh.

Perhaps the most striking feature of *Aster* is its remarkable morphological plasticity ranging from tiny depauperate non-flowering plants one or two cm high in grazed salt marsh swards to robust freely flowering plants up to 180 cm high in optimum growing conditions. The latter seem to be associated with lime-rich marshes on soils rich in silt where salinity is generally not above 2 per cent, as in upper estuarine marshes on the Humber estuary, Yorkshire. The early studies of Montfort and Brandrup (1927) and Schratz (1934) indicated that the salinity of the parental habitat influenced seed size and seedling growth rates.

Close environmental 'tracking'

Chapman (1960) found that *Aster* seeds germinated most freely in fresh water, at about half the fresh-water rate in cultures at 2 per cent salinity, and not at all in seawater. However, Chater (in Clapham *et al* 1942) reports plants in inland salines surviving 4·6 per cent salinity and there is evidently genetic adaptation to high salinity in some races of this highly variable species. Indeed Gray (1971) has demonstrated marked physiological and morphological distinctions which are very localized in different *Aster* populations according to their position on a particular marsh.

The short-lived perennial exemplified by *Aster tripolium* illustrates well Ehrlich and Raven's (1969) conception of selection favouring close 'tracking' of the environment and co-adapted genetic combinations related to environmental factors changing with time. Apart from survival selection, its generation time is sufficiently long for environmental modification to interact with the gene complex, but sufficiently short to enable it to adapt more closely to specific environmental conditions at a time and place than longer-lived perennials. The latter must be less specialized to survive the greater vicissitudes of change operating over the longer periods of time they are established at particular locations.

Forms of *Aster* especially adapted to growth on submergence marsh have more numerous air spaces in the rhizome than those adapted to growth on emergence marsh according to Iverson (1936).

Response to grazing

The succulent leaves of *Aster* are attractive to both herbivorous wildfowl like the Brent goose (Ranwell and Downing 1959), and sheep (Ranwell 1961), but plants are capable of surviving in the semi-hemicryptophyte state (normally adopted during the winter), all the year round in grazed pastures. Vegetative propagation by detachable axillary buds still enables plants to reproduce although non-flowering, but continued persistent grazing probably accounts for the absence of this species on some Scottish salting pastures e.g. in some Argyllshire marshes.

Dispersal

Although seeds of *Aster tripolium* are supplied with pappus hairs, they tend to stick together in the capitulum and only some are partially dispersed over relatively short distances by wind; the remainder fall to the ground where they are dispersed by water.

Bearing in mind the limited extent of the salt marsh habitat and the wastage which would occur to unsuitable habitats either side of the shoreline if wind dispersal were not restricted, this compromise seems a very effective adaptation for providing *Aster* with the means of rapidly colonizing open ground within the confines of the salt marsh. Both this and the compromise between the annual and perennial strategy equip *Aster* to behave like a particularly well-adapted weed species (Gray 1971) and in emergence marsh it is frequently a temporary colonist of gaps created by drought (Fig. 31) or by tidal litter. As with most weeds it seems intolerant of shade

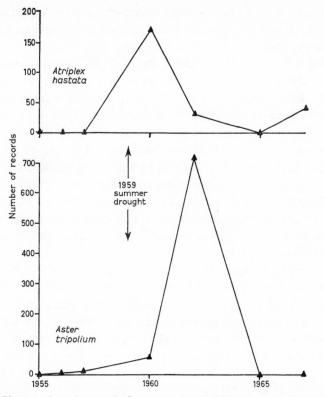

Fig. 31. Changes in salt marsh flora associated with summer drought. Note the peaking of the annual (*Atriplex hastata*) and the short-lived perennial species one year, and two years respectively, after the drought in 1959. Results derived from point quadrat records over a 12 year period in a grazing exclosure at the *Festuca rubra* marsh level, Bridgwater Bay, Somerset.

and is usually sparse in dense or tall communities such as *Spartina* or *Phragmites* marsh. Although an abundant colonist of reclaimed agricultural land temporarily salinized at the time of a sea flood in S.E. England (Hughes 1953), it was unable to persist as a weed element once the salt had leached and the land was again restored to agriculture.

Herbaceous Perennial Strategies

Consequence of longevity

Unlike the more ephemeral strategies discussed above, the herbaceous perennial strategy must cater for persistence at a location on the salt marsh for several decades. During this time the initial conditions operating on the seedling at the time of establishment change as a result of accretion and soil maturation. These produce distinctly different living conditions for the aged mature plant.

Judging from easily visible clonal patterns and known rates of growth individual clones of *Spartina anglica* commonly survive for 50 years or more (Hubbard 1965). While undoubtedly many plants live for much shorter time, available evidence suggests that very little recruitment of perennials by newly established seedlings occurs within the body of the salt marsh. For example, Boorman (1967) found seedlings of *Limonium vulgare* only very occasionally in the field and these usually in areas outside its optimal range, although mature plants were abundant in his study area. Again although *Spartina anglica* seedlings occur scattered beneath mature swards in early spring they do not survive beneath the shade of tall summer growths at Bridgwater Bay in Somerset, and rarely occur at all in the denser growths of Poole Harbour, Dorset.

Grasses are by far the commonest type of herbaceous perennial in most salt marshes. The relatively few species found such as *Spartina anglica, Puccinellia maritima, Festuca rubra, Agrostis stolonifera* and *Phragmites communis* are extremely widespread, at least in the northern hemisphere. In spite of their importance they have received comparatively little autecological study until recently.

Adaptations of *Spartina*

Very few species have succeeded in spanning survival from the absolute seaward limit of salt marsh growth on open high level mudflats to the landward limit of salt marsh growth at high water equinoctial tides, and from fully saline to brackish water conditions. The recently evolved *Spartina anglica* has achieved this. Longer established species of *Spartina* on American marshes (Mobberly 1956) have become specialized for growth in particular zones within this range but only *Spartina anglica* has the capacity to span the whole range. It has achieved this through a type of polyploidy (see Marchant 1967) which confers vigorous growth, large size, and high fertility, enabling it to dominate other species and reproduce extremely rapidly. At the same time it has developed unusually high phenotypic plasticity. This enables it to elongate stems as much as 10 or 15 cm a year to grow up through accreting mud in pioneer marsh and at a later stage in its life to adjust to accretion between one tenth and one twentieth of this rate in fully mature marsh. As Bradshaw (1965) has pointed out, 'where changes in environment occur over very short distances, adaptation by the formation of genetically different populations may be precluded. In these conditions very spectacular types of plasticity may be evolved'. The salt marsh habitat and *Spartina anglica* exemplify this.

Adaptations to survival at the seaward limit of submergence marsh include: a relatively large seed with considerable food reserves; rapid rate of shoot and root growth; development of deep, stout, anchor roots, and shoots well supplied with air spaces.

Taylor and Burrows (1968) have shown that some establishment does occur by fragments, but this seems to be of minor importance compared with seedling establishment except perhaps in long distance establishment via the tide-line to new sites. One of the putative parent species, *Spartina maritima*, sets little or no fertile seed (Marchant 1968). Even in favoured sites (e.g. Foulness, Essex), only widely scattered isolated clones develop from the occasional established fragment. *Spartina anglica* by contrast, rapidly fills in gaps with seedlings once pioneer clones have established. This enables it to develop a continuous sward over large areas in about 20 years.

Experimental studies have shown that *Spartina anglica* plants are tolerant of salinities up to 9 per cent in culture. Even in Emergence marsh where higher salinities than sea water develop salinity is unlikely to limit growth. Summer drought probably limits seedling establishment at higher levels, but it is often the density of its own tidal litter which kills out plants near the strandline and finally defeats its growth (Ranwell 1964 *b*). Grazing reduces flowering, but increases tillering to produce short dense swards (Ranwell 1961).

Adaptation of *Puccinellia*

Puccinellia maritima also spans a very wide range of the salt marsh habitat, but it is distinguished from *Spartina anglica* by much smaller size and much greater reliance on vegetative, as opposed to sexual reproduction. In common with *Spartina anglica* it is tolerant (but to a lesser extent), of water-logging, high salinity and high accretion rates of up to 5 cm per year. It too exhibits considerable phenotypic plasticity and pioneer forms are charac-terized by stolons up to 50 cm long, while under intense sheep grazing a tight mat-like growth little more than 1 cm high develops.

A vegetative propagation strategy is favoured in this species by tendencies to apomictic seed development (Hubbard 1968) and by sheep grazing which produces quantities of discarded fragments (much in evidence on the strandline of salting pastures), which root readily when heeled into damp marsh surfaces by sheep treading. In an experimental study of sheep grazing at Bridgwater Bay, Somerset, tread-planting was particularly noticeable where a period of grazing was followed by a big tide flooding the plots so irrigating the newly 'planted' *Puccinellia* and aiding its establishment.

A distinctive growth of narrow-leaved, widely spaced, upright shoots of *Puccinellia maritima* is characteristic of ungrazed marsh at Dengie, Essex, a marsh which is subject to surface scour erosion. This and other distinctive forms are in cultivation at the Coastal Ecology Research Station, Norwich to discover their phenotypic and genotypic relationships. *Puccinellia maritima* is not entirely apomictic and some sexual reproduction occurs, so one would expect greater variation in genotype on ungrazed marshes where seed propagation is likely to occur and greater uniformity on grazed marshes where vegetative reproduction would result in propagation of the few initially established types.

Adaptations in *Agrostis* and *Phragmites*

Spartina anglica and *Puccinellia maritima* have adapted to pioneer growth on water-logged saline silt liable to accretion, in ungrazed and grazed conditions respectively. Their counterparts in the brackish zone, *Phragmites communis* in ungrazed, and *Agrostis stolonifera* in grazed salt marsh, play a similar role and show similar adaptations related to tolerance of waterlogging, rapid powers of horizontal spread, and capacity for vertical adjustment. They might be expected to differ principally from the first two species in their tolerance of saline conditions, and this proves to be so. Field measurements (Ranwell 1964) and culture experiments (Taylor 1939 and Gray 1971) indicate that both *Agrostis stolonifera* and *Phragmites communis*, in temperate zones at least, are restricted to estuarine marshes where chlorinity of the soil solution does not rise much above 1 per cent. This does not necessarily mean that chlorinity is the limiting factor at the seaward limit for these species and Hannon and Bradshaw (1968) give evidence suggesting that it is not in the case of *Agrostis stolonifera*.

All four species are likely to be limited to landward by competition for soil moisture with more drought tolerant species or by shade in the case of the shorter species. Experimental studies are needed to determine these tolerance limits and in the case of drought, with and without association with other species.

Woody Perennial Strategies

Adaptations in *Limonium*

We can take *Limonium* species as representative of the woody perennial strategy as recent studies by Boorman (1967, 1968) have added considerably to knowledge of the autecology of *Limonium vulgare* and *L. humile*. They both possess a stout woody rootstock and deep tap root and are tolerant of salinities in excess of sea water. In fact pre-treatment with sea-water followed by fresh water may actually enhance germination in *Limonium humile* compared with that in fresh water alone, (Fig. 32). Boorman suggests that sea water pre-conditions the embryo for germination and has an osmotic shock effect which weakens the seed coat and stimulates subsequent germination in fresh water. As in the case of *Aster*, seed size and early environmental history play a part (in addition to genetic control), in variations in germination response to different treatments. Germination is reduced by low oxygen levels and the seaward limit of *Limonium vulgare* is related to tidal flooding frequency, while the landward limit of both species seems to be controlled by competition for light or soil moisture with other species.

Both species are very susceptible to trampling damage by grazing animals, and sheep bite young buds off *L. vulgare* in spring. This rapidly leads to its disappearance. Both species are insect-pollinated and clearly likely to

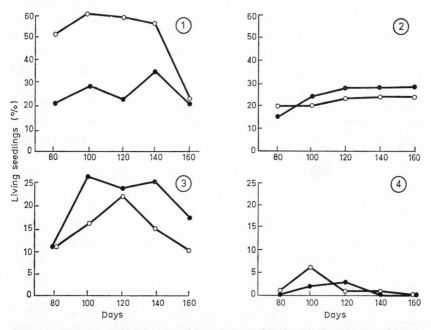

Fig. 32. Seedling establishment of *L. vulgare* and *L. humile*. Percentage of living seedlings after 160 days in an unheated greenhouse. 1. Fresh water and sand. 2. Fresh water and mud. Sea water/fresh water and sand. 4. Sea water/fresh water and mud. *L. vulgare* ○, *L. humile* ● (from Boorman 1968).

be left unpollinated if populations are so reduced that bees and other insects are no longer attracted to them. It may be a combination of intense sheep grazing and depressed insect activity in the cooler climate of Scotland, rather than a simple direct climatic factor alone, which has prevented both species from penetrating into more northerly Scottish marshes.

Advantages of high density growth in Emergence marsh

Boorman (1967) found that the vertical range of *L. humile* was restricted to one third of its potential range when in competition with *L. vulgare* and to one half its potential range when other species were present in high density. Rhizomes are little more than 5 cm long and it is evident that in contrast to Submergence marsh, where long rhizomatous species or ephemeral species occur, Emergence marsh favours short rhizome plants and dense or tufted growths. Most Emergence marsh species have dense woody rootstocks (e.g. *Armeria maritima, Halimione portulacoides, Inula crithmoides, Limonium* sp. and *Plantago maritima*). Others while not woody, tend to have compact short rhizomatous growth (e.g. *Festuca rubra, Juncus gerardii, Juncus maritimus* and *Triglochin maritima*). The latter are less sensitive to trampling than the brittle woody perennials and persist better in grazed marsh.

There is obviously selective advantage in relatively impenetrable dense growth in Emergence marsh. This is presumably related to the increasing competition that develops as the marsh vegetation becomes diversified and closes up. It is clearly shown in air photographs of *Spartina anglica* where the original rounded clone structure becomes compressed into polygonal clonal boundaries in more mature marsh. Marchant (1967) notes that *Spartina anglica* derivatives thought to be of polyhaploid origin have a much higher tiller density, about double that of the parent. It is noteworthy that these high density *Spartina* forms are particularly found in the upper Emergence marsh levels in Poole Harbour, Dorset and elsewhere. There is little root layering in salt marsh soils because of the limits on respiration imposed by water-logging not far below the surface. Competition for moisture and nutrients at the 5 to 10 cm level is likely to be keen at the upper limits of Emergence marsh especially on more coarse particled substrata.

Problems of distinguishing limiting factors

Autecological studies of the type described above help to sort out master factors controlling the strategies appropriate to different salt marsh zones. Within the major zones, limiting factors may sometimes be too closely confounded for statistical approaches like the partial component analysis employed by Dalby 1970, to distinguish them. The solution of these prob-

lems must lie in laboratory study and field experimental study at critical
seasons of growth and at both actual and potential limits of growth.

Limited knowledge of animal autecology on salt marshes

It should not be assumed that animals are of negligible importance in salt
marshes because they receive so little mention here. This is due mainly to
lack of knowledge.

The dominant influence of animals on salt marshes is vertebrate grazing
but very little is known about animal behavioural patterns influencing this.
Invertebrate influences tend to be localized to particular sub-habitats of
limited area such as creeks, pans, tidal litter and the rather limited epifauna
associated with certain plant species. With some exceptions such as Dahl's
(1959) outstanding autecological studies on Scandinavian Ephydridae
(Diptera), much of the work on salt marsh invertebrates remains at the
taxonomic and distribution stage of study. There is great scope for autecological study of invertebrate adaptations to life on salt marshes and
speciation arising from this.

Some attempt to balance the largely plant ecological emphasis of this
chapter, by reference to animal population studies, is made in the next
chapter concerning synecology.

7 Salt Marshes: Structure and Function of Communities

The primary constraint on the types and numbers of organisms found on a salt marsh is the availability of the organisms themselves, that is the composition of evolved biological material at any particular place at any particular time.

The next constraint is the energy level imposed particularly by the climatic factors temperature and light. As we have seen in Chapter 1 these are primarily responsible for determining the regional type of marsh vegetation found.

Subordinate to these higher orders of restraint are water and particularly water quality (especially salinity) and oxygen availability. In other words this amounts to position on landward to seaward gradients and degree of submergence or emergence in relation to that position.

The ultimate level in the hierarchy of environmental constraints is nutritional and dependent not only on physical and chemical factors but also on the biological material which is itself energetic and can in turn generate the evolution of new biologic material.

This chapter concerns the arrangement of biological material, its movement, and the energy flowing through it in the salt marsh ecosystem. It is not concerned with the floristic or faunistic composition of different salt marsh communities except so far as they illustrate relation between structure and function. The presence or absence of most species in a habitat is irrelevant to the great majority of other species (including man) in the habitat. The dimensions, population size, and behaviour of a few species, and the degree of diversity of the remaining species (rather than their particular type), seem to be the more significant biological elements of the ecosystem. It is worth keeping in mind in the approach to the complexities of community study that, as Odum (1961) points out, 'basic work which is functional in approach is almost immediately practical . . . description alone, no matter how detailed, does not bring understanding.'

Plant Populations

Haline zones and plant distributions

Beeftink (1962) has produced a conspectus of phanerogamic salt plant communities in the Netherlands and considers that their zonation coincides very well with the classification of saline waters known as the Venice system (Final Resolution of the Symposium on the Classification of Brackish Waters, 1959) i.e.:

Zone	% Chlorinity (mean values at limits)
Euhaline	1·65 – 2·2
Polyhaline	1·0 – 1·65
Mesohaline	0·3 – 1·0
α - mesohaline	0·55 – 1·0
β - mesohaline	0·3 – 0·55
Oligohaline	0·03 – 0·3
Fresh water	0·03 – or less

To the extent that some of these limits coincide approximately with boundaries of some of the more abundant species controlling the character of certain communities these divisions seem of practical value in relation to British habitats also.

In particular there is a small group of highly salt tolerant species (e.g. *Halimione portulacoides, Limonium vulgare*) which do not normally penetrate beyond the up-estuary limit of the polyhaline zone. There are others which penetrate seaward just so far as the down estuary limit of the Polyhaline zone (e.g. *Agrostis stolonifera* and *Phragmites communis*). The limit of tidal woodland growth (e.g. *Alnus glutinosa, Salix cinerea* spp. *atrocinerea*) lies close to the down estuary limit of the oligohaline zone. Too many other considerations affect distribution to press these relationships too hard, but a competent ecologist should be able to deduce the halinity zone from the spectrum of species or vice versa quite reliably.

Sub-habitats of the salt marsh ecosystem

There are 10 quite distinctive sub-habitats (Fig. 33) found in most salt marshes and each provides distinctive growing conditions for the communities that occupy them. Teal (1962) has attempted to sum the proportions of sub-habitats on a complete marsh and find out how they equate with the total populations of the more abundant species occupying them. High quality air photographs which are now available should enable this type of analysis to be carried out quite readily, and it seems a useful basis for rapid survey of wildlife resources over large areas comparable to that developed by Poore and Robertson (1964).

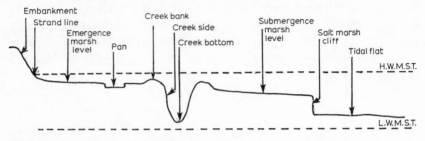

Fig. 33. Sub-habitats of the salt marsh ecosystem.

While it is true that a sizeable area of a salt marsh consists of level marsh, the other component sub-habitats may together make up an even greater area on much dissected marshlands. Yet the distinctive communities of these sub-habitats have been subject to very little individual study. Much of what follows therefore concerns level marsh communities. However, as Odum (1961) points out, because of the importance of tidal action in nutrient cycling and production, the entire estuarine system must eventually be considered as one ecosystem or productive unit. This means that the sub-systems based on plankton, benthos, and marsh-detritus food economies and the sub-habitats with which they are associated, must be analysed separately and ultimately related, before the system as a whole can be understood.

Transitional habitats

Salt marshes normally develop as relatively narrow belts adjoining sheltered coasts. Consequently they have extensive boundaries adjoining other systems where transitional habitats between the two are developed. In smaller marsh systems, transitional habitats may be more extensive in area than the pure salt marsh system itself.

Transitions to wet land, dry land, shingle and cliff tend to be relatively sharp with fairly steep salinity gradients near the top of the marsh in which many of the less common and more locally distributed species find a home. Transitions to sand dune may be much less sharp owing to the mobility of sand in wind and water.

In coastal sectors which have been reworked by wave action, horizontal and vertical mixtures of contrasting particle size; clay, silt, sand or shingle, impose patterns of transitional habitat type on the more typical salt marsh habitat.

Formation of the plant communities

The threshold level for salt marsh plant growth on a tidal flat often develops quite suddenly, and new colonization over a comparatively large surface area may occur very rapidly. West (1956) also finds that 'colonization of a mud flat (by mangrove) is not gradual but sudden and this results in stepwise bands of even age growth adjoining the coast'.

This threshold level varies in height in relation to the tidal regime and in accordance with stability, turbidity, and the light climate as we have seen. If this threshold happens to be low in level there is likely to be rapid colonization by a very pure community of the lowest growing pioneer species (e.g. *Salicornia* or *Spartina*); if it is higher then the amount of emergence may be sufficient for most of the main marsh species to colonize almost simultaneously and a mixed marsh community develops. In the intermediate case it depends very much on the proportions of annuals and perennials as pioneers whether diversification takes place early or late in marsh development, for the entry of new species depends very much on available space.

The subsequent vegetational history of the marsh is a product of interacting physical and biological boundaries. These are developed in horizontal and vertical planes and become diversified in time. Consequently it is of vital importance, to measure the rate at which the various interfaces and boundaries are changing to understand the plant and animal community transformations which both accompany, and at the same time, modify them.

Types of population change

What is becoming evident is that whether a pure dominant marsh community (like *Spartina anglica* marsh) or a mixed marsh community (e.g. *Triglochin, Plantago, Limonium, Puccinellia* marsh) develops initially, it may be relatively stable in composition for decades. Changes occur either in the vicinity of significant vertical changes in level (e.g. cliffs, creeks, pan edges or accretion to some new critical threshold level) or, where vertical changes in height of the vegetation are imposed by grazing, cutting or the invasion of taller species which can over-shade shorter ones.

Minor population changes are associated with physiographic development

I

of creeks, pans and cliffing. More far-reaching ones are associated with management interferences with the surface growths. The primary population changes which are perhaps of more fundamental interest will depend on the pioneer species growing and accreting silt to a level at which their reproductive performance is sub-optimal, and a new threshold for change in the flora has been reached.

There are surprisingly few studies of population changes on salt marsh though there are many assumptions in the literature implying that zonation can be equated with succession. Chapman (1959) has provided a valuable series of maps showing plant community changes over a period of 25 years at Scolt Head Island, Norfolk. But one has only to look at the slumped clods of main marsh level communities doomed to die in the bottom of a creek to realize that the probabilities of any particular square metre of salt marsh turf taking part in uninterrupted text-book succession may be very low indeed. Just what these probabilities are from site to site remains to be worked out.

Successional processes

Studies of population changes in mature *Spartina* marshes have helped to illustrate some of the general points made above and perhaps at the same time throw a little light on the successional processes.

In the Bridgwater Bay marsh it was found that at least three processes were involved in replacement of *Spartina* marsh by other species in mesohaline zones near the landward limit of *Spartina*, (1) suppression of *Spartina* growth by accumulation of its litter, (2) accretion towards a less saline and drier zone which favoured reproduction and growth of such invading species as *Agropyron pungens, Scirpus maritimus* and *Phragmites communis* and depressed reproduction and growth of the *Spartina* and, (3) shading out of *Spartina* beneath vegetative ... ... taller growths (Ranwell 1964 b). It was found that *Spartina* retained dominance for about 20 years, but in the subsequent 12 years about 50 per cent of the *Spartina* had been replaced by the invading species along the 2 mile (1·6 km) landward edge of the marsh. It was noted also that the build-up of levels suitable for growth of the invading species occurred more rapidly than they could be utilized. This was demonstrated by experimental transplants of the invading species well beyond their natural limits within *Spartina* marsh where they survived in competition with *Spartina*.

Yet another successional process, involving frost damage to *Spartina* growth near its upper limit, became apparent after the 1962–1963 cold winter in the Keysworth marsh in Poole Harbour. Patches of

Spartina killed back by frost together with suppression of growth locally by patches of litter, opened up the marsh surface for colonization by invaders similar to those at Bridgwater Bay (Hubbard and Stebbings 1968).

The younger marsh at Bridgwater Bay is still relatively lower in relation to tidal flooding than that at Keysworth and invasion is still largely linear in association with litter along the landward boundary. By contrast at Keysworth, litter is more widely scattered over an older and relatively higher marsh and *Spartina* is being invaded in irregular patches over the whole surface because it has all reached the new threshold level for such a transformation. It looks as though succession occurs in sudden jumps after long periods of relative stability and that it is the loss of vigour of the original species in sub-optimal growth conditions that results in its withdrawal to make room for the next phase.

Invasion boundaries

Fig. 34 shows a typical profile of one of many linear invasion boundaries subsequently mapped over a number of years by plane table mapping. The profile shows a distinctive pattern in which the *invading* species (*Phragmites*) grades quite gradually from high to low in height or biomass from landward to seaward i.e. from near optimal to sub-optimal growth conditions. By contrast the *invaded* species (*Spartina*) shows a characteristic

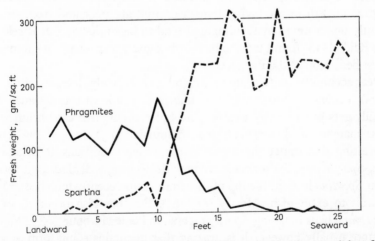

Fig. 34. Invasion boundary. Note the gradual increase in shoot weight of the invading species (*Phragmites*) and the sudden decrease in shoot weight of the invaded species (*Spartina*) from seaward to landward across the boundary. Poole Harbour, Dorset.

sudden decline and eventual extinction, within the taller growths of the invading species. This pattern was similar in boundaries between *Spartina* and other invaders such as *Scirpus maritimus* or *Agropyron pungens*.

It was found that if shoots were removed reciprocally at points across a mixed boundary of *Spartina* and *Phragmites*, *Spartina* maintains, but does not increase, its density in the absence of *Phragmites*, but can be extinguished by *Phragmites* growths of density 150 shoots per metre or more. By contrast, the removal of *Spartina* had no significant effect on *Phragmites* at the mid-point of the boundary.

Crude as this experiment is, it illustrates the susceptibility of *Spartina* near its landward survival limit. It is of interest that reciprocal shoot removal experiments in main marsh communities recently carried out at Scolt Head Island (Woodall *pers comm.*) show very little adjustment between species which implies much greater stability in these populations, at present in the middle rather than near the limit of their vertical range of growth.

Influence of grazing and fire

Grazing and exclosure experiments (Ranwell 1961 and 1968) show that very rapid readjustments in population balances can be induced by such wholesale alterations of the habitat. Recent studies in oligohaline marshes on the Fal estuary have demonstrated that it is possible for ungrazed salt marsh to succeed to tidal woodland without major isostatic change, but conditions for tree growth in the badly drained ground are poor and trees are frequently undermined by flooding and tend to be short-lived. It is relevant that Reid (1913) found trees to be mostly quite young in age in submerged forest beds around the British coast.

Peat accumulation (e.g. up to 2 ft (60 cm) of slowly decaying litter in 8 years), occurs in *Spartina patens* marsh in south east Louisiana. This usually burns down in dry weather and fire prevents tree establishment on these marshes so they remain grass-dominated (Lynch *et al* 1947). It is interesting that under the highly nutrient-rich conditions at Bridgwater Bay, *Spartina anglica* marshes are now developing a distinct peat formed from *Spartina* litter at the top of the shore. This recently took fire and was difficult to extinguish (Morley (*in litt.*)). Fire has also occurred in the *Phragmites* beds invading *Spartina* marsh in Poole Harbour.

More usually however it is grazing that maintains some form of grass marsh whether it be by sheep and cattle in Europe; cattle in North America; camels in the Red Sea marshes (Kassas 1957), or marsupials and rabbits in Australia or New Zealand.

Truncated development

Polyhaline marshes tend to form abrupt saline to non-saline boundaries with adjoining coasts since by their nature they are remote from ameliorating influences of fresh-water. They are more prone to disturbance from wave action and tend to be coarse-particled as they are also remote from river-borne silt sources. There is some evidence (Guilcher and Berthois (1957)) that their more readily erodable sandy-silt may tend to re-cycle and plant communities on them may not undergo significant directional succession. Human activities of course frequently truncate the development of marshland before it can reach its final stages.

Animal Populations

Numbers and biomass

Apart from vertebrate grazers there seems to have arisen a general belief that animals are of minor significance in the salt marsh habitat. Chapman (1960) for instance devotes less than two pages to them in a 350-page book on salt marshes and salt deserts. In fact it is only in the last decade or so since Chapman wrote that the abundance and significance of animals in salt marshes has come to be realized.

Paviour-Smith (1956) obtained the astounding figure of 7,631,460 animals per m^2 from a closely rabbit-grazed salt marsh turf in New Zealand with a soil (admittedly highly organic in character) only 20 cm deep over almost pure sand. Her figures for biomass show that animals represent only about 2 per cent of the value for plant biomass:

	mg/m^2 dry wt.
Total zoomass (max.)	32,436
Phytomass (bacteria)	10
(higher plants)	1,680,000
	1,712,446

Of particular interest also are her figures for organic matter. They immediately suggest the importance of detritus and hence of detritus feeders in the salt marsh economy:

	g/m^2 organic matter dry wt
Dead	17,374·4
Live plants	760·9
Live animals	25·6
	18,160·9

Origins of animal groups

Teal (1962) examined the terrestrial and aquatic macro-invertebrate fauna of a salt marsh in Georgia, U.S.A. (Fig. 35) and found it was distributed as follows:

(a) Terrestrial species	(1) General marsh levels
	(2) Upper limits of marsh
(b) Aquatic species	(1) Seaward edge of marsh
	(2) Creek sides
	(3) General marsh levels
(c) Marsh species (aquatic derived origin)	(1) Planktonic in larval stage
	(2) Marsh-living throughout the life cycle

Terrestrial groups formed nearly 50 per cent of the marsh fauna, but aquatic groups were found to be more important in the energetics of the system. He also found there was only slight adaptation to marsh conditions

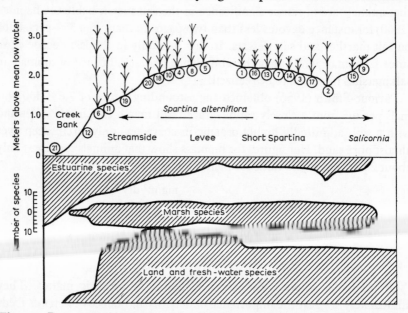

Fig. 35. Representative section of a Georgia salt marsh with horizontal scale distorted non-uniformly. Sample sites indicated by circled numbers. Site 2 represents the beginning of a drainage channel, not an isolated low spot. Symbols for grass are drawn to correct height for average maximum growth at those sites. The number of species of animals of 3 groups listed in Table 1* are plotted against sample sites. Names of marsh types used herein are also indicated (from Teal, 1962, by permission of the Duke University Press).

* Not given here.

Table 15. Ordinal composition of sets of ten samples taken in five types of salt marsh vegetation in the summer of 1960. Newport river estuary, North Carolina, U.S.A. From Davis and Gray, 1966, by permission of Duke University Press).

Stations	Mean percentage composition							Average number of insects per sample
	Homoptera	Diptera	Hemiptera	Orthoptera	Coleoptera	Hymenoptera	Other orders	
Spartina alterniflora								
Bogue Banks★	75·15	9·27	12·31	2·05	0·46	0·61	0·08	1,316
Piver's Island	53·47	40·28	0·70	0·70	2·78	2·08		288
Beaufort Channel	55·09	30·94	5·28	3·02	3·02	2·26	0·38	265
Bell Creek★	87·74	10·20	0·16	1·22	0·26	0·37	0·05	1,893
Harlowe Creek★★	95·73	3·07	0·68	0·13	0·21	0·16	0·02	11,095
Lennoxville Point	31·65	52·23	3·16	7·91	2·22	2·53	0·32	316
All stations	90·11	6·72	1·76	0·66	0·38	0·37	0·04	2,529
Spartina-Salicornia-Limonium								
Bogue Banks	78·10	13·41	3·89	2·67	0·98	0·73	0·24	411
Juncus roemerianus								
Bogue Banks	85·61	5·30	1·52	5·30		2·27		132
Core Creek	30·00	15·00	20·00	20·00		10·00	2·27	20
Nelson Bay	73·17	7·32	1·22	15·85	1·22	1·22		82
Bell Creek	16·66	50·00		22·22	11·11	11·11		18
All stations	72·22	9·92	2·78	11·11	0·79	2·78	0·40	63
Distichlis spicata								
Lennoxville Point	60·83	13·64	21·83	2·35	0·51	0·78	0·06	1,782
Core Creek	72·29	14·13	9·45	0·39	3·04	0·62	0·08	1,281
Nelson Bay	38·41	40·71	14·60	1·50	3·54	1·15	0·09	1,130
Harlowe Creek	54·32	10·12	30·19	2·36	1·85	1·18	0·08	1,186
All stations	57·32	18·66	19·18	1·17	2·04	0·91	0·07	1,345
Spartina patens								
Bogue Banks	41·06	25·17	17·22	2·65	9·27	3·31	1·32	115
Piver's Island	19·90	61·22	4·59	2·04	3·07	7·65	1·53	196
Beaufort Channel	28·65	40·00	10·81	3·24	5·41	10·81	1·08	185
Harlowe Creek	43·90	31·22	6·83	4·39	1·95	11·22	0·49	205
Lennoxville Point	22·04	54·69	6·94	2·45	3·67	9·39	0·80	245
All stations	30·41	43·88	8·78	2·96	4·39	8·78	1·02	196

★ *Prokelisia marginata* (Homoptera) estimated in two samples.
★★ *P. marginata* estimated in four samples.

under flood, most climbing to escape (e.g. spiders) or trapping air (e.g. ants). Certainly one of the most dramatic and enlightening experiences the author has had was in watching the mass escape of terrestrial animals by flying, crawling up stems, swimming, or walking over the water surface supported by surface tension, one quiet evening on the equinoctial flood of the Fal marshes in Cornwall.

The basically terrestrial nature of the fauna of these marshes was confirmed by Stebbing's (1971) findings that, 'in general the faunal species recorded were representative of any marshland ecosystem in southern Britain and were not indicative of saline or brackish conditions'.

Distribution of insects on marshes

Davis and Gray (1966) found some 250 species of insects on North Carolina salt marshes and concluded they were abundant in both variety and quantity. They studied the distribution of insect groups above ground with respect to plant zones of increasing elevation (Table 15). Most of the insect species spend the winter in the egg state either in dead *Spartina* stems or in the ground. They found that shelter and food are factors that affect the size of insect groups more than tidal influences. For example the grass *Distichalis spicata* was rich in insects as it provided much cover and food, while the slender tough stems of the rush *Juncus roemarianus* attracted *Orthoptera* which are characteristic of open stands of coarse vegetation and can utilize tough plant tissues for food better than most insects. *Homoptera* decreased with increasing elevation, but ants, common in *Spartina patens*, were excluded by the tide at lower levels.

Dahl (1959) has made a special study of the distribution of species and numbers within species of Diptera Brachycera in salt marsh and dune habitats on the coasts of Norway and Sweden. Six sample surfaces of each sub-habitat were recorded and proportions of the more abundant species common to determine in which sub-habitat particular species were dominant. Studies on the biology of the different species reveal their preferences and adaptations. Work on the species – habitat relationships of wide ranging groups of closely related species of this type are of particular value because they show how the capacity for dominance may be altered by climate or other environmental factors.

It will be of absorbing interest to watch the build up of the marsh fauna on the relatively new *Spartina anglica* marshes in Europe. Preliminary studies on one of the oldest of these new marshes in Poole Harbour, Dorset show that the principal species at present include a herbivorous bug (*Euscelis obovata*), an omnivorous grasshopper (*Conocephalus dorsalis*) and a carnivore (*Dolichonabis lineatus*), a rather nice illustration of the balanced way in which this new animal community seems to be developing. *Euscelis* feeds on *Spartina*, *Conocephalus* on *Euscelis* and *Spartina*, and *Dolichonabis* on *Euscelis* (Payne 1972).

Trophic Levels and Relationships

Paviour-Smith (1956) first outlined some basic trophic relationships on a salt marsh (Fig. 36).

Marples (1966) has recently utilized radio-isotopes to clarify the food

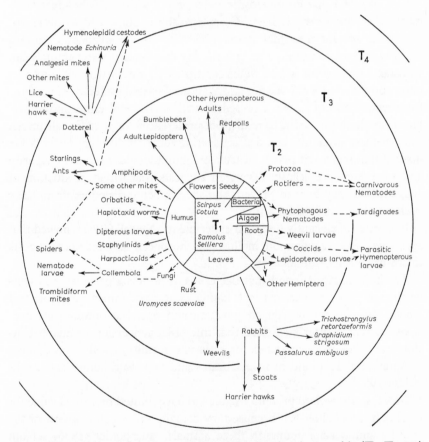

Fig. 36. Foodweb of the salt meadow community showing trophic (T$_1$, T$_2$ etc.) levels. The producer organisms are enclosed in boxes, and succeeding trophic levels are enclosed in succeeding concentric circles. Solid lines represent known relationships and broken lines assumed relationships. Hooper's Inlet, Otago Peninsula, New Zealand. (After Paviour-Smith 1956.)

chains of Arthropods. He labelled *Spartina* and detritus-rich sediment surfaces with the Phosphorus isotope P^{32}. He sampled standing crops and used sweep netting to capture insects to record their distribution and changes in their radioactivity with time (Fig. 37).

Results showed that four species of insects were dominant grazing organisms (one *Orthoptera*, two *Hemiptera* and one *Homoptera*). Species in two families of Diptera (*Dolichopodidae* and *Ephydridae*) and *Littorina* snails were dominantly detritus feeders. Spiders were the important carnivores and obtained their energy from both the detritus and the grazing food chains.

Luxton (1964) has examined the zonation of *Acarina* on the grazed salt marshes of the Burry estuary, Glamorganshire. Some species were restricted to specific intertidal zones, others occurred in all zones, even into the seawardmost *Spartina anglica* zone. He showed that these animals can withstand immersion in sea water for up to 12 weeks without apparent harm and that neither larvae nor adults showed special preference for salt or fresh water conditions when presented with a choice of either in culture. However these mites did have distinct preferences for specific salt marsh fungi as food, so salinity could affect acarine zonation through the food. He noticed that many salt marsh Acarina exhibited viviparity or ovoviviparity and since eggs are readily dislodged suggests that direct production of active larvae may help to prevent the species being dislodged from their preferred habitats by tidal action.

In a series of elegantly designed experiments, Newell (1965) showed that *Hydrobia ulvae* (a common mollusc on European salt marshes) digests micro-organisms, but not organic debris.

Taschdjian (1954) found that bacteria and protozoa participate in conversion of *Spartina* extracts to a higher content of mixed vegetable and animal protein. Studies on community and bacterial decomposition of Spartina marsh litter suggested that microbial conversion in marsh benthos was a key to maintenance of estuarine fertility, notably production of Vitamin B 12 found in invertebrates and fish (Burkholder and Burkholder 1956).

Spartina alterniflora proteins (Table 16) have limited biological value for marine fish and shell-fish because they contain only small amounts of the specific amino acids found in these animals. Burkholder (1956) set out cages of *Spartina* marsh litter in creeks and found that about 50 per cent of the dry matter disappeared after a period of about 6 months. About 11 per cent (dry wt. basis) of the annual crop of marsh grass may be rapidly converted to bacteria, but microbial utilization of crude fibre takes place more

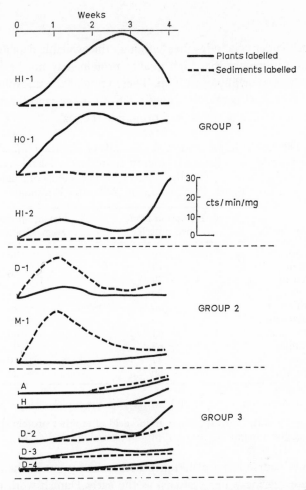

Fig. 37. Uptake curves of 10 animal populations based on mean weekly activity density for 4 weeks following the labelling of plants. (*Spartina alterniflora*) and sediments with P^{32}.

Group 1 includes three species (in descending order, *Trigonotylus* sp., *Prokelisia marginata* and *Ischnodemus badius*) which became highly labelled within 1 or 2 weeks after the grass was labelled. These species were judged to be primarily grazing herbivores.

Group 2 includes the group of highly related Dolichopodid flies and the *Littorina* snails which became highly labelled when the sediments were labelled, but less so when the grass was labelled.

Group 3 includes those Anthropods (Arachnida, Hymenoptera: Ichneumonidae, Braconidae, Chalcidae and Scelionidae, *Oscinella insularis*, *Chaetopsis apicalis* and *C. aenea* and *Hoplodicta*) which did not become highly labelled in either quadrant or became labelled only after 3 to 4 weeks. These groups were judged not to be actively feeding on either the growing grass or the detritus, or to be predators, in the case of delayed uptake. Sapelo Island marshes, Georgia (from Marples, 1966, by permission of the Duke University Press).

slowly. Burkholder concludes that 'although the available data are too few, still the indications are that high quality protein may not be formed by either marsh grass or phytoplankton. There remains the unexplored possibility that microbial conversion may act like a huge transformer to step up the potential value of the pool of protein in the sea'.

Table 16. Deviation* in per cent of amino acids of mature terminal leaf stalks of *Spartina alterniflora* (collected in August from Sapelo Island area, Georgia, U.S.A.), above ($+$) or below ($-$) the amino acids in proteins of fish and average *Graminae*. Data from Block, 1945 and Lugg 1949 (after Burkholder 1965).

Amino acids	Deviation from fish muscle	Deviation from average Gramineae
Arginine	$- 78$	$- 90$
Leucine	$- 73$	
Isoleucine	$- 79$	$\}- 56$
Lysine	$- 24$	$+ 7$
Methionine	$- 90$	$- 76$
Phenylalanine	$- 75$	$- 55$
Tryptophane	$- 41$	$- 60$
Histidine	$- 63$	$- 93$
Valine	$- 77$	$- 60$
Threonine	$- 50$	$- 24$

* Per cent deviation $= \dfrac{x - y}{y}$. 100, where x is the amino acid of one protein (*Spartina*) and y is the corresponding amino acid of another protein the values of x and y being given in gm. per 100 g of protein, based upon $N = 16\%$.

The sea of course has a plankton-based economy but in the marsh and near-shore estuarine water systems, as the early Danish work on *Zostera* (Petersen 1915, 1918) suggested, detrital food chains are likely to be of greater importance. These unlike the direct plant/herbivore consumer food chain are much more complex. Both of these food chains are operative in most ecosystems, but often in widely different proportions (Odum 1963). It is largely thanks to Odum and his co-workers that we are at last beginning to understand how a salt marsh nutritional system really works, largely through the concept of energy flow.

Energy Flow

Odum and Smalley (1959) showed how numbers tend to overemphasize, and biomass to underemphasize, the importance of small organisms in the community (see Paviour-Smith's figures above), while the reverse tends to be true of large organisms. Numbers and biomass can be integrated by a consideration of energy flow. These relationships were compared in two species (*a*) a herbivore and (*b*) an omnivore in *Spartina* marsh.

These workers obtained data by seasonal sampling, respirometry and calorimetry, of *Spartina alterniflora*, the herbivorous grasshopper *Orchelimum fidicinium*, and the omnivorous mollusc *Littorina irrorata*. They found that energy flow fluctuated only two-fold while numbers and biomass fluctuated five- or six-fold (Fig. 38). They noted that there was synchronization of the energy flow peak with medium numbers of median sizes (i.e. stages of active growth) of the secondary producers rather than with maximum numbers or maximum biomass. Food availability was related to periods of high energy flow and operated over a longer period for the mollusc than the grasshopper (Fig. 39).

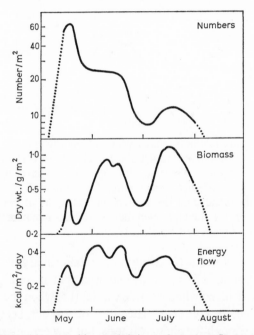

Fig. 38. Numbers, biomass (dry weight), and energy flow per square metre (1 kcal. = 4186 J) in a population of salt marsh grasshoppers (*Orchelimum fidicinium*) living in low-level *Spartina alterniflora* marsh, Sapelo Island, Georgia, U.S.A. (from Odum and Smalley 1959).

Role of benthic algae

Now benthic algae have a high production all the year round in Georgia, U.S.A. at least and these and detritus were considered to be the principal food of the mollusc *Littorina*. Pomeroy (1959) found that net production of

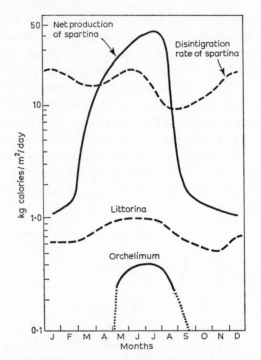

Fig. 39. Comparison of the annual pattern of energy flow (1 kcal = 4186 J) in *Littorina* and *Orchelimum* populations in relation to certain potential food sources. Net production of *Spartina alterniflora* in low level marsh is the sole source of food energy for *Orchelimum* while the disintegration of dead *Spartina* through the entire marsh and the subsequent transport of detritus (including associated microflora) to the high level marsh provides one potential food source for *Littorina* (from Odum and Smalley 1959).

'mud-algae' makes a major contribution to total primary production of the salt marsh ecosystem. His work also showed that in summer, maximum photosynthesis occurred when the tide was in, (i.e. when the marsh was not desiccated); in winter it occurred when the tide was out, i.e. when temperatures were high enough for photosynthesis, but low enough not to desiccate the algae.

It is of interest to note here in relation to the above that the herbivorous Brent Goose was found to synchronize its feeding at Scolt Head Island, Norfolk on tidal flat algae in winter (where temperatures even at these latitudes favour active growth of algae) and on the salt marshes in spring (Ranwell and Downing 1959). We begin to see why the tidal flats are so productive for waders and wildfowl during winter months in the northern hemisphere.

On a larger scale of course, productivity is also related to regional climate. One study on the mollusc faunas of *Spartina-Salicornia* marshes illustrates this. The local, seasonal and latitudinal variations in their faunas were analysed quantitatively in 11 marshes ranging over 20° of latitude on the North American Pacific Coast by Macdonald (1969). He found that the standing crop of the living animals increases considerably from north to south, suggesting that available resources increase at lower latitudes.

Grazing and detrital pathways

Odum (1962) and Teal (1962) found that major energy flow between autotrophic and heterotrophic levels on a marsh is by way of the detritus food chain rather than the grazing food chain. In Georgia estuaries dominated by *Spartina alterniflora*, organic detritus (more than 90 per cent of *Spartina* origin) is the chief link between primary and secondary produc-

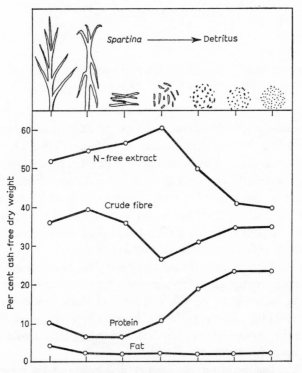

Fig. 40. The nutritive composition of successive stages of decomposition of *Spartina alterniflora* marsh grass, showing increase in protein and decrease in carbohydrate with increasing age and decreasing size of detritus particles. Sapelo Island, Georgia, U.S.A. (from Odum and Cruz 1967).

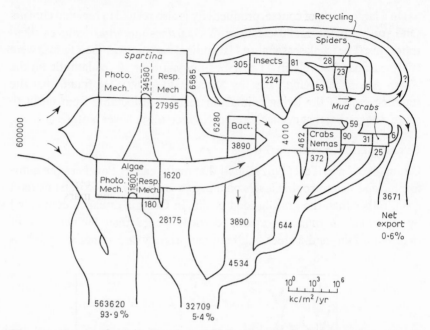

Fig. 41. Energy flow (1 K cal = 4186 J) diagram for a salt marsh. Sapelo Island, Georgia, U.S.A. (from Teal 1962, by permission of the Duke University Press).

tivity because only a small portion of the net production of the marsh grass is grazed while it is alive (Odum and de la Cruz 1967). These authors studied the seasonal changes in amounts of detritus by netting at a creek mouth, they examined the distribution of size and composition of particles, their origin, the decomposition rates of litter, its nutritive value and the metabolism of detritus particles under incubation. They conclude that bacteria-rich detritus is nutritionally a better food source for animals than the flesh *Spartina* from which it is derived (Fig. 40).

Pomeroy (1959) concludes that in water less than 2 m deep benthos is the more important energy converter; in water greater than 2 m deep phytoplankton are believed to be the principal primary producers. In fact, increasing turbidity due to pollution in inshore waters may reduce the possibilities for phytoplankton growth and be increasing the role of benthos in inshore water productivity.

Teal (1962) has measured the energy flow relations for a Georgia salt marsh (Fig. 41) and these are summarized in Table 17 which shows that 45 per cent of the net production of the marshes is exported to the estuarine waters where it is believed to largely support harvestable shrimps and crabs in waters too turbid for significant phytoplankton production. Clearly increasing turbidity may not merely modify the lower limit of salt marsh growth but also affect profoundly the balance in energy paths at critical junctions between ecosystems.

Table 17. Summary of salt marsh energetics derived from studies at Sapelo Island, Georgia, U.S.A. One kc = 4186 J (from Teal 1962 by permission of the Duke University Press).

Input as light	600,000 kcal/m²/year
Loss in photosynthesis	563,620 or 93·9%
Gross production	36,380 or 6·1% of light
Producer Respiration	28,175 or 77% of gross production
Net Production	8205 kcal/m²/year
Bacterial respiration	3,890 or 47% of net production
1° consumer respiration	596 or 7% of net production
2° consumer respiration	48 or 0·6% of net production
Total energy dissipation by consumers	4,534 or 55% of net production
Export	3,671 or 45% of net production

K

PART THREE   Sand Dunes

8 Sand Dunes: Formation and Differentiation of the Habitat

One thing that salt marsh and sand dune plants have in common, in spite of the striking differences between these two habitats, is the problem of establishing in a soil which is initially unstable. Foreshore sand washed daily by the tides on an open shore is in fact so unstable that no flowering plants or even macro-algae have yet succeeded in colonizing it. Even when sand is exposed for days at a time, it soon dries out in the wind and may still be blown about too frequently for plants to establish. Moreover, unlike silt on which salt marsh plants grow, sand is very deficient in plant nutrients and moisture (at least in the surface layers). Without nutrient income from the tide, sand would be unlikely to support much plant growth for long even if it were stable.

All three of these deficiencies; instability, lack of nutrients, and lack of soil moisture, are ameliorated by tidal litter, deposited at the top of the fore-shore in strandlines, and it is here that the process of dune formation can start.

The Strandline

Sand feeding to the strandline

Krumbein and Slack (1956) recognize four zones on sandy shores as shown in Table 18. To the extent that each zone feeds sand to the zone above, adequate sand supply in all of them is essential to the continued long term growth of dunes. But width, height and orientation of the backshore zone is of more immediate concern, as it is from this zone that the bulk of the sand is derived by wind action for dune building (Plate 9).

Coastal physiographers have carried out intensive studies of the sweep zone of open shores (see King 1972), but so far there has been little attempt to link these changes with rates of supply to dune systems, though studies on this are now in progress in Northern Ireland.

Sandy shores bordering estuaries or sounds are usually narrow, and being well protected from strong wave action tend to accumulate considerable quantities of tidal litter. This enables strandline plants to establish but there is usually insufficient sand supply to lead to significant dune formation.

In contrast sandy shores on the open coast are often wide and what tidal litter there is forms temporary surface accumulations above mean high water spring tide level. Litter sticking up from the sand reduces windflow near the sand surface and wind blown sand is deposited until the litter is buried. No further sand is likely to accumulate once a smooth surface is restored again, and the deposit is likely to be re-worked by the next tide to reach it.

Table 18. Sand shore zones (Krumbein & Slack 1956)

Shore Zone	Limits	Tidal relations	Agents of sand movement
1. Nearshore bottom	Mean low water to minus 9 m	Nearly always submerged	Currents and breaking waves
2. Foreshore	Mean low water to high tide line	Alternately submerged and exposed	Currents, breaking waves, occasional wind action
3. Backshore	High tide line to dunes	Nearly always exposed but occasionally submerged during storms or exceptionally high water	Breaking waves, wind action
4 Dunes	Above highest tide limit	Always exposed	Wind action

Colonization of the strandline

Hulme (1957) has shown (Fig. 42) how after the high tides of the spring equinox, falling high water levels leave a zone up to 11·5 m wide seaward of maximum high spring tide level at Longniddry, East Lothian. Annual strandline plants can colonize in this zone. The tidal litter contains or traps varying quantities of viable seeds. Tidal litter reduces daily temperature fluctuations in summer at the sand surface from 25°C in open sand to 7°C

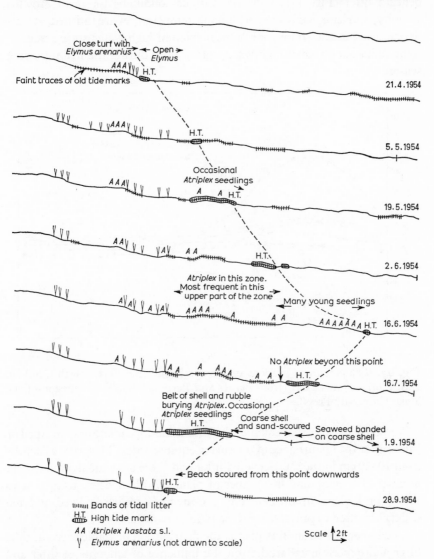

Profile of transect 16.7.1954

Close turf with
Elymus arenarius ← Open →
Elymus
A A A V V V H.T.
Faint traces of old tide marks

21.4.1954

V V V V A A A V V V V V H.T.

5.5.1954

Occasional
Atriplex seedlings
A A A V V V V V A A H.T.

19.5.1954

V V V A A V V V V A V A A H.T.

2.6.1954

Atriplex in this zone.
← Most frequent in this →
upper part of the zone
Many young seedlings
A V A V V A V A V A A A A A A A A A A A A A H.T.

16.6.1954

V V V A V V V V A A A A A A A A A A H.T.
No *Atriplex* beyond this point

16.7.1954

Belt of shell and rubble
burying *Atriplex*. Occasional
Atriplex seedlings
H.T. Coarse shell
and sand-scoured
Seaweed banded
on coarse shell

1.9.1954

V V V V V V V H.T.
← Beach scoured from this point downwards

28.9.1954

ıııııı Bands of tidal litter
H.T. High tide mark
A A *Atriplex hastata* s.l.
V *Elymus arenarius* (not drawn to scale)

Scale ↑2ft
→

Fig. 42. A permanent transect across the foreshore at Longniddry, East Lothian, charted at intervals throughout the summer. Note the downward extension of colonization by *Atriplex*, as the zone free from tidal scour (to left of dotted line) increases during the early part of the summer. (After Hulme, 1957).

beneath litter (Fig. 43). Thus the various conditions for plant growth; stability, nutrients, moisture and suitable temperatures are satisfied, at least temporarily, in the shore zone from maximum high water spring tides to some point above mean high water spring tides during the main growing season.

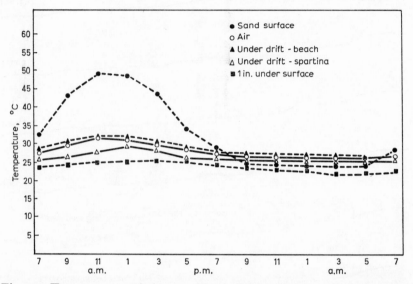

Fig. 43. Temperature variations on Piver's Island, Beaufort, North Carolina, U.S.A. on a summer day (from Barnes and Barnes, 1954, by permission of the Duke University Press).

The annual plants that colonize the strandline appear late (e.g. in April or May), after the disturbance of the spring equinox tides. They root at depths from 10–40 cm in the sand-covered litter and there are wide fluctuations in number of species, and in number of plants within species, from year to year (Cunningham in Burnett 1964). Growth is too short-lived and too widely scattered to promote significant dune growth.

The biology of strandline plants, the distribution of viable seeds in tidal litter and experimental studies on the influence of amounts of litter and seeds on the thresholds for embryo dune formation, all deserve further study.

The Embryo Dune

Perennial grass pioneers and accretion

Tidal litter and strandline plants accumulate sand to a level just above H.W.M.O.S.T. This is sufficient for perennial grasses like *Agropyron junceiforme* and *Elymus arenarius* to establish, and their growth laterally and vertically is sufficiently persistent to raise a dune a metre or two high. Bond (1952) found evidence of continued vegetative growth in *Elymus arenarius* in all months of the year except January at Aberdeen, but Nicholson (1952) found that *Agropyron junceiforme* was dormant during winter at the same latitude. Nevertheless even in winter the dead shoots of *Agropyron* are persistent and help to retain sand trapped in summer.

The inherent capacity of these plants and others like them elsewhere in the world (e.g. *Uniola paniculata*, North Carolina, U.S.A.) to bind sand lies in the ability to perennate and to develop extensive horizontal and vertical rhizome systems. Bond (1952) recorded vertical rhizomes 150 cm long in *E. arenarius* and noted that viable buds survived at depths of 60 cm. Viable buds of *Agropyron junceiforme* occur at depths of 60 cm but this species is not tolerant of accretion rates of more than 60 cm per year (Nicholson 1952). This is probably about the limit for both species, but it needs to be determined experimentally.

Agropyron junceiforme propagates readily by seed and within 10 days the seedling root has elongated 7 cm to more or less permanently humid sand. Rhizome fragments are also important in reproduction and according to Nicholson (1952) propagation from broken rhizomes is common. *Elymus arenarius* propagates rather less freely from seed in the field than *Agropyron* according to Bond (1952).

Seedling regeneration only becomes significant in *Elymus* when plants are abundant. Germination tends to be delayed by the presence in seeds and glumes of a water soluble germination inhibitor until spring, when seedlings have a better chance of survival. Seedlings can not withstand more than about 7·6 cm of sand burial (Clarke 1965).

Growth of *Agropyron* embryo dune

Gimingham (in Burnett 1964) gives a good account of the way in which *Agropyron junceiforme* forms a fore dune from a newly established seedling:

'The single primary root quickly extends to a depth of about 15 cm where a level of moisture content rather higher than that of surface layers is often maintained. The first lateral roots, however, extend horizontally closely below the sand surface. After a rosette of tillers has been established, short rhizomes are formed extending obliquely for distances of between 5 and 30 cm from the original plant giving rise to new groups of tillers (Fig. 44 A to C). This type of growth may continue for two seasons, but in time long horizontal rhizomes are produced greatly increasing the vegetative spread of the plant (Fig. 44 D). Their tips normally turn upwards in autumn, first breaking the surface, ready to produce a new group of shoots in spring. Development may continue indefinitely in this way if sand accumulation is only slight, for elongation of the shoots can bring them to the surface through layers not exceeding about 23 cm in depth. Where however, burial is more rapid, shoots are killed and rhizomes instead of extending laterally assume a vertical direction until the new surface is reached, when again tillering takes place. This sympodial development may keep pace with repeated sand deposition, often up to heights of 1·8 m and considerably more.'

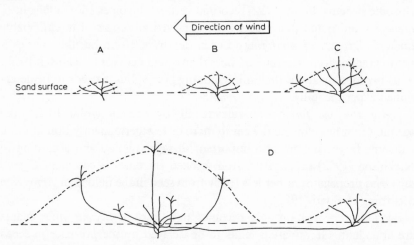

Fig. 44. Stages in colony development and formation of 'embryonic dunes' by *Agropyron junceiforme*. The upper broken line represents the surface of the dune. (from Nicholson, 1952).

Plant growth habit and dune formation

Although the occasional bud at depths of 60 cm in *Agropyron junceiforme* and *Elymus arenarius* may produce vertical growth to reach the surface, continuous accretion of this order per year would result in such sparse surface growth that plants would be unlikely to survive. Effectively they are limited to annual accretion zones of about 30 cm a year, and are incapable of building the really high dunes produced by *Ammophila* growth, and certain other species.

Cowles (1899) recognized two contrasting growth habits among dune-forming plants which are of fundamental importance in understanding their capacities and limitations. *Ammophila* species and *Agropyron junceiforme* both produce horizontal rhizomes of potentially unlimited growth. Others like *Elymus arenarius, Salix repens* and *Populus* species seem to lack the capacity for rapid horizontal spread, but do readjust to sand burial with oblique or vertical rhizome growth. In the case of the two shrub species the vertical rhizome growth may be virtually unlimited at acceptable accretion rates. Their tight growth form tends to produce rather steep-sided hummock dunes in contrast to the much broader dune units formed by the more widely spreading growth of *Ammophila.*

Limitations of the pioneer grasses

It is not clear whether or not *Agropyron junceiforme* and *Elymus arenarius* are simply overwhelmed by high accretion rates and/or shading (see Nicholson 1952) which *Ammophila* induces, or whether their moisture or nutrient requirements cannot be satisfied in high dunes. Gimingham (in Burnett 1964) concludes that since *Agropyron junceiforme* seldom has active roots below 60 cm and the water table may be over 1·2 m below the surface the roots are independent of it. However, they may be more dependent on organic matter and spray-borne nutrients than *Ammophila.* It may be significant also that *Elymus arenarius* does survive in high *Ammophila* dune at Durness, Sutherland where rainfall and spray are high compared with more southerly dunes. Clearly there is scope for experimental transplant studies and studies of moisture and nutrient requirements to help solve this problem.

We are now in a position to appreciate the special advantages which *Ammophila* species possess in dune building, namely potentially unlimited horizontal *and* vertical rhizome growth. No other species combine these two vital attributes and throughout the world it is either *Ammophila arenaria* or *Ammophila breviligulata* which have created the really high dune landscapes.

Establishment and Growth Patterns of *Ammophila*

Pioneer studies by Gemmell, Greig-Smith and Gimingham (1953) showed how *Ammophila arenaria* initiates dune building. They found that establishment by seedlings on the higher parts of the backshore at Luskentyre in the Outer Hebrides was sporadic. At Ainsdale, Lancashire establishment from rhizome fragments from the eroded coast dune occurred more commonly than seedling establishment.

Shoot tufts from rhizome fragments or seedlings were initially unbranched and created smooth dunes parallel with the upper shore like those formed by *Agropyron.* These leafy shoots were capable of growth through moderate accretion by leaf elongation. If leaves were buried, axillary buds developed to form vertical shoots with long internodes which produced new leafy shoots at the surface. Adventitious roots formed on the vertical rhizomes just below the surface and deeper horizontal rhizome connections gradually died. As the leafy shoots occasionally produced more than one vertical rhizome branching increased and dome-shaped tussocks developed.

Laing (1954) confirmed and amplified this picture with detailed studies of the American species *Ammophila breviligulata* on the inland dunes around Lake Michigan. He found this species regenerating mainly from eroded rhizome fragments on the beach. Seedling regeneration was confined to damp hollows or protected sites on the lee slopes of eroding dunes.

The evidence suggests that seedling establishment on shore or dunes depends on periods of heavy rainfall which gives both moisture and temporary stability and that where coastal dunes are eroding, rhizome fragments from toppled clumps are the principal means of re-establishment of a new embryo dune. Where erosion of a coast dune cuts back to forested dunes beneath which *Ammophila* has been shaded out, such regeneration may be prevented as at Holkham, Norfolk.

Laing (1954) found that shoot elongation occurs in spring, especially from buried vertical stems which at the onset of dormancy in the previous autumn had a fully formed blade but an incompletely elongated sheath and internode. Newly formed internodes of the current spring also develop and elongate. Buds of the continuous development type form only on vigorous shoots from depositing surfaces and only on those internodes which mature from late April to early June. Dormant buds form elsewhere and may be dormant for months or years. Branching of the vertical shoots creates a cluster of shoots around the parent shoot; loose open clumps in accreting surfaces, compact tufts on stable areas.

Dune stratigraphy

Both Laing (1954) and Olson (1958 *c*) have shown how past depositional patterns can be determined through measurement of internodal lengths which occur in response to burial (Fig. 45). Olson (1958 *c*) found that foredunes accrete only about 30 cm a year probably because shoot burial removes their power to hold more sand until new growth appears in the following year. He notes how the appearance of a new foredune effectively cuts off sand supply to the one to landward where dead growths persist, clumping becomes more compact and flowering diminishes markedly within 3 or 4 years of stabilization. These very swift reactions of *Ammophila* to changes in sand accretion indicate how greatly its vigour depends upon them. Both *Ammophila breviligulata* and *A. arenaria* have been shown (Laing 1954 and Ranwell 1958) to just tolerate an absolute limit of sand burial of 1 m per year, but density diminishes rapidly if these conditions persist. These high rates of accretion are especially characteristic of the higher lee slopes of dunes.

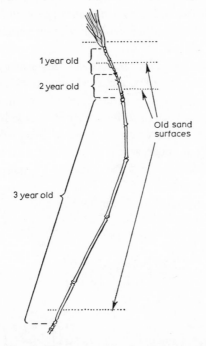

Fig. 45. Three annual growth cycles of a buried marram grass stem. Wide spacing of internodes occur in years following rapid deposition of sand in winter. Stabilization of the dune shown by sudden decrease in annual growth elongation (from Olsen 1958 *c*).

In order to understand the mechanics of dune building and development of the dune landscape it is necessary at this point to consider some fundamental principles relating to the effect of surface roughness in the form of vegetation on wind flow and sand movement.

Windflow, Sand Movement and Dune Vegetation

Bagnold (1941) has shown that sand moves by saltation, a process whereby the first grains moved by a sufficiently strong wind fall under gravity to the loose sand surface and bounce back into the wind at the same time setting other grains in motion by their impact. He showed that the impact gradient threshold varies approximately as the square root of the grain diameter. Above the impact velocity, about 10 miles per hour (4·5 m/s), rate of sand flow varies as the cube of the wind velocity. It follows that really substantial sand movement is only accomplished by high wind velocities.

Much remains to be learned about the frequency of movement of shore sand in relation to the incidence of rainfall and the special conditions operating on drying out sandflats with or without variously spaced pioneer growths of algae or higher plants.

Air flow over a smooth level surface decreases in velocity in a regular manner near to the surface. Over a curved smooth surface, the rate of velocity decrease increases near the surface especially at the point of maximum curvative. Surface roughness interferes with the smooth laminar flow of air and creates turbulence. As a result the profile of mean velocity $(\overline{V})$ as a function of height (Z) is not linear, as it is in laminar flow, but logarithmic. The logarithmic relationship implies that velocity decreases to zero at some height greater than zero (Z_0).

Bagnold (1941) showed that Z_0 can be related to height and spacing of

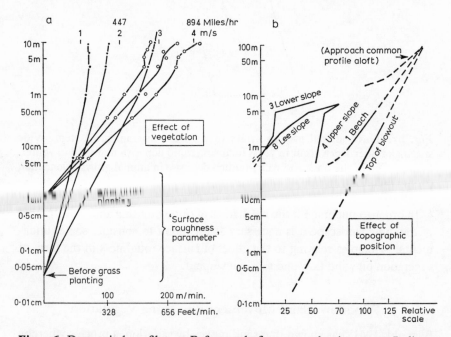

Fig. 46. Dune wind profiles. *a*, Before and after grass planting on an Indiana dune; *b*, comparable plotting of key profiles for a bare Michigan dune, after Landsberg and Riley 1943 (from Olsen 1958 *b*).

surface irregularities and he called it 'the surface roughness parameter'. For a given roughness (Z_0), the slope of velocity with respect to log Z increases as velocities aloft increase. This slope is proportional to the 'drag velocity' (V_*) which equals the square root of shear stress over air density. The proportionality constant is 5·75 when log Z is to base 10. Hence the relationship:

$$\overline{V} = 5{\cdot}75 \ V_* \ (\log Z - \log Z_0)$$
$$= 5{\cdot}75 \ V_* \log \frac{Z}{Z_0}$$

Using this relationship on anemometer measurements of wind velocity at series of heights above dune surfaces, Olson (1958 b) showed that the upper level of calm air near the surface (i.e. Z_0) was raised approximately thirty-fold from the bare sand value to the new value after the sand was planted with *Ammophila breviligulata* (Fig. 46).

A fairly low surface roughness (Z_0) around 0·03 cm seems to be a general characteristic of bare dune surfaces (Bagnold 1941, Landsberg and Riley 1943 and Olson 1958 b).

Now the threshold velocity for sand movement, 4·5 m/s must be exceeded at the 1 cm Z_0 level for sand to move from a vegetated surface. In fact Olson's results show that most dune-building vegetation reduces wind velocity at the sand surface well below this value, indeed to zero in an *Ammophila* plantation. As Olson points out we can see why most sand is trapped within a few metres of a vegetated edge. The effect is maintained by the fact that unlike other obstacles, dune-building vegetation regenerates surface roughness by growth.

Wind profiles over a dune

Ammophila keeps pace with sand accretion in the building phase as we have seen, but changes in dune shape themselves modify the overall air flow patterns. It is known from aerodynamics that laminar flow over an aerofoil crowds the streamlines and accelerates flow near the point of curvature. This produces the well-known half Venturi effect on which the lift factor of an aerofoil depends. Now an *Ammophila* dunelet or a mature coast dune, especially in regions where the prevailing and dominant wind is on shore, approximates an aerofoil shape and measurements over the profile show that wind profiles (Fig. 47) behave somewhat similarly to those over the aerofoil. The anatomy of a dune system with dunes and intervening slacks (Plate 12) is explicable in terms of these relationships.

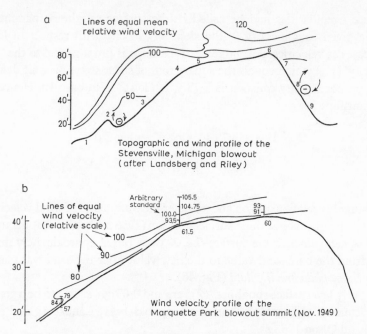

Fig. 47. Effects of topography on wind profiles over dunes. *a*, Michigan profile shows negative velocities behind small foredune ridge and large blowout dune, and crowding of high velocities very near dune surface at the upper slope (position 5); *b*, Indiana profile of present study (see table 1) shows similar crowding of high velocity near surface on windward slope. Velocities here are given relative to 3·34+ meter anemometer on the main tower, labelled 'arbitrary standard' (from Olson 1958 *b*).

Critical zones

Critical zones to bear in mind are (1) Protection in front of a big dune due to a 'stalling' effect (suggested by the spreading of the streamlines in Fig. 47); (2) Maximum wind velocity near the surface leading to maximum erosion near the crest of the windward face of the dune which according to exposure, wind and rain climate controls the height to which dunes can grow in any particular region; (3) the vortex behind the lee slope which creates calm for deposition in relation to winds flowing over the dune (and where non-prevailing winds have greater influence); (4) the extended shelter to leeward of the dune where a dune slack may be developed and (because the wind has deposited most of its sand load already on the lee slope) accretion is minimal and (5) the point beyond the shelter of the dune to landward (which is a function of the dune height) where higher wind velocities approach the sand surface carving down to non-erodable damp

1 *Arthrocnemum* marsh (sansouire) in the Camargue (Rhone delta). France. Note the open nature of the vegetation in this fully mature marsh in a climate where evapo-transpiration exceeds precipitation.

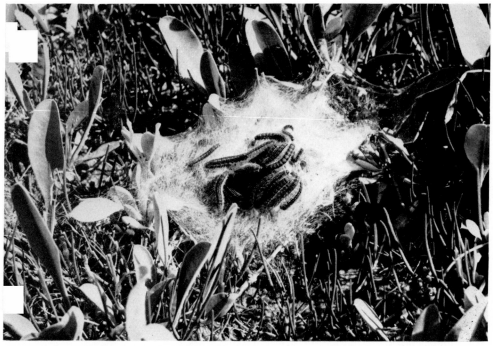

2 A 'nest' of caterpillars of the Ground Lackey moth (*Malacosoma castrensis*), one of the larger terrestrial invertebrates specifically adapted to living on salt marsh vegetation at the higher Emergence marsh level. This species has a very restricted distribution in Britain and is confined to ungrazed *Halimione* and *Limonium* marsh in south-east England. Havergate Island, Suffolk.

3 Pioneer growth form of *Puccinellia maritima* with stolons radiating onto open silt at Morecambe Bay, Lancashire. Sheep-grazing prevents flowering over most of these marshes and it is only in the more remote pioneer zones to seaward that sexual reproduction becomes important, and plants are more inherently variable. Note also the hummock form of growth which right at the start of marsh formation imposes local topographic point to point variation, later expressed as soil, moisture, and plant species variation in the fully colonized marsh.

4 Tidal litter (foreground on right) from *Spartina* marsh accumulates at the upper limit of the marsh and open up the dense *Spartina anglica* sward (foreground on left) allowing invaders like *Typha latifolia* (centre) to colonize. Bridgwater Bay, Somerset.

5 Oil pollution experiments on *Puccinellia maritima* marsh in the Burry estuary, Glamorganshire, South Wales. The plot shows the effect of chronic pollution with persistent applications of oil. Occasional pollution with oil has much less dramatic effects on the growth of salt marsh plants.

6 Sheep grazing experiments in progress at the upper limits of *Spartina anglica* marsh, Bridgwater Bay, Somerset. This is a critical transition zone where the *Spartina* marsh has reached maturity. Grazing favoured invasion by *Puccinellia maritima*, a short grass palatable to both sheep and wildfowl. The ungrazed marsh became invaded by tall growths of *Scirpus maritimus* and *Phragmites communis*.

7 Cattle walkway and flooded borrow pits in Gulf Coast marshland, Louisiana, U.S.A. These walkways are built so that man and animals can get in and out of marshes when they are flooded at high tide. The borrow pits from which silt has been dug to build the walkway provide habitat for wildfowl. (*Photograph by R. E. Williams.*)

8 Turf cutting experiment in *Festuca rubra* salting pasture at Bridgwater Bay, Somerset. This marsh has been undergrazed and sheep and wildfowl tend to avoid the tussocky *Festuca*. Turf has been cut to see if the succession can be put back to the earlier *Puccinellia* stage, as this grass is more palatable. Small amounts of *Puccinellia* are still present in the *Festuca* marsh, and in addition to the complete turf-cutting treatment, strips of marsh from which regeneration can take place are left in another treatment. The uncut control plots are also clearly visible. (*Photograph by P. G. Ainsworth.*)

9 Backshore zone of a sandy shore with abundant tidal litter. Unlike the foreshore (top left) which remains damp, the backshore sand readily dries out and it is from this zone that most shore sand is blown by the wind to feed dune vegetation (right). The tidal litter supplies nutrients for the growth of pioneer species *Agropyron junceiforme* and *Elymus arenarius*. Holy Island, Northumberland.

10 Coast dunes exposed to the maximum onslaught of prevailing and dominant winds at Morfa Dyffryn, Merionethshire, Wales. Once the dunes have grown to their maximum height they erode back from the shore. In the gaps so formed, strandline vegetation and embryo dunes start the cycle of dune building again. This shore is much trampled by tourists, but prickly Saltwort (*Salsola kali*) is avoided and scattered patches are developing in spite of the trampling.

11 *Salix repens* hummocks ('hedgehogs') at Newborough Warren, Anglesey. These very characteristic bio-topographic units are a common sub-habitat type in dunes in many parts of the world, although formed by different plant species. They are produced by alternating periods of accretion and erosion.

12 Dune slack colonized by *Salix repens* formed in the wake of a landward-migrating parabola dune (background) at Newborough Warren, Anglesey. Low-lying hollows like that in the foreground flood with fresh water in the winter.

13 Vigorous and free-flowering *Ammophila arenaria* among mobile dunes at Newborough Warren, Anglesey. This grass and the related *Ammophila breviligulata* are responsible for the build-up of dunes in many parts of the world.

14 De-pauperate growths of non-flowering *Ammophila arenaria* on stabilized dunes at Ross Links, Northumberland. The upright habit of growth persists but sand accretion has stopped, shoots topple and are very susceptible to damage from trampling at this stage.

15 A plantation of *Ammophila arenaria* protected by fishing netting pegged about 30 cm above the ground surface at Gullane dunes, East Lothian, Scotland. Sand movement at the surface is instantly stilled in the plantation. Nets prevent people trampling on sites planted to heal erosion scars and are visually unobtrusive.

16 A graded and hydraulically seeded dune at Camber, Sussex, showing good growth of introduced turf grasses. Hydraulic seeding is carried out by machine spray. Chopped straw is sprayed dry onto the bare sand to still the sand surface and provide a mulch. Seed and fertilizer are then sprayed on in a water mix. In this way a compensated environment for germination and growth is provided. Chestnut pale fencing protects the plantations and is an ideal permeable barrier for catching blown sand and helping to heal erosion gaps at the coast.

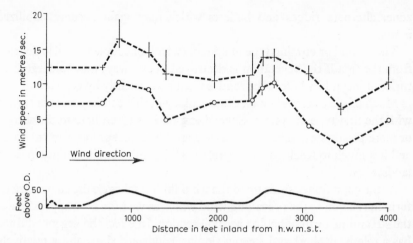

Fig. 48. Wind speeds recorded at 5 cm. (0—0) and 1m. (+—+) above the ground surface on T1 - T4 during a south-west gale of 40 knots (20 m/sec.) at Newborough Warren. The verticals on the curves show the range of speeds recorded at individual sites. The point where the dotted lines cut the verticals is the estimated average speed at the site (from Ranwell 1958).

sand just above the water table. The wind profile in Fig. 48 illustrates these relationships well.

Formation of the Dune and Slack System

Displacement of the coast dune

As we saw in Chapter 2, sand supply, orientation in relation to prevailing wind, and local topography, all greatly influence the type and extent of any particular dune system. But whatever type is considered, growth of the coast dune is initially in a linear or curvi-linear manner parallel with the strandline.

Here it may either stabilize at a low level, erode and re-cycle as in a small bay, or continue to accumulate in open coast sites where sand supply is abundant. One of two things can then happen to the coastal dune, either (1) a new coast dune forms to seaward e.g. where there are broad and high backshore levels and moderate onshore winds or (2) the coast dune grows to its maximum height and then erodes moving landwards e.g. where there are narrow backshore levels and prevailing and dominant winds are on shore.

The first or prograding type of system may simply add ridge on ridge which become stable *in situ* or, if there is more than one backshore

L

zone, alternate ridges and hollows which may again become stabilized *in situ*.

The second or eroding type of system (which of course may also develop from the first if the vegetation is destroyed in any way) may undergo centuries of instability before the sand is fixed permanently by vegetation.

Much of the earlier work on dune ecology in this country was concerned with the first type of system. Special emphasis is given here to the second or more plastic system because it has been the subject of more recent study and has much to teach us about problems of combating instability in dune landscapes.

As the coast dune builds up to the wind limit it takes on the characteristic form in relation to the prevailing wind which as we have seen approximates the streamline form of half an aerofoil section. In effect the vegetated dune has a relatively short and steeply sloping windward slope and a relatively long and gently sloping leeward slope. Now the non-vegetated barchan dune common in deserts has exactly the opposite. Taken together these facts imply that the natural tendency of a sand mound as big as a dune is to develop a shallow windward slope, but vegetation, and the growth of *Ammophila* in particular, modifies this tendency in the direction of a dune with a steep windward slope. Bearing in mind that the windward face of a vegetated coastal dune is rarely completely closed by vegetation it is clear that the vegetated coastal dune form is inherently unstable. This of course has been tacitly recognized in classical techniques of dune restoration where the aim is to create a more stable gently sloping windward face (see Steers 1964 p. 513 Fig. 108).

Seaward growth of the coast dune is restricted by the height of storm tides which can undercut the dune to form a near vertical seaward face. Once this condition develops in regions where there are strong onshore winds the coast dune windward face continues to erode sand which accumulates on the leeward slope. Thus the dune actually moves back from the shoreline while still continuing to build to its maximum height. Ultimately the crest of the dune may reach a critical height in exposed areas where *Ammophila* can no longer hold the sand and the entire seaward face and crest becomes bare eroding sand. Whole coastal dune ridges may move landward in this way (Plate 10) and on the western coast of Britain where prevailing Atlantic winds are on shore this is a natural phenomenon which occurs quite independently of human disturbance.

The highest dunes are usually found some way inland in sites where prevailing winds are directly onshore (Oosting 1954; Willis *et al* 1959). On the Atlantic coast of France or Spain the inland dunes may reach 70 or

80 m in height. On coasts where the prevailing wind is offshore maximum heights are likely to occur at the coast dune (e.g. on the east coast of the British Isles at Strathbeg, Aberdeen).

Rates of dune building and travel

In seeking to understand complex phenomena it is especially valuable to study situations in which particular effects are maximized. For example the seasonal mechanics of salt marsh accretion (see Chapter 5), only became readily apparent from the studies at Bridgwater Bay where accretion was at a maximum. In just the same way, the mechanics of mobile dune system development can be more readily understood by studying a maximal erosion situation where the prevailing and dominant wind has uninterrupted flow to a coastline exactly normal to its direction. Such a situation occurs at Newborough Warren, Anglesey. Landsberg (1956) found perfect correlation at this site between a calculated wind resultant and the orientation of parabola or U-shaped dunes (Plate 12) of which many parts of it are composed. Subsequently the rate of dune building and dune travel in a region where entire dune ridges were moving landward successively were measured by means of repeatedly levelled transects at this site (Ranwell 1958).

The theoretical point of maximum erosion was confirmed and in this case occurred about 18 m to windward of the crest of 15 m high dunes. Zones of maximum accretion varied from 0 to 18 m behind the crest in low stable dune sections to as much as 164 to 183 m to leeward of the crest in high unstable sections.

It was calculated that the coastal dune must take at least 50 years to build

Table 19. Some recorded rates of dune movement (from Ranwell 1958).

Place	Rate m/annum	Authority
Inland		
Indiana	1–2	Cowles (1911)
Lake Michigan	2–4	Gates (1950)
Coastal		
Kurische Nehrung	5·5–6·1	Care & Oliver (1918)
Gascony	9·1 (mean)	
Wales, Morfa Harlech	3·7 (max.)	Steers (1939)
Morfa Dyffryn	6·1 (max.)	
South Lancashire		
Great Crosby	1·1	Salisbury (1952)
Freshfield	5·5–7·3	
Norfolk coast	1·5	

to maximum height and its mean rate of travel inland near the coast was estimated at 6·7 m per year. It would therefore take at least another 20 years or so for the coast dune to travel landwards sufficiently for a new embryo dune system to develop. So the cycle could take some 70 or 80 years to complete. Failure to understand such time factors may result in costly, unnecessary and undesirable attempts to stabilize a system which ultimately achieves its own stabilization.

Some recorded rates of dune movement are given in Table 19.

The water table and slack differentiation

The wind ceases to erode a bare dune surface when some underlying non-erodable surface such as shingle, rock, clay or wet sand is reached. Most usually, dune slacks have either a freely-drained shingle base or a damp sand base.

As Willis *et al* (1959) have pointed out, a big dune system perched on low lying ground acts itself as an isolated catchment. They showed that water percolated through the dunes at Braunton Burrows, Devon and accumulated over impermeable sub-surface deposits to form a dome-shaped water table (Fig. 49).

They point out that steeper water gradients at the margins of the system

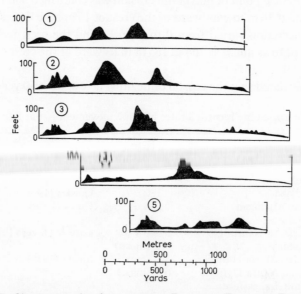

Fig. 49. Profiles across the dune system, Braunton Burrows, Devon. Heights obtained by survey are given in feet above O.D. (Newlyn). The sand above the water table of June 1952 is shown in black (from Willis *et al* 1959).

result from the fact that greater volumes of water (dependent on the greater catchment involved) percolate through the margins of the system compared with the centre of the system. They note the close correspondence of slack ground level with water table level and similar results were obtained at Newborough Warren, Anglesey (Ranwell 1959).

Parabolic dune units and cyclic alternation between dune and slack

It is rare for whole ridges to erode uniformly in the way described earlier for Newborough. Even on this system, ideally orientated for maximum uniform erosion, parts of the coast dune reach maximum height more rapidly than adjoining parts locally and this produces irregular erosion of ridges in the form of parabolic or U-shaped dune units (Fig. 50).

From the direct measurements of dune movement and studies of the growth and age patterns of *Salix repens* either side of mobile dunes, it was possible to demonstrate that there must have been cyclic alternation of dune

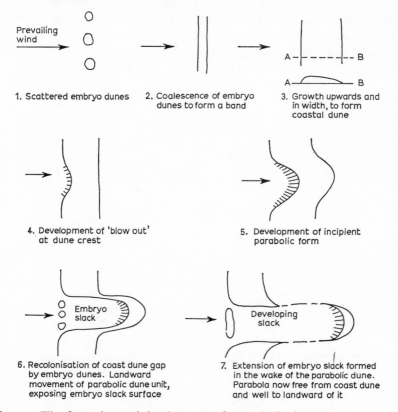

Fig. 50. The formation and development of a parabolic dune unit.

and slack at many points among the more mobile parts of the system. The period of this cycle was estimated at about 80 years and clearly corresponds to the period of the dune building cycle at the coastline (Ranwell 1960 *a*).

There is similar *a priori* evidence in N. American dunes as Oosting's (1954) graphic account testifies: 'When a dune moves over a forest the trees are buried as they stand and are preserved in the dune. Again and again "ghost" or "grave-yard" forests are reported where such long-dead trees have again been exposed as a dune moves on.' However there seems to have been no critical study of the dune and slack relationships in these American sites.

It is not implied of course that any particular point will alternate regularly, because once the dune ridge structure has become broken up complex local shelter effects play a part, and development becomes irregular.

Ultimately dunes are worn down and are sufficiently remote from coastal exposure and strong winds to become stabilized, often at some intermediate level between dune and slack. Only when this stage is reached can one really compare plant successional changes with those found on dunes that stabilize more or less *in situ* on a sheltered prograding coast.

9 Sand Dunes:
Sand, Water Relations and
Processes of Soil Formation

If initially the problem for growth of plants on salt marshes is too much water, for dune plant growth it is the reverse. Dune sand is not only remote from the permanent water table but also very low compared with silt, for example, in water-holding capacity. Plants and their dead remains increase the water-holding capacity of sand. Increasing organic matter increases the capacity of the soil to retain nutrients. This chapter concerns the properties of sand and especially its water relations. It is also concerned with the way sand is transformed into soil capable of supporting the many hundreds of plant and animal species found on dunes. The basic ideas on these subjects are still largely derived from the pioneer work of Salisbury (1952) and his results are quoted extensively. However, it is evident that on some of the more controversial points more data and more critical work with modern techniques is badly needed in both the study of water and nutrient relations on dune systems.

Properties of Sand

Particle size in dune sands

Salisbury (1952) concluded that the average particle size of dune sand has a general relationship to the average strength of the prevailing onshore winds, but this conclusion was derived from very limited data.

Subsequent studies (Cooper 1958 and Ritchie and Mather 1969) show that there is as much variation in either average or median particle size from site to site within a particular climatic region, or even within a dune system (Fig. 51), as there is from one major climatic region to another. The original source and sedimentation history of the shore sand of any particular dune system is probably of far greater significance in relation to particle size, than the wind strengths in the area. Ritchie and Mather (1969) define sand sizes in general terms as follows:

	Median particle diameter in microns
Coarse sand	> 600 to < 1100
Medium sand	< 600 to > 200
Fine sand	< 200

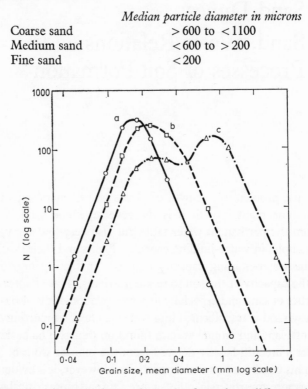

Fig. 51. Grading diagrams for sand samples from three different situations at Braunton Burrows. For each of the three samples the graphs show the proportion of sand having a particular grain size. This proportion is expressed by the parameter N, which is the percentage of the total sample which falls in a given fraction, divided by the difference between the logarithms of the maximum and minimum particle sizes in that fraction (*see* Bagnold 1941, p. 113 et seq.). The samples illustrated are as follows. (a) Fine sand from among *Ammophila* shoots on the lee slope of the main line of dunes. (b) Medium sand from the shore above high water mark. (c) Sand from the erosion face of a blow-out and containing two components, a coarse fraction left on the surface by wind sorting and a medium sand from below (from Willis *et al* 1959).

In their study of 16 dune sites in N.W. Scotland they found the median ranged from 192 to 496 microns and other studies confirm that most dune systems are composed of medium grade sand. At Newborough Warren, Anglesey particles of less than 20 microns (clay/ silt fraction) only contributed two per cent to the total. Particulate air pollution may well be augmenting this finer fraction on some of our dune systems now and this could well have far reaching effects on their water and nutrient holding capacity and consequently their flora.

Pore space

Measurements on dune soils at Braunton Burrows, Devon and Harlech, Merionethshire indicated a pore space around 40 per cent of the soil volume (Salisbury 1952). In the closest packing array the pore space between spherical particles would be 26 per cent of the volume. The difference is a measure of sand particle angularity and the extent to which particles are held apart by interstitial live and dead organic material. It is this organic matter which plays such a vital part in improving the water-holding capacity of sand.

Water Relations in the Dune

Field moisture capacity and availability

It is essential to keep in mind the changing weight to volume ratios which occur with soil maturation on a dune system. Old dune soils weigh only about half as much per unit volume as young dune soils.

Field moisture capacity may vary from 7 per cent (by volume) in young dune sand to 33 per cent in old dune sand (Salisbury 1952). In dry slack sand the field moisture capacity was between 25 and 30 per cent and in surface humus horizons of wet slacks as high as 50 per cent (by volume) at Newborough Warren, Angelsey (Fig. 52). Salisbury (1952) records minimum water contents of 1 per cent or less in dune sand and notes that water is no longer available to plants when it falls to values of 0·5 per cent, when wilting ensues. However, this does not necessarily mean the death of plants, for wilting cuts down the surface for evapo-transpiration and at least some dune plants can survive daily wilting (Oosting 1954).

Water content and plant requirements

The water content (by weight) to loss on ignition (corrected for carbon dioxide loss from carbonate) ratio is rather constant; usually from 1 to 2·5 (full range 0·15 to 3·48) Salisbury (1952). In general the water content of old dune soils is about twice that of young dune soils when the soils are at field capacity. This is clearly another indication of the changing weight to volume ratio referred to above and evidence that the water content is closely dependent on the organic matter content of dune soil.

The water content of the soil exploited by a plant of *Trifolium arvense*

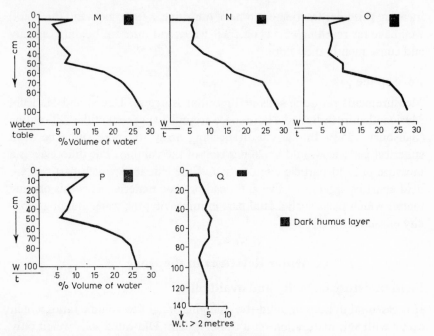

Fig. 52. Soil moisture profiles, Newborough Warren.
M & N beneath fixed dry slack *Agrostis tenuis – Festuca rubra* turf associes.
O & P beneath fixed dry slack *Salix repens* associes.
Q beneath semi-fixed dune *Salix repens* associes (Ranwell 1959).

would be used up in less than 4 days by evapo-transpiration in dry weather but the species can survive apparently unharmed on dunes up to 6 weeks without rain (Salisbury 1952). In general the water content at any one time in young dune soils is only enough for plants growing in it to survive for 2 to 5 days.

To resolve this apparent anomaly we must consider the distribution of soil moisture within the dune and the ways in which this moisture can be augmented other than by rainfall.

Soil moisture distribution within the dune

Several studies in open dune communities have shown that soil moisture augments to depths of about 60 cm below the dune surface and then tends to fall off to a more constant level (Salisbury 1952, Ranwell 1959 and Willis *et al* 1959). This is usually at about 1 m below the surface (Fig. 52). Live roots of plants characteristic of the open dune such as those of *Euphorbia portlandica* or *Ammophila* penetrate to depths of about 1 m, but not significantly below this.

In closed dune communities light rainfall is absorbed and held near the surface by organic matter to give a reversal of the soil moisture gradient characteristic of open dune soils. The water content of sand at depths between 60 to 90 cm in dry seasons is lower beneath dry dune pasture than beneath *Ammophila* on a high dune. In August 1955 at Braunton Burrows for example the values were 1 per cent and 4·9 per cent respectively (Willis *et al* 1959). However, it is still true that the establishment of seedlings in the surface layers of an open dune is very much dependent on the incidence of rainfall because the top few centimetres heat up and dry out daily in hot dry weather. In artificially stabilized mobile dunes where there has not been time for organic matter to build up it seems likely that serious moisture deficiencies might occur limiting the establishment of other species, and this would be worth investigating.

Sources of water for dune plants

Olsson-Seffer (1909) showed that the capillary rise of water from a free water surface even in very fine sand 30 to 50 microns particle size was not more than about 40 cm. The water table in a dune only 3 or 4 m high can therefore make no direct contribution to the moisture requirements of plants rooting to depths of only 1 m. In really high dunes the water table lies many metres below the surface and has no significance for plant growth at the dune surface.

The primary source of water for dune plants comes from rainfall, and in particular that proportion of it held as pendular water dependent on the moisture-holding capacity of the sand. But as Salisbury's studies have shown there must be some other source of water to carry plants through long periods of dry weather. Olsson-Seffer (1909) was the first to suggest a possible source: 'It must be remembered that the diurnal and nocturnal temperature variations are considerable on an open sand formation, on which the radiation factor is one of considerable moment. Such fluctuations in soil temperature . . . are sufficient to cause periodical condensation of water vapour in the soil.'

Salisbury (1952) demonstrated that the average water increment from dew was 0·9 ml per 100 ml soil per night in cloudless conditions, and transpiration measurements showed that this was sufficient to maintain plants exploiting that soil volume in rainless periods. Salisbury believed that warm moisture-laden air from above the adjacent sea after sunny days was drawn into the pore spaces of the sand 'as a concomitant of the upward convection currents maintained especially on the southern face and crest of the dune after dusk', where it was deposited on cold grains as internal dew.

Willis *et al* (1959) point out that at night the temperature gradient in the soil (Fig. 53) is favourable for an *upward* movement of water vapour from the warm and wetter layers of the sand below and this is so even when the upper layers do not fall below the dew point of the external air. The actual moisture contents found by Salisbury (Table 20) seem to preclude the possibility of drainage of dew from surface condensation. But as Willis *et al* (1959) point out, the greatest increase of moisture content after dew formation recorded by Salisbury (Table 20) occurred at a depth of 36 in (0·9 m) where the temperature is very unlikely to fall below the dew point. The problem clearly requires further study, perhaps with the aid of tracers, and one would like to know more about the distribution of moisture in the various components of the soil including that imbibed by micro-organisms which possibly undergo diurnal/nocturnal migration in the soil.

Table 20. Water content of sand after and before dew formation. Blakeney Point, Norfolk (from Salisbury 1952).

		Water contents by weight		
	Sample depth (cm)	27/7/38 Night samples %	27/7/38 Day samples %	Gain night-day
Single samples from the side of a pit	7	0·59	0·18	+ 0·41
	30	0·99	0·35	+ 0·64
	90	3·80	1·94	+ 1·86
Composite samples	7	0·71	0·53	+ 0·18
	30	1·31	1·18	+ 0·13

Water Relations in the Slack

Very little work has been published on the ecology of dune slacks or low-lying flat areas where growth is influenced by the proximity of the water table although they may occupy up to half the area of some dune systems.

Shape of the water table and drainage

As we have seen, the overall shape of the water table in a large isolated dune system is dome-shaped (Fig. 49). This means that peripheral slack communities are particularly likely to have nutrient enriched ground water derived from lateral seepage outwards from the centre of the dune system. It also explains why permanent dune lakes often occur at the landward side of the dune system where hinterland and dune system drainage meets.

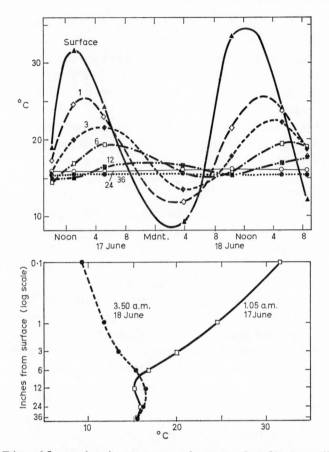

Fig. 53. Diurnal fluctuations in temperature down a sand profile. An undisturbed profile about 40 in (1 m) deep was exposed by digging a pit in the top of a bare dune. Resistance thermometers were inserted without delay into the profile at 36, 24, 12, 6, 3 and 1 in from the surface, and the excavated sand was restored as far as possible in its original position. After 2 days, periodic measurements of temperature were made, and are shown in the upper diagram. The temperature at the surface was recorded by means of a mercury-in-glass thermometer. The lower diagram shows the maximum extent of the fluctuation against a logarithmic scale of depth. Times are given in G.M.T. Braunton Burrows, Devon (from Willis *et al* 1959).

The ground surface closely follows the shape of the water table from slack to slack indicating the limit to which wind deflation of the dunes can occur. At the edge of a slack, the water table rises slightly, but does not follow the steep contours of the dune. Any one slack therefore has a saucer-shaped water table unit tilted slightly downwards towards the periphery of the dune system.

In most dune systems with well developed wet slacks impermeable clay or rock underlies the sand and holds the water up. Where they are built on permeable shingle slacks tend to be dry.

Tidal effects on the water table

Sea water does not readily penetrate into the ground water zone through a coastal dune (unless a reverse gradient is created by ground water extraction). The positive drainage gradient out from the dune system normally prevents this. Consequently, no fluctuation of the water table with respect to tide is found within the larger hindshore dune systems like Braunton Burrows, Devon or Newborough Warren, Anglesey (Willis et al 1959, Ranwell, 1959). Where a large part of the dune system is surrounded by sea water and dunes are built on shingle, tidal fluctuations of the fresh water table floating on salt water among the permeable shingle can occur (Hill and Hanley 1914). Brown (1925) showed that the fresh water body beneath small pervious islands capped with dunes is lens-shaped, and floats upon the convex salt ground water surface.

Seasonal fluctuations of the water table

In a wet year there may be widespread flooding in dune slacks at Newborough Warren, Anglesey from November to April. The water table falls from April to August and recovers the high winter levels during autumn rains. As Fig. 54 shows there is close correlation in this seasonal pattern with the distribution of rainfall. The rapid fall of the water table in April and May coincides with the leafing of deciduous plants like Salix repens (dominant in the slacks) and the autumn rise with the leaf fall in mid-October.

A ten year study of water level and rainfall fluctuations at Braunton Burrows, Devon enabled Willis et al (1959) to estimate the extent and duration of recent flooding at any point on the site from a knowledge of its land height and water level. They found that the slopes of lines for the regression of water level on rainfall were nearly proportional to the mean heights of the water table at each sampling point. They also calculated an index of flooding which could be related to different plant communities.

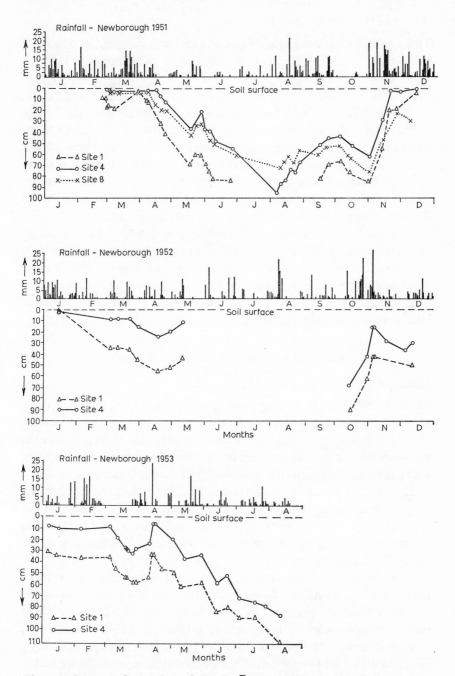

Fig. 54. Seasonal fluctuation of the free water table at selected sites in wet slacks with *Salix repens* associes, and daily rainfall 1951–1953 at Newborough Warren, Anglesey (from Ranwell 1959).

This was defined as the average numbers of months in a year for which the site is under water, from 0, free of flooding, to 12, permanently flooded.

Water table range

Willis *et al* (1959) concluded from their study that maximum annual range of the water table occurred near the flatter centre of the dome-shaped water table and smaller ranges occurred at the more steeply sloping water table of the peripheral sites. This relationship was not confirmed at Newborough Warren where a rock ridge running through the centre of the system may complicate the pattern of water movements. In both studies the annual range of the water table was of the order of 1 m and this probably depends on the total annual rainfall which was similar in both areas. In drier climates as at Winterton, Norfolk the annual range of the water table is reduced to about 0·5 m and the possible vertical range of communities dependent on the water table must be telescoped accordingly. Clearly there is an analogy here with the vertical range of salt marsh communities in relation to the vertical range of the tide.

Soil Development in Dunes and Slacks

Changes in soil properties with time

Striking differences in soil properties of young dunes compared with those of increasing age were detected by Salisbury (1925). He recorded an increase in organic matter paralleled by a decrease in pH value of the soil solution and a decrease in the calcium carbonate content of dunes with increasing age at Blakeney Point, Norfolk and Southport dunes, Lancashire.

These trends depend upon decrease in mobility of dunes as they become fully vegetated and accumulate organic matter and the time they are exposed to the leaching effects of rainfall. This dissolves carbonate in the soluble bicarbonate form and carries it downwards to the water table where it may flow out of the system.

The opposing agencies favouring nutrient accumulation and nutrient depletion interact with the changing soil properties in a rather complicated way as we shall see. Also the trends may be obscured in systems with high initial carbonate content (Gimingham in Burnett 1964), or persistent mobility (Ranwell 1959, and Willis *et al* 1959). Nevertheless, Salisbury's conception of this basic pattern of soil development is generally applicable to dune systems wherever they occur.

Differences in soil moisture in young and old dune and slack soils have already been discussed. Right from the start this effectively controls the oxidation of organic matter so that young slack soils start with twice the amount of organic matter that comparable aged dune soils contain (Ranwell 1959). In addition, gravity favours the accumulation of nutrients in the slacks at the expense of the bank of nutrients in dunes. As Olson (1958 a) succinctly puts it, 'the rich system gets richer and the poor system poorer', at least until wind deflation brings the two systems together so closely at the dry slack level that the systems interact as in a chalk heath situation where shallow-rooted plants live in an acid soil side by side with deeper rooted plants tapping base rich soil below (Fig. 55 Profile EF).

Particle size changes

Perhaps because the initial silt and clay contents of dune sand are so low as to be almost unmeasurable, little attention has been given to changes in the finest fractions of dune and slack soil. However Olson's (1958 a) work on the ancient inland dune systems of Indiana, U.S.A., has shown that these finer particle fractions do accumulate with time as a result of weathering *in situ* and accumulation of airborne dust. The exchange capacity of the sand will be increased by clay accumulation but is of course decreased by hydrogen ion replacement as leaching proceeds with age.

Rates of change in carbonate content

The evidence from a number of dune systems with an initial carbonate content of not more than 5 per cent (by weight) shows that most free carbonate is lost from the first decimetre of surface dune soil within 300 to 400 years (Salisbury 1952, Olson 1958 a, Ranwell 1959). Under the prevailing weather conditions, Olson (1958 a) found that it takes about 1,000 years for carbonate to leach out of the first 2 metres of dune soil in the Indiana dunes. The rate of carbonate loss was found to be proportional to the amount of cabonate left at any point in time. Salisbury (1952) points out that calcium may be replenished at the surface in three ways: by wind blow of shell fragments from mobile dunes, by re-cycling via plant roots and leaves, and by the burrowing activity of rabbits. Ultimately however it seems from Olson's studies that leaching wins in the end, even where forest cover is developed as on the Indiana dunes. Similarly Ovington (1950) found in studies of the afforested Culbin dunes that nutrients are lost from the soil at a greater rate than they are being made available. He points out that if an allowance were made for the nutrients in the trees there would be an overall increase of nutrients in the afforested areas, but these of course will be removed at felling.

M

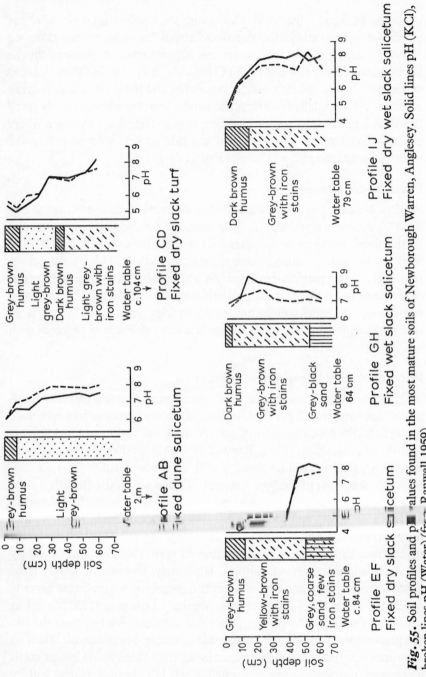

Fig. 55. Soil profiles and pH values found in the most mature soils of Newborough Warren, Anglesey. Solid lines pH (KCl), broken lines pH (Water) (from Ranwell 1959).

Profile AB
Fixed dune salicetum

Grey-brown humus
Light grey-brown
Water table 2 m

Profile CD
Fixed dry slack turf

Grey-brown humus
Light grey-brown
Dark brown humus
Light grey-brown with iron stains
Water table c. 104 cm

Profile EF
Fixed dry slack salicetum

Grey-brown humus
Yellow-brown with iron stains
Grey, coarse sand few iron stains
Water table c. 84 cm

Profile GH
Fixed wet slack salicetum

Dark brown humus
Grey-brown with iron stains
Grey-black sand
Water table 64 cm

Profile IJ
Fixed dry wet slack salicetum

Dark brown humus
Grey-brown with iron stains
Water table 79 cm

Rates of organic matter and nitrogen changes

Salisbury (1925) found that organic matter augments slowly at first, but appreciably faster after about 200 years in the dunes especially in the higher rainfall climate at Southport, Lancashire.

In contrast Wilson (1960) found very rapid increase in organic matter in the very lime-deficient dunes at Studland, Dorset. This he attributes to early invasion by *Calluna* which is largely responsible for the rapid litter accumulation, and possibly also accelerated leaching of what little carbonate there is present initially, by means of humic acids as well as carbonic acid. Under the rapidly developing acid conditions litter breakdown is inhibited and organic matter accumulation promoted (Fig. 56). Optimum organic matter accumulation was found at the limit of winter flooding at Newborough Warren. Olson (1958 *a*) found that organic carbon increases about three times faster at the surface compared with 10 cm depth on the Indiana dunes. Even in soils believed to be about 500 years old not more than 2 per cent organic matter accumulated at depths of 20 to 25 cm at Newborough Warren (Ranwell 1959).

Carbon to nitrogen ratios were found to vary from 10:1 in young dune

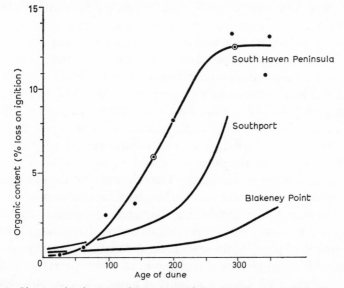

Fig. 56. Changes in the organic content of dune surface soil (0 to 5 cm depth) with age at South Haven Peninsula, Dorset. The ringed points represent overall means for the second and third dune ridges from the coast. Salisbury's (1925) curves for the Southport, Lancashire and Blakeney Point, Norfolk dune systems have been inserted for comparison (from Wilson 1960).

grassland soils, to 20:1 in old forest dune soils in the Indiana dunes (Olson 1958 a). A balance between gain and loss of nitrogen seems to be reached at about 1000 years following stabilization of the dune surface.

Cation exchange capacities

The cation exchange capacity of the slack soils at Newborough rose from 2–3 m E per cent in young dry slack soils to 15 to 20 m E per cent in older wet slack soils (Ranwell 1959). Olson (1958 a) found low values in very ancient dunes at Indiana: 5·3 m E per cent in 8,000 year old dunes and 6·5 to 8 m E per cent in 10,000-year-old dunes. In contrast Ovington (1950) found quite high values in the humus layers at Tentsmuir, Fife up to 25–30 m E per cent and these were probably due to the presence of *Calluna* litter, the dominant species in the area examined.

Biological influences on soil formation

The initial organic matter supplied to the shore in tidal litter forms a relatively rich nutrient medium for the growth of strandline plants. It is processed by temporary faunas including abundant amphipods and mites (McGrorty *pers comm.*). Brown (1958) found little evidence of fungi in tide-washed sand, but Gunkel (1968) has recently demonstrated that oil-decomposing bacteria are present in shore sand and pollutant products decomposed by bacteria may well be enriching not only the shore, but also the sand being blown onto coastal dunes at the present time.

Prior to the advent of serious shore pollution, the switch from the relatively rich tidal litter-based nutrient economy of the shore to the nutrient deficient high level *Ammophila* dune sand must clearly have presented serious nutritional problems for the inhabitants of the open dune community. Webley *et al* (1952) developed a technique whereby the microfloras of the open sand, the rhizosphere, and the root surface of *Agropyron* and *Ammophila* could be compared. They showed that the rhizosphere of these sand dune plants contains abundant bacteria which are present only in very low numbers in intervening sand areas. Hassouna and Wareing (1964) have demonstrated by experimental cultures that nitrogen is limiting for the growth of plants of the open dune and that the growth of root-surface sterilized *Ammophila* seedlings exhibited much poorer growth than those inoculated with bacteria capable of fixing nitrogen (providing carbon sources, possibly derived from exudates, are adequate). The regular association of fungi e.g. *Inocybe* species with *Ammophila* suggests that mycorrhizal symbiosis may also be important in the supply of nitrogen.

Webley *et al* (1952) also demonstrated that the bacterial flora of the early stages of dune fixation increased to the dune pasture stage, but decreased markedly where dune heath was developed. At this stage the fungal flora, which like the bacterial flora augmented with increasing fixation, became more abundant than the bacterial flora (Table 21). However, it should be borne in mind that the values are given on a weight basis.

Table 21. Microbiological analyses of dune soils on a transect through the Newburgh dunes, Aberdeenshire, 8 September 1948 (from Webley *et al* 1952).

Sample (depth 5–15 cm)	Moisture content (% of dry wt. of sample)	pH	Bacteria per g oven-dried material	Fungi per g oven-dried material
(1) Open sand	3·5	6·80	18,000	270
(2) Yellow dunes, *Ammophila arenaria*	3·7	6·68	1,630,000	1,700
(3) Early fixed dunes *Ammophila arenaria* with grasses, etc.	1·5	5·14	1,700,000★	69,470
(4) Dune pasture	7·1	4·80	2,230,000	109,780
(5) Dune heath	16·8	4·27	127,000	148,190

★ Just over 50 % were actinomycetes.

Gimingham (in Burnett 1964) notes that legumes increase in the later stages of stabilization and shrubs like *Hippophaë rhamnoides* also develop root nodules with bacteria which have been shown to be capable of nitrogen fixation (Bond *et al* 1956).

We are still very ignorant of the nutrient pathways in sand dune habitats, but it does seem evident that there is a distinct switch from the bacterial-based economy of the younger or more base-rich dune soils to a fungal-based economy on the older or more base-deficient soils dominated by *Calluna* or conifer plantations where litter accumulates. No information seems to be available on the biological influences on soil formation in dune slacks, but those that flood late into spring have an additional source of production from algal blooms contributing to their enrichment. Shields (1957) has demonstrated high levels of amino nitrogen in algal lichen surface crusts compared with sand at 15 cm depth in New Mexico desert soils. Similar crusts formed by congeneric species occur in young lime-rich dune slacks and probably engender a continually renewable supply of soil nitrogen. In fact it has been demonstrated with the use of labelled nitrogen that blue-green algae in dune slacks fix atmospheric nitrogen and that such labelled nitrogen is taken up by mosses and higher plants from the soil and assimilated (Stewart 1967).

10　Sand Dunes: Structure and Function of Dune Communities

Dunes are immensely rich in species of plants and animals in contrast to salt marshes. Unlike a salt marsh with exacting constraints imposed by salt-dominated relatively level ground, dune habitats are highly variable. They range from mobile to fixed dunes of varying aspects and from ground-water dependent, to ground-water independent levels. This complex mosaic of habitats is further diversified at the surface by the plant and animal components which both inhabit and help to create the environment in which they live.

Ecologists were rather mesmerized by this wealth of diversity and, until recently devoted much of their time to lengthy descriptive studies and rather little to behavioural study and experiment. As Elton (1966) puts it, 'One wishes that some of the very elaborate European investigations of dune faunas had given less time to statistical abstractions and cryptic classical terminologies, and more to finding out what the animals do and where they do it, in relation to the rather obvious patterns of habitat structure and climate.' This is equally true of the study of dune floras and dictates limits to the accounts of the dune and slack communities given in this and the next chapter. The emphasis is therefore primarily on structure and rather less on function, but it is hoped that the accounts will encourage future study on function of the component parts of the dune system, such as the ecology of the *Ammophila* tussock, the *Salix repens* hummock, or *Hippophaë* scrub.

The Dune Flora and Fauna

Species diversity

Taking British dune systems as a whole, i.e. dune and slack complexes, Salisbury (1952) notes there are about 400 species of vascular plants. It is clear that this represents only the truly native flora, for a recent tally of native and introduced vascular plants on 43 of the more important dune systems in Great Britain shows that over 900 species occur on them. Many of these additional species are associated with the forestry plantations developed on dunes over the past 100 years. More than half the species of vascular plants growing on British dunes at the present time were probably introduced there directly or indirectly by man or by birds (especially gulls, see below). It has always been accepted of course that the dune flora contains a large element derived from the weed flora of agricultural land. This element of heterogeneity from site to site in the dune flora presents classification problems for classical phytosociologists. Floristic assemblages are often as unstable as those on a rubbish dump. Bearing out Darwin's conclusion that the indigenous plants of a district are not necessarily those best suited to it, Westhoff (1952) points out that no less than 31 species in the *Hippophaë – Ligustrum* community on Dutch dunes are exotics.

There are in addition several hundred species of lichens, bryophytes, fungi and algae on our dune systems and no doubt an equally rich microflora. It would be a formidable task to develop floristic classification of the dune floras of the world let alone the fact that species have not even been listed for such major European dune systems as the Coto Doñana in Spain for example.

No figures are available for the animal species found on a whole sand dune system. Heerdt and Morzer Bruyns (1960) found 368 species of arthropods in the open dune communities on the island of Terschelling off the Dutch coast. Hincks *et al* (1951–1954) recorded over 2,000 species of invertebrates (between one fifth and one quarter of the British fauna) on the sand dune and salt marsh complex at Spurn Head, Yorkshire in an area of less than 1 square mile (less than 200 ha). Duffey (1968) found no less than 188 species of spiders alone in systematic sampling on the lime-rich dunes of Whiteford Burrows, Glamorgan and the more lime-deficient dunes at Tentsmuir, Fife.

He points out that the relatively low total of only 54 species of spiders found on Terschelling by Heerdt and Morzer Bruyns (1960) is partly due to the fact that the collections were limited to a particular time of the year (August) and partly to the limited area within each vegetation type sampled. The sampling intensity is particularly important, because even with spring and summer sampling at Whiteford Burrows, Cotton (1967) found only 25 per cent of Duffey's total of spider species for that site.

Coleoptera, Hymenoptera and Diptera seem to be the best represented insect groups in the dune habitat.

Communities

Biological spectra

Raunkiaer's system of life form groups as modified by Braun-Blanquet (1932) is based on the position of the perennating organs during the unfavourable season, i.e. during cold winter or hot dry summer, and it is a useful way of analysing complex floras.

Böcher (1952) gives results for a series of sand ridges on shingle at Isefjord, Denmark (Table 22). The flora of dunes and slacks were analysed separately at Newborough (Table 23).

Both analyses clearly emphasize the dominance of the hemicryptophyte habit i.e. plants with perennial shoots and buds close to the earth's surface, and this is reinforced by the fact that the abundant cryptogams of dune systems also are to be classified as hemicryptophytes. Also notable is the importance of therophytes (annual species) in the open habitats of the early stages of succession in Böcher's figures and the high preponderance of this group in both dunes and slacks at Newborough, a west coast dune system with a high degree of mobility and hence extensive areas of open ground.

Nobuhara (1967) has studied the way in which proportions of life form types change zonally and seasonally in the Japanese strand flora.

Analytical studies

Much of the European literature on sand dune ecology is dominated by subjective classification of vegetation types which appear relatively homogeneous to the observer. Often they are accompanied by somewhat arbitrarily chosen measurements of habitat factors, but the information contained in them is not readily applicable to functional aspects of the vegetation groups or usable in relation to modern management requirements. More recently their value as a basis for vegetation mapping, which as Westhoff (1952) points out is of value to the dune landscape architect in enabling him to see what will grow where and maintain itself in competition with existing species, has been demonstrated by such studies as those of Martin (1959) in America and Boerboom (1960) and Maarel and Westhoff (1964) in Holland. At the same time attempts are being made to draw together classifications of dune associes and selected environmental factors for dune systems in several European countries (Wiemann and Domke 1967).

More objective methods of purely floristic analysis such as the association analysis developed by Williams and Lambert (1960) have been applied to dune floras in Holland (Maarel 1966), in Australia (Welbourn and Lange

Table 22. Biological spectra of dune ridges at Isefjord, Denmark.
Figures refer to numbers of species in each group (from Böcher 1952)

	Phanerophyte	Chamaephyte	Hemicryptophyte	Geophyte	Therophyte
Strandline	0	0	33	18	48
Coast ridge	3	0	56	19	22
2nd ridge	8	0	68	11	13
3rd ridge	12	2	65	12	9
4th ridge	10	9	70	5	5
5th ridge	17	5	63	5	9
Landward dune	11	7	64	7	11
Heath	13	13	70	4	0

Table 23. Biological spectra of dunes and slacks at Newborough Warren, Anglesey.
Figures refer to numbers of species in each group (from Ranwell 1959).

	Phanerophytes	Chamaephytes	Hemicryptophytes	Geophytes	Helophytes	Therophytes	Total species
Dunes	4	11	40	5	0	40	122
Slacks	0	9	57	9	9	16	109

1969) and in England (Moore 1971). In addition Maarel (1966) has sought to combine classification and ordination techniques and to correlate directly vegetation and environmental types (analysed separately) in a unified system.

Study of the Island beach dune spit in New Jersey led Martin (1959) to conclude that the dune system consisted of a zoned mosaic dominated by topographically determined environmental features. Topography and vegetation were interrelated and interacting. Most community types could occur on more than one topographic facet and topographic facets could support more than one community type.

The hummock is a good example of a biotopographic unit which maintains integrity as a habitat unit in dune systems in many parts of the world. Thus Osborn and Robertson (1939) writing of New South Wales dunes, Australia note 'that mat plants (*Mesembryanthemum aequilaterale, Scaveola suaveolens* and *Stackhausia spathulata*) may persist, building the sand into rounded hummocks a metre or more in height, long after wind erosion has removed the low dune on which they had been growing'. Ramaley (1918) describing San Francisco dunes in California, U.S.A. notes that, 'Distributed throughout the dune area are many small mounds 2 to 4 m high capped with willow (*Salix lasiolepis*).' Yano (1962) in Japan speaks of clonal hummocks in unfixed dune, and Duffey (1968) notes that at Whiteford Burrows, South Wales *Salix repens* hummocks 2 to 3 m high form small steep-sided dunes which have earned the local name 'hedgehogs' (Plate 11).

The point to be made here is that clonally based pattern is of such universal significance as a module of plant and animal community structure that it must become more widely utilized in the study of dune ecology if functional aspects are to be successfully unravelled.

Duffey (1968) points out that 'phytosociological concepts are of limited value to the ecologist studying animal associations on dunes and habitat classification is proposed based mainly on structural characteristics of the vegetation cover' (Fig. 57). He finds that the more distinctive spider faunas

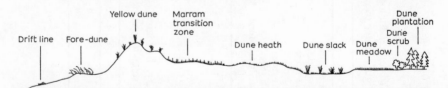

Fig. 57. Diagrammatic representation of habitats on a dune system (from Duffey 1968).

are associated with the more specialized open dune and dune heath habitats compared with other dune habitat types and notes close similarity in dune heath and inland heath spider faunas.

Ardö (1957) found that the dipterous fauna of sand dunes was 'overwhelmingly rich'. He distinguished a eurytope group of species and a stenotope group. In the latter a close relationship was demonstrated between thermal preference and choice of zone. Drought resistance and light preference were also important.

The main factors affecting distribution of invertebrates include: mechanical damage by flying sand particles; physical injury by desiccation and salt content of onshore wind; shelter; and food according to Heerdt and Morzer Bruyns (1960). They note that few species can survive seaward of the main coast dune ridge and that this is therefore a principal boundary for invertebrates of the open dune areas they studied.

Primary biotopographic units of the dunes

The primary biotopographic units of dunes are those associated with orientation, particularly in regard to incidence of direct insolation and incidence of dominant winds. Boerboom (1964) as we saw in Chapter 1, has recorded the microclimatic differences due to aspect of dune slopes. In many continental studies plant community analyses are related to aspect in a general way. However, we are a long way from understanding precisely how *Empetrum nigrum* becomes dominant on a shade slope and how its establishment seems to be prevented completely on a sun slope as on Terschelling, for example. Primary topographic units include:

(1) Dune plateaux
(2) Solar slopes
(3) Shade slopes
(4) Windward slopes
(5) Leeward slopes
(6) Intermediate slopes
(7) Dune hollows

The ecology of any one of these major units would be worth studying on its own in relation to the zonal gradients of a dune system.

Secondary biotopographic units of dunes

Superimposed on the plateaux or orientated slopes of dunes are secondary units ranging from physiographically dominated units like blow-outs, through biotopographic units like tussocks, and hummocks, gulleries, warrens, burrow mouths, ant hills and pathways to patterned plant shape and height arrangements which themselves create diverse topography on otherwise level ground.

Once again one would like to see studies orientated more specifically on these individual secondary biotopographic units of the dune system and already the trend towards this type of study is starting. For example, Ardö (1957) studied the microclimate of *Elymus* dunes in Scandinavia in relation to Diptera, Heerdt and Morzer Bruyns (1960) the microclimate of *Ammophila* tussocks in Holland in relation to the fauna, while Elton (1966) gives us a fascinating insight into the oasis-like character of this habitat from observations on the Daymer dunes, Cornwall.

The clonal hummock habitat is of particular interest because the plants that create it frequently can only originate in a slack where there is adequate moisture for germination. Subsequently they keep pace with accretion from the advancing dune and ultimately come to lie at the dune summit (e.g. *Salix repens* at Newborough Warren, *Populus alba* in the Coto Doñana, Spain). This fundamental form has received very little specialized study and offers particularly attractive opportunities for comparative study in discrete units in a great variety of orientations, vertical heights, and horizontal zones from seaward to landward.

Animal-controlled biotopographic units are just beginning to receive detailed study. Work is in progress for example on the South Walney Island dunes, Lancashire where the largest Lesser Black-backed Gull colony in Europe has transformed the dune vegetation over considerable areas from open *Ammophila* dune to a distinctive lush carpeting growth of annual weed species such as *Stellaria media*. Trampling by gulls has been observed to destroy robust *Ammophila* tussock growth at Newborough Warren, Anglesey but to so enrich the dune sand with guano locally that *Dactylorchis* species (normally confined to slacks), grow in lush turf among the high level dunes. Gillham (1964) records that the commonest means of arrival of viable weed seeds in off shore island sites with gulleries was in the pellets which gulls eject from their crops. Single plants of weed species such as *Brassica sinapis*, *Plantago lanceolata* and *Stellaria media* were found on perching hummocks where regurgitation pellets also occurred at Newborough Warren.

The activities of grazing animals (especially rabbits) on dunes have not yet received the systematic study they deserve. We are aware in a general way of the profound effects that rabbit grazing has had on the dune flora, especially following the striking changes that have occurred since myxomatosis. But we do not have any critical experimental data and nor has there been any serious attempt to relate specific population densities of rabbits to plant community types. Rabbit population density and grazing intensity varied enormously from site to site on any particular dune system prior to myxomatosis. Intensively warrened areas were particularly associated with the better vegetated more landward parts of the dune system which are frequently worn down to a level intermediate between the dune and dry slack level. On larger dune systems with extensive areas of highly mobile dunes to seaward, rabbit density and grazing intensity was much reduced in these seaward parts. On smaller more stable systems such as that at Blakeney, Norfolk, rabbit grazing evidently did occur extensively at the coast and White (1961) records much improved growth and flowering of *Agropyron junceiforme* in embryo dunes following loss of rabbits from myxomatosis. The general changes he recorded on transect studies at Blakeney are similar to those found in dry slack transect studies at Newborough Warren, Anglesey described in the next chapter.

Both grazing and wind exposure have profound effects on the structure of vegetation of dunes and it is useful at this point to consider the vertical layering of vegetation.

The Vegetation Layers

Boerboom (1960) points out that deviations in the correlated occurrence of the respective vegetation layers may lead to anomalies in classification and suggests that more attention should be given to their separate analysis. It is interesting here to note that no correlation was found between the distribution of species of filamentous algae on a salt marsh and the species of higher plants in a recent (unpublished) study of a Norfolk coast marsh. Stewart and Pugh (1963) found a similar lack of correlation between blue-green algae and the dominant flora at Gibraltar Point, Lincolnshire. Similarly one would expect that shade tolerant bryophytes with wide edaphic tolerance might well prove to be indifferent to what species of plant provides the shade so long as it has the right structure. Experimental work with artificial structures could soon clear up this point. Such studies are incidentally of direct relevance to the colonization of erosion scars after their treatment with dead brushwood.

The ground carpet layer

One of the most noticeable features of dune vegetation in the later stages of stabilization is the abundance of bryophytes and lichens. There has been very little study of the growth of dune lichens, but interesting work has been carried out on bryophytes. Richards (1929), and Ducker (in Steers 1960), demonstrated their zonation at Blakeney Point, and Scolt Head Island, Norfolk respectively, and Birse and Gimingham (1955) have studied growth form in relation to increasing stability. Pioneer species like *Tortula ruraliformis* on open sand are of the acrocarpous type with an upright growth habit capable of growing through small amounts of accreting sand. In more stable areas pleurocarpous mosses with a spreading habit of growth like *Hypnum cupressiforme* are found.

In moss transplant experiments (Birse *et al* 1957) there was no emergence of 8 species transplanted into *Ammophila* zones subject to 4 to 5 cm sand accretion in 10 months. In more stable *Ammophila*, 3 species emerged through 3 cm accretion and only where accretion was less than 1 cm in 10 months did all 8 species survive. In pot burial experiments several species emerged through 4 cm burial and none from deeper burial. The ability to produce rhizoids in overlying sand and the rapidity of upward growth were important in the ability to survive burial.

Robertson (1955) demonstrated the importance of shade by transplant experiments and found, with the exception of two species which were indifferent, the order in which transplants to a sunny site died out was in the same order as the level of shading in which they normally grew. North-field (1968) found that pioneer bryophytes at Studland, Dorset were always in well protected sites associated with other plants and only began to move out into open sand with the invasion of *Calluna* which occurs at an early stage on this lime-deficient dune system. Lichens tend to become more abundant in dry rabbit-disturbed ground than bryophytes. With the general growth of grasses since myxomatosis, bryophytes at first increased in the formerly lichen-rich areas, but are now decreasing as shade increases and litter isolates them from the sand surface.

Alvin (1960) has recorded the lichen zonation on Studland dunes (Fig. 58) and compares his results with Böcher's (1952) study of lichen zonation on the island dunes at Laesø, Denmark. Differences were believed to be primarily due to climatic factors as both are lime-deficient dune systems. Brown and Brown (1969) found that lichens at Blakeney, Norfolk were well represented in arid areas less favourable to higher plant growth and Robertson (1955) found that on dry eminences at Ross Links, Northumberland, lichen mats break into polygons especially where turf death attributed to drought due to rabbit burrows close to the surface occurs. Such areas were especially prone to erosion.

Dune annuals are a very characteristic element of the dune flora occurring on the ground layer among lichens and especially in the sheltered mouths of old rabbit burrows. Salisbury (1952) has shown that these are

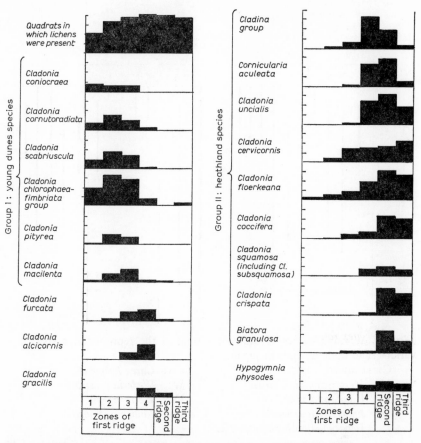

Fig. 58. Histograms representing the distribution of the main lichen species in six zones of the dunes as determined by their occurrence in 100 random quadrats in each zone. One division of the vertical scale represents 25 occurrences. The top left histogram shows the number of quadrats in which any lichens occurred. South Haven Peninsula, Dorset (from Alvin, 1960).

shallow-rooted plants which mostly germinate in autumn and are able to grow in the warmer days of winter at a season when moisture is adequate. Lichen rich sites are 'hot-spots' and winter temperatures are adequate for growth. In summer the winter annuals pass the unfavourable season in seed.

The grass/herb layer

It is of particular interest that in addition to many of the hummock species, such dominant plants of the dunes as *Carex arenaria* can also only establish from seed in damp hollows. Unlike the hummock formers which

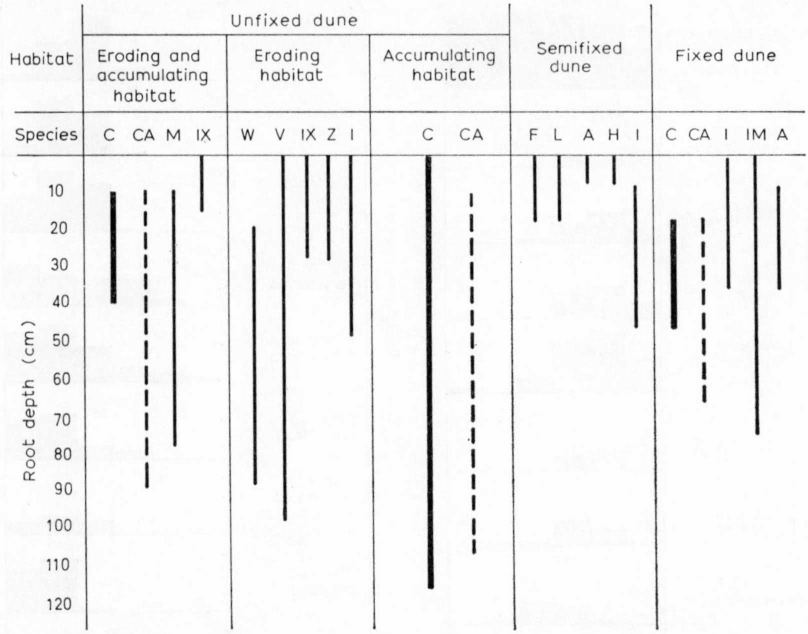

Fig. 59. Working ranges of the root system of the representative species in various sand dune habitats in Japan.

C: *Calystegia soldanella*   CA: *Carex kobomugi*
M: *Messerschmidia sibirica*   W: *Wederia prostrata*
V: *Vitex rotundifolia*   IX: *Ixeris repens*
F: *Fimbristylis sericea*   L: *Linaria japonica*
I: *Ischaemum anthephroides* var.
        eriostachyum
IM: *Imperata cylindrica* var. *koenigii*   Z: *Zoysia macrostachya*
A: *Artemisia capillaris*   H: *Heteropappus arenarius*

(from Yano 1962)

have rather limited horizontal, as opposed to vertical powers of growth, this species spreads widely onto dunes by means of rapidly extending horizontal growth. In relatively dry systems like that at Holkham or Blakeney, Norfolk, *Carex arenaria* may well be of uniform clonal origin over very large areas. It would be interesting to apply Harberd's (1961) technique of clonal analysis to see if this can be demonstrated. Certainly White's (1961) observation that *Carex arenaria* is holding its own, but not spreading to new areas at Blakeney Point since myxomatosis implies problems of establishment.

Those biennial or perennial species which do regenerate at the dune level to become part of the herb layer like *Euphorbia paralias* or *Cyno-*

glossum officinalis tend to be large seeded and capable of very rapid root extension down to moist layers at 15 cm depth within a week of germination. Thus their occupancy as seedlings of the tricky arid ground layer is cut down to a minimum. Yano (1962) has studied root formation of Japanese dune plants in relation to depth, root area, morphology, and propagation across the dune zones. He found that plants with well developed rhizomes rooting deeply over a wide area, formed large clones on mobile dunes. On fixed dunes plants had poorly-developed rhizome systems, were generally shallow-rooted over more limited areas, and formed small clones (Fig. 59).

The striking change in the growth form of *Ammophila* species from the vigorous close tussock habit of mobile dunes (Plate 13) to the sparse depauperate isolated shoots of fixed dunes (Plate 14) has been variously interpreted as due to drought, mineral deficiency, toxicity or senescence (Marshall 1965). Olson (1958 *c*) was the first to suggest that normal internodal elongation in *Ammophila breviligulata* on a stable surface raises the meristem into surface dry sand which prevents normal development of adventitious roots. However Laing (1954) produced experimental evidence that mineral deficiency and toxicity were not associated with decline in vigour of *Ammophila breviligulata* and found that sand burial alone was sufficient to restore vigour. Marshall (1965) reached similar conclusions (see also Hope-Simpson and Jefferies 1966) with regard to decline of both *Ammophila arenaria* and *Corynephorus canescens* (Fig. 60). In a nice demonstration using split root-culture technique he found that new adventitious roots in *Corynephorus canescens* were more efficient in water and nutrient uptake than nine-month-old roots. The interest of these studies lies in the emphasis they give to inherent morphological, growth, and senescence characteristics of dune dominants in relation to successional changes of plant pattern. This tendency for *Ammophila* to literally grow out of the ground in stable dune surfaces is well illustrated in the toppling of *Ammophila* shoot tufts in response to trampling (Plate 14).

With the development of really fine, detailed studies of the types just mentioned one is forcibly reminded of Watt's (1947) vision in his classical paper on 'Pattern and process in the plant community'. We begin to see the possibilities of, as he puts it, 'fusing the shattered fragments into the original unity.' But we have a long way to go in understanding the complex interacting patterns of the dune grass/herb layer. As Olson (1958 *a*) points out, 'successions in the dunes are going off in different directions and have different destinations according to the many possible combinations of independent variables which determine the original site and subsequent

N

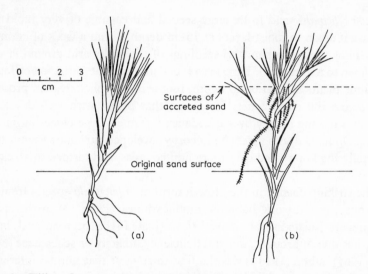

Fig. 60. Tillers from two plants of *Corynephorus canescens* growing approximately 20 cm apart. In plant (a) the site of adventitious root production was above the sand surface and the roots failed to develop. Plant (b) was partially covered with sand by rabbits. The site of adventitious root production was below the sand surface and the new roots, which have not been drawn to their full extent, had developed. Note the difference in diameter of the new roots in comparison with the older roots and also the presence of root hairs on the former (from Marshall, 1965).

conditions for development.' He emphasizes the value of multivariate techniques of analysis such as Maarel (1966) has recently applied to the Voorne dune environments in Holland, in helping us to understand these complex relationships.

The shrub and woodland layers

Partly for reasons of space and partly for lack of detailed study it is not possible here to deal adequately with the woody components of the dune flora. In Europe at the present time we are witnessing a resurgence of scrub on dune systems as a result of myxomatosis. In many areas these developing communities have not yet achieved a stable equilibrium with the environment, and especially with the human part of it.

An attempt to analyse some of the problems associated with the development of a particular type of dune scrub, *Hippophaë rhamnoides*, which is transforming many areas of dune grassland in Europe has recently been made by a group of Nature Conservancy biologists (Ranwell (ed.) 1972).

Some discussion of the dwarf shrub community formed by *Salix repens* in dune slacks is given in the next chapter, and of afforestation in the last chapter. Dwarf shrub communities anyway tend to be associated with dune slacks and those landward parts of the dune system where erosive and accumulative processes draw together the dune and slack levels to a plateau level somewhat intermediate between the two. Native woodland is a rather rare phenomenon on dunes and the accounts that do exist are primarily of a general descriptive character (e.g. Osborn and Robertson 1939; Westhoff 1947 and 1952; Lambinon 1956; Olson 1958; Boerboom (1960)). If the study of the ecology of dune scrub is in its infancy, that of the afforested dunes has scarcely yet begun and it offers challenging opportunities for work relating to the changing communities associated with fire and felling-recovery sequences of considerable practical interest.

Perhaps one might end this chapter with a plea that instead of directing attention to the generalized zonal trends that are more or less universal and fairly well known in dunes throughout the world but which tend to obscure what goes on in time at a particular spot in a particular dune system, we should turn our attention to the more detailed study of the unit 'fragments' of the ecosystem, the better to eventually understand the whole.

11 Sand Dunes:
Structure and function of slack communities

Surprisingly little work has been carried out on the ecology of dune slacks outside the British Isles and Holland. This may be because these damp or wet hollows among the dunes are much more restricted in distribution than dunes and are sparsely represented in the more arid parts of the Mediterranean climatic zone for example. Slacks are however a very characteristic feature of large dune systems underlain by impervious deposits in the more humid Temperate zones, and it would be valuable to have fuller accounts than we have at present of slack systems in American and Australasian sites to say nothing of the still largely undescribed magnificent slack communities of the Coto Doñana in Spain.

Apart from their intrinsic interest as floristically and faunistically rich sites, their study is vital to an understanding of dune communities because many species of the dunes regenerate either more freely or solely at damp slack levels. The study of plant growth in the vicinity of the water table is also of considerable significance to both agriculturalists and water engineers concerned with cropping water-logged land, or water extraction.

In many ways a dune slack with its level surface; often influenced by salt in the early stages of formation; generally influenced by moderate accretion; and subject to the opposing influences of submergence or drought seasonally or at different stages of its development over longer periods of time, has much in common with a salt marsh. Certainly in transitional zones between the two, the sandy salt marsh and the saline dune slack merge so completely that they become indistinguishable.

It is not possible with the present state of knowledge to give a balanced account of dune slack ecology for we know little about the biology of most dune slack plants and have scarcely begun to study their animal communities. It is hoped that the somewhat fragmentary account given here will nevertheless stimulate further study of this neglected habitat.

Species Diversity

The biological spectrum given in Table 23 shows that in a site where slacks form nearly half the area of the dune system, they are almost as rich in vascular plants as the dunes. When we take into account the cryptogamic flora, and especially bryophytes which are particularly abundant, there is little doubt that in some sites the dune slack flora is the richer of the two. This forms a striking contrast with the relative poverty of the salt marsh flora and indicates optimum conditions in the dune slack for plant establishment, though not necessarily as we shall see, for plant growth.

We have no data on the relative species diversities of dunes and slacks so far as animals are concerned, but from general observations, the cooler climate of slacks, and the unpredictable tendencies towards flooding or surface desiccation from season to season it seems likely that fewer species of animals will have become adapted to them than to the dunes. Arthropods and molluscs (on lime-rich systems) are the most abundantly represented groups of the larger invertebrates, and annelids form a small but important section of the soil fauna in older slacks as at Newborough Warren. On machair, annelids are especially found in association with dung pats (Boyd 1957). The soil macrofauna of fully vegetated slacks at Newborough is sufficient to attract moles in quite large numbers in winter (e.g. 80 fresh mole hills noted in an area of less than $350\,m^2$ in December 1953 at Newborough.

Prior to myxomatosis, rabbits exerted a controlling influence on the vegetation of dry slacks and a more indirect influence on that of wet slacks (see section on grazing below).

Analytical Studies of Slack Vegetation Gradients

Much of what has already been said about the analysis of the dune flora in Chapter 10 is applicable also to the flora of slacks, but there is one important series of papers (Crawford and Wishart 1966, 1967 and 1968), devoted to the analysis of the dune slack flora of Tentsmuir, Fife. This provides an objective analysis which is enlightening. A grid of quadrats were examined for floristic cover and abundance, analysed by association analysis, and the groupings compared for similarity (Crawford and Wishart 1966). Results gave a spatially orientated series which was meaningful in relation to the

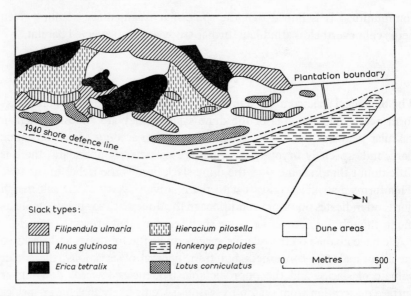

Fig. 61. Distribution of slack types determined by association analysis. Data from Tentsmuir, Fife (from Crawford and Wishart 1966).

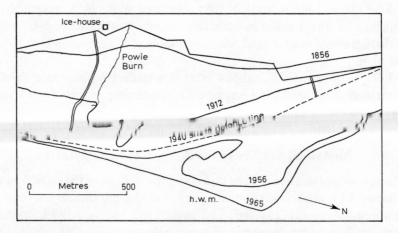

Fig. 62. Coastal changes at Tentsmuir from 1856 to 1965. All the coastlines except the most recent are taken from the unpublished report of Grove, A.T. (1953) Tentsmuir, Fife; soil blowing and coastal changes. Nature Conservancy, Edinburgh (from Crawford and Wishart 1966).

temporal development of this prograding dune system (Fig. 61 and 62). It was found that seasonally high salinity was correlated with the floristic groups associated with seawardmost slacks, while water level and soil activity were correlated with distinctive groupings in landwardmost slacks.

In a further treatment of this data (Crawford and Wishart 1967), a multivariate technique based on coincidence of occurrence and species interaction distinguished fewer groups than the original analysis and showed that many were ecotonal in character (Fig. 63) as might be expected in rapidly changing vegetation of this type. In their final paper (Crawford and Wishart 1968), an agglomerative method is used following the original divisive process to check for misclassification and secondly a means of representing the variance both within and between the terminal groups of an ordination procedure. It is then shown how the potential of any quadrat for membership of any classified type can be used to give computer maps of varying group potential, rather than discrete vegetation boundaries. Significantly the authors point out that, 'While it is always possible to draw a boundary marking the distribution of one particular species . . . no boundary can be drawn with any precision for any vegetation type that is defined on the basis of the probable occurrence of a number of species.' Objective studies of this type provide valuable confirmation of the

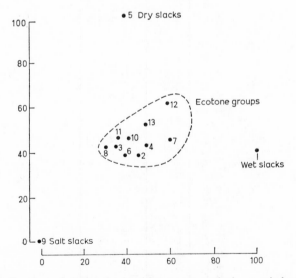

Fig. 63. Ordination of slacks obtained by group analysis; x axis based on types 9 and 1, y axis on types 9 and 5. Data from Tentsmuir, Fife (from Crawford and Wishart 1967).

Table 24. Soil analyses of samples from five different stands in the transition from sand dune to salt marsh. Each value represents the mean of five samples as expressed as g/100g oven dry weight. Mairiut District, Egypt (after Rezk 1970).

Soil type	Hygroscopic moisture	Loss on ignition	Org. C	Loss on acid treatment	Exchangeable Ca	Total soluble salts	Soluble chlorides	Soluble sulphates
Dune sand	0·12	2·7	0·033	99·0	20·29	0·11	0·004	0·001
Partly stabilized dune	0·2	2·8	0·080	98·1	18·31	0·10	0·004	0·001
Stabilized dune	0·2	5·0	0·156	95·3	15·71	0·14	0·004	0·007
Transition to salt marsh	1·2	5·7	0·138	86·1	16·29	0·23	0·015	0·009
Salt marsh	1·2	15·1	0·306	76·5	23·14	1·31	0·424	0·351

significance of trends hitherto distinguished primarily by more subjective approaches.

Westhoff *et al* (1961), Freijsen (1967) and Rezk, M. R. (1970) have
studied dune slack to salt marsh transitions including relationships between
plant associes and physico-chemical soil properties (Table 24).

On the dune to slack gradient most of the environmental changes are
dependent solely on the change in water relations, and the gradient contains
a mixture of species from each habitat, but none confined to the gradient
zone. In contrast, at the salt marsh to sand dune slack gradient environmental changes are much more profound and involve changes in soil type,
in salinity, *and* in water relations. Many species are more or less confined to
the intermediate gradient zone (e.g. *Blysmus rufus, Centaurium littorale,
Frankenia laevis, Limonium bellidifolium* and, though also associated with
damp shingle, *Suaeda fruticosa*). This 'sandwich zone' as it might be called
from the characteristic alternating soil types deserves special study in its
own right as a separate habitat complex.

Maarel and Leertouwer (1967) used ordination and classification of contiguous quadrats on a dune gradient at Schiermonnikoog, Holland based on
an index distinguishing floristic difference between adjacent quadrats.
This showed continuous variation of vegetation which was correlated with
variation in pH value and vertical height of the ground (Fig. 64). The
remarkable pH gradient they found from *Drosera* areas on soil with pH 4 to
Schoenus areas on soil of pH 7 over a very short distance is clearly similar to
that in the dune heath situation studied at Newborough (Ranwell 1959).

While it is true that these studies emphasize the continuum nature of
dune slack transitions, Leeuwen (1965) points out that the presence of a
fluctuating water table near the surface marks out a zone on the gradient
between dune and slack which is characterized by instability (in regard to
the water factor) in time. This gives a specialized habitat which appears to
suit orchids for example which are characteristic of (though not necessarily
confined to) gradient situations like this and path sides. Freijsen's (1967)
work (see below) shows that *Centaurium littorale* is best developed where
the fluctuating influence of the water table is maximal.

For practical purposes it is necessary to draw boundaries and preferably
ones which can be readily distinguished on the ground or on aerial photographs. Crawford and Wishart (1968) note the distinctive appearance of
certain physiognomic dominants like *Erica tetralix, Glyceria maxima,
Carex nigra* or *Juncus effusus* on photographs of the Tentsmuir dune slacks.
Individual species of this type have special value for mapping when it comes
to monitoring the rapid vegetation changes that occur in coastal systems.

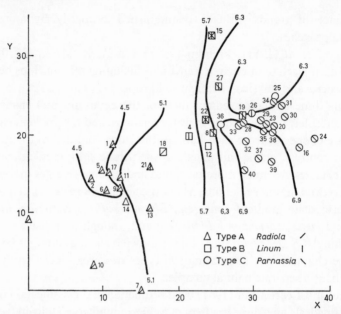

Fig. 64. Ordination of 40 quadrats in a 10 × 4 m transect laid down in the transition between *Schoenus nigricans* associes on base-rich ground at low elevations, and *Drosera rotundifolia* associes on base-deficient ground at slightly higher elevations, with isonomes of pH superimposed. Species number was taken as a measure of species diversity and was found to be related to range of pH and height. Results suggest a continuum-like variation in vegetation types mainly governed by pH variation itself governed by variation in height (from Maarel and Leertouwer 1967).

Similarly we need practical and workable divisions of the apparent continuum from the aquatic habitat to the dune in the vertical plane, and the next section outlines a system suitable for this purpose.

Water Table Limits as a Basis for Defining Slack Plant Community Limits

Studies at Newborough Warren and subsequent observations suggest that four distinctive levels of plant growth in relation to the water table can be distinguished (Ranwell 1959 and 1960 *a*). They are levels which appear to be significant in a number of ways which are biologically meaningful, but it is highly desirable that their delineation should be based on more objective criteria. In particular, one would like to see comparative study of the rooting depths of all species and study of the nutrient economy within and between the different zones. At the present time the literature on sand dune vegetation seems especially confusing in relation to the levels variously referred to as 'dune pasture', 'dune grassland', 'fixed dune', and 'grey dune'. Judging from the species composition and descriptions, many of these landscape types have more in common with what is defined below as the dry slack level than they do with the dune level. Perhaps the following classification may serve as a useful basis for clearing up such problems:

(1) *Semiaquatic habitat*

The water table is never more than 0·5 m below the soil surface and floods the surface from autumn to spring or later; plant roots are almost permanently waterlogged. Amphibious hydrophytes like *Littorella uniflora, Polygonum amphibium* or *Ranunculus aquatilis* are represented in the flora.

(2) *Wet slack habitat*

The water table never falls below 1 m below the soil surface and plants have their roots within reach of adequate moisture supplies at all seasons. Bryophytes are particularly abundant, the bulk of the flora is mesophytic and relatively few grass species occur.

(3) *Dry slack habitat*

The water table lies between 1 and 2 m below the surface at all seasons. Shallower rooted species are beyond the influence of the water table, but deeper rooted species benefit from its influence in summer drought. Phreatophytes and grasses are especially abundant and under rabbit-grazed conditions lichens may be locally abundant.

(4) *Dune habitat*

The water table never rises above 2 m below the surface and most of the plant growth is independent of it and wholly dependent on pendular water. Xerophytes and therophytes are common and vegetation tends to remain open.

In connection with the paucity of grasses in wet slacks, Jones and Etherington (1971) found from pot experiments that the dune grasses (*Agrostis stolonifera* and *Festuca rubra*) showed reduced tiller production and stunted roots in water-logged conditions. Growth of sedges (*Carex flacca and Carex nigra*) was less affected by water-logging.

It is true that Boerboom (1963) found that the presence of moisture indicator plants was found to be ordered by the quality (humus content) of the topmost soil layer rather than by the depth of the groundwater level and concluded that the field moisture capacity of the soil surface layers during drought was a better standard for the presence of moisture indicators than total pore space or the moisture content at various tensions. It is also true that as Vose *et al* (1957) showed there may be a higher moisture retentiveness in the surface layers in more humid areas such as the Tiree machairs off the western seaboard of Scotland. Also species like *Empetrum nigrum* normally dependent on groundwater survive at higher levels on north slopes (Westhoff 1947). Nevertheless, the broad distinctions outlined above seem to hold in European dunes at least, and it is very much easier to determine the approximate position of the water table within 2 m of the surface at any season with an auger than it is to measure field moisture capacities in drought periods.

Goethart *et al* (1924) have worked out the vertical ranges in relation to the water table of 91 species of flowering plants in several Dutch dune systems, but this work has been overlooked by most later workers.

Minor slack habitats

Within the main slack levels which are generally flat, secondary biotopographic units may be developed locally. They include: wet flushes; man-made pools and turf or peat cuts; low hummocks associated with clonal patches of such species as *Agropyron junceiforme* and *Salix repens*; mole-hills; ant-hills; and rabbit-disturbed ground. Each of these surface irregularities may show zonal sequences with characteristic communities varying according to salinity, moisture and physico-chemical soil factors. They are minor habitats found again and again in different dune systems wherever dune slacks occur, and they are worthy of detailed comparative study. To take one example, Freijsen (1967) has made a special study of the low *Agropyron junceiforme* hummocks of the Boschplat on the island of Terschelling. These form characteristic circular or horseshoe-shaped isolates on the floor of coastal slacks. He investigated the performance and regeneration of *Centaurium littorale*, a plant characteristic of the wet-dry gradient, on these hummocks. His results (see below) are of considerable interest in helping us to understand the problems of plant establishment and growth in this sub-habitat of dune slacks. These *Agropyron* hummocks are especially characteristic of rapidly prograding phases of dune systems and are also found at Tentsmuir, Fife; Morrich More, Ross; Towyn Burrows, Carmarthen, and Newborough Warren, Anglesey.

Establishment and Growth in the Slack Habitat

Migration into the slack

Salisbury (1952) concluded that the flora of wet slacks is chiefly composed of marsh plants commonly found outside the dune system. Very few species are confined to the dune slack habitat. Apart from being a relatively rare habitat, slacks are isolated among the drier dunes and only in direct communication with other wet habitats such as a salt marsh during relatively short periods when they are formed at the coast or with other fresh-water bodies via temporary streams during flooding. Once the slack is isolated by the growth of dunes, migration into it must come largely via wind-borne seeds, by birds, or by human activities.

The open damp slack surface exposed in the wake of eroding dunes becomes warm and moist in late spring or early autumn and ideal for seedling establishment, but only for very short and irregular periods. Where the slack surface is level, Martin (1959) failed to find any obvious environmental gradients of soil moisture, salinity, or soil physico-chemical factors in Island Beach, New Jersey. Yet there were striking differences from point to point in the vegetation (e.g. locally pure stands of *Dryopteris thelypteris* up to 40 m in diameter). Blanchard (1952) found similar point to point variation and large pure stands of a variety of species in a relatively young slack at Ainsdale, Lancashire. Martin concluded that chance factors of migration and establishment must play a big part in the colonization of slacks to account for the variety found. At Newborough Warren a few large clones of *Juncus maritimus* occur in certain landward slacks. During a 20 year period of observation only one new seedling of this species became established in these slacks. The seeds of this species are small enough to be carried in mud on the feet of birds, but unlikely to be distributed far by wind. Now there is a 200 acre (80 ha) *Juncus maritimus* marsh within a distance of 3 flight miles (4·48 km) of these slacks. This example suggests that bird-induced migration of plant species into slacks is likely to be of very rare occurrence indeed, a conclusion also reached by Westhoff (1947) in relation to colonization of the West Friesian Islands off the Dutch coast. Westhoff concluded that cattle were an important agent of dissemination within dune systems in addition to the main agents, water and the wind.

Establishment problems

The presence of such relict salt marsh species as *Glaux maritima* which establish in seaward slacks and persist in landward ones long since cut off from the sea, often gives the impression that there is a persistent saline influence in landward slacks operating through the water table. This is not necessarily so and many authors (Lambinon 1956, Ranwell 1959, Martin 1959, Duvigneaud 1947) have confirmed that the saline groundwater influence is limited to coastal slacks affected by tidal influence either by occasional tidal flooding or via percolation through a permeable shingle base. Pioneer species like *Centaurium littorale, Agrostis stolonifera* and *Juncus articulatus* are able to tolerate temporary periods of high salinity and even *Salix repens* can germinate in 25 per cent sea water (Ranwell 1960 *a*).

Submergence in wet slacks limits the period of establishment of most species to late spring or summer when the flood waters recede. Freijsen (1947) found that *Centaurium littorale* occurs on a level just reached by the capillary fringe (c. 55 cm above the water table). Germination in this species occurred when the mean afternoon temperature exceeded the critical temperature for germination (13°C) and was at a maximum when the temperature reached 24°C. The effect of the sun's altitude is important in autumn when slack surfaces become warmer than north slopes. Shallow water acts as a heat reservoir during the night and warms slacks to slope temperatures in spring. Experimental sowings of *Centaurium littorale* showed that germination was inhibited where the surface soil was saturated (Freijsen).

The lower limit of many species in slacks appears to be controlled by submergence though precisely how is not clear. Blanchard (1952) made detailed observations of the duration of fresh-water submergence in dune slacks at Ainsdale, Lancashire.

Birse (1958) carried out experiments on the tolerance of mosses to flooding and showed that species characteristic of dry slacks like *Ceratodon purpureus* and *Climacium dendroides* could tolerate up to 4 months flooding and survive. Westhoff (1947) found that in dune slacks with open water the strip along the shores is almost always water-logged, while elsewhere the soil is drier even though the water table is at the same depth. As Freijsen (1967) points out this is because the capillary rise is higher in wet than in dry soil where large pore spaces limit the rise of capillary threads. Westhoff observed that species requiring water-logged soil (e.g. *Littorella uniflora* can only thrive in the neighbourhood of open water and hence are particularly sensitive to drainage.

The density of vegetation in fully-vegetated slacks is persistently very high and this makes it difficult for other plants to establish. The only sites where *Calluna vulgaris* seedlings were found at Newborough were in turf cut areas where the vegetation had been temporarily opened up. *Calluna* does not enter the succession until a late phase at Newborough where leaching provides a sufficiently acid soil. There is of course no such problem for this species in lime-deficient dune slacks such as Good (1935) described at Studland, Dorset as *Calluna* can enter the slacks in the open phase.

Freijsen (1967) demonstrated how populations of *Centaurium vulgare* (syn. *Centaurium littorale*) oscillated in their vertical distribution from year to year according to the depth of the soil water table in spring (Fig. 65). Drought was clearly limiting both germination and establishment at the upper vertical limit of the populations. At the wetter, lower limit *Centaurium* showed delayed development up to three years though it is normally a biennial plant. As in *Aster* we have here another good example of the 'close-tracking' of the environment (see Chapter 6) shown by a short-lived perennial.

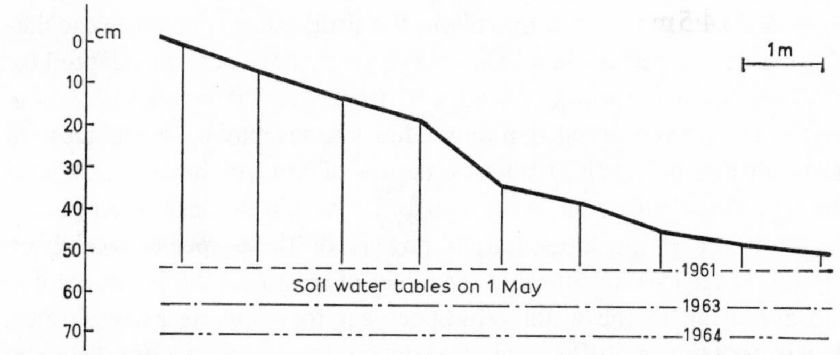

Sample plot	A1	A2	B1	B2	C1	C2	D1	D2	
length in cm	18	—	11	—	3	—	4·5	—	⎫
fruits (av.)	5·3	—	2·1	—	1	—	1	—	⎬ 1961
plants on 2m²	170	—	375	—	350	—	130	—	
fruits on 2m²	885	—	800	—	370	—	130	—	⎭
length in cm	15	14	13	10	4	6	0	0	⎫
fruits (av.)	15	8	4	4·3	1	1	0	0	⎬ 1963
plants on 2m²	1	19	42	33	10	3	0?	0?	
fruits on 2m²	15	153	170	141	10	3	0	0	⎭
diameter of rosettes (mm)	0	0	15	8	5	5	2	2	⎫ 1964
plants on 2m²	0	0	120	2500	1250	1250	250	100	⎭

Fig. 65. Variations in properties of *Centaurium vulgare* (syn. *C. littorale*) populations across a transect in a dune slack on Terschelling, West Friesian Islands, Netherlands (from Freijsen 1967).

It is of interest that these gradient environments favour the development of hybrids between *Agrostis stolonifera* (which occurs in wet slacks and semi-stable dune) and *Agrostis tenuis* (confined to drier sites) on the older dry slacks at Newborough (Bradshaw 1958). Anderson and Stebbins (1964) have pointed out the significance of habitat gradients for survival of hybrids.

Species of dune slack plants show very extreme morphological modifications in reaction to excess or deficiency of water. Non-flowering and very flaccid-leaved forms of *Myosotis scorpioides* occur in slacks submerged until summer. Reduced terrestrial forms of aquatic species like *Polygonum amphibium* occur in areas normally flooded but exposed in drought. As we have seen, submergence causes dwarfing in *Centaurium littorale* and *Salix repens* while as Salisbury (1952) demonstrates, drought has a similar effect on *Samolus valerandi* and *Plantago coronopus*. It is not surprising that with the two opposed extremes of too much and too little water constantly oscillating that very few species like *Centaurium littorale* have become adapted for growth specifically in the gradient zone between wet and dry slacks.

Westhoff (1946) observed that only a few species may have contact with the groundwater or capillary zones to depths of 3 m. At the dry slack level (as defined above) many species do so and it would be desirable to know more about the evapo-transpiration powers of these species. Robinson (1952) quotes the extraordinarily high figure of an annual discharge equivalent to a 2 m fall in the water table per year for *Tamarix* growing on a shallow water table at Safford Valley, Arizona. By contrast where the water table depth is 4·5 m the annual water loss from transpiration is equivalent to a fall in the water table of only 5 cm. There is no doubt that with the spread of such species as *Hippophaë rhamnoides* since myxomatosis, wet slacks will dry out and marsh species will suffer, but this effect has not yet been measured.

Community Transformations

It may seem a surprising omission that diagrams showing how plant communities of salt marsh or sand dunes are linked to one another to form successional series are completely absent from this book. There are two reasons: first, it is a fact that there is extraordinarily little direct evidence based on frequent and long term observations of marked plots in support of the assumptions made in such diagrams; second, two-dimensional diagrams are inadequate for the expression of the complexity of communities that can arise at any one location according to its history and subsequent treatment.

Successional diagrams not only oversimplify the many directions in which a particular community can develop, but they tend to falsify the reality of the situation in the minds of student ecologists. Successions do not end at the point where man's influence becomes dominant, they are simply modified by it. Many of the earlier accounts of dune succession stop at the first fence-line and ignore the fact that beyond it in the sandy pastures, the golf links or the conifer plantations, a high proportion of the dune flora and fauna continues to exist and develop under the imposed conditions of management. Some account of these various forms of more intensive management are discussed in the last chapter.

Physiographic changes (Chapter 8) and soil changes (Chapter 9) in space and time have already been discussed. These exert primary control on the type of communities present at any particular time and in any particular place on a dune system. As we have seen, the seaward edge of a dune system tends to undergo alternating change from the strandline community through embryo to open dune community and back again. Within the mobile dunes another type of alternation or cycle may occur from the open wet slack community to a more species rich, but still open dune community which erodes right down to damp bare sand to start the next phase in the cycle. And finally only when the dunes are worn down at the landward side of the dune system to near the dry slack level is there persistent stability. Here fully closed vegetation maintained as turf with dwarf shrubs under grazing, or developing towards some type of woodland, can develop.

Thus as in an estuarine series of marshes, we must think in terms of several quite distinct successional series operating persistently at different points in the system and not in terms of units of the spatial sequence from seaward to landward succeeding one another in time.

Coastal slacks

These are usually very transient features liable to sea water flooding or to obliteration by the growth of embryo dunes. They usually contain very open communities of scattered strandline species and a few salt marsh plants tolerant of well-drained soils. Where the dune system is prograding in alternating bands of low dunes and intervening coastal slacks they can develop more stable communities in which individual clones of halophytic and wet dune slack perennials close up to form a mosaic. The development of these communities has received little study and it would be interesting to establish long term observations on such sites as Morrich More, Ross or Tentsmuir, Fife to see how persistent the halophytic elements are with time and to find out just how perennials characteristic of later stages establish.

Blanchard (1952) made a detailed map of semi-aquatic plant communities associated with a coastal slack in Ainsdale dunes, Lancashire. She

o

found these formed a mosaic, the elements of which were evidently laid down at the time of establishment and subsequently formed a pattern of very persistent form. It is interesting that although this slack has been cut off from the sea for many years, now some 20 years after Blanchard's study the sea is threatening to break through again. If this is allowed to happen the existing vegetation of tall fresh water marsh species may well be destroyed leaving a bare surface for a new pattern, stemming from chance factors affecting establishment, to be set up.

Wet slacks

Where these are created by the erosion of a mobile dune as at Newborough, Anglesey, each new crescent of newly exposed wet sand in the wake of the eroding dune carries a slightly different seed complement from that of the previous year. Consequently banded communities commonly occur across the slacks often at slightly different levels according to the depth of the water table and the intensity of wind erosion at the time of their formation.

Among mobile dunes these slacks may persist with relatively open vegetation for 50 years or more. It was interesting to find at Newborough Warren that even with the reduction in rabbit grazing following myxomatosis that the existing vegetation of these wet slacks remain short although the flowering of many species (especially terrestrial orchids) was much improved. Evidently the adverse effects of summer drought for some species and winter flooding for others and not grazing are the main factors restricting growth.

However Westhoff (1946) records that since about 1910 the Dutch government has been active in controlling rabbits, and scrub has come up in the dune slacks. This led Westhoff to conclude that biotic rather than climatic factors have limited the spread of dune woodland in the past. Tansley (1949) suggested that the lack of tree seed parents in the neighbourhood of the coast was mainly responsible for absence of native forest on coastal dunes.

Now of course we are witnessing the post-myxomatosis transformation and *Alnus* and *Salix* are developing extensively in wet slacks and especially where they are close to afforested areas where rabbits were controlled prior to myxomatosis. Nevertheless in some of the bigger systems still remote from tree seed parents, tree seedlings have not yet appeared in wet slacks.

Dry slacks

Open vegetation communities at the dry slack level, like coastal slacks, are usually very transient habitats. They occur either at the base of the lee slope of advancing mobile dunes or occasionally over wider areas where shifts in the dune contours have led to re-erosion of a low dune area. Hummocks of *Salix repens, Ligustrum vulgare* or other shrub species are especially characteristic of such sites and they usually carry a rather sparse associated flora in which annual species are common, at least in the more stable areas.

The dune system comes to rest at the closed dry slack to dune level, and it is here that biological, as opposed to other environmental influences, become paramount in controlling community changes.

Prior to myxomatosis it was shown that there was strong evidence from sequences in the mosaic of vegetation that turf and dwarf shrub communities alternated with one another in time at Newborough Warren, Anglesey (Ranwell 1960 *a*). In this particular example a defoliating beetle (*Lochmea capreæ*) and the drought effect from rabbit-burrowing beneath *Salix repens* were believed to be responsible for its death. The occasional chance establishment of *Salix* seedlings in rabbit-disturbed turf started the cycle of shrub growth and ultimate death and decay again.

In this more stable zone it is legitimate to equate seral relations in time and space in local areas. From a study of serally related transects on dry slack turf at Newborough before and three years after myxomatosis, it was shown that while no seral trends were reversed, significant changes did occur in the frequency of species which were serally static. In particular there was a marked increase in the growth and flowering of most grasses and sedges. Turf 1 cm high grew to 15 cm in 3 years, low growing herbs and lichens were much reduced, but mosses remained abundant (Ranwell 1960 *b*). Now 15 years later the grassland has formed a 'rough' 40 to 50 cm high, mosses are much reduced, lichens are absent and scattered shrubs are overtopping the grassland.

Even more dramatic effects are evident on the dunes where rabbits no longer graze in any numbers. The vastly increased seed output has filled up the gaps in many formerly mobile dune areas and effectively locked the moving dunes into place.

The future clearly lies with the newly developing shrub communities, especially those associated with *Hippophaë rhamnoides* in European systems, unless active management takes a hand.

PART FOUR   Human Influences

12 Management of Salt Marsh Wildlife Resources

Salt marshes are the product of land erosion and therefore an expanding resource. It is no accident that the greater part of the world's population derives its food from the great deltas, largely in the form of fish and rice. No other habitat has sufficient natural fertility to support it. According to Grist (1959) possibly over 600 million people in Asia derive 50 per cent or more of their food calories from rice.

For centuries human beings have settled at the head of deltas and estuaries and expanded cropping and port facilities in pace with the seaward thrust of siltation. Yet it is extraordinary how even today in the most highly civilized countries this elementary geographical process seems to catch unawares the local authorities or other coastal landowners who suddenly find that their creek or tidal flat frontages are no longer open but clothed with salt marsh vegetation. Similarly, the significance of the dredger off-shore or the coastal engineering works on the other side of the estuary is rarely grasped by those whose coastal facilities will suffer in 10, 20 or 50 years time, until it is too late to do anything about it.

Rather more subtle changes associated with isostatic adjustment may be equally significant over periods of 50 or 100 years in those areas where the rate of coastal sinking is nearly balanced by the rate of salt marsh accretion. As we have seen this appears to be happening on parts of the south and south-east coasts of England at the present time.

Human influence on the salt marsh environment is increasing. The ecologist and the physiographer have an important responsibility to inform themselves of the directions and time scales of change relating to salt marsh formation, development and destruction. They also have the responsibility to pass on their knowledge in intelligible form to those who need to act on it.

An excellent account of human influences on general estuarine processes and the animals inhabiting estuaries is given by Cronin (in Lauff 1967); the following is chiefly concerned with human influence on salt marsh vegetation, and its management.

External Human Influences

Catchment activities

Land cultivation and mining activities have big effects on water and silt inflow into estuarine basins and hence on the life cycle of salt marshes.

It is claimed that the hydraulic mining in operation from 1850 until it was banned in 1884 added a metre of silt to the Suisan and San Pablo parts of San Francisco Bay (Gilliam 1957).

If silt is added in quantity to an estuary it increases the turbidity and raises the lower vertical limit to which salt marsh plants can grow. At the same time the rate of accretion of the levels which can support marsh growth will increase. These opposing effects result in a tendency to extensive cliffing at the seaward edge of the marsh which is very persistent even after the silt input is subsequently reduced. No one has measured these effects yet recent changes in land cultivation have been on a vast scale and must have had a profound influence on salt marsh development. Equally if cultivation demands improved drainage, then a greater volume of fresh water enters the estuary and this on meeting tidal waters will cause an increase in the height to which the tide will rise and consequently a reduction in the depth at which salt marsh can establish.

The need for data relating to these input factors is now recognized in relation to current studies on estuarine barrage schemes (Anon 1966 *a* to *c*, 1967, and 1970 *a*).

Pollution

In addition to the relatively innocuous effects of increased water and sediment input there may come along with it a frighteningly complex array of chemical substances derived from agricultural operations, industry, and sewage. This pollution approaches the salt marshes from landward and seaward. There is also a vertical component from air pollution.

In industrialized estuaries the sediment of which marshes are built may contain a high proportion of man-made detritus. Cinders, siliceous and metallic fly ash, slag, and coal were found in the sand-size fractions from the top 35 cm of a core in bottom sediment from the centre section of the Hudson estuary, New York State (McCrone 1966).

With the possible exception of oil, we are again very ignorant of both the nutritive or toxic effects of these substances on the life of salt marshes. No one has measured for example changes in the deathline for salt marsh growth in heavily polluted estuaries due to the combined effect of all these influences close to centres of civilization. It has been shown that overall productivity of macro-algal communities on the Adriatic coast remains unimpaired right up to the deathline where macro-algal growth suddenly fails (Golubic 1970). Significantly as this point is approached, the species diversity is reduced from many to only two algal species (*Ulva lactuca* and *Hypnea musciformis*) and one larger animal, the sea hare *Aplysia fasciata*. Beyond this point persistently anaerobic organic-rich mud forms a foul-smelling 'bacterial soup' virtually devoid of higher forms of life.

One of the most noticeable changes in southern English salt marshes over the past 20 years is the extensive growths of green algae (*Enteromorpha* and *Ulva* species) which have developed around the seaward edges of salt marshes. They occur particularly in the more sheltered bays where sewage or industrial effluents in built up areas, or fertilizer outwash in arable farming areas, are likely to accumulate. Now these algae are capable of utilizing nitrogen in the ammonium form and these various effluents must contribute substantial quantities of organic or ammonium nitrogen, which would normally be converted to readily assimilated nitrite and nitrate. But it is significant that under anaerobic conditions, the conversion of organic nitrogen stops with the step of ammonium formation (Black 1968). It seems likely that accumulation of ammonium nitrogen may preferentially benefit algal, rather than salt marsh plant growth. The growths are so extensive that in sheltered bays which could act as nutrient traps in the Blackwater estuary, Essex, or Poole Harbour, Dorset, for example, they appear to smother salt marsh growth and replace it locally. Studies are in progress to test the truth of this hypothesis and to determine the ultimate fate of the algal growths in chronic pollution conditions.

Chronic pollution from oil refinery effluent has much the same effect and the line between apparently normal live *Spartina anglica* marsh and dead marsh at Fawley in Southampton Water for example was found to be very sharp indeed when the site was visited in 1962. Boorman (*pers. comm.*) notes that *Limonium* species disappear from salt marsh in heavily polluted estuaries. It is important that studies should be made of the more subtle effects of pollution: sub-lethal damage, nutritional disturbance and, in the case of invertebrates, behavioural disturbance due to chemo-sensitivity, but there is much to be said for concentrating first on gross effects of total pollution as described above.

Heavy but isolated oil pollution may be tolerated without serious harm by salt marsh plants like *Spartina anglica* (Ranwell and Hewett 1964), indeed marsh growth forms a valuable trapping surface for oil in estuaries and strains it from the tidal water where it is so harmful to birds. However, most vegetation including salt marsh is rapidly killed by emulsifiers used to disperse oil (Ranwell and Stebbings 1967), so it is pointless to use them on an oiled salt marsh.

A recent bibliography by Nelson-Smith (1968) gives a valuable key to the literature on oil pollution and outstanding contributions have been made on the effects of oil (Plate 5) and emulsifiers on salt marsh plants and salt marshes by Baker (1970 *a* to *i*). This work is incidentally a model example of the experimental approach and its presentation. It has demonstrated the relatively high resistance of *Puccinellia* marsh turf to repeated oil sprayings, clearcut differences in the tolerance of different salt marsh species to oil pollution, and a (possibly indirect) nutritive effect of oil on salt marsh vegetation.

Baker (1970 *c*) also tested the effect of emulsifiers used to disperse oil pollution on *Puccinellia maritima/Festuca rubra* turves and found that emulsifiers in current use killed plants in concentrations above 10 per cent (Fig. 66). In a field trial where emulsifier (B.P. 1002) was used to clean oil, no decrease in damage to *Puccinellia* or *Spartina* marsh was noted and it was concluded that oiled salt marshes are best left to recover naturally (Baker 1970 *i*).

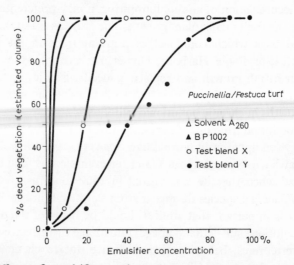

Fig. 66. Effects of emulsifiers and a solvent on *Puccinellia maritima/Festuca rubra* turf (from Baker 1970 *c*).

The effects of air pollution on salt marshes are probably minimal because of regular tidal flooding. However, there is evidence (McCrone 1966) that algae and silt accumulate radio-isotopes and Preston (1968) has shown that radionuclide concentrations decrease exponentially with depth from the surface in silt cores taken from the Ravenglass estuary, Cumberland. By contrast there was little significant change in radionuclide concentrations, in cores taken in nearby beach sands.

Introduced species

One of the most powerful human influences on salt marshes in Europe has been the deliberate introduction of *Spartina anglica* to particular sites and its subsequent uncontrolled spread to other sites from them (Ranwell 1967 a). This plant has also been established in Australia, Tasmania and New Zealand and recently planted in Puget Sound, Washington State, U.S.A. where it seems to be flourishing (Table 25). It has partially replaced *Zostera* and algal communities on high level mudflats and temporarily reduces variety where it becomes dominant in salt marshes. The rationale of many of the introductions is questionable and many attempts have been made to eradicate it locally. In most cases they have failed because of the high reproductive potential of this species. Currently work is in progress in Northern Ireland and elsewhere to determine the population level at which effective control can be achieved at reasonable cost.

Table 25. World resources of *Spartina anglica* marsh (from Ranwell 1967).

Country	Date of first record*	Area	
		Acres	Hectares
Great Britain	1870	30,000	12,000
Ireland	1925	500–1,000	200–400
Denmark	1931	1,230	500
Germany	1927	1,000–2,000	400–800
Netherlands	1924	9,800–14,300	4,000–5,800
France	1906	10,000–20,000	4,000–8,000
Australia	1930	25–50	10–20
Tasmania	1927	50–100	20–40
New Zealand	1913	50–100	20–40
United States	1960	< 1	< 1
Total		52,400–68,500	21,000–27,700

* Dates refer to the first recorded appearance, or first known introduction, to a country. All British material before 1892, when the fertile form was first recorded, is of the sterile form. Area estimates are of ground covered 50 % or more by *Spartina* and must be considered as very approximate.

The introduction of *Tamarix gallica* from the Mediterranean to the salt marshes of the southern United States has had more serious consequences. Martin (1953) records that its uncontrolled spread from wind and water dispersed seed has interfered with drainage, promoted flooding, reduced the value of grazing and waterfowl habitat, and resulted in extensive losses of irrigation water through evapo-transpiration. The latter has the effect of increasing ground water salinity in brackish areas. This limits the extent of rice cultivation and other salt-sensitive crops in the delta areas. The growth of deep-rooted phreatophytes like *Tamarix* is primarily a problem associated with marshlands in the warmer and more arid parts of the world.

Much of the literature on this subject relates to inland growths of *Tamarix*. Fletcher and Elmendorf (1955) for example quote annual water losses of up to 5 acre – feet due to *Tamarix* in the Pecos river delta, New Mexico. They give a useful review of the significance of phreatophytes in water control and the effect of attempts to limit their growth.

Internal Human Influences

The mildest forms of human influence on salt marshes result from sporadic direct cropping of the plants and animals which live on them (e.g. the gathering of 'samphire' (*Salicornia* sp.) or wildfowling). Indirect cropping with domestic grazing animals has a stronger influence as it changes the physical environment and the species composition. Draining and spraying activities produce even more profound changes in hydrological, chemical and biological parts of the environment. Both the creation and extermination of salt marshes may be caused by coast protection activities, reclamation, or other coastline modifying activities such as estuarine barrage or airport construction.

It is useful to consider these activities as given above in the sequence of increasingly strong human influence and we have to bear in mind there in often a hidden legacy from past activities, such as salt panning or derelict reclamation schemes which have left their mark on the marsh. Directly or indirectly, the character of most salt marshes throughout the world today has been largely determined by human activities past or present just as in other habitats.

Direct cropping

Spartina marshes on the north-east coast of North America were formerly mown for hay and Burkholder (1956) records an amusing energy chain from Georgia, U.S.A. where 'in former years marsh grass was harvested as the sole feed for mules that were used to haul fuel for the wood-burning steam locomotives on the Old Brunswick and Florida Railroad.' *Spartina patens* was formerly cut for hay in Delaware and *Spartina pectinata* (said to be dominant over some 28,000 acres (11,3000 ha) of marsh around the Bay of Fundy, Nova Scotia) is under investigation at the present time for use as hay and pasture (Nicholson and Longille 1965). Hubbard and Ranwell (1966) demonstrated that it was possible to cut *Spartina anglica* marsh in dry weather using a light tractor at Bridgwater Bay, Somerset and to make palatable and digestible silage for sheep. No information has been found on the effect of regular mowing of salt marshes on their botanical composition. It seems unlikely that mowing was practised in the native short grass or herb-rich marshes on European coasts, though reed (*Phragmites*) cutting is still an important activity in the larger deltas like that of the Danube.

Most of the *Spartina anglica* planting stocks used in different parts of the world were derived from a small bay in Poole Harbour, Dorset (Ranwell 1967) and seed stocks of *Festuca rubra* are currently harvested from Lancashire marshlands. Both this species and *Agrostis stolonifera* are being propagated for use on embankments on the German North Sea coast (Wohlenberg 1965). The selection and breeding of coastal grasses for use in specialized habitats of this type has hardly begun, and there is great scope for further work in this field and for their use as pasture plants on inland salinized soils.

Turf cutting is practised on the sheep-grazed Lancashire and Solway marshes. Usually 2 in (5 cm) strips are left between cuts to improve regeneration and within 5 years the same areas may be cut again. Experiments are in progress in the Bridgwater Bay National Nature Reserve, Somerset to determine the botanical changes of this cycle and to see if it is possible to reverse succession from coarse and relatively unpalatable *Festuca rubra* marsh to *Puccinellia* marsh, more palatable for wildfowl (Plate 8).

Wintering flocks of wildfowl on tidal marshes have been cropped for centuries. While in general this has developed in an uncontrolled manner particularly in Europe, the controlled cropping of wildfowl and muskrat on Delaware marshes has been combined with the application of sophisticated habitat management techniques. These include the excavation of flight pools, the planting of wildfowl foods, and spraying or burning to control tall marsh growths (Lynch 1941; Schmidt 1950 and Steenis *et al* 1954).

There is another less tangible 'crop' of increasing importance from salt marshes and that is the education and recreation derived by students, naturalists, yachtsmen and anyone who seeks to explore the life of the marshes or derives pleasure from the subtle contours and colours of their remote landscapes.

Indirect cropping

By far the most widespread use of salt marshes has involved indirect cropping by open range grazing with domestic animals. On the Gulf and Atlantic coasts of North America cattle graze the coarse *Spartina* marsh growths and older breeds of sheep do so in the British Isles. Williams (1955, 1959) has shown how access to the marshes can be improved by provision of cattle walkways (Plate 7). These are ridges of spoil bull-dozed from the marsh and spaced half a mile (0·8 km) apart where they provide refuge for cattle at high tide. The borrow pits from which the soil is dug, flood, and attract wildfowl. *Spartina* and *Distichalis* marshes will support a cow for every 2 to 4 acre (0·8 to 1·6 ha) during the 6 month grazing season. Burning is practised widely by stockmen to stimulate succulent new growth, but during drought, fire can reach plant crowns and severely damage the marsh vegetation (Williams 1955).

Salt marshes of the European seaboard are used for cattle, but more generally for sheep-grazing. Very extensive salting pastures are found in Northern France (e.g. the Baie de St. Michel) and on a smaller scale in most of the estuaries and bays of the west coast of England and Wales from the Solway to the Bristol Channel. European saltings are composed of three principal grasses, *Agrostis stolonifera*, *Festuca rubra*, and *Puccinellia maritima*. They support 2 to 3 sheep to the acre (0·4 ha) for most of the year when the marshes are free of tides. It has been shown that high level *Spartina anglica* marsh can be converted to *Puccinellia maritima* marsh by sheep grazing (Ranwell 1961). Experimental studies (Plate 6) indicate that on high level *Spartina* marsh growing on firm silt this can be achieved in about 5 to 10 years. With the development of intensive agriculture and loss of inland pastures for folding sheep at high tide, or in mid winter, sheep grazing has declined on many coast marshes in southern England. This has led to the spread of unpalatable tufted growths of *Festuca rubra* or *Agropyron pungens* which accrete silt more rapidly than close-grazed salting, quickly replacing succulent *Puccinellia* marsh. Chippindale and Merricks (1965) have shown how gang-mowing can help to maintain reclaimed salting pasture at times when sheep are in short supply. Wohlenberg (1965) records that turf cutting on salting pasture on the West German coast may enable *Agropyron pungens* to establish. Once established this coarse, unpalatable species can rapidly invade high level salting pasture.

There is a very critical stage near the upper limit of *Puccinellia* growth where coarser grasses can invade but at this level sheep-trampling helps to offset the very small but significant accretion brought by the few tides that reach these high level salting pastures. This compaction, aided by the normal settlement due to drying, can hold the marsh at a level suitable for *Puccinellia* growth for decades longer than it would otherwise be able to survive, providing it continues to be hard-grazed by sheep (Ranwell 1968 *a*).

Drainage

Large scale residential development near tidal marshes in the warmer parts of the world invariably promotes activities associated with mosquito control; in particular drainage and spraying.

Bourn and Cottam (1950) record that ditching for mosquito control began in New Jersey in 1912; greatly expanded in 1933 when relief labour (organized as a result of the economic depression) became available, and by 1938 had encompassed 90 per cent (562,500 acre (227,700 ha)) of the original tidewater lands lying between Maine and Virginia. Inevitably there was a clash with sporting and conservation interests, but by the time this became vociferous enough to achieve action most of the marshes had been criss-crossed by a network of drainage channels.

Taylor (1937) testified to the effectiveness of mosquito control on newly ditched marshes in comparison with unditched marshes and concluded from a superficial study of the vegetation that the only significant changes were in the development of secondary vegetation on ditch banks, notably the spread of *Iva ovaria*. However Bourn and Cottam (1950) carried out a much more detailed study over a period of 12 years on ditched Delaware marshes and found that shrubby growths of *Baccharis halimifolia* and *Iva Frutescens* had largely replaced the marshes natural grass associations and resulted in serious reductions in populations of marshland invertebrates important as food for wildfowl and waders. There is no mention of reduction in grazing or hay cutting on these marshes with the advent of ditching, but inevitably this would result from reduced access due to the ditches and must have contributed to the spread of taller vegetation. In addition to the serious loss of wildlife habitat, Bourn and Cottam (1950) note that mosquito control has not been effective in many areas due to lack of maintenance on the ditches.

A great deal of literature exists relating to the use of brackish water for crop irrigation in coastal areas (see Gallatin *et al* 1962 and numerous publications of the U.S. Salinity Laboratory, Riverside, California), but very little study has been given to the effects of changing water quality on the wildlife of tidal marshlands. However, valuable studies have been carried out on this subject in the Camargue marshes of the Rhône delta, France by biologists at the Tour du Valat Biological Station. For example, Aguesse and Marazanof (1965) have studied changes in salt marsh and brackish water populations of invertebrates over a period of some 30 years in relation to climate, the effects of irrigation for rice cultivation, and habitats modified by salt production. Of particular interest is their conclusion that all the changes observed are reversible. But one should not assume that this would be true for larger vertebrates. As we have seen the spread of phreatophytes like *Tamarix* species may contribute to increasing the salinity of ground water, while the development of desalination plants will increase the salinity of superficial waters flooding estuarine marshes. Presumably this will result in a partial reversal of the normal salinity gradient in estuaries and encourage the spread of more salt tolerant species further up the estuary.

Spraying

In the past 30 years insecticide or herbicide spraying has been used increasingly on coastal marshes for management purposes in relation to wildlife cropping. Spraying has been used also for mosquito control, for oil pollution decontamination purposes, and in mangrove swamp for clearance for military purposes.

In general the use of herbicides for wildlife management is a responsible activity carried out or supervised by well-informed people who are primarily interested in protecting wildlife rather than destroying it. Certain herbicides like Dalapon (sodium salt, 2, 2 – dichloropropionic acid) are not known to be significantly harmful to life on tidal marshes other than the grass species like *Spartina* or *Phragmites* they are used to control. However, it is not possible to use sprays effectively in marshland washed daily by the tides and in the control of *Spartina anglica* in such sites the use of pelleted substituted urea compounds such as Fenuron (3-phenyl-i, i-dimethylurea) has been found effective (Ranwell and Downing 1960). These of course are soil sterilents and non-specific. It would be desirable to know more about their side effects on invertebrates and the risks of promoting erosion before they are used on a wide scale.

The aerial spraying of tidal marshland for mosquito control has had serious consequences and Springer and Webster (1951) have demonstrated the more immediate effects of aerial spraying on experimental plots in the New Jersey marshes. Plots were 50 acre (20 ha) or 100 acre (40 ha) and were treated with dosages ranging from 0·2 (0·09 kg) to 1·6 lb (0·7 kg) DDT per acre (0·4 ha) and results measured against untreated controls. Birds were not obviously affected, but heavy losses of fish were recorded in dosages above 0·8 lb per acre (0·36 kg/ha) and crabs were almost completely killed, these effects being greater in ponds than in creeks or ditches. Effects on smaller invertebrates were variable; shrimps and amphipods were seriously affected, insects, spiders and worms less so, and mites and molluscs not apparently harmed.

Now of course, we are aware of the more subtle dangers that accrue through the build up of chlorinated hydrocarbon residues from substances like DDT in food chains. Haderlie (1970) records the death of hundreds of fish-eating marine birds and some sea lions, believed to have accumulated lethal doses of DDT off the Monterey Bay coast, California. He is currently studying the accumulation of this substance and its derivatives in the estuary of the Salinas River draining the Salinas valley. Here, during the past 10 years it is estimated that 125,000 lb (56,700 kg) of DDT has been sprayed on agricultural land each year.

Tschirley (1969) estimates that the regeneration of mangrove forest to its original condition following defoliant spraying in Vietnam for military purposes with 2, 4–D and 2,4,5–T (normal butyl esters of 2,4–dichlorophenoxy – acetic acid and 2,4,5 – trichlorophenoxyacetic acid) or with triisopropanolamine salts of 2,4–D and picloram (4 – amino – 3,5,6 – trichloro-picolinic acid) will require about 20 years. Fish yields have increased during a period of intensive defoliation, but this could be a temporary phenomenon due to release of nutrients.

Reclamation and coastal transformation

Reduction in the tidal area of Poole Harbour, Dorset through natural siltation and reclamation is estimated to have increased within the past 150 years to a rate 12 times that of the previous 6,000 years (May 1969). This gives some idea of the accelerated pace at which salt marshes are being diminished. In San Francisco Bay less than a quarter of the original marshland survives (Harvey 1966). Much depends on how the reclamation is achieved, and there is convincing evidence that embankment of marshland around the Wash in England has in the past stimulated the formation of new salt marsh to replace that reclaimed (Inglis and Kestner 1958 a and Kestner 1962). Dalby (1957) estimates that some 80,000 acre (32,400 ha) have been embanked around the Wash since the seventeenth century and estimated that embankment could continue at a rate of some 15 000 acre (6 100 ha) per century. This reclaimed land has produced some of the most highly fertile agricultural soils in the world, but only at a controlled rate of reclamation which does not exceed the rate of new marsh formation. In fact,

P

Inglis and Kestner (1958 *b*) give evidence which suggests that supplies of silt which had taken thousands of years to accumulate in the Wash may already be so depleted as a result of reclamation that little of the progressive silting expected seaward of a recent embankment has occurred.

The pace of salt marsh formation has been increased on the Dutch, German and Danish wadden coasts by means of ditched and groyned sedimentation fields and an excellent account of the techniques involved is given by Kamps (1962).

Unfortunately, in many industrialized estuaries, land prices are so high and the need for new land so urgent that it becomes economic and expedient to infill marshes with rubble and rubbish directly to make up the level at a rate faster than there is time for new marsh to form. Obviously this brings a serious risk of pollution especially if the tipping is not done behind bunds which effectively keep the sea from re-working the rubbish.

Reclaimed marshland used as pasture and intersected by drainage ditches may retain elements of the salt marsh flora for at least 100 years (Petch 1945). It provides grazing and roost for wildfowl at high tide and the dykes and ditches extend the habitat of many rare species normally localized at the salt marsh upper limit and in brackish flushes. This habitat has never received proper ecological study although it probably carries almost as high species diversity as the sand dune and slack gradient. The present trend towards arable farming is rapidly destroying reclaimed pastureland at a time when its wildlife potential is only beginning to be recognized and valued.

The needs of coastal protection, improved navigation and wholesale transformation for fresh water reservoirs behind estuarine barrages, or coastally sited airports, all result in re-structuring of coastal sediments and the marshes derived from them. It is not always appreciated that foreshore amenity may be lost in a few decades as a result of siltation and marsh formation at sites apparently remote from newly constructed works. For example the training of the low water channel to the south shore of the Dee Estuary, Flint is the indirect cause of the loss of coastal waterfront at Parkgate, Cheshire on the north shore.

Kestner (in Thorn 1966) has reviewed the effects of dredging, barrages and training walls, on the tidal and siltation regime in estuaries. He concludes that the most successful schemes have been those in which the estuary as a whole has been modified. Half measures have usually not been successful and have produced undesirable side effects.

Gilson (in Lowe-McConnell 1966) has discussed some of the biological implications of proposed barrages in Morecambe Bay, Lancashire and the

Solway Firth to the north of it. More specifically Gray (in Perring 1970) who has completed a two year study of the Morecambe Bay salt marshes, draws attention in an interim report to the hazards of ecological prediction and to the probably ill-founded assumption that the present ecological behaviour of a given species is a reliable guide to its reaction to new situations. Most likely it is not, and the explosive spread of *Typha* in possibly new genetic combinations on the pseudo-delta of the Niger estuary (Trochain *pers. comm.*) may well be a pointer to the sort of biological reactions we should expect.

Integrated Management

It should be apparent from this account that the human impact on the salt marsh environment has not in general been based on informed understanding or consideration for the wildlife resources it contains. It follows that we are not fully aware of the value of these resources. Somewhat frantic efforts are being made at the present time to bring to the attention of authorities a fuller understanding of what is being lost and what might be gained by combined planning for the use of existing resources and the deliberate design of new salt marsh resources. For example, the creation of the Rømo dam joining the mainland to the island of Romø in Denmark, has been foreseen to encourage the formation of new salt marshes in its sheltered angles. Their formation is actively aided by ploughing drainage ditches in high level mudflats to seaward so that salt marsh growth is improved on the intervening ridges.

The activities of the San Francisco Bay Conservation and Development Commission (Harvey 1966 *a* and *b*) are spreading wider understanding of the value of existing wildlife resources to the people that live around the shores of the Bay. Steenis *et al* (1954) have done the same for the Delaware marshes and Goodwin *et al* (1961) for Connecticut's coastal marshes where significant advances in legislation have provided valuable protection to these habitats.

Fresh water reservoir proposals in the inter-tidal zone of estuaries are under joint investigation by engineers, hydrologists, fisheries, biologists, limnologists and all who are directly concerned with the protection and production of wildlife. All these activities are leading towards integrated management proposals which should enable the living things on salt marshes space to exist and should no longer allow the marsh to be treated as a convenient potential rubbish dump.

But they cannot only exist. They must be made to produce in common with other land for our crowded societies. Work in the larger nature reserves must evolve new management techniques, the full value of marshes in coastal protection must be assessed and the value of a fully utilized marsh set against any reclamation proposals for other purposes.

One example of the seasonal cycle of use that might be more fully developed is as follows. In the spring when migratory wildfowl have left, marshes may be rested for a few weeks to allow vegetation to recover and resident marshland birds to breed. Turf cutting could commence on suitable sites and stock return to graze. In summer, marshland areas could be increasingly used for recreation and education at a time when least harm will be done to wildlife resources. Mowing can be carried out to preserve the quality of salting pasture and in preparation for autumn turf cutting. In winter the migratory wildfowl will take up residence and could be cropped on a regulated permit system as at Caerlaverock National Nature Reserve, Dumfries, or fully protected as in the case of diminishing species such as the Brent Goose as at Scolt Head Island, Norfolk.

Only when we have tried to dove-tail these various forms of management can we hope to set a proper value on the salt marsh.

13 Management of Sand Dune Wildlife Resources

Sand dunes, unlike salt marshes, are effectively a diminishing resource around the coasts of lowland Europe and North America. Not only is their regeneration limited by what is believed to be a diminishing bank of off-shore sand supplies, but their rate of destruction under development of various kinds is almost certainly exceeded by their rate of formation. Expansion in area of a dune system is a much slower process than that associated with salt marsh formation. No figures are available for the proportion of sandy prograding coasts where the rate of formation is maximal as opposed to systems where the coastline is static or eroding, but it seems likely that if dune coastline lengths were scored for these properties, prograding sandy coasts would be in the minority.

While a certain amount of re-cycling of material goes on, this is primarily of a very local nature and most of the sand of a dune system being above the inter-tidal zone is out of circulation anyway. So, while there may be considerable internal mobility, dune systems as a whole are much more static in position on the coastline than salt marshes. They also tend to be more isolated one from another than salt marshes and this accounts for the distinctiveness of each individual dune flora. This is well illustrated by the colour variants of *Viola tricolor* sub-species *curtisii* on European dunes. Only yellow-flowered forms may occur on one system, on another, both yellow and blue-flowered forms are found, presumably evidence of isolation in terms of gene flow.

As we have seen, the low fertility of dune soils coupled with much open ground for casual colonization produces an immensely rich flora. This, combined with the distinctive landscape and shorelines ideal for recreation, attracts people in ever increasing numbers.

Sand dunes were among the earliest of sites settled by primitive man.

They have often been used with little understanding and disastrous results when the dunes, re-mobilized by over-cropping, have overwhelmed adjoining land settlements. More enlightened management policies followed and the value of dunes in coast protection was recognized. Some of the larger systems were afforested in the eighteenth and nineteenth century. As land became scarce dune systems were levelled for industry, housing, and airport needs. Now we are beginning to realize the special virtues of the diminishing dune landscape for recreation and the need for protecting these resources from further despoliation.

External Influences

Water extraction

The effect of water extraction on the dune flora has received little study except in the Netherlands. Here, Westhoff (1964) records that the dune area has 'to a large extent been dried up by the extraction of drinking water'. The Wassenaar dunes near the Hague have been exploited as a catchment area since 1874 and from about 1885 onward this has caused a serious fall in the level of the ground water table (Boerboom 1960). Many moisture-loving plants disappeared and the plant communities dependent on a high water table level were almost destroyed except in a few small man-made hollows formerly used as wells. Even a small permanent fall in the water table of about 10 cm can be fatal especially to the plants and animals of sub-aquatic and wet dune slacks (Voo 1964). In their place, common species such as *Molinia caerulea* or *Calamagrostis canescens* have spread over these habitats in the Netherlands. Uncontrolled water extraction from sites close behind the coastal dune can also lead to contamination of fresh-water supplies with brackish water.

Fortunately the dangers have been recognized in time and artificial fresh-water infiltration has been started in the Wassenaar dunes since 1955. Doerboom (1966) has been recording the floristic changes as the water table began to rise again. These changes are not necessarily a straight reversal to the original damp and wet slack communities, partly because of loss of parent material and partly because rabbit-grazing has diminished so altering the floristic balance. Studies on changes due to falling water tables are urgently needed in British dunes and especially those where there is little immediate prospect of new slack formation at the coast (as at Ainsdale, Lancashire for example). Any new slacks would of course result from wind excavation down to the new water table level.

Pollution

In a low-lying country like the Netherlands, there is a serious problem in maintaining oligotrophic communities like those found in lime-deficient dune slacks for they are enriched by nutrients from fertilizer residues washed out of agricultural land. Westhoff (1964) points out that a high proportion of the rare flowering plant species found in European dune slacks are characteristic of leached soils developed in the Atlantic climate zone. These are the first to diminish as soil enrichment progresses. This enrichment effect is proceeding only slowly in the Netherlands according to Voo (1964). Nevertheless from samples of about 900 oligotrophic waters throughout the Netherlands, it was found that significant changes in communities attributed to enrichment occurred in 42 per cent of them. Much depends on the way drainage from the agricultural catchment impinges on the dune water table. High-lying arable land directly to landward of the dune system is likely to have the most serious effects. In mesotrophic dune systems, incipient oligotrophic dune heath develops at the landward edge of the system. Such areas, lying closest to cultivated land, are particularly susceptible. For this reason it is essential to control drainage or at least to have a buffer zone to landward where high fertility cultivation is discouraged if oligotrophic systems are to be preserved as nature reserves.

Oil pollution does not have such serious effects on dune systems as on salt marshes, but where it does reach coastal dune slacks such species as *Euphorbia paralias* may be damaged by combinations of oil and emulsifiers (Ranwell 1968 *b*). It has been observed that up to 10 per cent of wind blown sand grains may be contaminated with oil and emulsifiers (Elliston – *pers. comm.*) after a serious pollution incident. We have no measure of the background oil contamination levels on sandy shores, but this will be maximal at the backshore, the source of dune sand, where conditions may often be too dry for effective bacterial breakdown of oil residues.

An increasing quantity of litter of all types is brought to the shores by tides and into the dune system by tourists. Teagle (1966) has analysed the weekly quantities of litter collected at Studland dunes, Dorset over a two-year period and finds the summer values about ten times greater than the winter quantities with peak values of thirty times the winter values on public holidays. The bulk of the litter is paper, but food remains attract gulls, and empty milk bottles trap small mammals in alarming quantities e.g. 48 mammals in 15 bottles in 1 year.

The possible consequences of air pollution on the mineral deficient soils of dune systems has been referred to earlier, but remains open for study.

Voo (1964) notes that shelter belts have been planted along the borders of nature reserves in the Netherlands to reduce the effects of airborne pollution and Bernatsky (1969) has demonstrated the importance of design of protective plantations in reducing air pollution.

Introduced species

Because of the need to control sand dune movement species like *Ammophila arenaria* have been deliberately introduced from Europe to the United States, South Africa, Australia and New Zealand. *Hippophaë rhamnoides* has now been planted on more dune systems within the British Isles than there are in its native range. The presence of this species (frequently planted in gardens), within a radius of about 5 miles (8 km) of a dune system brings a persistent risk of invasion via the agency of birds. A vigilant management policy is needed to check sporadic appearances and subsequent spread if the dune flora is not to be shaded out by its growth. This is a serious problem in some sand dune native reserves (e.g. Ainsdale Lancashire and Gibraltar Point, Lincolnshire). The rare sterile hybrid grass *Ammocalamagrostis baltica* was widely planted to new stations on Norfolk and Suffolk coasts during a dune re-planting programme following damage to the coast by floods in 1953 (Ellis 1960).

Afforestation is by far the most powerful agent for introduction of new species on to sand dunes and Holder (1953) records that following afforestation at Ainsdale, Lancashire the flora became far richer than it was originally. Similarly at Newborough, Anglesey the introduction of trees and shrubs for stabilization purposes, the use of roadside verge cuttings and forestry 'brash' to still the sand, and the introduction of weeds with hop manure in nursery beds, increased the flowering plant species total of the system by at least one third in about 10 years.

Teagle (1966) found little evidence that increasing numbers of tourists had added to the introduced flora at Studland, Dorset but since 1953 the New Zealand alien, *Acaena anserinifolia* has become well established in car park areas and in heavily trampled pathways. This species has hooked burrs on the fruiting head and is readily transported on the fur of animals or on clothes. The burrs may so clog the feathers of fledgling ground-nesting birds that they are unable to move effectively and die of starvation. This has been observed at Holy Island dunes, Northumberland where *Acaena* is abundant in *Ammophila* dunes.

Garden rubbish dumping adds to the dune flora and bulb cultivation on the Isles of Scilly has produced a remarkable assortment of aliens on many of the small dune systems there.

Internal Influences

Direct cropping of sand

The sand itself is mined locally for mineral extraction or building purposes. Mineral-bearing sands are widespread on the shores and dunes throughout the New South Wales coast and also on the south and central Queensland coasts of Australia (Sless 1956). Sand-winning for building purposes occurs sporadically around the British coast e.g. at Ainsdale, Lancashire and Druridge Bay, Northumberland. In many areas it has been discontinued (e.g. at Rock dunes, Cornwall) because of the risks to coast protection and loss of amenity beaches.

Other direct cropping

With the exception of the cranberry bogs associated with some of the North America dune systems, there is little available evidence that dune floras have so far yielded plants of any significant economic value. However, it is interesting that *Elymus arenarius* has been successfully hybridized with wheat (Pissarev and Vinogradova 1944), and with barley (Tsitsin 1946). Tsitsin considers that the hybrids thus obtained are 'of very great importance indeed' and should lead to big increases in crop yield.

In the past, marram grass (*Ammophila arenaria*) was regularly cut for thatching as at Newborough Warren, Anglesey (Ranwell 1959), but with increased availability of straw and development of plastics this is now discontinued in most areas.

Sand dune-building plants (especially *Ammophila* species) are cropped for stabilization purposes, but only on a small scale as a few strong tussocks will produce a great many planting units (Plate 15).

Rabbit cropping

Sand dunes were used extensively in medieval times as rabbit warrens, at least in Britain. They have also been used for centuries as open range grazing for stock. Warrens were effectively managed at first, but wild populations established and spread without control. Tansley (1949) records that rabbits were little known in Scotland until as late as the nineteenth century when their numbers rapidly increased. The structure of sand dune communities in Europe prior to myxomatosis was effectively the product of intensive rabbit-grazing.

Stock cropping

There is little information about the effect of stock grazing on dunes and this has never received experimental study. Frame (1971) records that a cow's hoof exerts a pressure of 40 to 60 lb per in^2 and that an acre of pasture would be trodden some three or four times in a year at normal stocking. By contrast sheep hooves exert a pressure of about 25 to 35 lb per in^2 and tread an acre of pasture six to ten times in a year. It becomes immediately clear from this why sheep have been found to be particularly damaging to dune pasture. However the low-lying lime-rich dune pastures (machairs) of Scotland have a relatively high moisture-holding capacity and have supported sheep for centuries without serious erosion. Elsewhere the uncontrolled mobility of many European dune systems which developed in stormy periods was undoubtedly triggered off by over-grazing by rabbits and stock in the past. All forms of large mammal grazing have now declined in many dune areas though it is still possible to see the typical grazed sward flora in pockets where rabbits have survived. At Whiteford Burrows, Glamorgan, ponies graze the dunes (in addition to sheep) and with little apparent harm to the dune turf which they crop almost as closely as rabbits.

Golf links

The use of sand dunes as golf links involves heavy local fertilizing, extensive mowing, some drainage, and local shrub clearance. Small areas are intensively managed as greens, tees or bunkers, but for the most part a modified, fairly varied dune flora and fauna survives unharmed. Wallace (1953) recorded some 350 species of flowering plants on Dawlish Warren, Devon a small dune system of about 100 acre (c.40 ha) partly used as a golf links. Beeftink (1966) found no less than 220 species on only one hectare of the Heveringen dunes formerly grazed by horses and goats and afterwards used as a golf links. Experimental studies on the effects of mowing dune vegetation are now in progress in the Newborough Warren (Anglesey), and Holkham and Winterton (Norfolk) National Nature Reserves.

No one has yet brought together the very considerable practical experience obtained by golf links management on sand dunes. Ecologists need to relate this knowledge to the modified, but locally species – rich plant and animal communities produced. It may well help in the design of field experimental studies required for effective management of sand dune nature reserves. It is probably true to say that this relatively benign use has done more to preserve the dune flora and fauna near built up areas than any other factor. In doing so it has helped to keep open the lines of migration between one dune system and another for recruitment of flora and fauna.

Afforestation

The primary reason for planting trees on sand dunes has always been to protect the surface of shifting sands which in the past have overwhelmed coastal settlements in many parts of the world on more exposed dune coasts. Plantings have also been made for amenity purposes, as at Holkham, Norfolk. Afforestation is not the best means of protecting dunes from coastal erosion as the trees shade out *Ammophila* and other plants capable of recruiting new coastal dunes at the strandline. Timber production is only significant on the very largest dune plantations, and then only behind the shelter of protection forest consisting of wind-deformed trees, themselves useless for timber production.

At Les Landes in France 250,000 acre (101,075 ha) of dune were afforested during the nineteenth century mainly with *Pinus maritima* (Macdonald 1954). English (1969) has described the technique developed on this coast by the French engineer Bremontier. A shallow sloping littoral dune is created with fences and *Ammophila* planting, and behind this lies the protection forest itself protecting the production forest. In 1949 forest fires destroyed 200,000 acre (80,940 ha) of this woodland and 82 people died. However, the speed of the fire was so rapid that seeds survived intact in cones and pine regenerated in the burnt areas (English 1969).

In Denmark 75,000 acre (30,352 ha) of coastal dune have been afforested and are managed by the State primarily as amenity woodlands. *Pinus mugo* is used as both *Pinus nigra* and *Pinus maritima* (widely used on dunes elsewhere) were found to be attacked and destroyed by the fungus *Crumenula pinea* after 15 to 20 years growth. Careful attention is paid to thatching felled areas with cut heather or to planting with *Ammophila* before new plantations are started (Thaarup 1954). Trees on dunes are very deep-rooted and not readily subject to wind throw.

Some 10,000 acre (4,047 ha) have been planted chiefly with *Pinus nigra* var. *calabrica* and some *P. maritima* and *P. sylvestris* in Great Britain (Macdonald 1954).

The immediate effect of afforestation is to increase the diversity of flowering plant species largely through introduction as mentioned earlier. As the trees mature they shade out the ground flora almost completely although certain species like *Goodyera repens* at Culbin, Moray (not present in the unplanted dunes), are widespread in the plantations.

Ovington (1950 and 1951) has studied changes in the soil environment due to afforestation on dunes. He found that the water table was lowered by 17 cm in 20 year old conifer plantations compared with unplanted areas at Tentsmuir, Fife. At both Culbin and Tentsmuir, the nutrient content decreased with afforestation and the soil acidity increased (Fig. 67) while the organic matter at the surface and the manganese content increased in plantations over a 20 year period. Nutrients are bound up in the tree crop and when this is removed the impoverished soil is highly vulnerable to erosion.

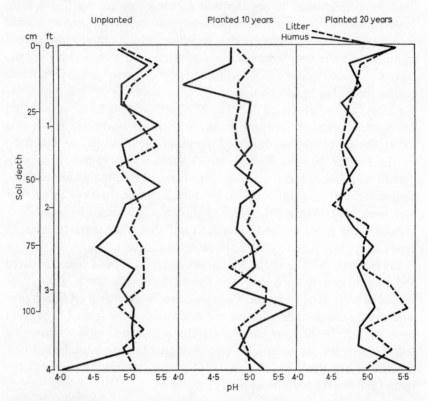

Fig. 67. The effect of Conifer planting upon soil pH at various depths in dune soil from Culbin Sands, Morayshire. Two profiles for each area are shown (from Ovington 1950).

Wright (1955) extended Ovington's studies to a wider variety of tree species and age classes at Culbin and recorded soil moisture and temperature in plantation soils using gypsum soil moisture blocks and thermistor techniques. The growth of trees dried out upper sand layers considerably although the surface organic layers of older plantations had a high moisture-holding capacity.

Little is known about the ecology of these dune forests or the young plantations. Where seedling pines invade dune nature reserves as at Tents-muir, Fife they have to be cut out regularly, to protect the native fauna and flora.

Coast protection and amenity use

Ever since the stormy periods of the fourteenth and fifteenth centuries *Ammophila* has been planted to stabilize sand surfaces. Brown and Hafen-richter (1948) in an important series of papers describe experiments on the influence of date of planting, density, and different combinations of fer-tilizers on the growth of *Ammophila breviligulata, A. arenaria* and *Elymus mollis*. Charlton (in Anon 1970 *b*) has also carried out fertilizer trials on the growth of *Ammophila arenaria* and *Elymus arenarius* in Scotland. Thornton and Davis (1964) have selected and propagated genotypes of *Ammophila breviligulata* and studied germination of this species. Organic material of various kinds (e.g. forestry trimmings, roadside verge cuttings) is regularly used to protect bare sand from erosion. Haas and Steers (1964) describe a latex spray technique for stilling sand surfaces and Zak (1967) experi-mented with the use of hydraulically sprayed mulches and seed mixtures for stabilization purposes (Plate 16).

There is now a very extensive world literature on dune stabilization techniques and as this is being reviewed elsewhere it is not appropriate to deal with it here. Perhaps of more direct interest to the ecologist is the effect of the treatments on the plants and animals, the effect that the recent upsurge in tourist use of dunes is having upon them, and the techniques being used to study this.

Hewett (1970) has recorded the re-establishment of the dune flora within a 100 acre (40 ha) *Ammophila* plantation at Braunton Burrows, Devon and found that 53 species of flowering plants, two mosses and one lichen had colonized the bare sand in 15 years or less. These were all plants charac-teristic of the existing dune system and included several of the less common species. *Festuca rubra* was beginning to close up the gaps in the plantations and leguminous species were becoming increasingly common 10 to 15 years after stabilization.

No studies have yet been made on grasslands established on dunes by hydraulic seeding using cultivated grass seed. Where this has been done successfully, at Camber, Sussex for example, the dunes have been arti-ficially graded before seeding to produce uniform slopes. Some habitat diversity has therefore already been lost and it may be many years before native species are able to reinvade. In fact this system of some 250 acre (100 ha), part of which is used as a Golf Links, may receive up to 17,000 people a day in summer and it seems likely there will be a constant need for repair of trampled turf by seeding and fertilizing. Shrub planting is now in progress and the system is clearly moving towards a very artificial habitat specifically designed for recreational use. Nevertheless it may still harbour many native species alongside the introduced ones.

Where human population pressures are rather lower as on parts of the East Lothian sand dune coast, dune restoration with native species, *Elymus arenarius* and *Ammophila arenaria*, and the judicious clearance of pathways through invasive growths of *Hippophaë rhamnoides*, help to retain much of the original character of the dune systems while still allowing large numbers of people access to the shores. (Tindall 1967 and Anon 1970 *b*.)

Low level aerial photography from a captive balloon coupled with quadrat ground survey has been used to record the distribution of people and plants at Whitesands and Yellowcraig, East Lothian (Duffield in 1970 *b*). Here a very detailed picture is being built up from which future changes can be measured.

Quinn (in Anon 1970 *b*) used conventional air photography to study recreational use over a 230 acre (85 ha) dune system at Brittas Bay, Wicklow, Ireland and recorded a maximum of 250 people per $50\,m^2$, falling to 120 to 80 people per $50\,m^2$ at 100 to 150 m distance from paths.

Goldsmith *et al* (1970) have studied the effect of trampling on dune vegetation in the Isles of Scilly. Schofield (in Duffey 1967) used electronic counters for monitoring the movement of people on dunes at Gibraltar Point, Lincolnshire, while Bayfield (1971) has shown how short soft metal wires can be set in paths and used to measure trampling by the proportion of wires that get bent flat.

These studies are just beginning, but it is clear that the ecologist is at last beginning to treat man as a highly significant animal in the dune landscape worthy of objective study.

Integrated Management

Because dune systems are now recognized as a valuable and limited resource not only for wildlife but also as recreational land, each country with dune resources clearly needs to develop a national plan for their protection and use. Such a plan would record the distribution and size of dune resources and designate those areas in which there is a priority for coast protection, recreational use or for protection of wildlife.

Any dune sites which are managed primarily for coast protection or recreation will still contain significant wildlife resources. Their protection is clearly relevant to the maintenance of the system for both these uses. Nevertheless the initiative to protect specific populations of rare or local species on such systems must lie with local naturalists or voluntary bodies. They can do much to help avoid unnecessary destruction by providing owners and planners with maps showing location of sites for which protection is desirable or by actually transplanting species to nearby safe areas from those which must be disturbed. The recording of such transplanting activities is clearly desirable.

Management for coast protection

Where coast protection is the primary aim any sand-winning activities should be gradually phased out, growth of trees should not be allowed to shade out dune-forming grasses near the coast and a regular maintenance commitment accepted at the coast. Air photography should be commissioned on a regular 3 to 5 year basis to record the success of management activities and to help understand the structural development of the system in relation to adjoining coastal changes. Instant stabilization can be employed in serious trouble spots with modern techniques referred to above. Elsewhere the principle of developing an aerodynamically stable shallow-sloping seaward face to the coast dune should be followed with conventional fencing and planting techniques using selected strains of appropriate grasses with use of fertilizers to aid establishment.

Management for recreation

Where recreational use is the primary object it is essential to provide convenient access to the shore where most people want to be, via specified pathways which effectively protect the sand from erosion. Where visitors are few natural vegetated pathways can be protected by rotational use. With increasing numbers of visitors fertilizing and regular repair of pathways by seeding becomes essential. Where large numbers of people need access to the shore artificially surfaced paths (plastic netting, wood, shells or gravel) must be provided.

The extent to which people penetrate back into the dunes from the shore is under active study at the present time. Many factors are involved here including the orientation of the dune coast, the freedom of the shore from pollution, the weather, and the type of vegetation on or behind the coast dune. Much could be done by judicious management of the grass/shrub balance to accommodate more people within dunes in relative privacy from one another, but there is a limit and at the present time we do not have the facts and figures which will tell us the optimum design for maximum acceptable densities.

While coast protection is primarily concerned with dune maintenance at the coast itself, a more comprehensive dune maintenance programme over the whole dune system is required where it is under intensive recreational use. Air photo monitoring may be required more frequently to detect changes in pathway patterns pointing to the need for closer access control or urgent restoration activities. Car park capacities must be related to holding capacity of the dune system for people and uncontrolled parking on dune turf is bound to lead to expensive control measures or ultimate abandonment of the site. The siting of car parks and caravan sites to the landward of the dunes should be designed to avoid releasing large numbers of people where the shore is narrow and sand supply for dune building minimal.

Management for wildlife protection

The objectives of management for coast protection and recreation are simply defined. They are to keep the sea out and to enable as many people as possible to enjoy the dune amenity without destroying it.

The objectives of management for wildlife protection are more complex and less easily defined and achieved. The British series of dune National Nature Reserves has been chosen to include representative physiographic and soil and climate-determined biological types throughout the country. Broadly speaking the objectives of management in these systems is to maintain the plant and animal communities for which they were originally selected, to utilize them for educational and research purposes and, where there is scope for this, to increase the diversity of habitats within them by controlled disturbance.

The maintenance of dune communities produced by a long history of intensive rabbit grazing, now much reduced since myxomatosis, presents special problems. It may be possible on one or two larger systems to enclose a captive rabbit population within rabbit-proof fencing. This would in fact be a return to the way in which these communities presumably started in specially created warrens. However, because of costs and the general undesirability of building up rabbit populations this could not be a universally acceptable policy. Cutting out of invasive trees and shrubs at least in selected areas is more generally acceptable and practicable where invasion is still in an early stage. This policy is already in practice in a number of reserves e.g. at Whiteford Burrows, Glamorgan where *Hippophaë* is removed and at Tentsmuir, Fife where unwanted pines are cut out.

Mowing could only be used on a limited scale and while it may help to maintain populations of certain low-growing species threatened by under-grazing. it will produce different communities to those characteristic of rabbit grazing. Carefully controlled sheep and pony grazing may be more generally applicable, but imply control of dogs which is not easily achieved near centres of population.

It seems inevitable that we must accept major changes towards scrub and woodland communities in some reserves where invasion is already well-advanced as at Ainsdale, Lancashire or Gibraltar Point, Lincolnshire. These new communities may eventually become as diverse and interesting as the species-rich dune grasslands they replace. However, it seems likely that they will themselves tend to be controlled by fire, as already happens at Studland, Dorset. It follows therefore, that specially designed fire-breaks will have to be created and maintained if fire control is not to become too destructive and lead to massive erosion.

As we have seen the problem of falling water tables can and has been tackled in Dutch dune reserves by active management of the water table. This again is costly and probably only applicable to few selected areas. The deliberate creation of pools by excavation can help to recreate late stage hydroseres where these have been lost by drying up or where as at Newborough Warren, Anglesey it was done to diversify the system. But this does bring the risk of attracting Herring Gulls which may in turn attack the young of other ground-nesting species such as terns. Wherever possible the natural formation of new slacks at the coast should be allowed to proceed unhindered to replenish those which in the normal course of development become drier as they mature.

Unlike the salt marsh habitat there is little opportunity for zoning different activities in time on dune systems, but there is a great deal to be gained from spacial zonation. The principle of resting sections from intensive educational or recreational use with temporary fencing can improve both coast protection and restoration of a trampled strand-line flora. Afforestation designed for recreational use can develop side by side with undisturbed wildlife sectors running from the coast to the landward limits in the bigger dune systems. Educational use can be separated from remoter research sites to cut down disturbance to the latter to a minimum.

It is already apparent in the British sand dune reserve series that systems showing a high recreational use are more appropriate for intensive educational use (e.g. Studland, Dorset) those readily accessible to research stations with lighter recreational use are more appropriate for research use (e.g. Holkham, Norfolk), while small remote systems with climatically distinctive communities (e.g. Invernaver, Sutherland) are best left undisturbed as much as possible.

We begin to see a pattern emerging which should be applicable not just to nature reserves, but to dune systems generally whatever their use: appropriate use of different systems; appropriate use of parts within the systems, joint care for the needs of people and of wildlife.

Q

References

ADAMS, D. A. (1963), 'Factors influencing vascular plant zonation in North Carolina salt marshes', *Ecology*, **44**, 445–456.

ADRIANI, E. D. (1945), 'Sur la Phytosociologie, la Synécologie et le bilan d'eau de Halophytes de la région Néerlandaise Méridionale, ainsi que de la Mediterranee Française.' *S.I.G.M.A.*, *Groningen*, **88**, 1–217.

AGUESSE, P. and MARAZANOF, F. (1965), 'Les modifications des milieux aquatiques de Camargues au cours des 30 dernières annés', *Ann. de Limiol.*, **1**, 163–190.

ALLEN, S. E., CARLISLE, A., WHITE, E. J. and EVANS, C. C. (1968), 'The plant nutrient content of rainwater'. *J. Ecol.*, **56**, 497–504.

ALVIN, K. L. (1960), 'Observations on the lichen ecology of South Haven Peninsula, Studland Heath, Dorset', *J. Ecol.*, **48**, 331–339.

ANDERSON, E. and STEBBINS, G. L. (1954), 'Hybridization as an evolutionary stimulus', *Evolution*, 8, 378–388.

ANON (1966 *a*), *Solway Barrage*, Water Resources Board Report, London: H.M.S.O.

ANON (1966 *b*), *Morecambe Bay Barrage*, Water Resources Board Report, London: H.M.S.O.

ANON (1966 *c*), *Morecambe Bay and Solway Barrages*, Water Resources Board Report, London: H.M.S.O.

ANON (1967), *Dee crossing study. Phase 1*. Ministry of Housing and Local Government Report, London: H.M.S.O.

ANON (1970 *a*), *The Wash: estuary storage*, Water Resources Board Report, London: H.M.S.O.

ANON (1970 *b*) *Dune conservation 1970*, North Berwick Study Group Rep, North Berwick: East Lothian County Council.

ANON (1970 *c*), *Modern Farming and the Soil*, London: H.M.S.O.

ARDÖ, P. (1957), 'Studies in the marine shore dune ecosystem with special reference to the dipterous fauna', *Opusc. ent. Suppl.*, **14**, 1–255.

ARNOLD, A. (1955), Die Bedeutung der Chlorionen für die Pflanze. Bot. Stud. 2. Jena.

AUGUSTINE, M. T., THORNTON, R. B., SANBORN, J. M. and LEISER, A. T. (1964),

'Response of American Beachgrass to fertilizer', *J. Soil and Water Consvn.*, **19**, 112–116.

BAGNOLD, R. A. (1941), *The Physics of Blown Sand and Desert Dunes*, London; Methuen.

BAKER, J. M. (1970 *a*), 'Oil and salt marsh soil', Institute of Petroleum Symposium on the ecological effects of oil pollution on littoral communities. London, Morning Session 1–10.

BAKER, J. M. (1970 *b*), 'Growth stimulation following oil pollution', *Ibid*, 11–16.
(1970 *c*), 'Comparative toxicities of oils, oil fractions and emulsifiers', *Ibid*, 17–26.
(1970 *d*), 'The effects of oils on plant physiology', *Ibid*, 27–37.
(1970 *e*), 'The effects of a single oil spillage', Institute of Petroleum Symposium on the ecological effects of oil pollution on littoral communities. London, Afternoon Session, 1–5.
(1970 *f*), 'Successive spillages', *Ibid*, 7–18.
(1970 *g*), 'Refinery effluent', *Ibid*, 19–29.
(1970 *h*), 'Seasonal effects', *Ibid*, 31–38.
(1970 *i*), 'Effects of cleaning', *Ibid*, 39–44.

BAKKER, D., TER BORG, S. J. and OTZEN, D. (1966), 'Ecological research at the Plantecology Laboratory, State University, Groningen', *Wentia*, **15**, 1–24.

BALL, P. W. and BROWN, K. G. (1970), 'A biosystematic and ecological study of *Salicornia* in the Dee estuary', *Watsonia*, **8**, 27–40.

BARKLEY, S. Y. (1955), 'The morphology and vegetation of the sands of Forvie with reference to certain related areas', Ph.D. Thesis, Aberdeen.

BARNES, B. M. and BARNES, R. D. (1954), 'The ecology of the spiders of maritime drift lines', *Ecology*, **35**, 25–35.

BAYFIELD, N. G. (1971), 'A simple method for detecting variations in walker pressure laterally across paths', *J. appl. Ecol.*, **8**, 533–535.

BEEFTINK, W. G. (1962), 'Conspectus of the phanerogamic salt plant communities in the Netherlands', *Biol. Jaarb. Antwerp*, 325–362.

BEEFTINK, W. G. (1965), De zoutvegetatie van ZW – Nederland beschouwd in Europees Verbaud. Wageningen.

BEEFTINK, W. G. (1966), 'Vegetation and habitat of the salt marshes and beach plains in the south-western part of the Netherlands', *Wentia*, **15**, 83–108.

BERNATZKY, A. (1969), Die Bedeutung von Schutzpflanzungen gegen Luftverunreinigungen. Air Pollution. Proc. 1st. Europ. Congr. on Influence of Air Pollution on Plants and Animals, Wageningen 1968, 383–395.

BERNSTEIN, L. and PEARSON, G. A. (1956), 'Influence of exchangeable sodium on the yield and chemical composition of plants. 1. Green beans, garden beans, clover and alfalfa', *Soil Sci.*, **82**, 247–258.

BIEDERMAN, E. W. Jr. (1962), 'Distinction of shoreline environments in New Jersey', *J. Sediment. Petrol.*, **32**, 181–200.

BIGOT, M. L. (1958), Les grands caractères écologiques des milieux terrestes de Camargue, 3° Congr. Soc. Sav., 533–539.

BINET, P. (1964 *a*), 'Action de la température et de la salinité sur la germination des graines de *Plantago maritima* L.', *Bull. Soc. bot. Fr.*, **111**, 407–411.

BINET, P. (1964 b), 'La germination des semences des halophytes', *Bull. Soc. Fr. Physiol. Vég.*, **10**, 253–263.

BINET, P. (1965 a), Etudes d'écologie expérimentale et physiologique sur *Cochlearia anglica* L. I Etudes dans l'estuaire de l'Orne.' *Oecol Planta.*, **1**, 7–38.

BINET, P. (1965 b), 'Action de la température et de la salinité sur la germination des graines de *Cochlearia anglica* L.', *Revue gen. Bot.*, **72**, 221–236.

BINET, P. (1965 c), 'Action de divers rhythmes thermiques journaliers sur la germination des semences de *Triglochin maritima* L.', *Bull. Soc. Linn. Normandie Series* 10, **6**, 99–102.

BINET, P. (1965 d), 'Action de la température et de la salinité sur la germination des graines de *Glaux maritima* L'., *Bull. Soc. bot. Fr.*, **112**, 346–350.

BINET, P. (1965 e), 'Aptitude a germer en milieu salé de trois espèces de *Glyceria*: *G. borreri* Bab., *G. distans*. Wahlb. et *G. maritima* Wahlb.', *Bull Soc. bot. Fr.*, **113**, 361–367.

BIRSE, E. L. and GIMINGHAM, C. H. (1955), 'Changes in the structure of bryophytic communities with the progress of succession on sand dunes', *Trans. Br. Bryol. Soc.*, **2**, 523–531.

BIRSE, E. L., LANDSBERG, S. Y. and GIMINGHAM, C. H. (1957), 'The effects of burial by sand on dune mosses', *Trans. Br. Bryol. Soc.*, **3**, 285–301.

BIRSE, E. M. (1958), 'Ecological studies on growth-form in Bryophytes. III. The relationship between the growth-form of mosses and ground-water supply', *J. Ecol.*, **46**, 9–27.

BLACK, C. A. (1968), *Soil-plant Relationships*. 2nd edn. Chichester: J. Wiley.

BLANCHARD, B. (1952), An ecological survey of the vegetation of the sand dune system of the South West Lancashire coast, with special reference to an associated marsh flora. Ph.D. Thesis, Liverpool.

BLOCK, R. J. (1945), 'Amino acid composition of food proteins', Adv. Protein Chemistry. **2**, 119–134.

BÖCHER, T. W. (1952), 'Vegetationsudvikling iforhold til marin akkumulation', *Bot. Tidsskr.*, **49**, 1–32.

BOERBOOM, J. H. A. (1960), 'De plantengemeenschappen van de Wassenaarse duinen', *Meded. LandbHoogesch. Wageningen*, **60**, 1–135.

BOERBOOM, J. H. A. (1963), 'Het verband tussen bodem en vegetatie in de Wassenaarse duinen', *Boor en Spade*, **13**, 120–155.

BOERBOOM, J. H. A. (1964), 'Microclimatological observations in the Wassenaar dunes', *Meded. LandbHoogesch. Wageningen*, **64**, 1–28.

BOLLARD, E. G. and BUTLER, G. W. (1966), 'Mineral nutrition of plants', *A. Rev. Pl. Physiol.*, **17**, 77–112.

BOND, G., MACCONNELL, J. T. and McCULLUM, A. H. (1956), 'The nitrogen nutrition of *Hippophaë rhamnoides*, L.', *Ann. Bot.* (*N.S.*), **20**, 501–512.

BOND, T. E. T. (1952), '*Elymus arenarius*. Biological Flora of the British Isles', *J. Ecol.*, **40**, 217–227.

BOORMAN, L. A. (1967, '*Limonium vulgare* Mill. and *L. humile* Mill, Biological flora of the British Isles', *J. Ecol.*, **55**, 221–232.

BOORMAN, L. A. (1968), 'Some aspects of the reproductive biology of *Limonium vulgare* Mill. and *Limonium humile* Mill.', *Ann. Bot.*, **32**, 803–824.

BOURN, W. S. and Cottam, C. (1950), Some biological effects of ditching tide-water marshes. U.S. Fish and Wildlife Service, Rep., **19**, 1–30.

BOYCE, S. G. (1954), 'The salt spray community', *Ecol. Mongr.*, **24**, 29–67.

BOYD, J. M. (1957), 'The Lumbricidae of a dune – machair soil gradient in Tiree, Argyll', Ann. Mag. nat. Hist., Ser. 12, **10**, 274–282.

BRADSHAW, A. D. (1958), 'Natural hybridization of *Agrostis tenuis* Sibth. and *A. stolonifera* L.', *New Phyt*, **57**, 66–84.

BRADSHAW, A. D. (1965), 'Evolutionary significance of phenotypic plasticity in plants', *Adv. Genet.*, **13**, 115–155.

BRAUN-BLANQUET, J. (1932), *Plant Sociology*, London: McGraw-Hill.

BRAYBROOKS, E. M. (1958), The general ecology of *Spartina townsendii* (*sic. S. anglica*) with special reference to sward build-up and degradation. M.Sc. Thesis, Southampton.

BRERETON, A. J. (1965). Pattern in salt marsh vegetation. Ph.D. Thesis, Univ. of Wales.

BRERETON, A. J. (1971), 'The structure of the species populations in the initial stages of salt-marsh succession', *J. Ecol.*, **59**, 321–338.

BROOKS, C. E. P. (1949), *Climate Through the Ages*. London: Ernest Benn.

BROWN, D. H. and BROWN, R. M. (1969), 'Lichen communities at Blakeney Point, Norfolk', *Trans. Norfolk Norwich Nat. Soc.*, **21**, 235–250.

BROWN, J. C. (1958), 'Soil fungi of some British sand dunes in relation to soil type and succession', *J. Ecol.*, **46**, 641–664.

BROWN, J. S. (1925), A study of coastal ground water. U.S. Geol. Survey Water Supply Paper 537, 16–17.

BROWN, R. L. and HAFENRICHTER, A. L. (1948), 'Factors influencing the production and use of beach-grass and dune-grass clones for erosion control. I. Effect of date of planting. II. Influence of density of planting. III. Influence of kinds and amounts of fertilizer on production', *J. Am. Soc. Agron.*, **40**, 512–521; 603–609; 677–684.

BROWNELL, P. F. (1965), 'Sodium as an essential micronutrient element for a higher plant (*Atriplex vesicaria*)', *Pl. Physiol.*, **40**, 460–468.

BURKHOLDER, P. R. (1956), Studies on the nutritive value of *Spartina* grass growing in the marsh areas of coastal Georgia', *Bull. Torrey bot. Club*, **83**, 327–334.

BURKHOLDER, P. R. and BURKHOLDER, L. M. (1956), 'Vitamin B_{12} in suspended solids and marsh muds collected along the coast of Georgia', *Limnol. Oceanogr.*, **1**, 202–208.

BURKHOLDER, P. R. and BORNSIDE, G. H. (1957), 'Decomposition of marsh grass by aerobic marine bacteria', *Bull. Torrey bot. Club*, **84**, 366–383.

BURNETT, J. H. (ed.) (1964), *The Vegetation of Scotland*. Edinburgh: Oliver and Boyd.

CAREY, A. E. and OLIVER, F. W. (1918), *Tidal Lands*. London: Blackie.

CHAPMAN, V. J. (1938), 'Studies in salt marsh ecology. Sections I–III', *J. Ecol.*, **26**, 144–179.

CHAPMAN, V. J. (1940), Succession on the New England salt marshes. *Ecology*, **21**, 279–282.

CHAPMAN, V. J. (1942), 'The new perspective in the Halophytes, *Q. Rev. Biol.*, **17**, 291–311.

CHAPMAN, V. J. (1944), 'Cambridge University expedition to Jamaica', *J. Linn. Soc.* (Bot), **52**, 407–533.

CHAPMAN, V. J. (1959), 'Studies in salt marsh ecology. IX. Changes in salt marsh vegetation at Scolt Head Island, Norfolk', *J. Ecol.*, **47**, 619–639.

CHAPMAN, V. J. (1960), *Salt Marshes and Salt Deserts of the World*. London: Leonard Hill.

CHAPMAN, V. J. and RONALDSON, J. W. (1958). The mangrove and salt marsh flats of the Auckland Isthmus. N.Z. Dept. Sci. and Indust. Res., Bull. 125, 1–79.

CHIPPINDALE, H. G. and MERRICKS, R. W. (1965), 'Gang-mowing and pasture management', *J. Br. Grassld Soc.*, **11**, 1–9.

CLAPHAM, A. R., PEARSALL, W. H. and RICHARDS, P. W. (1942), '*Aster tripolium*. Biological flora of the British Isles'. *J. Ecol.*, **30**, 385–395.

CLARKE, L. D. and HANNON, N. J. (1967), 'The mangrove swamp and salt marsh communities of the Sydney district. I Vegetation, soils and climate', *J. Ecol.*, **55**, 753–771.

CLARKE, L. D. and HANNON, N. J. (1969), 'The mangrove swamp and salt marsh communities of the Sydney district. II The Holocoenotic complex with particular reference to physiography', *J. Ecol.*, **57**, 213–234.

CLARKE, L. D. and HANNON, N. J. (1970), 'The mangrove swamp and salt marsh communities of the Sydney district. III. Plant growth in relation to salinity and waterlogging', *J. Ecol.*, **58**, 351–369.

CLARKE, S. M. (1965), Some aspects of the autecology of *Elymus arenarius* L. Ph.D. Thesis, Hull.

COTTON, M. J. (1967), 'Aspects of the ecology of sand dune arthropods', *Entomologist*, **100**, 157–165.

COOPER, W. S. (1958), 'Coastal sand dunes of Oregon and Washington', Geol. Soc. America Memoir, **72**. Baltimore.

COTTAM, C. and MUNRO, D. A. (1954), 'Eelgrass status and environmental relations', *J. Wildl. Mgmt*, **18**, 449–460.

COULL, J. (1968), 'Crofting townships and common grazings', *Agr. Hist. Rev.*, 16.

COWLES, H. C. (1899), 'The ecological relations of the vegetation on the sand dunes of Lake Michigan', *Bot. Gaz.*, **27**, 95–117; 167–202; 281–308; 361–391.

COWLES, H. C. (1911), 'A fifteen year study of advancing sand dunes', Rep. Br. Ass. 1911, 565.

CRAWFORD, R. M. M. and WISHART, D. (1966), 'A multivariate analysis of the development of dune slack vegetation in relation to coastal accretion at Tentsmuir, Fife', *J. Ecol.*, **54**, 729–743.

CRAWFORD, R. M. M. and WISHART, D. (1967), 'A rapid multivariate method for the detection and classification of groups of ecologically related species', *J. Ecol.*, **55**, 505–524.

CRAWFORD, R. M. M. and WISHART, D. (1968), 'A rapid classification and ordination method and its application to vegetation mapping', *J. Ecol.*, **56**, 385–404.

DAHL, R. G. (1959), 'Studies on Scandinavian *Ephydridae* (*Diptera, Brachycera*)', Opusc. ent. suppl., **15**, 1–224.

DALBY, D. H. (1962), 'Chromosome number, morphology and breeding behaviour in the British *Salicorniae*', *Watsonia*, **5**, 150–162.

DALBY, D. H. (1963), 'Seed dispersal in *Salicornia pusilla*', *Nature*, **199**, 197–198.

DALBY, D. H. (1970), 'The salt marshes of Milford Haven, Pembrokeshire', *Field Studies*, **3**, 297–330.

DALBY, R. (1957), 'Problems of land reclamation. 5. Salt marsh in the Wash', *Agric. Rev.*, **2**, 31–37.

DAVIS, J. H. (1940), The ecology and geologic role of mangroves in Florida. Carnegie Inst. Publ. 517, 303.

DAVIS, L. V. and GRAY, I. E. (1966), Zonal and seasonal distribution of insects in North Carolina salt marshes. Ecol. Monogr., **36**, 275–295.

DAY, J. H. (1951), 'The ecology of South African estuaries Pt. I. A review of estuarine conditions in general', *Trans. Roy. Soc. S. Afr.*, **33**, 53–91.

DEFANT, A. (1964), *Ebb and Flow*. New York: University of Michigan Press.

DUFF, S. and TEAL, J. M. (1965), Temperature change and gas exchange in Nova Scotia and Georgia salt marsh muds. Woods Hole Oceanographic Inst. Contrib. No. 1501, 67–73.

DUFFEY, E. (1967), The biotic effects of public pressure on the environment. Nature Conservancy, Monks Wood Experimental Station Symposium, **3**, 1–178.

DUFFEY, E. (1968), 'An ecological analysis of the spider fauna of sand dunes', *J. Anim. Ecol.*, **37**, 641–674.

DUVIGNEAUD, P. (1947), 'Remarques sur la végétation des pannes dans les dunes littorales entre La Panne et Dunkerque', *Bull. Soc. roy. Bot. Belg.*, **79**, 123–140.

EHRLICH, P. R. and RAVEN, P. H. (1969), 'Differentiation of populations', *Science*, **165**, 1128–1232.

ELLIS, E. A. (1960), 'The purple (hybrid) Marram, *Ammocalamagrostis baltica* (Fluegge) P. Fourn. in East Anglia', *Trans. Norfolk Norwich Nat. Soc.*, **19**, 49–51.

ELTON, C. S. (1966), '*The pattern of Animal Communities*'. London: Methuen.

ELZAM, O. E. and EPSTEIN, E. (1969), 'Salt relations of two grass species differing in salt tolerance. I. Growth and salt content at different salt concentrations', *Agrochimica*, **13**, 187–195.

ENGLISH, N. (1969), 'Les Landes', Nature Conservancy unpubld. typescript, 1–20.

EVANS, H. J. and SORGER, G. J. (1966), 'Role of mineral elements with emphasis on the univalent cations', *A. Rev. Pl. Physiol.*, **17**, 47–76.

FAEGRI, K. (1958), 'On the climatic demands of Oceanic plants', *Bot. notiser*, 3, 325–332.

FAEGRI, K. (1960), *The Distribution of Coast Plants*. Oslo: Oslo University Press.

FAIRBRIDGE, R. W. (1961), 'Eustatic changes in sea level', *Phys. Chem. Earth*, **4**, 99–185.

FLETCHER, H. C. and ELMENDORF, H. B. (1955), 'Phreatophytes – a serious problem in the West. U.S.', *Yearb. Agric.*, **1955**, 423–429.

FRAME, J. (1971), 'Fundamentals of grassland management. 10. The grazing animal', *Scottish Agric.*, **50**, 1–17.

FREIJSEN, A. H. J. (1967), *A Field Study of the Ecology of Centaurium vulgare* Rafn., Tilburg: H. Gianotten.

FOWDEN, L. (1959), *Physiologia Pl.*, **12**, 657–664.

GALLATIN, M. H., LUNIN, J. and BATCHELDER, A. R. (1962), 'Brackish water sources for irrigation along the eastern seaboard of the United States', *U.S. Dept. Agric. Prod. Resour Rep.*, **61**, 1–28.

GARRET, P. (1971), The sedimentary record of life on a modern tropical tidal flat, Andros Island, Bahamas. Ph. D. thesis John Hopkins Univ., Baltimore.

GATES, F. C. (1950), 'The disappearing Sleeping Bear Dune', *Ecology*, **31**, 386–392.

GEMMELL, A. R., GREIG-SMITH, P. and GIMINGHAM, C. H. (1953), 'A note on the behaviour of *Ammophila arenaria* (L.) Link in relation to sand-dune formation', *Trans. bot. Soc. Edinb.*, **36**, 132–136.

GIGLIOLI, M. E. C. and THORNTON, I. (1965), 'The mangrove swamps of Keneba, Lower Gambia river basin. I. Descriptive notes on the climate, the mangrove swamps and the physical conditions of their soils', *J. appl. Ecol.*, **2**, 81–103.

GILLHAM, M. E. (1957), 'Coastal vegetation of Mull and Iona in relation to salinity and soil reaction', *J. Ecol.*, **45**, 757–778.

GILLHAM, M. E. (1964), 'The vegetation of local coastal gull colonies', *Trans. Cardiff Nat. Soc.*, **91**, 23–33.

GILLIAM, H. T. (1957), *San Francisco Bay*. New York: Doubleday.

GILLNER, V. (1965), 'Salt marsh vegetation in Southern Sweden', *Acta Phytogeogr. Suecica*, **50**, 97–104.

GIMINGHAM, C. H. GEMMELL, A. R. and GREIG-SMITH, P. (1948), 'The vegetation of a sand dune system in the Outer Hebrides', *Trans. Proc. Bot. Soc. Edinb.*, **35**, 82–96.

GIMINGHAM, C. H. (1951), 'Contributions to the maritime ecology of St. Cyrus, Kincardineshire. Part II. The sand dunes', *Trans. Proc. Bot. Soc. Edinb.*, **35**, 387–414.

GIMINGHAM, C. H. (1953), 'Contributions to the maritime ecology of St. Cyrus, Kincardineshire. III. The salt marsh', *Trans. Proc. Bot. Soc. Edinb.*, **36**, 137–164.

GINSBURG, R. N., ISHAM, L. B., BEIN, S. J. and KUPERBERG, J. (1954), Laminated algal sediments of south Florida and their recognition in the fossil record: unpublished Rep. No. 54–21, Marine Laboratory, University of Miami, Coral Gables, Florida.

GINSBURG, R. N. and LOWENSTAM, H. A. (1958), 'The influence of marine bottom communities on the depositional environment of sediments', *J. Geol.*, **66**, 310–318.

GLOPPER, R. J. de (1964), 'About the water content and shrinkage of some Dutch lacustrine and marine sediments', *Neth. J. agric. Sci.*, **12**, 221–226.

GODWIN, H. SUGGATE, R. P. and WILLIS, E. H. (1958), 'Radiocarbon dating of the eustatic rise in ocean level', *Nature*, **181**, 1518–1519.

GOETHART, J. W. C., TESCH, P., HESSELINK, E. and DIJT, M. D. (1924), 'Cultuur-en waterleidingbelangen wittreksel uit het rapport inzake het verband tusschen wateronttrekking en plantengroei', *Meded. Rijksboschb Proefstn. s'Gravenhage*, 1/3, 5, 5–28.

GOLDSMITH, F. B., MUNTON, R. J. C. and WARREN, A. (1970), 'The impact of reacreation on the ecology and amenity of semi-natural areas: methods of investigation used in the Isles of Scilly', *Biol. J. Linn. Soc.*, **2**, 287–306.

GOLUBIC, S. (1970), 'Effect of organic pollution on benthic communities', Marine Pollut. Bull. 1 (N.S.), 56–57.

GOOD, R. (1935), 'Contributions towards a survey of the plants and animals of South Haven Peninsula, Studland Heath, Dorset. II General ecology of the flowering plants and ferns', *J. Ecol.*, **23**, 361–405.

GOOD, R. (1964), *The Geography of the Flowering Plants*. (3rd edn.) London: Longman.

GOODMAN, P. J. and WILLIAMS, W. T. (1961), 'Investigations into 'die-back' in *Spartina townsendii* agg. III. Physiological correlates of 'die-back', *J. Ecol.*, **49**, 391–398.

GOODWIN. R. H. (ed.) (1961), 'Connecticut's coastal marshes. A vanishing resource', *The Connecticut Arboretum Bull.*, **12**, 1–36.

GORHAM, A. V. and GORHAM, E. (1965), 'Iron, manganese, ash and nitrogen in some plants from salt marsh and shingle habitats', *Ann. Bot.*, **19**, 571–577.

GORHAM, E. (1958 *a*), 'Soluble salts in dune sands from Blakeney Point in Norfolk', *J. Ecol.*, **46**, 373–379.

GORHAM, E. (1958 *b*), 'The influence and importance of daily weather conditions in the supply of chloride, sulphate and other ions to fresh waters from atmospheric precipitation', Phil. Trans. Roy. Soc. Series B, **241**, 147–178.

GOTTSCHALK, L. C. and JONES, V. H. (1955), 'Valleys and hills, erosion and sedimentation', *Yearb. U.S. Dep. Agric.*, 135–143.

GRAY, A. J. (1971), 'Variation in *Aster tripolium* L., with particular reference to some British populations'. Ph.D. Thesis, University of Keele.

GREEN, F. H. W. (1964), 'A map of annual average potential water deficit in the British Isles', *J. appl. Ecol.*, **1**, 151–158.

GREEN, R. D. and ASKEW, G. P. (1965), 'Observations on the biological development of macropores in soils of Romney Marsh', *J. Soil. Sci.*, **16**, 342–349.

GREENSMITH, J. T. and TUCKER, E. V. (1966), 'Morphology and evolution of inshore shell ridges and mud-mounds on modern intertidal flats, near Bradwell, Essex', *Proc. Geol. Ass.*, **77**, 329–346.

GRIM, R. E. (1953), *Clay Mineralogy*. New York: McGraw-Hill.

GRIME, J. P. (1965), 'Comparative experiments as a key to the ecology of flowering plants', *Ecology*, **46**, 513–515.

GRIST, D. H. (1959), *Rice*, London.

GUILCHER, A. and BERTHOIS, L. (1957), 'Cinq années d'observations sédimentologiques dans quartre estuaires-témoins de l'ouest de la Bretagne', *Rev. de Géomorph. Dynamique*, **5–6**, 67–86.

GUNKEL, W. (1968), 'Bacteriological investigations of oil-polluted sediments from the Cornish coast following the Torrey Canyon disaster. The biological effects of oil pollution on littoral communities', *Field Studies 2, suppl.*, 151–158.

GUTNECHT, J. and DAINTY, J. (1968), 'Ionic relations of marine algae', *Oceanogr. Mar. Biol. Ann. Rev.*, **6**, 163–200.

HAAS, J. A. and STEERS, J. A. (1964), 'An aid to stabilization of sand dunes: experiments at Scolt Head Island', *Geogr. J.*, **130**, 265–267.

HADERLIE, E. C. (1970), 'Influence of pesticide run-off in Monterey Bay', *Mar. Pollut. Bull.* **1** (*N.S.*), 42–43.

HANNON, N. and BRADSHAW, A. D. (1968), 'Evolution of salt tolerance in two co-existing species of grass', *Nature*, **220**, 1342–1343.

HARBERD, D. J. (1961), 'Observations on population structure and longevity of *Festuca rubra*', *New Phytol.*, **60**, 184–206.

HARVEY, H. T. (1966 *a*), 'Marshes and mudflats of San Francisco Bay', San Francisco Bay Conserv. and Dev. Comm., San Francisco.

HARVEY, H. T. (1966 *b*), 'Some ecological aspects of San Francisco Bay', San Francisco Bay Conserv. and Dev. Comm., San Francisco.

HASSOUNA, M. G. and Wareing, P. F. (1964), 'Possible role of rhizosphere bacteria in the nitrogen nutrition of *Ammophila arenaria*', *Nature*, **202**, 467–469.

HEERDT, P. F. VAN and MÖRZER BRUYNS, M. F. (1960), 'A biocoenological investigation in the yellow dune region of Terschelling', *Tijdschr. Ent.*, **103**, 225–275.

HEIMANN, H. (1958), 'Irrigation with saline water and the ionic environment', 'Potassium-symposium'. 1958. Berne, 173–220.

HESSE, P. R. (1961), 'Some differences between the soils of *Rhizophora* and *Avicennia* mangrove swamps in Sierra Leone', *Pl. Soil*, **14**, 335–346.

HESSE, P. R. (1963), 'Phosphorus relationships in a mangrove swamp mud with particular reference to aluminium toxicity', *Pl. Soil*, **19**, 205–218.

HEWETT, D. G. (1970), 'The colonization of sand dunes after stabilization with Marram grass ' (*Ammophila arenaria*), *J. Ecol.*, **58**, 653–668.

HEWETT, D. G. (1971), 'The effects of the cold winter of 1962/63 on *Juncus acutus* at Braunton Burrows, Devon'. Devon Assoc. Adv. Sci. Lit. Art Rep. Trans., 1970, **102**, 193–201.

HIGGINS, L. S. (1933), 'An investigation into the problem of the sand dune areas on the South Wales coast', *Arch. Camb.*, June 1933.

HILL, T. G. and HANLEY, J. A. (1914), 'The structure and water content of shingle beaches', *J. Ecol.*, **2**, 21–39.

HINCKS, W. D., MICHAELIS, H. N., SHAW, S., BRAHAM, A. C., MURGATROYD, J. H. and BUTLER, P. M. (1951–4), 'The entomology of Spurn Peninsula', *Naturalist*, 1951: 75–86, 139–46, 183–90; 1952: 131–8, 169–76; 1953: 125–40, 157–72; 1954: 74–8, 95–109.

HINDE, H. P. (1954), 'Vertical distribution of salt marsh phanerogams in relation to tide levels', *Ecol. Mon.*, **24**, 209–225.

HITCHCOCK, A. S. (1904), 'Methods used for controlling and reclaiming sand dunes', U.S. Department of Agriculture, Bureau of Plant Industry Bull. No. 57.

HOLDER, F. W. (1953), 'Changing flora of the South Lancashire dunes', *N.West. Nat.*, **1** (N.S.), 451–452.

HOPE-SIMPSON, J. F. and JEFFERIES, R. L. (1966), 'Observations relating to vigour and debility in Marram grass (*Ammophila arenaria* (L.) Link)', *J. Ecol.*, **54**, 271–274.

HOPKINS, B. (1962), 'The measurement of available light by the use of *Chlorella*', *New Phyt.*, **61**, 221–223.

HUBBARD, C. E. (1968), *Grasses*. (2nd edn.), Harmondsworth: Penguin.

HUBBARD, J. C. E. (1965), '*Spartina* marshes in Southern England. VI. Pattern of invasion in Poole Harbour', *J. Ecol.*, **53**, 799–813.

HUBBARD, J. C. E. (1969), 'Light in relation to tidal immersion and the growth of *Spartina townsendii* (s.l.)', *J. Ecol.*, **57**, 795–804.

HUBBARD, J. C. E. (1970), 'Effects of cutting and seed production in *Spartina anglica*', *J. Ecol.*, **58**, 329–334.

HUBBARD, J. C. E. and RANWELL, D. S. (1966), 'Cropping *Spartina* salt marsh for silage', *J. Br. Grassld Soc.*, **21**, 214–217.

HUBBARD, J. C. E. and STEBBINGS, R. E. (1968), '*Spartina* marshes in Southern England. VII Stratigraphy of the Keysworth marsh, Poole Harbour', *J. Ecol.*, **56**, 707–722.

HUGHES, G. P. (1953), 'The effect on agriculture of the East Coast floods', Unpublished report by the National Agricultural Advisory Service, Ministry of Agriculture Fisheries and Food, 1–262.

HULME, B. A. (1957), 'Studies on some British species of *Atriplex* L.', Ph.D. Thesis, University of Edinburgh.

HUNT, O. J. (1965), 'Salt tolerance in intermediate wheatgrass *Agropyron intermedium*', *Crop Sci.*, **5**, 407–409.

INGLIS, C. C. and ALLEN, F. H. (1957), 'The regimen of the Thames Estuary as affected by currents, salinities and river flow', *Proc. Instn Civ. Engrs*, **7**, 827–878.

INGLIS, C. C. and KESTNER, F. J. T. (1958 a), 'Changes in the Wash as affected by training walls and reclamation works', *Proc. Instn Civ. Engrs.*, **11**, 435–466.

INGIS, C. C. and KESTNER, F. J. T. (1958 b), 'The long-term effects of training walls, reclamation, and dredging on estuaries', *Proc. Instn Civ. Engrs*, **9**, 193–216.

IVERSON, J. (1936), *Biologische Pflanzentypen als Hilfsmittel in der Vegetationsforschung*. Copenhagen: Medd. Fra. Skalling-Labor. Bd., 4.

IVERSON, J. (1954), 'The zonation of the salt marsh vegetation of Skallingen in 1931–4 and in 1952', *Meddr Skalling – Lab.*, **14**, 113–118.

JACOBSEN, N. K. (1960), 'Types of sedimentation in a drowned delta region', *Geogr. Tidsskr.*, **59**, 58–69.

JACOBSEN, N. K. (1964), 'Troek af Tøndermarskens naturgeografi med saerligt henblik på morfogenesen', *Folia Georgr. Dan.*, **7**, 1–350.

JAKOBSEN, B., JENSEN, K. M. and NIELSEN, N. (1955), 'Forlag til landvindingsarbejder langs den sømderjyske vadehavskyst', *Geogr. Tidsskr.*, **55**, 62–87.

JAKOBSEN, B. (1961), 'Vadehavets sedimentomsoetning belyst ved kvantitative målinger', *Geogr. Tidsskr.*, **60**, 87–103.

JAKOBSEN, B. (1964), 'Vadehavets morfologi', *Folia Geogr. Dan.*, **11**, 1–176.

JENNINGS, J. N. (1964), 'The question of coastal dunes in tropical, humid climates', *Z. Geomorph.*, **8**, 150–154.

JOHNSON, C. G. and SMITH, L. P. (Eds.) (1965). *The Biological Significance of Climatic Changes in Britain*. London: Institute of Biology and Academic Press.

JOHNSON, D. S. and YORK, H. H. (1915), The relation of plants to tide levels, Carnegie Institute Washington Publication, 206.

JONES, R. and ETHERINGTON, J. R. (1971), Comparative studies of plant growth and distribution in relation to water-logging IV. The growth of dune and slack plants, *J. Ecol.*, **59**, 793–801.

JOSEPH, A. F. and OAKLEY, H. B. (1929), 'The properties of heavy alkaline soils containing different exchangeable bases', *J. agric. Sci.*, **19**, 121–131.

KALLE, K. (1958), Sea water as a source of mineral substances for plants, Nature Conservation (London) Translation No. 11.

KAMPS, L. F. (1962), 'Mud distribution and land reclamation in the eastern Wadden shallows', *RijkswatSt. Commun.*, No. 4, 1–73.

KASSAS, M. (1957), 'On the ecology of the Red Sea coastal land', *J. Ecol.*, **45**, 187–203.

KELLEY, W. P. (1951), *Alkali Soils: their Formation, Properties and Reclamation*. Monograph No. 111. New York: Rheinhold.

KESTNER, F. J. T. and INGLIS, C. C. (1956), 'A study of erosion and accretion during cyclic changes in an estuary and their effect on reclamation of marginal land', *J. Agric. Engng. Res.*, **1**, 63–67.

KESTNER, F. J. T. (1961), 'Short term changes in the distribution of fine sediments in estuaries', *Proc. Instn. Civ. Engrs.*, **19**, 185–208.

KESTNER, F. J. T. (1962), 'The old coastline of the Wash', *Geogr. J.*, **128**, 457–478.

KESTNER, F. J. T. (1963), The supply and circulation of silt in the Wash. 10th Congr. International Association Hydraulic Research, London, 231–238.

KIDSON, C. and CARR, A. P. (1961), 'Beach drift experiments at Bridgwater Bay, Somerset', *Proc. Bristol Nat. Soc.*, **30**, 163–180.

KING, C. A. M. (1972), *Beaches and Coasts* (2nd edn.), London: Edward Arnold.

KRINSLEY, D. H. and FUNNELL, B. M. (1965), 'Environmental history of quartz sand grains from the Lower and Middle Pleistocene of Norfolk, England', *Q J. Geol. Soc. Lond.*, **121**, 435–461.

KRUMBEIN, W. C. and SLACK, H. A. (1956), 'The relative efficiency of beach sampling methods', *Tech. Memo. Beach Eros. Bd U.S.*, **90**, 1–34.

LAING, C. (1954), The ecological life history of the marram grass community on Lake Michigan dunes. Ph.D. dissertation, University of Chicago.

LAMB, H. H. (1969), 'The new look of climatology', *Nature*, **223**, 1209–1215.

LAMB, H. H. (1970), The variability of climate. Met. Office, Bracknell, unpublished typescript, 1–22.

LAMBINON, J. (1956), 'Aperçu sur les groupements végétaux du district maritime Belge entre La Panne et Coxyde', *Bull. Soc. Roy. Bot. Belg.*, **88**, 107–127.

LANDSBERG, S. Y. (1956), 'The orientation of dunes in relation to wind', *Geogr. J.*, **122**, 176–189.

LANDSBERG, H. and RILEY, N. A. (1943), Wind influences on the transportation of sand over a Michigan sand dune. Proceedings 2nd. Hydraulics Conference Bulletin 27, Univ. Iowa Studies in Engineering.

LARSEN, H. (1967), 'Biochemical aspects of extreme Halophilism', *Adv. Microb. Physiol.*, **1**, 97–132.

LAUFF, G. H. (ed.) (1967), Conference on estuaries. Jekyll Island (Ga.), 1964. Washington.

LEEUWEN, C. G. van (1965), 'Het verband tussen naturrlijke en anthropogene landschapsvormen, bezien vanuit de betrekkingen in grenzmilieu's', *Gorteria*, **2**, 93–105.

LINES, R. (1957), 'Estimation of exposure by flags', Report on Forestry Research, H.M.S.O. London 1957, 47–48.

LOPEZ-GONZALEZ, J. de and JENNY, H. (1959), 'Diffusion of strontium in ion-exchange membranes', *J. Colloid Sci.*, **14**, 533–542.

LOWE-McCONNELL, R. H. (ed.) (1966), *Man-made Lakes*. London: Institute of Biology and Academic Press.

LUGG, J. W. H. (1949), 'Plant Proteins', *Adv. Protein Chem.*, **5**, 230–295.

LUXTON, M. (1964), 'Some aspects of the biology of salt marsh Acarina', *Acaralogia*. C.R. 1er Congrès Int. d'Acaralogie, Fort Collins, Colorado, U.S.A. 1963, 172–182.

LYNCH, J. J. (1941), 'The place of burning in management of the Gulf Coast refuges', *J. Wildl. Mgmt.*, **5**, 454–458.

LYNCH, J. J., O'NEIL, T. and LANG, D. W. (1947), 'Management significance of damage by geese and muskrats to Gulf Coast marshes', *J. Wildl. Mgmt.*, **2**, 50–76.

MAAREL, E. VAN DER (1966), 'Dutch studies on coastal sand dune vegetation, especially in the delta region', *Wentia*, **15**, 47–82.

MAAREL, E. VAN DER and LEERTOUWER, J. (1967), 'Variation in vegetation and species diversity along a local environmental gradient', *Acta. Bot. Neerl.*, **16**, 211–221.

MAAREL, E. VAN DER and WESTHOFF, V. (1964), 'The vegetation of the dunes near Oostvoorne', *Wentia*, **12**, 1–61.

MACDONALD, J. (1954), 'Tree planting on coastal sand dunes in Great Britain', *Adv. Sci.*, **11**, 33–37.

MACDONALD, K. B. (1969), 'Quantitative studies of salt marsh mollusc faunas from the North American Pacific coast', *Ecol. Mongr.*, **39**, 33–60.

MACNAE, W. (1966), 'Mangroves in eastern and southern Australia', *Aust. J. Bot.*, **14**, 67–104.

MACNAE, W. (1968), 'A general account of the fauna and flora of mangrove swamps and forests in the Indo-West-Pacific Region', *Adv. Mar. Biol.*, **6**, 73–270.

MARCHANT, C. J. (1967), 'Evolution in *Spartina* (Graminae) I. The history and morphology of the genus in Britain', *J. Linn. Soc. (Bot.)*, **60**, 1–24.

MARCHANT, C. J. (1968), 'Evolution in *Spartina* (Graminae) II. Chromosomes, basic relationships and the problem of *S. x townsendii* agg.,' *J. Linn. Soc. (Bot.)*, **60**, 381–409.

MARPLES, T. G. (1966), 'A radionuclide tracer study of Arthropod food chains in a *Spartina* salt marsh ecosystem', *Ecology*, **47**, 270–277.

MARSHALL, J. K. (1965), '*Corynephorus canescens* (L.) P. Beauv. as a model for the *Ammophila* problem', *J. Ecol.*, **53**, 447–463.

MARTIN, A. C. (1953), 'Improving duck marshes by weed control. U.S. Fish and Wildlife Service Circular', **19**, 1–49.

MARTIN, W. E. (1959), 'The vegetation of Island Beach State Park, New Jersey', *Ecol. Mongr.*, **29**, 1–46.

MATTHEWS, J. R. (1937), 'Geographical relationships of the British Flora', *J. Ecol.*, **25**, 1–90.

MAY, V. J. (1969), 'Reclamation and shore line change in Poole Harbour, Dorset', *Proc. Dorset Nat. Hist. Archaeol. Soc.*, **90**, 141–154.

McCRONE, A. (1966), 'The Hudson river estuary. Hydrology, sediments and pollution', *Geogr. Rev.*, **56**, 175–189.

McROY, C. P. (1969), 'Eelgrass under Arctic winter ice', *Nature*, **224**, 818–819.

MOBBERLEY, D. G. (1956), 'Taxonomy and distribution of the genus *Spartina*', *Iowa St. J. Sci.*, **30**, 471–574.

MØLLER, J. T. (1963), 'Accumulation and abrasion in a tidal area', *Geogr. Tidsskr.*, **62**, 56–79.

MØLLER, J. T. (1964), *Fladkystems og Flodens Morfologiske Elementer*, Copenhagen: K. G. Wingstrand.

MONTFORT, C. and BRANDRUP, W. (1927), 'Physiologische und Pflanzengeographische Seesalzwirkungen II. Okologische Studien über Keimung und erste Entwicklung bei Halophyten', *Jb. Wiss. Bot.*, **66**, 902–946.

MOORE, P. D. (1971), 'Computer analysis of sand dune vegetation in Norfolk, England, and its implications for convservation', *Vegetatio*, **23**, 323–338.

MÖRZER BRUYNS, M. F. and WESTHOFF, V. (1951), The Netherlands as an environment of insect life. 9th Int. Congr. Entom., Amsterdam.

MYRICK, R. M. and LEOPOLD, L. B. (1963), 'Hydraulic geometry of a small tidal estuary', U.S. Geol. Survey Professional Paper, 422–B, 1–18.

NELSON-SMITH, A. (1968), *A Classified Bibliography of Oil Pollution*, Swansea: University College (typescript 1–51).

NEWELL, R. C. (1965), 'The role of detritus in the nutrition of two marine deposit feeders, the Prosobranch *Hydrobia ulvae* and the bivalve *Macoma balthica*, *Proc. Zool. Soc. Lond.*, **144**, 25–45.

NEWMAN, W. S. and RUSNAK, G. A. (1965), 'Holocene submergence of the Eastern shore of Virginia', *Science*, **148**, 1464–1466.

NICHOLSON, I. A. (1952), A study of *Agropyron junceum* (Beauv.) in relation to the stabilization of coastal sand and the development of sand dunes. M.Sc. Thesis, University of Durham.

NIELSEN, N. (1935), 'Eine methode zur exakten sedimentations-messung studien über die marschbildung auf der halbinsel Skalling. Danske Videnskabernes Selskab', *Biol. Meddr.*, **12**, 1–96.

NOBUHARA, H. (1967), 'Analysis of coastal vegetation on sandy shore by biological types in Japan', *Jap. J. Bot.*, **19**, 325–351.

NORTHFIELD, J. (1960), 'The bryophyte flora of Studland Heath', *Durham Colleges Nat. Hist. Soc. J.*, **7**, 38–45.

ODUM, E. P. (1961), 'The role of tidal marshes in estuarine production', N.Y. State Conservationist Information Leaflet.

ODUM, E. P. (1962), 'Relationship between structure and function in the ecosystem', *Jap. J. Ecol.*, **12**, 108–118.

ODUM, E. P. (1963), 'Primary and secondary energy flow in relation to ecosystem structure', Proceedings of XVI International Congr. Zool., **4**, 336–338.

ODUM, E. P. and CRUZ, A. A. de la (1967), 'Particulate organic detritus in a Georgia salt marsh – estuarine ecosystem'. Estuaries. Publication No. 83 American Association for the Advancement of Science, Washington, 383–388.

ODUM, E. P. and SMALLEY, A. E. (1959), 'Comparison of population energy flow of a herbivorous and deposit-feeding invertebrate in a salt marsh ecosystem', *Proc. Natn. Acad. Sci., U.S.A.*, **45**, 617–622.

OKUDA, A. and Takahashi, E. (1965), The role of silicon, in *Mineral Nutrition of the Rice Plant*, Ch. 10, 123–146 (Proc. Intern. Conf. Rice Res. Inst., Los Bañjos, Philippines, 1964. John Hopkins Press, Baltimore).

OLIVER, F. W. (1929), 'Blakeney Point Reports', *Trans. Norfolk Norwich Nat. Soc.*, **12**, 630–653.

OLSON, J. S. (1958 *a*), 'Rates of succession and soil changes on Southern Lake Michigan sand dunes', *Bot. Gaz.*, **119**, 125–170.

OLSON, J. S. (1958 *b*), 'Lake Michigan dune development. 1. Wind-velocity profiles', *J. Geol.*, **66**, 254–263.

OLSON, J. S. (1958 *c*), 'Lake Michigan dune development. 2. Plants as agents and tools in geomorphology', *J. Geol.*, **66**, 345–351.

OLSSON-SEFFER, P. (1909), 'Hydrodynamic factors influencing plant life on sandy sea shores', *New Phytol.*, **8**, 37–49.

OOSTING, H. J. (1954), Ecological processes and vegetation of the maritime strand in the United States. *Bot. Rev.*, **20**, 226–262.

OSBORN, T. G. B. and ROBERTSON, R. N. (1939), 'A reconnaissance survey of the vegetation of Myall Lakes', *Proc. Linn. Soc. N.S.W.*, **64**, 279–296.

OVINGTON, J. D. (1950), 'The afforestation of the Culbin sands', *J. Ecol.*, **38**, 303–319.

OVINGTON, J. D. (1951), 'The afforestation of Tentsmuir Sands', *J. Ecol.*, **39**, 363–375.

PACKHAM, J. R. and LIDDLE, M. J. (1970), 'The Cefni salt marsh, Anglesey and its recent development', *Fld Stud.*, **3**, 331–356.

PARHAM, M. R. (1970), A Comparative study of the mineral nutrition of selected halophytes and glycophytes. Ph.D. Thesis University of East Anglia.

PAVIOUR-SMITH, K. (1956), 'The biotic community of a salt meadow in New Zealand', *Trans. Roy. Soc. N.Z.*, **83**, 525–554.

PAYNE, K. T. (1972 – in press), 'A survey of the *Spartina* feeding insects in Poole Harbour, Dorset', *Entomologist's mon. Mag.*

PERKINS, E. J., WILLIAMS, B. R. H. and BAILEY, M. (1963), 'Some preliminary notes on the bottom currents of the Solway Firth and North East Irish sea', *Trans. Dumfries and Galloway Nat. Hist. and Antiq. Soc. Ser.* 3, **41**, 45–51.

PERKINS, E. J. and WILLIAMS, B. R. H. (1965), 'Some results of an investigation of the biology of the Solway Firth in relation to radioactivity', *Trans. J. Dumfries. Galloway nat. Hist. Antiq. Soc., Ser.* **3**, **42**, 1–5.

PERRING, F. (1970), 'The flora of a changing Britain', *Bot. Soc. British Isles Rep.* No. 11. Hampton, Middlesex.

PERRING, F. H. and WALTERS, S. M. (1962), 'Atlas of the British Flora', London: Nelson.

PESTRONG, R. (1965), 'The development of drainage patterns on tidal marshes', Stanford University Publication Geological Science, 10, 1–87.

PETCH, C. P. (1945), 'Reclaimed lands of West Norfolk', *Trans. Norfolk Norwich Nat. Soc.*, **16**, 106–109.

PETERSEN, C. G. J. (1915), 'A preliminary result of the investigations on the valuation of the sea', *Rep. Dan. biol. Stn.*, **23**, 29–32.

PETERSEN, C. G. J. (1918), 'The sea bottom and its production of fish food', *Rep. Dan. biol. Stn.*, **25**, 1–62.

PETTERSSON, O. (1914), 'Climatic variations in historic and prehistoric time', *Svenska hydrogr.-biol. Kommn. Skr.*, **5**.

PHILLIPS, A. W. (1964), 'Some observations on coast erosion studies at South Holderness and Spurn Head', *Dock Harb. Auth.*, **45**, 64–66.

PISSAREV, V. E. and VINOGRADOVA, N. M. (1944), 'Hybrids between wheat and *Elymus*', C.r. *Dokl. Proc. Acad. Sci. U.S.S.R.*, **45**, 129–132.

POEL, L. W. (1960), 'The estimation of oxygen diffusion rates in soils', *J. Ecol.*, **48**, 169–177.

POMEROY, L. E. (1959), 'Algal productivity in salt marshes of Georgia', *Limnol. Oceanogr.*, **4**, 386–395.

POORE, M. E. D. and ROBERTSON, V. C. (1964), An approach to the rapid description and mapping of biological habitats. International Biological Programme Publication. London.

PORTER, J. J. (1962), 'Electron microscopy of sand surface textures', *J. Sedim. Petrol.*, **32**, 124–135.

PRAEGER, R. L. (1913), 'On the buoyancy of the seeds of some Brittanic plants', *Proc. Roy. Dub. Soc.*, **14**, 13–62.

PRESTON, A. (1968), Radioactive waste disposal, radioecology and radiobiology. Annual Report Lowestoft Laboratory, Ministry of Agriculture Fisheries and Food, London. 108.

PRICE, W. A. and KENDRICK, M. P. (1963), 'Field model investigation into the reasons for silting in the Mersey estuary', *Proc. Inst. Civ. Engrs.*, **24**, 273–518.

PURER, E. A. (1942), 'Plant ecology of the coastal salt marshes of San Diego County, California', *Ecol. Mon.*, **12**, 81–111.

RAGOTSKIE, R. A. (1959), Proc. Salt Marsh Conf. Marine Inst. University of Georgia Publication, Athens, Georgia.

RAMALEY, F. (1918), 'Notes on dune vegetation at San Francisco, California', *Pl. Wld*, **21**, 191–201.

RANWELL, D. S. (1955), Slack vegetation, dune system development and cyclical change at Newborough Warren, Anglesey. Ph.D. Thesis, University of London.

RANWELL, D. S. (1958), 'Movement of vegetated sand dunes at Newborough Warren, Anglesey', *J. Ecol.*, **46**, 83–100.

RANWELL, D. S. (1959), 'Newborough Warren, Anglesey. I. The dune system and dune slack habitat', *J. Ecol.*, **47**, 571–601.

RANWELL, D. S. (1960 *a*), 'Newborough Warren, Angelsey. II. Plant associes and succession cycles of the sand dune and dune slack vegetation', *J. Ecol.*, **48**, 117–141.

RANWELL, D. S. (1960 *b*), 'Newborough Warren, Anglesey. III. Changes in the vegetation on parts of the dune system after the loss of rabbits by myxomatosis', *J. Ecol.*, **48**, 385–395.

RANWELL, D. S. (1961), '*Spartina* salt marshes in Southern England. I. The effects of sheep grazing at the upper limits of *Spartina* marsh in Bridgwater Bay', *J. Ecol.*, **49**, 325–340.

RANWELL, D. S. (1964 *a*), '*Spartina* salt marshes in Southern England. II. Rate and seasonal pattern of sediment accretion', *J. Ecol.*, **52**, 79–94.

RANWELL, D. S. (1964 *b*), '*Spartina* salt marshes in Southern England. III. Rates of establishment, succession and nutrient supply at Bridgwater Bay, Somerset', *J. Ecol.*, **52**, 95–105.

RANWELL, D. S. (1967), 'World resources of *Spartina townsendii* (*sensu lato*) and economic use of *Spartina* marshland', *J. Appl. Ecol.*, **4**, 239–256.

RANWELL, D. S. (1968 *a*), Coastal marshes in perspective. Regional studies Group Bull. Strathclyde No. 9, 1–26.

RANWELL, D. S. (1968 *b*), 'Extent of damage to coastal habitats due to the Torrey Canyon incident', Fld Stud., **2** (Suppl.), 39–47.

RANWELL, D. S. (ed.) (1972), The Management of Sea Buckthorn (*Hippophaë rhamnoides* L.) on selected sites in Great Britain. Nature Conservancy Report. London.

RANWELL, D. S., BIRD, E. C. F., HUBBARD, J. C. E. and STEBBINGS, R. E. (1964), '*Spartina* salt marshes in Southern England. V. Tidal submergence and chlorinity in Poole Harbour', *J. Ecol.*, **52**, 627–641.

RANWELL, D. S. and DOWNING, B. M. (1959), 'Brent goose (*Branta bernicla* L.) winter feeding pattern and *Zostera* resources at Scolt Head Island, Norfolk', *Anim. Behav.*, **7**, 42–56.

RANWELL, D. S. and DOWNING, B. M. (1960), 'The use of Dalapon and Substituted Urea herbicides for control of seed-bearing *Spartina* (Cord-grass) in inter-tidal zones of estuarine marsh', *Weeds*, **8**, 78–88.

RANWELL, D. S. and HEWETT, D. (1964), 'Oil pollution in Poole Harbour and its effect on birds', *Bird Notes*, **31**, 192–197.

RANWELL, D. S. and STEBBINGS, R. E. (1967), Report on the effects of Torrey Canyon oil pollution and decontamination methods in Cornwall and Brittany, March to April 1967. Nature Conservancy (London) Unpublished rep., 1–12.

RATCLIFFE, D. A. (1968), 'An ecological account of Atlantic Bryophytes in the British Isles', *New Phytol.*, **67**, 365–439.

REDFIELD, A. C. (1965), 'Ontogeny of a salt marsh estuary', *Science*, **147**, 50–55.

REDFIELD, A. C. and RUBIN, M. (1962), 'The age of salt marsh peat and its

R

relation to recent changes in sea level at Barnstable, Massachusetts', *Proc. natn. Acad. Sci. U.S.A.*, **48**, 1728–1735.

REID, C. (1913), *Submerged Forests*. Cambridge: University Press.

RENGER, M. (1965), 'Berechnung der Austanchkapazität der organischen und anorganischen Anteile der Böden', *Z. Pfl-ernähr. Düng. Bodenk.*, **110**, 10–26.

REYNOLDSON, T. B. (1955), 'Observations on the earthworms of North Wales', *N. West Nat.*, Sept./Dec., 291–304.

REZK, M. R. (1970), 'Vegetation change from a sand dune community to a salt marsh as related to soil characters in Mariut District, Egypt', *Oikos*, **21**, 341–343.

RICHARDS, F. J. (1934), 'The salt marshes of the Dovey estuary. IV. The rates of vertical accretion, horizontal extension and scarp erosion', *Ann. Bot.*, **48**, 225–259.

RICHARDS, P. W. (1929), 'Notes on the ecology of the bryophytes and lichens at Blakeney Point, Norfolk', *J. Ecol.*, **17**, 127–140.

RIDLEY, H. N. (1930), *The Dispersal of Plants throughout the World*, Ashford: L. Reeve.

RILEY, G. A. (1963), 'Organic aggregates in sea water and the dynamics of their formation and utilization', *Limnol. Oceanogr.*, **8**, 373–381.

RITCHIE, W. and MATHER, A. (1969), *The Beaches of Sutherland*, Aberdeen: Dept. Geography, Univ. of Aberdeen.

RITCHIE, W. and MATHER, A. S. (1971), 'Conservation and use: Case-study of Beaches of Sutherland, Scotland', *Biol. Consvn.*, **3**, 199–207.

ROBERTSON, D. A. (1955), The ecology of the sand dune vegetation of Ross Links, Northumberland with special reference to secondary succession in the blow-outs. Ph.D. Thesis, Durham University.

ROBINSON, A. H. W. (1966), 'Residual currents in relation to shoreline evolution of the East Anglian coast', *Mar. Geol.*, **4**, 57–84.

ROBINSON, T. W. (1952), 'Phreatophytes and their relation to water in Western United States. Symposium on Phreatophytes', *Trans. Am. geophys. Un.*, **33**, 57–61.

ROBSON, M. J. and JEWISS, O. R. (1968), 'A comparison of British and North African varieties of tall Fescue (*Festuca arundinacea*) II. and III.', *J. appl. Ecol.*, **5**, 179–190 and 191–204.

RORISON, I. H. (ed.) (1969), *Ecological Aspects of the Mineral Nutrition of Plants*, Oxford: Blackwell.

SAKAI, A. (1970), 'Freezing resistance in willows from different climates', *Ecology*, **51**, 485–491.

SALISBURY, E. J. (1925), 'Note on the edaphic succession in some dune soils with special reference to the time factor', *J. Ecol.*, **13**, 322.

SALISBURY, E. J. (1934), 'On the day temperatures of sand dunes in relation to the vegetation at Blakeney Point, Norfolk', *Trans. Norfolk Norwich Nat. Soc.*, **13**, 333–355.

SALISBURY, E. J. (1952), *Downs and Dunes*, London: Bell.

SCHMIDT, F. V. (1950), 'An evaluation of practical tidal marsh management on state and private marshes. Proceedings of the North-East Fish and Wildlife Conference.

SCHRATZ, E. (1934), 'Beiträge zur Biologie der Halophyten I. Keimungsphysiologie', *Jb. wiss. Bot.*, **80**, 112–142.

SENECA, E. D. (1969), 'Germination response to temperature and salinity of four dune grasses from the Outer Banks of North Carolina', *Ecology*, **50**, 44–53.

SETCHELL, W. A. (1920), 'Geographical distribution of the marine spermatophytes', *Bull. Torrey bot. Club.*, **47**.

SHAW, R. H. (Ed.) (1967), *Ground Level Climatology*. Baltimore: American Assocn. for Advancement of Science.

SHIELDS, L. M. (1957), 'Algal and lichen floras in relation to nitrogen content of certain volcanic and arid range soils', *Ecology*, **38**, 661–663.

SIIRA, J. (1970), 'Studies in the ecology of the sea shore meadows of the Bothnian Bay with special reference to the Limnika area', *Aquila Ser. Bot.*, **9**, 1–109.

SLATYER, R. O. (1967), *Plant-water Relationships*, London: Academic Press.

SLESS, J. B. (1956), 'Control of sand drift in beach mining', *J. Soil. Conserv. Serv. N.S. W.*, **12**, 164–176.

SLOET V. OLDRUITENBORGH, C. J. M. (1969), 'On the contribution of air-borne salt to the gradient character of the Voorne dune area', *Acta bot. neerl.*, **18**, 315–324.

SPARLING, J. H. (1967), 'The occurrence of *Schoenus nigricans* L. in blanket bogs. II. Experiments on the growth of *S. nigricans* under controlled conditions', *J. Ecol.*, **55**, 15–31.

SPRINGER, P. F. and WEBSTER, J. R. (1951), 'Biological effects of DDT application on tidal salt marshes', *Mosquito News*, **2**, 67–74.

STEARNS, L. A. and MACCREARY, D. (1957), 'The case of the vanishing brick dust', *Mosquito News*, **17**, 303–304.

STEBBINGS, R. E. (1971), 'Some ecological observations on the fauna in a tidal marsh to woodland transition', *Proc. Trans. Brit. Entom. Soc.*, **4**, 83–88.

STEENIS, C. G. G. J. VAN (1958), Discrimination of tropical shore vegetation. Proceedings of the symposium on humid tropics vegetation, 215–217, New Delhi, UNESCO.

STEENIS, J. H., WILDER, N. G., COFER, H. P. and BECK, R. A. (1954), 'The marshes of Delaware, their improvement and preservation. Delaware Board of Game and Fish Commissioners', *Pittman-Robertson Bull.*, **2**, 1–42.

STEERS, J. A. (1939), 'Sand and shingle formations in Cardigan Bay', *Geogrl. J.*, **94**, 209–227.

STEERS, J. A. (Ed.) (1960), *Scolt Head Island*, Cambridge: Heffer.

STEERS, J. A. (1964), *The Coastline of England and Wales.* (2nd edn.), Cambridge: University Press.

STEVENSON, R. E. and EMERY, K. O. (1958), Marshlands at Newport Bay, California. Allan Hancock Foundation Publication No. 20. Los Angeles.

STEWART, G. R., LEE, J. A. and GREBAMJO, T. O. (1972), *Nitrogen Metabolism of Halophytes.* I. Nitrate reductase activity in *Suaeda* maritima,' *New Phyt.* **71**, 263–167.

STEWART, W. D. P. (1967), 'Transfer of biologically fixed nitrogen in a sand dune slack region', *Nature*, **214**, 603–604.

STUBBINGS, H. G. and HOUGHTON, D. R. (1964), 'The ecology of Chichester Harbour', *Int. Rev. ges. Hydrobiol., Syst. beih.*, **49**, 233–279.

STOUTJESDIJKE, Ph. (1961), 'Micrometeorological measurements in vegetations of various structures', *Proc. K. ned. Akad. Wet., Amsterdam. section C*, **64**, 1–207.

TANSLEY, A. G. (1949), *The British Islands and their Vegetation*, Cambridge: University Press.

TASCHDJIAN, E. (1954), 'A note on *Spartina* protein', *Econ. Bot.*, **8**, 164–165.

TAYLOR, M. C. and BURROWS, E. M. (1968), 'Studies on the biology of *Spartina* in the Dee estuary, Cheshire', *J. Ecol.*, **56**, 795–809.

TAYLOR, N. (1937), 'A preliminary report on the relation of mosquito control ditching to Long Island salt marsh vegetation', *Proc. New Jers. Mosq. Exterm. Ass.*, **24**, 211–217.

TAYLOR, N. (1939), Salt tolerance of Long Island salt marsh plants. New York State Museum Circular No. 23, 1–42.

TEAGLE, W. G. (1966), Public pressure on South Haven Peninsula and its effect on Studland Heath National Nature Reserve, Nature Conservancy, Unpublished typescript, 1–89.

TEAL, J. M. (1962), 'Energy flow in the salt marsh ecosystem of Georgia', *Ecology*, **43**, 614–624.

THAARUP, P. (1954), 'The afforestation of the sand dunes of the western coast of Jutland', *Advmt. Sci. Lond.*, **11**, 38–41.

THORN, R. B. (1966), *River Engineering and Water Conservation Works*, London: Butterworth.

THORNTON, R. B. and DAVIS, A. G. (1964), Development and use of American Beachgrass for dune stabilization. Paper to American Society of Agronomy Meeting, Missouri, 1–21.

TINDALL, F. P. (1967), 'The care of a coastline', *J. Tn Plan. Inst.*, **53**, 387–392.

TROLL, C. (1963), *Seasonal Climates of the Earth. The Seasonal Course of Natural Phenomena in the Different Climatic Zones of the Earth. World maps of Climatology*, Berlin: Springer.

TSCHIRLEY, F. H. (1969), 'Defoliation in Vietnam', *Science*, **163**, 779–786.

TSITSIN, A. N. (1946), 'Perennial wheats', *Discovery*, **7**, 180.

TSOPA, E. (1939), La végétation des halophytes du nord de la Roumanie en connexion avec celle du reste du pays', *SIGMA*, **70**, 1–22.

TÜXEN, R. (1957), 'Die Pflanzengesellschaften des Aussendiechslandes von Neu werk', *Mitt. flor.-soz. Arbeitsgem. 6/7*

TYLER, G. (1971), 'Studies in the ecology of Baltic sea-shore meadows III. Hydrology and salinity of Baltic sea shore meadows', *Oikos*, **22**, 1–20.

VOO, E. E. van der (1964), Danger to scientifically important wetlands in the Netherlands by modification of the surrounding environment. Proceedings of the MAR Conference, I.U.C.N. Publication. N.S. **3**, 274–278.

VOSE, P. B., POWELL, H. G. and SPENCE, J. B. (1957), 'The machair grazings of Tiree, Inner Hebrides', *Trans. Proc. bot. Soc. Edinb.*, **37**, 89–110.

WALLACE, T. J. (1953), 'The plant ecology of Dawlish Warren Pt. 1, *Rep. Trans. Devon. Ass. Advmt. Sci. Lit. Art*, **85**, 86–94.

WATT, A. S. (1947), 'Pattern and process in the plant community', *J. Ecol.*, **35**, 1–22.

WEBBER, H. J. (1895), The two freezes of 1894–95 in Florida, and what they teach. U.S. Department of Agriculture Year Book 1895, 159–174.

WEBLEY, D. M., EASTWOOD, D. J. and GIMINGHAM, C. H. (1952), 'Development of a soil microflora in relation to plant succession on sand dunes, including the 'rhizosphere' flora associated with colonizing species', *J. Ecol.*, **40**, 168–178.

WELBOURN, R. M. E. and LANGE, R. T. (1969), 'An analysis of vegetation on stranded coastal dune ranges between Robe and Naracoorte, South Australia', *Trans. Roy. Soc. S. Aust.*, **92**, 19–25.

WEST, R. C. (1956), 'Mangrove swamps of the Pacific coast of Colombia', *Ann. Ass. Am. Geogr.*, **46**, 98–121.

WESTHOFF, V. (1947), The vegetation of dunes and salt marshes on the Dutch islands of Terschelling, Vlieland and Texel. S. Gravenhage.

WESTHOFF, V. (1952), Gezelschappen met houtige gewassen in de duinen en langs de binnenduinrand. Dendrol. Jaarbk. 1952, 9–49.

WESTHOFF, V. (1962), Plant species characteristic of wetland habitats in the Netherlands. Proceedings of the MAR Conference I.U.C.N. Publication. N.S., **3**, 122–129.

WESTHOFF, V., LEEUWEN, C. G. van and ADRIANI, M. J. (1961), 'Enkele aspecten van vegetatie en bodem der duinen van Goeree, in het bizonder de contactgordels tussen zout en zoet milieu', *Jaarb. Wet. Genot. Goeree-Overflakke*, 46–92.

WESTLAKE, D. F. (1968), The biology of aquatic weeds in relation to their management. Proceedings of the 9th British Weed Control Conference, 372–381.

WESTON, R. L. (1964), 'Nitrogen nutrition in *Atriplex hastata* L.', *Pl. Soil*, **20**, 251–259.

WHITE, D. J. B. (1961), 'Some observations on the vegetation of Blakeney Point, Norfolk, following the disappearance of the rabbits in 1954', *J. Ecol.*, **49**, 113–118.

WHITE, D. J. B. (1967), *An Annotated List of the Flowering Plants and Ferns on Blakeney Point, Norfolk.* (2nd edn) Norwich: The National Trust.

WIEHE, P. O. (1935), 'A quantitative study of the influence of the tide upon populations of *Salicornia europaea*', *J. Ecol.*, **23**, 323–333.

WIEMANN, P. and Domke, W. (1967), 'Pflanzengesellschaften der ostfriesischen Insel Spiekeroog', *Mitt. Staatsinst. Allg. Bot. Hamburg*, **12**, 191–353.

WILLIAMS, R. E. (1955), Development and improvement of coastal marsh ranges. *U.S. Year Book of Agriculture 1955*, 444–449.

WILLIAMS, R. E. (1959), Cattle walkways. U.S. Department of Agriculture Leaflet, 459, 1–8.

WILLIAMS, W. T. and LAMBERT, J. M. (1959), 'Multivariate methods in plant ecology I. Association-analysis in plant communities', *J. Ecol.*, **47**, 83–101.

WILLIS, A. J. (1963), 'Braunton Burrows: the effects on the vegetation of the addition of mineral nutrients to the dune soils', *J. Ecol.*, **51**, 353–374.

WILLIS, A. J., FOLKES, B. F., HOPE-SIMPSON, J. F. and YEMM, E. W. (1959),

Braunton Burrows: the dune system and its vegetation. I and II. *J. Ecol.*, **47**, 1–24 and 249–288.

WILLIS, A. J. and YEMM, E. W. (1961), 'Braunton Burrows: Mineral nutrient status of the dune soils', *J. Ecol.*, **49**, 377–390.

WILSON, K. (1960), 'The time factor in the development of dune soils at South Haven Peninsula, Dorset', *J. Ecol.*, **48**, 341–359.

WOHLENBERG, E. (1965), 'Deichbau und Deichpflege auf biologischer Grundlage', *Die Kuste*, **13**, 73–103.

WRIGHT, T. W. (1955), 'Profile development in the sand dunes of Culbin Forest, Morayshire I. Physical properties', *J. Soil Sci.*, **6**, 270–283.

YANO, N. (1962), 'The subterranean organ of sand dune plants in Japan', *J. Sci. Hiroshima Univ. Ser. B. Div. 2 (Botany)*, **9**, 139–184.

ZAK, J. M. (1967), 'Controlling drifting sand dunes on Cape Cod', *Massachusetts Agric. Expt. Stn. Bull.*, **563**, 1–15.

ZONNEVELD, I. S. (1960), 'The Brabantse Biesboch. A study of soil and vegetation of a freshwater tidal delta', *Bodenik Stud. No. 4. Wageningen.*

Additional References

These, for the most part, most recent references (not included in the text) are given to render the bibliography as up to date as possible.

BIRD, E. C. F. (1965), *A geomorphological study of the Gippsland Lakes*. Dept. of Geography Pubn. G/1. Australian National University, Canberra.

BIRD, E. C. F. (1971), 'Mangroves as land-builders', *Victorian Nat.*, **88**, 189–197.

BOSTON, K. G. (1971), The physiography of Anderson's Inlet, Victoria, with special reference to early stages in the establishment of *Spartina*. M. A. Thesis, University of Melbourne.

BOUGHEY, A. S. (1957), 'Ecological studies of tropical coastlines. I. The Gold Coast', *West Africa J. Ecol.*, **45**, 665–687.

CAMERON, G. N. (1972), 'Analysis of insect trophic diversity in two salt marsh communities', *Ecology*, **53**, 58–73.

CLARKE, L. D. and HANNON, N. J. (1971), 'The Mangrove swamp and salt marsh communities of the Sydney district. IV. The significance of species interaction', *J. Ecol.*, **59**, 535–553.

DENIEL, J. (1971), 'Un example d'utilisation de l'écologie et de la biometriesur un boisement de protection de l'environnement: La plantation de dunes de Cléder (Finistère)', *Penn Bed*, **8**, 147–159.

EBERSOLE, W. C. (1971), 'Predicting disturbances to the near and offshore sedimentary regime from marine mining'. *Water, Air, and Soil Pollution*, **1**, 72–88.

EVANS, G. (1965), 'Intertidal flat sediments and their environments and deposition in the Wash', *Q. Jl geol. Soc. Lond.*, **121**, 209–245.

FREIJSEN, A. H. J. (1971), 'Growth-physiology, salt tolerance and mineral nutrition of *Centaurium littorale* (Turner) Gilmour: Adaptations to its oligotrophic and brackish habitat', *Acta bot. neerl.*, **20**, 577–588.

GLUE, D. E. (1971), 'Saltmarsh reclamation stages and their associated bird-life', *Bird Study*, **18**, 187–198.

GRAY, A. J. (1972), 'The ecology of Morecambe Bay. V. The salt marshes of Morecambe Bay'. *J. appl. Ecol.*, **9**, 207–220.

GRAY, A. J. (1972), 'The ecology of Morecambe Bay. VI. Soils and vegetation of the salt marshes: A multivariate approach', *J. appl. Ecol.*, **9**, 221–234.

GRIMES, B. H. and HUBBARD, J. C. E. (1971), 'A comparison of film type and the importance of season for interpretation of coastal marshland vegetation', *Photogramm. Rec.*, **7**, 213–222.

JEFFRIES, R. L. (1972) *Aspects of salt-marsh ecology with particular reference to inorganic plant nutrition*. The Estuarine Environment, Barking, England: Applied Science Publishers Ltd., 61–85.

JENNINGS, J. N. (1965), 'Further discussion of factors affecting coastal dune formation in the tropics', *Aust. J. Sci.*, **28**, 166–167.

JONES, R. (1972), 'Comparative studies of plant growth and distribution in relation to waterlogging. V. The uptake of iron and manganese by dune and dune slack plants', *J. Ecol.*, **60**, 131–139.

JONES, R. (1972), *Ibid*. VI. 'The effect of manganese on the growth of dune and dune slack plants', *J. Ecol.*, **60**, 141–145.

JONES, R. and ETHERINGTON, J. R. (1971), *Ibid*. IV. 'The growth of dune and dune slack plants', *J. Ecol.*, **59**, 793–801.

LANGLOIS, J. (1971), 'Influence du rythme d'immersion sur la croissance et le métabolisme proteique de *Salicornia stricta* Dumort'. *Oecologia Plantarum*, **6**, 227–245.

McGUINESS, J. L., HARROLD, L. L. and EDWARDS, W. M. (1971), 'Relation of rainfall energy streamflow to sediment yield from small and large watersheds', *J. Soil Wat. Conserv.*, **26**, 233–234.

MORTON, A. (1970), A study of some factors affecting the structure of grassland vegetation, Ph.D. Thesis, University of Bangor, N. Wales.

MORTON, J. K. (1957), 'Sand dune formation on a tropical shore', *J. Ecol.*, **45**, 495–497.

NEWTON, L. E. (1965), Taxonomic studies in the British species of *Puccinellia*, M.Sc. Thesis, University of London.

OWEN, M. (1971), 'The selection of feeding site by White-fronted geese in winter', *J. appl. Ecol.*, **8**, 905–917.

OWEN, M. (1972), 'Some factors affecting food intake and selection in White-fronted geese', *J. Anim. Ecol.*, **41**, 79–92.

OWEN, M. (1971), 'On the autumn food of Barnacle geese at Caerlaverock National Nature Reserve', *Rep. Wildfowl Trust*, **22**, 114–119.

PEAKE, J. F. (1966), 'A salt marsh at Thornham in N.W. Norfolk', *Trans. Norfolk Norwich Nat. Soc.*, **19**, 36–62.

PETHICK, J. S. (1969), The ecology of the Lamas estuary, M.Sc. Thesis, University of Cambridge.

PETHICK, J. S. (1971), Salt marsh morphology, Ph.D. Thesis, University of Cambridge.

PONS, L. Z. and ZONNEVELD, I. S. (1965), *Soil ripening and soil classification.* Initial soil formation in alluvial deposits and a classification of the resulting soils. Wageningen: H. Veenman and Zonen, 1–128.

SiïRA, J. and HAAPALA, H. (1969), 'Studies in the distribution and ecology of *Puccinellia phryganodes* (Trin.) Scribn. and Merr. in Finland', *Aquilo, Serie bot.* **8**, 1–24.

SMITH, E. R. (1970), *Evaluation of a leveed Louisiana marsh.* Trans. N. Am. Wildl. Conf., No. 35, 265–275.

THALEN, D. C. P. (1971), 'Variation in some salt marsh and dune vegetations in the Netherlands with special reference to gradient situations', *Acta. bot. neerl.*, **20**, 327–342.

TYLER, G. (1971), 'Studies in the ecology of Baltic sea-shore meadows. IV. Distribution and turnover of organic matter and minerals in a shore meadow ecosystem', *Oikos*, **22**, 265–291.

VAN STRAATEN, L. M. J. (1961), 'Sedimentation in tidal flat areas'. *J. Alberta Soc. Petrol. Geol.*, **9**, 203–226.

WILLIS, A. J. and JEFFERIES, R. L. (1961), 'Investigations on the water relations of sand-dune plants under natural conditions. The water relations of plants', *Brit. Ecol. Soc. Symp. No. 3*. Oxford, 168–189.

Index

This index should be used in conjunction with the contents list at the beginning of the volume.